Communications
in Computer and Information Science   1835

Rationale

The CCIS series is devoted to the publication of proceedings of computer science conferences. Its aim is to efficiently disseminate original research results in informatics in printed and electronic form. While the focus is on publication of peer-reviewed full papers presenting mature work, inclusion of reviewed short papers reporting on work in progress is welcome, too. Besides globally relevant meetings with internationally representative program committees guaranteeing a strict peer-reviewing and paper selection process, conferences run by societies or of high regional or national relevance are also considered for publication.

Topics

The topical scope of CCIS spans the entire spectrum of informatics ranging from foundational topics in the theory of computing to information and communications science and technology and a broad variety of interdisciplinary application fields.

Information for Volume Editors and Authors

Publication in CCIS is free of charge. No royalties are paid, however, we offer registered conference participants temporary free access to the online version of the conference proceedings on SpringerLink (http://link.springer.com) by means of an http referrer from the conference website and/or a number of complimentary printed copies, as specified in the official acceptance email of the event.

CCIS proceedings can be published in time for distribution at conferences or as postproceedings, and delivered in the form of printed books and/or electronically as USBs and/or e-content licenses for accessing proceedings at SpringerLink. Furthermore, CCIS proceedings are included in the CCIS electronic book series hosted in the SpringerLink digital library at http://link.springer.com/bookseries/7899. Conferences publishing in CCIS are allowed to use Online Conference Service (OCS) for managing the whole proceedings lifecycle (from submission and reviewing to preparing for publication) free of charge.

Publication process

The language of publication is exclusively English. Authors publishing in CCIS have to sign the Springer CCIS copyright transfer form, however, they are free to use their material published in CCIS for substantially changed, more elaborate subsequent publications elsewhere. For the preparation of the camera-ready papers/files, authors have to strictly adhere to the Springer CCIS Authors' Instructions and are strongly encouraged to use the CCIS LaTeX style files or templates.

Abstracting/Indexing

CCIS is abstracted/indexed in DBLP, Google Scholar, EI-Compendex, Mathematical Reviews, SCImago, Scopus. CCIS volumes are also submitted for the inclusion in ISI Proceedings.

How to start

To start the evaluation of your proposal for inclusion in the CCIS series, please send an e-mail to ccis@springer.com.

Constantine Stephanidis · Margherita Antona ·
Stavroula Ntoa · Gavriel Salvendy
Editors

HCI International 2023 Posters

25th International Conference
on Human-Computer Interaction, HCII 2023
Copenhagen, Denmark, July 23–28, 2023
Proceedings, Part IV

Springer

Editors
Constantine Stephanidis
University of Crete and Foundation for
Research and Technology - Hellas (FORTH)
Heraklion, Crete, Greece

Margherita Antona
Foundation for Research and Technology -
Hellas (FORTH)
Heraklion, Crete, Greece

Stavroula Ntoa
Foundation for Research and Technology -
Hellas (FORTH)
Heraklion, Crete, Greece

Gavriel Salvendy
University of Central Florida
Orlando, FL, USA

ISSN 1865-0929   ISSN 1865-0937 (electronic)
Communications in Computer and Information Science
ISBN 978-3-031-36000-8   ISBN 978-3-031-36001-5 (eBook)
https://doi.org/10.1007/978-3-031-36001-5

This Springer imprint is published by the registered company Springer Nature Switzerland AG
The registered company address is: Gewerbestrasse 11, 6330 Cham, Switzerland

Foreword

Human-computer interaction (HCI) is acquiring an ever-increasing scientific and industrial importance, as well as having more impact on people's everyday lives, as an ever-growing number of human activities are progressively moving from the physical to the digital world. This process, which has been ongoing for some time now, was further accelerated during the acute period of the COVID-19 pandemic. The HCI International (HCII) conference series, held annually, aims to respond to the compelling need to advance the exchange of knowledge and research and development efforts on the human aspects of design and use of computing systems.

The 25th International Conference on Human-Computer Interaction, HCI International 2023 (HCII 2023), was held in the emerging post-pandemic era as a 'hybrid' event at the AC Bella Sky Hotel and Bella Center, Copenhagen, Denmark, during July 23–28, 2023. It incorporated the 21 thematic areas and affiliated conferences listed below.

A total of 7472 individuals from academia, research institutes, industry, and government agencies from 85 countries submitted contributions, and 1578 papers and 396 posters were included in the volumes of the proceedings that were published just before the start of the conference, these are listed below. The contributions thoroughly cover the entire field of human-computer interaction, addressing major advances in knowledge and effective use of computers in a variety of application areas. These papers provide academics, researchers, engineers, scientists, practitioners and students with state-of-the-art information on the most recent advances in HCI.

The HCI International (HCII) conference also offers the option of presenting 'Late Breaking Work', and this applies both for papers and posters, with corresponding volumes of proceedings that will be published after the conference. Full papers will be included in the 'HCII 2023 - Late Breaking Work - Papers' volumes of the proceedings to be published in the Springer LNCS series, while 'Poster Extended Abstracts' will be included as short research papers in the 'HCII 2023 - Late Breaking Work - Posters' volumes to be published in the Springer CCIS series.

I would like to thank the Program Board Chairs and the members of the Program Boards of all thematic areas and affiliated conferences for their contribution towards the high scientific quality and overall success of the HCI International 2023 conference. Their manifold support in terms of paper reviewing (single-blind review process, with a minimum of two reviews per submission), session organization and their willingness to act as goodwill ambassadors for the conference is most highly appreciated.

This conference would not have been possible without the continuous and unwavering support and advice of Gavriel Salvendy, founder, General Chair Emeritus, and Scientific Advisor. For his outstanding efforts, I would like to express my sincere appreciation to Abbas Moallem, Communications Chair and Editor of HCI International News.

July 2023   Constantine Stephanidis

HCI International 2023 Thematic Areas and Affiliated Conferences

Thematic Areas

- HCI: Human-Computer Interaction
- HIMI: Human Interface and the Management of Information

Affiliated Conferences

- EPCE: 20th International Conference on Engineering Psychology and Cognitive Ergonomics
- AC: 17th International Conference on Augmented Cognition
- UAHCI: 17th International Conference on Universal Access in Human-Computer Interaction
- CCD: 15th International Conference on Cross-Cultural Design
- SCSM: 15th International Conference on Social Computing and Social Media
- VAMR: 15th International Conference on Virtual, Augmented and Mixed Reality
- DHM: 14th International Conference on Digital Human Modeling and Applications in Health, Safety, Ergonomics and Risk Management
- DUXU: 12th International Conference on Design, User Experience and Usability
- C&C: 11th International Conference on Culture and Computing
- DAPI: 11th International Conference on Distributed, Ambient and Pervasive Interactions
- HCIBGO: 10th International Conference on HCI in Business, Government and Organizations
- LCT: 10th International Conference on Learning and Collaboration Technologies
- ITAP: 9th International Conference on Human Aspects of IT for the Aged Population
- AIS: 5th International Conference on Adaptive Instructional Systems
- HCI-CPT: 5th International Conference on HCI for Cybersecurity, Privacy and Trust
- HCI-Games: 5th International Conference on HCI in Games
- MobiTAS: 5th International Conference on HCI in Mobility, Transport and Automotive Systems
- AI-HCI: 4th International Conference on Artificial Intelligence in HCI
- MOBILE: 4th International Conference on Design, Operation and Evaluation of Mobile Communications

List of Conference Proceedings Volumes Appearing Before the Conference

47. CCIS 1836, HCI International 2023 Posters - Part V, edited by Constantine Stephanidis, Margherita Antona, Stavroula Ntoa and Gavriel Salvendy

https://2023.hci.international/proceedings

Preface

Preliminary scientific results, professional news, or work in progress, described in the form of short research papers (4–8 pages long), constitute a popular submission type among the International Conference on Human-Computer Interaction (HCII) participants. Extended abstracts are particularly suited for reporting ongoing work, which can benefit from a visual presentation, and are presented during the conference in the form of posters. The latter allow a focus on novel ideas and are appropriate for presenting project results in a simple, concise, and visually appealing manner. At the same time, they are also suitable for attracting feedback from an international community of HCI academics, researchers, and practitioners. Poster submissions span the wide range of topics of all HCII thematic areas and affiliated conferences.

Five volumes of the HCII 2023 proceedings are dedicated to this year's poster extended abstracts, in the form of short research papers, focusing on the following topics:

- Volume I: HCI Design - Theoretical Approaches, Methods and Case Studies; Multimodality and Novel Interaction Techniques and Devices; Perception and Cognition in Interaction; Ethics, Transparency and Trust in HCI; User Experience and Technology Acceptance Studies
- Volume II: Supporting Health, Psychological Wellbeing, and Fitness; Design for All, Accessibility and Rehabilitation Technologies; Interactive Technologies for the Aging Population
- Volume III: Interacting with Data, Information and Knowledge; Learning and Training Technologies; Interacting with Cultural Heritage and Art
- Volume IV: Social Media - Design, User Experiences and Content Analysis; Advances in eGovernment Services; eCommerce, Mobile Commerce and Digital Marketing - Design and Customer Behavior; Designing and Developing Intelligent Green Environments; (Smart) Product Design
- Volume V: Driving Support and Experiences in Automated Vehicles; eXtended Reality - Design, Interaction Techniques, User Experience and Novel Applications; Applications of AI Technologies in HCI

Poster extended abstracts are included for publication in these volumes following a minimum of two single-blind reviews from the members of the HCII 2023 international Program Boards. We would like to thank all of them for their invaluable contribution, support, and efforts.

July 2023

Constantine Stephanidis
Margherita Antona
Stavroula Ntoa
Gavriel Salvendy

25th International Conference on Human-Computer Interaction (HCII 2023)

The full list with the Program Board Chairs and the members of the Program Boards of all thematic areas and affiliated conferences of HCII2023 is available online at:

http://www.hci.international/board-members-2023.php

HCI International 2024 Conference

The 26th International Conference on Human-Computer Interaction, HCI International 2024, will be held jointly with the affiliated conferences at the Washington Hilton Hotel, Washington, DC, USA, June 29 – July 4, 2024. It will cover a broad spectrum of themes related to Human-Computer Interaction, including theoretical issues, methods, tools, processes, and case studies in HCI design, as well as novel interaction techniques, interfaces, and applications. The proceedings will be published by Springer. More information will be made available on the conference website: http://2024.hci.international/.

General Chair
Prof. Constantine Stephanidis
University of Crete and ICS-FORTH
Heraklion, Crete, Greece
Email: general_chair@hcii2024.org

https://2024.hci.international/

Contents - Part IV

Advances in eGovernment Services

eCommerce, Mobile Commerce and Digital Marketing: Design and Customer Behavior

Designing and Developing Intelligent Green Environments

(Smart) Product Design

Social Media: Design, User Experiences and Content Analysis

Ride-Hailing Services: An Analysis of Gojek's Security and Privacy Protection

Nida Amalia Aristya[✉] and Filosa Gita Sukmono

Department of Communication Studies, Faculty of Social and Politics, Universitas Muhammadiyah Yogyakarta, Kasihan, Indonesia
nida.amalia.isip19@mail.umy.ac.id, filose@umy.ac.id

Abstract. This study presents a literature analysis on ride-hailing services in Indonesia to enhance knowledge of the actions taken by Gojek as a super application in safeguarding user and partner data and to enlighten ride-hailing services efforts in delivering online transportation services with the complexity of ride-hailing services in Indonesia. This study employs a qualitative research method with a descriptive approach; data for this study is derived from digital data in the form of historical records. Gojek delivers features that prioritize data security for users and driver partners that aim to avoid crimes, mainly digital or cybercrime, by providing parts that are also Gojek's industry-leading selling factors. These findings contribute to the development of research on ride-hailing services, particularly in privacy and security, and serve to address shortcomings previously identified with ride-hailing services.

Keywords: Ride-Hailing Services · GOJEK · Security · Privacy

1 Introduction

The evolution of information communication and technologies has influenced human behaviour and way of life [1]. The internet growth is one of the elements that has facilitated the transition to smartphones as a means of communication [2]. New media has been sought after by people from all walks of life [3]. One of them employs the Ride-hailing service, a transportation service that uses an internet-based mobile application on a smartphone [4]. This service has been popular in almost every city in the world in a short time, such as Uber, Lyft, Bolt, Ola, Didi, Grab and Gojek [5]. ICT plays an essential role in the development of online transportation. Big Data is a valuable resource for ride-hailing operators in managing and financing transportation services [6]. Information technology is used to process data and store data to produce information that is relevant, accurate and timely [7]. The number of internet users in Indonesia continues to grow; based on the 2022 APJII survey, as many as 77.02% of Indonesia's population is connected to the internet. Several reasons for internet users, such as accessing social media, conducting online transactions, searching for information, entertainment content, to online transportation application services; the total percentage reaches 9.27% with two applications often used, namely Gojek with 40.65% and Grab 36.32%.

C. Stephanidis et al. (Eds.): HCII 2023, CCIS 1835, pp. 3–9, 2023.
https://doi.org/10.1007/978-3-031-36001-5_1

Urban areas that require speed and timeliness have selected smartphone application-based ride-hailing services as an innovation [8]. The high number of users registered in ride-hailing apps raises the possibility of data security and privacy violations. While information technology has many advantages, it also has certain drawbacks. These innovations give birth to new digital crimes known as new cybercrime. According to a survey by cyber security company Kaspersky, about 11.8 million or as much as 27.6% of internet users in Indonesia are endangered by online crime, making Indonesia the Southeast Asian nation with the highest online crime concerns [9]. In several previous studies on ride-hailing in Indonesia, acceptance of ride-hailing is influenced by social influences, acceptance habits, and price values [4]. Technology plays an essential role in marketing techniques, and factors that influence consumers are influenced by social media marketing [10]. Social media as a new media has unique characteristics, and Social media makes it possible for interactivity between content providers and parties exposed to content [11]. This research contributes to the development of ride-hailing services studies, especially on privacy and security, and serves to fill the limitations that have been done previously regarding ride-hailing services.

2 Theory

Ride-hailing is a transportation service that uses a mobile internet application [12]; this is part of the digital era's development of communication and information media [8]. Online-based ride-hailing services face the risk of data threat, so preventive protection is needed for the data collection; the data collected is the details of each trip, including location traces with identities [13]. Hence, safety is one of the most critical factors influencing a fundamental challenge of ride-hailing service providers [14]. The ride-hailing service system coordinates the passenger movement process by regulating the regulations through the data received by the ride-hailing service [15]. The ride-hailing service allows users to send user calling requests to driver-partners using transmitted data so that drivers pick up at rates adjusted to their area [8]. The Gojek services providers match data between driver-partners and users by protecting the privacy of encrypted user locations and their anonymity using random ID codes from ride-hailing service providers [16].

3 Methodology

This study used a qualitative research method with a descriptive approach. This approach analyses how Gojek provides protection and security for partners and users through the #AmanBersamaGojek campaign. Data collection in this research originates from digital data from historical documents and Gojek's monthly and annual reports. From the data collected, it becomes a data reference regarding Gojek's steps in campaigning for security and privacy.

4 Results and Discussion

These findings suggest that ride-hailing is becoming an innovation in the transportation sector [17]; Gojek is rapidly evolving with various services; however, multiple variables influence the data security and privacy of partners and Gojek users. According to the Institute for Development of Economics and Finance (INDEF) research, Gojek users are the most popular among Indonesian customers. Gojek had the highest percentage of users (82%), followed by Grab (57%), Maxim (19%), and InDriver (4%). As Lampe stated, Gojek is evolving from a mobile application to a super application, a multi-service platform with around 20 services, including the following (Fig. 1):

Fig. 1. Gojek Services

According to Malawani [18], Gojek is the leading technology platform that serves millions of users in Southeast Asia; this is consistent with research conducted by the Demographic Institute of the Faculty of Economics and Business, University of Indonesia, which discovered that the GoPay service is the most popular among users. GoPay is a digital wallet that may be used for various transactions, including paying for restaurants, groceries, and bills. The second frequently utilized service is GoFood. With 550,000 registered merchant partners in 74 Indonesian cities, it is simpler for customers to place orders without visiting the restaurant. The higher the interest of service users, the more likely it is that certain parties would misuse and are not responsible for utilizing the service. Following Wiryawan's findings [15], the system in the ride-hailing service governs the management of user movement through the data received by the ride-hailing service; in this example, Gojek utilizes a cloud computing system to store and manage incoming data on the server.

Figure 2 demonstrates that regulatory data settings in the Gojek ride-hailing system employ a server to accept customer assistance queries. Consumers first request services using the Gojek app, which sends data such as names, phone numbers, and the user's location to the Gojek server. Then, following ride-hailing services that enable user data to be shared with driver-partners, Gojek will submit the data so that driver-partners can

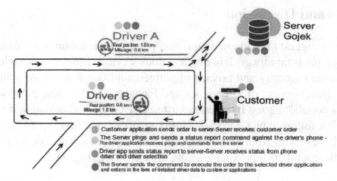

Fig. 2. The Flow Gojek Services

get it. There are options. According to Fahlevi and Firnanda [19, 20], modern internet crimes provide users unrestricted access to various information, giving rise to new crimes known as cybercrimes. This crime can manifest as data dumps, including usernames, phone numbers, passwords, order history, and user travels. In practice, this personal information might be used for fraud, online lending, or even getting into accounts that are harmful to the owner. As a result, the bigger the number of users, the higher the potential for data leakage from users and driving partners. Gojek offers preventative protection through fingerprint and faces verification features to secure financial data. This feature uses the biometric identification traits of each user, such as the user's fingerprints or face, to reduce misuse by others [21] (Fig. 3).

Fig. 3. Gojek Safety Feature (Doc. Gojek)

Gojek Security System	Function	Service
Smart Login feature	Utilizes each user's physiological characteristics consisting of fingerprints to verify every login attempt to the account	Gojek user accounts
Fingerprint & Face Verification Features	Security features that help verify GoPay transactions without using the user's PIN	GoPay, GoBill, GoPayLater, GoGive, GoInvest, GoSure

(continued)

(*continued*)

Gojek Security System	Function	Service
Phone Number Masking	There are disguised phone numbers of users and driver partners for convenience when communicating and ensuring the security of each other's data	GoRide, GoCar, GoSend, GoBox
Share Trip	Used to share trips in real-time • Pick-up location and destination • Driver information • Travel status and estimated time of arrival • Route traversed	GoRide, GoCar
Track Delivery	Track GoSend orders and deliveries in real-time; customers can ensure the delivery process without worrying about missing items	GoSend, GoBox

Source: www.gojek.com

According to Meng Li's statement [16], which requires the service provider to match driver partner data with the user, ride-hailing services are linked to the user's location to the user's telephone number information, creating a possibility for irresponsible persons to exploit personal data. In this situation, the criminal will pose as a Gojek partner and request a Time Password (OTP); with this OTP code, the criminal will be able to access the user's account until the user's e-wallet balance is depleted. Furthermore, Meng Li stated that it is possible with service providers to protect the privacy of the user's location and the random usage of anonymous ID [17]. Gojek has developed some masking tools to help avoid undesired crimes by anonymizing users and driving partners. This function can mask the user's actual phone number with a virtual number (VN), so the caller and recipient are unaware of the second number [22]. Gojek identifies which VN is active and distinct from the VN previously utilized to provide anonymity. The VN can only be used once while the order is being processed.

Circella [6] stated that ICT played a part in the development of technology to promote ride-hailing services, and one of the initiatives Gojek has made is to make the offered features become a selling point for Gojek to market the brand so that clients are more conscious of security and privacy when using Gojek's services. Gojek took the initiative to develop the #AmanBersamaGojek campaign, which focuses on education, technology, and protection, to enhance its commitment to preserving the security and privacy of consumers and partners. Education initiatives aim to improve community literacy to establish secure public areas. Gojek continues to develop in the technology department by delivering the newest technology in the form of features that work to secure customer and partner data security. Gojek travel insurance does not tolerate sexual violence and provides complete protection, including Gojek emergency unit services. According to Gojek's actions, this is reinforced by the Gojek campaign, which includes the hashtag

#AmanBersamaGojek in various Gojek content uploads on several Gojek official social media channels (Fig. 4).

Fig. 4. Content's Gojek (Doc. Twitter and Instagram Gojek)

5 Conclusion

Gojek created a super program to safeguard user and driver data. Gojek provides features emphasizing user and driver data security to avoid crimes, mainly digital or cybercrime. According to the findings in this research, these features include clever logins that employ fingerprints and facial IDs for security during transactions to verify users. In addition, Gojek has included a telephone number disguise tool to help users and driver-partners safeguard the privacy of personal data on user and driver-partner phone numbers. The following function is trip sharing and shipment tracking, which may be utilized to preserve user trust in driver partners in charge of services. These findings contribute to the advancement of ride-hailing service research, particularly in privacy and security, and fill previously identified gaps in ride-hailing service research. This article discusses Gojek's efforts to provide safety and privacy protection through cutting-edge technology, raising awareness among Gojek users and partners.

References

1. Selfira, B., Neltje, J.: Analysis of the legal protection of online transportation services users for unenjoyable actions by online Ojek drivers through social media according to law number 8 of 1999 concerning consumer protection (2022)
2. Nurhayati, S.S., Sukmono, F.G.: Gender advocacy, social media campaign to against sexual violence. In: Stephanidis, C., Antona, M., Ntoa, S., Salvendy, G. (eds.) HCII 2022. CCIS, vol. 1655, pp. 76–82. Springer, Cham (2022). https://doi.org/10.1007/978-3-031-19682-9_11
3. Kencana, W.H., Meisyanti, M.: The implementation of mass media digital platform in Indonesia. Komunikator **12**(2), 90–105 (2020). https://doi.org/10.18196/jkm.122038
4. Almunawar, M.N., Anshari, M., Ariff Lim, S.: Customer acceptance of ride-hailing in Indonesia. J. Sci. Technol. Policy Manag. **12**(3), 443–462 (2020). https://doi.org/10.1108/JSTPM-09-2019-0082

5. Wadud, Z.: The effects of e-ridehailing on motorcycle ownership in an emerging-country megacity. Transp. Res. Part A Policy Pract. **137**, 301–312 (2020). https://doi.org/10.1016/j.tra.2020.05.002
6. Circella, G., Pawlak, J., Mokhtarian, P.L.: Information and communication technologies (ICT), activity decisions, and travel choices: 20 years into the second millennium and where do we go next? May 2020
7. Pratiwi, M.R.: Peran ICT bagi organisasi media massa dan budaya masyarakat. J. Komun. **6**(1), 20–26 (2014). http://journal.umy.ac.id/index.php/jkm/article/view/212/174
8. Lampe, I., Alatas, R., Orynka, N., Saputra, G.B.R.: Local online courier and ride-hailing service social media marketing. Komunikator **13**(1), 66–77 (2021)
9. Clinten, B.: Awal 2022, Indonesia Hadapi 11 Juta Ancaman di Dunia Maya, 28 April 2022. https://tekno.kompas.com/read/2022/04/28/07000027/awal-2022-indonesia-hadapi-11-juta-ancaman-di-dunia-maya?page=all. Accessed 22 Oct 2022
10. Moslehpour, M., Ismail, T., Purba, B., Wong, W.K.: What makes GO-JEK go in Indonesia? The influences of social media marketing activities on purchase intention. J. Theor. Appl. Electron. Commer. Res. **17**(1), 89–103 (2022). https://doi.org/10.3390/jtaer17010005
11. Amalia, A., Sudiwijaya, E.: Yogyakarta tourism promotion using user-generated-content feature. Komunikator **12**(2), 136–145 (2020). https://doi.org/10.18196/jkm.122042
12. Nandi: The influence of online transportation application to the mobility and economic of the society (case study on using grab and Go-Jek in Bandung, Indonesia). In: IOP Conference Series: Earth and Environmental Science, vol. 286, no. 1, June 2019. https://doi.org/10.1088/1755-1315/286/1/012034
13. Rochet, F., Pereira, O.: PrivateRide: a privacy-enhanced ride-hailing service. Proc. Priv. Enhancing Technol. **2017**(2), 4–22 (2017). https://doi.org/10.1515/popets-2017-0013
14. Jing, P., Chen, Y., Wang, X., Pan, K., Yuan, D.: Evaluating the effectiveness of Didi ride-hailing security measures: an integration model. Transp. Res. Part F Traffic Psychol. Behav. **76**, 139–166 (2021). https://doi.org/10.1016/j.trf.2020.11.004
15. Wiryawan, I.W.G.: Urgency of employment protection regulation for online transportation driver. Sociol. Jurisprud. J. **3**(1), 34–42 (2020). https://doi.org/10.22225/scj.3.1.1319.34-42
16. Li, M., Gao, J., Chen, Y., Zhao, J., Alazab, M.: Privacy-preserving ride-hailing with verifiable order-linking in vehicular networks. In: Proceedings - 2020 IEEE 19th International Conference on Trust, Security and Privacy in Computing and Communications, pp. 599–606 (2020). https://doi.org/10.1109/TrustCom50675.2020.00085
17. Wang, Y., Gu, J., Wang, S., Wang, J.: Understanding consumers' willingness to use ride-sharing services: the roles of perceived value and perceived risk. Transp. Res. Part C Emerg. Technol. **105**, 504–519 (2019). https://doi.org/10.1016/j.trc.2019.05.044
18. Malawani, A.D., Salahudin, S., Qodir, Z., Loilatu, M.J., Nurmandi, A.: The evolution of "GO-JEK" as an Indonesian urban mobile ride hailing model study case: public and government regulatory responses on urban mobile ride hailing. In: Stephanidis, C., Antona, M. (eds.) HCII 2020. CCIS, vol. 1226, pp. 429–438. Springer, Cham (2020). https://doi.org/10.1007/978-3-030-50732-9_56
19. Firnanda, A.S., Junaedi, F., Sudiwijaya, E.: Digital content management of Twitter for climate change using hashtag. In: Stephanidis, C., Antona, M., Ntoa, S., Salvendy, G. (eds.) HCII 2022. CCIS, vol. 1655, pp. 18–24. Springer, Cham (2022). https://doi.org/10.1007/978-3-031-19682-9_3
20. Fahlevi, M., Saparudin, M., Maemunah, S., Dasih, I., Ekhsan, M.: Cybercrime business digital in Indonesia. https://doi.org/10.1051/e3sconf/201
21. GoPay: Your GoPay transactions is safer with the fingerprint & face ID feature. Gojek (2022). https://gopay.co.id/blog/fitur-touch-id-face-id
22. Jaiswal, A.: How we mask phone numbers to secure user identity. Gojek (2022). https://blog.gojek.io/how-we-mask-phone-numbers-to-secure-user-identity/. Accessed 12 Jan 2023

Representations of Health and Wellness on Instagram: An Analysis of Posting Behavior of Top-Ranked Health Influencers

Michelle Bak[1]([⊠]), J. Hunter Priniski[2], and Jessie Chin[1]

[1] University of Illinois Urbana-Champaign, Champaign, IL 61820, USA
chaewon7@illinois.edu
[2] University of California, Los Angeles, CA 90095, USA

Abstract. This study aims to investigate the prevalence of Health Influencers' Instagram content that could lead to negative impacts on mental health and body image. With the collected Instagram posts and associated metadata of top ranked Health Influencers, we performed content analysis on the most used hashtags, an unsupervised topic model to examine the semantic content and coverage of each theme discussed in the corpus, and an analysis on the audience engagement behavior by topics. Content analysis revealed posts composing of four broad themes: Fitness, Wellness, Self-Promotion, and Cosmetics and Appearance. In addition, well-known brands are prevalent among the hashtags suggesting product promotion is central to health content on Instagram. Topic modeling uncovered Health Influencers' posts as a mixture of content related to health and wellness as well as other potentially problematic topics (e.g., promoting brands that have spread unhealthy body ideals or associating cosmetic products with being healthy, etc.). We also found promotional posts have higher user engagement rates than non-promotional ones, which in part due to the differential incentives of engagement, and bias in health beliefs or algorithms. Current research suggests a large portion of content produced by Health Influencers likely contain factors that induce body dissatisfaction and other related issues among Instagram users.

Keywords: Social Media · Body Image · Mental Health

1 Introduction

Image-based social media is experiencing a significant increase in popularity among adolescents and young adults [1]. However, a large body of research suggests increased exposure to visual social media is correlated with mental health issues [2–6], which primarily affects adolescents [7] and women [8, 9]. Indeed, frequent Instagram use is positively correlated with appearance-related anxiety [10], dysmorphia [11], depressive symptoms [12], and low self-esteem [8]. Strikingly, some adolescent users have even reported developing eating disorders to take photos that get more likes [13].

A likely reason for these trends is that many images on Instagram promote Western beauty and thin-body ideals, which are known to induce body-image disturbances [14].

© The Author(s), under exclusive license to Springer Nature Switzerland AG 2023
C. Stephanidis et al. (Eds.): HCII 2023, CCIS 1835, pp. 10–20, 2023.
https://doi.org/10.1007/978-3-031-36001-5_2

Instagram Influencers, a class of Instagram users with the largest social reach on the platform, often promote a curated, stylized aesthetic which rarely represents diversity [15–18]. As a result, Instagram has become a medium composed largely of Western bodies [19] promoting Western ideals of beauty [20], inducing negative self-perceptions in many people not seeing themselves represented in their image feeds [21]. This mechanism is analogous to the effects of more traditional forms of popular Western media on mental health [22–25], which promotes thin-body ideals that lead to negative self-perceptions [14, 26]. Because millions of people, particularly adolescents, use Instagram daily, it is important to understand the sources of toxic content on the platform.

This paper analyzes the content of one of the most common types of Instagram Influencers, Health Influencers — users who promote physical and mental wellbeing by posting stylized photos of themselves engaged in health-related activities. Recent research suggests Health Influencers post content with negative health effects [10, 27–29]. We report a large-scale quantitative analysis of over 157,000 Instagram posts from 306 highly recognized Health Influencers to provide the comprehensive assessment of their posting behaviors. Specifically, we analyze the thematic analysis, unsupervised topic models, and statistical models to analyze the hashtags, posts, and engagement rates. Our studies should provide an overview of Health Influencers on Instagram and their potential impacts on their audience.

2 Data Collection

Data collection occurred in two phases. First, a collection of Health Influencer profiles was mined, and then their posts were extracted using the CrowdTangle platform [30].

2.1 Phase I: Extracting a List of Health Influencers

We curated a list of Health Influencers for analysis by mining the user profiles of 10,000 self-identified Health Influencers [31] from the website influence.co, a website designed for social media influencers to promote their online profiles to a broader audience [32]. We excluded any users with less than 10,000 followers and whose number of posts were less than 5 percentiles of all other Health Influencers (i.e., 34 posts) from later analysis. This selection cut-off was informed by social media expert opinion that influencers with 10,000 or more followers are "top-ranked" [33]. We then excluded data from the European Union following the General Data Protection Regulation (GDPR). We ended up having 306 top-ranked Health Influencers, with an average of 123,088 followers at posting and 512 posts from April 2017 to August 2020 [34].

2.2 Phase II: Mining Instagram Content

Using the CrowdTangle platform, we mined every available post from the selected list of 306 top-ranked Health influencers. This resulted in approximately 157,000 Instagram posts and associated metadata (e.g., username, public metrics of a post) of Health Influencers from April 2017 to August 2020. The present analyses only focused on text descriptions of the posts, because previous research indicates computer vision-based analyses of post images provide less insight [35].

3 Thematic Analysis of Common Hashtags

Analyzing hashtag use on social media can provide rich insight into the thematic content of the posts [36]. For instance, researchers can leverage hashtag statistics to structure a large corpora of social media data [37] and learn how the authors perceive their own messages, because hashtags can be treated as data annotations produced by the authors of the posts [38]. Furthermore, given that topic models do not have clear metrics for assessing overall fit and interpretability [38], analysis of commonly used hashtags is useful in validating topic modeling results (e.g., by comparing topic model results to the groupings induced by clustering commonly used hashtags).

3.1 Methods

We extracted the 500 most frequently used hashtags in our dataset and grouped them into categories based on their thematic content from two coders. First, both coders independently annotated each hashtag with respect to its thematic category. This process required searching Instagram for recent posts not in our dataset that were also labeled with the hashtag. These out-of-sample posts were used to inform us of the typical content associated with each hashtag, and guided the labels provided to them. Any annotation disagreement was resolved through discussions.

3.2 Results

The results revealed that posts fell into seventeen higher-level semantic categories (see Table 1) composing four broad themes: Cosmetics and Appearance, Self-promotion, Fitness, and Wellness. Cosmetics and Appearance refer to content about physical attributes, cosmetics products, beauty industry, or beauty-related trending keywords. Self-promotion pertains to content about advertisement, commercial brand, blog, or photo/place promotion. Fitness covers content about physical exercise or workout motivation. Wellness involves content about physical, mental, and social well-being.

Suggesting that a large portion of content is related to health and wellness, there is also a large body of content related to other factors as well (see Table 1). Indeed, the prevalence of hashtags related to self-promotion indicates that a substantial amount of content is devoted to promoting the Influencer's online presence ($N_{posts} = 41,433$; 26.25%). Furthermore, the prevalence of hashtags related to physical appearance and beauty ($N_{posts} = 16,720$; 10.59%) suggests that a large body of posts pertain to promoting specific appearances unrelated to health and wellbeing (e.g., #blondevibe, #wakeupand-makeup). Because research indicates Influencer identities do not represent the diversity of Instagram users [39], these contents are likely to distort many users' understandings of health and well-being, increasing the likelihood of self-comparison.

We further conducted descriptive analyses on the volume of each semantic category. As shown in Fig. 1, under wellness, posts containing emotion-related hashtags have the highest mean value. Given that some Influencers assure accomplishing ideal body shapes through using specific industry products as a key to happiness [29], this suggests Health Influencers who frequently include emotional terms in their posts may be discussing positive emotional outcome of certain health habits. The prevalence of hashtags

Table 1. Examples of themes and semantic categories of 500 most frequently used hashtags

Theme	Category	Example Hashtags
Cosmetics and Appearance	Appearance	#blondevibe, #nofilter
	Beauty	#makeupaddict, #wakeupandmakeup
	Fashion	#streetstyle, #bikini
Self-Promotion	Promotional	#ad, #sponsored
	Brand	#maccosmetics, #reeboksg
	Blog	#beautyblogger, #wellnessblogger
	Trend	#ootd, #intagood
Fitness	Fitness	#instarunners, #fitnessmodel
	Spirituality	#yoga, #mindbodysoul
Wellness	Food	#foodporn, #youarewhatyoueat
	Emotion	#positivethinking, #selflove
	Wellness	#healthylifestyle, #thenewhealthy

related to fashion and cosmetics, which indicates Health Influencers' proclivity for sharing posts that promote their style and aesthetic, also raises concern. Well-known brands and products such as Mac ($N_{posts} = 1,086$) and Reebok ($N_{posts} = 1,010$) are prevalent hashtags, suggesting product promotion is central to health content on Instagram. As product promotion is common among Instagram Influencers in general [29], it undermines the role of Health Influencers as authorities on health and well-being. Contents mainly focused on Western Educated Industrial Rich and Democratic (WEIRD) representations and Western-beauty norms might be disproportionately represented of all Instagram users [18].

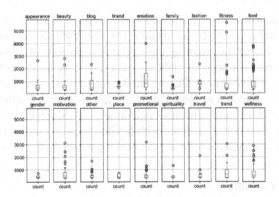

Fig. 1. Boxplots of number of posts containing each hashtag belonging to a semantic category

4   Topic Modeling Instagram Posts

We conducted unsupervised topic modeling to further analyze the posting behavior of Health Influencers. Additionally, we are interested in which lower-level topics may be presented within each of these four themes identified by the tagging behavior. To this end, we used the unsupervised topic modeling algorithm, latent Dirichlet allocation (LDA) [40], to assess which topics are most prevalent in the dataset.

4.1   Topic Modeling with LDA

LDA assigns documents (here, the description of a post on Instagram) to k predefined topics, where each topic is defined by a set of terms that best describe the documents in that topic. More generally, LDA assigns a k-length probability vector to each document where each element i represents the probability that the given document belongs to topic i. The probability values for a given document are determined by how many of topic k's "representative" terms appear in the document. We fitted our models with a Machine Learning for Language Toolkit (MALLET) wrapper of Gensim [41, 42] to the preprocessed post descriptions.

4.2   Preprocessing Text Descriptions

We preprocessed text descriptions using the Python package spaCy [43]. First, we lemmatized each word in the description and removed punctuation, whitespace, and stopwords. We kept terms whose part-of-speech was a noun, adjective, adverb, and verb. We then calculated term-frequency inverse-document frequency (TF-IDF) [44] representations of the bigrams and trigrams of each description. We used this final representation of the text descriptions to fit our topic models.

4.3   Topic Model Evaluation

Visual interpretations of a fitted topic model have been proposed to guide model selection [45]. Here, we used interactive visualization software [46] to interpret the fit of our topic model and to label the resulting topics (i.e., dimensions in a lower-dimensional embedding) with relevant semantic labels. Specifically, we used the Python package pyLDAvis [47], to transform our Gensim model into an interactive visualization [48] to guide model selection and assign labels to the learned topics. Furthermore, the final topic model reported the most semantically distinct, yet interpretable topics. However, other models (not reported) predefined with similar-but-different values of k returned similar topics, suggesting our results are not specific to the value of k we chose.

4.4   Topic Model Results

Our reported topic model showed the best results with nine topics (see Table 2). Topics and their associated keywords are in Table 2 and the proportion of the corpus categorized as each topic is shown in Fig. 2. Topic modeling revealed that Health Influencers post a mixture of content related to health and wellness as well as other — potentially problematic — topics. Specifically, topic modeling further expanded the results from the content analysis of hashtags suggesting Health Influencers post content varying along four main thematic dimensions: Cosmetics and Appearance, Self-promotion, Fitness, and General Wellness. Furthermore, the topic model provided greater detail into the semantic content of these broad themes as well as their coverage or frequency in the corpus. Both of these findings are discussed in more detail below.

First, topic modeling confirms that Health Influencers are prone to post promotional content: over one-third of the posts belong to a promotion-related topic. And while hashtag analysis indicated promotional content was common, the topic model shed further light on what types of promotional content is present in the corpus. Specifically, promotional content is composed of three distinct types of posts: promotion of the Influencer's online profile, their business and brand, and beauty products. These results are particularly informative given that some forms of promotion may be problematic. For instance, the promotion of certain fashion trends and styles, which are known to promote body dissatisfaction [48], may be inappropriate to develop positive body images of teen followers and requires intervention. Topic modeling also indicates content related to cosmetics is common among Health Influencers, confirming the finding that Cosmetics and Appearance is a common theme in health messages on Instagram.

While the majority (54.427%) of content pertains directly to health and wellbeing (e.g., Workout, Mental Health, and Physical Wellness), approximately one-third (36.021%) of content pertains to topics unrelated to health and likely to be harmful to some users (e.g., Business, Online Presence, and Beauty). Notably, the Beauty Promotion category has higher number of posts than other categories that are closely related to the primary definition of health (e.g., Physical Wellness and Mental Health). To examine this pattern, we hypothesized Health Influencers, who aim to increase online presence as the topic model reveals, are more likely to make promotional posts because promotional content receive higher audience engagement rate compared to non-promotional posts.

4.5 Audience Engagement by Topics

To examine the relationship between the promotional content and audience engagement metrics among posts of Health Influencers, we conducted t-tests to understand the differences in audience engagement (e.g., number of likes, views, and comments) between promotional and non-promotional content. The results show that compared to non-promotional posts (recipe, motivation, physical wellness, workout, mental health, or travel), promotional posts (business, online presence, or beauty) had significantly higher number of likes (313.54 more; $p < .001$), views (1515.2 more; $p < .001$), and comments (20.18 more; $p < .001$) on average. Figure 3 confirms higher audience engagement in promotional content of Health Influencers. This is particularly concerning given that promotion of certain styles is likely to promote body image distortion [49].

Table 2. Topics, associated keywords, and corresponding sample posts.

Topic Label		Keywords	Sample Post
Recipe		ingredient, oil, minute, egg, cheese, salt, bowl, pepper, tbsp	Anyone want desserts without feeling guilty? Here is the recipe for creamy vanilla cupcakes…
Motivation		change, thought, mind, dream, positive, power, opportunity	you can recover from anything. You can create yourself all over again. Nothing lasts forever
Physical Wellness		healthy, organic, clean, vitamin, energy, nutrient, natural	why is it important to stay hydrated? water is critical to our body…
Workout		fitness, exercise, training, muscle, gym, core, strength	who likes tabata workouts like I do?? exercise for 20 s and rest for the next 10 s
Mental Health (Spirituality)		love, happy, life, moment, heart, yoga, grateful, happiness	you have to love yourself because you matter. You are worth it. Then, give love to others around you
Travel		place, travel, world, local, nature, vacation, adventure	had to wake up early in the morning, took a train for more than 6 h to get here
Promotional	Business	link, code, order, box, www, event, brand, gift, free, page	*announcements* tomorrow night - birthday box sale!! we were sold out in 2 h last time…
	Online Presence	tag, post, comment, follow, share, picture, presentation	**giveaway alert** to enter the pool: follow me or tag a friend below…
	Beauty	pretty, hair, makeup, style, face, eye, ad, fashion, pink	spring is here!!! it's time to get ready for spring look…. Liquid eyeshadows, contour highlighter…

Note. Due to CrowndTangle's data confidentiality policy, we recreated sample posts that best capture the representative post for each topic

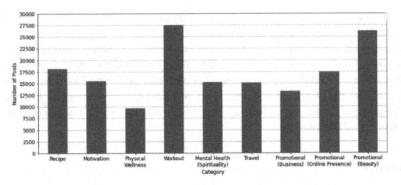

Fig. 2. Frequencies of posts belonging to each topic

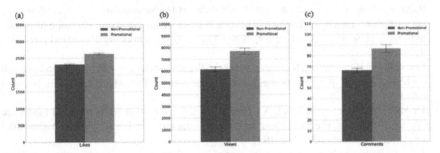

Fig. 3. Comparison in Audience Engagement Metrics in (a) likes, (b) views, and (c) comments.

5 Discussion

In this study, we performed a large-scale analysis of health-related content on Instagram. By focusing on content produced by Health Influencers, we took a first glimpse at how health and wellness are represented in millions of Instagram user's image feeds. The results suggest that a large portion of content produced by the Health Influencers has contained these factors, and covered these four themes: Cosmetics and Appearance, Self-promotion, Fitness, and General Wellness. While a topic model uncovered most posts belong to health-related topics, previous literature raise concern for certain aspects of health-related content, particularly those of fitness and recipe. For example, viewing fitspiration images leads to an increased level of body dissatisfaction [50, 51]. Similarly, fitness images containing a Health Influencer's bare chest can lead to lower body satisfaction in men [49]. Further, frequent exposure to curated food images stimulates unhealthy eating habits associated with obesity [52]. Further, we found higher audience engagement rate in promotional content than non-promotional content.

Higher rate of audience engagement may be related to a combination of reasons, such as material incentives to interact with the promotional posts (e.g., in exchange of free samples for posting comments), bias in health beliefs (e.g., associating active user participation with well-being [29]), and bias in algorithms leading to sustained biased promotion of certain content to the users. While Instagram reinforces user's existing belief through selective exposure of like-minded information [53], this algorithm-reinforced "filter bubble" could bias users who were initially motivated to engage with promotional posts by certain incentives (e.g., free sample) to continue to be exposed to the promotional posts. While this study is exploratory, it requires a closer investigation of how health is communicated by Health Influencers on Instagram. Future work should empirically establish the effects of different types of health-related content on (1) people's understanding of health and well-being and (2) the resulting real-life health effects from these conceptualizations.

References

1. Pew Research Center. https://www.pewresearch.org/internet/2018/05/31/teens-social-media-technology-2018/. Accessed 13 Mar 2023
2. Balta, S., Emirtekin, E., Kircaburun, K., Griffiths, M.D.: Neuroticism, trait fear of missing out, and phubbing: the mediating role of state fear of missing out and problematic Instagram use. Int. J. Ment. Heal. Addict. **18**(3), 628–639 (2018). https://doi.org/10.1007/s11469-018-9959-8
3. Feinstein, A., Hershenberg, R., Bhatia, V., et al.: Negative social comparison on Facebook and depressive symptoms: rumination as a mechanism. Psychol. Pop. Media Cult. **2**(3), 161–170 (2013)
4. JeriYabar, A., SanchezCarbonel, A., Tito, K., et al.: Association between social media use (Twitter, Instagram, Facebook) and depressive symptoms: are Twitter users at higher risk? Int. J. Soc. Psychiatry **65**(1), 14–19 (2019)
5. Nesi, J., Prinstein, M.J.: Using social media for social comparison and feedback-seeking: gender and popularity moderate associations with depressive symptoms. J. Abnorm. Child Psychol. **43**(8), 1427–1438 (2015). https://doi.org/10.1007/s10802-015-0020-0
6. Shensa, A., Escobar-Viera, G., Sidani, E., et al.: Problematic social media use and depressive symptoms among U.S. Young Adults: a nationally-representative study. Soc. Sci. Med. **182**, 150–157 (2017)
7. Frison, E., Eggermont, S.: Browsing, posting, and liking on Instagram: the reciprocal relationships between different types of Instagram use and adolescents' depressed mood. Cyberpsychol. Behav. Soc. Netw. **20**(10), 603–609 (2017)
8. Sherlock, M., Wagstaff, L.: Exploring the relationship between frequency of Instagram use, exposure to idealized images, and psychological well-being in women. Psychol. Pop. Media Cult. **8**(4), 482–490 (2019)
9. Tiggemann, M., Hayden, S., Brown, Z., et al.: The Effect of Instagram "Likes" on women's social comparison and body dissatisfaction. Body Image **26**, 90–97 (2018)
10. Fardouly, J., Willburger, K., Vartanian, R.: Instagram use and young women's body image concerns and self-objectification: testing mediational pathways. New Media Soc. **20**(4), 1380–1395 (2018)
11. Couture, B.C.: The looking glass selfie: Instagram use frequency predicts visual attention to high-anxiety body regions in young women. Comput. Hum. Behav. **108**, 106329 (2020)
12. Donnelly, E.: Depression among users of social networking sites (SNSs): the role of SNS addiction and increased usage. J. Addict. Prevent. Med. **02**(01) (2017)
13. Carrotte, R., Vella, M., Lim, S.: Predictors of "Liking" three types of health and fitness-related content on social media: a cross-sectional study. J. Med. Internet Res. **17**(8), e205 (2015)
14. Grabe, S., Ward, M., Hyde, S.: The role of the media in body image concerns among women: a meta-analysis of experimental and correlational studies. Psychol. Bull. **134**(3), 460–476 (2008)

15. Marengo, D., Longobardi, C., Fabris, A., et al.: Highly-visual social media and internalizing symptoms in adolescence: the mediating role of body image concerns. Comput. Hum. Behav. **82**, 63–69 (2018)

16. Marcella-Hood, M.: Instagram versus reality: the design and use of self-curated photo elicitation in a study exploring the construction of Scottish identity amongst personal style influencers on Instagram. Qual. Res. **21**(6), 865–889 (2020)

17. Yang, J., Hauff, C., Houben, G.-J., Bolivar, C.T.: Diversity in urban social media analytics. In: Bozzon, A., Cudre-Maroux, P., Pautasso, C. (eds.) Web Engineering. LNCS, vol. 9671, pp. 335–353. Springer, Cham (2016). https://doi.org/10.1007/978-3-319-38791-8_19

18. Brandt, J., Buckingham, K., Buntain, C., et al.: Identifying social media user demographics and topic diversity with computational social science: a case study of a major international policy forum. J. Comput. Soc. Sci. **3**(1), 167–188 (2020)

19. Hendrickse, J., Arpan, M., Clayton, B., et al.: Instagram and college women's body image: investigating the roles of appearance-related comparisons and intrasexual competition. Comput. Hum. Behav. **74**, 92–100 (2017)

20. Anixiadis, F., Wertheim, H., Rodgers, R., et al.: Effects of thin-ideal Instagram Images: the roles of appearance comparisons, internalization of the thin ideal and critical media processing. Body Image **31**, 181–190 (2019)

21. Feltman, E., Szymanski, M.: Instagram use and self-objectification: the roles of internalization, comparison, appearance commentary, and feminism. Sex Roles **78**(5–6), 311–324 (2018)

22. Benton, C., Karazsia, T.: The effect of thin and muscular images on women's body satisfaction. Body Image **13**, 22–27 (2015)

23. Cattarin, A., Thompson, K., Thomas, C., et al.: Body image, mood, and televised images of attractiveness: the role of social comparison. J. Soc. Clin. Psychol. **19**(2), 220–239 (2000)

24. Tiggemann, M.: Media exposure, body dissatisfaction and disordered eating: television and magazines are not the same! Eur. Eating Disorders Rev. Prof. J. Eating Disorders Assoc. **11**(5), 418–430 (2003)

25. Tiggemann, M., McGill, B.: The role of social comparison in the effect of magazine advertisements on women's mood and body dissatisfaction. J. Soc. Clin. Psychol. **23**(1), 23–44 (2004)

26. Agliata, D., TantleffDunn, S.: The impact of media exposure on males' body image. J. Soc. Clin. Psychol. **23**(1), 7–22 (2004)

27. Safarnejad, L., Xu, Q., Ge, Y., et al.: Contrasting misinformation and real-information dissemination network structures on social media during a health emergency. Am. J. Public Health **110**(S3), S340–S347 (2020)

28. Turner, G., Lefevre, E.: Instagram use is linked to increased symptoms of Orthorexia Nervosa. Eating Weight Disorders-Stud. Anorexia Bulimia Obes. **22**(2), 277–284 (2017)

29. Pilgrim, K., Bohnet-Joschko, S.: Selling health and happiness how influencers communicate on Instagram about dieting and exercise: mixed methods research. BMC Publ. Health **19**(1), 1054 (2019)

30. CrowdTangle. https://apps.crowdtangle.com/chrome-extension. Accessed 13 Mar 2023

31. Figshare. https://figshare.com/s/8b998ebe87eebb733860. Accessed 13 Mar 2023

32. Influence.co. https://influence.co/category/health. Accessed 13 Mar 2023

33. Boerman, C.: The effects of the standardized Instagram disclosure for micro- and meso-influencers. Comput. Hum. Behav. **103**, 199–207 (2020)

34. Figshare, https://figshare.com/s/25e5b0e91230fc40424d. Accessed 13 Mar 2023

35. Hosseini, H., Xiao, B., Jaiswal, M., et al.: On the limitation of convolutional neural networks in recognizing negative images. In: 2017 16th IEEE International Conference on Machine Learning and Applications (ICMLA), pp. 352–358. IEEE, Cancun, Mexico (2017)

36. Carrotte, R., Prichard, I., Lim, C.: "Fitspiration" on social media: a content analysis of gendered images. J. Med. Internet Res. **19**(3), e95 (2017)
37. Nazir, F., Ghazanfar, A., Maqsood, M., et al.: Social media signal detection using tweets volume, hashtag, and sentiment analysis. Multimed. Tools Appl. **78**(3), 3553–3586 (2019)
38. Argyrou, A., Giannoulakis, S., Tsapatsoulis, N.: Topic modelling on Instagram hashtags: an alternative way to automatic image annotation? In: 2018 13th International Workshop on Semantic and Social Media Adaptation and Personalization (SMAP), pp. 61–67. IEEE, Zaragoza (2018)
39. Abidin, C.: Aren't These Just Young, Rich Women Doing Vain Things Online? Influencer selfies as subversive frivolity. Soc. Med. +Soc. **2**(2), 205630511664134 (2016)
40. Blei, M.: Latent Dirichlet allocation. J. Mach. Learn. Res. **3**, 993–1022 (2003)
41. McCallum, K.: https://mimno.github.io/Mallet/index. Accessed 13 Mar 2023
42. Rehurek, R., Sojka, P.: Software framework for topic modelling with large corpora. In: Proceedings of the LREC 2010 Workshop on New Challenges for NLP Frameworks, pp. 46–50. University of Malta, Valletta, Malta (2010)
43. Honnibal, M., Montani, I.: spaCy 2: natural language understanding with Bloom embeddings, convolutional neural networks and incremental parsing (2017)
44. Aizawa, A.: An Information-theoretic perspective of TF–IDF measures q. Inf. Process. Manage. **21** (2003)
45. Chaney, B., Blei, M.: Visualizing topic models. In: Proceedings of the International AAAI Conference on Web and Social Media Association for the Advancement of Artificial Intelligence: pp. 419–422. AAAI, Dublin, Ireland (2012)
46. Sievert, C., Shirley, K.: LDAvis: a method for visualizing and interpreting topics. In: Proceedings of the Workshop on Interactive Language Learning, Visualization, and Interfaces, pp. 63–70. Association for Computational Linguistics, Baltimore, Maryland, USA (2014)
47. GitHub. https://github.com/bmabey/pyLDAvis. Accessed 13 Mar 2023
48. Figshare. https://figshare.com/s/f81fb94c038098dc12e0. Accessed 13 Mar 2023
49. Tiggemann, M., Anderberg, I.: Muscles and bare chests on Instagram: the effect of influencers' fashion and fitspiration images on men's body image. Body Image **35**, 237–244 (2020)
50. Prichard, I., Kavanagh, E., Mulgrew, E., et al.: The effect of Instagram #fitspiration images on young women's mood, body image, and exercise behaviour. Body Image **33**, 1–6 (2020)
51. Tiggemann, M., Zaccardo, M.: "Exercise to Be Fit, Not Skinny": the effect of fitspiration imagery on women's body image. Body Image **15**, 61–67 (2015)
52. Passamonti, L., Rowe, B., Schwarzbauer, C., et al.: Personality predicts the brain's response to viewing appetizing foods: the neural basis of a risk factor for overeating. J. Neurosci. **29**(1), 43–51 (2009)
53. Pariser, E.: The Filter Bubble: How the New Personalized Web Is Changing What We Read and How We Think. Penguin Books, London (2012)

Media Framing: An Analysis of the News on the Disaster of Football Riots in Indonesia

Puteri Cahya Safitriningati[✉], Erwan Sudiwijaya, Aly Aulia, and Fajar Junaedi

Department of Communication Studies, Faculty of Social and Politics, University of Muhammadiyah Yogyakarta, Yogyakarta, Indonesia
puterinevadaa07@gmail.com

Abstract. This study analyzes how the online media Detik and CNN Indonesia frame the Kanjuruhan tragedy according to their perspectives. The method used in this study is a qualitative method with a framing approach and uses the Nvivo 12 Plus software with chart analysis and word cloud features to analyze the data. Online media portals take sides in framing the media according to their views. Online media portals organize narratives in media content to trigger arguments that develop in society. This research shows that the two media portals have different framing related to the Kanjuruhan tragedy. Detik's structure is more on the point of view of how this event could have happened. At the same time, CNN Indonesia's frame is more aligned with the response from the institution responsible for football matches.

Keywords: Framing Analysis · Online Media · Football Riots · Indonesia

1 Introduction

Football is widely recognized as a competitive sport, so rivalries between football clubs are common. Numerous arguments and rivalries were discovered to have resulted in violence, as reported by victims; often, this violence was perpetrated by supporters and football club supporters against their opponents off the field; this violence constituted football hooliganism [1]. Team supporters, also known as supporters, will be present at every game to show their pride in the club. There are a variety of characters owned by supporters, one of which is a passionate supporter who can become a good friend when the team performs well and the worst enemy when they do not [2].

The incident at Malang's Kanjuruhan Stadium, which resulted in 754 casualties and 132 deaths, became one of the most significant events [3]. The tragedy of Kanjuruhan has captured the attention of the greater community. This is because numerous media outlets report it [4]. The news published in the media regarding the Kanjuruhan tragedy has influenced people's perceptions of football. The online media portals in the making news still take sides and corner one party, the online media portals organize published stories to spark growing arguments in society; the media coverage of the Kanjuruhan tragedy has influenced the public's perceptions of football. Numerous online media sources continue to take sides and isolate one party, online news portals organize published

C. Stephanidis et al. (Eds.): HCII 2023, CCIS 1835, pp. 21–27, 2023.
https://doi.org/10.1007/978-3-031-36001-5_3

stories to stimulate societal debate. In reporting emergencies, the media or newspapers should emphasize palliative rather than fear and death frames; the reader will become anxious if fear or death remains prominent in the news. Through the narratives or stories displayed, the media also construct information with varying levels of risk, come under the media also construct a perception of local and global risks [5].

According to previous research conducted by Nasario [6] shows the media, coverage is currently for public consumption, and if the online media reports news that is one-sided, it will cause unrest in society, such as between the supporters of the football clubs Persija and Persib, who have had a longstanding rivalry. Unlike previous research, [7] investigates how fanaticism affects behaviour. 21.1% aggressive behaviour. More adolescent supporters with high fanaticism (61%) and aggression (58%), with no correlation between gender, education, or favourite club and aggression. Research from Junaedi [8] explains that Ultras football fans attract a great deal of attention through choreographed and trained Ultras performances instead of merely being fans, Widyastuti [9] has discussed the role of media in disaster communication, and the presence of new media can serve as a framework for disaster communication in Indonesia. This research employs the media to mitigate a disaster's negative adverse effects and serve as an information hub for disasters. The research conducted by Prastya [10] revealed how the media provides information to PSS Sleman fans and readers, this research's subject is football fans' loyalty to their favourite team.

Based on prior research, emphazed is on how the media becomes a source of public consumption and information when disseminating news about disasters. Furthermore this study categorizes football fans' forms and types based on fanaticism percentages in supporting their favourite team. However, there currently needs to be research that exhaustively explains how the media frames the football tragedy. Therefore, the gap of this study focuses on how the tragedy at the Malang Kanjuruhan stadium was framed in online media. Consequently, is study aims to explain CNNIndonesia and Detik's framing of news about the Malang Kanjuruhan Stadium tragedy.

2   Theoretical Framework: Framing Media Online and Football Disaster

Framing is how individuals develop a specific conceptualization of a problem or redirect their thinking about it [11]; the frame enables the reader to be aware of the direction of the discussion and to concentrate on the issues and interests conveyed by the media. As part of society's efforts to communicate effectively about changing media frames, it is crucial to study the relationship between framing and media [12]. The media is essential in disseminating news that can be framed exaggeratedly. Furthermore, the media is crucial in describing an event [13]. The press has a non-regulatory role in education and training, providing only information services that are available and accessible to readers based on their interests. Online media platforms offer the public a constant flow of information and play a crucial role in disseminating news reports [14].

Disasters in football are analyzed to reveal the social, economic, and organizational tensions, political structures, and cultural practices that exist in various societies and football cultures around the globe [15]; the Kanjuruhan tragedy in the stadium exemplifies the risk of accidents and the concern for the safety of spectators in such circumstances. Supporters show various behaviour patterns in defending their favourite team, such as singing throughout the game and following every game out of town. It is common for supporters to mobilize tens, hundreds, or even thousands of individuals to support their team. This support typically results in extreme fanaticism and can lead to an overbearing attitude toward individual supporters. Alcohol can affect the behaviour, attitudes, and actions of fans watching the match, so many police in security will also prevent violence during games. Still, research shows that if this is excessive, aggressive policing can trigger fan violence [16].

3   Research Method

This study uses a qualitative method with a framing analysis approach to analyze how online media frames the Kanjuruhan events published in the news. This study employs the software NVIVO 12 Plus for data analysis. The data sources for this research are the online media Detik and CNN Indonesia and relevant journal articles. From October 2022 until November 2022, data will be collected from online media. This is because the Kanjuruhan tragedy was being discussed at the time by all elements, including the online media, each from their perspective. This study will compare the two online media and analyze how the two media frame the Kanjuruhan tragedy.

4   Result and Discussion

4.1   Framing Content Analysis of Kanjuruhan Stadium Tragedy

The data in Fig. 1 depicts the framing content on Detik and CNN Indonesia regarding the Kanjuruhan tragedy. Detik and CNN Indonesia are online media outlets that provide literacy services in the form of current news of various types, including disaster news. The framing content distributed by Detik and CNN Indonesia includes the terms "Witness," "Victim," "Police Action," and "Indonesian Football Association Response." From the perspective of the Indonesian Football Association Response, the content displayed by CNN Indonesia is more dominant, with a percentage of 50%.

. The witness and police action framing content distributed by the online media Detik is an example of a concentrated effort to raise the Kanjuruhan issue from a factual standpoint at the time of the incident. A witness or witness is a person who provides information about events or incidents for criminal investigation, prosecution, and trial [17]. The content of Detik appears superior in framing "witness" to demonstrate that an incident cannot be separated from the existence of witnesses who will serve as a source of information for determining who is responsible for the Kanjuruhan tragedy. The second framing category developed by Detik is from the perspective of the police with the efforts that had been made in handling the masses at that time through their actions, which the community viewed as having taken repressive actions; "the police's handling of the masses was frequently viewed as going too far." According to Detik, the use of tear gas at each stand deprived many spectators of oxygen and threw the situation into chaos. The media uses framing as a discourse tool to uncover interpretations, which

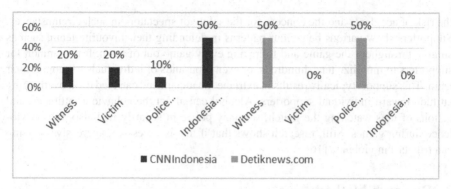

Fig.1. Content Category Framing Reporting on the Kanjuruhan Tragedy

assumes that the media displays news and meanings designed to influence how news content is interpreted and understood [18].

In contrast to the content published by CNN Indonesia, the response of Indonesian football association institutions is dominated by a 50% news presentation. The Framed by CNN highlight how Indonesian Football Association to be watch football tragedy in Kanjuruhan [19]. Figure 1 reveals that CNN Indonesia predominately frames the response of those with authority and responsibility for the match. Therefore, framing content analysis is a cognitive activity designed to describe, differentiate, and describe a media assumption that displays news containing facts, figures, and data. In the current digital era, online media is one of the informational platforms for society, and the existence of media influences the community's assessment of a case [20]. In the context of the Kanjuruhan tragedy, framing enables the reader to understand the direction of discussion, the focal point of the issues the media takes, and the interests it brings [14]. This pertains to how the media frames news stories from a biased perspective.

4.2 Framing Narrative Analysis of Kanjuruhan Stadium Tragedy

The use of technology in information dissemination efforts is currently crucial. Media narratives can be analyzed to determine the impact of social media on disseminating information. In their efforts to disseminate information about the Kanjuruhan tragedy, narrative analysis on the online news platforms Detik and CNNIndonesia share similarities. Detik and CNN Indonesia presented news narratives that elevated the categories of "witnesses," "association institutions," and "police action" concerning the football federation president.

Figure 2 depicts the results of a Word Cloud analysis of the two Indonesian online news sites, Detik and CNN Indonesia. According to the results of the preceding analysis, it consistently discusses narratives about Kanjuruhan's "witnesses." According to the data generated by Word Cloud, the narratives presented by Detik and CNN Indonesia tend to be dominated by "witnesses" Detik and CNN Indonesia published Suprapti, who claiming that many fans were already drunk before the riot. Still, Suprapti later apologized to Aremania, and the slandered deceased was a hoax [21]. The family referred to in this introductory paragraph was a victim of the Kanjuruhan tragedy, as evidenced

Fig. 2. Narrative of Kanjuruhan Tragedy Framing

by testimony published by Detik media regarding Emilia, who lost her husband and child in the Kanjuruhan tragedy. The supporters in question are Aremania supporters who watched the match of their pride team as witnesses and victims in the Kanjuruhan tragedy. When tear gas was fired into the field, followed by the stands, the fans interpreted throwing shoes as a sign that the supporters could not withstand the tear gas [22]. From the three data, Word Cloud concludes that framing narratives to witnesses needs to be confirmed by the public, and the truth is known. It describes how the incident occurred based on the testimonies of the victims who experienced the tragedy and the supporters who attended the match to watch their favourite team play [23].

The second category is the association institution accountable for the Kanjuruhan tragedy match. CNN Indonesia's online media frames the association as the individual responsible for every football match. The analysis results above pertain to the terms "PSSI" and "Iwan." PSSI is the Indonesian football association, or the Indonesian Football Association, which organizes all football sports in Indonesia [24]. PSSI and Iriawan/commonly known as Iwan Bule, have a connection, with Iwan serving as chairman of the Indonesian football association [25]. Iwan was mentioned in online media, CNN Indonesia and Detik, evading journalists after being questioned by Komnas HAM, and he was under pressure to resign his position [26]. PSSI should be able to regulate football in Indonesia and transform the sport so that safety, security, and comfort are prioritized.

The third category consists of police actions that garner public attention due to their actions in securing sporting events. Both online sources present a narrative in which "gas" appears in the Word Cloud, the gas in the introductory narrative is tear gas fired by security forces acting as a security agency during a soccer game. CNN Indonesia's framing narrative for the Kanjuruhan tragedy indicates that the institution should also be held accountable, this demonstrates that the abovementioned theory posits that police officers who are aggressively involved in securing matches can cause fan violence [16].

5 Conclusion

This study concludes that Detik and CNN Indonesia's framing of the Kanjuruhan Tragedy can influence the perspective of Indonesian readers. The two online news sources each publish news with a distinct emphasis. Detik framing is dominant for witness content and Police Action, whereas CNN Indonesia's framing is dominant for how the institutions of the Indonesian football association responded to this incident. In addition, CNN Indonesia and Detik disseminate framing narratives based on witnesses, police actions, and associations to sway public opinion. This research has a limitation because it only compares two online media, so the data obtained is still limited. Future researchers should therefore be able to utilize three online news media to get a broader perspective of news framing and a more comprehensive data comparison.

References

1. Ziaul, M.: The roots of violence in the rivalry between football club fans and supporters using the ABC triangle theory of galtung conflict. TEMALI: Jurnal Pembangunan Sosial **5**(2), 125–132 (2022)
2. Bilgiç, B., et al.: Functional neural substrates of football fanaticism: different pattern of brain responses and connectivity in fanatics. Psychiatry Clin. Neurosci. **74**(9), 480–487 (2020)
3. CNNIndonesia, Total Korban Tragedi Kanjuruhan Jadi 754 Orang, 132 di Antaranya Tewas (2022)
4. Putra, D.: Tujuh Tragedi Sepak Bola Dunia Paling Mematikan di Dunia, Indonesia Urutan Kedua (2022)
5. Lanang, I.G., Kharisma, A.: Framing analysis of the Kompas COVID-19 Coverage : January 2020 Edition Analisis Framing Pemberitaan COVID-19 pada Koran Kompas : Edisi Januari 2020, **5**(2), 219–231 (2020)
6. Nasario Wahyu Handoko, J.: Pembingkaian Rivalitas Persija Vs Persib (Analisis Framing Zhongdang Pan Dan Gerald M. Kosicky Di Media Online Bolasport.Com Pra-Pasca Pandemi Covid-19) (2021)
7. Aziz, H., Sitasari, N.W.: Suporter remaja sepak bola: Fanatisme mempengaruhi perilaku agresi ? JCA Psikol. **3**(1), 82–91 (2022)
8. Fuller, A., Junaedi, F.: Ultras in Indonesia: conflict, diversification, activism. Sport Soc. **21**(6), 919–931 (2018)
9. Widyastuti, D.A.R.: Using new media and social media in disaster communication. Komunikator **13**(2), 100–111 (2021)
10. Prastya, N.M.: The fan use of Football club official media (Descriptive Study of The Use of PS Sleman Official Media), Komunikator, vol. 12, no. 1, 2020
11. Chong, D., Druckman, J.N.: Framing theory. Annu. Rev. Polit. Sci. **10**, 103–126 (2007)
12. Molder, A.L., Lakind, A., Clemmons, Z.E., Chen, K.: Framing the global youth climate movement: a qualitative content analysis of Greta 'Thunberg's moral, hopeful, and motivational framing on Instagram. Int. J. Press. **27**(3), 668–695 (2022)
13. Tierney, K., Bevc, C., Kuligowski, E.: Metaphors matter: disaster myths, media frames, and their consequences in hurricane Katrina. Ann. Am. Acad. Pol. Soc. Sci. **604**(1), 57–81 (2006)
14. Selviani, T.M., Sunarto, S., Sunarto, S.: News framing analysis about sexual harassment on men in the work environment KPI on online media (detik.com and tribunnews.com). Budapest Int. Res. Critics Inst. Humanit. Soc. Sci. **5**(1), 7389–7400 (2022)
15. Darby, P., Johnes, M., Mellor, G.: Football disasters: a conceptual frame. Soccer Soc. **5**(2), 125–133 (2004)
16. Ostrowsky, M.K.: Sports fans, alcohol use, and violent behavior: a sociological review. Trauma, Violence, Abus. **19**(4), 406–419 (2018)
17. Harruma, I.: Kriteria Saksi dalam Perkara Pidana (2022)
18. Rahman, T.: Contextualizing jihad and mainstream Muslim identity in Indonesia: the case of Republika online. Asian J. Commun. **27**(4), 378–395 (2017)
19. Kumparan, "Induk Organisasi Sepak Bola Nasional adalah PSSI, Ini Sejarahnya (2022)

20. Susanti, E., Septrisulviani, R.: Analisis Kualitas Layanan Portal Media Online KOta Jogja.com Terhadap Pengguna Akhir Menggunakan Metode Webqual 4.0. J. Gaung Inform. **11**(2), 136–150 (2018)
21. Novelino, A.: Sosok 'Penjual Dawet' Kanjuruhan Muncul, Minta Maaf ke Keluarga Korban (2022)
22. CNNIndonesia, Komnas HAM: Gas Air Mata Pemicu Banyak Korban di Kanjuruhan (2022)
23. Assyaumin, M.I.B., Yunus, M., Raharjo, S.: Fanatisme Suporter Sepakbola Ditinjau Dari Aspek Sosio-Antropologis (Studi Kasus Aremania Malang). J. Sport Sci. **7**(1), 42–57 (2017)
24. PSSI, "PSSI SEJARAH, (2018)
25. Hamrun, T.: Profil dan Biodata Mochamad Iriawan atau Iwan Bule, Lengkap, Kelahiran, Pendidikan Hingga Sebagai Ketua PSSI (2022)
26. Budi, M.: Iwan Bule soal Desakan Mundur Usai Tragedi Kanjuruhan: Nanti Ada Jubir (2022)

Digital Ethnography in Mixed Reality (MR) Communities: Searching New Usage Scenarios

Hanah Correa(✉) ⓘ, Yuri Inhamuns ⓘ, Marcos Silbermann ⓘ, Lucas Almeida ⓘ,
and Janderson Viana ⓘ

Sidia Instituto de Ciência e Tecnologia, Manaus, AM 69055-035, Brazil
hanah.santos@sidia.com

Abstract. This article aims to present the results of digital ethnographic research we conducted within the XR communities, seeking to understand what are the main pains of users of extended reality today, how they see this technology on the rise, and what perceptions they have about the future of the XR.

From what we were able to analyze from the data collected in the digital ethnography, we were able to understand that XR technology is constantly evolving, but that it may soon reach a more accessible level within the market.

The XR is a great revolutionary promise within several scenarios such as education, health, industry, entertainment, and social, but the current XR technologies have different factors that still need to evolve, from their immature UX within their applications to the strong deficit in their Form Factor. For these reasons they end up hindering the constant use of this technology by users in their daily routines, leaving them to use these devices only in specific activities that don't require much effort. All these factors make the mass adoption of this technology slower.

Keywords: extended reality · virtual reality · augmented reality · communities XR · user research · user interview · technology adoption

1 Introduction

This research was born from a discussion shared by different projects in our research and development center called Sidia and located in the city of Manaus, Brazil. We are interested in producing useful knowledge for all projects involved in exploring experiences using mixed reality (XR) technologies. This paper is the result of a survey on views, values, and frustrations of end users of XR devices, and especially their use in productivity use scenarios. It builds a portrait of the users' view on the recent developments of mixed reality technologies, which aims to map important opportunities for the different projects of our institute that have been exploring this type of user experience.

Admittedly, large companies like Meta have presented as a business strategy the attempt to broaden the horizon of the use of mixed reality devices for productivity use scenarios. Offering their potential consumers applications that allow them to perform daily work tasks such as attending meetings and editing documents. Despite being a new

C. Stephanidis et al. (Eds.): HCII 2023, CCIS 1835, pp. 28–38, 2023.
https://doi.org/10.1007/978-3-031-36001-5_4

technology, XR promises to positively impact several areas such as Education, healthcare, industry, entertainment, and social. Furthermore, six possible categories have been identified for XR if adopted in the organizational environment: expected cost-benefit of XR technology, technology readiness, organizational readiness, security, environment-external pressure, and corporate climate (Chuah, 2018). In this sense, this article proposes to present from the results of ethnographic research in digital media with users of XR technologies, a mapping of their perceptions about the current releases of devices and new features recently presented by major manufacturers.

However, it is important to note that the proposition of a survey of XR users and specialists is challenging due to the difficulties in conducting user recruitment. In particular two important contextual aspects related to the market development itself for this type of technology and some geographical issues. First, the current expansion of the XR consumer market does not yet represent the consolidation of the market and the diversification of the consumer profile. Particularly, in our case, as a Brazilian research center, in our country this consumer market is even smaller, where the few users of these technologies find it difficult to acquire devices due to the high cost of purchase and import. Considering these factors related to the difficulty of recruiting participants for our user research, we defined as a research strategy the realization of an ethnography in digital media to observe discussions among users, as well as the formation of communities of users interested in sharing information and knowledge about this type of technology.

We believe that this was the best methodological strategy for us to solve these challenges related to forming a relevant sample of XR technologies users, in addition to allowing for primary data collection, participant observation allowed us to recruit users to be interviewed by our research team. Among our primary research interests were the use of HMDs in productivity scenarios, the knowledge and values attributed by users to experiences using the Passthrough feature, and their views on the development and application horizon of this everyday consumer.

This article presents the results of this research and is structured in three parts: research methodology, where we present and justify the choice of our research tools. Development of the fieldwork, in which we briefly discuss some references in the area and focus mainly on the details of ethnography in digital media, describing the process of data collection and analysis. Finally, we present the results of our research structured in two main axes of findings about the experiences of using XR devices in productivity scenarios: the notion shared by users that the UX of XR productivity applications is still immature, presenting many friction points and usability problems. As well as the users' view on advances and limitations related to the form factor of the devices, another factor hindering the adoption of HMDs into users' work routines. In the conclusion, we propose a critical reflection based on our findings, which we consider fundamental to form this portrait of the users' expectations and visions about the future of these technologies.

2 Research Methodology

We defined a qualitative approach composed of two research tools: digital ethnography and user interviews. The starting point for defining the ethnographic approach of the research is the verification of the existence of communities and other discussion forums about XR technologies on social media so that social media such as Facebook, LinkedIn, and Twitter are the place to start our ethnographic experience. In the construction of these communities and in discussions we find how these users produce knowledge about the use of HMDs, it is in social media that early adopters and experts on the subject produce definitions, discuss values, and spread knowledge about XR technologies and their development soon.

2.1 Digital Ethnography

Ethnography is an important tool and very well used mainly in the study area of Anthropology in field research. However, searching for users of XR technologies is a challenge due to two points: the lack of a consolidated market for these technologies and, especially, the scarcity of users in Brazil. In this sense, recruiting people with experience and knowledge about the use of this type of device is a challenge that our team continuously faces. The choice to conduct an ethnography in digital media (HINE, 2004), (HINE, 2015) and (SEGATA, 2016) is the strategy we found to access these users and observe how they produce knowledge and express their opinions about XR technologies. The following quote demonstrates how Hine (2015) reinforces how ethnography is an interesting tool for us to describe and understand in a complex and "multifaceted way "the ways people adopt and relate to new technologies.

"It is also very well suited to giving us a critical stance on over-generalized assumptions about the impact of new technologies. Taking a multi-faceted view, as ethnographers do, and focusing on how lives are lived, how technologies are adopted and adapted to our lives, and how social structures are made seems a promising way to capture what is distinctive about our contemporary way of life, and what is enduring about the challenges we face, and our means of coping with them." (HINE, 2015).

2.2 In-depth Interview

To deepen our knowledge on specific topics such as Productivity and Passthrough, but also the focus on users' lived experiences, we recruited eight people identified through our insertion in communities and debates about XR held on social media. These users were interviewed, and in our recruitment, we got an important variation between Brazilian and foreign users, coming from countries like Norway, Italy, and the United States. Each of these people had different levels of involvement and knowledge about XR technologies, as well as different consumer profiles, while some were professionals working in companies that develop or use HMDs, others fit the consumer and end-user profile. This phase was extremely important so that we could know the context in which these users were inserted and what were their insights regarding the use of XR in productivity scenarios, Passthrough use, and projections about the future of technology.

The sessions were conducted virtually with a duration of about 45 min. In our setup, one researcher played the role of interviewing the guest and two other researchers observed and took notes on a virtual board. At the end of each session, we held short 15-min Debriefing meetings to discuss the main insights identified during the interview.

3 Research Development

3.1 Literature Review

When we set out to research Emerging Technologies, such as Mixed Reality, we immediately identify a context full of controversies, in which actors such as companies, users, and developers seek to define the main concepts and ways of using these technologies. Some concepts from interdisciplinary areas of knowledge, such as the social studies of science and technology, helped circumscribe the object of our research by highlighting these fundamental aspects of emerging technology platforms: they are a constant object of discussion and controversy, and the ongoing attempt by companies and experts to establish almost definitively what this new technology platform is for. Conducting digital ethnography was a way for us to map and interpret these controversies set up in the social media environment.

Among the concepts that inspired our going to the field, as previously stated, they helped us to circumscribe the objects to be observed. First, Sociotechnical Controversies, just as the mixed reality directed to final consumers is in its historical moment of emergence, both scientific concepts and major technological systems are controversial objects. Authors such as Latour (1994) and Hughes et al. (2012) show how these moments are important for us to understand how their establishment does not work linearly, highlighting the historical and cultural aspects, on which their development depends. These authors signalize a context of complex emergence, in which the understanding of the development of a given technological platform cannot be told only from the technology itself. Researchers must understand the social, historical, and cultural aspects of this emergence.

These already classic concepts in the field of social studies of science and technology established the theoretical-methodological perspective from which we built our research in the digital field. Our focus became how, amid discussions and controversies, users of XR technologies try to define concepts and ways of using XR technology. Amid discussions and exchange of information about how to use the devices, we found condensed in the users' points of view their ways of understanding the technology, its main values, and problematic points.

3.2 Defining the Studied Platforms

Our focus was to map knowledge and information spaces about XR technology through the users' view, we identified six platforms that concentrated relevant discussions to the research: Twitter, Facebook, LinkedIn, Discord, Reddit, and Youtube. In defining these social media we relied on the support of a privileged informant who was knowledgeable about the places where questions about XR technology were discussed. In addition, we also mapped institutionalized communities, i.e., official XR communities in the country, such as XRBR. We were then able to find users, influencers, and experts in the area through Digital Ethnography in these networks.

3.3 Cataloging the Discussions

We created professional profiles on social media to reach the users that would be recruited later. Before we began cataloging the posts and discussions, we raised a series of questions to use in searching for and selecting content pertinent to our topics of interest. These questions helped us get a broad view of the knowledge discussed on the platforms, expanding our understanding of how concepts and understandings about XR technology are constructed in these dialogues:

- What are the main types of content published by the participants of these social media?
- What is the context of the making and development of these conversations?
- What are the main issues discussed?
- What are the main user profiles found in these communities?
- How is the Passthrough (VST) topic presented and discussed on the platforms?
- How is the topic of Productivity presented and discussed in the platform?

We understand that among the social media mapped some could concentrate a higher and better-structured level of knowledge than others because they already have numerous and consolidated communities. As would be the case of Youtube and Facebook where several users provide discussions and forums with considerable production of visual material and posts of great reach. For this reason, at an early stage, we decided to focus our efforts on YouTube and Facebook instead of other social media such as Instagram and Discord. Although these concentrate on knowledge and information about the field, they play a secondary role of influence within the XR industry due to the way discussions are structured on the platform and the number of people involved.

In the course of the research, we went on to study two other platforms, Twitter and LinkedIn. In each of these platforms, we sought to identify groups and communities with greater relevance defined by the volume of posts and their reach. When we came across discussions and posts with relevant topics we registered the screenshots and links of the pages in a database for later analysis.

3.4 Database Organization

To facilitate the analysis process we created a consistent database where we stored links and screenshots of posts from the explored social media We carried out a continuous process of improving and adding to the repository for each content studied. The categorization of the database worked as follows, we created folders for each of the platforms, with subfolders to organize the type of content identified while reading the forums, for example, one subfolder could be called Passthrough and another Productivity. We added to the subfolders the prints and links of that content that helped us to quickly access the shared knowledge (Figs. 1 and 2).

Fig. 1. Exemplary folder structure for Digital Ethnography platforms (Author's Compilation, 2023)

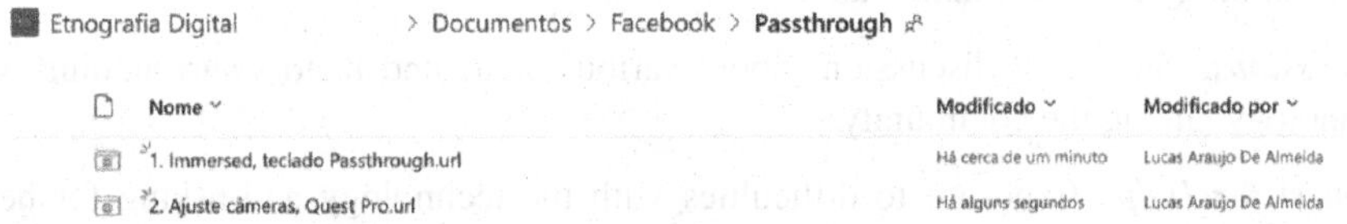

Fig. 2. Exemplary subfolder structure with Digital Ethnography themes and content (Author's Compilation, 2023)

3.5 Data Analysis

First Sights in the Field: Identifying Types of Content and Understanding Differences Between Platforms. We focused on the analysis of material collected from the three platforms with the highest volume of content production on the theme: Twitter, Facebook, and LinkedIn. They are responsible for concentrating on a wide variety of concepts, discussions, and opinions of users and professionals in the area. With this we started a general reading of the content, analyzing it by theme, for example, we tried to analyze all the content generated about Passthrough through all three platforms and so on. In this way, we consolidated our ideas and insights about a theme and could merge or compare the opinions that were formed on each platform, by different users' views. By analyzing the content shared on different applications we could see similarities and disparities, but many of the themes had topics in common.

In many moments the analyzed contents converge on the same topic or demonstrate opinions that talk to each other. However, because they are content from different platforms, the tone of the conversation could be more formal or informal. Initially, we categorized the posts on social media into the five most recurrent types that structured the dialog between users:

Tips, Doubts, and Pain Points. Tips for using the device or apps. Sharing pain points and other factors that have generated user dissatisfaction.

Reviews, News, and Curiosities About the Area. Product indications and reviews. Exposure to curiosities about XR technology and sharing of news and novelties in the area.

Promotion of a Product/Service and Sales. Promotion of products and services around XR technology and information about their sale.

Discussions. Survey of discussions about various areas and factors surrounding XR technology among the community.

Request for Help. Exposure to difficulties with the technology and asking for help afterward. The community is used to sharing its experiences and helping.

Platforms in Focus. By focusing the analysis on the content generated on Twitter, Facebook, and Linkedin we noticed the particularities and differences in the way knowledge about XR is produced on each of these platforms. Privileging differences in content that are related, generally, to authority arguments and definitions on topics about the technology used and its development, content aimed at establishing controversies and critics. Some people produce materials and products for XR, while others consume exclusively. There are different degrees of knowledge about the technologies and the device, as well as immersion and involvement regarding the applications created for XR. In the following we will briefly discuss these points encountered:

Twitter. In this social network, there are no specific XR groups. Everyone informally produces his content, bringing questions, positions, and news, mainly to promote discussion in the comments of the publication. In this network, people seek to express their opinions without many filters, that is, the language is almost always informal, and there is no defined structure with roles for each user. So, we observe the socio-technical controversies occurring more spontaneously and clearly, due to the lack of a presumed hierarchy among the participants of the threads. Even if we identify the attempt of certain participants to consolidate themselves as experts or more authoritative on the topic, the functioning of the platform does not happen around the structuring of the community with well-defined roles and hierarchies, because it is centered on the realization of the dialogue through the threads.

Facebook. It is important to note that Facebook works around the structuring of a community composed of members with different responsibilities and authority within the group. Some communities exist for about 10 years, adding different levels of experience and relevance to the observed posts. On Facebook, there are groups with very well-defined structures, adding users with different roles, such as administrator, moderator, group expert, and among other roles. The content generated by these groups is rich in posts by XR technology experts and enthusiasts. Bringing a voluminous content of opinions, questions, and requests for help to share pains and anxieties. However, it is the network in which we find a kind of "tag" of the posts, identifying those new participants of the group, who generally, join the community by taking questions from users considered experts" by the platform itself.

LinkedIn. The content shared on LinkedIn is mainly news shared recently in the world about the development of the XR and updates about recently held events. In addition to the positioning of realistic and enthusiastic profiles among the professional community. The content generally has a more formal tenor compared to other networks, since it is a network that connects professionals.

4 Results: What Do the Current Users Think About Using HMD to Work?

The main results found during the survey go in two different directions. First, for users, XR technologies suffer from two major impediments that make their adoption by the public unfeasible. The high cost of content production and the maturity of the available software still greatly restrict the quality of the experiences. Specifically, the expansion of experiences into productivity scenarios is hindered by form factor issues, i.e., for users, the devices are not yet comfortable enough to sustain long working hours. We present our findings in detail below:

4.1 UX Immaturity

During the questionnaire, we observed that users believe there are a variety of barriers in the UX for XR, which makes the best experience in the use of applications for this technology impossible. We noticed that for the research participants, the UX definitions are still immature, causing great frustration to these XR users, arguing that the UX for these platforms needs to be better developed. In this research we identified 3 main types of UX immaturity within XR applications:

- Friction between interactions
- Lack of feedback
- Software problems.

Friction Between Interactions. During the research, we identified that one of the main problematic points that users point out about UX in XR is the processes that require external equipment (computers, cell phones, etc.) for the XR devices. This occurs constantly when logging into productivity applications such as Horizon Workrooms and Immersed, making it very difficult to use these applications. Users denote this process of getting ready to use the applications as "friction" as one of the main points of frustration in their user experience. In contrast to their everyday flows of using smartphones and computers in their work routines to use HMD, they point out that this difference still makes them find their use laborious and unconvincing.

Lack of Feedback. According to the perception of the interviewed users, the goal of XR technology is to naturalize interactions that are common in the real world and that they are already used to. These are desirable points in virtual experiences. But the lack of feedback in interactions in a productivity scenario like writing remains one of the biggest UX challenges in the XR context, very present in some interactions using the hands, hand tracking is an XR input, which has a big deficit in lack of feedback. Users feel the need to reproduce physical sensations and perceive tactile feedbacks that they are already used to in other platforms (computers, smartphones, tablets, etc.), to better use XR applications.

Software Problems. Respondents consider that there is little content produced for XR technologies. Content production processes still need major investment. Without much content available and with software still considered immature in terms of quality, users consider that the UX of available applications is poorly developed. The democratization of this content can broaden market notions and drive new solutions in both software and UX.

4.2 Form Factor

The form factor of the HMD devices available on the market is pointed out by users as one of the main factors hindering the adoption of HMDs in their work routine. According to them, the weight of the device and the short battery life prevent them from being used continuously. However, there is a widespread impression that the Form Factor, as well as the hardware of the devices, has evolved a lot in recent years. Their perception is that the Platform is only a few steps away from reaching a stable and satisfactory device model:

- Discomfort
- Battery life
- Value in daily life
- Form Factor evolution

Discomfort. Users still point out that the XR glasses continue to be very uncomfortable, spending more than a few hours wearing the device can cause severe headaches, neck pain, and motion sickness. In addition, users also complain that they do not feel comfortable wearing the XR Glasses outside of the home, as they see that the technology is not designed for outdoor use, thus limiting the use of these devices in their daily lives. Finally, we understand that discomfort is one of the topics that generate resistance from users in joining the XR constant within their daily lives, they do not believe they are more comfortable and accessible than other devices they are already used to such as smartphones, computers, tablets, etc.

Battery Life. Another major technical problem is the battery life of the XR devices. The batteries in the XR devices cannot keep up with long user trials, discharging too quickly and overheating. When the device discharges, the user is forced to use the HMD with a charger plugged in, restricting it to a stationary position (AKYILDIZ, 2022), and limiting its ability to move. Depending on the application, this situation can deprive the user of having a full experience with the device.

Value in Daily Life. It was observed that some XR users do not see a great value that these devices can add to their daily lives, because of the limitations that this technology currently imposes on users. Although the form factor evolves in many ways with each new device, users receive these innovations more as demonstrations, not as something that has reached the desired level to be used in their routines.

Form Factor Evolution. The companies focused on the development in extended reality, perceive the Form Factor of XR devices as a major bottleneck in the acceptance of users, so this technology is seeking to adapt even more to the routine of a person, we can see this evolution more clearly comparing the devices Gear VR (2016) and Quest Pro (2022) of Oculus. Even if these improvements are not yet mature, the community notes that they are on the right track to being accepted. And that the hardware is the most promising point in this evolution.

5   Conclusion

It is important to finish this article by elaborating a critical reflection directed by the results of this ethnographic research and built from the variety of user perceptions mapped and presented here. When we overlap the two main axes of findings, the perception of great hardware evolution and its importance for adoption in productivity scenarios and, on the other hand, the clear perception that XR applications are still very immature in terms of usability, we have a broad view of how users perceive the future of this technological platform. As we noted, these two axes exist in a kind of contradiction that expresses the unstable presence of the technology, in the sense that there is not yet a defined and stable way of how the technology should be used or about its future applications to the daily life of average users.

We point out that this apparent contradiction must be understood as a diagnosis of this moment of the technological platform, a moment in which large corporations try to define the horizons of evolution of the technological platform by building new usage scenarios and trying to convince people that they can become consumers of these devices and integrate them into their daily lives. Just like other technological devices such as PCs and smartphones, which are already integrated in such a fundamental way in our daily lives and the most diverse contexts.

However, the findings of this research make it explicit that the industry will face long-standing challenges in convincing users of the usefulness of HMDs in corporate work. As long as users are immersed in the usage vocabularies of other devices that are pervasively involved in their routines, they will still find it difficult to identify value in using uncomfortable devices with many usability problems. We would like to end with a question: will we be able to think of XR device use experiences that do not replace smartphones and computers, but that work in a complementary way to other devices bringing convenience and comfort to users?

References

Chuah, S.: Why and who will adopt extended reality technology? Literature review, synthesis, and future research agenda (2018)

Akyildiz, I.F., Guo, H.: Wireless Extended Reality (XR): Challenges and New Research Directions (2022)

Hine, C.: Ethnography for the Internet: Embedded, Embodied and Every Day, 1st edn. Bloomsbury Academic, London (2015)

Hine, C.: Virtual Ethnography, 1st edn. Editorial Uoc, S.L., Spain (2004)

Segata, J., Rifiotis, T.: Ethnographic Politics in the Field of Cyberculture, 1st edn. Brazilian Anthropology Association – ABA, Brazil (2016)

Latour, B.: We were never modern, 1st edn. Editora 34, Rio de Janeiro (1994)

Hughes, T., Bijker, W., Pinch, T.: The Social Construction of Technological Systems, anniversary edition: New Directions in the Sociology and History of Technology, 1st edn. The MIT Press, Massachusetts (2012)

Investigating Longitudinal Effects of Physical Inoculation Interventions Against Disinformation

Niklas Henderson$^{(\boxtimes)}$, Oliver Buckley , and Helen Pallett

University of East Anglia, Norwich NR4 7TJ, UK
{N.Henderson,O.Buckley,H.Pallett}@uea.ac.uk

Abstract. This ongoing project investigates both the immediate and long-term effectiveness of the "Fake News" card game, a physical inoculation-based board game to counter disinformation, developed by the DROG group in collaboration with the University of Cambridge Social Decision-Making Lab. This extends previous research using the "Fake News" card game, incorporating a longitudinal element and a wider demographic. A pre-test post-test within-subjects study (N=54) was designed to test participants' persuasiveness and reliability judgements on fictional 'fake news' articles. 7-point Likert scales, as well as a number of qualitative, open-ended questions were delivered before playing the "Fake News" game, immediately after, and 9 weeks after the intervention. Qualitative analysis found participants critically analysing the author and writing style of 'fake news' articles with a high frequency and in more detail immediately after the intervention, with a skill fade over the subsequent 9 weeks to the longitudinal post-test. Contrary to this, quantitative testing found a significant decrease in persuasiveness and reliability judgements of 'fake news' articles exclusively in the longitudinal post-test. These quantitative results are in contrast to current literature around longitudinal effects of inoculation interventions, and if repeatable this may indicate stimulation of reflective learning in a way that digital gamified inoculation interventions have not achieved.

Keywords: Disinformation · Inoculation · Gamification · Longitudinal

1 Introduction

Increasing claims that we are in a 'post-truth' digital age have helped heighten public awareness of misinformation online. Despite this it remains a serious problem, with Russian and Chinese state disinformation campaigns proving effective on online social networks [2], impacting the wider UK political landscape. Many current solutions in fighting false information online have taken platform-specific approaches, with bot detection systems and false information classification challenges. These solutions have focused on the false information itself, rather than the human information consumer. Cognitive approaches are important as they

© The Author(s), under exclusive license to Springer Nature Switzerland AG 2023
C. Stephanidis et al. (Eds.): HCII 2023, CCIS 1835, pp. 39–46, 2023.
https://doi.org/10.1007/978-3-031-36001-5_5

can transcend single platforms or mediums. By helping the end user improve skills in detecting false information and build resilience to persuasive false information, they can apply skills to far wider contexts and share these skills with others around them.

1.1 Inoculation Theory

One cognitive-based approach is Inoculation Theory [3]. Inoculation theory follows the biological analogy, in that to increase resistance to persuasion the subject can be pre-exposed to a weakened version of a persuasive argument. An inoculation intervention can take many forms, with original research exploring different levels of participation (active or passive), and different types of intervention (supportive or refutational). Recent research has tied elements of active learning such as gamification to inoculation theory. Game-based inoculation interventions have yielded positive results [4], however many studies have not yet investigated the long term effectiveness of these interventions, especially outside of digital contexts.

2   Literature Review

One of the first gamified approaches to combat misinformation explored the effectiveness of inoculating through a physical game [1]. The approach tasked students with creating their own false narratives around a highly politicised area, while impersonating a pre-allocated biased character. Results showed some evidence that the "Fake News" card game reduced participants' susceptibility to fake news, however with a small sample size, and uneven balance of testing article political alignment, the authors encouraged results to be interpreted as preliminary. Subsequent approaches have also explored digital games' potential to inoculate against disinformation. The "Bad News" game [5] was created as an online game to get players to impersonate a disinformation creator within the context of social media and social media platforms. With the game being digital, a far larger participant pool of 15,000 users was possible. Again, this solution showed evidence of players' effectiveness in resisting misinformation increasing after taking part. Other digital systems such as "FakeYou!" [6] are mobile-based. This approach also uniquely generates game content by scraping articles and images from the web in real time. Repeat experiments using these games and platforms have not always seen positive results however. Some research has used games shown to be successful in pilot studies, however have in some instances not been able to recreate such promising results [7]. Other more recent approaches have yielded more success [8,9].

Within the research area, there is relatively little work understanding the skill fade/longitudinal decay of specifically gamified inoculation interventions [10]. Understanding how long the effects of an inoculation intervention can last with a participant are of significant importance, as a high decay may signal a need for "booster" interventions, or alternative approaches. Further research using the "Bad News" game has looked at longitudinal affects of the intervention [10]. Their work concluded that while there was an immediate positive effect after the intervention, this decayed significantly over a 2 month period. Much more research is required to understand how to decrease skill fade from inoculation interventions, and how potential 'booster' inoculation sessions may be utilised to decrease skill fade.

This preliminary research project looks to exploit the gap in longitudinal research in games to help protect people against false information. There exists no other work to date looking at skill fade of *physical* gamified inoculation interventions against false information, and we hope that this project will start to ignite more work here.

3   Method

To investigate the longitudinal effects of physical board game inoculation interventions, a pre-test post-test within-subject cross-sectional study was designed. Participants were tested immediately before the inoculation intervention (pre-test), immediately after the inoculation intervention (post-test), and 9 weeks after the day of the inoculation intervention (long post-test). This study design is closely related to previous inoculation research using the "Fake News" board game [1] and longitudinal work with the "Bad News" digital game [10], as it is hoped that extensions to this study with larger participant pools will allow comparisons between results of the three studies. This testing design is however different to the control-treatment methodology adopted in previous research using this game [1] to maximise participants in what is a very early-stage investigation.

3.1   The "Fake News" Card Game

The "Fake News Card Game" is a board game originally created by the Cambridge Social Decision-Making Lab in collaboration with DROG [1]. It was originally created in the early phases of this research area combining games and inoculation to help protect people against false information. Originally tested in a secondary public highschool in the Netherlands, the 'Fake News' game is a collaborative board game played in groups of 2–4. The game materials consist of 4 different character cards, a source card, and a set of paragraph templates. The aim of the game is to create a propaganda article from the provided paragraph templates, that best matches the groups given character motivation, aims, and disinformation techniques. A group is randomly assigned their character card, which details their chosen character's motivations, goals, and what methods they take to achieve this. The source card gives groups background information on background statistics (Fig. 1). For each article section, there are 4 template cards that groups can choose from; each card is suited to a different character. Groups work collaboratively through verbal discussion to choose the most suitable paragraph templates. The groups' score is calculated by totalling the number of correct paragraph templates chosen.

Fig. 1. The "Fake News" card game [1]. This group's character card is at the bottom (center), next to the source card (right). An article has been created with the paragraph templates.

3.2   Session Structure

Participants booked an hour-long session online, where basic demographic information was captured. Each session lasted 60 min, with 2–4 participants in each. Each session began with a broad introduction to the research project by the session lead, and an overview of the session structure. Each participant then completed the pre-test, supervised by the session lead. After an introduction to the game and game rules, groups then spent a maximum of 30 min playing the "Fake News" game, which was timed by the session lead. Groups were able to finish the game in less time if they wished, and those nearing the 30 min time limit were encouraged to finish by the session lead. The session ended with the post-test, also supervised by the session lead. 9 weeks after each session, participants were emailed with the final longitudinal post-test, to be completed unsupervised online. Participants were required to complete the final post-test within 7 days. Late longitudinal post-test submissions were discarded.

3.3   Testing Design

While the research of using inoculation games to help protect against disinformation is wide, there lacks a consistent method or agreed-upon framework for testing the effectiveness of gamified interventions. For consistency, participants were tested using the same method in original research [1], however using a pre-test post-test within-subjects methodology, rather than control and treatment groups.

Within each testing phase, participants read one of four (randomly selected) 'fake news' articles, after which they answered 3 quantitative and 3 qualitative questions on their opinions of the article. Articles used in the testing phases were written with a fixed number of literary techniques, including hyperbole, the 'common man appeal', 'arguments from authority', 'conspiratorial reasoning', 'demonisation of the out-group', whataboutism, and ad hominem. Each article also had a fixed structure, with both fictional and real names of people and institutions included. All articles also shared a common topic: immigration within the United Kingdom and the EU. To negate for political bias within groups, two articles were politically left-leaning, and two were politically right-leaning. Two of these articles were from original research [1], but adjusted to fit within a UK context. As this project included a further longitudinal testing stage, two more articles were written to ensure an even political balance. Both the pre-test, post-test, and longitudinal post-test all use the same testing method, however the individual article that participants read as part of the test was random (participants cannot be tested with the same article more than once). Once participants had read each article, they were asked to rank the article's persuasiveness, reliability, and personal agreement on a 7-point Likert scale. Participants were also asked 3 open-ended qualitative questions: "What do you think the writer is trying to convince you of?", "Which arguments did you find persuasive and non-persuasive?", and "Which arguments did you find reliable?" These quantitative and qualitative questions are the same as previous research [1].

4 Participant Pool

The game was tested on members of the public from the East of England through the University of East Anglia Paid Participant Panel Scheme. Demographic information on age, nationality, gender, education level and political leaning of participants was captured during registration for the study. Age of participants was skewed to a younger demographic with 40.7% of participants being between the age of 18 and 24. Most participants identified as Female (70.3%). Politically, most participants identified to have a more left leaning ideological belief, with the average leaning score at 37.47 (on a slider of values between 0 to 100, 0 being completely left-leaning, and 100 being completely right-leaning, with which participants self-identified). A total of 54 participants took part in this pilot study.

5 Results

Both the judged persuasiveness of articles, participants' personal agreement with articles, and judged reliability of articles shared a similar trend in mean value between the pre-test, post-test, and longitudinal post-test. In all participant judgements, mean article ratings between the pre-test and immediate post-test had little variation (change of -0.06 for judged persuasiveness, -0.15 for personal agreement, and -0.06 for judged reliability). All three participant judgements did however feature a significant drop between the immediate post-test, and the longitudinal post-test (change of -0.44 for judged persuasiveness, -0.75 for personal agreement, and -0.56 for judged reliability) (Fig. 2).

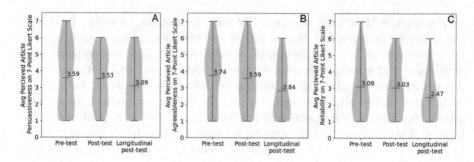

Fig. 2. Violin plots showing the mean and distribution of quantitative testing results from the pre-test, post-test, and longitudinal post-test. Panel A shows participant perceived persuasiveness. Panel B shows how much participants personally agreed with the article. Panel C shows the participant perceived reliability.

5.1   Critical Analysis of the Author

One theme that was identified within the open-ended qualitative questions, was participants' critical analysis of the article's writing, and the article's author. This critical analysis was collated and separated into pre-test, post-test, and longitudinal post-test groups.

Pre-test. critical analysis of the author found some identification of the article being an unbalanced, or opinionated piece. Participants also communicated a lack of trust in the article, especially with the ad hominem attacks. Key themes from the pre-test can be summarised as (a) opinion (adjectives including "waffle", "extreme", "informal"), (b) motive (descriptions of the article having "bias" or being "unbalanced"), and (c), a lack of trust. Some full quotes that represent these key themes are given below.

> *"The comments seem extreme so would find it difficult to find any of them reliable without balance."*
> *"All the arguments were unsubstantiated and were opinions."*

Immediate post-test. critical analysis found many more participants giving critical analysis of the author's writing style. Some analysis was also given from the perspective of the author: "If you don't balance your argument then you do not persuade." Key themes from the immediate post-test include (a) context (statements being labeled as "conjecture" or "misappropriated"), (b) motive, (c) tone (text being "sensationalist", "childish", "immature", having an "informal tone"), and similarly to the pre-test, (d) opinion (text having "gross generalisations", "speculation", being "subjective"). Some full quotes that represent these key themes are given below.

> *"All the insults make it childish and unpersuasive, saying only sane people think this or the man they're arguing against looks like emperor Palpatine doesn't help their actual argument at all."*

"What I found not persuasive was the informal tone regarding the president of the European union. it takes away from the integrity of the article and makes it seem immature."

Longitudinal post-test. critical analysis was not as extensive or detailed as the immediate post-test, however had a particular focus on the emotional tone of the article, more so than the pre-test or immediate post-test. Key themes can be summarised as (a) tone (being "sensationalist", "disrespectful", "unprofessional", having "scaremongering language"), and (b) opinion (text being "just a reaction", "emotive", "irrational", "personal"). Some full quotes that represent these key themes are given below:

"I didn't find the article persuasive. The writing was sensationalist and also personally disrespectful to Juncker. The tone of the article made me dismissive of the message."

6   Discussion and Conclusion

The results observed from this study are significant as they have found that participants' perceived reliability and persuasiveness of false articles did not change from pre-test to immediate post-test, but did improve (reduce) over 9 weeks to the longitudinal post-test. This is notable as these results differ from the typical skill fade seen in other cross-sectional studies on digital game inoculation interventions [10,11]. A novel feature of this study is an analysis of responses to qualitative open-ended questions during testing phases, that goes beyond sentiment analysis. Coding participant responses for critical analysis of testing articles delivers results that better align with current literature. Namely, an increase in frequency and detail between the pre-test and immediate post-test, with a decrease in frequency and detail for the longitudinal post-test that remains an improvement to the pre-test. This highlights the importance of using a variety of different testing methods and approaches, as changes in testing procedure and analysis may drastically alter results.

This gamified inoculation intervention differs from other digital approaches as (a) the "Fake News" card game is a *collaborative* game in which players communicate and work together during play, and (b) it is a *physical* board game, where players can physically see and touch game pieces. This may have facilitated a greater long-term cognitive effect on the player, as opposed to an alternative single-player, online intervention. It must be stressed however the sample size for this study was comparatively small, and we recommend that the reader see this work as exploratory in nature. The uncontrolled testing style between the pre- and post-test, and the longitudinal post-test may have also had a role to play in the change of results. The unsupervised nature of the longitudinal post-test may have also affected the attitudinal approach to the final stage of testing.

To continue this project, the research team hope to collect data from additional groups of participants in line with the outlined research method, as well as investigating more qualitative testing methodologies such as participant interviews to better understand the effect of gamified inoculation interventions on participants.

References

1. Roozenbeek, J., van der Linden, S.: The fake news game: actively inoculating against the risk of misinformation. J. Risk Res. **22**(5), 570–580 (2019). https://doi.org/10.1080/13669877.2018.1443491
2. Erlich, A., Garner, C.: Is pro-kremlin disinformation effective? Evidence from Ukraine. Int. J. Press/Politics **28**(1), 5–28 (2023). https://doi.org/10.1177/19401612211045221
3. McGuire, W.J.: Some contemporary approaches. Adv. Exp. Soc. Psychol. **1**(C), 191–229 (1964). https://doi.org/10.1016/S0065-2601(08)60052-0
4. Roozenbeek, J., van der Linden, S.: Breaking harmony square: a game that "inoculates" against political misinformation. Harvard Kennedy School Misinformation Review (2020). https://doi.org/10.37016/mr-2020-47
5. Roozenbeek, J., van der Linden, S.: Fake news game confers psychological resistance against online misinformation. Palgrave Commun. **5**(1), 1–10 (2019). https://doi.org/10.1057/s41599-019-0279-9
6. Clever, L., et al.: FakeYou! - a gamified approach for building and evaluating resilience against fake news. In: van Duijn, M., Preuss, M., Spaiser, V., Takes, F., Verberne, S. (eds.) MISDOOM 2020. LNCS, vol. 12259, pp. 218–232. Springer, Cham (2020). https://doi.org/10.1007/978-3-030-61841-4_15
7. Pimmer, C., Eisemann, C., Magdalena, M.: Fake news resilience through online games? tentative findings from a randomized controlled trial in higher education. In: 17th International Conference on Cognition and Exploratory Learning in Digital Age, CELDA 2020, August, pp. 387–390 (2020). https://doi.org/10.33965/celda2020_202014c055
8. Basol, M., Roozenbeek, J., Van Der Linden, S.: Good news about bad news: gamified inoculation boosts confidence and cognitive immunity against fake news. J. Cogn. **3**(1). https://doi.org/10.5334/joc.91
9. Jeon, Y., Kim, B., Xiong, A., Lee, D., Han, K.: ChamberBreaker: mitigating the echo chamber effect and supporting information hygiene through a gamified inoculation system. In: Proceedings of the ACM on Human-Computer Interaction, 5(CSCW2) (2021). https://doi.org/10.1145/3479859
10. Maertens, R., Roozenbeek, J., Basol, M., van der Linden, S.: Long-term effectiveness of inoculation against misinformation: three longitudinal experiments. J. Exp. Psychol. Appl. **27**(1), 1–16 (2021). https://doi.org/10.1037/xap0000315
11. Zerback, T., Töpfl, F., Knöpfle, M.: The disconcerting potential of online disinformation: persuasive effects of astroturfing comments and three strategies for inoculation against them. New Media Soc. **23**(5), 1080–1098 (2021). https://doi.org/10.1177/1461444820908530

An Actor-Network Theory Perspective on Harry Styles' Gender-Fluid Fashion in Twitter User Community

Alifya Ikhsanty Heryana[✉] and Wulan Widyasari

Department of Communication, Universitas Muhammdiyah Yogyakarta, Bantul Regency, Kasihan, Indonesia
alifya.i.isip19@mail.umy.ac.id

Abstract. This study aims to analyze the pattern of discussions created on Twitter among fans about the gender-fluid fashion worn by Harry Styles. Gender-fluid fashion campaigns have become an object of discourse on social media. This issue is related to gender equality campaigns because [1] there are stereotypes and stigma that divide clothing categories based on one's gender. This study found differences in the acceptance by three informants of the gender-fluid fashion worn by Harry Styles. The Actor-Network Theory confirm the relationship between fans and actants, which influences each other so that a network is created within them.

Keywords: Harry Styles · Gender-fluid fashion · New Media · Twitter

1 Introduction

Gender fluidity has been emphasized in fashion, where people are encouraged to express themselves freely without regard to socially created gender roles [2]. Bates views [3], gender-fluidity is a person who does not identify with the assigned gender. In addition, gender fluidity is related to the roles that are created by society's social construction of men and women; this construction can result in masculine or feminine stereotypes, which can shape a person's social identity. The masculine and feminine styles in clothing are intended for men and women, respectively. However, Belinda argues [2], the existence of a gender-fluid phenomenon in fashion displays opposition to values around gender and is an expression of gender equality and gender fluidity. Fashion, a form of popular culture, has evolved into a means of self-expression used in campaigns on gender issues, [4] Ardyatama clarify that the presence of cultural exchange through social media has led to many influencers and even pop artists making Indonesia as their market one of which is a gender-fluid fashion that is disseminated through the use of new media by celebrities.

This study analyses Harry Styles's fans' social media interactions. Harry Styles supports gender-fluid fashion in several ways, according to Singh [5], who claims that he is not restricted to wearing men's attire. He was the first male solo model for Vogue when

C. Stephanidis et al. (Eds.): HCII 2023, CCIS 1835, pp. 47–53, 2023.
https://doi.org/10.1007/978-3-031-36001-5_6

he appeared in the magazine wearing a Gucci dress. Harry Styles, who does not identify as a feminist in interviews, the press, or tweets, was also called a "proud feminist" by a magazine [6]. He also demonstrated his interest in gender-fluid through record artwork, music videos, and stage appearances. Harry Styles fans on Twitter discuss his gender-fluid fashion based on media content. According to Singgalen [7], new virtual identities have emerged due to increased user intensity and social media use. Fans complimented his outfit for various reasons, but some questioned people's supports for Harry Styles. He became the subject of fan conversation, and some said his support was due to his white-ness and social norms. This phenomenon shows how humans and non-human variables like technology coexist and affect each other, as described by Berry [8]. Twitter spreads ideas, discussions, and campaigns [9], reflecting pop culture. Smartphone users may also communicate faster due to the internet's expansion [10]. Ethnographic methods are best for studying online arguments because they create a social and cultural phenomenon in cyberspace [11]. The actor-network theory was used to study Chinese lesbian social media communities, [12] L-app connects all lesbians in China. Fan interactions and a gender-fluid fashion star community are not studied. Thus, this study seeks to explain the pattern of Harry Styles's admirers' discussions of his gender-fluid fashion in Twitter.

2 Overview of Literature

Actor-Network Theory has been employed in many ways, Singgalen views [7], ANT considers social media users as actors with unrestricted capacities to form virtual social networks. Twitter chats should consider feelings [13]. Based on Callon [14] there are four concepts: an actor, which can be human or non-human; an actant, which influences each factor in it; a network, which is made up of parts that interact and affect each other; and a connection, which specifies the particular link between each actant. ANT and affordances are used to classify current electronic media [15]. According to Fuchs [16], contemporary media creates cyberculture by mutually generating habits and structures that employ computer technology networks to build and reproduce thinking (ideas, val-ues, affects, meanings, and tastes) and bodies. Users' skills, technology's material form, and technology usage context are all changing [17]. In Western culture, *gender* defines as male and female. However, this includes non-binary (an umbrella word for identities other than binary), gender-fluid, and Indigenous populations. Gender expression is how a person expresses their gender to others by their behaviour, appearance (haircut and dress), and cultural expectations of social rank, attributes, and sexual behaviour. Gender identity is essential [3], which is caused by how gender discrimination in fashion creates power dynamics, social structures, and sociological reasons [18]. Belinda also views, [2] the gender-fluid phenomena in fashion industry is a form of nonverbal communication that represents gender-based fashion through silhouettes, colours, and other categories.

3 Method

This study uses ethnography and qualitative descriptive methods to determine Twit-ter culture. Netnography is reinventing social science approaches by combining ethno-graphic research with new digital and network data collection, analysis, and represen-tational study [19]. Actor-Network Theory shows how discourse analysis and ANT are used in media studies to analyze a collection of texts with restrictions caused by social asymmetry or technology, culture, or society [20]. This study uses qualitative methods to confirm ANT use [21]; by passive participant observation, in-depth interviews with informants, and data gathering through documentation studies [22].

4 Result and Discussion

Actor-network theory explains how Harry Styles' gender-fluid fashion is accepted and discussed on Twitter [23]. Gender fluidity reflects the majority standards; as Diamond views [24] social media and the internet give everyone access to complex gender narratives worldwide. The finding shows informants are part of actor, as Latour views [25] an actor is something that acts, it also can be anything provided to be the source of action. Table 1 shows informants 1, 2, and 3's opinions on Harry Styles' fashions. Informant 1 wanted Harry Style to dress usually. According to informant 2, Harry Styles' fashion indicates LGBTQ + but not determines gender or sexuality. In informant 3, whatever Harry Styles' clothing choices still suit him.

Table 1. Tweet by Informants

Informant 1 (@cmntek)
October 4, 2022
Tweet 1: And also, I miss Harry Style' fashion when he had a long hair + wearing shirt/coat, or with a short hair style + shirt/t-shirt [attached photo of Harry Styles]
Tweet 2: Is it okay if Harry's style going back to normal again, he's very good looking if he wears normal clothing
Tweet 3: Let's make your hair long [Mentioning @Harry_Styles]

Informant 2 (@nowwhatw)
September 30, 2022
Tweet 1: 48k followers but minding an artist's sexual orientation, imagine in Indonesia that thing is sensitive, then what about other developed countries? [Quoted Tweet by @littleukiyo]
Tweet by another (@littleukiyo): You think a very private person like Tae, who booked a restaurant long before, being honest that he watched Call Me by Your Name and recommended that on vLive, being supportive to LGBTQ artists, will be that careless? He is the type to shout his love at the top of his lungs and protect his dear one. He was not hiding it
[1 reply]
Example reply by others (@Ruruarmy2): Even if the dating issue is not correct, that does not mean to claim to have an interest in women straightly. Anyways, that is his right to like anyone. Why would you decide that alone?
Example reply by informant (@nowwhatw): Harry Styles presents the world of LGBTQ + by his fashion, his song, and other things, but no one forbids him to go on a date with a woman. Or none of his fans told him to be gay

Informant 3 (@alkanfl)
September 16, 2022
Tweet 1: Harry Styles wearing any fashion will always make him look good

Fig. 1. Tweets by Informants

The informant's motivations in evaluating Harry Styles' gender-fluid fashion are expressed through rejection by informant one and support by informants 2 and 3. The acceptance of gender-fluid fashion by informant 1 (see Fig. 1) is prompted by beliefs that are impacted by social construction in society towards fashion style [18], which state that a person's fashion must be based on their gender, through masculine for men and feminine for women. Unlike informant 2 (see Fig. 1), whose background includes the belief that clothing style is unrelated to one's gender and sexual orientation [3], one's gender identity may not be the same as sex and may exist outside of the male/female dichotomy. The third informant believed that the environment affected acceptance; an environment considered it every day, but not everyone could accept [1]; this was related to the gap in acceptance gender-fluid fashion due to the prevalence of male values in contemporary society.

Informant 1.

"Information about fashion from Harry Styles is usually obtained through the Timeline on Twitter, apart from that Harry Styles' name also entered trending and you can see posts about him on the Timeline."

Informant 1 discovered the issue from Twitter's Trending feature, which enables users to respond autonomously to current events by following hashtags, trending, like, and retweeting anything [26].

Informant 2.

"I usually get information about the fashion she wears via Twitter and through base accounts that provide celebrity information or news, for example, the Twitter account @Popbase."

According to informant 2, information is obtained through accounts that provide information about popular culture [4] through Twitter; the exchange of information about culture occurs where users can interact.

Informant 3.

"I learned about Harry Styles' gender-fluid clothes when one of my Twitter mutuals liked a photo of him performing on stage. His costume looked feminine but yet fit Harry Styles. YouTube, music videos, concerts, etc. He wears odd clothes that fit him well."

Informant 3, the tweet suggestion tool shows relevant tweets from friends' interactions [26]. Twitter helps Harry Styles' fans learn about his gender-fluid fashion. Figure 2 shows how (1) is @Popbase's Tweet about Harry Styles' wardrobe difficulties. (2) shows a tweet contrasting Sam Smith's and Harry Styles' gender-fluid fashion. (3) shows Harry Styles' look from a fashion magazine. Based on this, each informant obtained information about gender-fluid fashion by Harry Styles' through Twitter and other users who provided the contents.

Fig. 2. Twitter as Actant

Twitter mediates all discussions about Harry Styles' gender-fluid fashion [27]; twitter requires to provide actors in a network to relate to one another. Through the use of Twitter, networks are built within the frameworks of knowledge about the topic, [26] to generate meaning, empathetic reactions to produce affiliation, and attention consolidation to create interest. See Fig. 3; (1) Twitter provide a suggestion tweet based on user's previous liked post, (2) Twitter provide a user to see the following's retweet, and (3) Twitter provide a suggestion tweet based on the related topic. Based on Fig. 2, the informants have the same pattern to understanding Harry Style' gender-fluid fashion.

Fig. 3. Twitter Provides Actors

Figure 1–3 show that the informants had the same pattern in interpreting Harry Style's gender-fluid fashion [23]; The discussion about gender-fluid fashion refers to actors' movement, and this study discovered that each informant interacted with Harry Style's fashion-related posts and tweeted about them. From this perspective, the gender-fluid fashion by Harry Styles' issue allows users and Twitter to have a connection,

[27] actions are driven by the interconnection between various 'actors' in the network. Therefore, this study uses ANT to propose the existence of actors' discussion on Twitter about gender-fluid fashion worn by Harry Styles in a complex social network. It also can be observed that each informants acts to actively showed their perspectives on the issue. In ANT, each informant is connected as users of Twitter and influences each other. This research also shows that the content containing Harry' Styles' gender-fluid fashion is the potential actant to cause the whole discussion about it based on actor-network perspective.

5   Conclusion

This article stated that the gender-fluid fashion worn by Harry Styles is a form of representation of gender expression used to break the division of gender roles in fashion. We underline that gender-fluid fashion is motivated by a dominant ideology in society, a form of division of dress styles based on one's gender, where men must wear a masculine style and women wear a feminine style. We can confirm that the actor-network theory sees the discussion among Twitter users and finds the differences in informants' acceptances. ANT sees fans as actors who interact with each other to give opinions. At the same time, Twitter allows fans to exchange information about the gender-fluid fashion worn by Harry Styles through hashtags, tweets, likes, and retweets, thus creating an interconnected network.

References

1. Savitri, E., Syarief, A., Laksemi, S.K.: The Concept of gender-fluid clothing based on the views of urban society. J. Seni Reka Ranc. **4**(2), 271–287 (2022)
2. Belinda, B.C.: Persepsi Dan Reaksi Generasi Z Terhadap Fenomena Gender Fluid Dan Gaya Fesyen Androgini **5**(2) (2022)
3. Bates, N., Chin, M., Becker, T.: Measuring Sex, Gender Identity, and Sexual Orientation (2022). https://doi.org/10.17226/26424
4. Ardyarama, R., Junaedi, F., Sukmono, F.G.: The cross-cultural acceptance of japanese animation, analysis of social media. Commun. Comput. Inf. Sci. (CCIS) **1654**, 249–256 (2021). https://doi.org/10.1007/978-3-031-19679-9_31
5. Singh, O.: Harry styles opens up about his fluid sense of style and why he doesn't like 'limiting' himself to only men's clothing. Insider.com (2020). https://www.insider.com/harry-styles-gender-fluid-fashion-style-clothing-vogue-interview-2020-11
6. Feasey, R.: Masculinit (ies) and the male celebrity feminist. Men Masc. **20**(3), 283–293 (2017). https://doi.org/10.1177/1097184X17718587
7. Singgalen, Y.A.: Actor-network theory and sentiment analysis on regional development issues and politics in social media. J. Komun. **13**(1), 89 (2021). https://doi.org/10.24912/jk.v13i1.9627
8. Berry, C.R.: Under surveillance: an actor network theory ethnography of users' experiences of electronic monitoring. Eur. J. Criminol. **18**(6), 817–835 (2021). https://doi.org/10.1177/1477370819882890
9. El Ishaq, R., Mahanani, P.A.R.: Social media, public space, and culture 'pop.' ETTISAL J. Commun. **3**(1), 15 (2018). https://doi.org/10.21111/ettisal.v3i1.1928

10. Nurhayati, S.S., Sukmono, F.G.: Gender advocacy, social media campaign to against sexual violence. Commun. Comput. Inf. Sci. (CCIS) **1655**, 76–82 (2021). https://doi.org/10.1007/978-3-031-19682-9
11. Juariah, S., Setiaman, A.: Studi Etnografi Virtual Pesan Nonverbal tentang Prinsip Menikah Muda dalam Instagram @ nikahasik. Komunikator **9**(1), 57–68 (2017)
12. Chen, F., Zhang, Y.: Constructing Chinese lesbian online community through social media: an actor-network theory-based discussion (2021)
13. Papacharissi, Z.: Affective Publics (Sentiment, Technology, and Politics), 2015th ed. New York (2016)
14. Callon, M.: The sociology of an actor - network : the case of the electric vehicle. Mapp. Dyn. Sci. Technol., 19–34 (1981)
15. Scarlett, A., Zeilinger, M.: Rethinking affordance, pp. 1–48 (2019)
16. Fuchs, C.: Internet and Society, 2008th ed. Taylor & Francis, New York (2008). https://www.ptonline.com/articles/how-to-get-better-mfi-results
17. Evans, S.K., Pearce, K.E., Vitak, J., Treem, J.W.: Explicating affordances: a conceptual framework for understanding affordances in communication research. J. Comput. Commun. **22**(1), 35–52 (2017). https://doi.org/10.1111/jcc4.12180
18. Akdemir, N.: Deconstruction of gender stereotypes through fashion. Eur. J. Soc. Sci. Educ. Res. **5**(2), 185 (2018). https://doi.org/10.26417/ejser.v5i2.p185-190
19. O'Donohoe, S.: Netnography: doing ethnographic research online, vol. 29, no. 2 (2010). https://doi.org/10.2501/S026504871020118X
20. Spöhrer, M., Ochsner, B.: Applying the Actor-Network Theory in Media Studies, pp. 1–314, August 2016. https://doi.org/10.4018/978-1-5225-0616-4
21. Brancati, D.: Social scientific research. In: Social Scentific Research, 1st ed., SAGE Publications, Inc., New York (2018)
22. Barker, C.: Cultural studies, theory & practice. In: Ketujuh, M. Kasihan, B. (eds.) KREASI WACANA (2000)
23. Rath, S., Swain, P.K.: The interface between political ecology and actor–network theory: exploring the reality of waste. Rev. Dev. Chang., 097226612211225 (2022). https://doi.org/10.1177/09722661221122553
24. Diamond, L.M.: Gender fluidity and nonbinary gender identities among children and adolescents. Child Dev. Perspect. **14**(2), 110–115 (2020). https://doi.org/10.1111/cdep.12366
25. Latour, V.B., Rip, L.: On actor-network theory. vol. 4, no. 1996, pp. 369–381 (2013)
26. Senbel, S., Seigel, C., Bryan, E.: Religious violence and twitter: networks of knowledge, empathy and fascination. Religions **13**(3) (2022). https://doi.org/10.3390/rel13030245
27. Heinsch, M., Sourdin, T., Brosnan, C., Cootes, H.: Death sentencing by zoom: an actor-network theory analysis. Altern. Law J. **46**(1), 13–19 (2021). https://doi.org/10.1177/1037969X20966147

#MataramIsLove on Twitter: Indonesian Football Fan Activism Towards the Kanjuruhan Tragedy

Anggita Indah Pramesti[✉], Muhammad Muttaqien, and Filosa Gita Sukmono

Department of Communication, Yogyakarta Muhammadiyah University, Kasihan, Indonesia
{anggita.indah.isip19,muttaqien,filosa}@umy.ac.id

Abstract. This study aims to identify Indonesian football supporters' Digital Movement of Opinion activities through #MataramIsLove using the Social Network Analysis (SNA) method on the social media Twitter from October 8 - October 16, 2022. This research uses a descriptive qualitative method with an analysis WordStat. Based on the study's findings, the supporter movement with the Digital Movement of Opinion activity hashtag #MataramIsLove through Twitter social media is an act of solidarity and peace with a collective and solid mass of supporters against the Kanjuruhan tragedy. This finding argues that Twitter hashtags can become part of the digital movement and media of public aspirations.

Keywords: Digital Movement of Opinion · Hashtag · Twitter · Football · Riot

1 Introduction

Social media has become increasingly influential in expressing one's opinion online [1]. Beside that, social media is now an online platform that people use to share content in photos, videos, experiences, and comments [2]. In the new digital environment, social media strongly supports transforming the notion of public Opinion towards a combination of general discussion and collective voice [3], social media can change how people socialize and communicate by providing opportunities to express themselves and voice their opinions [4]. The idea of public Opinion is purposeful to seek socio-political support and suggestions for conveying aspirations and as an act of social protest or political movement.

Digital movement of Opinion (DMO) is one of the public opinions through social media. DMO is a form of active expression of digital public Opinion that arises as a reaction to social issues, thereby creating a new social movement [3]. Twitter is a platform for discussions and activities on various social problems [4], one form of public opinion on social media, Twitter, was carried out by Indonesian football supporters regarding the Kanjuruhan tragedy which killed 131 people including children and women who were victims of the riots [5].

DMO uses the hashtag function on Twitter as a facilitator to create a social movement [7]. Hashtags are essential for social movement mobilization because they link specific

C. Stephanidis et al. (Eds.): HCII 2023, CCIS 1835, pp. 54–60, 2023.
https://doi.org/10.1007/978-3-031-36001-5_7

words or phrases, make online content easy to search for and share in bulk and act as a discursive frame that can be used to create a shared collective identity [8]. Football riots and violence have been global problems for decades [9], fan Violence usually occurs in domestic football matches of the highest national championship leagues [10]. It is known that Ultras fan groups play a vital role in football, which often carries out fandom violence in post-reform Indonesia. Ultras fan groups have free time to support their club – either through being in the stadium or through social media campaigns [11], including by social movement or expressing solidarity with other actors against incidents of soccer violence [12]. Therefore, preventive measures are needed to anticipate riots between football fans in Indonesia.

Previous research on the DMO in the solidarity and peace movement for football supporters in Indonesia has yet to be found. Previous research was conducted by Olesen [13] discussing the protest movement of football supporters against ticket prices from the English football club Liverpool FC through the hashtag #walkouton77, which can. Arianto [14] explained the digital protest movement by Sleman supporters by utilizing social media against the arrest of one of their supporters with the hashtag #BebaskanYudhiAtauBoikot. Other studies demonstrate the analysis of the expressions and responses of football fans via Twitter to the anti-Semitic and social issues anti-homophobia rainbow laces campaign [15, 16].

2   Overview of Literature

Social media is an online platform sufficient as the primary public information source, coordinates and is used by people to build social networks or social relations with others. It mobilizes the DMO, creating virtual networks between users to comment [17–19]. DMO aims to create a virtual network between users to express and comment spontaneously by following technological developments, especially new media found on social media [20]. Twitter as a social media has many opportunities for the public to participate, including creating content, tagging, sharing content, and following hashtags, which can facilitate the public to be more informed and involved [21]. Hashtags are the main elements of Twitter that are useful for the formation of social movements, serve as a means to increase awareness and discussion to stimulate engagement between the activities of social organizations and the public, passively invite mentioned actors to change their roles and actively respond or contribute to discussions and intensify public discourse [22]. Social Network Analysis (SNA) is a network analysis that is useful for visualizing the activity and strength of connections between users in social networks as well as steps to identify interactions in sharing knowledge by combining qualitative and quantitative approaches where the numerical data from the web is converted into a graphical visualization, followed by an explanation of the pattern in detail-narrative and network structure [23].

3   Methodology

This study uses a qualitative method with a descriptive approach. This approach analyses how the DMO formed a solidarity and peace movement for football supporters against the Kanjuruhan tragedy through #MataramIsLove. Data collection uses the data analysis application Wordstat which functions to describe data about preventive steps by football supporters to prevent future Indonesian football riots. Data collection was taken from October 8 to October 16, 2022. The data source for this research is #MataramIsLove, with tweet text and tweet date data to form a DMO.

4　Results and Discussion

These findings indicate that Twitter as social media is a platform for carrying out social movement activities on various social issues [5]. Based on the investigation, this study outlines that football fans in Indonesia use Twitter to carry out social movement actions against the riots in Kanjuruhanwith hashtags#MataramIsLovewhich was carried out after the tragedy of the riots occurred. It can be seen from the data below that DMO with hashtags #MataramIsLove was widely used during the period October 8 – October 16, 2022; 213 tweets were using the hashtag #MataramIsLove. See Fig. 1; the highest frequency count has obtained the highest frequency count on October 8 with 70 tweets. This graph proves the existence of the DMO activity towards the Kanjuruhan tragedy. This data shows that #MataramIsLove is a collective social movement. The public knows that #MataramIsLove is a DMO by supporters to express solidarity with supporters from other fandoms against football riots.

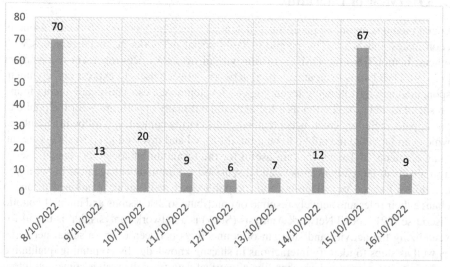

Fig. 1. Frequency of using hashtag' #MataramIsLove October 8 – October 16, 2022 (Source: WordStat 2022.0.1 Software)

According to Sinpeng [8], hashtags are essential for social movements, making online content easily searchable because they link to specific words or phrases. Based on an analysis conducted using WordStat on social media Twitter, in addition to using #MataramIsLoveThe table below also shows topics related to the Kanjuruhan tragedy. Table 1 shows the topics used to express and form a DMO. " Investigate thoroughly" is the highest topic that is widely used, with a case percentage of 65.00% and a total of 195 cases; this topic has keywords like investigate thoroughly, love, thoroughly investigate the tragedy of usut tuntas, love, investigate the Kanjuruhan tragedy, mataramislove, from solo with love, brajamusti batam, paseopati batam, and from batam. Other topics such as "Kanjuruhan Stadium," "Mataram", and "Be a witness" are other phrases used as Digital movements of Opinion. In line with the hashtag element, these topics are phrases used and shared en masse to create a collective identity.

Table. 1 Other topics and keywords used by the Digital Movement of Opinion for the Kanjuruhan tragedy (Source: WordStat 2022.0.1 Software)

No	Topic	Keywords	Cases	% Cases
1	Usut tuntas (Investigate thoroughly)	Usut tuntas (Investigate thoroughly), Love, Usut tuntas tragedi kanjuruhan (Investigate the Kanjuruhan tragedy), MataramIslove, From Solo With Love, BrajamustiBatam, Paseopati Batam, From Batam	195	65.00%
2	Stadion Kanjuruhan (Kanjuruhan Stadium)	Stadion (Stadium), Kanjuruhan, Stadion Kanjuruhan (Kanjuruhan Stadium), Solo Adem Ayem (Serene Solo city)	28	9.33%
3	Mataram	Mataram, Kanjuruhan, Mataramislove	22	7.33%
4	Menjadi Saksi (Be a witness)	Prayforkanjuruhan, MataramIslah, MataramIslove, Menjadi Saksi (Be a witness)	18	6.00%

The Digital movement of Opinion using virtual networks through hashtags on social media Twitter is carried out with the aim of spontaneous expression and commentary [20]. Through #MataramIsLove, supporters participate by creating content, sharing and tagging content, and retweeting other actors' content hashtags so the public can be directly involved and form a discussion. This can be seen from some of the content of supporters on Twitter, and it was found that there were discussions between supporters which facilitated the public to be directly involved and more informed. Fill in the debate in the tweet text like-supporters agree to make peace with anyone and are determined that there will be no more rivalry outside the match, peaceful action to commemorate the Kanjuruhan tragedy, and uphold unity and brotherhood. The hashtag function on Twitter is proper as a DMO facilitator for various social issues [7]. Table 2 proves that social movements can be voiced through tweet text using hashtags to discuss with each other. Supporters are free to express their voices through social movement campaigns on Twitter social media [11] and express bonds of solidarity with other supporters [12].

Table. 2 DMO of football supporters via Twitter #MataramIsLove vulnerable time October 8 – October 16, 2022 (Source: WordStat 2022.0.1 Software).

Tweet Text
All Indonesian football fans agreed to make peace and promised that there would be no rivalry between fans outside of football matches. Three football fandoms in Indonesia with a long history of rivalry, namely Persis Solo, PSIM Yogyakarta, and PSIS Sleman, have agreed to make peace #MataramIsLove
Mataram is a form of unity from the regions of Jogja, Solo, and Sleman, which are brothers to each other #MataramIsLove
#MataramIsLove sings anthems to each other to voice peace
Prayers from #MataramIsLove for all the victims of the Kanjuruhan tragedy
Several elements of football supporters, namely Brigata Curva Sud, Curva Nord Famiglia, Brajamusti, Pasoepati, and The Jakmania, carried out a peaceful action to commemorate the Kanjuruhan tragedy at the Maguwoharjo Stadium #MataramIsLove

Fig. 2. The frequency of words about the Kanjuruhan tragedy

Figure 2 shows that many still use the hashtag #MataramIsLove on Twitter social media to coordinate or build social networks and mobilize DMOs to create virtual networks [17–19]. This is one of the movements using the hashtag so that people care about the incidents of football riots in Indonesia. The words used to show much content related to things often discussed in the Kanjuruhan tragedy, such as the emergence of the word love, illustrate that through DMO activities, supporters can channel a sense of solidarity and peace.

5 Conclusion

This finding confirms the activities of supporters of the Digital Movement of Opinion towards the Kanjuruhan tragedy through hashtags. The results show that DMO activities using the hashtag #MataramIsLove on social media Twitter is considered successful in creating bonds of solidarity and peace between football fans in Indonesia. This success can be seen from the influence of the Digital Movement of Opinion, which can form a solid collective movement. This research implies that the DMO is a movement that can change social and political issues. of Public Opinion on social media. This study also confirms that WordStat, as an analytical tool, can reduce data from hashtags on Twitter to describe data in text, images, charts, and tables. The researcher hopes there will be further research to discuss the supporter movement with the DMO regarding socio-political issues in football, which is still a global problem through social media so that this movement can bring change to better conditions.

References

1. Kim, Y., Song, D., Lee, Y.J.: #Antivaccination on Instagram: a computational analysis of hashtag activism through photos and public responses. Int. J. Environ. Res. Public Health **17**(20), 1–20 (2020). https://doi.org/10.3390/ijerph17207550
2. Nurhayati, S.S., Sukmono, F.G.: Gender advocacy, social media campaign to against sexual violence. Commun. Comput. Inf. Sci. (2021). http://link.springer.com/book/10.1007/978-3-030-90179-0%0A, http://link.springer.com/book/10.1007/978-3-030-90176-9
3. Barisione, M., Michailidou, A. (eds.): Social Media and European Politics. PSEPS, Palgrave Macmillan UK, London (2017). https://doi.org/10.1057/978-1-137-59890-5
4. Susanti, D., Hantoro, P.D.: Indonesian Netizens' digital self and identity creation on social media. Komunikator **14**(2), 104–113 (2022). https://doi.org/10.18196/jkm.16541
5. Firnanda, A.S., Junaedi, F., Sudiwijaya, E.: Digital content management of twitter for climate change using hashtag anisa. Commun. Comput. Inf. Sci. (2021). http://link.springer.com/book/10.1007/978-3-030-90179-0%0A, http://link.springer.com/book/10.1007/978-3-030-90176-9
6. Mutia, A.: "Update: Daftar 131 Korban Meninggal Tragedi Stadion Kanjuruhan, 39 Korban Usia Anak (2022). https://databoks.katadata.co.id/datapublish/2022/10/05/update-daftar-131-korban-meninggal-tragedi-stadion-kanjuruhan-39-korban-usia-anak
7. Barisione, M., Michailidou, A., Airoldi, M.: Understanding a digital movement of opinion: the case of #RefugeesWelcome. Inf. Commun. Soc. **22**(8), 1145–1164 (2019). https://doi.org/10.1080/1369118X.2017.1410204
8. Sinpeng, A.: Hashtag activism: social media and the #FreeYouth protests in Thailand. Crit. Asian Stud. **53**(2), 192–205 (2021). https://doi.org/10.1080/14672715.2021.1882866
9. Newson, M.: Football, fan violence, and identity fusion. Int. Rev. Sociol. Sport **54**(4), 431–444 (2019). https://doi.org/10.1177/1012690217731293
10. Brechbühl, A., Schumacher Dimech, A., Schmid, O.N., Seiler, R.: Escalation vs. non-escalation of fan violence in football? Narratives from ultra fans, police officers and security employees. Sport Soc. **20**(7), 861–879 (2017). https://doi.org/10.1080/17430437.2016.1221932
11. Fuller, A., Junaedi, F.: Ultras in Indonesia: conflict, diversification, activism. Sport Soc. **21**(6), 919–931 (2018). https://doi.org/10.1080/17430437.2017.1300392

12. Perasović, B., Mustapić, M.: Carnival supporters, hooligans, and the "Against Modern Football" movement: life within the ultras subculture in the Croatian context. Sport Soc. **21**(6), 960–976 (2018). https://doi.org/10.1080/17430437.2017.1300395

13. Olesen, M.: #walkouton77;Football fan activism in Premier League. MedieKultur **34**(65), 117–137 (2018). https://doi.org/10.7146/MEDIEKULTUR.V34I65.104550

14. Arianto, B.: Gerakan protes digital para suporter sleman. Kalijaga J. Commun. **3**(1), 1–16 (2022). https://doi.org/10.14421/kjc.31-01.2021

15. Hansen, M., Kavanagh, E., Anderson, E., Parry, K., Cleland, J.: An analysis of responses on Twitter to the English Premier League's support for the anti-homophobia rainbow laces campaign. Sport Soc. 1–15 (2022). https://doi.org/10.1080/17430437.2022.2028774

16. Seijbel, J., van Sterkenburg, J., Oonk, G.: Expressing rivalry online: antisemitic rhetoric among Dutch football supporters on Twitter. Soccer Soc. **23**(8), 834–848 (2022). https://doi.org/10.1080/14660970.2022.2109800

17. Akram, W., Kumar, R.: A Study on positive and negative effects of social media on society. Int. J. Comput. Sci. Eng. **5**(10), 351–354 (2017). https://doi.org/10.26438/ijcse/v5i10.351354

18. Eriyanto, E..: Hashtags and digital movement of opinion mobilization: a social network Analysis/SNA study on #BubarkanKPAI vs #KamiBersamaKPAI Hashtags. J. Komun. Indones. **8**(3) (2020). https://doi.org/10.7454/jki.v8i3.11591

19. Widyastuti, D.A.R.: Using new media and social media in disaster communication. Komunikator **13**(2), 100–111 (2021). https://doi.org/10.18196/jkm.12074

20. Irawan, V.D.Y., Usman, O.: Digital movement of opinion mobilization for football tournament fans in Indonesia: sna study #Pialamenpora2021 Vs #Persijaday. J. Econ. Bus. Govern. Challen. **4**(2), 105–120 (2021). https://doi.org/10.33005/ebgc.v4i2.196

21. Bosch, T.: Twitter activism and youth in South Africa: the case of #RhodesMustFall. Inf. Commun. Soc. **20**(2), 221–232 (2017). https://doi.org/10.1080/1369118X.2016.1162829

22. Wonneberger, A., Hellsten, I.R., Jacobs, S.H.J.: Hashtag activism and the configuration of counterpublics: dutch animal welfare debates on Twitter. Inf. Commun. Soc. **24**(12), 1694–1711 (2021). https://doi.org/10.1080/1369118X.2020.1720770

23. Damayanti, A.: Paracrisis and social media: a social network analysis of hashtag #uninstallbukalapak on Twitter. Komunikator **12**(1) (2020). https://doi.org/10.18196/jkm.121032

Analyzing Consumer Experience of Autonomous Vehicles Using Topic Modeling

Jinu Jung⬤, Xinyu Wang⬤, Jiaojiao Ge⬤, Jingrui Niu⬤, and Seonglim Lee⁽⊠⁾⬤

Department of Consumer Science, Convergence Program for Social Innovation, Sungkyunkwan University, Seoul, South Korea
clothilda@skku.edu

Abstract. There have been many studies on consumer acceptance and perception of autonomous vehicles. In contrast, scant research has been conducted on the user experience of autonomous vehicles. This study explored the user experience of autonomous vehicles and investigates consumer problems and issues related to autonomous vehicles from the consumer perspective. Vehicle users share information and opinions and discuss various vehicle-related topics in online communities. We collected their online posts published between February 2014 and December 2022. Applying LDA topic modeling analysis was conducted as a method for text data analysis. Considering the coherence score and interpretability, we derived five topics. Each of the topics was specified as "Perceived risks," "Knowledge share," "Reasons to purchase," "Arbitrary hardware mounting," and "Arbitrary software manipulation." First, consumers are concerned about lane departure and possible accidents. Second, consumers built up knowledge about autonomous driving technology by sharing information on and discussing the technical aspects of autonomous vehicles. Third, long-distance driving or commuting was the primary driver to purchase autonomous vehicles. Fourth, some consumers were active rather than passive in using autonomous driving technology in terms of both hardware and software manipulation. They mounted an auxiliary device to a non-autonomous vehicle and converted it into an autonomous one. They manipulated the default setting of the autonomous deriving system reflecting their own speeding or distancing preferences. Since autonomous vehicles are sensitive and complex structures, arbitrary mounting and manipulation can cause fatal accidents. Guidelines for using autonomous driving technology and legal and administrating measures are necessary for the safe use of autonomous driving technology. Customizing hardware and software which satisfy individual consumers' need and want may reduce the risk of arbitrary manipulation.

Keywords: Autonomous Vehicle · Topic Modeling · User Experience · Arbitrary Manipulation

1 Introduction

An autonomous vehicle is referred to as a self-driving car equipped with all required sensors, including GPS, IMU, cameras, and sensors [1]. The capacity of an intelligent system to perform certain tasks under the uncertainty of the system and its surroundings

C. Stephanidis et al. (Eds.): HCII 2023, CCIS 1835, pp. 61–67, 2023.
https://doi.org/10.1007/978-3-031-36001-5_8

is known as autonomy [2]. The higher a system's level of automation is in carrying out a particular activity, the more equipped it is to deal with uncertainty while requiring little to no human intervention. The Society of Automotive Engineers (SAE) defines 6 levels of driving automation ranging from 0(fully manual), 1(driver assistance), 2(partial automation), 3(conditional automation), 4(high automation) to 5 (fully autonomous) [3]. The automation level of autonomous vehicles (AVs) has been steadily rising in recent years, driving a desire for more advancements.

The market trend of autonomous vehicles is also widely watched. Many industry experts around the world have predicted market trends for autonomous vehicles, with Boston Consulting Group (BCG) predicting a 12% market for autonomous vehicles by 2025 and 25% by 2035; what's more, Navigant Research predicts the market for autonomous vehicles will reach as much as 75% by 2035 [4]. As the first country to commercialize 5g communication technology, Korea applies this technology to autonomous vehicle communication, navigation, etc. [5]. In addition, the Korean government has decided to complete road infrastructure and related legal systems to commercialize fully autonomous by 2027 [6].

The use of autonomous vehicles brings many benefits to urban mobility and city design, such as increasing vehicle safety, decreasing cities' congestion, and required space for parking [7]. Due to the benefits brought about by the use of autonomous vehicles, consumer acceptance and usage are increasing. Previous research on autonomous driving has focused on the benefits and costs of autonomous vehicles as well as the safety and dangers of autonomous driving technology [8–10]. Many studies have been conducted to examine consumers' acceptance and intention to use autonomous vehicles and found that social influence, perceived risk, hedonic and other factors are the significant variables to affect consumers' acceptance and intentions to use autonomous vehicles [11–15].

Though some levels of autonomous technologies are now widely spread in Korea and commercialization is progressing rapidly, there is a lack of substantive investigation into the user experience of autonomous vehicles. Since some drivers using autonomous technologies posted a large number of comments on online communities, it is possible to examine users' perceptions and experiences of autonomous vehicles. Therefore, this study aims to provide useful implications to policymakers and the auto industry based on the user experience of autonomous vehicles. Specifically, this study explores users' experiences and viewpoints about autonomous vehicles to understand the actual reaction of users. We analyze text data from the online platform by applying text mining analysis.

2   Method

2.1   Data Collection

This study examined the consumer experience with autonomous vehicles using online community posts. Data about the consumer experience with autonomous vehicles were collected from Korean online communities, specifically, Naver-cafe and Bobaedream, using the Python selenium package. A total of 17,113 posts were collected, covering the period from February 2014, when discussions on the consumer experience with autonomous vehicles first emerged in Korea, to December 2022.

2.2 Data Cleaning

The collected online community posts were transformed into structured data for text mining. Using the Python KoNLPy package, we extracted the nouns as the unit of analysis. The data were then cleaned by correcting spelling errors and removing unnecessary words, symbols, and punctuation marks that did not add meaning or context to the text.

2.3 Data Analysis

This study applied Latent Dirichlet Allocation (LDA) topic modeling analysis to identify the main topics and corresponding keywords related to the consumer experience of autonomous vehicles. LDA analysis is a statistical algorithm that can reveal hidden topics in unstructured data, such as text corpora [16]. The algorithm identifies the structure of documents and latent variables from the words used in them, generating a specified number of topics through the distribution of Dirichlet over the words in the document set [16]. To determine the optimal number of topics, this study calculated the coherence score, which evaluates the semantic consistency of a topic, for each topic model using the Python 'gensim' package. After considering both coherence score and interpretability, we selected the model with 5 topics.

3 Result

3.1 Results of Topic Modeling

The results of the LDA topic modeling analysis are shown in Table 1. Each of the 5 topics contains consumer experiences and opinions on autonomous vehicles that are currently being discussed.

First, In Topic 1, various terms associated with the driving risk of autonomous vehicles, including "Accident," "Risk," "Anxiety," "Curve," and "Derail," were identified. Moreover, through the keywords "Situation" and "Experience," the topic was found to revolve around the risks encountered while driving. As such, we have assigned the label "Perceived Risk" to Topic 1.

Second, Topic 2 pertains to the sharing, acquiring, and accumulation of knowledge regarding autonomous driving. The discussions revolve around the future development of technology, which is evident through the keywords such as "Future," "Technology," and "Development." Furthermore, Topic 2 is composed by the anticipation of how technological advancements would transform the application of self-driving cars, which is indicated by the use of keywords such as "Transformation," "Application," and "Expectation." As a result, Topic 2 has been labeled as "Knowledge share."

Third, Topic 3 explores the reasons behind consumer preference for autonomous vehicles. The advantages of autonomous vehicles are discussed in-depth, with keywords such as "Fuel efficiency," "Long distance," "Commute," and "Advantage" being commonly used. Additionally, keywords such as "Choice," "Purchase," and "Satisfaction" indicate that the benefits of autonomous vehicles play a crucial role in consumer decision-making and lead to their purchase. Therefore, Topic 3 was labeled as "Reasons to purchase."

Table 1. Results of topic modeling

	Topic 1	Topic 2	Topic 3	Topic 4	Topic 5
	Perceived risks	Knowledge share	Reasons to purchase	Arbitrary hardware mounting	Arbitrary software manipulation
1	Accident	Technology	Choice	Problem	Brake
2	Safety	Future	Satisfaction	Road	Operation
3	Curve	Development	Fuel efficiency	Setting	Distance
4	Necessity	Improvement	Downtown	National road	Forward
5	Assistance	Corporation	Long distance	Lane center	Preceding vehicle
6	Risk	Market	Concern	Frontal visual focus	Camera
7	Situation	Sale	Distance	Mark	Lane
8	Derail	Transformation	Advantage	Auxiliary Device	Acceleration
9	Anxiety	AI	Commute	Installation	Sensor
10	Experience	Data	Sufficient	Company	Deceleration
11	Basic	Green	Upgrade	Water bottle	Adjustment
12	Criteria	Application	Indoor	Independent automotive repair shop	Warning
13	Beware	Expectation	Tiredness	Instrument panel	Crash
14	Steering	Lidar	Purchase	Phenomenon	Departure
15	Update	Service	Stability	User	Automatic

Fourth, Topic 4 indicated that discussions around the installation of hardware in the vehicles as a solution to some challenges faced by consumers during autonomous driving. The topic identifies issues such as "Lane center", "National road", and "Problem" where the vehicle fails to follow the center of the lane or operate smoothly on national roads. To relieve these challenges, drivers install additional devices or modify default settings as evidenced by keywords such as "Setting", "Auxiliary device", "Water bottle", "Independent automotive repair shop", and "Installation". The term "Water bottle" in this context refers to the practice of mounting a water bottle on the steering wheel during autonomous driving to deceive the system into thinking that the driver's hands are on the wheel when they take off. Therefore, the topic is named "Arbitrary Hardware Mounting".

Finally, similar to Topic 4, Topic 5 also revealed that consumers manipulate the software related to autonomous driving to relieve the inconvenience experience during autonomous driving. Although "Coding" did not appear among the top 15 keywords, consumers were changing the software default values. The keywords such as "Preceding vehicle", "Distance", "Camera", "Acceleration", and "Warning" indicated that consumers were adjusting the software by changing the distance from the preceding vehicle, adjusting the speed in front of the speed camera, or turning off the warning light. Therefore, Topic 5 has been labeled as "Arbitrary software management".

4 Conclusion

The study used LDA topic modeling to identify and label five distinct topics related to consumer experiences with autonomous vehicles. Topic 1 pertains to consumers' perceived risks associated with autonomous vehicles, and Topic 2 revolves around the sharing and acquisition of knowledge regarding self-driving technology among auto consumers. The knowledge-sharing practice plays a crucial role in helping each other be informed about autonomous driving technology. By exchanging knowledge and experiences collectively, consumers can gain a comprehensive understanding of the benefits and limitations of autonomous vehicles [17]. This, in turn, enables informed consumers to make better decisions about using this emerging technology [18]. Topic 3 represented the preference for and reasons behind purchasing autonomous vehicles. The perceived benefits influence consumers' purchase decision-making about autonomous vehicles. In contrast, Topic 4 and Topic 5 highlight consumers' arbitrary hardware mounting and software management practices to add convenient autonomous services or to relieve inconveniences during autonomous driving. The arbitrary manipulation of hardware and software raises significant safety concerns. Since autonomous vehicles are sensitive and complex structures, arbitrary mounting and manipulation can cause fatal accidents [19]. Therefore, the arbitrary installation of hardware modifications and the adjustment of software settings without proper authorization pose a risk to both the vehicle occupants and other road users [20].

Industry stakeholders and policy-makers need to recognize the urgency of the consumers' arbitrary manipulation and take appropriate action to ensure the safe and responsible use of autonomous vehicles. To reduce the risk of arbitrary manipulation, automakers may provide customized autonomous driving experiences incorporating individual consumers' wants and needs in the product design and manufacturing processes [21], and guidelines for software customization. Currently, relevant regulations are not established in Korea that guide the safe management and use of autonomous driving devices [22], It is necessary to build up necessary legal and administrative measures to ensure the safe and responsible use of autonomous vehicles, including regulating (or standardizing) manipulation of the hardware and software.

References

1. Samuel, M., Hussein, M., Mohamad, M.B.: A review of some pure pursuit based path tracking techniques for control of autonomous vehicle. Int. J. Comput. Appl. 135(1), 35–38 (2016)

2. Wang, J., Huang, H., Li, K., Li, J.: Towards the unified principles for level 5 autonomous vehicles. Engineering **7**(9), 1313–1325 (2021)
3. Society of Automotive Engineers: Taxonomy and Definitions for Terms Related to Driving Automation Systems for On-Road Motor Vehicles (2021)
4. National Information Society Agency: Autonomous driving opens the door to the automotive industry (2017)
5. Park, S.U., Lee, S.W., Lee, J.S.: 5G is opening the world of autonomous driving. Broadcast. Media Magaz. **24**(1), 23–32 (2019)
6. Ministry of Land, Infrastructure and Transport: A pan-ministerial cooperative autonomous driving technology development project to achieve a first-class autonomous vehicle country has begun in earnest. http://www.molit.go.kr. Accessed 5 March 2023
7. Santana, E.F.Z., Covas, G., Duarte, F., Santi, P., Ratti, C., Kon, F.: Transitioning to a driverless city: evaluating a hybrid system for autonomous and non-autonomous vehicles. Simul. Model. Pract. Theory **107**, 102210 (2021)
8. Canitez, F.: Transition to autonomous vehicles: a socio-technical transition perspective. Alphanum. J. **9**(2), 143–162 (2021)
9. Litman, T.: Autonomous vehicle implementation predictions: Implications for transport planning. Victoria: Victoria Transport Policy Institute (2022)
10. Qian, L., Yin, J., Huang, Y., Liang, Y.: The role of values and ethics in influencing consumers' intention to use autonomous vehicle hailing services. Technol. Fore-cast. Soc. Change **188**, 122267 (2023)
11. Jing, P., Xu, G., Chen, Y., Shi, Y., Zhan, F.: The determinants behind the acceptance of autonomous vehicles: a systematic review. Sustainability **12**(5), 1719 (2020)
12. Meyer-Waarden, L., Cloarec, J.: "Baby, you can drive my car": Psychological antecedents that drive consumers' adoption of AI-powered autonomous vehicles. Technovation **109**, 102348 (2022)
13. Park, J., Han, S.: Investigating older consumers' acceptance factors of autonomous vehicles. J. Retail. Consum. Serv. **72**, 103241 (2023)
14. Ribeiro, M.A., Gursoy, D., Chi, O.H.: Customer acceptance of autonomous vehicles in travel and tourism. J. Travel Res. **61**(3), 620–636 (2022)
15. Tan, H., Zhao, X., Yang, J.: Exploring the influence of anxiety, pleasure and subjective knowledge on public acceptance of fully autonomous vehicles. Comput. Hum. Behav. **131**, 107187 (2022)
16. Blei, D.M., Ng, A.Y., Jordan, M.I.: Latent dirichlet allocation. J. Mach. Learn. Res. 993–1022 (2003)
17. Sharma, I., Mishra, S.: Quantifying the consumer's dependence on different information sources on acceptance of autonomous vehicles. Transport. Res. Part A: Policy Pract. **160**, 179–203 (2022)
18. Ward, C., Raue, M., Lee, C., D'Ambrosio, L., Coughlin, J.F.: Acceptance of automated driving across generations: the role of risk and benefit perception, knowledge, and trust. In: Kurosu, M. (ed.) HCI 2017. LNCS, vol. 10271, pp. 254–266. Springer, Cham (2017). https://doi.org/10.1007/978-3-319-58071-5_20
19. Serter, B., Beul, C., Lang, M., Schmidt, W.: Foreseeable Misuse in Automated Driving Vehicles-The Human Factor in Fatal Accidents of Complex Automation, No. 2017-01-0059. SAE Technical Paper (2017)
20. Adelsbach, A., Huber, U., Sadeghi, A.R., Stüble, C.: Embedding Trust into Cars—Secure Software Delivery and Installation. In Third Workshop on Embedded Security in Cars (escar 2005), Cologne, Germany (2005)

21. Scott-Sharoni, S.T., Fereydooni, N., Walker, B.N., Jeon, M., Riener, A., Wintersberger, P.: To customize or not to customize-is that the question?. In: 13th International Conference on Automotive User Interfaces and Interactive Vehicular Applications, Proceedings, pp. 156–159. ACM, Online (2021)
22. Ministry of Land, Infrastructure and Transport: Ethical Guidelines for Autonomous Vehicles. http://www.molit.go.kr/. Accessed 5 March 2023

A Sentiment Analysis of User Attitudes Toward Information Cocoons in Short Video Apps

Lili Liu[1], Jinbi Yang[2(✉)], Zhaoying Ding[1], Shanjiao Ren[1], and Chuanmin Mi[1]

[1] College of Economics and Management, Nanjing University of Aeronautics and Astronautics, Nanjing, China
{lili85,joy9971}@nuaa.edu.cn
[2] School of Digital Economics and Management, Wuxi University, Wuxi, China
yangjinbi@jiangnan.edu.cn

Abstract. Applying personalized recommendation technology to short video APPs may create information cocoons, where users are exposed to homogeneous information and hardly hear different opinions. Existing studies focus on the negative consequences of information cocoons (e.g., group polarization), few scholars have investigated individuals' mental mechanism regarding information cocoons, such as their attitudes. We first crawl discussions regarding information cocoons in TikTok from a popular Chinese social media, and conduct a sentiment analysis to identify users' different attitudes towards information cocoons in short video apps. Thereafter, we adopt the deep learning algorithm model – BERT model to classify users' attitudes toward information cocoons into three categories: negative (breakthrough attitude), positive (retention attitude) and neutral. This study not only enriches our knowledge on information cocoons and user attitudes, but also provide important practical insights for short video apps' managers regarding the utilization of personalized recommendation technology.

Keywords: Information cocoons · Sentiment analysis · Information cocoons retention attitude · Information cocoons breakthrough attitude

1 Introduction

Short video APPs (i.e., TikTok), which serve as a tool for people to entertain, socialize and obtain information, has become increasingly popular. By the end of June 2022, 91.5% Chinese internet users have registered for short video Apps, which are approximately 962 million users [1]. Internet users have spent ever-increased time on short video APPs. On average, a user would spend more than 2 h on short video APPs per day [2], surpassing the time he/she spends on other social media applications (e.g., Weibo, WeChat, etc.) [3]. In other words, short video apps have become the main sources where internet users obtain information. The short video Apps continuously tracks and records users' participation behavior, such as browsing history, retweeting, commenting, frequency and the duration of use, in order to capture users' preference and interests. Based on the archive data, personalized recommendation technology generalize and deliver personalized content

© The Author(s), under exclusive license to Springer Nature Switzerland AG 2023
C. Stephanidis et al. (Eds.): HCII 2023, CCIS 1835, pp. 68–74, 2023.
https://doi.org/10.1007/978-3-031-36001-5_9

to users. On one hand, the personalized recommendation technology delivers the content that matches the user's interests, thus enhance user experience. On the other hand, the personalized recommendation technology may filter out valuable information that users do not prefer, restricting users' access to heterogeneous information, making them "hear only the information they choose, that is comfortable and enjoyable to them", thus easily been trapped in information cocoons [4].

Short video app users who are aware of information cocoons may generate different attitudes toward information cocoons [5, 6]. Personalized recommendation technology may quickly deliver contents that match users' interests and satisfy their information needs, improve their pleasure and enjoyment, users thus generate positive attitude and may choose to actively stay in the information cocoons. On the contrary, users may be tired with homogeneous information provided by the personalized recommendation system, and feel that they are surrounded by unwanted and useless information (e.g., news that is not interesting but highly popular), thus generate negative attitude (e.g., fatigue) and seek to break through the information cocoons.

Limited research has paid attention to user attitudes toward information cocoons. In order to fill the gap, this study crawls social media user discussions on information cocoons, and adopt BERT (Bidirectional Encoder Representations from Transformers) pre-training model based on NLP (Natural Language Processing) to identify and classify users' different attitudes toward information cocoons. Based on a sentiment analysis, this study seeks to provide suggestions to short vide app operators, that is, how they can improve the personalized recommendation technology, in order to reduce the negative impact of information cocoons while satisfying users' information needs.

2 Theoretical Background

Social media users post their opinions on various issues, generating massive amounts of user generated text contents. Text sentiment analysis is the use of natural language processing techniques to analyze users' text posts, identify their sentiment tendencies, and then clarify user's emotional attitudes [7]. Sentiment analysis based on deep learning is able to autonomously acquire and classify semantics via pre-trained models. BERT pre-trained models perform good in emotion classification tasks, resulting in high classification accuracy. For instance, Munikar et al. [8] complete fine-grained sentiment classification tasks on the Stanford Sentiment Treebank data set by fine-tuning the BERT pre-training model with better accuracy than more complex architectures, such as recursive, recyclic and convolutional neural networks, demonstrating the transfer learning capability of BERT models in NLP. Araci et al. [9] propose an improved BERT model, FinBERT, further improves 15% accuracy in the financial sentiment classification task based on the Financial Phrasebank dataset. Xu et al. proposed an extended model of BERT, DomBERT, which has been applied to aspect-based sentiment analysis of low-resource environments [10]. Zhao et al. apply the BERT-based sentiment analysis and key entity detection method to conduct online financial text mining and social media opinion analysis, and the results outperforms SVM, LR, NBM and BERT on both financial sentiment analysis and key entity detection data sets [11]. In short, the fine-tuned BERT pre-training model is suitable and applicable for sentiment classification.

3 Research Methodology

3.1 Data Collection and Processing

We seek to identify and distinguish short video app users' different attitudes toward information cocoons based on text analysis. Since there are limited discussions on information cocoons in short video Apps, we collect data from a popular Chinese social media Weibo. Using "information cocoons" and "short video apps" as keywords to search in Weibo, we are able to find a great number of original discussions, which reflect users' real feelings and attitudes toward information cocoons in short video apps. In this study, we adopted Python language to write the crawler program, in order to crawl the original posts regarding "information cocoons" and "short video apps" on Weibo. We crawled the posts on Weibo from September 1, 2021 to September 30, 2022. In total, 24,265 posts have been collected, the information included user nicknames, texts, and posting times.

The original text data was pre-processed, in order to exclude the misspellings, emoji abuse and other irregularities, which ultimately improve the text data quality. Since there was lack of information cocoons related sentiment annotation data set in the natural language processing, we had manually annotated the sentiment categories for the subsequent learning and training of the BERT model. Considering the labor and time costs of manual annotation, 40% of the posts (7510 items) were manually annotated with sentiment categories in this experiment. The labeling rules were depicted in Table 1. If the statements were subjective and had obvious sentiment tendency, the sentiment polarity is recognized as negative or positive; if the statements were objective and had no obvious sentiment tendency, the attitude was neutral.

Subsequently, we adopted the hold-out method to divide the labeled data as training set, validation set and test set. The proportion of negative, active, and neutral data in the training set, validation set and test set were consistent, in order to avoid the potential bias caused by unbalanced data division. The three data sets were divided according to the 8:1:1 proportion, and the distribution of each data set was shown in Table 2. The training set consisted of 6610 text data, which was used to obtain the sentence semantics and its relationship with sentiment classification, and to adjust the model-related parameters to further optimize the sentiment classification accuracy. The validation set consisted of 750 text data, which was used to verify the training results of the test model and record the F1 evaluation metrics of each training round. The test set with a total of 750 text data was used to evaluate the classification accuracy of the model based on various evaluation metrics.

Table 1. Examples of Manual annotation rules

Text Examples	Tags	Label Explanations
How can we break through the information cocoons in TikTok?	0	Statements are subjective and emotional Negative: There is a breakthrough, aversion or other negative attitude toward the information cocoons
I hope we can all escape from the information cocoons in TikTok and bravely embrace the world		
Hate the information cocoons in TikTok, every time it takes a long time to escape from it		
Consciously focus on different people and consciously try to break through the information cocoons in TikTok		
I want to stay in my information cocoons and only read the recommended contents in TikTok	1	Statements are subjective and emotional Positive: There is a positive attitude towards information cocoons, such as actively create information cocoons and stay in it
Live in information cocoons that you have created, and only listen to what you want to hear and only see what you want to see in TikTok		
I love big data, I want to stay in the information cocoons and TikTok for a lifetime		
Spend a lot of money to buy some happy Internet surfing, just build an information cocoon room, then I can stay happy in TikTok forever		
I often wonder what is information cocoons when using TikTok	2	Statements are objective and has no obvious attitude tendency, just mention "information cocoons" in the text
Information cocoons in TikTok: Brush how handsome you are riding a motorcycle, brush how bad you fell		
Liu Xiang's new summary "Cultural Picnic" is very good, one minute, this period of information cocoons, find it on TikTok		

Table 2. Distribution of each data set

Emotional category	Training set	Validation set	Test set
Negative	3310	413	413
Active	1770	221	221
Neutral	930	116	116
Total	6610	750	750

3.2 Sentiment Classification Based on BERT Model

We adopted the BERT pre-trained model and PyTorch framework to conduct the sentiment classification [12], in order to quantitatively identify users' different attitudes toward information cocoons. First, the training set data was input into the pre-training model for training, and the experimental parameters of the BERT model were configured and showed in Table 3.

Table 3. Experimental parameters configuration

Parameters	Parameter Meaning	Parameter Value
do_train	Whether to do training	true
do_eval	Whether to do verification	true
do_predict	Whether to make predictions	true
num_train_epochs	Number of iterations	25
train_batch_size	Training the size of the batch	16
Optimizer	Optimizer Selection	Adam
learning_rate	Learning Rate	2e-5
max_seq_length	Maximum sentence length	200

The effectiveness of the trained model should be further evaluated by several metrics. Accuracy, Precision, Recall, and the F1-score were set as evaluation metrics. The formula formulation involved the meaning of the symbols for the calculation of the confusion matrix, as shown in Table 4.

Table 4. Confusion Matrix

Predicted value / Actual value	Positive	Negative
Positive	TP (True Positive)	FN (False Negative)
Negative	FP (False Positive)	TN (True Negative)

Finally, the accuracy of the model was 0.8387, and the results of other evaluation indexes were shown in Table 5. Among the three emotional labels, the values of label 0 (negative) and label 1 (positive) indicators were greater than the values of label 2 (neutral) indicators. The overall evaluation of the model had achieved an acceptable level.

Table 5. Model evaluation results

Label	Precision	Recall	F1
0	0.8668	0.8689	0.8679
1	0.8688	0.8348	0.8514
2	0.6810	0.7315	0.7054
Macro avg	0.8055	0.8117	0.8082
Weighted avg	0.8421	0.8409	0.8413

The trained BERT model had accurate and stable autonomous scoring and classification ability, which could be applied to predict the non-manually annotated data sets. The non-annotated 11431 text data was then imported into the BERT text sentiment classification model, and each text data was labeled with sentiment attitude. Finally, the non-manually and manually annotated dataset were aggregated, and the number of negative, positive, and neutral samples were counted. The final emotional attitudes toward information cocoons proportion was shown in Fig. 1.

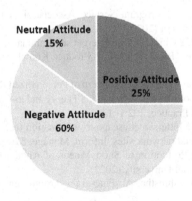

Fig. 1. Emotional attitude distribution of the total sample

As shown in Fig. 1, the total number of posts on Weibo with negative attitude towards the information cocoons in TikTok was 11,237, accounting for 60% of all samples, the total number of posts with positive attitude towards information cocoons in TikTok was 4,708, accounting for 25% of all samples, while the total number of posts on Weibo with neutral attitude towards the information cocoons in TikTok was 2,830, accounting for 15% of samples.

4 Conclusions

Findings of the sentiment analysis confirm the assumption that users might generate different attitudes toward information cocoons in short video apps. Furthermore, approximately 60% of the users hold negative attitude toward information cocoons and would like to break through the restriction of information cocoons by switching to other websites or short vide apps. Only 25% of users hold positive attitude towards information cocoons and would like to stagnate in the information cocoons. In other words, except for a small number of people who maintain a neutral attitude towards information cocoons, majority (85%) of short video apps' users hold more extreme emotional attitudes toward information cocoons, that were, the information cocoon retention attitude and the information cocoon breakthrough attitude.

This study provides implications for both academics and practitioners. Theoretically, we conduct a quantitative to identify users' different attitudes toward information cocoons in short video apps. Our findings enrich our knowledge on information cocoons and user attitudes. Practically, our findings provide important insights for the sustainable operation of short video apps. In particular, our findings suggest that short video app managers need to pay close attention to the negative effect of personalized recommendation technologies, such as information cocoons. A possible solution is to optimize the recommendation systems, in order to avoid information homogenization, and deliver more diverse, useful information to users.

References

1. China Internet Network Information Center: The 50th Statistical Report on the Development of Internet in China (2022)
2. China Network Audiovisual Program Service Association: China Network Audiovisual Development Research Report (2021)
3. QuestMobile (2022). 2022 China Mobile Internet semi-annual report
4. Sunstein, C.R.: Infotopia: How Many Minds Produce Knowledge. Oxford University Press (2006)
5. Yujiao Yang, Qinjian Yuan. The Hidden concern of Personalized Recommendation: An Analysis of Information Cocoons Based on Grounded Theory and its Causes and Consequences[J]. Information Theory and Practice, 202:1–14
6. Cheikh-Ammar, M.: The bittersweet escape to information technology: an investigation of the stress paradox of social network sites. Inform. Manage. 57(8), 103368 (2020)
7. Chao, M.: Research on Promotion of Short Videos of Ancient Books Based on Emotion Analysis. Shanghai Normal University (2022)
8. Munikar, M., Shakya, S., Shrestha, A.: Fine-grained Sentiment Classification using BERT (2019)
9. Araci, D., Genç, Z.: Financial Sentiment Analysis with Pre-trained Language Models (2020)
10. Xu, H., Liu, B., Shu, L., et al.: DomBERT: Domain-oriented Language Model for Aspect-based Sentiment Analysis. arXiv (2020)
11. Zhao, L., Li, L., Zheng, X., et al.: A BERT based sentiment analysis and key entity detection approach for online financial texts. In: 2021 IEEE 24th International Conference on Computer Supported Cooperative Work in Design (CSCWD), 1233–1238 (2021)
12. Paszke, A., Gross, S., Massa, F., et al.: PyTorch: An imperative style, high-performance deep learning library. Advances in Neural Information Processing Systems, p. 32. Curran Associates, Inc. (2019)

Social Media and Information Dissemination of Indonesia as G20 Presidency

Ali Maksum[1]($\boxtimes$), Ahmad Sahide[2], Tan Bee Wah[3], Hilman Mahmud Akmal Ma'arif[2], and Sitti Zarina Alimuddin[2]

[1] Department of International Relations, Universitas Muhammadiyah Yogyakarta, Yogyakarta, Indonesia
`ali.maksum@fisipol.umy.ac.id`
[2] Master of International Relations, Universitas Muhammadiyah Yogyakarta, Yogyakarta, Indonesia
[3] College of Business, Universiti Utara Malaysia, Sintok, Kedah, Malaysia

Abstract. This research aimed to investigate the dissemination of information about Indonesia's G20 presidency in 2022, particularly through the social media platform of Twitter (Web.2.0), which allows interaction between the providers and other users. A qualitative methodology was employed with content analysis of social media discussions, specifically Twitter. Furthermore, computer-assisted qualitative data analysis software (CAQDAS) was used, namely NVivo 12 Plus (QSR International, Burlington, Massachusetts, USA), which can generate data for sentiment analysis, top influencers, dominant hashtags, top mentions, and dominant words. The Twitter data were collected during the G20 summit on 15–16 November 2022 using the keywords "#G20Indonesia" and "KTT G20". The two keywords were selected since they were becoming a trending topic. The results found that using the "KTT G20" keyword, a message on Indonesia's G20 presidency was widely distributed and received positive sentiment from locals. The use of the hashtag "#G20Indonesia", the presidency attracted international attention while generating additional negative sentiment.

Keywords: information · Twitter · Indonesia · G20 · the presidency

1 Introduction

Understanding the dissemination of information about the G20 Summit in Bali is critical, particularly for the Indonesian government. President Joko Widodo (Jokowi) stated that Indonesians should be proud of the G20 presidency. According to the President, becoming the first developing country to hold the G20 Presidency is significant because it shows respect, value, and development. The Indonesian people should overcome their "colonized" mindset and become more confident before other countries [1]. The election of the G20 Presidency [2] is meaningful because it raises various hopes for strategic benefits. With the theme "Recover Together, Recover Stronger", Indonesia hopes to gain at least three advantages, namely (1) economic - driving domestic consumption, (2) social development - increasing vaccine production and distribution, and (3) political - demonstrating Indonesia's success in implementing the Job Creation Law and the Sovereign Wealth Fund (SWF) [3].

The question is, "How is the information dissemination in Indonesia as G20 Presidency at the general public level?" amid high expectations from the government. To respond to this query, it is vital to conduct social media research to understand the spread of information and identify the issues that the general public is debating concerning the G20 Presidency. Twitter is a social media platform that has gained popularity and is a useful tool for comprehending the social discourse taking shape. However, the unrestricted nature can also propagate hoaxes or false information, as was the case with the Covid-19 pandemic [4].

The majority-Muslim nation understands the idea of *"tabayyun"* or confirmation as a crucial means of halting the spread of false information and ensuring integrity. A research found that most respondents did not conduct *"tabayyun"* or confirm the news heard [5]. Since Twitter (Web.2.0) allows interactions between information disseminators and other users, this research intended to evaluate the online dissemination of the G20 presidency in 2022. It unpacks the information about the influencers, the most popular hashtags, and sentiment analysis concerning the G20 presidency. The analysis can serve as a policy recommendation to the government, the primary party responsible for realizing the concept. Therefore, the following paragraphs will discuss ICT and Twitter as public diplomacy.

2 Literature Review

2.1 ICT and Public Diplomacy

Public diplomacy was still conventional before the rapid development of ICT. Diplomacy is carried out using a variety of methods, such as cultural diplomacy as practiced by Korea [6], the United States [7], Turkey [8], and Taiwan [9], as well as efforts to establish diplomatic relations at the regional government level or paradiplomacy [10].

The emergence of social media, which falls under the Web 2.0 umbrella, is one of the key advances in ICT. This indicates that the pattern of information dissemination has changed dramatically compared to earlier technologies. For instance, it seems to be a monologue, and there is no interactivity on the website platform (Web 1.0). In contrast, social media (Web 2.0) is more interactive because it involves direct two-way dialogue between information suppliers and recipients [11].

The existence of social media platforms such as Twitter has compelled policymakers to adapt to these changes in information dissemination. Direct contact with the general public also influences the pattern of diplomacy. Therefore, social media is a reality that the government should deal with to manage information and communicate with the public directly. Other countries recognize that social media should be utilized to communicate and gain public support for policies. For instance, public diplomacy using social media is carried out by China [12], Russia [13], India [14], the United States [15], and others. The construction of the literature that examines social media and public diplomacy especially related to the G20 Presidency, is still relatively minor.

2.2 Twitter as a Public Diplomacy

Several experts researched Twitter's use in public diplomacy. For example, the Chinese government strongly encourages diplomats to engage with the global community through this social media [16]. As a result, sentiment analysis is generally positive, indicating widespread public support for the Chinese government's diplomacy. The same tendency exists in Turkey, where Twitter supports the government's diplomatic policies. The Turkish government has used this strategy to popularize news information sources that are becoming increasingly popular, such as The Republic of Turkiye Directorate of Communications, TIKA, Yunus Emre Institute, and TRT [17]. Even Twitter is useful for spreading propaganda during the South China Sea crisis, which involved numerous accounts from the US, China, and India [18]. It is also used successfully in many cases of public diplomacies, such as Iran – US relations [19], US – Cuba relations [20], and Indonesia [21]. This research is expected to provide a fresh perspective on Twitter and public diplomacy studies, which have received little attention from academics.

3   Methodology

A qualitative approach was employed with content analysis of discussions about Indonesia's G20 presidency on social media, particularly Twitter. The data were collected during the G20 summit on 15–16 November 2022 using the keywords "#G20Indonesia" and "KTT G20" and utilized computer-assisted qualitative data analysis software (CAQDAS), namely NVivo 12 Plus (QSR International, Burlington, Massachusetts, USA). The two keywords were selected since they were becoming a trending topic on Twitter. Additionally, each of the two keywords represented different segments, namely "#G20Indonesia" for the global and "KTT G20" for the local audience. Once the dataset was collected, NVivo 12 Plus was used to conduct the coding process and generate sentiment analysis, top influencers, dominant hashtags, top mentions, and dominant words. Furthermore, the research strategy of Ahmed, Vidal-Alaball, Lopez Segui, and Moreno-Sánchez [22] on the Twitter analysis was adopted. The protocol of this research can be described in the following Fig. 1.

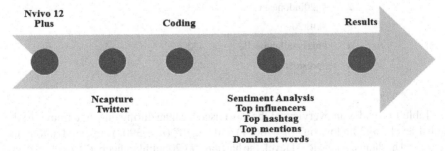

Fig. 1. Data Analysis Process

4 Findings

Twitter has given several pieces of information about Indonesia's G20 presidency. After the coding process using NVivo 12 Plus, the subsequent paragraphs present specific analyses from a Twitter discussion on those particular issues. Using #G20Indonesia the sentiment tends to negative (>55%), while searching keyword "KTT G20" the sentiment tends to positive (>68%). This indicates that on the global level, Indonesia's G20 presidency was dominated by negative sentiment. In contrast, this achievement was greatly appreciated at the local level. Jokowi's desire to make Indonesia proud of the G20 presidency has prevailed, and the positive sentiment shows the information disseminated effectively across society. The differences in sentiment analysis correlated with the received message of the audience both at the global and local levels. Measuring Twitter hashtags is crucial to understand the message with the same subject. In this case, NVivo 12 Plus has generated top hashtags for the two different keywords, as shown in Table 1.

Table 1. Top Hashtags on Indonesia's G20 Presidency

Top five hashtags using #G20		
No.	Hashtag	Number of references
1	#g20indonesia	8651
2	#g20	3902
3	#ﺍﻟﺪﻭﻟﺔ_ﺳﻴﻴﺮ	1813
4	#ﻗﻤﺔ ﻋﻠﺸﺮﻳﻦ	1636
5	#uae	1150
Top five hashtags using KTT G20		
No.	Location	Number of references
1	#g20pulihlebihcepat	1980
2	#g20indonesia	873
3	#kttg20	541
4	#masyaallahgiselle	432
5	#presidensig20	420

Table 1 provides an overview of the most used hashtag during this time frame. At the global level, "#g20indonesia" ($n = 8651$) and "#g20" ($n = 3902$) appeared among the most used hashtags. At the local level, the hashtag "#g20pulihlebihcepat" ($n = 1980$) was ahaead of #g20indonesia ($n = 873$), #kttg20 ($n = 541$), #masyaallahgiselle ($n = 432$), and #presidensig20 ($n = 420$). Indeed, among the top, irrelevant hashtags constantly appeared, such as "#uae" ($n = 1150$) and "#masyaallahgiselle" ($n = 432$). The hashtag

in Arabic also appeared as " "رئيس_الدولة#"" (ref: head of state) ($n = 1813$) and "
"قمة العشرين#"" (ref: G20 summit) ($n = 1636$). The hashtag "#masyaallahgiselle" is
irrelevant since it is the celebrity-related hashtag of a girls' band, namely JKT48, which
went viral due to one of the members wearing a hijab. The emergence of various hashtags
conveys that even though the G20 discourse is held in Indonesia and globally, it also
benefits many parties.

Related to influencers, during G20 Summit in Bali, there were Twitter accounts
that deliberately influenced the social media discussion. Interestingly, there are significant differences in the influencers in the two keywords, with the global influencers
using #G20Indonesia being international figures or institutions who are influential and
relevant to the theme. According to Table 2, the top five influencers are @forsan_uae
(UAE media & news agency), @bkksnow (a Thai academic), @g20_india (Indian G20
secretariat), @rishisunak (UK Prime Minister), and @thestanislawski (Ukrainian Jour-
nalist). Meanwhile, domestic influencers include @jokowi (President of Indonesia),
@narendramodi (Prime Minister of India), and @cakiminow (Indonesian politician).
Anonymous influencer accounts, namely @ndagels and @txtdarihi, emerged on Twitter
and influenced the Indonesian G20 presidency discourse. This demonstrates that international Twitter accounts truly control the flow of information on the G20 presidency.
Table 2 provides a listing of the numerous most influential individuals. A huge number
of followers does not ensure that other users will positively receive a Twitter account.

Table 2. Top Influencer on Indonesia's G20 Presidency

Top five influencers using #G20

No.	Twitter account name	Account type	Number of references	Followers
1	@forsan_uae	Media & news agency of UAE	1895	587,845
2	@bkksnow	Academia from Thailand	1194	345,445
3	@g20_india	Unofficial Indian G20 account	857	536,486
4	@rishisunak	Prime Minister of the UK	801	1,785,988
5	@thestanislawski	Ukrainian Journalist	791	11,376

Top five influencers using KTT G20

No.	Twitter account name	Account type	Number of references	Followers
1	@jokowi	President of Indonesia	1351	19,070,311
2	@ndagels	Indonesian anonymous influencer	589	388,186
3	@txtdarihi	Indonesian anonymous influencer	561	139,746
4	@cakiminow	Indonesian Politician	345	237,670
5	@narendramodi	Prime Minister of India	341	85,170,928

President Jokowi (@jokowi) was consistently the most-mentioned account on Twitter among domestic users, surpassing other well-known domestic accounts, as seen in Table 3. However, the popularity of the accounts lags far behind compared to others, such as @g20org (India's G20 Presidency), @mohamedbinzayed (President of the UAE), @narendramodi (Prime Minister of India), and @uaeembassyjkt (UAE Embassy Jakarta). This gap appears to correspond with the posting locations, as seen in Table 3. Referring to Table 3, foreign Twitter accounts predominate from the dominance of hashtags, influencers, and user locations. The Indonesian account performs exceptionally when the tweet contains the keyword "G20 Summit", but the outcomes differ when "#G20Indonesia" is used. This indicates that Indonesian Twitter users' conversations are still not very intense, affecting how information spreads worldwide. Instead, Twitter users dominate conversations using the keyword "G20 Summit", probably because it is more well-liked and accepted than #G20Indonesia. However, among the mentioned accounts, the official Twitter of Indonesia's G20 Presidency, namely @Indonesia_G20, is absent in all categories.

Table 3. Top Five Users Most Mentioned on Indonesia's G20 Presidency

Most mentioned Twitter accounts using #G20				
No.	Twitter account name	Account type	Number of references	Followers
1	@g20org	India's G20 Presidency	4147	536,546
2	@mohamedbinzayed	President of the UAE	1973	4,833,759
3	@narendramodi	Prime Minister of India	1536	85,170,928
4	@uaeembassyjkt	UAE Embassy Jakarta	1509	2,509
5	@jokowi	Indonesian President	850	19,070,311
Most mentioned accounts using KTT G20				
No.	Twitter account name	Account type	Number of references	Followers
1	@jokowi	President of Indonesian	895	19,070,311
2	@g20org	Indian G20 Secretariat	461	536,546
3	@erickthohir	Indonesian politician	445	474,522
4	@ridwankamil	Indonesian politician	361	5,424,082
5	@kemenbumn	Indonesian government	259	726,038

In terms of word distribution, it closely aligns with the data presented above. For example, when the keyword #G20Indonesia is used, the NVivo 12 Plus auto-coding results showed that the hashtag is dominant, as evidenced by the bold print on the word-cloud image followed by "https", indicating a high intensity of the website. Similarly, the keyword "G20 Summit" dominates the spread of words in word-cloud images, followed by "https" printed in bold. Therefore, Twitter has a limited number of characters for sending messages, and users frequently provide additional information through the website URL. The primary aim is for users who intend to learn more about the G20 presidency to log on to related links that provide more detailed information (Fig. 2).

#G20Indonesia   KTT G20

Fig. 2. Word-Cloud Analysis

Besides the limited number of characters, Twitter conversations are highly dynamic and can be altered. Concerning the limitations, it only covers the period between 15 and 16 November 2022, the day of the G20 Summit. Future research should be able to dismantle data about the G20 leadership throughout various periods. The content analysis only addresses one component of information distribution, which is quite simplistic. However, this has not delved deeper into the Twitter conversation's themes as a research on the 2017 French presidential election [23]. Keywords can also be added in future research, as evidenced by the hashtags for anti-vaccine propaganda [24]. The NVivo 12 Plus software greatly aided this research, and the results may differ. For example, the visualization and display of the results are more appealing and complete when using alternative software, such as NodeXL, Python, and R Programming.

5   Conclusion

This research discovered that information dissemination related to Indonesia's G20 presidency significantly contributed to the literature on digital diplomacy. It uncovered how Twitter data represented information disseminated to the public among Indonesians and the global community. Indeed, using local keywords such as "KTT G20", a message was widely distributed and received positive sentiment from the locals. Using the hashtag "#G20Indonesia", the presidency drew international attention and gained more negative sentiment. Despite being one of the largest social media users, Indonesia's Twitter influencers remain untold compared to global influencers. In the future, the government should focus on improving digital diplomacy in cyberspace, which is critical for a country's public diplomacy.

Acknowledgement. The authors would like to thank the Indonesian Ministry of Education, Culture, Research, and Technology for funding this research through DRTPM Research Grants.

References

1. Sekretariat Kabinet Republik Indonesia: Menjadi Presidensi G20, Presiden Jokowi Ingin WNI Bangga pada Indonesia (2021). https://setkab.go.id/menjadi-presidensi-g20-presiden-jokowi-ingin-wni-bangga-pada-indonesia/
2. Munira, S., Jatmika, S.: Assessing policies, practices and impact of actions and policies in handling Covid-19 pandemic: comparative studies of Bangladesh and Indonesia. J. Islam. World Polit. **6**(1), 46–58 (2022)
3. CNN Indonesia: 3 Manfaat Presidensi G20 bagi Indonesia (2022). https://www.cnnindonesia.com/ekonomi/20220117173120-537-747721/3-manfaat-presidensi-g20-bagi-indonesia
4. Ahmed, W., Vidal-Alaball, J., Downing, J., López Seguí, F.: COVID-19 and the 5G conspiracy theory: social network analysis of Twitter data. J. Med. Internet Res. **22**(5), e19458 (2020)
5. Reza, I.F.: Counteracting Hoax in social media through Tabayyun by Islamic student community. Ta'dib **24**(2), 269–279 (2021)
6. Dhawan, R.K.: Korea's cultural diplomacy: an analysis of the Hallyu in India. Strateg. Anal. **41**(6), 559–570 (2017)
7. Ratzlaff, A.: Birds of a feather?: Lessons on U.S. cultural diplomacy from Walt Disney during the Good Neighbor Policy. Int. J. Cult. Policy 1–16 (2022)
8. Özkan, A.: Strategic practices of public diplomacy policies in educational field and Turkey's potential for cultural diplomacy. Procedia Soc. Behav. Sci. **176**, 35–43 (2015)
9. Rawnsley, G.: Soft power rich, public diplomacy poor: an assessment of Taiwan's external communications. China Q. **232**, 982–1001 (2017)
10. Burksiene, V., Dvorak, J., Burbulytė-Tsiskarishvili, G.: City diplomacy in young democracies: the case of the Baltics. In: Amiri, S., Sevin, E. (eds.) City Diplomacy. PMSGPD, pp. 305–330. Springer, Cham (2020). https://doi.org/10.1007/978-3-030-45615-3_14
11. Fesharaki, M.N., Fetanat, A., Shooshtari, D.F.: A conceptual model for Socio-Pragmatic Web based on activity theory. Cogent Educ. **7**(1), 1797979 (2020)
12. Sun, W.: Chinese language digital/social media in Australia: diaspora as 'double agents' of public diplomacy. In: Kennedy, L. (ed.) Routledge International Handbook of Diaspora Diplomacy, p. 12. Routledge, London (2021)
13. Crilley, R., Gillespie, M., Willis, A.: Tweeting the Russian revolution: RT's #1917LIVE and social media re-enactments as public diplomacy. Eur. J. Cult. Stud. **23**(3), 354–373 (2019)
14. Garud-Patkar, N.: India's mediated public diplomacy on social media: building agendas in South Asia. In: Association for Education in Journalism and Mass Communication Annual Conference (2019)
15. Zhong, X., Lu, J.: Public diplomacy meets social media: a study of the U.S. Embassy's blogs and micro-blogs. Public Relat. Rev. **39**(5), 542–548 (2013)
16. Anindita, A.N., Elias, R.A., Kibtiah, T.M., Miranda, E., Permana, A.: High-engagement Chinese digital public diplomacy on Twitter. In: Yang, X.-S., Sherratt, S., Dey, N., Joshi, A. (eds.) ICICT 2022. LNNS, vol. 464, pp. 437–448. Springer, Singapore (2023). https://doi.org/10.1007/978-981-19-2394-4_40
17. Alanka, Ö., Çimen, Ü.: Twitter as a digital channel of public diplomacy in Turkey. In: Elitaş, T. (ed.) Maintaining International Relations Through Digital Public Diplomacy Policies and Discourses Hershey, pp. 176–189. IGI Global (2023)
18. Nip, J., Sun, C.: Public diplomacy, propaganda, or what? China's communication practices in the South China sea dispute on Twitter. J. Public Dipl. **2**(1), 43–68 (2022)
19. Duncombe, C.: Twitter and transformative diplomacy: social media and Iran–US relations. Int. Aff. **93**(3), 545–562 (2017)
20. Valencia, R.J., Moscato, D.: Navigating #ObamainCuba: how Twitter mediates frames and history in public diplomacy. Place Brand. Public Dipl. **17**(2), 168–179 (2021). https://doi.org/10.1057/s41254-020-00162-7

21. Madu, L.: Twitter diplomacy @Kemlu_RI: a case study of Bali democracy forum 2019. J. Hub. Internasional **10**(1), 31–43 (2021). https://doi.org/10.18196/jhi.v10i1.11566

22. Ahmed, W., Vidal-Aballl, J., Lopez Segui, F., Moreno-Sánchez, P.A.: A social network analysis of tweets related to masks during the COVID-19 pandemic. Int. J. Environ. Res. Public Health **17**(21), 8235 (2020)

23. Downing, J., Ahmed, W.: #MacronLeaks as a 'warning shot' for European democracies: challenges to election blackouts presented by social media and election meddling during the 2017 French presidential election. Fr. Polit. **17**(3), 257–278 (2019). https://doi.org/10.1057/s41253-019-00090-w

24. Khadafi, R., Nurmandi, A., Qodir, Z., Misran: Hashtag as a new weapon to resist the COVID-19 vaccination policy: a qualitative study of the anti-vaccine movement in Brazil, USA, and Indonesia. Hum. Vaccin. Immunother. **18**(1), 2042135 (2022)

Recognizing Emotions in the Discourse of Women in Power Positions in Social Networks via Sentiment and Content Analysis

Stefanie Niklander(✉)

Universidad Autónoma de Chile, Av. Pedro de Valdivia 425, Santiago, Chile
stefanie.niklander@uautonoma.cl

Abstract. Understanding people's emotions is one of the biggest challenges today. From the last decades, the study of emotions has been one of the most emerging research areas from social science to computer science. Indeed, emotions are recognized as a vital element in the relationships between people and computers. Human computer interaction (HCI) is the discipline that deals with the design, evaluation, and implementation of the interaction between people and computing systems. For an adequate interaction between the computer and people, the computer must be able to have some perception of the emotional state of the human being with whom it interacts. The computer be only able to obtain the perception of people emotions through the lexical expressions communicated in his speech. Emotions are present in most forms of communication and can change the meaning of the message transmitted. In this work, we take different Instagram accounts from well-known mass media (CNN, Deutsche Welle among others) to analyze the emotions contained in the representations of women in positions of power. We combine sentiment and content analysis to help you understand sentiment in briefings, including irony and mixed language. Interesting results were obtained to understand the feelings involved in information about women in positions of power.

Keywords: HCI · content analysis · sentiment analysis · women in power position

1 Introduction

Women's equal participation and leadership in politics and public life are critical to achieving the Sustainable Development Goals by 2030. Although the gender gap in the workplace continues to narrow on a daily basis, women who manage to reach top executive positions must face not only the challenges of being a leader in a company, but sometimes also the challenge of managing men who are not accustomed to working with women in positions of power [1]. However, data show that women are underrepresented at all levels of decision making around the world. Therefore, gender parity in politics is still far from being achieved.

C. Stephanidis et al. (Eds.): HCII 2023, CCIS 1835, pp. 84–87, 2023.
https://doi.org/10.1007/978-3-031-36001-5_11

In this article we will focus on all those women who have managed to overcome the obstacles and have been able to reach positions of power and are made visible by the media. The representation of women in the mass media has been a topic of discussion and debate for a long time. We cannot deny that there have been advances in the inclusion of women in the media, however, there are challenges and barriers to be overcome.

One of the main concerns is the way in which the female gender is represented in the media. Information about this gender is stereotyped and limited, focusing on their physical appearance rather than their abilities and achievements. This situation is of great concern, as it can perpetuate gender stereotypes and limit women's aspirations. Another concern is the lack of representation of women in leadership positions in the media.

For this purpose, news about women in positions of power published on the Instagram accounts of CNN, Deutsche Welle and El Mundo in January and February 2023 will be studied. Based on Content and Sentiment Analysis, this research analyzes the media's representation of women in positions of power. In addition, we will be able to analyze whether in representing the female gender it is done through positive, neutral or negative emotions.

Content analysis is a research technique used to analyze and study the content of texts, images, audio and video. This research technique performs the identification and categorization of significant elements in the study material. In the case study, (texts and images from social networks) themes, keywords, language patterns, tone, style and other important elements can be identified [2].

This paper is organized as follows: Sect. 2 presents the problem, results, and discussion. Conclusions and some lines of future directions are given at the end. Please note that the first paragraph of a section or subsection is not indented. The first paragraphs that follows a table, figure, equation etc. does not have an indent, either.

2   Discussion and Results

In this research they analyzed all the posts between January and February of CNN Chile, DW_es and El Mundo. The first thing that stands out is the scarce presence of women in positions of power in the media. In CNN Chile, the presence of the female gender in the case studied was only 3.8%, while in DW_es it was 2.14%. The presence increases slightly in El Mundo, where it was 6.82%.

We could observe that women working in the political area had a 52% presence, while those working in the artistic area had a 43% presence. Only 5% of them did so from a sports sphere.

It is noteworthy that there were no women in managerial positions in private companies.

On the DW_en site, the situation of the presence of women in positions of power is quite similar. From the political sphere, 44% were represented, 44% from the artistic sphere and 11% in managerial positions in companies. However, we should point out that the 11% above referred to the fact that the CEO of Youtube was leaving her position. In the case of El Mundo, the situation is practically the same, except that the presence of women in positions of power within the artistic sphere was notoriously higher with 70.37% and in the political sphere only 29.63%.

In short, we could observe that the analyzed media only publish news about women in positions of power if they belong to the artistic or political sphere. Sports or company directors, it seems, are still relegated to the male gender for the analyzed media.

We also observed that in some of the information published, reference was made to women's clothing. This situation occurred in the political sphere. In the artistic sphere, women were repeatedly mentioned due to the couple conflicts they were experiencing.

It should be noted that there was no diversity in the representation of women in the media. Women in positions of power from different ethnic, cultural, religious and socioeconomic backgrounds were marginalized and excluded from the media.

After applying the Content Analysis, a sentiment analysis was carried out on the headlines of the analyzed news (using SentiStrength). Positive sentiment strength ranges from 1 (not positive) to 5 (extremely positive) and negative sentiment strength from -1 (not negative) to -5 (extremely negative). Through sentiment analysis, we can recognize if a text is positive, negative or neutral (Table 1).

Table 1. Polarity statistics in the news of women in positions of power

Positive	20%
Negative	55%
Neutral	25%

If we apply emotional computing to the titles of the information on Instagram, we can observe that 55% of them were rated as negative. 20% were positive captions and the remaining 25% were neutral.

3   Conclusions

With the application of content analysis, we were able to understand and interpret the different texts of the analyzed Instagram accounts. We were able to identify a trend: the spheres where the analyzed media report on women in a position of power were mainly artistic and political. The sentiment analysis showed that 55% of the headlines had a negative connotation.

It is important that the mass media work on the inclusion of women in all areas, from politics, economics, and sports. It is also crucial to pay attention to how women are portrayed and to promote fair and realistic representation.

References

1. Maritano, O., Bonavitta, P.: Análisis comparado de legislación, políticas públicas e instituciones orientadas hacia el logro de la equidad de género. Aposta: Revista de ciencias sociales (88), 158–168 (2021)
2. Kim, H., Lee, H.: Understanding user experience in online social networks: a content analysis approach. J. Interact. Mark. **50**, 1–14 (2020)

Social Media Movement: Indonesian Fundraising Movement in Football Disaster

Meri Noviyanti[✉] and Filosa Gita Sukmono

Department of Communication Studies, Faculty of Social and Politics, Yogyakarta
Muhammadiyah University, Kasihan, Indonesia
Merinoviyanti12@gmail.com, filose@umy.ac.id

Abstract. The purpose of this study is to explain the fundraising movement by the Indonesian army using Twitter for the victims of the Kanjurhan Malang Stadium football supporters tragedy. This study uses a qualitative method. This study uses NVIVO12 Plus to analyze data. The findings of this study The intensity of Twitter use determines the effectiveness in fundraising, as evidenced by the high activity of the Indonesian army on Twitter, which has managed to attract attention. Then, the dominant content distributed by the Indonesian army on Twitter related to fundraising for the Kanjurhan Stadium tragedy was army solidarity. So it can be seen that the dissemination of content coupled with the high intensity of Twitter usage makes fundraising in digital media very effective.

Keywords: Social Movement · Fundraising · Football Disaster

1 Introduction

Social movements can be conducted in numerous ways, including through social media. There are multiple types and purposes of social events, but fundraising is the most popular [1]. Social conduct has also evolved as social media usage has increased [2]. In the digital age, internet platforms have been utilized as social movement facilities, one type of event fundraising [3]. Twitter is a historically and sociologically popular platform for social advocacy and conversation. Twitter, one of the most extensively used mass media, facilitates social contact by spreading information, which may reduce inequality in a community [4].

The tragic football riot at the Kanjuruhan stadium in Malang involved supporters and police, resulting in fans' suffering. Undoubtedly, the death of an Indonesian football fan is a part of history that cannot be forgotten. According to the statistics obtained, 132 individuals perished [5]. Indonesia-based Army Indonesia is a BTS fan club (Utami&Winduwati,2020).Through its Twitter account @Wingsofbangtan, the Indonesian army was able to raise donations for the victims of the Kanjuruhan stadium disaster in Malang through donation activities that were more creative and exciting [6].

Scholar has classified a new form of social movement in social media research from [7] Explained that digital funding is a form of program management that can assist individuals in fully supporting their efforts because it simply requires an internet connection and provides money. Similarly, studies from [8]. Explained that BTS fans also play an active and productive role in fundraising, likewise, with research from [9]. The donation campaign can be run online or offline to establish personal branding in the fundraising effort. Current This innovation focuses mainly on fundraising, which is particularly useful for offline and online fundraising and makes it easy to support or donate. According to pertinent explanations from prior research, crowdfunding is more about raising funds through social media by sustaining existing initiatives. However, more research on community fundraising on social media needs to be done. Consequently, this study's originality centers on the Indonesian military's Twitter-based fundraising campaign.

2 Overview of Literature

Social movement' refers to an action group undertaken by social actors, including individuals, groups, and organizations, to affect social change and unite political movements. This collective identity is articulated in an outburst of social and political transformation based on ambition, freedom, and democracy [10]. Social movements motivate several individuals to take action; typically, social movements are carried out freely by emphasizing sympathy and empathy [11]. Social movements are renowned for their organizational abilities, which include developing and applying unusual methods and using existing networks to spread new ideas [12].

In contrast to the old social movements, a new social activity focuses on symbolically and culturally related topics of identity [13]. This movement serves as the foundation for the growth of digital social activities on social media, like Twitter and others [14]. An ancient social movement depending on political ideology Social movements are novel and tolerant of various perspectives, with a propensity to develop pragmatic attitudes and establish systems of political engagement [13]. Social movements rely on the dedication of their activists, but support from other individuals and groups is also crucial, given that support from others can mobilize feelings to achieve movement objectives [15].

Fundraising is one of the models of fundraising that may organize large groups of people. With the aid of social networks, fundraising seeks to collect funds for recurring investments. The fundraising mechanism solicits funds for product orders before the product's fabrication (pre-order) [16]. Therefore, the term Fundraising is used to refer to fundraising operations conducted via social networks. Fundraising is a paradigm that demonstrates how social media may present opportunities to anyone who wishes to become a fundraiser (Hidayanto et al., 2022). This reservoir of diverse capital is not the primary purpose of the Fundraising initiative. The development of the fundraising movement in Indonesia is well underway, with the value of social solidarity integrating the community in mutual aid through social participation based on technology innovation and communication linked through social networks and interactivity on social media [17].

3 Research Methods

This study employs a qualitative descriptive approach by evaluating social movements in the form of Twitter-based fundraising efforts by the Indonesian army for victims of the Kanjuruhan tragedy. The Twitter account @wingsofbantan_ provides the data for this study. Because the account serves as a conduit for the BTS ARMY Indonesia charity event, this project will collect data between October 1, 2022, and October 25, 2022, since the Kanjuruhan catastrophe occurred on October 1, 2022. For data analysis, this study employs the Nvivo 12 Plus program. Crosstab Query is the feature used by Nvivo 12 Plus [18, 19].

4   Discussion Result

4.1   Fundraising Intensity Analysis on Twitter

Analysis of new social movements influenced by solidarity groups and social actors, including individuals, groups, And organizations, For influence change social And unifying political movements [10]. According to the findingsHarlow, Summer [11], a social movement is an activity in that several people accompany to do something, usually done voluntarily by getting someone's sympathy and empathy. The new social movement differs from the old social movement, which focuses on symbolic topics. The new social movement is demonstrated through fundraising activities on social media based on community social connections to encourage fan groups to raise funds. In the tragedy of the football riot that occurred at the Kanjuruhan stadium, the Twitter account @wingsofbantan_ was used for a fundraising social movement.

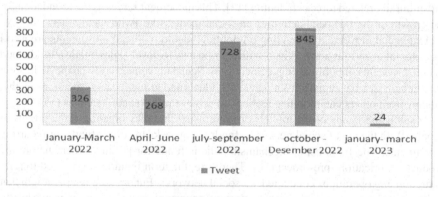

Fig. 1. Tweet intensity by account

Figure 1 shows the tweets on the @wingsofbantan account increasing in July-September, October, and December. The increase in tweets is based on a continuous fundraising movement. Wingsfobantan, through the BTS community, is carrying out a fundraising movement for the kanjuruhan tragedy. From these findings [20]. Explain the existence of open solidarity due to mutual need for one another and being part of the struggle to fight various repressive actors such as oligarchs and corporations that abuse power. With an increase in the intensity of tweets, it shows that social movements occur in a fundraising activity carried out by several people. The results of tweets from @Wingsofbangtan showed significant differences in the content of fundraising after the Kanjuruhan tragedy. This is to Bhawika's findings [16], the purpose of fundraising is to raise money with the help of social networks, so in this finding, the social movement in the Kanjuruhan tragedy uses a fundraising model that is open and provides opportunities for anyone to raise funds.

4.2 Fundraising Content Analysis on Twitter

As one of the popular mass media, Twitter serves to increase social interaction through the dissemination of information, which can reduce inequality within a community [21, 22]. According to the findings of Hidayanto, Syahrul Tofani [24], fundraising is a model that shows social media that is open to opportunities for anyone who becomes a fundraiser. The role of actors in social media has been used as a social movement activity, one form of which is fundraising for an event. The Twitter account @Wingsofbangtan analysis shows a very significant difference in the fundraising content data after the kanjuruhan tragedy.

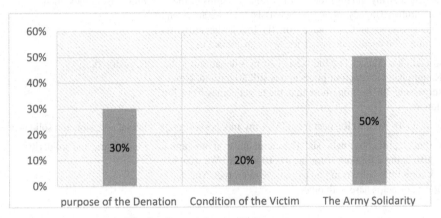

Fig. 2. Content data on Twitter accounts

The results are shown in Fig. 2, it shows. That the content on the Twitter account of the social movement shows information that there are three reasons, namely donating, the condition of the victim, and ARMY solidarity. The most effective content is intensified in posting on the @wingsofbantan account, which is about 50% ARMY solidarity. Other content, such as the purpose of donating,is 30%, and the victim's condition is 20%; this shows that the impetus that makes followers of the @wingsofbantan account donate is the strong bond between Indonesian ARMY members. So the fundraising movement for the victims of the Kanjuruhan tragedy received great enthusiasm in line with the findings of Morador and Vasquez [12]. There are new movements that organizations frequently employ to create and apply unorthodox ways informally and to further utilize existing networks for the dissemination of novel concepts. This is evident from the frequent statistical indications, with solidarity showing the most significant increase. According to these statistics, Twitter accounts are highly active in solidarity-related fundraising efforts.

4.3 Fundraising Tweet Data Analysis

The Tweet analysis results on the Twitter account provide suggestions for fundraising after the recommendation. The use of social media as a fundraising tool can work effectively if it is carried out significantly and regularly, with many donors knowing about fundraising through various social media platforms. The results of the analysis carried out by the Twitter account there are various forms and purposes for raising funds through the Tweet [25]—Table 1 describing from Twitter Account Tweets.

Table 1. Some Tweets from several Wingsofbangtan Twitter accounts

Examples	Tweet categories and functions
@(BTS_ArmyHelpCenter) let us pray for the victims and those affected for a moment	Calling solidarity
@ (Light ArmyMalang) for friends who are victims of the Kanjuruhan Tragedy and need legal assistance, we are open to legal assistance and assistance from the Indonesian army; for victims who need legal assistance, you can contact us	Fundraising movement
@ (Zulfikar Akbar) The Indonesian Army's donation for the Kanjuruhan victims four hours ago is still 80 million. Now surpassing 200 million, more than the target comes from 7707 donors	Crowdfunding
@ (Call To Action) Respect for BTS Army Indonesia friends	Social cohesion and solidarity
@(bubblepuffiebby) hello sis! The community on our campus is also doing a fundraiser for the award victims. We want to ask for a little help from you to achieve our target. You can donate or help share with others	Fundraising and solidarity

Table 1 illustrates that tweets from the Wingsofbangtan Twitter account have successfully supported fundraising efforts. After the kanjuruhan tragedy, this Twitter account has presented funding options. Through a variety of social media sites, several donors are aware of the fundraising campaign. Following the conclusions of Bin-Nashawa, Saeed Awadh Al-Daihani, and Meshari [1], Using social media as a fundraising tool can be executed more efficiently and consistently. As a result, the number of tweets that have been utilized has reached a very high amount, which undoubtedly aids more social movements in their efforts to generate funds for occupational disaster this movement also elevates the benefits and cons of the community. With the Fundraising model, it has been demonstrated that social media can provide fundraising opportunities to everybody participating in such activities [24]; this is very important to determine the dissemination of information and effectiveness in gathering information.

5   Conclusion

This study concludes that Twitter is an important facility used by the Indonesian army community in carrying out fundraising social movements related to the Malang Kanjuruhan Stadium tragedy. The intensity of Twitter usage determines the effectiveness of fundraising, as evidenced by the high activity of the Indonesian army on Twitter, which has managed to attract attention. Then, the dominant content distributed by the Indonesian military on Twitter related to fundraising for the Kanjurhan Stadium tragedy was army solidarity. So it can be seen that the dissemination of content coupled with the high intensity of Twitter usage makes fundraising in digital media very effective. The social movement carried out by the Indonesian army is proof that there is a new space for fundraising activities in the current era, namely digital media. Then, this study has limitations, namely, only using one Twitter social media. Therefore recommendations for further research can use other social media, such as Facebook so that data.

References

1. Bin-Nashwan, S.A., Al-Daihani, M.: Fundraising campaigns via social media platforms for mitigating the impacts of the Covid-19 epidemic. J. Islam. Mark. **12**(3), 576–597 (2020)
2. Dewantara, R.W., Widhyharto, D.S.: Aktivisme dan kesukarelawanan dalam media sosial komunitas kaum muda Yogyakarta. J. Ilmu Sos. Dan Ilmu Polit. **19**(1), 40 (2016)
3. Sulhan, M.: Deliberative democracy and the new social movement: a case from the Bojonegoro media. Komunikator **11**(1), 51–66 (2019)
4. Susanti, D., Hantoro, P.D.: Indonesian netizens' digital self and identity creation on social media. Komunikator **14**(2), 104–113 (2022)
5. Junaedi, F.: Rusuh Suporter Sepakbola vs Polisi dalam Bingkai Berita: Mempersoalkan Akurasi dan Verifikasi Berita, pp. 1–16 (2014)
6. Rodrigo Garcia Motta, G.N.J., Link, A., Bussolaro, V.A., et al.: Analisis Pengambilan Keputusan Untuk Berdonasi Pada Platrom Crowfunding. Pesqui. Vet. Bras. **26**(2), 173–180 (2021)
7. Kade Galuh, I.G.A.A.: Media sosial sebagai strategi gerakan Bali tolak reklamasi. J. Ilmu Komun. **13**(1), 73–92 (2016)
8. Sumunarsih: Produktivitas Fandom Army Dalam Kegiatan, p. 8 (2020)
9. Sespiani, K.A., Apilia, M., Miftajanna, S.: Studi Literatur Pelaksanaan Crowdfunding Oleh Public Figure Melalui Platform Kitabisa.Com. Jurnal Ilmu Komunikasi Dan Media Sosial **1**(2), 84–96 (2021)
10. Rane, H., Salem, S.: Social media, social movements and the diffusion of ideas in the Arab uprisings. J. Int. Commun. **18**(1), 97–111 (2012)
11. Harlow, S.: Social media and social movements: Facebook and an online Guatemalan justice movement that moved offline. New Media Soc. **14**(2), 225–243 (2012)
12. Morador, F.F., Vásquez, J.C.: New social movements, the use of ICTs, and their social impact. Rev. Lat. Comun. Soc. **71**, 398–412 (2016)
13. Fuadi, A., Tasmin, T.: Gerakan Sosial Baru di Ruang Publik virtual. Hanifiya J. Stud. Agama-Agama **1**(1), 48–60 (2019)
14. Susilowati, L.S., Sukmono, F.G.: Digital movement of opinion Terhadap Hastag #Kesehatan-Mental di Twitter Selama Pandemi Covid 19. Komuniti J. Komun. Dan Teknol. Inf. **13**(2), 124–146 (2021)

15. Stern, P.C., Dietz, T., Abel, T., Guagnano, G.A., Kalof, L.: A value-belief-norm theory of support for social movements: the case of environmentalism. Hum. Ecol. Rev. **6**(2), 81–97 (1999)
16. Bhawika, G.W.: Risiko dehumanisasi pada crowdfunding sebagai akses pendanaan berbasis teknologi di Indonesia. J. Sos. Hum. **10**(1), 47 (2017)
17. Sidiq, R.S.S., Jalil, A., Willya, R., Achmad, W.: Virtual world solidarity: how social solidarity is built on the crowdfunding platform Kitabisa.Com. Webology **18**(1), 192–202 (2021)
18. Nurfitriana, A., Sukmono, F.G., Sudiwijaya, E.: Social media consistency analysis ministry of state-owned enterprises in Indonesia during the Covid-19 pandemic. In: Stephanidis, C., Antona, M., Ntoa, S., Salvendy, G. (eds.) HCII 2022. CCIS, vol. 1655, pp. 63–68. Springer, Cham (2022). https://doi.org/10.1007/978-3-031-19682-9_9
19. Nurcahyani, M.T., Junaedi, F., Sudiwijaya, E.: Digital literacy: how social media prevent misinformation during pandemic. In: Stephanidis, C., Antona, M., Ntoa, S., Salvendy, G. (eds.) HCII 2022. CCIS, vol. 1655, pp. 56–62. Springer, Cham (2022). https://doi.org/10.1007/978-3-031-19682-9_8
20. Nofrima, S., Qodir, Z.: Gerakan Sosial Baru Indonesia: Studi Gerakan Gejayan Memanggil 2019. J. Sosiol. Reflektif **16**(1), 185 (2021)
21. Baharuddin, T., Salahudin, S., Sairin, S., Qodir, Z., Jubba, H.: Kampanye Antikorupsi Kaum Muda Melalui Media Sosial Twitter. J. Ilmu Komun. **19**(1), 58 (2021)
22. Subekti, D., Nurmandi, A., Mutiarin, D.: Mapping publication trend of political parties campaign in social media: a bibliometric analysis. J. Polit. Mark. 1–18 (2022)
23. Pernikasari, D.A., Sukmono, F.G.: Utilization of social media in handling and preventing violence against women and children case study: Indonesia. In: Stephanidis, C., Antona, M., Ntoa, S., Salvendy, G. (eds.) Hcii 2022, vol. 1655, pp. 83–88. Springer, Cham (2022). https://doi.org/10.1007/978-3-031-19682-9_12
24. Hidayanto, S., Tofani, A.Z., Pratiwi, A.P., Rahmah, S., Christian, P.: Aksi Sosial Di Internet: Peran Social Media Influencer Sebagai Aktor Dalam Crowdfunding Di Media Sosial. Jurnal Komunikasi Masyarakat dan Keamana **4**(1), 13–29 (2022). Ilmu Komunikasi, Universitas Bhayangkara Jakarta Raya 13. Issn: 2656-6125
25. Avan, A.: Pemanfaatan media sosial sebagai sarana komunikasi, vol. 2, no. 2, pp. 90–108. Kompas.Com (2022)

Analysis of Political Polarization Discourse on Social Media Ahead of the 2024 Election

Elita Putri Pradipta[(⊠)], Taufiqur Rahman, Filosa Gita Sukmono, and Fajar Junaedi

Department of Communication, Universitas Muhammadiyah Yogyakarta, Kasihan, Indonesia
elitaputripradipta@gmail.com, {taufiqurrahman,filosa,
fajarjun}@umy.ac.id

Abstract. This study intends to investigate the polarizing discourse that has developed on social media before the 2024 elections. This study used a qualitative research method with a descriptive approach, data retrieval in research derived from digital text mining data using WordStat to translate the data clearly by grouping topics, word frequency, and text tweets. The results of this study indicate that political polarization can take on a variety of shapes. The results of the frequency-intensity analysis divide the form of polarization into the fragmentation of support groups. The study shows that the topic produces an identity group based on the condition of the sentiment and issues that develop, and the categorization of tweets produces a form of political polarization that is not only divided into two large patterns but also based on the category that was made. These results contribute to the study of political polarization discourse, particularly in analyzing digital data on social media. They fill a research gap on political polarization in the virtual sphere.

Keywords: Discourse Analysis · Political Polarization · Social Media · Elections

1 Introduction

In the age of new media, when the media has become a place where information can be shared, the audience is no longer just a passive receiver of the information that is given to them. The media does not limit itself to merely informing but also engages the public in constructing discourse within the context of democratization [1]. Democracy is the same thing as the development of public space as a place for mediation between the public and the government, where the public is the private manager of public opinion [2]. The internet and new media have the potential to produce a political discourse that can polarize the public [3].

Polarization is characterized by sociocultural developments that retard the public's response to political issues. Polarization results from a solid devotion to a culture, ideology, or candidate that can increase the division between groups [4]. Polarization can cause a group to seek information that validates their beliefs and rejects information that contradicts their understanding, such as motivated reasoning theory. In addition, polarization might be the outcome of a shift in the framing of political communication

© The Author(s), under exclusive license to Springer Nature Switzerland AG 2023
C. Stephanidis et al. (Eds.): HCII 2023, CCIS 1835, pp. 95–102, 2023.
https://doi.org/10.1007/978-3-031-36001-5_13

brought about by the speech of discussion - critical discourse in the virtual public sphere [5].

The concept of a virtual sphere is one of the distinguishing features of traditional media and new media adaptations, such as social media with interaction columns. So that the idea of a "virtual public sphere" [1] can be established, the public can respond, criticize, and even send in data. Political polarization on social media can result from problems that gain prominence on social media, hence dividing public opinion [4]. 68% of people trust information from social media as a reference source. In 2017, it was predicted that there were 132.7 million internet users in Indonesia, with 92 million using social media [6].

Social media has been used in Indonesia to argue and exchange opinions [7]. Social media is vital in life, including political determination and dialogue [8]. Political polarization has indeed occurred in Indonesia's electoral process and strengthened at the regional level. Some voters in these elections seem to be split into two camps that do not agree on anything [9]. Multiple variables, including the cultural component, influence the discourse of political polarization in Indonesia. In addition, there are several other causes of political polarization in Indonesia, ranging from the identity of the candidate to the character and ideology of the party, which can also be the cause of the public being polarized in providing support, where the public will choose based on the background of the party that delegates the candidate to the leader.

In recent years, the concept of the virtual sphere has been examined, such as the virtual sphere conversation in research conducted by Papacharissi [3], which demonstrates the existence of new public spaces produced by the internet and technology directed toward political conversations. Virtual sphere discourse can strengthen democracy and facilitate democratic discussion and the exchange of ideas and perspectives. Other research indicates that involvement and contact in the virtual realm result from data transfers geared toward economic profit [10]. In line with previous research, this study demonstrates that the internet is a site for virtual engagement in reaction to reality [1]. Virtual sphere discourse can strengthen democracy and facilitate democratic discussion and the exchange of ideas and perspectives. Other research indicates that involvement and contact in the virtual realm result from data transfer geared towards economic profit. In line with previous research, this study demonstrates that the internet is a site for virtual engagement in reaction to reality.

2 Overview of Literature

Habermas first developed the concept of the public sphere in 1962 with the perspective that it should highlight rational characteristics and the freedom of the people to express their ideas and concepts [11]. Habermas (1987: 200) explains that each person has the same and equal right to enter the public sphere with the guarantee of freedom and without fear of pressure from any party [12]. According to Habermas' concept of the public sphere, the public sphere was constructed by the bourgeoisie against the regulatory structure of civil society and governmental regulation [13]. Currently, the public sphere is adapting to the emergence of the internet as a new medium to reflect the reality of the virtual sphere. The public is open to having dialogues [14], as social media significantly shares progressive views and ideas more broadly and diversely.

Traditional media, such as television, radio, and conventional publishing media, such as newspapers, do not include the virtual domain. The virtual sphere provides a forum for the public to discover new means of interaction and to discuss political, economic, and social issues [1]. Fragmentation of dialogue and polarization are consequences of chronic critique in virtual space [10]. One virtual public space provides a forum for political discourse and can strengthen democracy [3]. The efficiency of the virtual sphere can also be affected by an institution's or government's policies because each government has distinct formal and unwritten regulations [15].

3   Research Method

This study employs a qualitative approach [16] by analyzing text using WordStat tools [17]. The function of WordStat as qualitative data analysis software is to interpret social media cloud data. Collecting data from October to December of 2022. Data collection using the search terms "Anies Baswedan," "Ganjar Pranowo," and "Prabowo Subianto." By adopting the viewpoint of [18], we employ Wordstat to analyze text-mining data. Wordstat facilitates data interpretation in qualitative research by categorizing topics, word frequency, and tweet text. This strategy is compatible with a virtual sphere approach based on the translation and interpretation of Wordstat data.

4   Result and Discussion

4.1   Positive and Negative Sentence Frequency Analysis

Our study shows the fragmentation of political perspectives influences political polarization on social media. The study revealed the frequency with which the names Anies Baswedan, Ganjar Pranowo, and Prabowo Subianto were mentioned. Anies Baswedan has a high positive frequency but a dominant negative frequency of 100, whereas Ganjar Pranowo has both a low positive and negative frequency, see Fig. 1. These findings imply that the frequency of positive and negative phrases builds the discourse of political polarization [19], with social media playing a significant role in establishing political discourse.

The results indicate a communication pattern that leads to a form of polarization based on the frequency intensity of the three names mentioned, with a significant positive frequency for Prabowo Subianto and a dominantly negative frequency for Anies Baswedan. According to Nasrullah [1] explain that polarization cannot be demonstrated, the intensity of positive and negative social media frequency reveals polarization. According to Gustomy [9], political polarisation can result from strengthening positive and negative public opinion dominance, which can polarise two sides. Positive and negative discourses become fragmented based on the public's disposition towards each name. Positive sentences are associated with the desire to select the future president, and each has its own words, such as "Calon Presiden," "Presiden RI," and "Jadi Presiden," as well as varying intensities. Negative statements are based on the challenges of each individual's name and preferences. It has the potential to polarize Indonesian society based on their political opinions regarding every candidate they support or oppose.

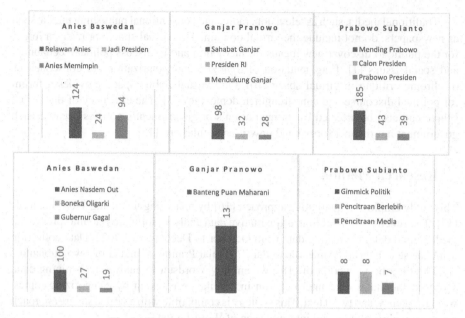

Fig. 1. Positive and Negative Sentence Frequencies

4.2 Topic Analysis

The classification of themes about Anies Baswedan, Ganjar Pranowo, and Prabowo Subianto that came from using categorized keywords revealed an exchange of ideas and political viewpoints. These data imply that polarizing discourse contacts constitute the groups of Anies Baswedan, Ganjar Pranowo, and Prabowo Subianto, as determined by Susanti's [20] conclusion that identity groups influence interactions. See Table 1, for the themes and keywords associated with each name. The resultant topic also includes a frequency, depending on the number of tweets and retweets containing the topic's keywords.

Keyword-based topic analysis reveals that polarization shapes images and public opinion. Referring to Jati [21], political polarization can be established based on identity background. These findings imply that identity background influences subjects that are the outcome of the management of the developing issue of identity. Several elements, such as identity, reputation for performance in prior leadership, philosophy, and policies of the supporting party, might contribute to the formation of political division. The issue of discussion regarding Anies Baswedan is the public's dissatisfaction with his leadership as governor of DKI Jakarta and the party's choice to declare Anies Baswedan's candidacy as a presidential candidate with a distinct philosophy from the party. While Ganjar Pranowo garnered public acclaim for his leadership of Central Java, the frequency of positive criticism of Ganjar Pranowo's accomplishments was greater than that of the other two.

Meanwhile, Prabowo Subianto's image as an electable presidential contender has improved. Annas [4] that strengthening public issues can lead to political polarization,

Table 1. Topics Formed

	Topic	Keyword	Coherence	Eigenvalue	Freq
Anies Baswedan	Tenggelamkan Nasdem	Tenggelamkananiesnasdem; Goodbyenasdemanies; Aniesgabenerpembohong;	0,647	10,36	1419
	Gubernur DKI Jakarta	Berhasil; Anies Boneka Oligarki; Kursi Gubernur DKI; Kursi Presiden Ri;	0,698	11,18	722
Ganjar Pranowo	Merapatkan	Mendukung; Kegiatan; Sahabatganjar; Untuk; Ganjarpranowo; Sahabat; Mendatang; Periode;Figur;	0,653	6,97	1439
	Gubernur Jawa Tengah	Gubernur Jateng; Diwakili Puan Maharani; Fokus Menjadi Gubernur Jawa Tengah; Simbol Banteng; Pelayanan Publik;	0,703	6,89	299
Prabowo Subianto	Posisi	Posisi; Elektabilitas; Mendingprabowo; Capres; Jadi Presiden;	0,783	9,89	664
	Elektabilitas	Prabowo Subianto; Calon Presiden; Partai Gerindra; Elektabilitas Tinggi;	0,980	10,29	119

this is in line with the results of this study, which show that political polarization is caused by how public opinion shapes the topic of a developing problem and that the issue can be a firm commitment that gives the community its identity, which in turn affects the polarization of society.

4.3 Tweet and Retweet Analysis

Categories of tweets produce a political polarization that is not solely focused on positive and negative fragmentation. The public has its approach to social media usage. Takikawa [22] observed that the political orientation of each Twitter user is reflected in their tweet copy. This conclusion examines how tweets and retweets from Twitter users might be categorized. The examination of tweet and retweet findings is tagged as Support, Interactivity and self-expression, Branding and Community, and Polarized and In-Group, see Table 2. Each name in the Interactivity and Self-Expression category includes the tweet category.

This study demonstrates that the classification of texts dictates the limits of interpersonal connections. Himelboim [23] generates an information flow network when people and groups tweet, retweet, and reply. According to these findings, the information network categorizes the text. We divide the Support tweets category into compelling tweets

Table 2. Tweet Category Analysis

Tweet	Retweet	Followers	Category
RT @An_Kiiim: Yang Ingin Pak Anies Baswedan jadi Presiden RI 2024, kasih tanda ❤https://t.co/Mkk bhvuG06	755	821	Support
RT @ChusnulCh: Anies adalah Gubernur 0 persen, yang cuma indah di kata-kata dan rencana.Setuju dengan Penyataan pak @gembong_warsono	461	1882	Interactivity and Self-Expression
Loyalitas tanpa batas…Dukungan Ulama, Tetua Adat serta para Tokoh di Sumbar untuk Pak Ganjar Pranowo. https://t.co/HEvDqko1JR	15	3572	Interactivity and Self-Expression
Mas Ganjar Pranowo adalah pilihan terbaik untuk meneruskan kerja nyata Pak Jokowi setelah 2024.Selain tidak pernah melakukan politisasi agama dan selalu berkomitmen menjaga kebhinekaan Indonesia, kinerjanya juga sudah teruji di Jawa Tengah. https://t.co/ 8NXpF7m8Ci	7	9862	Branding and Community
Krn partai pendukungnya pun dipimpin Pak Prabowo, bukan partai mak banteng, yg mendukung krn kepentingan pribadi.. https://t.co/ EKBf0Ut1BK	5	1521	Polarized and in-group
@OposisiCerdas Makin kesini makin aneh pak Prabowo, apa gak pernah mendengar keluhan rakyatnya ya	2	918	Interactivity and Self-Expression

describing a support type. Interactivity and self-expression According to Smith [24], the retrieval and distribution of messages are factors in online interaction. Interactivity and Self-Expression As a form of interaction and self-expression of social media users demonstrating interest in a topic, the retrieval and distribution of messages factors in online exchange. The Branding and Community category relates to tweets rebranding a person or organization. In contrast, the Polarized and in-group category focuses on tweets that establish a group through praise and criticism. By tweet category, examining these findings examined the emerging form of polarisation on social media.

5 Conclusion

This study found that political polarisation is created through social media interactions. In the discourse of presidential candidates in the 2024 elections, positive sentences tend to support Anies Baswedan, Ganjar Pranowo, and Prabowo Subianto, but negative sentences tend to take the shape of thoughts on negative issues that develop about each name. In addition, the topic generates a form of public sentiment based on differing perspectives regarding the performance and contributions of each participant. The classification of tweets according to categories, namely Support, Interactivity and Self-Expression, Branding and Community, and Polarized and in-group demonstrates that political polarisation develops in various ways, depending on the user's perspective. This study demonstrates that Twitter has become a virtual venue for public discourse ahead of the 2024 elections. However, our study was constrained by the early and brief data retrieval period. Thus, subsequent studies can utilize data collected over a longer time and closer to the 2024 elections to enhance data coverage.

References

1. Nasrullah, R.: Internet dan Ruang Publik Virtual, Sebuah Refleksi atas Teori Ruang Publik Habermas. Jurnal Komunikator **4**(1), 26–35 (2012)
2. Kadarsih, R.: Demokrasi dalam Ruang Publik: Sebuah Pemikiran Ulang untuk Media Massa di Indonesia. J. Dakwah **IX**(1), 1–12 (2008)
3. Papacharissi, Z.: The virtual sphere. Inf. Soc. Read. **4**(1), 379–392 (2020). https://doi.org/10.4324/9780203622278-36
4. Annas, F.B., Petranto, H.N., Pramayoga, A.A.: Opini Publik Dalam Polarisasi Politik Di Media Sosial. J. PIKOM (Penelitian Komun. dan Pembangunan) **20**(2), 111 (2019). https://doi.org/10.31346/jpikom.v20i2.2006
5. Karim, A.G.: Mengelola Polarisasi Politik dalam Sirkulasi Kekuasaan di Indonesia: Catatan bagi Agenda Riset. Polit. J. Ilmu Polit. **10**(2), 215 (2019). https://doi.org/10.14710/politika.10.2.2019.200-210
6. Lim, M.: Freedom to hate: social media, algorithmic enclaves, and the rise of tribal nationalism in Indonesia. Crit. Asian Stud. **49**(3), 411–427 (2017). https://doi.org/10.1080/14672715.2017.1341188
7. Nurfitriana, A., Sukmono, F.G., Sudiwijaya, E.: Social media consistency analysis ministry of state-owned enterprises in Indonesia during the COVID-19 pandemic. In: Stephanidis, C., Antona, M., Ntoa, S., Salvendy, G. (eds.) HCII 2022. CCIS, vol.1655, pp. 63–68. Springer, Cham (2022). https://doi.org/10.1007/978-3-031-19682-9_9
8. Firnanda, A.S., Junaedi, F., Sudiwijaya, E.: Digital content management of Twitter for climate change using hashtag. In: Stephanidis, C., Antona, M., Ntoa, S., Salvendy, G. (eds.) HCII 2022. CCIS, vol. 1655 pp. 18–24. Springer, Cham (2022). https://doi.org/10.1007/978-3-031-19682-9_3
9. Gustomy, R.: Pandemi ke Infodemi: Polarisasi Politik dalam Wacana Covid-19 Pengguna Twitter. JIIP J. Ilm. Ilmu Pemerintah. **5**(2), 190–205 (2020). https://doi.org/10.14710/jiip.v5i2.8781
10. Goldberg, G.: Rethinking the public/virtual sphere: the problem with participation. New Media Soc. **13**(5), 739–754 (2011). https://doi.org/10.1177/1461444810379862
11. Pembayun, J.G.: Rekonstruksi Pemikiran Habermas Di Era Digital. J. Komun. dan Kaji. Media **1**(1), 1–14 (2017). https://www.ptonline.com/articles/how-to-get-better-mfi-results

12. Pratama, H.N., Sadewo, F.S.: Harrys Nanda Pratama FX Sri Sadewo Abstrak. Soc. Netw. Syst. Sebagai Public Sph. Polit. Era Postdemokrasi Kampanye Pilpres **03**, 1–8 (2015)
13. Thompson, B.: The theory of the public sphere. Theory Cult. Soc. **10**, 173–189 (1989)
14. Benson, R.: Shaping the public sphere: habermas and beyond. Am. Sociol. **40**(3), 175–197 (2009). https://doi.org/10.1007/s12108-009-9071-4
15. Dekker, R., Bekkers, V.: The contingency of governments' responsiveness to the virtual public sphere: a systematic literature review and meta-synthesis. Gov. Inf. Q. **32**(4), 496–505 (2015). https://doi.org/10.1016/j.giq.2015.09.007
16. Davi, A., et al.: A review of two text-mining packages a review of two text-mining packages: SAS TextMining and WordStat. Am. Stat. **59**(1), 37–41 (2005). https://doi.org/10.1198/000 313005X22987
17. Pollach, I.: Software review: WordStat 5.0. **14**(4), 741–744 (2011). https://doi.org/10.1177/ 1094428109356713
18. Udoh, E., Rhoades, J.: Mining documents in a small enterprise using WordStat, pp. 1–4 (2006)
19. Gilardi, F., Gessler, T., Kubli, M., Müller, S.: Social media and political agenda setting. Polit. Commun. **39**(1), 39–60 (2022). https://doi.org/10.1080/10584609.2021.1910390
20. Susanti, D., Hantoro, P.D.: Indonesian netizens' digital self and identity creation on social media. Jurnal Komunikator **14**(2), 104–113 (2022). https://doi.org/10.18196/jkm.16541
21. Jati, M.I.: Manajemen Media sebagai Intervensi dalam Menanggulangi Isu Provokatif di Medsos. J. Ilmu Kepol. **13**(2), 16–29 (2019). http://mail.jurnalptik.id/index.php/JIK/article/ view/106
22. Takikawa, H., Nagayoshi, K.: Analysis of the 'Twitter political field' in Japan. In: 2017 IEEE International Conference on Big Data, pp. 3061–3068 (2017). http://arxiv.org/abs/1711.06752
23. Himelboim, I., Smith, M.A., Rainie, L., Shneiderman, B., Espina, C.: Classifying Twitter topic-networks using social network analysis. Soc. Media Soc. **3**(1) (2017). https://doi.org/ 10.1177/2056305117691545
24. Smith, B.G.: Socially distributing public relations: Twitter, Haiti, and interactivity in social media. Public Relat. Rev. **36**(4), 329–335 (2010). https://doi.org/10.1016/j.pubrev.2010. 08.005

A User-Based Evaluation of Jodel's Hashtag Feature: User Information Behavior and Technology Acceptance of Social Tagging in an Anonymous Hyperlocal Community

Katrin Scheibe[✉], Franziska Zimmer, and Aylin Imeri

Department of Information Science, Heinrich Heine University, Düsseldorf, Germany
{katrin.scheibe,franziska.zimmer,aylin.imeri}@hhu.de

Abstract. Jodel is a mobile-only application that establishes hyperlocal communities within a 10 km radius. Its hashtag function was analyzed using the survey methodology. Most of the 146 survey participants are from Germany and German-speaking countries, and fit Jodel's primarily user base. The main results indicate that Jodel's hashtag functionalities such as searching and indexing is seen as easy to use and somewhat useful. Hashtags are mainly applied to tag humorous content and few participants use hashtags to highlight serious topics. Measured on usage frequency, commenting hashtags and the hashtag retrieval functionality is used the least; clicking on hashtags and using hashtags in posts is performed more frequently. This study highlights that even if the different hashtag functionalities on Jodel are mostly perceived as easy to use and (somewhat) useful, the information content varies. Users agreed that they use hashtags to display the thematic content of a post, resulting in the observation that users are to some extent indexing the content they create. Further, one important aspect is the usage frequency of the hashtag functionalities, since most activities (retrieval, clicking, posting, and commenting) are rarely done daily. Therefore, the context of using hashtags on Jodel may depend on individual needs that are not commonplace.

Keywords: Social Tagging · Hashtags · Information Behavior · Technology Acceptance · Anonymity

1 Introduction

Many social media services, such as Facebook, Twitter, Pinterest, YouTube, and Twitter make use of social tagging (also known as collaborative tagging), to enable users to categorize user-generated content, making it retrievable and searchable [13]. Social tagging as information and classification technology is easily implementable, inexpensive, and easy to apply for users (e.g., [11]). Posts can usually be indexed by user-defined keywords [13], using a hash symbol (#) followed by a term – so called hashtags (e.g., [2, 4]). Hashtags play a special role in communication [15] and are used as "an instrument for creative self-expression and language play" [5, p. 51]. Sometimes, hashtags even

C. Stephanidis et al. (Eds.): HCII 2023, CCIS 1835, pp. 103–110, 2023.
https://doi.org/10.1007/978-3-031-36001-5_14

become part of a social movement, e.g., *#MeToo* to provide a community for victims of sexual abusement and harassment or rape [19] resulting in a so-called hashtag activism [20].

The mobile-only app Jodel, launched in 2014, also utilizes social tagging and hashtags (Fig. 1, No. 2). Jodel is a location-based social media application, whereby a user remains anonymous. It establishes local communities within a 10 km radius of the user. Users can change the location of the community (Fig. 1, No. 1) by changing their actual location, or, by paying for a Jodel Plus membership. The app is mainly adopted by users from European countries and the Middle East [9]. Posts on Jodel may include a text of up to 250 characters, images, or videos [16] and can be tagged with a hashtag. Some hashtags have a special function: e.g., the hashtag *#frage* (German for *question*) only allows serious comments for the post and the hashtag *#feedback* allows Jodel's users to give feedback about the app Jodel to the Jodel administration [7].

According to Nowak, Jüttner, and Baran [14], Jodel did not utilize a search tool for hashtags when it was first released. Social tagging, and clicking on hashtags of a post was the only possibility to search for and find posts tagged with the same hashtag. The app and its features have improved over time, whereby a search function for channels was implemented in 2018 [6] and later one for hashtags and text [8]. Taking a look at Fig. 1, users first have to click on the channel overview icon (No. 3), followed by the search box (No. 4), and, finally, on "Hashtag" (No. 5) to search for hashtags. Users may also search for channels and texts, however, only posts from the displayed location-based community of the last 365 days are shown. Further, trending hashtags of the week are presented to users (No. 6) and users can find a list of their published post on their profile page (No. 7).

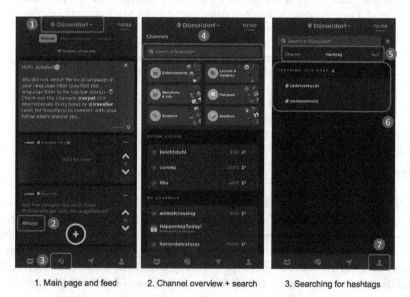

    1. Main page and feed   2. Channel overview + search   3. Searching for hashtags

Fig. 1. Screenshots of Jodel's 1. Main page, 2. Channel overview and search tool, and 3. Hashtag search. Important elements of the app's hashtag function are explained with numberings.

Apart from studies considering Jodel's quality as an information system [14], an evaluation of the hashtag functions on Jodel was not conducted in earlier studies yet. To understand user's information behavior on Jodel, the present study investigates the adaption and acceptance of social tagging in an anonymous location-based service. Since users can not only categorize content by adding hashtags but also make it retrievable, the hashtag usage behavior is part of information behavior research. Information behavior according to Wilson [18, p. 49] is "the totality of human behavior in relation to sources and channels of information, including both active and passive information seeking, and information use." Considering the recently introduced hashtag search function and the lack of studies focusing on the hashtag function, the present research investigates if users apply the (new) search function. Therefore, the present study will answer the following questions:

RQ1: Do users of Jodel know about hashtags and the hashtag search function?
RQ2: How often do users on Jodel use hashtags and the hashtag search function?

Schumann and Stock [17] developed a comprehensive heuristic model to evaluate information systems and its functions – The Information Service Evaluation (ISE) model. The model considers five different dimensions of an information system: the information service quality, the information user, information acceptance, information environment, and time. The service's functionalities as well as the perceived service quality are aspects of the information system dimension. Users' acceptance of a technology can be investigated following the Technology Acceptance Model (TAM) by Davis [3]. It considers the perceived usefulness, perceived ease of use, and the actual use of a technology as well as the users' behavior.

There are four separate functions in regard to hashtags on Jodel: 1. Searching: 1.1 clicking on a hashtag, 1.2 using the retrieval function to search for posts with the corresponding hashtag; 2. Indexing: 2.1 writing a post including hashtags, 2.2 writing a comment including hashtags (to tag another user's post). In line with perceived information service quality and TAM, this research further answers the following research questions:

RQ3a: To what extent are Jodel's hashtag functions perceived as easy to use?
RQ3b: To what extent are Jodel's hashtag functions perceived as useful?

Users of Jodel mainly use the app because of boredom, for fun, and to read funny posts [10]. According to Bauer [1], sometimes hashtags are used as insider jokes on Jodel and for humorous reasons. Further, Reelfs et al. [16] found that hashtags also reflect meme's content (popular humoristic posts circulating on social media). Nevertheless, besides being used for humorous content, hashtags also reference (local) phenomenon or (local) events. Since hashtags can be used with different intentions, especially considering the information behavior, it should be kept in mind, that on Jodel hashtags can be used for classification, to assign the post to a special topic, or to ask a serious question (via *#frage*) as well. Therefore, the following research question arises:

RQ4: What are users' motives to use hashtags on Jodel?

2 Methods

To answer the research questions, data was collected by applying survey methodology. An online survey was distributed from January 13th 2023 until February 20th 2023 via Jodel and was regularly posted on the main page in different cities in Germany, Austria, Switzerland, Liechtenstein, and Luxembourg to reach many German-speaking Jodel users as they comprise its biggest user group and Jodel was first released in Germany. The survey was composed in German and created on Qualtrics[1]. A total of 171 Jodel users started the survey, but only 146 finished the questionnaire.

At first, attendees were asked whether or not they use Jodel. If they do not use Jodel, the survey was terminated. Afterwards, survey participants were asked, for example, how long they had been using Jodel, how often they use Jodel, what they are doing on Jodel (lurking, posting, commenting, voting, chatting) and whether they are aware of the Jodel's hashtag feature and search feature. For the four separate hashtag-based activities (searching for hashtags, clicking on hashtags, using hashtags when posting, and using hashtags when commenting), users were asked how often they perform these activities.

The main questions of the survey are based on the Technology Acceptance Model by Davis [3], asking users for perceived ease of use, usefulness, and fun of the four separate hashtag functions on Jodel using a 5-point Likert scale [12]. Statements regarding the hashtags were presented (e.g., "Clicking on hashtags on Jodel posts to find posts tagged with the same hashtag is useful.") while possible answers ranged from "I totally disagree (1)" via "neutral (3)" to "I totally agree (5)." Users always had the option to answer "No indication." Additionally, users were asked why they use hashtags on Jodel to get insights about their motivation to use hashtags on an anonymous location-based app. In the end, survey attendees have been asked for demographic aspects including gender, age, country of residence, and highest level of education.

3 Results

From the 146 study participants, most are from Germany (N = 119), followed by Austria (N = 12), Switzerland (N = 8), and other countries (N = 7). Fifty-eight survey participants stated they are male and 82 are female. Additionally, three answered to be diverse, two identify themselves with another gender, and one person did not want to answer. The median age of the survey attendees is 25 and the mean age is 27 (N = 144). Most participants have a university degree (N = 51) or graduated high school (N = 42).

Nearly 10% (8.40%; 14 of 166 participants) did not know about the search function and around 3% (5 of 165 participants) did not know about hashtags and social tagging on Jodel.

When looking at the results to answer RQ2 (Table 1), and estimating the usage frequency of Jodel's hashtag functions, a few differences can be observed. The most striking result is that many users seem to never comment hashtags on other one's posts (29%; 44 of 151 participants) and only three users search for hashtags daily, either by using the search tool or by clicking on hashtags in a post. Further, thirty participants

---

[1] https://www.qualtrics.com

Table 1. Usage frequency of Jodel's hashtag functions (retrieval, clicking, posting, commenting).

	Retrieval (N = 149)		Clicking (N = 149)		Posting (N = 152)		Commenting (N = 151)	
	Abs.	Rel.	Abs.	Rel.	Abs.	Rel.	Abs.	Rel.
Daily	3	2%	3	2%	9	6%	4	3%
A few times a week	8	5%	22	15%	13	9%	19	12%
About once a week	6	4%	**26**	**17%**	17	11%	13	9%
A few times a month	22	15%	22	15%	**37**	**24%**	21	14%
About once a month	18	12%	23	15%	20	13%	12	8%
A few times a year	**31**	**21%**	19	13%	26	17%	13	9%
Less	30	20%	16	11%	11	7%	25	16%
Never	**31**	**21%**	18	12%	19	13%	**44**	**29%**

stated they use the search function less than a few times a year (62%; 92 of the 149 participants use it a few times a year or never). When it comes to the use of hashtags when creating a post, most of the users do so a few times a month (24%; 37 of 152 participants) and click on hashtags in posts once a week on average (17%; 26 of 149 participants).

Table 2. Perceived usefulness and ease of use of Jodel's hashtag search and index functions.

			Min	Max	Mean	Med.	SD	Var.	N
Searching	Retrieval	Easy to use	1.00	5.00	3.78	4.00	1.03	1.05	109
		Useful	1.00	5.00	3.94	4.00	0.83	0.69	111
	Clicking	Easy to use	1.00	5.00	4.47	5.00	0.76	0.58	121
		Useful	1.00	5.00	4.11	4.00	0.93	0.86	122
Indexing	Posting	Easy to use	1.00	5.00	4.39	5.00	0.85	0.72	129
		Useful	1.00	5.00	3.96	4.00	0.83	0.69	129
	Commenting	Easy to use	2.00	5.00	4.46	5.00	0.75	0.56	104
		Useful	1.00	5.00	3.90	4.00	0.85	0.72	105

Results on user's perceived usefulness of hashtags and if they are easy to use, can be obtained from Table 2. Here, when looking at the search function, clicking seems to be perceived as easy to use (mean 4.47) and useful (mean 4.11) by most participants. Retrieval is seen less favorable but still mostly positive (easy to use: mean 3.78, useful: mean 3.94). For the indexing function, posting and commenting hashtags are seen as easy to use (mean 4.39 and 4.46, respectively) by most users. Comparatively, they are seen as less useful (mean 3.96 and mean 3.90, respectively).

What are Users' Motives to Use Hashtags on Jodel?
The question was answered by 59 participants (Table 3). Tagging for humorous reasons seems to be favored, as most use hashtags when posting content for fun and to make (insider) jokes (total 22; 37.29%). A total of 20 participants (33.90%) answered they use hashtags to display the thematic context of a post. Only 13.56% (8 participants) use hashtags for serious topics. Other reasons stated by six participants are aesthetics, reaching a target audience, opinion sharing, no intention, or simply because it is common practice on Jodel.

Table 3. Motives to use hashtags on Jodel (N = 59). Sometimes multiple assignments.

Category	Absolute frequency	Relative frequency
Fun/(Insider) jokes	22	37.29%
Displaying the thematic context of a post	20	33.90%
Asking questions (#question)	16	27.12%
Linking similar posts	15	25.42%
Categorization	12	20.34%
Highlighting serious topics	8	13.56%
Supporting my post	3	5.08%
Other	6	10.17%

4   Discussion

This study approached the hashtag functionality and user's acceptance of a mobile-only location-based social media application, Jodel. The special feature of the app is its anonymous hyperlocal community. To this end, an online survey was distributed on the main page of different cities from German-speaking countries (Germany, Switzerland, Austria, Liechtenstein, and Luxembourg) as Jodel's biggest user group is located in this area. The survey is based on the Information Service Evaluation (ISE) model by Schumann & Stock [17], which also includes TAM by Davis [3]. A total of 146 participants completed the survey. The majority of the participants were from Germany, Switzerland, and Austria. The main findings indicate that many of Jodel's users know about hashtags on Jodel as well as about the hashtag search function (only 10% did not know about the search function and 3% did not know about social tagging on Jodel). Concerning the usage frequency of Jodel's hashtag functions, many users seem to never use hashtags when commenting on other users' posts and rarely use the retrieval function to search hashtags. Clicking on hashtags to see other posts including the hashtags and using hashtags in one's own posts are done more frequently. Overall, Jodel's hashtag functions (retrieval, clicking, posting, commenting) are perceived as rather positive by the majority of the users, with clicking on hashtags and commenting hashtags being the most easy to use functions. Users appreciate Jodel for its humorous content [1, 10, 16] which is reflected in their hashtag use, as the majority of participants state that their hashtags are mainly related to humor. Considering users' hashtag usage behavior it is interesting to see that only eight participants use hashtags to highlight serious topics even if 20 participants stated that they display the thematic context of a post with the help of a hashtag.

During the distribution of the survey link, we received some feedback regarding the hashtag function on Jodel. Some users reported they do not use hashtags anymore, because Jodel posts older than 365 days cannot be found (anymore) via the retrieval system. Other users mentioned that they did not know the search function and therefore are not taking part in the survey. This investigation confirmed that it is necessary to differentiate between different hashtag usage behaviors, especially between posting and commenting. Both are activities where new content is developed but with two different aims. Since one is used to answer actively to a previous Jodel and tag another one's Jodel (which includes positioning, offering information/answers, and sharing an opinion) the other one includes a new creation of content. Considering this sample, creating an own post and tagging it with a hashtag is frequently more done than using hashtags when commenting. This study also enables to critically think about retrieval functionalities, that it might not be sufficient to integrate new functionalities (such as the retrieval function) but that it is also necessary to introduce and highlight the new functionalities, especially since some Jodel users mentioned to be not aware of the functionality. Further, 21% of participants of the survey mentioned to never use the retrieval hashtag function, and additional 41% use it a few times a year or less. It would be crucial to investigate the motivational reasons.

This study has some limitations. First, the survey was answered by a small sample size. Additionally, only German-speaking users of Jodel took part in the survey. It therefore cannot comprehensively reflect Jodel's user base but it can offers first insights and therefore future research directions to thoroughly continue research. Other apps on which users are anonymous could present different results. Future research may look at those apps (e.g., Reddit) to generate comparable results. Further, since it is an anonymous social media application the age is not transparent and might have an influence on the overall information behavior and hashtag usage behavior. Additionally, Jodel has also channels associated with a hashtag, such as #Corona. In the future, it could be interesting also to differentiate between content found in Jodel's Channels and Jodel's main page, since the topic predefined by the channel can influence the hashtag usage behavior as well.

References

1. Bauer, M.J.: Anonymisierung und Hyperlokalität der Studierenden-App "Jodel": Eine Fallstudie zu Funktionsweise und Anwendungsmöglichkeiten des sozialen Netzwerks am Beispiel der Studierendenwerke. In: Matrisciano, S., Hoffmann, E., Peters, E. (eds.) Mobilität - Wirtschaft - Kommunikation. EKW, vol. 33, pp. 317–332. Springer, Wiesbaden (2021). https://doi.org/10.1007/978-3-658-32370-7_17
2. Chang, H.-C.: A new perspective on Twitter hashtag use: diffusion of innovation theory. Proc. Am. Soc. Inf. Sci. Technol. **47**, 1–4 (2010). https://doi.org/10.1002/meet.14504701295

3. Davis, F.D.: Perceived usefulness, perceived ease of use, and user acceptance of information technology. MIS Q. **13**(3), 319–340 (1989). https://doi.org/10.2307/249008

4. Halavais, A.: Structure of Twitter: social and technical. In: Weller, K., Bruns, A., Burgess, J., Mahrt, M., Puschmann, C. (eds.) Twitter and Society, pp. 29–41. Peter Lang, New York (2014). https://doi.org/10.3726/978-1-4539-1170-9

5. Heyd, T., Puschmann, C.: Hashtagging and functional shift: adaptation and appropriation of the #. J. Pragmatics **116**, 51–63 (2017). https://doi.org/10.1016/j.pragma.2016.12.004

6. Jodel Support (2021). https://support.jodel.com/hc/en-us/articles/360001037414-Channels-. Accessed 13 Jun 2023

7. Jodel Guidelines (n.D.). https://jodel.com/en/guidelines/. Accessed 13 Jun 2023

8. Jodel Support (2022). https://support.jodel.com/hc/en-us/articles/360001048194-Hashtag-Search. Accessed 13 Jun 2023

9. Lafitte, B.: Shifting from ads to in-app subscription-led revenue generation with Tim Schmitz (Jodel). Purchasely [blog] (2022). https://www.purchasely.com/blog/shifting-from-ads-to-in-app-subscription-led-revenue-generation-with-tim-schmitz-jodel. Accessed 13 Jun 2023

10. Jüttner, K., Nowak, P., Scheibe, K., Zimmer, F., Fietkiewicz, K.J.: The faceless vicinity: who uses location-based anonymous social networks like Jodel and why? In: Meiselwitz, G. (ed.) HCII 2021. LNCS, vol. 12774, pp. 54–73. Springer, Cham (2021). https://doi.org/10.1007/978-3-030-77626-8_4

11. Kroski, E.: The hive mind: folksonomies and user-based tagging. InfoTangle [blog] (2005). https://web20bp.com/13z2a6019/wp-content/uploads/2013/03/The-Hive-Mind-Folksonomies-2005.pdf. Accessed 07 Mar 2023

12. Likert, R.: A technique for the measurement of attitudes. Arch. Psychol. **22**(140), 5–55 (1932)

13. Nam, H., Kannan, P.K.: The informational value of social tagging networks. J. Mark. **78**(4), 21–40 (2014). https://doi.org/10.1509/jm.12.0151

14. Nowak, P., Jüttner, K., Baran, K.S.: Posting content, collecting points, staying anonymous: an evaluation of Jodel. In: Meiselwitz, G. (ed.) SCSM 2018. LNCS, vol. 10913, pp. 67–86. Springer, Cham (2018). https://doi.org/10.1007/978-3-319-91521-0_6

15. Rauschnabel, P.A., Sheldon, P., Herzfeldt, E.: What motivates users to hashtag on social media? Psychol. Mark. **36**(5), 473–488 (2019). https://doi.org/10.1002/mar.21191

16. Reelfs, H., Mohaupt, T., Hohlfeld, O., Henckell, N.: Hashtag usage in a geographically-local microblogging app. In: WWW 2019 Companion, pp. 919–927. ACM, New York (2019). https://doi.org/10.1145/3308560.3316537

17. Schumann, L., Stock, W.G.: The information service evaluation (ISE) model. Webology **11**(1), 1–20 (2014). http://www.webology.org/2014/v11n1/a115.pdf

18. Wilson, T.D.: Human information behavior. Informing Sci. **3**(2), 49–55 (2000). https://doi.org/10.28945/576

19. Xiong, Y., Cho, M., Boatwright, B.: Hashtag activism and message frames among social movement organizations: semantic network analysis and thematic analysis of Twitter during the #MeToo movement. Public Relat. Rev. **45**(1), 10–23 (2019). https://doi.org/10.1016/j.pubrev.2018.10.014

20. Yang, G.: Narrative agency in hashtag activism: the case of #BlackLivesMatter. Media Commun. **4**(4), 13–17 (2016). https://doi.org/10.17645/mac.v4i4.692

"Like! Points Application" Enables Exchange of Positive Messages in the Workplace

Takeaki Shionome[✉]

Faculty of Science and Engineering, Teikyo University,
1-1 Toyosatodai, Utsunomiya, Japan
shionome@ics.teikyo-u.ac.jp
http://www.ics.teikyo-u.ac.jp/~shionome/

Abstract. In this paper, we present a study on the usage patterns and social functions of a mobile app that allows users to exchange and accumulate "Like! Points" with their colleagues in the workplace. User interviews were conducted, and log data were analyzed to identify common uses of the app, such as expressing gratitude, sharing information, and building social connections. The findings of this study can inform the development of similar apps and contribute to the growing body of research on communication and collaboration in the workplace.

Keywords: Workplace depression · Mental health · Simulation · Organization assesment · Social isolation · "Like! Points app."

1 Introduction

Mental disorders such as depression, anxiety, and burnout are prevalent among employees, and if left untreated, they can lead to long-term economic, mental, and physical burdens for the employees themselves, as well as result in socioeconomic losses for the organization. In 2021, Japan recorded 2,346 workers' compensation claims for mental disorders, emphasizing the necessity of a predictive approach to protect employees and reduce losses caused by workplace depression.

Social isolation within an organization can lead to symptoms resembling depression and anxiety disorders, making it a potent stressor [1]. Stress can negatively impact brain function, including cognitive and emotional processing, and the interpretation of messages from others can determine an individual's emotional and physical response, ultimately affecting their actions [2,3].

As such, it's crucial to acknowledge how the quality of communication in an organization can impact employees' mental health. An approach that may prove effective in preventing workplace depression is to utilize an organization simulator to monitor isolated individuals and take proactive measures.

In this paper, we introduce the "Like! Points app.," which allows employees to express gratitude towards one another by sending points within the company. We

C. Stephanidis et al. (Eds.): HCII 2023, CCIS 1835, pp. 111–118, 2023.
https://doi.org/10.1007/978-3-031-36001-5_15

provide details on the app's usage, the information available to administrators, and also introduce an app that visualizes the exchanges through log data. We also conducted an interview survey targeting app users to investigate the app's usability and its impact on communication within the company.

2   Related Works

Digital health interventions are a promising alternative to face-to-face treatment, especially in the context of the COVID–19 pandemic [5]. However, as noted by Philippe et al., there is still a need for further research to fully understand the efficacy and appropriateness of these interventions for patients with understudied mental health conditions and those who are marginalized and may lack access to digital health tools [5].

Firth et al. demonstrated that psychological interventions delivered through smartphone devices can lead to a reduction in anxiety [6]. They recommended that future research focus on developing practical approaches to implement smartphone-based support for individuals with anxiety, and also compare the effectiveness of these interventions to traditional face-to-face psychological care.

Mohr et al. presented the outcomes of a technical expert panel assembled by the Agency for Healthcare Research and Quality and the National Institute of Mental Health. The panel was tasked with reviewing current research on behavioral intervention technologies (BITs) in mental health and identifying the top research priorities [7]. The study also suggests that with the large amounts of data generated by BITs, improvements in the collection, storage, analysis, and visualization of big data will be necessary.

Wu et al. presented a comprehensive survey to characterize the visual analytics area and summarize the state-of-the-art techniques for analyzing social media data [8]. They showed that node-link diagrams are perhaps the most common way to visually represent a social network.

We conducted a study on using an organization simulator as a way to prevent workplace depression [4]. The simulator, which is based on "Message Theory" and incorporates a communication model, provides a display of human relationship behaviors. The simulation results revealed that the personal and organizational statuses, such as the position of individuals, mean distance, and mean mental health index, vary depending on the initial conditions.

Stachl et al. found that communication and social behavior are most predictable through the collection of smartphone data, highlighting the benefits and dangers of smartphone data collection [9].

Observing the exchange of messages and changes in human relationships in actual workplace environments is extremely challenging. However, in recent years, there is a company that have been utilizing a "Like! Point app." within the workplace to practice positive message exchanges. Analyzing the usage of this app can contribute to the revitalization of communication in the workplace and the development of apps for that purpose.

3 "Like! Points App." Point Exchange Application

3.1   Overview

The "Like! Points app."(TSK Wallet) is an internal app where employees can anonymously give points to each other as a sign of gratitude or recognition for good behavior. It has been in operation since 2021. Each user can send up to 100 points at a time, and once a certain number of points have been accumulated, they can be converted to cash at an internal ATM (Fig. 1).

Users can attach a mini-message (e.g. "Good job", "Thank you", "You were a great help", "Well done") when sending points, and the sender can check the history of who they sent points to. The recipient can only confirm the receipt of the points and message, and it is not possible to identify the sender within the app. Users can send up to 100 points once a day, and any unused points will expire at the end of the day. The cost of sending points is covered by the company.

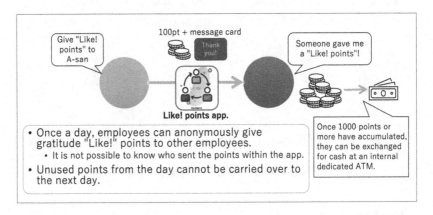

Fig. 1. Overview of "Like! Points App."

3.2   Usage

This section provides an overview of how to use the "Like! Points app.".

1. To log in to TSK Wallet, enter users' email address as the login ID and users' password on the login screen (Fig. 2(a)).
2. The main menu includes icons for News, Homepage, Videos, Like! Points, Like! Point List, and Work Calendar (Fig. 2(b)).
3. On the card selection screen, users can choose the amount of points to send and select from a variety of short messages such as "Thank you" or "Good job" before sending (Fig. 2(c)).
4. On the recipient list screen, users can select recipients from a list of employees. It is possible to search for a recipient by entering a part of their name in the search bar (Fig. 2(d)).

5. When user send an "Like! points", the sending result and the name of the recipient are displayed (Fig. 2(e)).
6. In the "Like!" list screen, user can check the transmission status (recipient and message) and reception status (latest received point, cumulative received point, etc.) of the "Likes" (Fig. 2(f)(g)).
7. When converting points to cash, users can display a QR code on the app and scan it at a designated ATM (Fig. 2(h)).

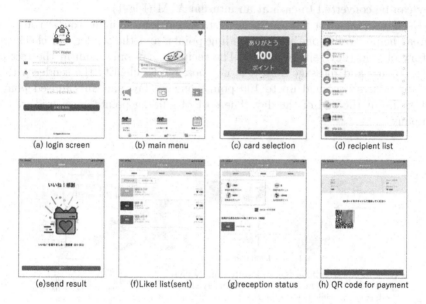

(a) login screen   (b) main menu   (c) card selection   (d) recipient list

(e)send result   (f)Like! list(sent)   (g)reception status   (h) QR code for payment

Fig. 2. Screenshots of "Like! Points app."(TSK Wallet)

3.3   Benefits

For users, this app allows them to easily express gratitude towards their colleagues. They can check their sending history and review who they sent points to, while recipients can receive points anonymously without knowing who the sender is, making it a safe and comfortable experience.

For management, this app provides a multi-dimensional evaluation of employees as they exchange points with each other. As shown in Fig. 3, the administrator dashboard provides information not only about individual point balances, but also about the connections between individuals and departments. This can lead to better support for employee development and provide more appropriate support to enhance employee performance.

Administrators have access to dedicated screens that allow them to view and confirm the network of each employee and department (Fig. 3). Administrators can also view and confirm the activity status of "Like! points" for each employee within and across departments. In addition, administrators can view and confirm the activity status of "Like! points" across departments.

3.4 Log Data and Visualization

The data on the exchange of "Like! Points app." includes the following information: date and time, sender's department and name, receiver's department and name, and the number of points (fixed at 100).

In FY2021, we collected data on approximately 250 individuals and recorded around 14,000 point exchanges. Regarding the use of the data, we have signed a non-disclosure agreement with both the company and the university.

We used the collected data to create a visualization that highlights the frequency of point exchanges between the employees, as shown in Fig. 4. Through this visualization, we were able to identify several interesting patterns and trends related to the volume of point exchanges. These findings can be used to pinpoint areas for improvement or opportunities for further development of the point exchange system. With this information, we can continue to refine and optimize the system to better meet the needs of the users and promote positive interactions within the organization.

From the log data, it can be concluded that there is a cyclic message exchange between employees, especially within their own department. This suggests the presence of strong intra-department communication and personal relationships between employees. Additionally, the log data shows that there are some departments with only two employees, indicating a close working relationship between those individuals. These insights can help to inform future policies and initiatives aimed at fostering positive workplace relationships and improving communication within and between departments.

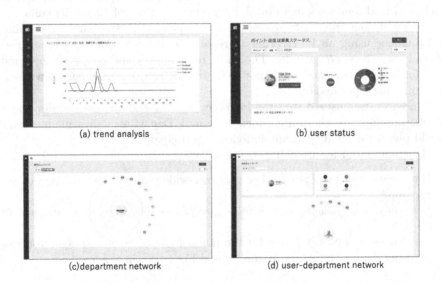

(a) trend analysis

(b) user status

(c)department network

(d) user-department network

Fig. 3. Screenshots of administrator dashboard.

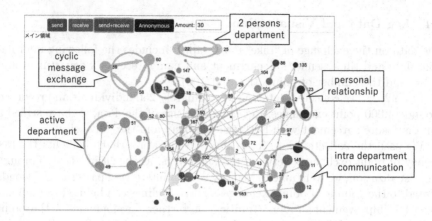

Fig. 4. Log data visualization. (a) Monthly trend of sent, received, and settled points; (b) Status of user points; (c) Display of user's department and its connections with other departments; (d) Display of user's connections with other departments.

4   User Interview

4.1   Overview

The purpose of this interview is to gather feedback from users and obtain basic data for improving the "Like! Points app." to promote more active usage. We conducted the interviews with a group of three people for approximately 45 min each, and held four sessions in total, interviewing a total of 12 participants.

To clarify our interview procedures, we explained to the participants that we would be using an IC recorder to record the conversation for the purpose of analyzing the survey results. The audio recordings would be transcribed and used for analysis only, and would not be shared with any external parties without obtaining prior permission.

Moreover, we ensured that the interview content and analysis results would not be presented to the Management Planning Department in a manner that would reveal the identity of any individual participant.

The main inquiries are delineated as follows.

- Have you noticed any personal or company-wide changes since starting to use the app?
- How do you feel when you receive or give points, and what motivates you to do so?
- Do you have any preferences for the number of points or messages you can send per day, or any other features you'd like to see in the app?

4.2   Data Analysis

The interviews conducted were recorded and transcribed into text format. The transcribed data was analyzed using KH Coder [10]. The analysis results presented in this study were originally written in Japanese and translated into English by the authors

Figure 5 shows the co-occurrence network of frequently used terms during user interviews. For example, "Send", "People", "point", "message", etc. are ranked high. These words are related to the main functions of messaging apps, such as sending and receiving messages and exchanging points. The co-occurrence network generated six subgraphs, which can be classified into (1) app usage and changes, (2) sending points and work-related connections, (3) messages and emotions that can be sent through the app, (4) point settlement, and (5)–(6) interview-related topics.

Furthermore, some of the highlighted words in the graph may have positive connotations depending on how they are used. For instance, words such as "thank you", "well done", "be helpful", and "happy" can express gratitude and empathy towards the recipient and may have the potential to facilitate smoother communication.

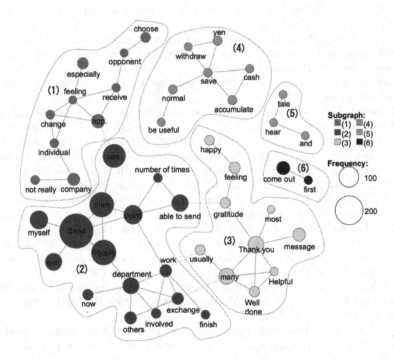

Fig. 5. Co-occurrence network of interview utterances.

5 Discussion

Our analysis of the visualization of "Like! points" revealed various patterns, including personal connections between individuals, frequent exchanges within specific departments, as well as cyclic exchanges among three individuals (Fig. 4).

These findings suggest that "Like! points" are used for both personal and professional purposes within the company.

In the interview survey conducted, the results showed a clear correlation between the level of work-related interactions and the frequency of point exchanges. This suggests that the more an individual engages in work-related activities, the more likely they are to actively participate in point exchanges through the application.

Overall, our analysis suggests that visualizing "Like! points" can provide valuable insights into the dynamics of communication and collaboration within a company. By identifying which departments and individuals are most engaged, companies can take steps to promote a more collaborative and supportive workplace culture.

References

1. Beck, A.T.: Thinking and depression: II. Theory and therapy. Arch. Gen. Psychiatry **10**, 561–571 (1964)
2. Matsumoto, K., Pinna, G., Puia, G., Guidotti, A., Costa, E.: Social isolation stress-induced aggression in mice: a model to study the pharmacology of neurosteroidogenesis. Stress **8**(2), 85–93 (2005)
3. Lazarus, R.S.: Psychological Stress and the Coping Process. McGraw-Hill, NewYork (1966)
4. Shionome, T.: A study on organization simulator as a means to prevent workplace depression. In: Stephanidis, C. (ed.) HCI 2018. CCIS, vol. 851, pp. 444–450. Springer, Cham (2018). https://doi.org/10.1007/978-3-319-92279-9_59
5. Philippe, T.J., et al.: Digital health interventions for delivery of mental health care: systematic and comprehensive meta-review. JMIR Ment. Health **9**(5), e35159 (2022). PMID: 35551058. PMCID: PMC9109782. https://doi.org/10.2196/35159
6. Firth, J., Torous, J., Nicholas, J., Carney, R., Rosenbaum, S., Sarris, J.: Can smartphone mental health interventions reduce symptoms of anxiety? A meta-analysis of randomized controlled trials. J. Affect. Disord. **218**, 15–22 (2017)
7. Mohr, D.C., Burns, M.N., Schueller, S.M., Clarke, G., Klinkman, M.: Behavioral intervention technologies: evidence review and recommendations for future research in mental health. Gen. Hosp. Psychiatry **35**(4), 332–338 (2013)
8. Wu, Y., Cao, N., Gotz, D., Tan, Y., Keim, D.A.: A survey on visual analytics of social media data. IEEE Trans. Multimedia **18**(11), 2135–2148 (2016). https://doi.org/10.1109/TMM.2016.2614220
9. Stachl, C., et al.: Predicting personality from patterns of behavior collected with smartphones. Proc. Natl. Acad. Sci. **117**, 17680–17687 (2020). https://doi.org/10.1073/pnas.1920484117
10. Higuchi, K.: A two-step approach to quantitative content analysis: KH coder tutorial using Anne of green gables (part II). Ritsumeikan Soc. Sci. Rev. **53**(1), 137–147 (2017)

Information Everywhere! Cognitive Load, Elaboration, and Knowledge Gain from Consuming Social Media News Posts

Preeti Srinivasan[✉]

University of Connecticut, Storrs, CT, USA
`preeti.srinivasan@uconn.edu`

Abstract. Information such as news is ubiquitously obtained through online and social media. However, news is competing with attention from other stimuli such as posts from friends, ads on social media and other content. The cognitive load theory proposes that extraneous load is affected by the number of elements present in a stimulus. The cognitive mediation model posits that cognitive elaboration mediates the relationship between media attention and learning. In this study, we combine the modality effects paradigm of the CLT with the cognitive elaboration model to understand if presentation modality (text only, video only, video with text) and topic (Health- low cognitive load vs. Science- High cognitive load) influences attention, cognitive elaboration, and knowledge. To test our hypotheses and research questions, a 3 × 2 between-subjects experimental design with presentation modality and topic was conducted with N = 152 young adult users of Facebook news. Participants were asked to view a news story while eye-tracking was used to measure users' visual attention allocation. They were then asked to engage in a thought listing activity to measure elaboration. Lastly, they were presented with a 3-question knowledge check based on the news story they viewed. Our preliminary analyses suggests that attention as measured by fixation count and fixation duration using the eye-tracking device does predict knowledge. We also find some modality effects for knowledge. Analysis for the elaboration variables is underway. We provide implications for social media news design, theoretical implications for cognitive load theory, and applications of eye-tracking technology to triangulate self-report and behavioral data.

Keywords: cognitive load · knowledge · attention · information · social media

1 Introduction

Social media and especially Facebook, continue to be a popular source of information for young adults all around the world [10]. Information and news on social media differs from other online sources such as news websites because information is often interspersed with social content on these platforms and is also presented using different modalities. For example, some stories could be presented as a hyperlinked article, while some others as a video, or video containing embedded text. Despite this, users receive a large chunk of

C. Stephanidis et al. (Eds.): HCII 2023, CCIS 1835, pp. 119–125, 2023.
https://doi.org/10.1007/978-3-031-36001-5_16

their information from these platforms because of their convenience and ease of access [3]. The multi-modal nature of information on social media can increase perceptions of salience and might thus prompt users to use these platforms for information. [3, 9]. Therefore, it is important to understand how this information should be presented to users. This study combines the modality effects paradigm [14] with the Cognitive mediation model (CMM) [4] to understand how presentation modality and story topic affect visual attention and knowledge.

An eye-tracking device was used to measure visual attention. Eye-tracking is a tool that traces the patterns of eye movements as a user engages with elements on the interface [12], and is often combined with self-report data. A fixation refers to the unique resting of the eye on an interface and saccade refers to the pattern of the eye as it move from one point to the other on the interface. For this study, we use fixation count (number of unique resting of the eye on an interface element) and fixation duration (time in seconds for each fixation) as measures of visual attention.

1.1 Theoretical Background

Modality effects paradigm. Extraneous and intrinsic load are identified as two types of cognitive load within the CLT. (A third type of cognitive load- germane cognitive load was also identified in this theory but was excluded from this study). Extraneous load refers to the interface design elements (ex. Hyperlinks, text, video, subtitles) and intrinsic load pertains to the complexity of the content presented. The higher the number of elements on an interface, the greater will be the cognitive load experienced. The modality effects paradigm of the cognitive load theory predicts that presenting informational content using audio and visual medium will be more effective than just visual text [14]. CLT posits that extraneous cognitive load should be reduced to promote better memory outcomes. There is mixed literature on whether richer media promote learning compared to leaner media. In fact, the presence of more interactive elements might promote motivation and learning [13].

[1] describes intrinsic cognitive load in terms of the complexity of the topic. Based on this, we chose to operationalize intrinsic cognitive load with a health story (low intrinsic load) and a science story (high cognitive load). Science stories might contain more technical content that might be unfamiliar to users and might thus impose heavier cognitive load.

Multi-modal content is also perceived to be more effective and credible compared to text or static content [15], even though larger number of interface elements might lead to more cognitive load. However, intrinsic load can moderate this relationship such that conditions of low intrinsic load (less complex content) will make processing information under conditions of high extraneous load easier [5]. Based on this, the following hypothesis is proposed:

> **H1: Extraneous and intrinsic load will interact such that conditions with low intrinsic load (health) and high extraneous load (video and video with text) will lead to higher knowledge score.**

Cognitive mediation model. The CMM [4] was proposed in the context of understanding how users gain knowledge from information on social media. The key tenet of the theory proposes that elaboration mediates the relationship between attention to information and knowledge. Elaboration refers to the process of reflecting on information and can benefit users in terms of laying the foundation for greater engagement with content [9]. This is because it increases users' involvement with the content and thus leads to deeper processing [6]. Based on this, we can predict that attention to content will predict elaboration which will in turn predict knowledge gain. For this study, we operationalize depth of elaboration as the total number of thoughts listed by the user.

H2: Attention to informational content will positively predict knowledge score.

H3: Depth of elaboration will mediate the relationship between attention and knowledge.

This study further expands on both the modality effects in cognitive load theory and the cognitive mediation model to understand how modality might affect attention, elaboration, and knowledge. However, analyses combining the CLT and CMM are beyond the scope of this extended abstract.

2 Methods

2.1 Sample and Procedures

$N = 150$ young adult users of Facebook news were recruited for this study. A 3 (Presentation modality: text only, video only, video with text) X 2 (Story topic: Health, Science) between-subjects experimental design was used. 60% of the sample identified as female, and the average age was 19 years. Participants visited the lab where they were asked to complete a few questionnaires that assessed their self-reported attention to news. They were randomly assigned to view one of 6 news stories while eye-tracking was used to measure users' visual attention allocation. They were then asked to engage in a thought listing activity to measure elaboration. Lastly, they were presented with a 3-question knowledge check based on the news story they viewed.

2.2 Stimuli

We selected six news stories from popular news outlets such as BBC, CNN, Buzzfeed, AAS Science, as these continue to be popular sources of news and information for audiences around the world. The six stories selected varied by story topic (Health or Science) and presentation format (text, video only, video with text). The lengths of the video conditions were equivalent to eliminate time effects.

2.3 Thought Listing Activity

After viewing the news story, participants were asked to list all thoughts that occurred to them as a measure of cognitive elaboration. They were asked to list as many thoughts as possible. Two independent coders who have no prior knowledge of the research coded all thoughts. Based on a predetermined codebook, thoughts were classified as follows:

A. Types of thoughts: Thoughts about story, platform, news source
   A paired samples t-test showed was significant and showed that participants had the most number of thoughts about the story ($M = 6.58$, $SD = 4.88$), followed by the platform ($M = .61$, $SD = 1.21$), and then the source ($M = .28$, $SD = .70$).
B. Valence of thoughts: Positive, negative, or neutral
C. Originality of thoughts
   a. Originated externally: recreating a statement from the story
   b. Modified externally: Thoughts that reflect on the story
   c. Generated internally: Thoughts not relevant to the story (add charts of number of thoughts)

   Cohen's k was run to determine the agreement between the two coders. There was high agreement between the coders. K = .80, p < .001 Additionally, the total number of thoughts was used as a measure of depth of elaboration ($M = 8.69$, $SD = 5.48$, Range = 0–20).

2.4 Measures

Knowledge was measured using three items that were constructed specifically for each news story. Participants viewed three questions related to the story they viewed and were scored based on the correct responses ($M = 1.92$, $SD = 0.98$).

Eye-tracking Measures. Fixation count refers to the total number of unique fixations falling within a certain interest area. Fixations refer to each unique resting of the eye when engaging with an interface element ($M = 343.67$, SD $= 176.52$).

Fixation duration refers to the sum of the time for all fixations in a particular interest area. This was measured in milliseconds and converted to seconds for further analysis ($M = 126.12$, $SD = 61.17$).

Control Measures. Self-reported attention was borrowed from [11] and measured using 6 items on a 7-point scale ($M = 5.31$, $SD = 1.14$, $\alpha = .91$). Example items include, "I keep up with current events, I like to know about what is going on in the world."

Issue Salience. This was measured on a 7-point semantic differential using four items. ($M = 5.12$, $SD = .91$, $\alpha = .89$). Example items include, "Irrelevant-Relevant."

3   Results

H1 predicted that extraneous and intrinsic load will interact such that conditions with low intrinsic load (health) and high extraneous load (video and video with text) will lead to higher knowledge score. A univariate ANOVA was conducted with extraneous load and intrinsic load as the fixed factors and knowledge score as the dependent variable. Self-reported attention and issue salience were added as covariates in the model. The main effect for extraneous load on knowledge was significant $F(2, 142) = 17.73, p <$

.001, and the interaction of extraneous and intrinsic cognitive load $F(2, 142) = 6.01, p < .001$ were significant. However the main effect for intrinsic load $F(1, 142) = 2.52$, $p = .12$, n.s. was not significant. Neither of the two covariates were significant in the model (Fig. 1).

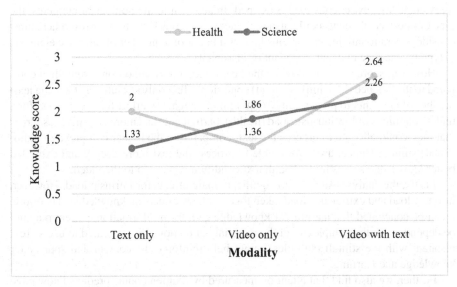

Fig. 1. Interaction of extraneous and intrinsic load on knowledge scores

H2 predicted that attention (measured using eye-tracking) will positively predict knowledge gain. A regression analysis with fixation count and fixation duration as predictors and knowledge score as the dependent variable was conducted. Fixation count emerged as a significant predictor of knowledge score $\beta = .23, t(149) = 1.95, p < .05$, $R^2 = .07, F(2, 147) = 5.08, p < .01$. However, fixation duration was not a significant predictor in the model.

H3 predicted that elaboration will mediate the relationship between attention and knowledge gain. Two separate mediation analyses with fixation count and fixation duration as predictors, elaboration (total number of thoughts) as the mediator and knowledge score as the outcome were conducted. Both the analyses were not significant. Thus, we find no evidence for H2.

4 Discussion and Implications

This study used the CLT and the CMM to understand how cognitive load affects attention, elaboration, and knowledge gain from information content on social media. The results from this study provides some support to the modality effects paradigm of the CLT. Results from H1 indicate that under conditions of low intrinsic cognitive load, even stimuli with high extraneous cognitive load (a greater number of interface elements), will lead to higher knowledge scores.

Firstly, the video with text conditions had the highest knowledge scores despite being highest in extraneous load. This is because text resonant with content presented in video and audio format tends to reinforce learning [2]. Even though subtitles or text add an additional element on the interface, they may actually reduce cognitive load when the text is consonant with the audio/video [8]. These findings might also help us evaluate how extraneous load is defined. In addition to the number of elements, the type of interface elements could also influence extraneous load. Further reserchers must consider operationalizing extraneous load as a factor of a. number of interface elements b. type of interface element (resonant or dissonant).

However, scores were lowest for the health video only condition, even when compared to the Science (high intrinsic load) conditions. Text only stimuli may have the least number of elements to process, may require more cognitive effort for users. Therefore, under conditions of low intrinsic load (health), participants had more cognitive resources that they could allocate to process the text, compared to the higher complexity (audio-visual) stimuli. Hence, users were able to process the text more deeply and exhibited better knowledge scores in the health text condition compared to the video.

Lastly, the analyses suggest no significant main effects for intrinsic load. However, intrinsic load and extraneous load taken together have effects on knowledge. Therefore, it can be concluded that learning or knowledge gain from information content may not be dependent on the complexity of the material but on how it is presented to users. Text resonant with the stimuli (subtitles) might help reinforce the content and spur better knowledge and learning.

Further, we also find that attention measured by fixation counts predicts knowledge score, but fixation duration does not. Therefore, the intensity with which a user's processes stimuli may be more important to information processing than how long the user views the content. However, we find no evidence of elaboration mediating the relationship between attention and knowledge scores. Whether the addition of cognitive load to this equation affects attention and knowledge, needs to be explored in more detail.

Overall, these results taken together provide support to the modality effects paradigm of the CLT. High extraneous load conditions lead to better information processing under conditions of low intrinsic load. Furthermore, the importance of text in information processing is also underscored. Video combined with resonant text might help users learn from the content better. Social media content designers can incorporate these findings to help users understand the content better and create better online user experiences.

References

1. Ayres, P.: Impact of reducing intrinsic cognitive load on learning in a mathematical domain. Appl. Cogn. Psychol. Official J. Soc. Appl. Res. Memory Cogn. **20**(3), 287–298 (2006)
2. Black, S.: The potential benefits of subtitles for enhancing language acquisition and literacy in children: an integrative review of experimental research. Transl. Cogn. Behav. **4**(1), 74–97 (2021)
3. Diddi, A., LaRose, R.: Getting hooked on news: Uses and gratifications and the formation of news habits among college students in an Internet environment. J. Broadcast. Electron. Media **50**(2), 193–210 (2006)

4. Eveland, W.P., Jr.: The cognitive mediation model of learning from the news: evidence from nonelection, off-year election, and presidential election contexts. Commun. Res. **28**(5), 571–601 (2001)
5. Ginns, P.: Meta-analysis of the modality effect. Learn. Instr. **15**(4), 313–331 (2005)
6. Kim, B., Barnidge, M., Kim, Y.: The communicative processes of attempted political persuasion in social media environments: the mediating roles of cognitive elaboration and political orientations. Inf. Technol. People **33**(2), 813–828 (2020)
7. Kiousis, S., Dimitrova, D.V.: Differential impact of Web site content: exploring the influence of source (public relations versus news), modality, and participation on college students' perceptions. Public Relations Rev. **32**(2), 177–179 (2006)
8. Lin, J.J., Lee, Y.H., Wang, D.Y., Lin, S.S.: Reading subtitles and taking enotes while learning scientific materials in a multimedia environment: cognitive load perspectives on EFL students. J. Educ. Technol. Soc. **19**(4), 47–58 (2016)
9. McGill, A.L., Anand, P.: The effect of vivid attributes on the evaluation of alternatives: the role of differential attention and cognitive elaboration. J. Consum. Res. **16**(2), 188–196 (1989)
10. Newman, N., Fletcher, R., Robertson, C., Eddy, K., Nielsen, R.K.: Reuters Institute Digital News Report (2022). https://reutersinstitute.politics.ox.ac.uk/sites/default/files/2022-06/Digital_News-Report_2022.pdf
11. Oeldorf-Hirsch, A., Srinivasan, P.: Reflecting on Facebook news posts: Effects of active reflection strategies on knowledge. In: 68th Annual Conference of the International Communication Association (ICA) (2018)
12. Poole, A., Ball, L.J.: Eye tracking in HCI and usability research. In: Encyclopedia of Human Computer Interaction 2006, pp. 211–219. IGI global (2006)
13. Skulmowski, A., Xu, K.M.: Understanding cognitive load in digital and online learning: a new perspective on extraneous cognitive load. Educ. Psychol. Rev. **34**(1), 171–196 (2021). https://doi.org/10.1007/s10648-021-09624-7
14. Sweller, J.: Element interactivity and intrinsic, extraneous, and germane cognitive load. Educ. Psychol. Rev. **22**, 123–138 (2010)
15. Zhou, X., Liang, W., Kevin, I., Wang, K., Shimizu, S.: Multi-modality behavioral influence analysis for personalized recommendations in health social media environment. IEEE Trans. Comput. Soc. Syst. **6**(5), 888–897 (2019)

Electronic Simple European Network Services (e-SENS) Social Media Analysis for Interoperability on Twitter

Wahdania Suardi[1]([✉]), Achmad Nurmandi[1], Titin Purwaningsih[1], and Zarina Zulkifli[2]

[1] Doctoral Program of Government Affairs and Administration, JusufKalla School of Government, Universitas Muhammadiyah Yogyakarta, Brawijaya Street, Yogyakarta City 55183, Indonesia
`w.suardi.psc22@mail.umy.ac.id`
[2] School of Government, Universiti Utara Malaysia, 06010 Sintok, Kedah, Malaysia

Abstract. Over the last two decades, research on e-Government found that e-government is a strategy to increase the effectiveness of public service policies and programs. Public policy is effective because it encourages citizens and business sectors to access government information 24 h daily. The use of e-government improves government performance in public services through economization and efficiency and reduces transaction costs. The success of e-government depends on the ability of government organizations to integrate data and information across borders. This study examines the Electronic Simple European Network Services (e-SENS) Social Media Analysis for Interoperability on Twitter. E-SENS is a pilot project aimed at facilitating the mobility of citizens. E-SENS will consolidate, improve and extend technical solutions, which will affect the quality of public services. E-SENS covers different aspects of ICT applied in several cross-border electronic use cases in numerous domains such as e-health, e-justice, e-procurement and business setup. This study uses a qualitative research method with a QDAS (Qualitative Data Analysis Software) approach. The data sources in this study came from Twitter (e-SENS). This study indicates that e-SENS on Twitter social media can consolidate, improve, and expand technical solutions to support implementing electronic-based public services by integrating one data. It enables an Interoperability framework for service delivery and communication between administrative authorities, businesses and citizens. This can be seen from the narrative built by e-SENS through Twitter media with digital and service dominance. The results of these findings can be a benchmark for maturity in a government organization for electronic-based and integrated public services.

Keywords: Electronic Simple European Network Services (e-SENS) · social media · Interoperability · Twitter

1 Introduction

Digital government, E-Government, and E-governance: all of which are terms that have become synonymous with the use of information and communication technologies in government agencies [1–3]. Despite the label, digital governance has become a key

© The Author(s), under exclusive license to Springer Nature Switzerland AG 2023
C. Stephanidis et al. (Eds.): HCII 2023, CCIS 1835, pp. 126–132, 2023.
https://doi.org/10.1007/978-3-031-36001-5_17

strategy for government administration reform [3–9]. E-Government continues to be recognized as a key strategy for improving government services and the effectiveness of public policies and programs [9]. A key component of e-government initiatives is the ability of multiple governmental and non-governmental organizations to share and integrate information across the boundaries of their traditional organizations. To summarize, e-government means using information and communication technology (ICT) to improve governance procedures and the interests of citizens, organizations and the government [10].

Over the past two decades, research on e-Government has found that e-government is a strategy to improve the effectiveness of public service policies and programs [9, 11–14]. The effectiveness of public policy is because it encourages citizens and sector businesses to access government information 24 h a day [15]. The use of e-government improves government performance in public services through economy and efficiency and lowers transaction costs [16, 17].

The success of e-government depends on the ability of government organizations to integrate data and information across borders [18]. E-Government integration is establishing a larger unit of the government entity, temporary or permanent, to merge processes and/or share information [19]. By combining processes or sharing information, decision-making will be easier and more efficient [20].

E-government is a tool to promote the modernization and integration of fragmented systems in forming technological infrastructure capable of supporting the improvement of services to the community, such as reducing or eliminating the need to access several institutions to receive information or services[21]. This can encourage efficiency in government administration that can reduce administrative costs, overcome corruption, and reduce transaction costs [22].

Based on the background presentation above, it was found that one of the successes in public services is based on e-government by prioritizing data integration. Therefore, the study aims to examine the Electronic Simple European Network Services (e-SENS) social media. E-SENS is a pilot project aimed at facilitating the mobility of citizens. E-SENS will consolidate, improve and expand technical solutions, which will affect the quality of public services. E-SENS covers various aspects of ICT applied in several cross-border electronic use cases across domains such as e-health, e-justice, e-procurement, and business settings.

2 Literature Review

2.1 Interoperability

Mapping the interoperability roadmap starts with information technology and Administrative Reform. Pertama, it can be claimed that most of the evidence presented in the analysis comes from studies of government IT applications before the 1990s when the Internet became a major force [14]. Secondly, it is possible to demonstrate the transformation of business organizations that used IT during the dot.com explosion and argue that similar changes could affect governments. Both are fair observations and deserve a corresponding response. That notable change occurred between the 1990s and the present, which may be related to the application of IT to specific tasks within a government organization and not to changes specific to a particular technology. This systematic study refutes the hypothesis in a fundamental way that is relevant not only for the thirty years of study but, more generally, until the 1990s. Studies conducted since then (e.g., Fountain, 2002) corroborate the basic findings of previous work—IT has not yet reformed public administration. The argument that recent experience in business proves the power of IT to reform organizations deserves careful consideration.

E-government seems to follow a more or less predictable development pattern ranging from the stage where interaction is limited to what is displayed on the screen to where there is two-way communication. Financial services and transactions can be completed with a satisfactory level of protection of personal privacy [23]. Today, e-government in almost all cities studied is merely an extension of government, with potential benefits in speed and accessibility. The argument is based on the issue of service-based e-government development by looking at several major e-Service categories: Web, Grid, and P2P services. This category provides a roadmap for improving government services that will enable the successful establishment of integrated service-based distributed applications[24].

One of the integrated service concepts through the development of a set of tools for use in assessing capabilities on a multidimensional basis versus maturity level approach in ITIM and Capability Maturity Models [18]. Modifications intended for the ITIM approach may include dimensions as an extension of these other models. However, the Plan for further development of the dimensional-based approach described here includes examining the possibility of including components such as thresholds or maturity in the design. The development can be seen from the system integration and interoperation framework in e-Government. The framework proposes projects by examining objectives, limitations, constraints, processes and outcomes of integration and operation in electronic governance.

3   Method

This research uses qualitative methods with a QDAS (Qualitative Data Analysis Software) approach [25]. The data source in this study comes from Twitter (e-SENS). Data for this study were collected using the Ncapture Feature [26]. NCapture is a web browser addon that records web content, including website content, social media, and other content documentation, such as scientific articles and opinion collections from online media and social media observers. In this study, the Ncapture tool on the Nvivo 12 Plus was mainly used to collect data on Twitter social media related to themes or issues studied on social media twiter e-Sens. The data obtained are then imported, encoded, and analyzed finding answers to research questions. To identify what material dominates the narrative discussed about introperability. Word cloud analysis and project maps will be used to analyze the dominant narrative and relationships between themes.

4   Result and Discussion

The e-SENS project aims to provide a coherent interoperability architecture with the consolidation of reusable building blocks for implementing digital services in Europe [27]. In summary, e-SENS gathers methodologies, specifications, and implementations from previous eID projects in a unique architecture. The e-SENS project ("Electronic Simple European Networked Services") is a new Large-Scale Pilot in the ICT Policy Support Program (ICT PSP) under the Competitiveness and Innovation Framework Program (CIP). The project aims to facilitate the cross-border deployment of digital public services through common and reusable technical components based on the building blocks of a Large-Scale Pilot. It defines the required capabilities for promoting interoperability as a set of Solution Architecture Templates (SATs) such as e-ID, e-Signatures, e-Delivery, e-Payment, and e-Documents. It will support the creation of a Digital Single Market by facilitating the delivery and use of electronic public services.

Electronic identity (eID) and electronic signature (e-Signature) are important supporters of e-government solutions in Europe[28]. This supports the main citizen-to-government (C2G) transactional services that are secure and privacy-preserving. eID is considered an important success factor for e-government to enable secure and reliable citizen identification or authentication in online services. Furthermore, signatures, to recognize this identity and be able to use it, especially in cross-border cases, is a complex and important thing. E-Delivery for cross-border e-Justice improves the efficiency of multilateral processes by supporting the electronic exchange of documents and data. The building blocks of e-Payment provide the necessary information to the end user to correctly identify the costs to be paid and use the nationally defined payment system to make payments. This project's purpose became a discussion topic on social media, Twitter e-SENS. This can be seen as follows:

Fig. 1. Themes Related to Interoperability on e-SENS Social Media

Figure 1 shows that the dominant theme is the theme of e-SENS, followed by public, Digital, Service, Project, Digital, e-Gov, business and several other themes discussed on social media Twitter e-Sens. The distribution of the themes above can be seen in the picture below.

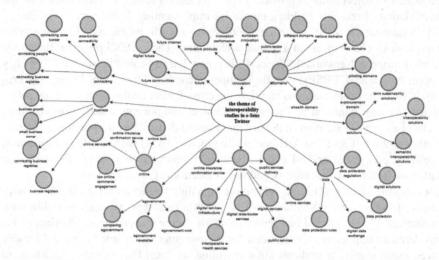

Fig. 2. The Theme of Studies of Interoperability in e-SENS Twiter

Based on the picture above, it can be seen that ten clusters are the theme of the conversation on social media, Twitter e-SENS. The first theme is about data consisting of data protection regulation related to the name of requested files, date and time of the request, Transferred data quantity, error status and IP address of requesting computer. Furthermore, domains consisting of pilotins domain themes become important because they relate to each other and serve integrated public services. The pilotins phase aims to test digital communications with public administrations in Europe. A broad spectrum of domains, such as e-Health, e-Justice, e-Procurement, Business Lifecycle, and others, is the focus of the e-SENS pilot [29]. This phase provides knowledge about the maturity of the service with the interoperability of the e-service.

Furthermore, the theme of innovation is often identified with the use of new ways by profit organizations to obtain the effectiveness and efficiency of both products, services, and methods in the face of business competition [30]. This innovation is also related to future communication, digital features and the Internet. Other things that are not explained in detail can be seen in Fig. 2 by looking at the connection between the themes studied.

5   Conclusions

Based on the background explanation above, it can be concluded that e-sens Twitter social media is a platform for consolidating the level of maturity in a government organization for electronic-based and integrated public services. To promote interoperability as a set of Solution Architecture Templates (SAT) such as e-ID, e-Signatures, e-Delivery, e-Payment, and e-Documents. It enables an Interoperability framework for service delivery and communication between administrative, business, and civil authorities. E-SENS on Twitter social media can consolidate, improve, and expand technical solutions to support implementation in electronic-based public services by integrating a single data. It enables an Interoperability framework for service delivery and communication between administrative, business, and civil authorities. The narrative constructed by e-SENS through the medium of Twitter with digital and service dominance. The limitations of this study are that the information obtained in the e-Sens tweet is limited, considering that the last e-sens account was actively discussing interoperability in 2017. With these limitations, the author only analyzed e-sens tweets from 2012 to 2017.

References

1. Van Overeem, A., Witters, J., Peristeras, V.: An interoperability framework for Pan-European E-Government Services (PEGS). In: Proceedings of Annual Hawaii International Conference on System Science (2007)
2. Gottschalk, P.: E-Government Interoperability and Information Resource Integration: Frameworks for Aligned Development (2009).https://doi.org/10.4018/978-1-60566-648-8.ch005
3. Gascó, M.: Approaching e-government interoperability. Soc. Sci. Comput. Rev. **30**(1), 3–6 (2012)
4. Karantjias, A., Stamati, T., Martakos, D.: Advanced e-government enterprise strategies and solutions. Int. J. Electron. Gov. **3**(2), 170–188 (2010)
5. Lamharhar, H., Chiadmi, D., Benhlima, L.: How semantic technologies transform e-government domain: a comparative study and framework. Transforming Govern. People Process Policy **8**(1), 49–75 (2014). https://doi.org/10.1108/TG-07-2013-0023
6. MacKenzie, R., Crompton, M., Wallis, C.: Identity management in e-governmnet. Priv. Secur. IEEE. **6**, 51–57 (2008)
7. Sowa, J.: Conceptual Graphs for Representing Conceptual Structures, pp. 101–136 (2009)
8. Xiao, Y., Xiao, M., Zhao, H.: An ontology for e-government knowledge modeling and interoperability. In: 2007 International Conference on Wireless Communication Network Mobile Computing WiCOM 2007, pp. 3605–3608 (2007)
9. Pardo, T.A., Nam, T., Burke, G.B.: E-government interoperability: interaction of policy, management, and technology dimensions. Soc. Sci. Comput. Rev. **30**(1), 7–23 (2012)
10. Marian, S., Bogdan, G.-M.: E-government in Romania – a case study. J. e-Govern. Stud. Best Pract. **2020**, 1–12 (2020). https://doi.org/10.5171/2020.608643
11. Dawes, S.S.: The evolution and continuing challenges of E-governance. Public Adm. Rev. **68**(SUPPL.) 1, (2008)
12. Hoetker, G., Fountain, J.E.: Building the virtual state: information technology and institutional change. Acad. Manag. Rev. **27**(4), 619 (2002)
13. Bekkers, V.: Reinventing government in the information age. International practice in IT-enabled public sector reform. Public Manag. Rev. **5**(1), 133–139 (2003)
14. Kraemer, K., King, J.L.: Information technology and administrative reform: will e-government be different? Int. J. Electron. Gov. Res. **2**(1), 1–20 (2006)
15. Yuhefizar, A.H., Gunawan, I., Hariyanto, E.: Naskah Akademik dan Rancangan Peraturan Daerah tentang Pengelolaan E-Government di Provinsi Sumatera Barat: Membangun E-Government (2017)
16. Oktavya, A.A.: Penerapan (Electronic Government) E-Government Pada Kantor Pelayanan Pajak Pratama Dalam Pemberian Pelayanan Di Kota Bontang. J. Ilmu Pemerintah. **3**(3), 1437 (2015)

17. Wirawan, V.: Penerapan E-Government Dalam Menyongsong Era Revolusi Industri 4.0 Kontemporer di Indonesia. J. Penegakan Huk. dan Keadilan **1**(1), 1–26 (2020)
18. Cresswell, A.M., Pardo, T.A., Canestraro, D.S.: Digital capability assessment for e-government: a multi-dimensional approach. In: Wimmer, M.A., Scholl, H.J., Grönlund, Å., Andersen, K.V. (eds.) Electronic Government. LNCS, vol. 4084, pp. 293–304. Springer, Heidelberg (2006). https://doi.org/10.1007/11823100_26
19. Scholl, H.J., Klischewski, R.: E-government integration and interoperability: framing the research agenda. Int. J. Public Adm. **30**(8–9), 889–920 (2007)
20. Haryati: Katalog Dalam Terbitan Prosiding Seminar Pemanfaatan Teknologi Informasi dan Komunikasi (TIK) dalam Meningkatkan Nilai Tambah Pelayanan Publik Guna Mewujudkan Editor Haryati Penata Letak & Desain Cover One Indraretnani. In: Balai Pengkajian dan Pengembangan Komunikasi dan Informatika (BPPKI) Bandung Badan Litbang SDM Kementerian Komunikasi dan Informatika RIPengembangan Komunikasi dan Informatika (BPPKI) Bandung Badan Litbang SDM Kementerian Komunikasi dan Informatika RI (2012)
21. dos Santos, E.M., Reinhard, N.: Electronic government interoperability: identifying the barriers for frameworks adoption. Soc. Sci. Comput. Rev. **30**(1), 71–82 (2012)
22. Mensah, I.K.: Factors influencing the intention of university students to adopt and use e-government services: an empirical evidence in China. SAGE Open. **9**(2), 215824401985582 (2019)
23. Torres, L., Pina, V., Acerete, B.: E-government developments on delivering public services among EU cities. Gov. Inf. Q. **22**(2), 217–238 (2005)
24. Tsalgatidou, A., Koutrouli, E.: E-services interoperability analysis and roadmap actions. In: CamarinhaMatos, L.M., Afsarmanesh, H., Ortiz, A. (eds.) Collaborative Networks and Their Breeding Environments. ITIFIP, vol. 186, pp. 455–464. Springer, Boston (2005). https://doi.org/10.1007/0-387-29360-4_48
25. Misran, A.N., Sutan, A.J.: Penggunaan Media Sosial Dalam Penyebaran Narasi Hak Asasi Manusia Di Indonesia (The Use of Social Media in Spreading Human Rights Narration in Indonesia). J. Gov. Sci. **2**(1), 40–50 (2021)
26. Khadafi, R., Nurmandi, A., Qodir, Z., Misran: Hashtag as a new weapon to resist the COVID-19 vaccination policy: a qualitative study of the anti-vaccine movement in Brazil, USA, and Indonesia. Hum. Vaccin. Immunother, p. 3 (2022)
27. Berbecaru, D., Lioy, A.: On the design, implementation and integration of an attribute provider in the Pan-European eID infrastructure. In: Proceedings of IEEE Symposium Computer Communication, vol. 2016-August, pp. 1263–1269 (2016)
28. Marsalek, A., Zefferer, T., Reimair, F., Karabat, Ç., Soykan, E.U.: Leveraging the adoption of electronic identities and electronic-signature solutions in Europe. In: Proceedings ACM Symposium Application Computer, vol. Part F1280, pp. 69–71 (2017)
29. E-SENS: Real-life piloting. E-SENS (2017)
30. Ridlowi, R., Himam, F.: Inovasi pada Organisasi Pemerintah: Tahapan dan Dinamika. Gadjah Mada J. Psychol. **2**(1), 22 (2018)

Before and After Images on Social Media: The Impact on Female Body Dissatisfaction of Getting Only Half the Picture

Mark Turner[(⊠)] [iD] and Antonia Ray

Department of Psychology, University of Portsmouth, Portsmouth, UK
{Mark.Turner,Antonia.Ray}@port.ac.uk

Abstract. Social media content can negatively influence body esteem in young women through the idealized forms of physical appearance that are portrayed. A recent social media trend has been a growth in posting images depicting side-by-side posed and un-posed photographs showing a natural self-representation alongside an altered version of the same individual. This study investigated the effects of viewing such 'before and after' style social media images on young women's mood and body dissatisfaction. Participants were 162 young women (aged 17–29 years old) who were randomly allocated to view either 15 idealized ('fitspiration') images, 15 'before and after' comparison images, or 15 images which depicted the 'after' only component of the same images. Results showed that exposure to 'before and after' comparison images led to improved mood and reduced body dissatisfaction in young women, compared to when viewing the 'after' only component or fitspiration images. Exposure to fitspiration-style images and 'after' only images increased body dissatisfaction and negative mood. This study suggests individuals may process and respond to images differently when viewed side-by-side compared to when the 'after only' version of the same image is shown on its own. Further research is needed to investigate the threshold of exposure to 'before and after' images embedded within social media needed for viewers to experience protective effects for body image.

Keywords: Social Media · Body Dissatisfaction · Body image · Comparison images · fitspiration · Body Acceptance

1 Introduction

1.1 Background

Social media content can negatively influence body esteem in young women through the idealized forms of physical appearance that are portrayed [1]. For example, the *#fitspiration* trend on social media has been used by young women who wish to identify with a greater drive for living fit and healthy lives emphasizing thinness, beauty and sexuality [2]. One previous experience sampling study based on self-reported exposure, estimates that women typically see an average of 9.5 fitspiration images over

© The Author(s), under exclusive license to Springer Nature Switzerland AG 2023
C. Stephanidis et al. (Eds.): HCII 2023, CCIS 1835, pp. 133–140, 2023.
https://doi.org/10.1007/978-3-031-36001-5_18

the course of a week [3]. Whilst fitspiration images ostensibly promote exercise, good nutrition and adopting healthy lifestyles, a growing body of research has demonstrated exposure to such images are linked to a range of negative psychological outcomes in female observers, including increased appearance-related anxiety, body dissatisfaction and objectification; and decreased self-esteem [4]. Prichard et al. [5] investigated the effect of different forms of fitspiration images, either functional (performing exercise) or non-functional (posed selfies), finding body satisfaction decreased and negative mood increased following exposure to both image types. This was contrary to the expectation that images which focused on body functionality would be viewed as less objectifying, and so result in more positive body image outcomes. Since social media users are known to favor posting images in which they look thin and attractive in order to enhance their self-presentation online [6], it follows that the appearance standards often communicated via social media may not reflect everyday appearance. However, existing academic literature is yet to fully consider the range of social media images women are typically exposed to.

A more recent social media trend has been a growth in posting 'Before & After' personal comparison images. Such images typically depict side-by-side, posed and unposed photographs showing a natural self-representation alongside an altered version of the same individual, with captions such as *"the photo on the left is staged as hell... These are the type of images we compare ourselves to everyday. Our bodies are glorious from every angle. Posed or un-posed."* The main aim of such posts is to highlight the unrealistic social media images and appearance ideals and encourage others to be confident about their bodies [7]. Such images may therefore be regarded as part of the wider body positive movement on social media, which seeks to challenge typical beauty ideals and promotes acceptance all body types [8].

Some studies have demonstrated that exposure to various forms of body positive images and written phrases can lead to improved body image outcomes [7, 9]. Exposure to idealized images of women wearing makeup have also been shown to lead to greater facial appearance concern in females compared to viewing images of women with no makeup [10]. Viewing digitally manipulated (retouched and reshaped) Instagram selfies has been found to directly lead to poorer body image, compared to viewing the original versions of the same images [11], whilst viewing humorous, parody versions of celebrities' idealized Instagram posts was found to increase body satisfaction and positive mood compared to viewing the authentic versions of the same posts [12]. There have been few empirical studies which have directly explored the effects of 'Before & After' style comparison images specifically. One exception, by Tiggemann and Anderberg [13] compared side-by-side social media photographs, where one side showed an idealized female image and the other side showed a more natural depiction of the same person. These effects of side-by-side images were compared to viewing either side of the image alone. Viewing side-by-side images, or viewing the natural depiction side of the images alone resulted in decreased body dissatisfaction relative to viewing the idealized size of the images. However, no comparison with other forms of social media image were included in their study.

1.2 The Present Study

Previous research suggests exposure to body positive content online, specifically authentic self-presentation where a person shows their 'true self', may help to reduce the negative impacts on body image of idealized social media imagery. In this study, the effects of 'Before & After' comparison images compared to fitspiration images are explored. Although past studies have investigated the effects of fitspiration images, their impact on young women's mood and body dissatisfaction relative to comparison images (depicting more realistic body representations and flaws alongside posed or edited images) have not been explored.

Hypothesis 1. Female body satisfaction will be greater when exposed to 'Before & After' images on Instagram, relative to viewing purely the 'after' part of the same images, or fitspiration images alone.

Hypothesis 2. Females exposed to fitspiration images, or the 'after' (posed-only part) of images, will show greater increases in negative mood compared to those who view the full 'Before & After' comparison images.

2 Method

2.1 Participants and Design

Participants were 162 young women (aged 17–29 years old; $M = 19.27$; $SD = 1.77$). All were active social media users, recruited through a research participation scheme at our institution, or directly through social media. All were experienced users of Instagram, as indexed by their number of followers $(M = 745.1; SD = 538.5)$, and number of posts made at the time of the study $(M = 117.5; SD = 206.4)$. BMI data for the sample indicated this to be in the 'normal/healthy' range $(M = 22.78; SD = 3.93)$.

A 3x2 (Image condition) x (pre/post exposure) mixed experimental design was used where participants were randomly allocated to view either 15 idealized fitspiration images, 15 'Before & After' comparison images, or 15 images which depicted the 'after' only component of the same images. These images were interspersed with five neutral images (depicting scenery) in a mock social media browsing task. All images were taken from publicly accessible pages on Instagram. The fitspiration images were sourced from Instagram using the hashtags *'#fitspiration', '#gymlife', '#gymmotivation'*. All fitspiration images showed single, white females in sports clothing, either posed selfies in gym or outdoor locations, or engaging in physical exercise, with fitness inspired captions (e.g. *"First work out of the New Year. Time to build"*). The 'Before & After' comparison images all showed one side of the image depicting more realistic (natural) body representations, besides the second (posed) side of the image, which had been taken to conceal appearance flaws. Both sides of the image showed the same person in the same item of clothing, which included underwear, swimwear or leisurewear. For these images, the written captions were adjusted to ensure these were still consistent with image content when the 'after' part of the image only was shown (e.g. *"Confidence nowadays. LOVE it!"*).

2.2 Measures

State mood and body dissatisfaction were recorded using Visual Analogue Scales (VAS). Participants rated how they were feeling "right now" by moving a sliding pointer to the appropriate place on a horizontal line with endpoints labelled "not at all" (0) and "very much" (100). Participants rated the following items: depressed, anxious, angry, confident (reverse coded), and happy (reverse coded), which were combined to form an overall measure of negative mood, and the items physically attractive (reverse coded), fat, satisfied with your facial appearance (reverse coded), and satisfied with your body size and shape (reverse coded), which formed a measure of state body dissatisfaction. These measures were taken pre and post exposure to each image condition. The Cronbach's alpha values for the mood items were 0.747 (pre) and 0.785 (post) and for body dissatisfaction were 0.796 (pre) and 0.864 (post) suggesting the scales to have acceptable internal consistency. To disguise the purpose of the study and reduce the salience of the body-related questions, participants also reported on their satisfaction with their romantic relationship, financial status, housing situation, and social life.

2.3 Procedure

The study was completed online using the *Qualtrics XM* research platform. In order to ensure people were attending to the images, participants were told prior to seeing the images that they would be given a memory test about their content at the end of the study. Participants were then exposed to 20 images in their allocated condition, presented serially in a random order. Participants were given unlimited time to look at each image but after an image had been viewed they could not go back and view it again. A hidden timer recorded the time spent looking at the images ($M = 4.65$ s per image). In addition, to ensure active engagement with the images, participants were asked to rate the extent to which each image made them feel positive or negative (using a 10-point rating scale from very negative (0) to very positive (10). The study was ethically approved by the relevant ethics committee at our institution. Participants with body-disturbance conditions or who felt they may have potentially become upset when viewing the image content were advised not to take part, prior to consent being taken at the start of the study. Sources of further support regarding body image and appearance issues were also provided in the debriefing at the end of the study.

3 Results

3.1 Hypothesis 1: Does Image Type Influence Body Dissatisfaction?

A 3×2 mixed factorial ANOVA was used to examine the influence of image exposure on body dissatisfaction. A significant interaction occurred between image type and time ($F(2, 162) = 12.40, p < .001, \eta^2_p = .133$) (Fig. 1). Pairwise comparisons with Bonferroni adjustment showed in the 'Before & After' image condition, body dissatisfaction was significantly lower ($p = .031$) after exposure to the images ($M = 50.53$, 95% CI [44.04, 57.03]) compared to before exposure ($M = 53.27$, 95% CI [47.26, 59.28]). However, a significant increase ($p = .005$) was found in body dissatisfaction when viewing the 'after' only images ($M = 58.32$, 95% CI [51.82, 64.81]) compared to before exposure to these images ($M = 54.78$, 95% CI [48.77, 60.78]). A significant increase in body dissatisfaction was also found ($p < .001$) after viewing fitspiration images ($M = 59.97$, 95% CI [53.48, 66.47]) compared to before viewing these images ($M = 54.19$, 95% CI [48.18, 60.19]). These results are consistent with the explanation that exposure to fitspiration images increased body dissatisfaction, whereas Before & After images decreased body dissatisfaction, supporting Hypothesis 1.

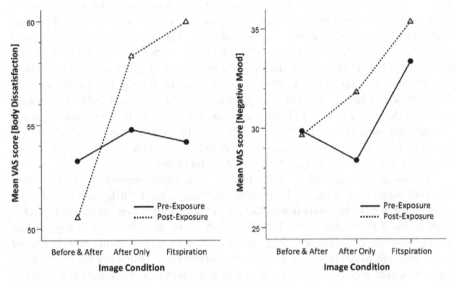

Fig. 1. Mean VAS scores for body dissatisfaction (left) and negative mood (right) pre and post exposure for the three image conditions.

3.2   Hypothesis 2: Does Image Type Influence Overall Mood?

A 3x2 mixed factorial ANOVA was used to examine the influence of the images on overall negative mood. No significant main effect of image condition was observed ($F(2,162) = 1.37, p = .258$ ns, $\eta^2_p = .017$) and no interaction effect was found between time and condition on overall negative mood ($F(2,163) = 2.46, p = .089, \eta^2_p = .029$). A main effect of time was found, with negative mood being significantly higher after exposure compared to before ($F(1,163) = 6.66, p = .011, \eta^2_p = .040$) (Fig. 1). Pairwise comparisons with Bonferroni adjustment were used to examine pre and post exposure differences. These suggested the main effect of time was accounted for by a significant increase ($p = .004$) in negative mood in the 'after only' image condition from before ($M = 28.39$, 95% CI [24.14, 32.64]) compared to after ($M = 31.82$, 95% CI [27.10, 36.53]) exposure, which did not occur in the 'Before & After' image condition ($p = .859$ *ns*), or fitspiration condition ($p = .088$ *ns*). Hypothesis 2 was therefore, not fully supported.

4 Discussion

Exposure to 'before and after' comparison images led to improved body satisfaction in young women, compared to viewing the 'after' only part of the same images or viewing fitspiration images, both of which decreased body satisfaction. The findings are consistent with previous studies [5, 13], and suggest that viewing the 'after' only part of images which are typically intended to idealize self-presentation and conceal flaws is as detrimental to body image as viewing fitspiration images. Exposure to the 'after' only component of images also led to increases in negative mood, which did not occur in the case of exposure to 'before and after' images or fitspiration images. This may be explained by the fact that both 'before and after' images and fitspiration images, to some extent, may additionally possess characteristics which serve to motivate or inspire the viewer [13, 14]. The current data suggest individuals may process and respond to photographs differently when similar images are viewed side-by-side to highlight the ease with which appearance can manipulated, compared to when only an enhanced version of the image is seen in isolation. Given that exposure to 'ideal' body types is so prominent on social media, there may be some protective value of viewing honest depictions of body shape and progression over time, or examples of how the perception of the same body can be changed for users of social media.

Previous research has indicated that disclaimer messages presented below Instagram images of attractive women, emphasizing that the images had been digitally edited, were not effective at reducing body dissatisfaction in viewers and often led to less favorable impressions of the profile owner [15]. The findings of the current study suggest that being able to see how appearance has be visually manipulated, rather than just being told it has, will have contrary outcomes as a strategy for addressing the body image consequences of social media. It may be speculated that exposure to idealized body types accompanied with written disclaimers may still induce negative appearance comparisons that lead viewers to feel less adequate; for example, since viewers may believe that even with similar editing of their own images, they would not be able to achieve the same appearance outcomes. By contrast, being exposed to a normal and enhanced version of the same image may facilitate a more positive perception that appearance change is possible for all individuals, thereby providing a more effective means of empowering body confidence and acceptance.

A potential limitation of the current study was that whilst 'before and after' images were used, the women shown in these photographs were still all relatively thin. Even the more realistic (un-posed) parts of these images, may then still have presented an attractive comparison target to observers given that the appearance flaws depicted could be considered relatively minor (e.g. examples of cellulite on otherwise toned bodies, rounded stomachs whilst seated). Previous research has shown that exposure to images of thin women may produce opposite effects on body confidence to those seen when viewing plus-size models [16], and it is not clear to what extent the size of the women in the photographs used in the current study may have limited, or contributed to, the observed effects. Future research could usefully explore the dynamics between the before and after components of images to better understand exactly what changes are required to produce positive body image outcomes.

The present study used no fixed time limit for how long participants were required to observe images. Instead, participants were asked to respond to a question about how each individual image made them feel, and given a post-exposure memory test as safeguards to ensure engagement. This resulted in a minimum exposure time of no less than 4 s per image for any participant. Whether this duration could be considered typical of normal social media browsing on sites such as Instagram remains unclear. One possibility is that the total number of images social media users are exposed to in a short space of time, rather than the absolute time spent considering individual images may have greater consequences for female body image. It is common for browsing behavior to involve rapid exposure to many images as users sift quickly through content [3]. An interesting option for future research may be to consider how varying the volume of images users are exposed during browsing affects their overall body dissatisfaction, as an alternative to current experimental approaches which typically use fixed image sets.

Overall, this study contributes to the body of research surrounding the effects of different types of social media images and their impact on body image. The study demonstrates the unique consequences of seeing 'normal and enhanced' comparison images side-by-side as a positive motivator of body image, which does not occur when seeing only the 'enhanced' version of the same person from the same image.

References

1. Vandenbosch, L., Fardouly, J., Tiggemann, M.: Social media and body image: recent trends and future directions. Curr. Opin. Psychol. **45**, 101289 (2022). https://doi.org/10.1016/j.copsyc.2021.12.002
2. Carrotte, E.R., Prichard, I., Lim, M.S.C.: "Fitspiration" on social media: a content analysis of gendered images. J. Med. Internet Res. **19**(3), e95 (2017). https://doi.org/10.2196/jmir.6368
3. Griffiths, S., Stefanovski, A.: Thinspiration and fitspiration in everyday life: an experience sampling study. Body Image **30**, 135–144 (2019). https://doi.org/10.1016/j.bodyim.2019.07.002
4. Cataldo, I.: Fitspiration on social media: Body-image and other psychopathological risks among young adults. a narrative review. Emerg. Trends Drugs Addict. Health **1**, 100010 (2021). https://doi.org/10.1016/j.etdah.2021.100010
5. Prichard, I., McLachlan, A.C., Lavis, T., Tiggemann, M.: The impact of different forms of #fitspiration imagery on body image, mood, and self-objectification among young women. Sex Roles **78**(11–12), 789–798 (2017). https://doi.org/10.1007/s11199-017-0830-3
6. Pounders, K., Kowalczyk, C.M., Stowers, K.: Insight into the motivation of selfie postings: impression management and self-esteem. Eur. J. Mark. **50**(9/10), 1879–1892 (2016). https://doi.org/10.1108/EJM-07-2015-0502
7. Cohen, R., Fardouly, J., Newton-John, T., Slater, A.: #BoPo on Instagram: an experimental investigation of the effects of viewing body positive content on young women's mood and body image. New Media Soc. **21**(7), 1546–1564 (2019). https://doi.org/10.1177/1461444819826530
8. CwynarHorta, J.: The commodification of the body positive movement on Instagram. Stream Cult. Politics Technol. **8**(2), 36–56 (2016). https://doi.org/10.21810/strm.v8i2.203
9. Nelson, S.L., Harriger, J.A., Miller-Perrin, C., Rouse, S.V.: The effects of body-positive Instagram posts on body image in adult women. Body Image **42**, 338–346 (2022). https://doi.org/10.1016/j.bodyim.2022.07.013

10. Fardouly, J., Rapee, R.M.: The impact of no-makeup selfies on young women's body image. Body Image **28**, 128–134 (2019). https://doi.org/10.1016/j.bodyim.2019.01.006
11. Kleemans, M., Daalmans, S., Carbaat, I., Anschütz, D.: Picture perfect: the direct effect of manipulated Instagram photos on body image in adolescent girls. Media Psychol. **21**(1), 93–110 (2018). https://doi.org/10.1080/15213269.2016.1257392
12. Slater, A., Cole, N., Fardouly, J.: The effect of exposure to parodies of thin-ideal images on young women's body image and mood. Body Image **29**, 82–89 (2019). https://doi.org/10.1016/j.bodyim.2019.03.001
13. Tiggemann, M., Anderberg, I.: Social media is not real: the effect of 'Instagram vs reality' images on women's social comparison and body image. New Media Soc. **22**(12), 2183–2199 (2020). https://doi.org/10.1177/1461444819888720
14. Raggatt, M., Wright, C.J.C., Carrotte, E., et al.: "I aspire to look and feel healthy like the posts convey": engagement with fitness inspiration on social media and perceptions of its influence on health and wellbeing. BMC Public Health **18**, 1002 (2018). https://doi.org/10.1186/s12889-018-5930-7
15. Fardouly, J., Holland, E.: Social media is not real life: the effect of attaching disclaimer-type labels to idealized social media images on women's body image and mood. New Media Soc. **20**(11), 4311–4328 (2018). https://doi.org/10.1177/1461444818771083
16. MorenoDomínguez, S., ServiánFranco, F., ReyesdelPaso, G.A., CepedaBenito, A.: Images of thin and plus-size models produce opposite effects on women's body image, body dissatisfaction, and anxiety. Sex Roles **80**(9–10), 607–616 (2018). https://doi.org/10.1007/s11199-018-0951-3

Text Mining Analysis of User Reviews of Mobility Service

Jaeyoung Yoo[1] (iD), Xu Li[2] (iD), and Hyesun Hwang[1](✉) (iD)

[1] Department of Consumer Science, Convergence Program for Social Innovation,
Sungkyunkwan University, Seoul, South Korea
h.hwang@skku.edu
[2] Department of Consumer Science, Sungkyunkwan University, Seoul, South Korea

Abstract. Information and communications technology (ICT) has been applied to the mobility industry, enabling the provision of real-time information based on location. This functionality demonstrates an early form of smart city materialization through immediate access to consumer transportation facilities, and contributes to the development of Mobility as a Service (MaaS) based on a user-centric approach. This study aimed to examine the user experience of mobility service apps in Korea. We collected 17,335 consumer reviews of three mobility service apps offered by Kakao Mobility for their taxi, bus, and subway services. These apps provide various additional services affiliated with Kakao Talk, a popular social media messaging app in Korea. We examined the relationship between the characteristics of transportation services using Structural Topic Modeling (STM), which led to the extraction of eleven topics. First, three topics concern the primary purpose of mobility service apps—providing relevant traffic information, such as timetables and estimated times. Second, four topics reflect negative experiences caused by problems related to technical and functional aspects of the apps, such as interface, connection, and update issues. Third, four topics are related to consumer problems with the taxi app, such as cancellations or service refusal. The results of this study confirmed that the failure of the service was noticeable in taxis that provide privacy services according to consumer demand and that functional and technical problems were found in all services. This study contributes to the development of information-based services in a consumer-oriented direction, which is essential in the development of MaaS.

Keywords: Smart city · Mobility as a service · Structural topic modeling

1 Introduction

The widespread adoption of smartphones and the development of smartphone apps have greatly transformed consumer lifestyles, particularly in the realm of mobility [1, 2]. Mobile apps based on GPS technology provide real-time information on public transportation, such as subways, buses, and taxis, making mobility more convenient than ever before [3]. In recent years, there has been growing interest in integrated and seamless mobility; to achieve this goal, Mobility as a Service (MaaS) has emerged as a new trend

C. Stephanidis et al. (Eds.): HCII 2023, CCIS 1835, pp. 141–148, 2023.
https://doi.org/10.1007/978-3-031-36001-5_19

in the mobility industry [4]. MaaS can be categorized into levels (from 0 to 4) depending on how diverse and integrated the transportation services provided by mobility apps are [5]. However, in areas where MaaS is in the early stages of implementation or being piloted, consumers complain of inconvenient services due to relatively undeveloped transportation infrastructure and high usage costs [6, 7].

South Korea has achieved a high level of information and communications technology (ICT) development; it is considered to have a high mobile device penetration rate [8] and relatively good transportation infrastructure [6, 7]. Therefore, South Korea has favorable conditions for the provision of MaaS and is considered to have high potential for the development of such services [6, 7]. However, consumer responses to apps that provide information about mobility services in South Korea are only partially positive [9, 10]. The failures experienced by consumers in such apps mainly relate to the lack of real-time traffic information [9]; furthermore, their accuracy or responsiveness is regarded as insufficient.

Considering these issues against the background of Korea's preparation for MaaS, it is essential to understand how Korean consumers react to critical mobile app services for subways, buses, and taxis [11, 12]. Therefore, this study aims to analyze consumer reviews using text-mining techniques to understand consumer perceptions of relevant mobile apps. We also hope to provide foundational information for a user-centered approach to MaaS development.

2   Literature Review

2.1   Mobility Services in Korea

In South Korea, several private companies such as Naver, Kakao, and Daum offer mobile-based mobility services [13]. Among them, Kakao started as a social media messaging service called Kakao Talk, which has a vast network effect as most Koreans use it for everyday messaging [14]. Consequently, Kakao has been able to provide mobility services more easily to consumers [14]. Specifically, Kakao T (taxi app) holds a 90% share of mobile taxis operating in Korea, making it an essential app for this kind of mobility [10]. As mentioned above, examining Korean consumer perceptions of user-friendly mobility services is essential for the future development of MaaS based on a user-centered approach. Therefore, this study analyzes consumer reviews of Kakao's mobility services (subway, bus, and taxi) using text-mining methods.

2.2   Topic Modeling

Large-scale text analysis of data such as online reviews can be achieved through natural language processing [15, 16]. Topic modeling allows for identifying topics within textual data and analyzing their relationships [17]. Various topic modeling methods exist, such as Latent Semantic Analysis (LSA), Latent Dirichlet Allocation (LDA), and Structural Topic Modeling (STM). Among these, LDA is the most commonly used [18–25]; it assumes that topics are independent, making it challenging to simultaneously analyze text alongside other information, such as review ratings and authors' gender [25]. Contrastingly, STM recognizes interactions between topics and allows for analysis of the differences in topics based on factors such as the date and review ratings [26]. Therefore, this study uses STM to examine what consumers discuss when using subway, bus, and taxi apps and how their perceptions differ according to transportation mode. The study also aims to explore positive and negative reactions to the identified topics.

3 Method

3.1 Data Collection and Data Cleaning

This study collected consumer reviews written on Google Play Store for the mobility services offered by Kakao, namely, Kakao Bus, Kakao Subway, and Kakao T (taxi app) from their respective launch dates until December 2022 using Python. The collected data consisted of 13,917 reviews for Kakao T (March 2015–December 2022), 5,812 reviews for Kakao Bus (April 2016–December 2022), and 4,999 reviews for Kakao Subway (June 2016–December 2022). The data were then processed by excluding stop words and non-app-related reviews. Subsequently, 10,193 reviews for Kakao T, 3,815 reviews for Kakao Bus, and 3,327 reviews for Kakao Subway, totaling 17,335 reviews, were used for STM analysis.

3.2 Data Analysis

This study utilized the KoNLPy package in Python to extract nouns and adjectives from the consumer review data using the Okt dictionary [27], which is considered appropriate for analyzing consumer reviews. For the STM analysis, the STM package in R programming was employed. To determine the optimal number of topics, SearchK (coherence, exclusivity, likelihood, residuals) [26] analysis was conducted while considering interpretability; ultimately, an 11-topic model was selected.

4 Results

4.1 Words Frequency

We extracted the top 50 most frequently used words. Words such as "Call," "Location," "Notification," and "Comfortable" were frequently mentioned, indicating that consumers were discussing the convenience of mobility apps. However, words such as "Discrepancy," "Pass," and "Late" also appeared frequently, suggesting that mobility services sometimes provide inaccurate information, inconveniencing consumers. In addition, words related to errors in the mobility service system, such as "Update," "Setting," and "Error," were also frequently mentioned.

4.2 Results of Structural Topic Modeling

Topic Modeling. Topic modeling results are shown in Table 1. First of all, Topic 1 related to mobility services' failure to provide accurate bus and subway information; it consisted of words such as "Schedule," "Discrepancy," "Bus station," and "Subway station." We named it "Misinformation."

Table 1. Result of Structural Topic Modeling

Topic	Word
Topic 1	Schedule, Discrepancy, Bus-S, Arrival, Information, Sub-S, Accord, Missed, Transfer, Mark
Topic 2	Cancellation, Driver, Com-M, Report, Fee, Fabulous, Mistake, Reservation, Contact, Penalty
Topic 3	Location, Arrival, Noti-F, Departure, Setting, Get-off, Precise, Check, Close, Appointment
Topic 4	Call, Cost, Deluxe-taxi, Area, Money, Town, AC, Nearby, Regular-taxi, Possible
Topic 5	Ride, Commute, Circuitous, Directions, Late, Morning, Map, Guide, Route, Tardiness
Topic 6	OTB, Betterment, Payment, Download, Error, Request, Check, Matter, Connection, Auto-M
Topic 7	Catch, Distance, Difficult, Near, Long-D, Money, Refusal, Selective, GAT, Urgent
Topic 8	Update, Inconvenient, MA, Function, Altered, Previous, Route, Search, Added, selection
Topic 9	Driver, Ride, PAX, DEST, Comfortable, Hospitable, Money, IFH, Convenient, Assessment
Topic 10	Wait, Pass, Allocation, Car, Ride, System, Direction, NC, Seat, Opposite
Topic 11	Irksome, Thinking, Deleted, Service, Urgent, KT, Corporation, MP, DN, Acquaintance

Notes. Bus-S = Bus station; Sub-S = Subway station; Com-M = Communication; Noti-F = Notification; AC = Additional cost; OTB = On the blink; Auto-M = Automation; Long-D = Long distance; GAT = Getting a taxi; MA = Metropolitan area; PAX = Passenger; DEST = Destination; IFH = In front of the house; NC = Not coming; KT = Kakao Talk; MP = Mobile phone; DN = Do not

Six topics related to taxi mobility services were derived. Topic 2, consisting of words such as "Cancellation," "Driver," "Communication," and "Report," was named "Reservation Cancellation." Topic 4, consisting of words such as "Call," "Deluxe-taxi," "Additional cost," and "Possible," was named "Premium Service." Topic 5, consisting of words such as "Ride," "Commute," "Circuitous," and "Directions," was named "Circuitous Route." Topic 7, consisting of words such as "Catch," "Distance," "Selective," and "Getting a taxi," was named "Selective Acceptance by Drivers." Topic 9, consisting of words such as "Driver," "Ride," "Passenger," and "Destination," was named "Calling Taxi Discrimination." Topic 10, consisting of words such as "Wait," "Pass," "Allocation," and "Car," was named "Taxi Delay."

Finally, four topics related to using apps were derived. Topic 3, consisting of "Location," "Notification," "Setting," and "Precise," was named "Informativity Enhancement of App." Topic 6, consisting of words such as "On-the-blink," "Payment," "Error," and "Connection" was named "App Error." Topic 8, consisting of words such as "Update," "Inconvenient," "Function," and "Added" was named "App Update." Topic 11 was named "App Withdrawal," consisting of "Irksome," "Deleted," "Service," and "Urgent."

Sentiment Analysis. In this study, sentiment analysis was conducted for each topic based on star ratings in online consumer reviews, divided into positive (4–5 points) and negative reviews (1–3 points). The results are shown in Fig. 1. Informativity Enhancement of App (Topic 3), Premium Service (Topic 4), and Calling Taxi Discrimination (Topic 9) were identified as positive topics. These positive features result from the development of ICT and near-universal penetration of smart devices, leading to new services such as information search, reservation, and payment through mobile apps, which reduce the uncertainty of traditional services. In addition, this result can be interpreted as representing demand from consumers for additional enhancements of these features and functions, which have become frequently used since the introduction of mobility services.

On the other hand, Misinformation (Topic 1), Reservation Cancellation (Topic 2), Circuitous Route (Topic 5), App Error (Topic 6), Selective Acceptance by Drivers (Topic 7), Taxi Delay (Topic 10), and App Withdrawal (Topic 11) were identified as negative topics. Finally, App Update (Topic 8) was identified as a neutral topic. The negative topics show the possibility that mobility services may actually hinder consumer mobility

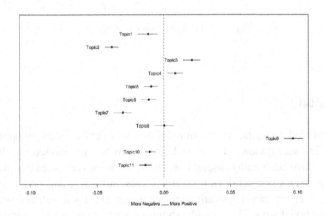

Fig. 1. Sentiment Analysis (Negative vs. Positive)

if problems arise and they do not function effectively. Therefore, developing consumer-oriented MaaS apps through sophisticated technology based on precise user location settings and real-time traffic information is necessary.

Topic Correlations Analysis. The relationships between the topics identified through STM are shown in Fig. 2. Misinformation (Topic 1), Circuitous Route (Topic 5), and Taxi Call Delay (Topic 10) are highly connected, while Informatively Enhancement of App (Topic 3), App Error (Topic 6), and App Update (Topic 8) show strong connections. Additionally, Reservation Cancellation (Topic 2), Premium Service (Topic 4), Driver Selective Acceptance (Topic 7), Calling Taxi Discrimination (Topic 9), and App Withdrawal (Topic 11) exhibit strong connections with each other. This suggests that consumers have positive and negative experiences with the convenience of taxi apps.

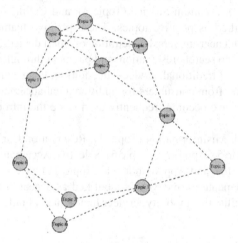

Fig. 2. Topic Correlations Analysis

5   Conclusion

This study analyzed consumer perceptions of mobility service apps by applying STM analysis to online user reviews. The main findings can be summarized as follows.

First, there have been many discussions about the inconveniences consumers experience when using mobile services related to buses, subways, and taxis, such as subway information errors, taxi reservation cancellations, taxi route detours, selective taxi acceptance, and taxi delays. These results show dissatisfaction with taxi services that are different from the inconvenience felt when using mobility services related to buses or subways. In particular, since taxi service is an individualized service provided based on individual demand, the range of factors that determine the quality of service inevitably fluctuates greatly. In this regard, it is necessary of mobility service providers to make efforts to standardize the quality of taxi services.

In addition, for taxis, there has been discussion about the cost of premium services and differentiation in taxi services. With the emergence of mobile taxi apps, consumer convenience has been improved by resolving problems frequently experienced in traditional taxi services, such as uncertainty and difficult interactions. However, despite the advancement of these services, the results show negative topics about taxi services, which indicates the need for quality control according to the advancement of services.

Finally, there has been discussion about technological issues such as server environments, including app errors and requests for enhanced functionality in common mobility app environments. When consumers use mobility services, they access them through mobile apps and thus demand basic app functionality and stability. Therefore, the development of MaaS implies the need for service providers to consider mobility characteristics and establish sufficient server security and system stability for app usage.

This study is significant in that it explores the problems experienced by Korean consumers using mobility services and their functional and technological requirements. It can provide basic data for Korea's development of MaaS. However, this study only analyzed mobility services (subway, bus, and taxi) provided by Kakao, and did not investigate consumer perceptions of mobility services provided by other companies, which may relate to different modes of transportation. Therefore, further research is needed to examine consumer perceptions from a broad perspective, including new mobility services that have recently attracted attention [28, 29].

References

1. Wong, Y., Hensher, D., Mulley, C.: Mobility as a service (MaaS): charting a future context. Transp. Res. Part A Policy Pract. **131**, 5–19 (2020)
2. Li, X., Yoon, D., Ding, Y., Hwang, H.: Consumer intention to accept ai-based products and services. In: Stephanidis, C., Antona, M., Ntoa, S., Salvendy, G. (eds.) HCII 2022, CCIS, vol. 1655, pp. 632–640. Springer, Virtual (2022)
3. Wu, W., Ng, W., Krishnaswamy, S., Sinha, A.: To taxi or not to taxi?-Enabling personalised and real-time transportation decisions for mobile users. In: 2012 IEEE 13th International Conference on Mobile Data Management, pp. 320–323. IEEE, Bengaluru (2012)
4. Kim, Y., Kim, E., Jang, S., Kim, D.: A comparative analysis of the users of private cars and public transportation for intermodal options under mobility-as-a-service in Seoul. Travel Behav. Soc. **24**, 68–80 (2021)
5. Sochor, J., Arby, H., Karlsson, I., Sarasini, S.: A topological approach to mobility as a service: a proposed tool for understanding requirements and effects, and for aiding the integration of societal goals. Res. Transp. Bus. Manag. **27**, 3–14 (2018)
6. Ko, E., Kwon, Y., Son, W., Kim, J., Kim, H.: Factors influencing intention to use mobility as a service: case study of Gyeonggi Province. Korea. Sustain. **14**(1), 218 (2022)
7. The Seoul Institute Homepage. https://www.si.re.kr/node/61730. Accessed 23 Mar 2023
8. Li, X., Kim, B., Yoon, D., Hwang, H.: Differences in smartphone overdependence by type of smartphone usage: decision tree analysis. In: Arai, K. (ed.) FICC 2022, LNNS, vol. 438, pp. 12–21. Springer, Virtual (2022)
9. Lee, J., Ryu, Y., Hwang, J.: Development of guidance app for public transportation. J. Digital Contents Soc. **18**(1), 115–121 (2017)
10. Lee, E.J., Kim, S.I.: A study on user experience of Kakao Taxi. J. Digital Converg. **16**(9), 359–364 (2018)

11. Vij, A., Ryan, S., Sampson, S., Harris, S.: Consumer preferences for Mobility-as-a-Service (MaaS) in Australia. Transp. Res. Part C Emerg. Technol. **117**, 102699 (2020)
12. Caiati, V., Rasouli, S., Timmermans, H.: Bundling, pricing schemes and extra features preferences for mobility as a service: sequential portfolio choice experiment. Transp. Res. Part A Policy Pract. **131**, 123–148 (2020)
13. So, J., An, H., Lee, C.: Defining smart mobility service levels via text mining. Sustainability **12**(21), 9293 (2020)
14. Han, S., Li, X., Hwang, H.: Analysis of news data on 'super app' using topic modeling. In: Stephanidis, C., Antona, M., Ntoa, S., Salvendy, G. (eds.) HCII 2022, CCIS, vol. 1655, pp. 33–39. Springer, Virtual (2022)
15. Li, X., Lim, H., Yeo, H., Hwang, H.: Text mining of online news, social media, and consumer review on artificial intelligence service. Fam. Environ. Res. **59**(1), 23–43 (2021)
16. Kim, B., Li, X., Yoon, D., Hwang, H.: How are the issues of poverty changing with COVID-19 in South Korea? In: Arai, K. (ed.) FICC 2022, LNNS, vol. 439, pp. 501–516. Springer, Virtual (2022)
17. Blei, D.M.: Probabilistic topic models. Commun. ACM **55**(4), 77–84 (2012)
18. Li, X., Lim, H., Hwang, H.: Daily life with "Clova" smart speaker: topic modeling of "Clova" review data. In: Proceedings of the XX International Conference on Human Computer Interaction, pp. 1–2. Association for Computing Machinery, Donostia (2019)
19. Li, X., Yeo, H., Hwang, H., Kim, K.: 5G service and discourses on hyper-connected society in South Korea: text mining of online news. In: Arai, K., Kapoor, S., Bhatia, R. (eds.) FICC 2020, AISC, vol. 1130, pp. 892–897. Springer, San Francisco (2020)
20. Lim, H., Li, X., Yeo, H., Hwang, H.: Semantic network analysis of Korean virtual assistants' review data. In: Ahram, T., Karwowski, W., Vergnano, A., Leali, F., Taiar, R. (eds.) Intelligent Human Systems Integration 2020. AISC, vol. 1131, pp. 633–639. Springer, Cham (2020). https://doi.org/10.1007/978-3-030-39512-4_98
21. Lee, Y., Li, X., Hwang, H.: Understanding agendas of unmanned stores: the case of South Korea. In: Stephanidis, C., Antona, M., Ntoa, S., Salvendy, G. (eds.) HCII 2022, CCIS, vol. 1654, pp. 267–274. Springer, Virtual (2022)
22. Han, J., Li, X., Hwang, H.: A study on the consumer boycott participation experience: using text mining analysis and in-depth interview. J. Korea Contents Assoc. **22**(2), 88–106 (2022)
23. Kim, M., Hwang, H.S., Li, X.: Research trends of consumer education using topic modelling. Consum. Policy. Educ. Rev. **16**(2), 83–115 (2020)
24. Hwang, H., Li, X., Xiang, M., Kim, K.O.: Consumer experiences of the world's first 5G network in South Korea. In: Stephanidis, C., Antona, M. (eds.) HCI International 2020 - Posters. CCIS, vol. 1224, pp. 445–449. Springer, Cham (2020). https://doi.org/10.1007/978-3-030-50726-8_58
25. Hu, N., Zhang, T., Gao, B., Bose, I.: What do hotel customers complain about? Text analysis using structural topic model. Tour. Manage. **72**, 417–426 (2019)
26. Roberts, M., et al.: Structural topic models for open-ended survey responses. Am. J. Polit. Sci. **58**(4), 1064–1082 (2014)
27. Choi, S., Li, X., Hwang, H.: A study on the types of consumer issues in C2C transactions: using a text mining approach. J. Consump. Cult. **25**(4), 1–26 (2022). https://doi.org/10.17053/jcc.2022.25.4.001
28. Li, X., Yeo, H., Hwang, H.: Detecting themes related to public concerns and consumer issues regarding personal mobility. In: Stephanidis, C., Antona, M. (eds.) HCI International 2020 - Posters. CCIS, vol. 1224, pp. 161–166. Springer, Cham (2020). https://doi.org/10.1007/978-3-030-50726-8_21
29. Choi, S., Li, X., Yoo, J., Hwang, H.: 5G based autonomous vehicle issue analysis: text mining South Korean news data. In: Arai, K. (ed.) FICC 2023, LNNS, vol. 651, pp. 619–629. Springer, Virtual (2023)

Multi-platform Distribution of Video Content: An Analysis of Video Content Cross-Posted by YouTubers on Bilibili

Hantian Zhang[1]([✉]) [iD] and Katrin Scheibe[2] [iD]

[1] Sheffield Hallam University, Sheffield S1 1WB, UK
Hantian.Zhang@shu.ac.uk
[2] Heinrich Heine University, Universitätsstraße 1, Düsseldorf, Germany
katrin.scheibe@hhu.de

Abstract. Among YouTube content creators from the Western culture, it is becoming more and more present to upload their YouTube content on the Chinese video-sharing platform Bilibili. YouTubers may adjust their video content and uploading strategies when cross-posting to Bilibili. However, research on the cross-posting behavior of YouTube creators between YouTube and Bilibili is lacking but will give insights into platform-specific practices. In this work-in-progress paper a qualitative content analysis is performed, to compare video content cross-posted from YouTube to Bilibili by the same creators, their uploading behaviors and the utilization of user interface features associated with the videos. Results show adjustments of video content, especially regarding textual elements and outro design. All in all, adjustments to content and platform-exclusive content uploaded are targeted at Chinese viewers, who represent a potentially large audience group on Bilibili with a different cultural background. The present research is an initial step to form a contribution to the literature that seeks to understand the role of culture and platform affordances played in multi-platform content distribution, specifically in the Chinese-Western context.

Keywords: Cross-posting · Multi-platform · Content analysis · YouTube · Bilibili

1 Introduction

Cross-posting and, thus, uploading identical content on various social media platforms is nothing new. The procedure is common for user-generated text and images, especially by professional users [1]. When it comes to short-video content, multi-platform distribution is typically found across TikTok, Instagram Reels, and YouTube Shorts [2]. In recent years, YouTube creators started posting their content on Bilibili, a Chinese video-sharing platform. Recent research about Chinese creators posting on multiple platforms indicates adjustments to the same content posted [e.g., 3], but does not go into detail about the made adjustments. Considering the platform differences between YouTube and Bilibili (e.g., user base, interface elements), YouTubers may alter their content and strategies

C. Stephanidis et al. (Eds.): HCII 2023, CCIS 1835, pp. 149–156, 2023.
https://doi.org/10.1007/978-3-031-36001-5_20

when cross-posting on Bilibili. However, research on the cross-posting behavior between YouTube and Bilibili by YouTube creators is lacking. This paper aims to compare videos cross-posted to Bilibili by YouTubers, the utilization of user interface features associated with the videos, and YouTube creators' uploading behavior on YouTube and Bilibili. The research questions are:

RQ1: What differences can be observed between the content cross-posted by YouTubers from YouTube on Bilibili?

RQ2: How do YouTubers utilize the platform's interface features on Bilibili when cross-posting their content, in comparison to YouTube?

RQ3: What differences between YouTubers' uploading behaviors on YouTube compared to Bilibili can be observed?

The present research is an initial step to form a contribution to the literature that seeks to understand the role of culture and platform affordances played in multi-platform content distribution, specifically in the Chinese-Western context.

2 Related Literature

Farahbakhsh, Cuevas, and Crespi [1] investigated the cross-posting activity of professional users on the online social networks Facebook, Twitter, and Google+. Results showed that content is frequently cross-posted by professional users, especially between Facebook and Twitter. Ma, Gui, and Kou [4] found that platform prioritization, synchronization of content across multiple platforms, and audience management are important practices in creator ecology. Meng and Nansen [3] uncovered Chinese content creators not only produce and circulate videos across multiple platforms but also consider their self-presentation and online identity management and formation. Cross-platform sharing is performed to increase the creator's visibility and reach a greater audience. However, platforms are used following their respective aims, leading to platform-specific practices including platform-specific management of identity and self-presentation practices.

Some studies explored the differences between user-generated content (UGC) across multiple social media platforms regarding the same topic. Smith, Fischer, and Yongjian [5] compared the customers' UGC related to two brands across YouTube, Facebook, and Twitter, and found significant differences. For example, customers are more likely to upload self-promotional content on YouTube, tweet brand-centered content on Twitter, and respond to marketer action via UGC on both Twitter and Facebook. Later research by Roma and Aloini [6] compared the brand-related UGC across the three platforms and discovered updated evidence regarding the UGC differences. For example, they found that while YouTube still features more self-promotional UGC from customers than Facebook and Twitter, Facebook has closed the gap with YouTube due to the inclusion of features that allow more visually rich content. The results also found customers reacted to the brand campaign differently on three platforms depending on the brands, further arguing that in addition to the platforms' differences, how the brands use social media to engage customers is also important to determine the content posted.

Instead of specific brands, Zhan et al. [7] analyzed the content relating to the same product across Reddit, Twitter, and product online forums. Similar to Smith, Fischer, and Yongjian [5] and Roma and Aloini [6], the results showed that the product-related content is presented differently based on the platform's characteristics. For example, the posts on Reddit are broader due to their comprehensive nature, while Twitter is more specific on debates regarding the product.

Overall, the above research indicated content on different social media platforms may be presented differently, even if they evolve around the same topics. However, existing research has not focused on comparing the content created by the same creator cross-posted on multiple platforms, and they did not focus on comparing platforms that are built for video-sharing like YouTube and Bilibili. They also did not compare the content created by the same creator and cross-posted on other platforms, especially platforms that are within different cultural domains.

Recent research by Zimmer, Scheibe, and Zhang [8] found different utilizations and inclusions of the gamification elements (e.g., donating, commenting, linking, chatting, sending a digital gift) on popular video streaming apps used in countries like China, Germany, and the United States, with a noticeable difference between the design of gamification features in Chinese and Eastern country apps and the one usually used in the Western countries. While the research did not compare content on different platforms, the results still imply that like other social media sites, video-sharing or streaming platforms are also built differently for user groups in different cultural domains. This is in line with Levian and Arriaga's [9] argument that different social media platforms offer the contributors various forms of capital from the content they posted, such as ratings, featuring, social network position, and attention. Therefore, when the same group of creators cross-posts from one video platform to another, especially if the platforms are focusing on viewer groups with different cultural backgrounds like Bilibili and YouTube, the content and the utilization of the platform features may be altered by the creators to maintain the same level of the benefits or capitals received. However, existing research rarely has explored the creators' cross-posting behaviors on Bilibili and YouTube.

3   Methodology

A qualitative content analysis was performed by observing the content of the same videos uploaded to Bilibili and YouTube by creators who have an official account on both platforms, but first started content creation on YouTube. The YouTube creators Viva La Dirt League (VLDL; entertainment content) and Pamela Reif (fitness content) have been considered for analysis. Both YouTube channels started posting their content on Bilibili in 2020 and are still actively uploading content on both platforms. The sample videos were the most viewed one on Bilibili, the first video that was uploaded to Bilibili and was also available on YouTube, and one was randomly chosen. In total, twelve videos (six videos per YouTube creator; three videos on each platform) have been observed regarding the video content, whereby everytime the same video has been watched on YouTube and on Bilibili. Furthermore, the video uploading behavior of both content creators has been observed by examining the uploading date of the same videos on both platforms as well as by checking whether content has solely and especially been uploaded to one of the platforms.

The conventional approach [10] was applied to arrive at the content categories, therefore the themes emerged during the analysis. The authors watched the videos independently, whereby one researcher observed the videos of Pamela Reif and one of VLDL. The emerging topics were discussed during a meeting. The authors watched different videos to arrive at a codebook. In general, a content analysis allows qualitative as well as quantitative results, whereby the results presented in this study are qualitative by presenting the coded themes.

4   Results

4.1   Video Content

The results found six areas of differences between the content of the videos on YouTube and the ones cross-posted to Bilibili: on-screen texts, subtitles, thumbnail design, outro design, ads, video quality, and watermarking.

On-screen texts are texts YouTubers added to their video as part of the content. For Pamela Reif, the name of each workout movement is presented in all her workout videos. For VLDL, the title of each episode is shown at the beginning of each short story in the video that contains multiple episodes. Both creators have changed on-screen texts from English to Chinese while maintaining a similar text style on Bilibili. This may be due to their aim to make the video more accessible to Chinese viewers.

The observation shows that the videos uploaded by VLDL to Bilibili have Chinese *subtitles* embedded, but no embedded subtitles in the original YouTube videos. This can be the creators' technique to further enhance the accessibility of their videos for Chinese viewers. This does not apply to Pamela Reif as all her videos in the sample are workout videos with no dialogues but music playing in the background.

Thumbnail design refers to the video thumbnails presented on YouTube and Bilibili. Both YouTubers have changed the English texts on the original thumbnail to Chinese, with similar colors and styles. The images most of the time remain the same (design style) across both platforms. This again reflects the practice of YouTubers trying to enhance the accessibility of their videos.

The *outro design* is also different between both platforms. For VLDL, at the end of a video on Bilibili, they added an outro graphic that matches the buttons on the Bilibili interface, including likes and shares. On YouTube, however, the outro includes a YouTube "subscribe" button asking for subscriptions. For Pamela Reif, the original video on YouTube includes the promotion of the workout music playlist (on certain platforms that are not accessible in China), which was cut out in the cross-posted version in Bilibili. Thus, both creators seem to alter their outro to accommodate the platforms or overall environment and accessibility of viewers.

Advertising includes ads added by the platform during the video and ads included as promotions by the creators. It was found that videos on Bilibili do not have ads that interrupt the viewers. On YouTube, however, there are ads in the videos (the users can also remove ads by buying a membership). Pamela Reif's YouTube videos however further included ads by the creator which were highlighted by a small note saying "Ad" at the beginning of the video, which was not displayed in the video uploaded to Bilibili.

For *video qualities*, on YouTube, viewers can change available qualities without restrictions. However, on Bilibili, the video was played in low quality by default. Users need to log in to access high-quality selection, with the highest quality locked behind a Bilibili membership payment. This may be due to policy differences between the platforms instead of the choice of the uploaders.

Watermarking is a unique element of Bilibili. In both creators' videos, there are watermarks in the form of the channel names and a Bilibili Logo. Only Pamela Reif's first video on Bilibili does not have a watermark, which may be due to being at an early stage of uploading. This is perhaps due to plenty of YouTube videos from YouTube creator were directly reuploaded to Bilibili by users without the creators' permission, leading to both creators adding watermarks to the video to prevent copying and copyright infringements. However, based on the similarity of the watermark format, it could be a requirement by the Bilibili platform as well.

4.2 Utilization of the User Interface Elements

Five differences between the utilization of user interface features on YouTube and Bilibili by the creators were discovered, which are related to the function of video titling, donation, commenting, copyright statement, and video description.

For *video titling*, the results showed that both YouTubers utilize Chinese video names (or English and Chinese combined) when they cross-post their videos. The titles are not always directly translated from English to Chinese. It seems like the YouTube creators not only try to lower the language barrier but also make the video titles more understandable to Chinese viewers.

Donation refers to the function on both platforms that allows viewers to donate money to the creators. On YouTube the videos from VLDL all have the donation, or "thanks" function enabled. Pamela Reif, on the other hand, does not enable the donation function on YouTube. On Bilibili, there are two possibilities to donate to the creators on the video interface, named "giving coins" and "charging." Both functions will grant the creators virtual currencies that can be exchanged for real money or to buy virtual items. Among those, the charging function can be enabled or disabled by the creators. The analysis showed that both donation functions on Bilibili are present for both creators. This can be the practice in which the creator adopts the business models of the Bilibili platform.

For *commenting*, the results show that comment sections are all enabled under the videos on YouTube and Bilibili. On YouTube, VLDL sometimes directly interacts with viewers by liking their comments. Pamela Reif added her own comments on top of the comment section, directly under the videos by making "pinned" comments. On Bilibili, there is no interaction between VLDL and the viewers' comments. However, Pamela Reif still utilizes the pinned comments, but in Chinese, to connect with her Chinese viewers. Bilibili also has a function called Danmaku, through which the viewers can input comments on the exact moment (timestamp) in the video and let it move across the screen for other viewers to see. All observed videos cross-posted to Bilibili from YouTube have Danmaku in them.

Copyright statement is a unique function of Bilibili. Creators can choose to turn on the copyright statement when they upload the video. The statement, besides the video title, indicates other users cannot reupload or redistribute the video unless authorized by the original creator. Both creators have this function turned on for all the videos they cross-posted to Bilibili. This is perhaps due to the situation in which there are YouTube videos directly reuploaded by other users to Bilibili.

Video descriptions are extra information displayed below the video added by the creators. Both creators have English descriptions under their original videos on YouTube. On Bilibili, the descriptions are in Chinese (sometimes combined with English), but also have different content than the English version. For example, one video from VLDL has a Chinese description of the video content on Bilibili, while the original YouTube video has a longer description with video content and promotion of the YouTubers (e.g., social media, product range). In Pamela Reif's first video on Bilibili, in addition to describing the video content in Chinese, she added that she hopes her Chinese is correct (in English). So, it seems like the creators all tailored their descriptions for their Bilibili uploads.

4.3 Creator's Uploading Behaviors

Finally, the results showed that the uploading behaviors of the creators are different when they start cross-posting videos to Bilibili, mainly regarding the uploading schedule and exclusive content.

For the *uploading schedule*, the results showed that the creators' accounts on Bilibili are uploading slower than on YouTube. The original videos on YouTube are usually uploaded weeks or months earlier than the cross-posted version on Bilibili. It can be explained by the post-production they need to do before posting the content from YouTube to Bilibili, including adding Chinese subtitles and replacing on-screen text as well as translating the thumbnail's text.

We also found that there is *exclusive content* posted by the creators that are specifically created for the platform's viewers. For example, one video on Pamela Reif's Bilibili channel was made for the Chinese Lunar New Year, in which she briefly speaks Chinese (Mandarin) in the video. There is also another video she made in partnership with the Chinese online retailer Jingdong. Those videos were not uploaded to YouTube. However, on YouTube, some videos are not uploaded to Bilibili either, especially those workout videos that are older than the first video she cross-posted to Bilibili. VLDL also made exclusive content for Bilibili's audience. The first upload found on their Bilibili channel is a promotional video for the Chinese viewer base and is solely available on Bilibili. In the video, the main members of VLDL introduce themselves in Chinese. On YouTube, they also uploaded an introduction video for YouTube's audience when they started the channel, which is a skit and music video. Similar to Pamela Reif, some of their earlier content is not cross-posted to Bilibili.

5 Discussion

The present study sheds light on the multi-platform distribution of video content cross-posted by YouTubers on the Chinese video-sharing platform Bilibili. The results reveal that YouTubers have made changes to the content they have cross-posted on Bilibili. Especially by changing the textual content of the video and thumbnail from English to Chinese and by adding Chinese subtitles, the video is more accessible to Chinese viewers. However, some changes may be caused by the affordability of the platform, such as the video quality options, and the cut outro or the new outro design for Bilibili. Meng and Nansen [3, p. 37] argue it "is a form of *platform migration*, in order to create optimal conditions for their videos to spread and be viewed." Other studies identified differences in the content posted by different users across multiple platforms regarding the same topic [5–7]. Our results are partially in line with the existing research, which revealed that content types regarding the same topic are different across different UGC platforms. However, with the focus on YouTube and Bilibli, our research proposes there are also changes applied to the content cross-posted from the original platform to the one in another cultural environment by the same creator, due to the platform features and the viewer demographics on those platforms.

Previous research uncovered creators' behaviors for audience engagement on YouTube including the use of comment sections for participation [11–13] and fulfilling viewers' needs of seeking information [14] by, for example, using descriptions on YouTube. Our research added to those studies and found that YouTubers also try to utilize similar features on Bilibili when cross-posting to engage their viewers. However, our research indicates that YouTubers also alter their way of using those functions to further accommodate the viewers' demographics on Bilibili, such as using Chinese comments and video descriptions. In addition to similar functions, our research found some other unique implementations of the user interface on Bilibili including the inclusion of a copyright statement. This is in line with existing research (e.g., [8]) that uncovered different or similar interface elements of the online streaming platform. However, we have further discovered that when the same creators cross-post content from one streaming platform to another, there will also be similarities and differences between their utilizations of those functions.

Further, the results show that the creators have considered the Bilibili demographics intentionally to market their channels in a different way than they do on YouTube. While some of the results are in line with the research that discovered the differences between user behaviors across different platforms, such as the content they are posting regarding the brands and topics [5, 6], our results further indicate that the creators may alter their strategies to engage their audience when cross-posting between different platforms with the same functionality (e.g., video sharing), especially when the platforms are in different cultural domains (e.g., Chinese vs Western).

Some limitations of this work-in process study must be mentioned. It should be highlighted that the number of YouTube channels as well as the number of analyzed videos is rather low and only content in the field of fitness (Pamela Reif) and entertainment (VLDL) was considered. Further videos from creators of other topics should be included in future analyses (e.g., food, fashion, lifestyle). In addition, at least two researchers will have to watch the same videos to be able to calculate an inter-coder reliability score [15] for the validity of the results.

References

1. Farahbakhsh, R., Cuevas, A., Crespi, N.: Characterization of cross-posting activity for professional users across Facebook, Twitter and Google+. Soc. Netw. Anal. Min. **6**(33), 1–14 (2016)
2. Abidin, C.: Mapping internet celebrity on TikTok: exploring attention economies and visibility labours. Cult. Sci. J. **12**(1), 77–103 (2021)
3. Meng, Z., Nansen, B.: Chinese video creator identities – a cross-platform social media perspective. Platform J. Med. Commun. **9**(1), 24–42 (2022)
4. Ma, R., Gui, X., Kou, Y: Multi-platform content creation: the configuration of creator ecology through platform prioritization, content synchronization, and audience management. In: 2023 CHI Conference on Human Factors in Computing Systems (CHI 2023), vol. 5, CSCW2, Article 429. ACM (2023)
5. Smith, A.N., Fischer, E., Yongjian, C.: How does brand-related user-generated content differ across YouTube, Facebook, and Twitter? J. Interact. Mark. **26**(2), 102–113 (2012)
6. Roma, P., Aloini, D.: How does brand-related user-generated content differ across social media? Evidence reloaded. J. Bus. Res. **96**, 322–339 (2019)
7. Zhan, Y., Liu, R., Li, Q., Leischow, S.J., Zeng, D.D.: Identifying topics for e-cigarette user-generated contents: a case study from multiple social media platforms. J. Med. Internet Res. **19**(1), e24 (2017)
8. Zimmer, F., Scheibe, K., Zhang, H.: Gamification elements on social live streaming service mobile applications. In: Meiselwitz, G. (ed.) Social Computing and Social Media. Design, Ethics, User Behavior, and Social Network Analysis. LNCS, vol. 12194, pp. 184–197. Springer, Cham (2020). https://doi.org/10.1007/978-3-030-49570-1_13
9. Levina, N., Arriaga, M.: Distinction and status production on user-generated content platforms: using Bourdieu's theory of cultural production to understand social dynamics in online fields. Inf. Syst. Res. **25**(3), 468–488 (2014)
10. Hsieh, H.F., Shannon, S.E.: Three approaches to qualitative content analysis. Qual. Health Res. **15**(9), 1277–1288 (2005)
11. Burgess, J., Green, J.: YouTube: Online Video and Participatory Culture, 2nd edn. Polity Press, Cambridge, Medford (2018)
12. Tarnovskaya, V.: Reinventing personal branding building a personal brand through content on YouTube. J. Int. Bus. Res. Market. **3**(1), 29–35 (2017)
13. Zhang, H.: Behind the scenes: exploring context and audience engagement behaviors in YouTube vlogs. In: Meiselwitz, G. (ed.) Social Computing and Social Media. LNCS, vol. 13315, pp. 227–244. Springer, Cham (2022)
14. Khan, M.L.: Social media engagement: what motivates user participation and consumption on YouTube? Comput. Hum. Behav. **66**, 236–247 (2017)
15. Krippendorff, K.: Reliability in content analysis: some common misconceptions and recommendations. Hum. Commun. Res. **30**(3), 411–433 (2004)

Virtual Community Security Focused on Social Media

Xiaowen Zhang(⊠)

DePaul University, Chicago, IL 60604, USA
XZHAN111@depaul.edu

Abstract. We know that the security of the physical community is crucial to the quality of human life. Security communities can make people feel privacy protection and physical and mental health. Compared with community security, virtual community security can also affect people's quality of life. Virtual community security via social media refers to the concepts of private security and health security using social media, which enables users to interact securely with each other via social media. With the increasing popularity of virtual community technology, more and more people hope to share and publish their interesting, knowledgeable, and valuable personal life through social media and establish connections with others. Does social media provide virtual community security for users? There are three main threats to posting personal information and talking about your personal life via social media. First, users lack awareness of personal information security when using virtual communities through social media. Second, companies can track, collect, and analyze users' personal information without users' permission. Third, Internet Security Threats. How improving users' security in the social media virtual community? The findings suggest that increasing awareness of social media hazards and improving safety techniques for virtual communities are key points for designers and developers of social media virtual communities to help maintain user security and enhance the social media user experience. Therefore, I would like to propose two effective protection methods that can increase users' security when using social media virtual communities.

Keywords: Virtual Community · Social Design · Service Design · Privacy and Online Security · HCI Theories and Methods · User Experience

1 Introduction

As virtual community technology becomes more and more convenient, virtual communities established through social media are becoming more and more common in human life. Social media becomes an extension of a person's real life, including a detailed record of all aspects of a person's information [3]. More and more people also want to share and publish their thoughts through virtual communities on social media. I found that most users were unaware of the threats of posting through social media virtual communities, and only a minority were aware of the threats of posting through social media virtual communities; however, some of them were not concerned about virtual community security via social media.

© The Author(s), under exclusive license to Springer Nature Switzerland AG 2023
C. Stephanidis et al. (Eds.): HCII 2023, CCIS 1835, pp. 157–162, 2023.
https://doi.org/10.1007/978-3-031-36001-5_21

There are three threats to posting personal information and talking about personal life in social media virtual communities. First, users may unknowingly lose their identity. Users may or may not be aware of the dangers of using virtual communities through social media, but when they do, they lose some privacy and face security threats. Second, social media can utilize, collect, and analyze user data. Social media can collect and analyze users' personal information through virtual communities without their permission. Third, social media based on the Internet environment may leak users' personal information because cloud security and network security are not secure. So, being aware of the dangers of social media and improving virtual community security technology is the focus of company design and developers to help users protect themselves and improve user protection in the risky Internet through social media. Therefore, it is important to provide effective protection methods to improve the security awareness of users when using social media virtual communities. In the end, I would like to introduce two effective protection methods that can increase the security of users when using social media virtual communities.

2 The Three Threats to Publishing Personal Information and Talking About Personal Life in the Social Media Virtual Community

2.1 Lack of Virtual Community Security Awareness via Social Media

First, users may lose privacy security and health security without knowing it. Personal email addresses and birthdays, for example, are left behind when users sign up for social media and use virtual communities to publish their life. Sharing such personal information without awareness shows blind trust in these social media platforms, which is not a good thing. Users lack the security awareness of virtual communities via social media, not only losing privacy security but also losing health security. For example, users spend too much time in virtual communities via social media. Users are addicted to virtual communities via social media and have no time to communicate with family and friends in real life. Users may then develop health and mental illnesses. According to "using social media before bed can harm your sleep duration and sleep" [2], it is necessary to control the user's nighttime use of social media and avoid staying up too late to use social media virtual communities. Therefore, users need to raise their security awareness when using virtual communities and not blindly trust social media.

2.2 Malicious Use of Users' Personal Information in Social Media Virtual Communities

In addition to the lack of virtual community security awareness via social media, personal information maliciously used by companies can decrease the security of using virtual communities via social media. Social media can utilize, collect, and analyze users' data from a virtual community. I researched the security of customer transaction information on e-commerce websites, which exposed the same problem of user privacy loss due to the company's failure to care about the security of user privacy data. Although user data is the most important resource used by the company, social media companies only care about the revenue from using big data. For example, LinkedIn earns profits from advertising, subscribers, and selling data to third parties. Users will no longer trust social media virtual communities if virtual communities cannot provide users with a secure user experience. Therefore, designers and developers should design social media virtual communities by improving virtual community security technology and security awareness.

2.3   Internet Risks the Security

Social media based on the Internet environment may leak users' privacy and cause user security threats because cloud security and network security are not safe. Therefore, it cannot be guaranteed that no criminals will take advantage of the situation and threaten the security of users. For example, a hacker can defraud a social media user by obtaining user information in a virtual community. Therefore, designers and developers of social media companies need to protect user security by raising awareness of technology and risks in virtual communities.

3   The Two Solutions Improving the Security of Users in the Social Media Virtual Community

3.1   Sending Alert Messages for Users' Security Protection

The first method is the social media application of protection and early warning features, which means sending an alert notification when users' security is threatened in the virtual community. This can be achieved by focusing on the dangerous behavior of users. When users use social media communities to trigger dangerous behaviors, protection, and early warning services will quickly remind users. For example, when users receive phishing danger information and are attacked by hackers, the social media application can automatically set up protection warning messages for users. The diagram below shows how alert messages can be used to protect users accessing virtual communities via social media (see Fig. 1).

Users in the virtual community can be aware of dangerous signals by receiving warnings from the social media platform, thereby avoiding users' losses.

3.2   Setting Specific Mode for Protecting Users' Security

Another method is security mode. Security mode supports specific settings according to the needs of different users. With the growing popularity of social media, the user base has expanded from teens and young adults to those over 50. Different users can customize their security mode settings according to their needs. Users use social media applications for more than two hours on average every day. Long-term use of social media is harmful to the physical and mental health of people, so the security mode can protect the security of users.

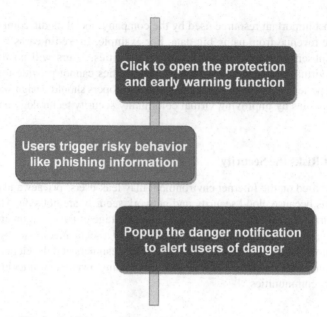

Fig. 1. Sending alert information for users' security protection

Teenagers can set the usage time of the virtual community within 2 h, which can better protect teenagers from indulging in social media. The diagram below shows how teens in virtual communities using social media can be protected by setting teen security mode (see Fig. 2).

Adults can set it to automatically lock the virtual community 2 h before going to bed to avoid using social media before going to bed and causing poor spirits and lack of sleep the next day. The image below shows how to protect user security by setting sleep security mode (see Fig. 3).

Limiting the number of time users spend on social media virtual communities, which not only to avoid users from wasting too much time on social media but also prevents health problems caused by their addiction to social media. Therefore, the security mode is an effective method to prevent users from using the virtual community for a long time to improve security awareness.

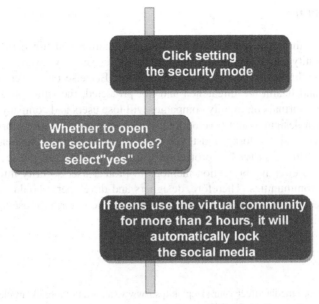

Fig. 2. Setting teen security mode for protecting users' security

Fig. 3. Setting sleep security mode for protecting users' security

4 Conclusion

There are three threats to publishing personal information and life narratives in the virtual community via social media. Improving users' security awareness in virtual communities is the key to avoiding security threats. Because once users realize that their privacy and health are threatened and not protected, the situation will be very serious, because virtual community companies will lose users and company reputation. Therefore, when designing and developing virtual community functions through social media, designers and developers must well cover the technology in the field of private security and health security. The protection warning function and the security mode function are two effective protection methods to protect user security through social media virtual communities. Therefore, designers and developers should continuously improve the security of social media users. Protecting the security of users can build a high-quality virtual community.

References

1. How does social media affect your sleep? https://www.sleepstation.org.uk/articles/sleep-tips/social-media/. Accessed 21 Oct 2022
2. Method of improving the information security of virtual communities in … (n.d.). https://ceur-ws.org/Vol-2392/paper3.pdf. Accessed 19 Mar 2023
3. Tsikerdekis, M.: Social interaction design for social media: the. case of groupthink and aggression. Social Interaction Design for Social Media: The Case of Groupthink and Aggression, 1 January 2012. https://is.muni.cz/th/messf/fithesis.pdf
4. Wang, Z.: On virtual community management of Wechat from the. perspective of public security. On Virtual Community Management of Wechat from the Perspective of Public Security, Location, 6 April 2018

How Do the Perceived Factors of Internet Community Charity Affect User Stickness? Consider the Mediating Role of Perceptual Ease of Use Value and Perceived Affective Value

Qingying Zhou[✉]

Tongji University, Shanghai, China
zhouqingying0816@163.com

Abstract. Community charity has a positive impact on the public, but the public's enthusiasm for community charity is not high. Based on SOR theory, this study establishes a research framework to explore the design factors that enhance the stickness of community charity users. Based on a survey of 369 respondents, our research provides significant evidence that feedback timeliness, interactivity, immersion, and pleasure are key factors that influence the stickness of community charity users. In addition, we demonstrate the mediating role of perceived ease of use and perceived emotional value. Enhance community philanthropy by exploring key design factors.

Keywords: Internet Community charity · user stickness · Perceived value · Structural model

1 Introduce

Community charity is a charitable non-profit organization based on local communities. Its main task is to create the well-being within the community by raising, holding, investing and distributing local and personal resources [1]. Furthermore, with the progress of technology, "public welfare digitalization" has also become a hot spot of the year. The combination of charity and technology can greatly expand the scope of charity projects and the spread of charity culture.

However, more and more people show low enthusiasm for community charity. Most users are short- term participants in the online community. When they get the social support they want, they will leave the online community [2]. For example, Burk and others found that charities in the UK and the United States are facing a crisis of reduced public stickiness to charities. After the first donation, Many charities lost up to 60% of their participants [3].

Many researchers focus on research and development on the behavior of community charity users. Adrian and others explored the factors influencing the loyalty of charity donors from the perspective of marketing. The research shows that (1) perceived service quality (2) common beliefs (3) perceived risks (4) the existence of personal connections with organizations (5) trust and commitment can increase the loyalty of charitable donors [38]. Existing researches have studied how to enhance the enthusiasm of the public for community charity from different perspectives, but few have explored the influencing factors of user stickness of Internet community charity from the design field.

This study aims to explore the influence of design factors on the user stickness of Internet community charity. Based on the theory of perceived value proposed by Zeithaml and Stimulus-organism-response theory (SOR theory), In order to solve the above problems, we adopted the PLS-SEM modeling and SOR theory to determine the influence relationship of various factors in the model.

2   Literature Review and Research Hypotheses

2.1   Literature Review

Stimulus-organism-response Theory (SOR Theory). SOR psychological model, also known as "stimulus-body-response" model, is an important research model in the field of cognitive psychology and educational psychology. Study of human behavioral outcomes through a three-stage process in which the perception of external or environmental stimuli (S) influences an individual's emotional and cognitive state (O), thereby stimulating conscious or unconscious human behavior (R) [4].

At present, SOR model has been widely used to study how environmental character-istics affect user mental state and user behavior. Based on SOR model, Zhou Tao takes community quality and social support as stimulus factors to study the virtual sense of community as the emotional experience of users and the behavioral mechanism process of business users [5]. Chen Zhigang and others used the SOR model to study the pur-chase intention of game players for virtual items [6]. Therefore, this study takes it as the theoretical basis for studying the stickness of charitable users in Internet communitie.

Framework Structure. Based on SOR model, we propose a framework the user stick-ness of community charity under the Internet. (Fig. 1) This framework takes into account the interactivity, feedback timeliness, immersion, and pleasure as Stimulus (Stimulus), the perceived ease of use value and perceived affective value as individual affective per-ception (Organism), the user stickness of community charity as the external behavior Response after the stimulus and organism changes (Response).

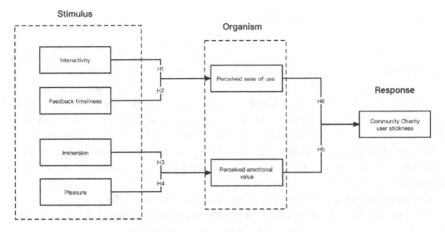

Fig. 1. Research model and hypotheses

2.2 Hypothesis

Interaction and Feedback Timeliness. With the vigorous rise of charity, community charity has become one of the developing trends of charity. However, users are tired of the traditional community charity activities. Sedig believe that the important factor of change is interaction[7]. Research believe that Internet interaction is one of the key factors affecting consumers' online experience, perceived enjoyment and psychological status [9].

Yang found through research that response speed has a positive impact on patient satisfaction [9]. Dong verified through the perceived value theory combined with the expectation theory that the feedback timeliness can reduce the perceived cost and improve the perceived ease of use value of users, thus affecting users' willingness to continue using [10].

When conducting community charity activities on Internet, users can quickly understand and recognize charity activities through interaction. The community charity activities on Internet can also attract users' attention and enhance the authenticity of charity activities through feedback timeliness, increase users' interest and sense of trust, thus affecting users' perceived ease of use and increasing the user sticknes. Therefore, based on the above summary, we propose the following hypothesis:

H1: Interaction has a positive effect on perceived ease of use value.

H2: feedback timeliness has a positive effect on perceived ease of use value.

Immersion and Pleasure. Immersive experiences (immersion) have a positive impact on consumer ratings. For example: VR users often experience a sense of concentration and lack of distractions in a VR environment. [11] Studies have shown that a combination of immersion, interactivity or vividness increases the sense of reality in the image-generated world known as telepresence [12]. Heeter demonstrated that consumers with high (low relatively) immersion can show positive (negative relatively) consumer evaluations [13].

Pleasure refers to the user's positive feelings towards the product, such as happiness and joy for the situation caused by environmental stimulus [14]. Lavie believe that good aesthetic design is more likely to have the favor of users and enhance their emotional investment in the online retail environment [15]. Hassanein believe that there is a positive relationship between positive emotions and purchase intention [16]. In the field of Internet community charity, it can be understood that the more pleasant users feel after experiencing Internet community activities, the more likely they are to do Internet community charity activities again. Therefore, we decide to examine the following hypotheses:

H3: Immersion has a positive effect on perceived emotion value.

H4: Pleasure has a positive effect on perceived emotion value.

Mediation Effect of Perceived Ease of Use Value and Perceived Emotion Value. Zeithaml explored from the perspective of users' psychological characteristics that perceived value can improve users' purchase intention [17]. According to the study of Davis, perceived ease of use is the degree to which individuals feel comfortable using intelligent medical services [18]. The Perceived Value Acceptance Model (VAM) is based on the perceived value theory proposed by Ceithaml and the TAM model proposed by Davis [19]. Kim et al. constructs the perceived value acceptance model. Based on the perspective of value maximization, it is built for users' willingness to use Internet [20]. Based on the Internet perspective, this model verifies that perceived value plays a mediating role in users' intention to use.

Perceived ease of use is the features of a product that can help users understanding quickly and easily. Kaifeng Liu verified that perceived ease of use has a positive effect on users' behavioral intention [21].

Many studies have examined the relationship between perceived emotional value, attitude, and intention [22]. Ashidin verified that sentimental value has a positive impact on users' purchase intention [23]. Desny verified that emotional value can improve users' purchase intention from the perspective of visual packaging of cosmetics [24].As a result, we put forward to hypotheses:

H5: Perceived emotional value has a positive effect on the stickness of community charity users.

H6: Perceived ease of use has a positive effect on the stickness of community charity users.

3   Methods

3.1   Data Collection and Sample Characteristics

To verify the theoretical framework assumed we proposed, we conducted an online questionnaire survey. At the beginning of the questionnaire, the definition of community charity on Internet platform is described. The online questionnaire is divided into two parts. One is to investigate the influencing factors involved in the framework. Two is collect basic personal information, including user's gender, age, frequency of using Internet charity products, etc. 369 responses were collected during the two-week online survey. Meanwhile, in order to check whether the participants were paying attention and making meaningful answers, we set a simple question in the middle of the questionnaire (please select "don't know"). Answering any other answer would reflect carelessness of the tester. 1 participant who failed this test would be filtered from the subsequent analysis. 368 qualified samples were used for analysis (Table 1.). The personal information of participants in this study is as follows. Among them, 178 (56.4%) were male and 190 (51.6%) were female.

Table 1. Characteristic variables of respondents.

Characteristics		N	%
Gender	Female	190	51.6%
	Male	178	56.4
Age/year	<18	24	6.5%
	18–29	186	50.5%
	30–39	101	27.4%
	40–49	34	9.2%
	50–59	14	3.8%
	≥60	9	2.4%
Education	High school and below	59	16%
	Junior college	149	40.5%
	Undergraduate	123	33.4%
	Graduate and above	37	10.1%
Experience/month	<3	83	22.5%
	3–6	89	24.2%
	6–12	93	25.3%
	12–36	55	14.9%
	>36	48	13%

Note: N = Frequency; % = Percentage

3.2 Variable Description

In the measurement scale, all the variables were used in the previous research, and we made some modifications for the actual project to adapt to the current research, as shown in the table2.. Respondents first need to familiarize with the definition of Internet community charity. According to the definition of understanding, items related to interactivity, feedback timeliness, immersion, pleasure and perceived value are measured to obtain more accurate factors influencing the stickness of Internet community charity users. The questionnaire in this survey used a scale from 1 to 5 (1 = strongly disagree; 5 = strongly agree) of the five-point Likert scale to measure each variable of the item. We verified the questionnaire through a preliminary study on 33 interviewees and evaluated the comprehensibility of the questionnaire contents. We made slight changes to the wording of the questionnaire, according to the opinions collected. Besides, this preliminary study suggests that the questionnaire is suitable for larger studies. The specific item of the research is shown in Table2.

Table 2. List of constructs and their items

Constructs	Items	Scale	Source
Feedback timeliness	FT1: The community charity mutual aid system can actively respond to the user's operation FT2: Questions or inquiries in the community charity support system can be answered quickly FT3: When using it, the system usually provides me with relevant information in a timely manner	A 5-point scale	Huangwulan etal[25]
Interactivity	IN1: I think the design of community charity mutual aid system is more flexible, human-computer interaction is strong IN2: The community's mutual aid system is designed to be simple and friendly	A 5-point scale	Shu Chiung Lin[26]
Immersion	IM1: Time seems to fly when I use the community charity system IM2: Most of the time, I'm immersed when I use the system IM3: The community charity system is very attractive to me	A 5-point scale	Mark Yi-Cheon Yim[27]
Pleasure	PL1: The community charity system is interesting to me PL2: Using the community charity system makes me feel relaxed PL3: Overall, I think the innovative form of community charity mutual aid system is interesting	A 5-point scale	Ducoffe [28]
Perceived ease of use	PEU1: It is easy for me to learn to use the community charity system PEU2: Quickly learned to apply this system PEI3: It's easy for me to get what I need from the community charity system	A 5-point scale	Hwang etal. [29]

(*continued*)

Table 2. (*continued*)

Constructs	Items	Scale	Source
Perceived emotional Value	PEV1: The experience of using the system was new and different for me PEV2: It's a pleasure to use the community charity system PEV3: I had a satisfying experience using the community charity system PEV4: I think the community charity system gives me a sense of self-satisfaction	A 5-point scale	Sweeney&Soutar[30]
Community Charity user stickness	US1: In my free time, I often use the community charity system US2: I would strongly recommend other community members to use the community charity system US3: Whenever there is a need for use, I will think of the community charity mutual aid system US4: I will reuse the community charity system	A 5-point scale	Yu X[31]

4 Data Analysis and Results

Based on The SEM method, analyzing the study framework through SmartPLS 4.0, which is a technique of verifying both the structural model and the measurement model [32]. Partial least squares (PLS) is a modular structural equation modeling (SEM) technique [33]. In recent years, many empirical studies take PLS - SEM as a reliable statistical tool for research and analysis. Hair proposed a two-step approach for PLS analysis, first evaluating the measurement model and then analyzing the structural model [34].

4.1 Measurement Model

In this study variables: the mean value, standard deviation (SD), standardized factor loading, average variation extraction value (AVE), comprehensive reliability (CR) and Cronbach's values (Table 3.).

Integrated Reliability(CR)of all variables[35, 36] and Cronbach's Alpha are greater than the threshold value 0.7 numerically (see Table 3.), indicating that the structure meets the reliability standard. It is worth noting that the Cronbach's Alpha for general acceptance of UE structure is 0.914 and CR is 0.915, and this indicates our above considerations are appropriate. To be specific, measures of feedback timeliness, interaction, immersion and pleasure could reflect user stickness and have acceptable internal consistency reliability.

Table 3. Scales for reliability and validity of measurement model.

Construct	Item	M	SD	FL	α	CR	AVE
Feedback timeliness	FT1	2.815	1.640	0.466	0.720	0.863	0.628
	FT2	3.584	1.343	0.920			
	FT3	3.519	1.416	0.906			
Interactivity	IN1	3.611	1.363	0.899	0.773	0.774	0.815
	IN2	4.000	1.398	0.906			
Immersion	IM1	3.511	1.505	0.902	0.883	0.886	0.810
	IM2	3.334	1.494	0.895			
	IM3	3.473	1.439	0.903			
Pleasure	PL1	3.489	1.518	0.878	0.870	0.870	0.794
	PL2	3.549	1.515	0.904			
	PL3	3.519	1.443	0.859			
Perceived ease of use	PEU1	3.478	1.567	0.902	0.894	0.895	0.758
	PEU2	3.540	1.457	0.882			
	PEU3	3.571	1.420	0.890			
Perceived emotional Value	PEV1	3.538	1.472	0.870	0.855	0.860	0.775
	PEV2	3.554	1.390	0.883			
	PEV3	3.511	1.414	0.848			
	PEV4	3.503	1.347	0.881			
Community Charity user stickness	UE1	3.361	1.556	0.901	0.914	0.915	0.796
	UE2	3.410	1.497	0.885			
	UE3	3.467	1.496	0.891			
	UE4	3.516	1.564	0.891			

Note: M = mean; SD = standard deviation; FL = factor loading; α = Cronbach's alpha; CR = composite reliability; AVE = average variance extracted

On the part of convergent validity, the average variance extracted (AVE) and factor loading were assessed (see Table 3.), with factor loading above the recommended threshold of 0.5 for all items [37]. If the square root of the discriminative validity AVE is larger than the correlation coefficients of other structures, it indicates that the model has good discriminative validity [38]. The square root of AVE value of each construct in this study is larger than the correlation coefficient between the construct and other constructs, indicating that the scale in this study has high discriminant validity [39]. In terms of discriminating validity, according to the example of Fornell and Larcker [40], where the square root of AVE should transcend its highest correlation with items in different structures (see the diagonal elements of the correlation matrix (Table 4.). In addition, the cross-load results of each item on variables also show that the scale has good discriminant validity. Therefore, this scale has great reliability, validity and discriminant validity.

Table 4. Discriminant validity and Correlation Matrix

	FT	IM	IN	PEU	PEV	PL	US
Feedback timeliness	0.793						
Immersion	0.329	0.900					
Interactivity	0.508	0.461	0.903				
Perceived ease of use	0.468	0.334	0.511	0.891			
Perceived emotional Value	0.469	0.486	0.451	0.578	0.871		
Pleasure	0.445	0.529	0.416	0.299	0.510	0.881	
user stickness	0.374	0.377	0.429	0.574	0.591	0.372	0.892

Note: FT = Feedback timeliness, IM = Immersion, IN = Interaction, PL = Pleasure, PEU = Perceived easy of use, PEV = Perceived emotional value US = user stikness

4.2 Structural Model and Hypothesis Test

In the structural model evaluation phase, we used SmartPLS guided resampling technology to randomly generate 5000 samples to test our structural model. According to the prediction ability of the model, the path coefficient, the significance of the major influences of the structural model, and the R-square value were evaluated, (see Fig. 2 and Table 5.). The results of PLS algorithm obtained the R-squared values of three endogenous variables: perceived ease of use (0.320), perceived emotional value (0.325), user stickness (0.430), more than 0.20, indicating a large explanatory power (Ajamieh et al., 2016). The second was perceived affective value ($\beta = 0.299$, $p< 0.001$) and user stickness ($\beta = 0.350$, $p< 0.001$). Perceived ease of use ($\beta = 0.430$, $p< 0.001$) and perceived emotional value ($\beta = 0.389$, $p< 0.001$) have a strong positive effect on charitable user stickness; Meanwhile, feedback timeliness and interactivity have significant influence on perceived ease of use. Pleasure and immersion also have positive effects on perceived emotional value. In summary, the above results show that the hypotheses in the model (H1, H2, H3, H4, H5, H6) are verified.

To further verify the structural relationship of model, we examined mediating factors to determine whether the relationship between independent and dependent variables is direct or indirect [39]. This study hypothesizes that perceived ease of use and perceived emotional value mediate the effects of user stickness. (see Table 6.).

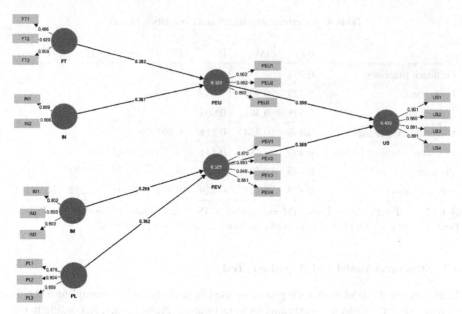

Fig. 2. Structural Model Results

Table 5. The results of hypothesis testing

Hypothesis	Path	Dependent Variable	R2	β	P Value	Hypothesis Supported
H1	IN - > PEU	PEU	0.320	0.282	0.000	YES
H2	FT - > PEU	PEU		0.367	0.000	YES
H3	IM - > PEV	PEV	0.325	0.299	0.000	YES
H4	PL - > PEV	PEV		0.352	0.000	YES
H5	PEU - > US	US	0.430	0.350	0.000	YES
H6	PEV - > US	US		0.389	0.000	YES

Note: FT = Feedback timeliness, IM = Immersion, IN = Interaction, PL = Pleasure, PEU = Perceived easy of use, PEV = Perceived emotional value US = user stickness

Table 6. The results of mediating factors

Indirect effects	Path	Dependent Variable	P Value	Hypothesis Supported
PEU	IN - > PEU - > US	US	0.000	YES
PEV	PL - > PEV - > US	US	0.000	YES
PEU	FT - > PEU - > US	US	0.000	YES
PEV	IM - > PEV - > US	US	0.000	YES

Note: FT = Feedback timeliness, IM = Immersion, IN = Interaction, PL = Pleasure, PEU = Perceived easy of use, PEV = Perceived emotional value US = user stickness

5 Discussion and Implication

From the perspective of SOR theory, this study proposes how design factors can improve user stickness under the background of Internet community charity. Specifically, the proposed structural model considers the effects of feedback timeliness, interactivity, immersion, and pleasure on user stickness, and examines the mediating role of perceived ease of use and emotional value. The empirical results show that feedback timeliness and interactivity have a positive impact on perceived ease of use, and immersion and pleasure have a significant direct impact on perceived emotional value. It also verifies that perceived ease of use and perceived emotional value have a significant mediating effect on user stickness. Further and specific discussions are as follows:

5.1 Discussion of the Results

First, we find that feedback timeliness and interactivity are key factors to improve perceived ease of use, and immersion and pleasure are key factors to improve perceived emotional value. This requires the community charity workers to update the information of Internet charity activities in a timely manner and improve the interaction between community charity activities and users. On the other hand, studies have also found that immersion and pleasure significantly affect perceived emotional value. This indicates that the Internet community charity platform should consider users' sense of immersion and pleasure when setting charity activities. To reduce the boring information displayed to users, reduce the perceived cost, and improve the perceived value.

Perceived ease of use has a significant mediating effect on the user stickness of Internet community charity. Previous studies have also shown that perceived ease of use affects users' intention to use it. Empirical data show that perceived ease of use has a positive impact on user stickness of Internet community charity, which is consistent with previous studies. Therefore, in the design of the Internet community charity platform, it is necessary to improve the user's ease of use and reduce the user's cognitive cost. Thus, to effectively improve the stickness of community charity users and promote the development of community charity.

The perceived emotional value also has a significant positive impact on the user stickness of Internet community charity. The experimental results effectively verify the mediating effect of perceived emotional value. Users can feel emotional experience in nternet community charity, which can significantly improve their emotional, and users can participate in it more positively and optimistically, thus improving their user stickness.

5.2 Theoretical and Practical Implications

This study provides some theoretical contributions that add to our understanding of Internet community. There are a few researches on user stickness of Internet community charity in the past, but there is still no research on the influence of perceived ease of use and emotional value on user stickness. Therefore, we put forward this new acceptance model for research. Our model explores feedback timeliness, interaction and immersion, and pleasure, including perceived ease of use and emotional value, to research the design factors that improve user stickness.

Our research results show that feedback timeliness, interaction and immersion, and pleasure are important factors affecting the stickness of community charity users. In addition, among the mediating effects of perceived ease of use and emotional value on user stickness, the mediating effect of perceived emotional value is stronger. In summary, this study broadens the research on the stickness of charitable users in Internet communities, and also provides a new, more granular perspective on how to improve user stickness.

In addition, this study also provides some practical meaning, such as some strategies for the development of Internet community charity. The results show that feedback timeliness and pleasure are the key factors affecting Internet community charity, and perceived ease of use and emotional value play a significant mediating role. Therefore, in the design and development of Internet community charity platforms, decision makers should pay attention to the design of experience and emotional strategies to improve users' sense of pleasure and use.

5.3 Limitations and Future Research

This study has still some limitations. Firstly, the Internet community charity platform has not commercialized, so we only inquired users about their potential attitudes. Thus, there may be a possibility that some of the causes may change over time. Additionally, from a design perspective, we only considered certain variables: interactivity, feedback timeliness, immersion, and pleasure, which means that future research could examine the impact of various types of design factors on user stickness. Finally, based on using online queries for data collection, we may have a potential sampling offset. The subjects were relatively young social media users who scored high on computer self-perception. Therefore, our sample may not meet the representativeness of all Internet community charity platform users, but our research objects have the opportunity to represent the target users. Future studies could survey more representative samples of users.

6 Conclusion

Understanding the public's psychological impact on the Internet community charity platform can make the user's expectations consistent with the development of the future design of the Internet community charity platform. Therefore, the influence of design factors on it is worth studying. Our results show that with improved feedback timeliness and interactivity, as well as increased pleasure and immersion, users will frequently use the Internet community charity platform, therefore increasing user stickness.

References

1. Wu V C S. The geography and disparities of community philanthropy: A community assessment model of needs, resources, and ecological environment[J]. VOLUNTAS: International Journal of Voluntary and Nonprofit Organizations, 2021, 32(2): 351–371. Author, F., Author, S.: Title of a proceedings paper. In: Editor, F., Editor, S. (eds.) CONFERENCE 2016, LNCS, vol. 9999, pp. 1–13. Springer, Heidelberg (2016)
2. Chen, A., Lu, Y., Wang, B.: Customers' purchase decision-making process in social commerce: a social learning perspective. Int. J. Inf. Manag. 37(6), 627–638 (2017)
3. Bryman, A., Burgess, R.G.: Analyzing Qualitative Data, Routledge. London (1994). (Burk, P. (2003). Donor Centred Fundraising, Cygnus Applied Research Inc/Burk and Associates Ltd, Chicago)
4. Mehrabian, A., Russell, J.A.: A verbal measure of information rate for studies in environmental psychology. Environ. Behav. 6, 233–252 (1974)
5. Tao, Z., Kexin, C.: Research on behavioral mechanism of social business users based on SOR model. Modern Inf. 38(3), 51–57 (2018). (in Chinese)
6. Chen, Z.G., Pan, F.: Study on the influence factors of game short video based on SOR model on players' virtual item purchase intention. Operation and management
7. Author, F.: Contribution title. In: 9th International Proceedings on Proceedings, pp. 1–2. Publisher, Location (2010)
8. LNCS Homepage. http://www.springer.com/lncs. Accessed 21 Nov 2016
9. Akar, E., Topçu, B.: An examination of the factors influencing consumers' attitudes toward social media marketing. J. Internet Commer. 10, 35–67 (2011)
10. Yang, H., Guo, X., Wu, T.: Exploring the influence of the online physician service delivery process on patient satisfaction. Decis. Support Syst. 78, 113–121 (2015)
11. Dong, Q., Zhou, X., Mao, F., Zhang, B.: an investigation on the users' continuance intention in online health community based on perceived value theory. Modern Intell. 39(03), 3–14+156 (2019)
12. Slater, M., Linakis, V., Usoh, M., Kooper, R.: Immersion, presence, and performance in virtual environments: an experiment with tri-dimensional chess. In: 1996 Virtual Reality and Software and Technology Conference, Hong Kong (1996)
13. Steuer, J.: Defining virtual reality: dimensions determining telepresence. J. Commun. 42(4), 73–93 (1992)
14. Heeter, C.: Communication research on consumer VR. In: Biocca, F., Levy, M.R. (eds.) Communication in the Age of Virtual Reality, pp. 191–218. Lawrence Erlbaum Associates, Hillsdale (1995)
15. Vanwesenbeeck, I., Ponnet, K., Walrave, M.: Go with the flow: how children's persuasion knowledge is associated with their state of flow and emotions during advergame play. J. Consum. Behav. 15(1), 38–47 (2016)
16. Lavie, T., Tractinsky, N.: Assessing dimensions of perceived visual aesthetics of web sites. Int. J. Hum. Comput. Stud. 60(3), 269–298 (2004)
17. Hassanein, K., Head, M.: The impact of infusing social presence in the web interface: An investigation across product types. Int. J. Electron. Commer. 10(2), 31–55 (2005)
18. Zeithaml, V.A.: Consumer perceptions of price, quality, and value: a means-end model and synthesis of evidence. J. Mark. 52(3), 2 (1988). https://doi.org/10.2307/1251446

19. Davis, F.D., Bagozzi, P.R.: Wasrshaw. user acceptance of computer technology: a comparison of two theoretical models. Manage. Sci. **35**(8), 982–1003 (1989)
20. Davis, F.D.: Perceived usefulnes, perceived ease of use, and user acceptance of information technology. MISQ. **13**(3), 319–340 (1989)
21. Kim, H.W., Chan, H.C., Gupta, S.: Value-based adoption of mobile internet: an empirical investigation. Decis. Support Syst. **43**(1), 111–126 (2007)
22. Liu, K., Tao, D.: The roles of trust, personalization, loss of privacy, and anthropomorphism in public acceptance of smart healthcare services. Comput. Hum. Behav. **127**, 107026 (2022)
23. Alam, S.S.: Is religiosity an important determinant on Muslim consumer behaviour in Malaysia ? J. Islamic Mark. **2**(1), 83–96 (2011)
24. Prabowo, D.S.P., Aji, H.M.: Visual packaging and perceived emotional value: a study on Islamic branded cosmetics. South East Asian J. Manage. **15**(1), 4 (2021)
25. Wulan, H., Zhang, T.: Research on user experience of mobile library based on structural equation model -- a case study of mobile library of Changzhou University. Libr. J. **4**(4), 80–89 (2017). https://doi.org/10.13663/j.carolcarrollnkilj.2017.04.013
26. Lin, S.-C., Tseng, H.-T., Shirazi, F., Hajli, N., Tsai, P.-T.: Exploring factors influencing impulse buying in live streaming shopping: a stimulus-organism-response (SOR) perspective. Asia Pac. J. Mark. Logist. **35**(6), 1383–1403 (2022). https://doi.org/10.1108/APJML-12-2021-0903
27. Yim, M.Y.C., Chu, S.C., Sauer, P.L.: Is augmented reality technology an effective tool for e-commerce? An interactivity and vividness perspective. J. Interact. Mark. **39**(1), 89–103 (2017)
28. Ducoffe, R.H.: Advertising value and advertising on the web. J. Advert. Res. **36**(5), 21–35 (1996)
29. Hwang, G.J., Wu, P.H., Chen, C.C.: An online game approach for improving students' learning performance in web-based problem-solving activities. Comput. Educ. **59**(4), 1246–1256 (2012)
30. Sweeney, J.C., Soutar, G.N.: Consumer perceived value: The develop- ment of a multiple item scale. J. Retail. **77**(2), 203–220 (2001)
31. Yu, X., Roy, S.K., Quazi, A., et al.: Internet entrepreneurship and "the sharing of information" in an Internet-of-Things context: the role of interactivity, stickiness, e-satisfaction and word-of-mouth in online SMEs' websites. Internet Res. **27**, 74–96 (2017)
32. Ringle, C.M., Wende, S., Becker, J.M.: SmartPLS 3. Boenningstedt: SmartPLS GmbH (2015)
33. Wold, H.: Soft modelling by latent variables: The non-linear iterative partial least squares (NIPALS) approach. J. Appl. Probab. **12**(S1), 117–142 (1975)
34. Hair, J.F., Hult, G.T.M., Ringle, C., Sarstedt, M.: A Primer on Partial Least Squares Structural Equation Modeling (PLS-SEM). Sage Publications, Thousand Oaks (2016)
35. Bagozzi, R.P., Yi, Y.: On the evaluation of structural equation models. J. Acad. Mark. Sci. **16**(1), 74–94 (1988)
36. Urbach, N., Ahlemann, F.: Structural equation modeling in information systems research using partial least squares. J. Inf. Technol. Theory Appl. **11**(2), 5–40 (2010)
37. Fornell, C., Larcker, D.F.: Structural Equation Models with Unobservable Variables and Measurement Error: Algebra and Statistics. Sage Publications Sage CA, Los Angeles (1981)
38. Hair, J.F., Black, W.C., Babin, B.J., Anderson, R.E.: Multivariate Data Analysis, 7th edn. Prentice-Hall, New Jersey, NJ (2010)
39. Iacobucci, D., Saldanha, N., Deng, X.: A meditation on mediation: evidence that structural equations models perform better than regressions. J. Consum. Psychol. **17**(2), 139–153 (2007)
40. Sargeant, A., Woodliffe, L.: Building donor loyalty: The antecedents and role of commitment in the context of charity giving. J. Nonprofit Public Sect. Mark. **18**(2), 47–68 (2007)

Advances in eGovernment Services

Electronic Government in the Municipalities of Perú: A Challenge Towards Digital Transformation

Ricardo Rafael Díaz Calderón[1]([⊠]) [iD], Carmen Graciela Arbulú Pérez Várgas[1] [iD], Nilton César Aroni Salcedo[1] [iD], Rosa Eliana Adrianzen Guerrero[1] [iD], Juanita Corina Barrantes Carrasco[1], Luis Jhonny Dávila Valdera[2] [iD], Madeleine Espino Carrasco[3] [iD], Jefferson Walter Díaz Lazarte[4] [iD], Hipatia Arlet Torres Serna[1] [iD], Ana Maria Alvites Gasco[5] [iD], and Daniel Jesús Castro Vargas[6] [iD]

[1] Cesar Vallejo University, Pimentel, Perú
rdiazcal@ucvvirtual.edu.pe
[2] Santo Toribio de Mogrovejo Catholic University, Lambayeque, Perú
[3] Sipán University, Pimentel, Perú
[4] Antenor Orrego Private University, Trujillo, Perú
[5] Chiclayo University, Pimentel, Perú
[6] National Autonomous University of Chota, Cajamarca, Perú

Abstract. The objective of this research work was to design an electronic government model that promotes citizen participation and the empowerment of digital citizenship in public management, identifying and addressing technological, social and cultural barriers that may limit their access and use in the Peru, based on the theory of modernization. To find out the perception of the exercise of digital citizenship, a sample of 175 users was randomly selected, including 22 public servants and 153 external users from a municipality. In addition, a survey was used for data collection and a Likert-type rating scale was applied to measure digital citizenship and e-government. The results showed that the majority of users had a regular or low level of knowledge about digital citizenship, which indicates a lack of knowledge of the digital environment. Regarding electronic government, a low and regular level was identified, which indicates a deficient provision of electronic services. Consequently, it is concluded that both users and public servants have deficiencies in the use of technologies and a model is proposed that promotes a greater proximity of citizens to the state. In addition, a significant and direct relationship was found between the levels of digital citizenship and electronic government. Therefore, it is necessary to implement a digital transformation policy to improve the efficiency and effectiveness of public services, as well as encourage greater citizen participation in decision-making.

Keywords: Electronic government · digital citizenship · municipal users

© The Author(s), under exclusive license to Springer Nature Switzerland AG 2023
C. Stephanidis et al. (Eds.): HCII 2023, CCIS 1835, pp. 179–186, 2023.
https://doi.org/10.1007/978-3-031-36001-5_23

1 Introduction

At the global level, the authentic digital revolution recognizes that digital citizenship is a fundamental element for the exercise of the democratic rights of citizens in the 21st century. Consequently, digital citizenship has already acquired a real existence, although its distribution remains uneven. (Clastornik 2019). However, the essential condition to be a digital citizen is to be connected to the Internet, which implies not only having access to it, but also enjoying an adequate quality of service. (Avila 2016).

In Latin America and the Caribbean, 73% of the countries have a digital government strategy on their agenda. However, according to recent research from the Inter-American Development Bank, less than 30% of transactions can be carried out entirely online and only 7% of citizens complete their final paperwork with the government online. That is, they still face barriers such as the use of paper or credentials (Porrúa 2019).

Electronic government has been the subject of study since the beginning of the century, municipal portals in Latin America have just passed the initial phase of digital government, according to research by Martínez (2017). Colombia has shown interest in promoting e-government strategies, but faces global trends and widespread expectations, which limits its development and progress in terms of accountability (Líppez and García 2016), its development could be the essential path for modernization of nations, even in territories with low connectivity and "digital divide" such as Latin America, according to Jijena (2016). The Electronic Government seeks to create innovation channels for government and citizen communication, where information flows with greater transparency and equitable participation, allowing the search for joint solutions and collegiate decision-making (Amoroso 2020).

"In Peru, electronic government seeks to reduce corruption and increase transparency in government processes in an accessible and affordable way (UNC 2020). The COVID-19 pandemic has led to an unprecedented push in the digitization of the Peruvian government, including electronics. Judicial and administrative procedures, as well as the implementation of electronic windows and boxes in various public entities (Chávez 2020). This has provided opportunities for both the government and citizens in the use of certain digital portals that offer government services (Téllez 2017). Although the municipalities of the Cajamarca region recognize the importance of an inclusive and transparent government in terms of public information, they face a lag in the public management of Information Technology services due to the lack of a modern and internationally regulated electronic government model. Adapted to their needs to guide policies and good practices, as well as the need for users to develop skills and competencies".

"That is why this research raises the following question: What is the theoretical model of electronic government that could promote the active participation and empowerment of digital citizenship in decision-making processes and public management, taking into account the Technological, social and cultural barriers that may limit its access and use? For this, the objective was set, to design an electronic government model that promotes citizen participation and the empowerment of digital citizenship in public management, identifying and addressing technological, social and cultural barriers that may limit their access and use in the Peru. To contribute to the above, the following have been considered as specific objectives: (a) Analyze the theoretical assumptions that explain the electronic government paradigm for the construction of Digital Citizenship. (b) Determine the level of electronic government and digital citizenship in a district municipality of Peru. (c) Determines the relationship between electronic government and digital citizenship district municipality in Peru. (d) Design the theoretical model of electronic government with incidence in the construction of the Digital Citizenship of the users in a district municipality of Peru. (e) determine the validity of the theoretical model of electronic government with incidence in the construction of the Digital Citizenship of the users in a district municipality of Peru".

2 Dimensions

Regarding the electronic government variable, the OCDE, cited by (Villoria and Ramírez 2013) describes it as the use of Information and Communication Technologies, especially the Internet, to achieve optimal government administration. According to Riascos et al. (2008) Electronic government is a set of procedures and tools that facilitate access to government services for both internal system administrators and external users, as well as allowing remote consultation and processing of information. In addition, Ganga and Águila (2008) observe that electronic government is considered an innovative form of governance and government, which is developed exclusively through the use of Information and Communication Technologies (TIC). The Economic Commission for Latin America and the Caribbean (CEPAL 2011) defines electronic government as a change in public administration that implies the extensive use of ICT in the organization and operational management in public management.

Regarding the digital citizenship variable, the United Nations Educational, Scientific and Cultural Organization (cited by Agesic and UNESCO Montevideo 2019), digital citizenship refers to a set of skills that enable citizens to access, choose, investigate, understand, value and use information in innovative ways. The Electronic Government Agency and the Information and Knowledge Society (Agesic 2020) indicates that the creation of citizenship in the digital sphere requires the collaboration of the State, university institutions, organizational entities, civil society and the population in general. Likewise, Rojas et al. (2022) argue that it is necessary to establish political guidelines with the aim of promoting awareness and awareness to achieve improvements.

3 Method

To address this research, the quantitative approach was used, which according to Hernández et al. (2014), consists of probative and sequential processes that are developed systematically, defining objectives and research questions, under a non-experimental design, following Hernández and Mendoza (2018), which allowed the observation of the phenomenon in a natural way, without changing the variables. Of a basic type that according to the National Council of Science, Technology and Technological Innovation (CONCYTEC 2020) in its fifth article, it is stated that basic research has the purpose of increasing scientific knowledge without addressing practical issues, the scope was correlational, transversal and a proposal for an electronic government model was built for the construction of Citizenship within the framework of digital transformation in district governments.

In this case, two different populations were identified: the 22 internal workers of the municipality and the 253 external users of the district municipality. To select a representative sample from each population, a probabilistic sampling technique with a finite formula was used. The data collection technique used was the survey, which consisted of 20 items to measure digital citizenship and 12 items to measure electronic government. The reliability of the instrument was determined by Cronbach's alpha coefficient, which indicated that the instruments were 89.3% and 90.9% reliable, respectively (Table 1).

4 Results

Table 1. Level of exercise of digital citizenship in a district municipality in Peru

Level	Frequency	Percentage
Low	78	44,6%
Regular	97	55,4%
High	0	0,0%
Total	175	100.00%

44.6% consider that they have a low level of digital citizenship exercise, while 55.4% qualify it as regular. This implies that respondents have difficulties in selecting, analyzing, comparing and processing the information on the municipality's website. In addition, they do not appreciate the importance of the data and do not understand that the municipality is aware of the risks that can arise on the Internet and how to manage or avoid them. They also fail to recognize that the municipality has the ability to create and participate in valuable digital content, respect copyrights and licenses, and communicate effectively in the digital environment (Table 2).

Table 2. Electronic government level of the district municipality in Peru

Level	Frequency	Percentage
Low	63	36,0%
Regular	112	64,0%
High	0	0,0%
Total	175	100.00%

A user survey was carried out and it was found that 36% of them consider that electronic government has a low level, while 64% qualify it as regular. This implies that not enough is being done to improve online communication between public administration, citizens and organisations. In addition, there are no specialized web portals for electronic public information and services, and common methods are not used to achieve the expected results through the communication and exchange of information between two or more systems. There is also a lack of social use of social networks and insufficient openness and accountability.

Table 3. Relationship between digital citizenship and electronic government

| | Kolmogorov-Smirnova | | |
	Statistics	gl	Sig
Electronic government	.242	175	.000
Digital Citizenship	.166	175	.000

Table 3 shows that the electronic government and digital citizenship variables have a probability of occurrence of less than 5%, which indicates that they do not follow a normal distribution (Table 4).

Table 4. Variable relationship

	Variable Electronic government	Variable. Digital Citizenship
Electronic government	1	
Digital Citizenship	.763**	1

The relationship between digital citizenship and e-government of a district municipality in Peru is very strong and significant, with a value of 0.763** or 98.5% at the bilateral 0.01 level. This indicates that the municipality is not adequately developing its electronic government, which is reflected in the lack of development of digital citizenship. Therefore, the evidence supports the hypothesis that an e-government model is necessary to build the digital citizenship of users.

5 Model

With the results obtained, we proceed to represent the electronic government model for the construction of digital citizenship of the users of a municipality in Peru (Fig. 1).

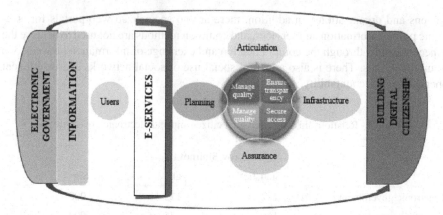

Fig. 1. Electronic government model for the construction of the Digital Citizenship of the users of a district municipality in Peru

6 Conclusions

There is a significant gap between the level of electronic government and digital citizenship in the district municipality of Peru. To address this gap, it is necessary to develop a theoretical model of electronic government that takes into account the theoretical assumptions of the electronic government paradigm, such as transparency, citizen participation, effectiveness and efficiency in the provision of public services, and accountability. This theoretical model should focus on building digital citizenship, which means helping citizens acquire the digital skills and competencies necessary to actively participate in political, social and economic life online.

The relationship between electronic government and digital citizenship in the district municipality in Peru is evident in the survey results. Respondents indicated that they have difficulties selecting, analyzing, comparing and processing the information on the municipality's website, which suggests that e-government still has a lot of room for improvement. In addition, respondents do not adequately value the importance of data and do not recognize the municipality's ability to create and participate in valuable digital content. Therefore, the construction of digital citizenship in a district municipality of Cajamarca depends to a large extent on the improvement of electronic government.

In order to design a theoretical model of electronic government with an impact on the construction of digital citizenship adapted to the needs of district municipalities in Peru, the development of policies and strategies that allow improving the quality of information and services must be taken into account, technology education to promote digital inclusion and address the lack of digital skills of citizens, electronic audiences.

He validity of the theoretical model of electronic government was confirmed by 5 experts on the subject, who validated the instruments and the proposal through a scale, obtaining positive results for its application. However, to achieve a real improvement in the quality of electronic public services and encourage citizen participation, it will be necessary for local authorities to properly implement the model and commit to its success.

In addition, the model must be monitored and evaluated to measure its effectiveness and make adjustments if necessary.

References

Clastornik, J.: El ciudadano digital está aquí: ¿están preparados los gobiernos? (2019). Recuperado de https://apolitical.co/es/solution_article/elciudadano-digital-esta-aqui-estan-preparados-los-gobiernos

Ávila, P.: Construcción de ciudadanía digital: un reto para la Educación. Suplemento SIGNOS EAD, 1 (2016)

Porrúa, M.A.: La Agenda Digital en América Latina: Un avance a distintas velocidades (2019). Recuperado de https://blogs.iadb.org/administracionpublica/es/la-agenda-de-gobierno-digital-en-america-latina

Martínez, F.: Gobierno Electrónico en América Latina. Estudio Comparativo de Portales Web de Administraciones Locales de México, Chile, Colombia y Uruguay (2017). Recuperado de http://ri.uaemex.mx/bitstream/handle/20.500.11799/67959/FMR_Tesis%20Maestria_Portales%20Web%20Locales.pdf?sequence=1

Líppez, S. y García, R.: Ciudadanos y gobierno electrónico: la orientación al ciudadano de los sitios Web municipales en Colombia para la promoción de la participación. Javeriana 22, 23 (2016)

Jijena, R.: Gobierno Electrónico, Transformación Tecnológica del Gobierno y Derecho (2016)

Amoroso, Y.: Gobierno Electrónico. Concepto y reflexiones (2020). Recuperado de https://icj.pe/2020/05/27/gobierno-electronico-concepto-y-reflexiones/

Universidad Nacional de Cajamarca (2020). Plan estratégico de gobierno electrónico 2018–2020. Recuperado de http://transparencia.unc.edu.pe/Documentos/ObtenerArchivo?codigo=000000034

Chávez, D.: El gobierno digital y el derecho de petición en el Perú (2020). Recuperado de https://canalti.pe/el-gobierno-digital-y-el-derecho-de-peticionen-el-peru/

Tellez, E.: Ciudadanía digital (2017). Recuperado de https://www.researchgate.net/publication/332752264_CIUDADANIA_DIGITAL

Villoria, M., y Ramírez, A.: Los modelos de gobierno electrónico y sus fases de desarrollo. Un análisis desde la Teoría política. Gestión y política pública 9–103 (2013)

Riascos, S., Martínez, G., Javier, O.: El gobierno electrónico como estrategia de participación ciudadana en la administración pública en Suramérica. Casos Colombia y Uruguay. Libre Empresa 5(1), 143–157 (2008). Recuperado de https://revistas.unilibre.edu.co/index.php/libreempresa/article/view/2910

Ganga, F., Aguila, M.: Percepción de los proveedores del Sistema electrónico "Chilecompra" en la Xa región-Chile. Revista Venezolana de Información Tecnología y Conocimiento. Gale. Universidad del Valle (2008)

Comisión Económica para América Latina y el Caribe (CEPAL). (2011). El gobierno electrónico en la gestión pública. Recuperado de https://www.cepal.org/es/publicaciones/7330-gobierno-electronico-la-gestionpublica

Agesic & UNESCO Montevideo. (2019). Estrategia de Ciudadanía Digital . Amoroso, Y. (2020). Gobierno Electrónico. Concepto y reflexiones. Recuperado de https://www.icj.pe/2020/05/27/gobierno-electronico-concepto-y-reflexiones/

Agencia de Gobierno Electrónico y Sociedad de la Información y del Conocimiento (Agesic). (2020). Cómo se construye Ciudadanía Digital Recuperado de https://www.gub.uy/agencia-gobierno-electronico-sociedad-informacionconocimiento/herramientas-ciudadania/construir-ciudadania-digital

Rojas, L., Reyes M., Espino, K., ArbulÚ, C., Gomez, A.: Effectiveness of the Electronic Government of the Public Administration. Case: José Leonardo Ortiz District Municipality – Peru. Springer International Publishing (2022).https://doi.org/10.1007/978-3-031-06391-6_52

Consejo Nacional de Ciencia, T. e. (s.f.). *concytec.gob.pe.* https://portal.concytec.gob.pe/images/renacyt/reglamento_renacyt_version_final.pdf

Sanchez, A.V., Manzuoli, C.H., Bedoya, É.D.: Digital Citizenship: A Theoretical Review of the Concept and Trends (Abril de 2019)

Hernández, R., Fernández, C. y Baptista, M. . (2014). Metodología de la investigación (6ta ed.). . México D. F.: Mc Graw-Hill Education

Hernández-Sampieri, R., Mendoza, C.: Metodología de la investigación. Las rutas cuantitativa, cualitativa y mixta (2018)

Information Management for Decision Making: Public Hospitals. Peru Case

Danicsa Karina Espino Carrasco[1](✉) [ID], Carmen Graciela Arbulú Pérez Vargas[1] [ID],
Moises David Reyes Perez[2] [ID], Luis Eden Rojas Palacios[3] [ID],
Jhoselit Lisset Facho Cornejo[4] [ID], Luis Jhonny Dávila Valdera[5] [ID],
Madeleine Espino Carrasco[6] [ID], Ana Maria Alvites Gasco[7] [ID],
and Jefferson Walter Díaz Lazarte[6] [ID]

[1] Cesar Vallejo University, Pimentel, Peru
despinoc@ucvvirtual.edu.pe
[2] General Studies Academic Unit, Norbert Wiener University Private S.A., Lima, Peru
[3] Tecnológica del Perú University, Chiclayo, Peru
[4] San Martin de Porres University, Pimentel, Peru
[5] Santo Toribio de Mogrovejo Catholic University, Chiclayo, Peru
[6] Señor de Sipan University, Pimentel, Peru
[7] Particular de Chiclayo University, Pimentel, Peru

Abstract. The pandemic caused by Covid -19 teaches us a great lesson that the health sector is not prepared to undergo drastic changes, which leads to a resumption in the conceptualization of the environment. BANI (fragile, anxious, non-linear and incomprehensible) in what describes the reality lived in these times. The general objective of this article is to design a Theoretical Model based on environments (BANI) that favor the experiences of doctors and nurses in decision-making in response to the needs of the patient, based on the electronic medical record, within the framework of the information management. Specific objectives: i) Reveal the experiences in decision-making of doctors and nurses in chaotic contexts; ii) Characterize clinical histories from the experiences of doctors, nurses and patients; iii) Understand and interpret the results of the experiences and processes that doctors and patients went through in BANI contexts, due to Covid-19 when making decisions based on medical records; iv) Determine the axes that support the BANI Model articulated to the management of electronic medical records, within the framework of information management in a hospital in the Lambayeque Region. The design was non-experimental at the basic - interpretive level with a qualitative approach, with a phenomenological - hermeneutic design. The population consisted of health professionals, doctors (3), nurses (3) and patients (2). For the collection of information, the semi-structured interview was used as a technique, and the interview script was also used as an instrument. Interview. It is concluded that the experiences and processes of medical and nursing staff during Covid-19 in a BANI context, occurred in a chaotic environment, making decision-making difficult due to the lack of medical records during emergencies, causing delays in care.., which leads medical and nursing staff to act immediately in the face of crises caused by this changing world.

C. Stephanidis et al. (Eds.): HCII 2023, CCIS 1835, pp. 187–194, 2023.
https://doi.org/10.1007/978-3-031-36001-5_24

Keywords: Information management · decision making · electronic medical records · BANI environment

1   Introduction

1.1   Problematic Reality

Quality of care means using medical technology and science to maximize benefits for hospital institutions, which face enormous challenges to increase user satisfaction with services and detect errors and make improvements. (Gavilánez 2020).

The World Health Organization (OMS) established a regulation on digital transformation, inviting different countries to promote technologies in order to increase universal health coverage and sustainable development (World Health Organization [OMS], 2018). Such is the case of Peru, where Law No. 30024 is approved, which consists of creating the National Registry of Electronic Medical Records (Government of Peru 2017; Congressional News Center, 2022).

In this regard, the hospitals of the Social Security of Health (EsSalud) since 2019 they have a health services management system called EsSI (Smart Health Service), which includes, among other elements, electronic medical records. The purpose of this system is to significantly reduce the attention time in all EsSalud institutions nationwide through electronic medical records, becoming one of the first innovative institutions in the management of its administrative and care services at the national level. Which includes, among other elements, electronic medical records. The purpose of this system is to significantly reduce the attention time in all EsSalud institutions nationwide through electronic medical records, becoming one of the first innovative institutions in the management of its administrative and care services at the national level (Global 2022), assuming the need to generate guidelines related to policies for continuous improvement (Rojas et al. 2022).

In the public hospitals of the Ministry of Health of the Lambayeque Region, a great demand of citizens insured by the Comprehensive Health Insurance is served and also in a particular way, there are some deficiencies in the care provided to patients, as well as in the information included in clinical histories, because they are on physical support (paper), these are created as requested by the user in the different health establishments, when a good filter of the user's clinical history record is not carried out by the administrative staff working in the admission area, it is duplicated in more than one health establishment nationwide, registering patient information in each of them, which will mean that said information will never be integrated due to the lack of technological support.

Likewise, in all hospitals, medical records are lost and deteriorate due to limitations such as lack of space, which is why they are piled up on scaffolding, passageways, and even outside the archiving area; on the other hand, paperwork Documentaries that are made are very extensive where people wait their turn for an indeterminate time to access an appointment or medical care, generating a negative perception on the part of the patient about the management of medical records. In public hospitals in the Lambayeque Region, electronic medical records have not been implemented due to the existence of administrative discrepancies and personal interests, despite the fact that there are laws, policies and regulations in force, progress has not been made in determining the management and use of this source of information.

1.2 Literature Review

Electronic Government as the Basis of Contemporary Public Administration. Information and communication technologies (ICT) have been perfected for the benefit of the health sector at an international level, in order to optimize the quality of life and well-being of people (Harrington et al. 2020). In Spain, the standardization of medical records has been considered a serious issue, despite its territorial expansion and different problems, it has managed to establish an efficient and centralized system. (Gavilánez 2020). Regarding the management of health information, it is a discipline dedicated to the study of health records and taxonomy, it works to guarantee patients that the use of their information is worked properly (Fenton et al. 2017). In this way, information management serves as an indispensable instrument for health organizations, which contextualizes information to evaluate, compare and determine data in a timely manner and that is available when required. (Gu et al. 2017).

Due to what happened in the pandemic, the world suffered drastic changes in 2020, bringing with it the transformation of concepts or tools that help make sense of the current reality, these models allow us to respond adequately to an uncontrollable world, so in In this environment of confusion and uncertainty, the BANI concept (fragile, anxiety, non-linear, incomprehensible) is taken up again, created by Jamais Cascio in 2016, which has the meaning of describing the characteristics of the current reality and from there designing new strategies and values, directed at us and companies (Martins and Chagas 2021; Prasad 2022).

Objectives. General objective: Design a Theoretical Model based on BANI environments that favor the experiences of doctors and nurses in decision-making in response to the needs of the patient, based on the electronic medical record, within the framework of the management of the information. The following specific objectives: i) Reveal the experiences in decision-making of doctors and nurses in chaotic contexts; ii) Characterize the clinical histories from the experiences of doctors, nurses and patients; iii) Understand and interpret the results of the experiences and processes that doctors and nurses went through in fragile, anxious, non-linear and incomprehensible contexts, due to Covid-19 when making decisions based on medical records; iv) Determine the axes that support the BANI Model articulated to the management of electronic medical records, within the framework of information management in a hospital in the Lambayeque Region.

Method. The present study called Management of information for decision-making: Electronic clinical history in a hospital of the Ministry of Health, Lambayeque, is a basic-interpretative investigation, because the researcher seeks to understand the meaning that the phenomenon has for the patient. Object of study. Who have a vision of the participants for the achievement of sustainable development through the modernization of the State.

With the present investigation, the experiences of medical personnel and nurses regarding information management and decision-making in Minsa hospitals were revealed and interpreted; Likewise, limitations that this problem has in public management were determined; Finally, likewise, a proposal was made to minimize its effects and work towards a Theoretical Model based on BANI environments for proper decision-making by doctors and nurses, based on the electronic medical record.

According to Heidegger (1989) hermeneutic phenomenology is responsible for interpreting the world based on a description of lived experiences, according to this perspective it seeks to understand how people experience their world, besides Gadamer (2007) He argues that in order to understand people, a means of communication such as conversation, dialogue, and interview is needed, and this is how the fusion of horizons is achieved, achieving an understanding through linguistics.

2 Results

Reveal the Experiences in Decision-Making of Doctors and Nurses in Chaotic Contexts. According to the results of the experiences of doctors according to decision-making in chaotic contexts, they reported that for decision-making, clinical histories did not help much when making decisions regarding patient care during an emergency, because the information in relation to the previous antecedents, they are filed in these physical medical records, so the doctor is limited to making decisions based on what the patient himself or the relatives express, that is why it is very important that the doctor in the evolution doctor take a good history. In addition, if there were interconnection between institutions, it would no longer be necessary to use physical medical records, because all the information obtained would be available in real time for better emergency care.

"…there is no automated system, we do not have computers so that we can get the information quickly and at the moment". (D3, personal communication, October 21, 2022).

"The physical histories have their limitations, one of the limitations is that at the Las Mercedes hospital on holidays or non-working days, we do not have the physical medical histories because there is no activity in the admission service, we only have what the relatives or the patient himself tell us." (D2, personal communication, October 21, 2022).

On the other hand, the nurses interviewed mentioned that when making decisions, the physical medical records are very important, because they are helpful if a good record is made during emergency care, this allowed immediate decisions to be made for the timely care of the patient.

"Yes, it helps us, because I repeat it again, the signs are already graphed so as not to waste those little minutes in immediate patient care". (N1, personal communication, October 21, 2022).

"…During an emergency we can have access to a medical history that can be done at the time but not have access to specific data that the patient may have, such as an allergy to a specific medication, but if at the time of the In an emergency, we can collect the data that the patient himself can provide us according to the diagnosis or how he arrives, according to his degree of priority or the data that accompanying third parties come with the patient". (N3, personal communication, October 21, 2022).

From another perspective, according to the experiences in decision-making by doctors, they mention that there were limitations, because they depended a lot on the adequate reception of the clinical history, there were delays when it was requested, lack of personnel in the archiving area, for which they mostly fill out the medical history in simple sheets to determine the current status of the patient.

"…They can't be found and if you ask for a story, they even take up to two or three days, even on normal days, or sometimes they can't find them, they are mixed up or they are lost". (D3, personal communication, October 21, 2022).

The results found in Hospital Las Mercedes on the revelations of the experiences in decision-making of doctors and nurses in chaotic contexts, are related to what was found by Kharrazi et al. (2018), who in their article, reach the result that hospitals are decades away from fully implementing sophisticated applications that provide decision support in electronic medical records, so it will not reach maturity since there are no changes in the policies of your country.

Characterize Clinical Histories from the Experiences of Doctors, Nurses and Patients. Regarding the characterization of the clinical histories from the experiences of the doctors according to the answers, there is no availability of the clinical histories in their work area on holidays, Sundays and/or during the night shift, because there is no staff assignment in the filing area during those shifts to provide the requested medical history.

"There is a lack of personnel, a lack of management, automation and carelessness of our authorities to reach our current century, we are two centuries behind, it is time for this to improve". (D2, personal communication, October 21, 2022).

"No, there is no availability on any day, because if it were a holiday or non-holiday, it would be difficult for them to bring you the medical history, this is due to not having the personnel who fulfill this type of affinities or functions." (D1, personal communication, October 21, 2022).

As for the nurses, they also mention that there is no such availability of medical records in their work area on holidays, Sundays and/or during the night shift, highlighting that not having this information delays patient care. Patient.

"…There is not that facility to have the clinical history here in the hospital, it will be by administrative means, lack of personnel, like every hospital that sometimes happens, there are many limitations". (N2, personal communication, October 21, 2022).

"No, access to medical records on holidays and night shifts is limited, since the file personnel where the physical records are located, do not work on holidays or night shifts, they only work on business days, not This information is available when the patient suddenly arrives and some type of extra information is needed to be able to provide the respective care". (N3, personal communication, October 21, 2022).

Regarding the patient, they report that the doctor during the shift in which they were treated in an emergency did provide correct information about the patient's health status, mentioning that to be treated they have to wait for the doctor to solve the problems of critical patients first and then care for patients with minor emergencies, it was also detailed that there is no type of discrimination for emergency care.

"…In my person I have no problems with the doctor because it has been good care both in medicine and in his person letting me know about my condition". (P2, personal communication, October 23, 2022).

"One also has to wait because not only in emergencies one arrives at the moment that one wants to attend, but there are also others with the same or more serious problems, however the attention has been positive, the doctor very kind and waiting for them to give with the appropriate prescription for the patient, when the dose has been finished they have evaluated me and told me how I am, that is satisfying for me because I see that this professional is concerned with his patients" (P1, personal communication, October 23, 2022).

The lived experience of the patient when the medical history was opened in emergencies is that they came to observe that the medical staff only dedicates themselves to asking questions and writing as if there were no emergency, likewise they compared the current hospital system with that of the hospital. Private sector, where he stressed that the patient can be treated without any complications in different parts of the country.

The patients have had the opportunity to carry out procedures in the filing area, where they have been able to observe that the environment is in a chaotic state, in addition, it does not have adequate conditions for storing medical records, likewise the care is not good when some procedure is carried out in the archive area.

"...where these stories are thrown away, they are piled up in an environment that is not properly correct, exposed to losing patient information and the environment where all people pass and manage to see that they are in this state" (P1, personal communication, October 23, 2022).

Determine the axes that support the BANI Model Articulated to the Management of Electronic Medical Records, within the Framework of Information Management in a Hospital in the Lambayeque Region.

According to the experience of doctors and nurses on the influence of information management during decision-making at the time of diagnosis and patient care, it was found that in difficult situations this management fails because there is no digitized system, Likewise, they have the need to verify the clinical history because it contains information on all the auxiliary tests performed on the patient, on the other hand, despite not having the support of the file, the doctors and nurses provided comprehensive care.

"Here in this hospital we have many limitations due to the way it is mechanized, because in the end the information is lost." (D1, personal communication, October 21, 2022).

"At this time, at our Las Mercedes regional teaching hospital, we do not have this information, but in any case, we do not stop making efforts to provide better quality care and warmth, so that our users receive adequate care." (N1, personal communication, October 21, 2022).

The results found according to the axes that support the BANI Model articulated to the management of electronic medical records, within the framework of information management in a hospital in the Lambayeque Region, these results are similar to studies where in another context on public hospitals lack information technology and support in medical services, are similar to what was found by Valencia (2021), who concludes that in order to reach a BANI environment, good planning must be available that includes skills and tools of according to the needs of the organization.

3   Conclusions

1. The experience in decision-making in chaotic contexts according to the doctors was that there is no internal management design in terms of information management, this being a negative aspect as an organization, however, for nurses despite not having adequate management, consider the information obtained during the emergency relevant to make timely decisions on care.
2. According to the characterization of the clinical histories from the experiences of the doctors and nurses, they detailed that they do not have access to them on holidays, Sundays or during the night shift, likewise, the patient explained that they are in an inadequate and deteriorated environment, Therefore, the study subjects agree that the hospital should be modernized with an information system for medical records.
3. It was interpreted that the experiences and processes of the medical and nursing staff during Covid-19 in a BANI context, took place in a chaotic environment, making decision-making difficult due to not having medical records during emergencies, causing delays in care., which leads medical and nursing staff to act immediately in the face of crises caused by this changing world.
4. The axes that support the BANI Model articulated to the management of electronic medical records, within the framework of information management are the fragility, the anxious, the non-linear and incomprehensible that develop in a context where organizations will have to adapt to the new guidelines, carrying out innovative transformations in terms of leadership, to continue surviving in chaotic times.

References

Fenton, S., Low, S., Abrams, K., Butler, K.: Health Information Management: Changing with Time. IMIA and SchattauerGmbH (2017)

Gadamer, H G.: Sandhed og metode: Grundtræk af en filosofisk hermeneutik. : Sys-time Academic (2007)

Gavilánez, N.F.: Master's degree in health services management topic: standardization of health clinical records in the city of Guayaquil - 2020. [Master's Thesis Catholic University of Santiago de Guayaquil] UN Institutional Repository (2020). http://repositorio.ucsg.edu.ec/han-dle/3317/14221

Global. SDG value chains program (2022). Retrieved on May 24 from https://sdgvaluechains.undp.org/content/sdgvaluechains/es/home.html?gclid=EAIaIQobChMIsvP1oJT59wIVbEFIAB2rTwPcEAAYASAAEgLAs_D_BwE

Government of Peru. They approve the Regulation of Law No. 30024, Law that cre-ates the National Registry of Electronic Medical Records. 32–45 (2017). https://www.administracion.usmp.edu.pe/institutoconsumo/wp-content/uploads/Reglamento-de-la-Ley-N°-30024-Ley-que-crea-el-Registro-Nacional-de-Historias-Clinics

Gu, D., Li, J., Li, X., Liang, C.: Visualizing the knowledge structure and evolution of big data research in healthcare informatics. Int. J. Med. Inf. **98**, 22–32 (2017)

Harrington, C., Marie, L., Rogers, W.: Design of health information and communica-tion technologies for older adults. ScienceDirect 341–363 (2020). https://doi.org/10.1016/B978-0-12-816427-3.00017-8

Heidegger. The ontological difference in the work of Heidegger In: Phenomenology and Hermeneutics. Merida (2009)

Kharrazi, H., Gonzalez, C., Lowe, K., Huerta, T., Ford, E.: Forecasting the matura-tion of electronic health record functions among US hospitals: Retrospective analysis and pre-dictive model. J. Med. Internet Res. **20**(8), 1–11 (2018). https://doi.org/10.2196/10458

Martins, C., Chagas, A.: (2021, 16 de Marzo) . After VUCA, The transformation to a BANI World. LLYC. https://ideasen.llorenteycuenca.com/2021/03/16/after-vuca-the-transf ormation-to-a-bani-world/

Rojas, L., Reyes, M., Espino, D., Arbulú, C. Gómez, A.: Effectiveness of the electronic government of the public administration. Case: José Leonardo Ortiz District Munici-pality – Peru. International Conference on Human-Computer Interaction (2022). https://doi.org/10.1007/978-3-031-06391-6_52

Valencia, H.: Application of agile methodologies in organization of telecommunications in a VICA context. [Final specialization work, University of Buenos Aires]. Postgradu-ate economics UBA repository (2021). http://bibliotecadigital.econ.uba.ar/download/tpos/1502-2151_Vale nciaLozanoHD.pdf

World Health Organization [WHO] (2018). Global Strategy on Digital Health 2020–2025. Retrieved on May 23, 2022. https://www.who.int/docs/default-source/documents/200067-lb-full-draft-digital-health-strategy-with-annex-cf-6jan20-cf-rev-10-1-clean-eng.pdf?sfvrsn= 4b848c08_2

Technology Readiness of e-Government in the Use of Poverty Data for Social Assistance in Indonesia

Rijalul Fikri[1,2](✉) , Eko Priyo Purnomo[1] , Ulung Pribadi[1] ,
and Nur'Jila Binti Mohammad[3]

[1] Doctoral Program of Government Affairs and Administration, Jusuf Kalla School of Government, Universitas Muhammadiyah Yogyakarta, Brawijaya Street, Yogyakarta 55183, Indonesia
`rijalul.fikri@soc.uir.ac.id`
[2] Universitas Islam Riau, Pekanbaru, Indonesia
[3] School of Government (SOG), Universiti Utara Malaysia, Kedah, Malaysia

Abstract. The use of e-government in the processing of poverty data is very important to concentrate the beneficiaries of social assistance on target. Technology readiness is still an obstacle in the application of e-government in processing poverty data for the distribution of social assistance. Technological knowledge is another gap for the poor in utilizing e-government to get social assistance. This study looked at the response from the public to the readiness of e-government technology in the use of poverty data for social assistance, especially in the Indonesian poverty data application, namely SIKS-NG (Social Welfare Information System-Next Generation). This research uses Nvivo 12 Plus software to analyze qualitative data, which presents cross tab analysis and visual analysis. The stages in using Nvivo have five stages including; data collection, data import, data coding, data classification, and data presentation. The data that Nvivo had processed was then continued for qualitative analysis. The data source was obtained from the Twitter data set. The findings of this study found that the readiness of e-government technology in the use of poverty data for social assistance is still constrained in the aspect of receiving technology for its users, so that e-government in the use of poverty data for social assistance still requires many parties involved in it. In the aspect of technological knowledge, it is also an obstacle so that e-government in the use of poverty data for social assistance in Indonesia is not entirely done electronically / online but there are still conventional ones. This research's limitation is that this research only discusses the technological readiness form two aspect are Technology knowledge and Technology acceptance. The recommendation for further research is the compatibility of technologies that should also be looked at in the application of e-government to the poor.

Keywords: Technology Readiness · E-Government · Poverty Data

C. Stephanidis et al. (Eds.): HCII 2023, CCIS 1835, pp. 195–202, 2023.
https://doi.org/10.1007/978-3-031-36001-5_25

1 Introduction

Poverty is still a serious problem in Indonesia, the poverty rate in Indonesia reached 9.54% or around 26.36 million people live below the poverty line [1]. There have been many attempts to alleviate poverty by the government, which are applied in the form of policies and programs, both direct and indirect. Direct policies, which are in the form of programs that are directly given to the poor, for example; direct cash assistance (BLT), rice for the poor (RASKIN), while indirect policies, for example the public health insurance program, IDT program, BOS School Operational Assistance, Smart Indonesia Card [2].

The Social Assistance Program is motivated by efforts to maintain the level of consumption of Target Families (RTS) as a result of economic problems. To optimize the target of social assistance recipients, the Indonesian government utilizes e-government, known as the Social Welfare Information System–Next Generation (SIKS-NG). The function of the SIKS-NG application is to provide accurate and integrated poverty data. However, in its implementation, problems arise such as data validity [3], there are also people who have not received social assistance [4].

The use of this application in determining social assistance targets raises public reactions in the form of opinions, because this application involves many actors in it from the central government to local governments and village governments [5]. People who receive social assistance use this application to see whether they are recipients of assistance or not. From these problems, researchers are interested in seeing the readiness of the application by looking at public opinion on social media and then analyzing it.

2 Literature Review

2.1 E-Government Satisfaction

The development of electronic government is one of the initiatives to increase the effectiveness and efficiency of public services [6]. In other words, through optimizing the use of information and communication technology, e-government management systems and work processes in the government environment are carried out [7].

There is no consensual definition of e-government citizen satisfaction. Researchers defined e-government citizen satisfaction as a service provider-customer relationship, with the government serving as the service provider and people serving as the consumers [8]. Therefore, e-government citizen satisfaction can also be considered as customer satisfaction. Apart from service ratings, satisfaction is also determined by an individual's comparison of net benefits with other customers; if the comparison is judged to be fair, consumers are satisfied [9].

One of the first studies to analyze e-government satisfaction in relation to government trust was [10]. He defined e-government satisfaction as "an overall rating of the influence (positive or negative) of e-government on government operations. Part of the issue is that satisfaction is an undefinable, "you know it when you see it" idea [8]. In general, e-government researchers agree on three key factors that have been derived from information systems literature: (1) system quality criteria, which indicate the quality of information processing (user friendliness, website design, dependability, and interactivity) [11]. (2) Information quality factors assess the perceived worth of the website's information, which includes (security, content, accuracy) (Parasuraman in [12]; [13]), and (3) Service quality components include SERVQUAL conceptions (Parasuraman in [8]), trust, support, and efficiency [14].

2.2 Public Value of e-Government

Understanding e-government and the value it is meant to provide need knowledge of public sector management. Despite the fact that both public and private organizations seek to serve people, their interests are distinct [15]. Private sector seek to maximize profit by serving people as consumers, whereas government organizations serve people as constituents. As a result, government organizations are not only concerned with profitability, but must also take into account "public value".

The concept of public value provides a more fruitful route for addressing the complex socio-political consequences of ICT adoption in the public sector [16]. According to Castelnovo and Simonetta [17] and [18], policies for e-government may be assessed based on their potential to expand the capacity of public administration to provide public value for people as consumers, customers, policymakers, and operators of public administration. In the context of ICT-enabled public sector reforms, Bannister and Connolly [19] studied the effect of ICTs on public sector values and proposed that "public sector value" be understood and translated into a behavioral form in which ICT has the ability to change or transform. That is, creating "public value" in e-government should be regarded as e-government systems' potential to increase government efficiency, citizen services, and societal ideals such as inclusion, democracy, transparency, and participation [15, 20].

3   Research Methods

This research uses the Nvivo 12 Plus software and web analytics. Nvivo 12 Plus is used to evaluate qualitative data, which includes crosstab and visual analysis. There are five phases in utilizing Nvivo: data collection, data import, data coding, data categorization, and data display. Nvivo's processed data is then continued for qualitative analysis. And with web analytics we can see trends that occur on certain topics.

4   Discussion and Results

The dynamics of social assistance distribution in Indonesia has always been a topic of discussion. Via Google Trends, headlines from 2020–2022 have always been a subject for online communication media discussion. The distribution of news related to social assistance is widely discussed, especially on the big islands in Indonesia such as Java, Sumatra and Kalimantan. (See Fig. 1).

Fig. 1. Distribution of social assistance topics in online media by area in 2020–2022 (Source: Google Trends [21]

4.1 System Quality Criteria

System quality criteria in e-government refer to the standards and guidelines that ensure the development and implementation of effective and efficient e-government systems. SIKS-NG as e-government to support the distribution of social assistance in several regions is trying to be integrated with other information systems owned by the region. As happened in Gunung Kidul Regency where SIKS-NG was tried to be integrated with other systems [5] (Table 1).

Table 1. The Non-Human Actors. Source: [5]

Tehcnogram	Actors
the non-human actors	• Data processing instrument (application/software): SID BERDAYA, SIKAB, SIKS-NG, SIKS-droid • Internet networks and information technology tools: village computers and the Kominfo Office server • Various reference documents, such as statutory regulations, data collection forms, and data collection guidelines

However, the Ministry of Social Affairs continues to feel that a centralized information system, such as SIKS-NG, will benefit the regions more. It is not necessary for villages and regions to develop their own apps. They can use the budget funds they have for other purposes. So that villages and regions are not confused, the poverty data gathering system has been integrated with SIKS-NG. The data belongs to the villages and regions, hence the security system has been established as well [5].

4.2 Information Quality

Information quality in e-government refers to the accuracy, completeness, relevance, timeliness, and accessibility of the information provided by government agencies through digital channels. The SIKS-NG application is expected to provide accurate information regarding social assistance recipients in Indonesia.

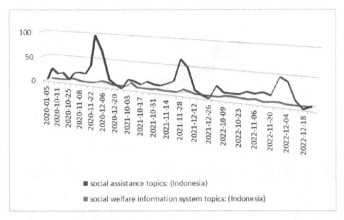

Fig. 2. A comparison of the discussion trends of social assistance topics and social welfare system topics on social media in Indonesia 2020–2022 [21]

People are more interested in discussing social assistance information, according to the trend (Fig. 2). In comparison to talks about the Social Welfare Information System (SIKS-NG), which is not frequently discussed. This is related to the availability of the SIKS-NG application, which the public still does not understand its role and utility.

4.3 Service Quality

E-government refers to the use of information and communication technologies (ICTs) to deliver government services to citizens and businesses. Service quality is a critical aspect of e-government, as it determines the extent to which citizens and businesses are satisfied with the services provided. Some of the features provided by the SIKS-NG application include: 1) Beneficiary data management such as personal data, family data, and data on assistance received. 2) Monitoring and evaluation of social welfare programs. 3) Determination and distribution of social assistance. 4) Reporting on activities and performance achievements. In use, SIKS-NG can be accessed by social welfare program managers at the Ministry of Social Affairs or by beneficiaries who already have an account in the system.

When looking at (Fig. 3) basically the number of visitors to the SIKS-NG application is quite large where in access from November 2022 to February 2023 the average application was accessed 58,489 times. However, in practice there are still negative sentiments from the implementation of social assistance distribution in Indonesia despite using e-Government. (see Fig. 4).

Based on the picture below, we can see that conversations on social media, especially twitter, related to social assistance still tend to have negative sentiments. This is because there are public complaints related to the distribution of social assistance that is not on target, and the problem of poor people who have not been recorded in the SIKS-NG application. In the aspects of content, accuracy, and timeliness, the level of satisfaction is very low for these three aspects, while for the aspects of format and ease of use, the

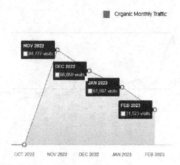

Fig. 3. Traffic Overview https://siks.kemensos.go.id/ oct 2022 – feb 2023 (Source: ubersuggest [22])

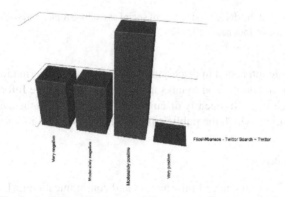

Fig. 4. Sentiment Result of social assistance #bansos on twitter

level of satisfaction is at a fairly satisfied level with the next-generation social welfare information system (SIKS-NG) [3].

5   Conclusion

The readiness of e-government technology in utilizing poverty data for social assistance in Indonesia has several challenges in terms of system quality, information quality and service quality. User opinion shows that SIKS-NG and applications to support social assistance in the future must have this public value so that e-government is consistent with its objectives. This research also concludes that e-government must be open to all forms of interoperability that may occur in its development.

References

1. Indonesian Statistics Center, "Statistical Yearbook of Indonesia 2023, Badan Pus. Stat. vol. 1101001, p. 790 (2023). https://www.bps.go.id/publication/2020/04/29/e9011b3155d45d7 0823c141f/statistik-indonesia-2020.html

2. Murdiyana, M., Mulyana, M.: Policy analysis on poverty alleviation in Indonesia. J. Polit. Pemerintah. Dharma Praja **10**(1), 73–96 (2017). https://doi.org/10.33701/jppdp.v10i1.384

3. Gobel, U.T., Katili, M.R., Polin, M.: Evaluation of the SIKS-NG user satisfaction level using the EUCS method in bone Bolango Regency. Diffus. J. Syst. Inf. Technol. **2**(1), 143–149 (2022). https://ejurnal.ung.ac.id/index.php/diffusion/article/view/13423

4. Haromin, Andriyansah, D.: The Effectiveness of E-government implementation through the next generation social welfare information system (Siks-Ng) as a poverty data processing application In Lamajang Village, Pangalengan Sub-District, Bandung District Haromin1. J. JISIPOL Ilmu Pemerintah. Univ. Bale Bandung **6**(3), 34–56 (2022)

5. Wijoyono, E.: The utilization of village-information system for integrated social welfare data management: actor-network theory approach in Gunungkidul regency. J. Teknosains **11**(1), 13 (2021). https://doi.org/10.22146/teknosains.60798

6. Valle-Cruz, D.: Public value of e-government services through emerging technologies. Int. J. Public Sect. Manag. **32**(5), 473–488 (2019). https://doi.org/10.1108/IJPSM-03-2018-0072

7. Robbins, P.S.: Organization Theory: Structure, Design, and Application. Arcan, Jakarta (2015)

8. Nguyen, T.T., Phan, D.M., Le, A.H., Nguyen, L.T.N.: The determinants of citizens' satisfaction of e-government: an empirical study in Vietnam. J. Asian Financ. Econ. Bus. **7**(8), 519–531 (2020). https://doi.org/10.13106/JAFEB.2020.VOL7.NO8.519

9. Seetharaman, A., Saravanan, A.S., Patwa, N., Bey, J.M.: The impact of property management services on tenants' satisfaction with industrial buildings. J. Asian Financ. Econ. Bus. **4**(3), 57–73 (2017). https://doi.org/10.13106/jafeb.2017.vol4.no3.57

10. Welch, E.W., Hinnant, C.C., Moon, M.J.: Linking citizen satisfaction with e-government and trust in government. J. Public Adm. Res. Theor. **15**(3), 371–391 (2005). https://doi.org/10.1093/jopart/mui021

11. Santos, J.: E-service quality: a model of virtual service quality dimensions. Manag. Serv. Qual. An Int. J. **13**(3), 233–246 (2003). https://doi.org/10.1108/09604520310476490

12. Buyle, R., Van Compernolle, M., Vlassenroot, E., Vanlishout, Z., Mechant, P., Mannens, E.: Technology readiness and acceptance model' as a predictor for the use intention of data standards in smart cities. Media Commun. Theor. Reflections Case Stud. **6**(4), 127–139 (2018). https://doi.org/10.17645/mac.v6i4.1679

13. Papadomichelaki, X., Mentzas, G.: E-GovQual: a multiple-item scale for assessing e-government service quality. Gov. Inf. Q. **29**(1), 98–109 (2012). https://doi.org/10.1016/j.giq.2011.08.011

14. Warkentin, M., Gefen, D., Paul Pavlou A., Gregory Rose M.: Encouraging Citizen adoption of e-government by building trust. Electron. Mark. **12**(3), 157–162 (2002)

15. Twizeyimana, J.D., Andersson, A.: The public value of e-government – a literature review. Gov. Inf. Q. **36**(2), 167–178 (2019). https://doi.org/10.1016/j.giq.2019.01.001

16. Cordella, A., Bonina, C.M.: A public value perspective for ICT enabled public sector reforms: a theoretical reflection. Gov. Inf. Q. **29**(4), 512–520 (2012). https://doi.org/10.1016/j.giq.2012.03.004

17. Castelnovo, W., Simonetta, M.: A public value evaluation of e-Government policies, ECIME 2007 Eur. Conf. Inf. Manag. Eval. **11**(2), 63–70 (2007)

18. Castelnovo, W.: A stakeholder based approach to public value. In: Proceedings of 13th European Conference on Egovernment, pp. 94–101 (2013)

19. Bannister, F., Connolly, R.: The fourth power: ICT and the role of the administrative state in protecting democracy. Inf. Polity **23**(3), 307–323 (2018). https://doi.org/10.3233/IP-180072

20. Othman, M.H., Razali, R.: Electronic government systems interoperability model. J. Telecommun. Electron. Comput. Eng. 9(3–4), 1–9 (2017). Special Issue. https://www.scopus.com/inward/record.uri?eid=2-s2.0-85041738812&partnerID=40&md5=b8b28bedbb851541b5fa3fb0bfbc6368

21. Google, T.: Google Trends Indonesia Soscial Assitance Topics, google (2023). https://tre
    nds.google.com/trends/explore?date=2020-01-012022-12-31&geo=ID&q=bantuansosialdi
    indonesia,sisteminformasikesejahteraansosial&hl=en
22. Ubersuggest, Traffic Overview : https://siks.kemensos.go.id/, Ubersuggest (2023). https://
    app.neilpatel.com/en/traffic_analyzer/overview?domain=https%3A%2F%2Fsiks.kemensos.
    go.id%2F&lang=id&locId=2360&mode=domain

Exploration Organizational Interoperability in Smart Governance in Indonesia and Malaysia

Rudi Hardi[1](✉) [iD], Achmad Nurmandi[2], Titin Purwaningsih[3] [iD],
and Halimah Binti Abdul Manaf[4] [iD]

[1] Government Science Study Program of Doctoral Program, Universitas Muhammadiyah
Yogyakarta, Universitas Muhammadiyah Makasssar, Yogyakarta, Indonesia
rudi.hardi.psc22@mail.umy.ac.id
[2] Department of Government Affairs and Administration, Jusuf Kalla School of Government,
Universitas Muhammadiyah Yogyakarta, Yogyakarta, Indonesia
[3] Government Science Study Program of Doctoral Program, Universitas Muhammadiyah,
Yogyakarta, Indonesia
[4] School of Government, Universiti Utara Malaysia, Kedah, Malaysia

Abstract. Organizational interoperability increases efficiency, improves service delivery to citizens, and facilitates better decision-making. Achieving interoperability requires a holistic approach involving technical solutions, policies, procedures, change management, and the involvement of stakeholders, government officials, and the community. The objective of this research is to explore the interoperability frameworks that organizations use to share information and exchange data in intelligent governance. The involvement of stakeholders, including government officials, community members, and representatives in private sector organizations, has also been explored. This approach uses a multi-criteria decision analysis structure based on AHP (Analytic Hierarchy Process). The Nvivo app is then used to visualize connections and find themes and patterns. Additionally, SmartPLS (Partial Application Least Squares Structural Equation Modeling) is used to analyze comparisons of relations between countries. Key components explored from the interoperability framework include data signatures, exchange of data from one organization to another, data management procedures, data quality, processes business, identity management, and technical infrastructure (hardware, software, and networks that organizations use to share information and exchange data). The results of the study reveal that interoperability frameworks in Indonesia and Malaysia implement smart governance, which is carried out using existing standards and protocols or by adopting new regulations based on the demands of public services. Flexible, adaptive, and actionable framework over time in response to technological and organizational changes. So that the organizational interoperability work structure becomes inclusive and open to the involvement of all stakeholders, including the government, the commercial sector, and citizens. Citizens.

Keywords: Organizational Interoperability · Smart Governance · share information · exchange data

C. Stephanidis et al. (Eds.): HCII 2023, CCIS 1835, pp. 203–210, 2023.
https://doi.org/10.1007/978-3-031-36001-5_26

1 Introduction

Today, almost all governments in the world are changing the way their services become remote and online public services and realizing that these two digital technology services can change the face of government administration allowing for more customized and proactive public services and enabling more innovative solutions to be provided (1). In fact, since the late 1990s, governments at all levels in Europe have launched electronic government projects to provide electronic information and services to citizens. (2). Then, since 2014, OECD (The Organisation for Economic Co-operation and Development) member states have officially adopted digital governance as a strategic driver to create an open, participatory, trustworthy public sector that brings together government and non-government actors (3).

Interoperability enables timely, efficient, and effective service completion, as well as the discovery of new, smarter, and more adaptive services (4). E-government architecture model for the deployment of interoperable systems from government to government. Responsiveness to risk is closely related and the main determinant is the dimensions of Organization, Management, and Interoperability (5).

In Indonesia (Bandung City) (which also won the Smart City Award 2015 held by the magazine Asia's Tech Ecosytem(6)), Smart City applications can form public trust by improving application quality, satisfaction, reliability and community empowerment. However, the number of people who use smart city applications is still small. Therefore, the culture of using such applications needs to be encouraged to help build citizen trust in the government and improve urban quality (7). Citizens need to be reassured that their data is protected, and confidentiality is ensured. Not only to convince the public of goodwill, but also to ensure the involvement of citizens in the success of smart city projects. Therefore, the state (government) needs to present a clear narrative about why the government needs to transform into a smart city or what might happen if the government fails to become a smart city (8).

2 Literature Review

2.1 Smart Governace

For much of the 20th century, the idea that a city could be intelligent was portrayed in the popular media as science fiction, but suddenly the potential for a city to be intelligent, even alive, has become a new reality (9). The smart city concept is increasingly popular, and almost all cities in the world label their cities as smart cities (10). Initially, this concept emerged as a response to the challenges of urbanization in the 21st century. Planning and building smart urban districts is an aim of the smart city concept, where technology is integrated into infrastructure and used to control and manage city functions innovatively (11).

Smart Governance according (12) reflected in aspects of community participation in government as well as services to the community such as its administrative functions. Smart governance is reflected through online public services, supporting infrastructure, and open government (government transparency) ((13). To observe smart governance, there are 4 (four) indicators, namely, 1) participation in policy making, 2) online services (online procedures), 3) infrastructure (HR capabilities, wifi coverage, diversity of sensors), and 4) open governance (data sets and open data).

Smart governance: It is described mainly by effective and efficient public administration, quality of public services and and the participation of residents in making decisions about the city. Information and communication technologies are used in e-administration, to improve democratization and services delivery, as well as support decisions made by public authorities (14).

2.2 Organization Interoperability

The concept of interoperability was used for the first time in the military field circa 1977, defined as "The ability of a system, unit or force to provide services and receive services from other systems, units, or forces and to use the services that are exchanged to enable them to operate effectively together. Same."(15), (16), (17). Accordingly, this concept is also interpreted as interoperability is the ability of two or more systems or components to cooperate despite differences in functionality, language, and implementation framework (18).

Interoperability is characterized as an organization's ability to interact with many other organizations across data, systems, and processes in order to achieve common goals (19). Interoperability solutions are critical to enabling the transfer of data and assets for the deployment of innovative applications, both within private enterprises and government agencies. Interoperability which aims to enable the system to connect services and open the possibility of data exchange to provide better services to stakeholders. Interoperability can increase advanced functionality for future applications and revolutionize the design principles of technology governance (20).

Aspects (attributed) Organization Interoperability determines the level (level) of interoperability of smart government. There are 9 (Nine aspects that are the indocators of interoperability organizations, namely: 1) Design Process, 2) Government Process Alignment, 3) Compatibility with policies and regulations, 4) Interaction with users, 5) Service Consumption, 6) Reuse and sharing, 7) Interoperability at national-international level, 8) Change Management, and 9) Governance (21).

3 Research Methods

This approach uses a multi-criteria decision analysis structure based on AHP (Analytic Hierarchy Process). The Nvivo app is then used to visualize connections and find themes and patterns. Additionally, SmartPLS (Partial Application Least Squares Structural Equation Modeling) is used to analyze comparisons of relations between countries. Key components explored from the interoperability framework include data signatures, exchange of data from one organization to another, data management procedures, data quality, processes business, identity management, and technical infrastructure (hardware, software, and networks that organizations use to share information and exchange data).

4 Discussion and Results

Organizational interoperability in smart governance refers to the ability of different organizations to exchange information effectively and efficiently and coordinate their activities to achieve common goals in an intelligent governance ecosystem. Smart governance involves the use of advanced technology and data analytics to improve decision-making, increase transparency, and increase citizen participation in government activities.

In Indonesia and/or Malaysia, interoperability is often associated with other terms, such as interconnectivity, Connectivity, Openness, Communication, Data exchange, Data integratio, Data collaboration, atau Data sharing. Figure 1 shows the past year's search interest in the word's "interoperability" and "data sharing" in google trends.

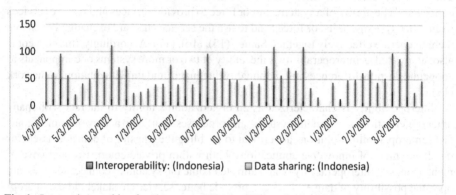

Fig. 1. Interest in searching for "interoperability" and "data sharing" in Indonesia in the last year (Source: Google Trends)(22)

Similarly, in Malaysia, search interest for the words "interoperability" and "data sharing" appears in (See Fig. 2).

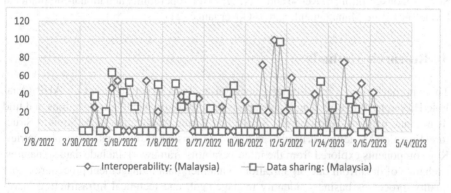

Fig. 2. Interest in searching for "interoperability" and "data sharing" in Malaysia in the last year (Source: Google Trends)(23)

Achieving interoperability between public administration in Indonesia and Malaysia is an important factor for efficient, cost-effective, and transparent public service delivery. However, there are many challenges and limitations that must be faced, due to technical, semantic, legal, and organizational factors. The importance of organizational interoperability to information integration has been known for many years. Today, it is still a challenge and is undoubtedly gaining momentum due to the complexity of organizational aspects as public organizations move towards inter-organizational governance as well as due to the enforcement of new policies such as One Data and Open Data.

Di Malaysia, interoperability (perkongsian data) means the disclosure of data from one or more of the organizations to another, or the sharing of data between different departments/divisions within an organization.

Design Process Interoperability
The design process in interoperability requires a series of stages to ensure that different systems or organizations can work together smoothly and effectively. In Malaysia, the design of the interoperability process is contained in the achievement strategy interoperability (*pengkongsian data*). The strategy formed is the result of the combination of each core and the EDGE framework (See Table 1). This is to ensure that the strategy under each core is comprehensive. The aim is to create an integrated and conducive data sharing environment in Malaysia to support data value creation for the public sector, private sector, and the people.

Table 1. Strategy Achievement of Interoperability in Malaysia (24)

Framework	Purpose	Strategy Direction
E Establish	Basics of control mechanisms and structures necessary for a conducive data sharing environment	Accountability and control mechanisms to strengthen the transmission in the system based on related acts/policies
D Develop	Existing controls and structures to be empowered to enable more conducive data sharing	Guidelines and resources to ensure smooth access, use, control, and governance rights for all data types
G (Guide)	Public sector, private sector, and people on proper understanding for data sharing	Stakeholders in intra-sectoral/cross-industry or sector data sharing for value creation
E Enable	Public sector, private sector and people to share data for value creation, especially through innovation	An environment that promotes the construction of data governance strategies and effective implementation plants

To realize interoperability, Malaysia built an interoperability management platform, namely Malaysian Government Central Data Exchange (MyGDX) A data sharing platform consisting of a collection of standards, tools, components, repositories, and registries that enable the sharing of data from various agency sources to the target agency in an agreed data format. MyGDX is a data sharing platform that provides data integration services across agencies to facilitate the provision of End to End (E2E) online services.

Currently, in Malaysia MyGDX users are Government agencies registered with MyGDX consisting of federal, state, local government, and statutory agencies. The implementation of integration through MyGDX began 25 May 2018. As of February 2021, a total of 120 Application Programming Interface (API) has been developed for data sharing purposes involving 26 public sector agencies.

In Indonesia, Data Interoperability Services (LID) are services provided by certain agencies in accordance with their duties and authorities in order to share Data between Electronic Systems using certain mechanisms to ensure reliability, accountability, and security. Data interoperability or data and information exchange services is the process of sending and receiving data or information from two or more devices connected in a network, both local and global such as the internet.

Data exchange procedures in Indonesia are carried out by 1) Electronic Data Interchange/EDI can be done by sending documents in electronic format over a computer network. 2) System-to-System Data Exchange can be done by connecting one system to another system through a computer network. 3) Device-to-Device Data Exchange can be done by connecting one device to another device through a computer network or without a computer network, and 4) Application-to-Application Data Exchange can be done using applications that support data exchange.

5 Conclusion

To ensure that various systems or organizations can coexist harmoniously and productively, the planning process for interoperability necessitates a number of steps. In Malaysia, the achievement strategy interoperability contains the design of the interoperability procedure (pengkongsian data). Malaysia established the Malaysian Government Central Data Exchange (MyGDX), an interoperability management platform, to accomplish interoperability. MyGDX is a platform for sharing data that consists of various standards, tools, elements, repositories, and registries that permit the sharing of data from various agency sources to the destination agency in an accepted data format.

Interoperability frameworks in Indonesia and Malaysia implement smart governance, which is carried out using current standards and protocols or by implementing new laws based on the demands of public services. An adaptable, practical, and flexible framework that can be adjusted to changing organizational and technological requirements. so that the organizational interoperability work framework can be used by all stakeholders, including the government, the business community, and citizens.

References

1. Härmand, K.: Digitalisation before and after the Covid-19 crisis. ERA Forum **22**(1), 39–50 (2021). https://doi.org/10.1007/s12027-021-00656-8

2. Torres, L., Pina, V., Acerete, B.: E-government developments on delivering public services among EU cities. Gov. Inf. Q. **22**(2), 217–238 (2005)
3. OECD. Digital Government Strategies for Transforming Public Services in the Welfare Areas. OECD [Internet]. 63 (2016). http://www.oecd.org/gov/digital-government/Digital-Govern ment-Strategies-Welfare-Service.pdf
4. Albouq, S.S., Sen, A.A.A., Almashf, N., Yamin, M., Alshanqiti, A., Bahbouh, N.M.: A survey of interoperability challenges and solutions for dealing with them in IoT Environment. IEEE Access **10**, 36416–36428 (2022). https://ieeexplore.ieee.org/document/9741799/
5. Casalino, E., Bouzid, D., Ben Hammouda, A., Wargon, M., Curac, S., Hellmann, R., et al.: COVID-19 Preparedness among emergency departments: a cross-sectional study in France. Disaster Med. Public Health Prep. **16**(1), 245–253 (2022)
6. Mursalim, S.W.: Implementasi kebijakan smart city di Kota Bandung. Jurnal Ilmu Administrasi: Media Pengembangan Ilmu dan Praktek Administrasi. **14**(1), 126–138 (2017)
7. Herdiansyah, H.: Smart city based on community empowerment, social capital, and public trust in urban areas. Global J. Environ. Sci. Manage. **9**(1), 113–128 (2023)
8. Cole, A., Tran, É.: Trust and the smart city: the Hong Kong Paradox. China Perspectives.(2022/3), 9–20 (2022)
9. Batty, M., Axhausen, K.W., Giannotti, F., Pozdnoukhov, A., Bazzani, A., Wachowicz, M., et al.: Smart cities of the future. Eur. Phys. J. Special Top. **214**(1), 481–518 (2012)
10. Borsekova, K., Koróny, S., Vaňová, A., Vitálišová, K.: Functionality between the size and indicators of smart cities: a research challenge with policy implications. Cities **78**, 17–26 (2018)
11. Nooringsih, K., Susanti, R.: Implementation of smart city concept for sustainable development in Semarang old town area. In: IOP Conference Series: Earth and Environmental Science vol. 1082, no. 1 (2022)
12. Anthopoulos, L., Janssen, M., Weerakkody, V.: A unified smart city model (USCM) for smart city conceptualization and benchmarking. Int. J. Electron. Gov. Res. **12**(2), 77–93 (2016)
13. Baslé, M.: Smarter cities' attractiveness. testing new criteria or facets: "data scientists" and "data platforms." J. Knowl. Econ. **12**(1), 268–278 (2016). https://doi.org/10.1007/s13132-016-0398-0
14. Kozlowski, W., Suwar, K.: Smart city: definitions, dimensions, and initiatives. Eur. Res. Stud. J. **XIV**(Special Issue 3), 509–520 (2021)
15. Secretary of defense Washington DC. Standardization and interoperability of weapons systems and equipment within the North Atlantic treaty organization [Internet]. vol. 4. (1977). https://apps.dtic.mil/sti/citations/ADA270295
16. Kubicek H, Cimander R, Scholl HJ. Organizational Interoperability in E-Government [Internet]. Berlin, Heidelberg: Springer Berlin Heidelberg; 2011. Available from: http://link.spr inger.com/https://doi.org/10.1007/978-3-642-22502-4
17. Bayraktar, H., Bayar, D.Y., Bilgin, G.: Making cities interoperable in TURKEY. The international archives of the photogrammetry, Remote Sensing and Spatial Information Sciences [Internet]. XLVI-4/W5-(4/W5–2021), 91–6 (2021). Available from: https://www.int-arch-pho togramm-remote-sens-spatial-inf-sci.net/XLVI-4-W5-2021/91/2021/
18. Dinh, T.T.A., Datta, A., Ooi, B.C.: A Blueprint for Interoperable Blockchains Tien. arXiv [Internet]. 189–90 (2019). https://arxiv.org/abs/1910.00985v3
19. Kruger, B.: Interoperability – the key enabler of e- government. The Interoperable Europe Academy [Internet]. 8–10 (2022). https://joinup.ec.europa.eu/node/705192
20. Bokolo, A.J.: Exploring interoperability of distributed ledger and decentralized technology adoption in virtual enterprises. information systems and e-business management [Internet]. (2022). https://doi.org/10.1007/s10257-022-00561-8

21. Margariti, V., Stamati, T., Anagnostopoulos, D., Nikolaidou, M., Papastilianou, A.: A holistic model for assessing organizational interoperability in public administration. Government Inf. Q. [Internet]. **39**(3), 101712 (2022). https://doi.org/10.1016/j.giq.2022.101712

22. trends.google.co.id. Interest Over Time [Internet]. 2023. p. 3–5. https://trends.google.co.id/trends/explore?geo=MY&q=interoperability,Datasharing&hl=id

23. Trends.google.co.id. Interest Over Time [Internet]. 2023. p. 6–8. Available from: https://trends.google.co.id/trends/explore?geo=ID&q=interoperability,Datasharing&hl=id

24. Kementerian Komunikasi dan Multimedia Malaysia. Dasar Perkongsian Data Nasional (NDSP) [Internet]. (2022). https://drive.google.com/file/d/1cm5ekxYxVK_A_wQo1TuB dVH-MaP2OBvt/view

Sentiment Analysis of the Community of Nusa Tenggara Barat (NTB) on NTB Care

Imansyah[1]([✉]), Achmad Nurmandi[2], Misran[1], and Dimas Subekti[1]

[1] Department of Government and Administration, Universitas Muhammadiyah Yogyakarta, Yogyakarta, Indonesia
{imansyah.psc22,misran.psc20}@mail.umy.ac.id
[2] Department of Government Science and Administration Science, Jusuf Kalla School of Government, Muhammadiyah University, Yogyakarta, Indonesia
nurmandi_achmad@umy.ac.id

Abstract. This study aims to analyze the sentiments of the people of West Nusa Tenggara towards the Peduli NTB Application. This study uses a qualitative approach. Sentiment data was taken from the NTB Care website and media, the data taken was public opinion on the NTBCare application and complaints submitted through NTB Care and processed using the NVivo 12 plus software. This study uses sentiment analysis indicators to determine positive, negative and neutral sentiments in the NTB Care application. The result of this research is positive sentimentreached 43%. On average those who give this positive sentiment are people who submit complaints and have been responded to by NTB Care and feel very satisfied with the work that has been done by NTB Care, negative sentiment reaches 14%, and those who give negative sentiment are people. Who are dissatisfied with NTB Care services, as well as people who have raised concerns but have not been responded to by NTB Care, and neutral sentiment has reached 43%, on average people who give neutral sentiment are people who have conveyed or have not given a good response to their performance conducted by NTB Care.

Keywords: E-Government · E-reports · Electronic Services · Sentiment · NTB Care Application

1 Introduction

The rapid development of Technology, Information and Communication, as well as the public's need for easy access to public services, has encouraged the Government to offer online-based services, with online public services expected to be more effective and efficient. in accessing public service information systems [1]. Maximizing the use of ICT resources opens opportunities for governments to implement new ways of providing public services in a transparent, effective, efficient and accountable manner. This also has implications for the Community Complaint Commission organized by the government [2].

© The Author(s), under exclusive license to Springer Nature Switzerland AG 2023
C. Stephanidis et al. (Eds.): HCII 2023, CCIS 1835, pp. 211–218, 2023.
https://doi.org/10.1007/978-3-031-36001-5_27

E-Government is an information technology system developed by the Government to improve public services by providing choices to the public for easy access to public information [3]. These policies and strategies are regulated together in Presidential Decree No. 3 of 2003 concerning National Policy and Strategy for E-Government Development at all levels of government [4]. Activities at this stage include making information pages in every government office, developing human resources, preparing Information Technology Infrastructure, supporting the E-Government implementation process, and disseminating Information sites both inside and outside the Government environment for E-socialization.. -Government is carried out consistently and continuously by providing knowledge to the public, because the community does not yet understand what e-government is, how it works, and its benefits [5].

Sentiment analysis uses are covered by several interesting scientific and commercial fields, such as opinion mining, recommendation systems, and event detection [6]. Sentiment analysis is the process of understanding, extracting and processing textual data [7]. Automatically to get sentiment information contained in an opinion sentence [8]. Sentiment analysis is carried out to see opinions or opinion trends on a problem or object that is carried out by someone, whether they tend to be natural, positive, or negative opinions [9].

There have been several previous studies (Cruz, 2021) Analyzing Community Concern Responses to the Formulation of Procedures and Laws using Sentiment Analysis through the VADER Application, The findings of this study are that the VADER sentiment analysis module is effective in distinguishing positive, neutral, and negative tweets. The results of the VADER Sentiment Analysis module were then evaluated using a test data set collected using the Twitter Scraper tool through the confusion matrix and yielded an accuracy of 80.71% and an F-Score of 84.33.Further research was also submitted by [11] The Relational Graph Attention Network for Aspect-Based Sentiment Analysis, the research findings indicate that the relationship between aspects and opinion words can be better constructed with the R-GAT, and as a result, the performance of GAT and BERT improves significantly. We also conducted ablation studies to validate the role of the new tree structure and relational heads. Lastly, error analysis was performed on the examples of incorrect predictions.

From the several research references above, the authors found that the research above was to find sentiment analysis assessments of several problems or research objects, while the research that the authors examined discussed advances in information technology in government and people's evaluation of e-government products issued by the government. (NTB Care Application).

NTB Governor Regulation No.4 of 2015 states that Electronic Government (e-Government) is an information technology system owned by the provincial government that changes the shape of relationships with citizens, the private sector, and/or government work units to encourage citizen empowerment, improve service delivery, strengthen accountability, increasing transparency, and improving government efficiency, ICT has permeated every area of work, from administrative work, planning, management, monitoring, and evaluation, to strategic functions in leadership decision-making [12].

The NTB Cares application is also a government service to get closer and always interact with the people of NTB and the NTB Cares service is also regulated inNTB

Governor Regulation Number 14 of 2022 Concerning Management of Community Complaints Through NTB Services in West Nusa Tenggara Province, as a form of reference in making complaints and solving existing problems [13].

Therefore this study aims to analyze the sentiments of the NTB people towards the NTB Care Application.

2 Literature Review

2.1 E-Government

E-Government is generally described as involving several different uses of ICT across government agencies and public administration, with e-Government frameworks providing change in the overall functioning of the public sector in terms of culture, values, structure, and ways of doing business. Done, and tasks.carried out by the government- Given, there is much significant potential associated with ICT as a key driver of public performance and change in government or institutions [14].

E-government is defined as the use of Information Technology to transform relations with citizens, businesses and other government agencies [15]. The application of E-government in government activities continues to increase. This is an implication of the global call to reform the public sector to improve service delivery. E-government was introduced in Indonesia in the 1990s when government websites were developed to facilitate communication [16]. According to The World Bank Group, E-Government is an effort to use information and communication technology to increase government efficiency and effectiveness, transparency and accountability in providing better public services [17].

2.2 Electronic Services

The latest technological developments in the world of computers and the internet have brought about changes and transformations in both the public and private sectors, the main purpose of using new technologies such as new applications in this sector is to increase the effectiveness of service delivery, in this case, public organizations have started using communication technology. Information., in particular, e-services, to improve the efficiency of their organizations and to raise service quality standards on behalf of citizens(Incirkuş and Cass, 2019).

Electronic services (E-Service) is a very general term, usually referring to the provision of services via the internet, so electronic services can also include internet commerce, and can also include non-commercial (online) services, which are usually provided by governments [19]. Service quality E-Service is defined as a public service website that enables more effective and efficient services. Consumers must rely on ICTs to obtain public services and e-services aimed at satisfying users regardless of social status [20].

2.3 E-Report

E-Lapor is a social media application that involves community participation and is two-way in nature, which is used as a tool for monitoring and verifying development program achievements as well as public complaints regarding the implementation of national development programs [21]. E-report has been designated as a National Public Service Complaint Management System (SP4N) based on Presidential Regulation Number 76 of 2013 and Minister of State Apparatus Empowerment and Bureaucratic Reform Regulation Number 3 of 2015 [22].

3 Research Methods

This study used a qualitative method, and the data source for this research was the NTB Cares Application. Sentiment data was taken from the NTB Care website and media, the data taken was public opinion on the NTBCare application and complaints through NTB Care. The data taken are (Table 1):

Table 1. Complaints from the NTB Community from 1 January to 8 November 2022

Complaint type	Number of Complaints	Being processed	Approved	Finished
Social	61 cases	10 cases	11 cases	40 cases
Health	220 cases	70 cases	40 cases	110 cases
Infrastructure	66 cases	0 cases	31 cases	35 cases
Cleanliness	20 cases	1 case	6 cases	13 cases
Natural disasters	25 cases	1 case	5 cases	19 cases
Criminal	6 cases	0	3 cases	3 cases
Environmental destruction	4 cases	0	1 case	3 cases
Agriculture	4 cases	0	2 cases	2 cases
Education	4 cases	0	1 case	3 cases
Total	410 cases	82 cases	100 cases	228 cases

Then the data is processed using the sentiment analysis tool available in the NVivo 12 plus research application, to determine each Negative, Positive or Neutral opinion from the people of NTB towards the NTB Cares Application. Researchers will present the results of the NVivo process to find out a comparison of public opinion using the NTB Care Application.

4 Results and Discussion

4.1 Complaints from the People of NTB from 1 January to 8 November 2022

From the data table for filing complaints as of January 1 to November 8 2022, there have been 410 cases processed, reaching 82 cases, 100 cases approved, and cases resolved reaching 228 out of 410 cases that have become complaints from the people of NTB. Cases of social complaints reached 61 cases, and the number of complaints currently being processed was 10 cases, approved reached 11 cases, and 40 cases have been resolved, many of these social cases including cases related to poverty and social assistance. Health complaints are complaints that many people complain about in NTB, reaching 220 cases of complaints that are being processed, 70 cases are approved, 40 cases are completed in the mancala process, and 110 cases, these cases cover various diseases experienced by the community. There are 66 infrastructure cases, the number of complaints received being processed as much as 0, 31 cases were approved and 35 cases resolved. Infrastructure cases are the second case that receives the most complaints from the people of NTB after health cases reaching 220 cases. Complaints related to cleanliness reached 20 cases being processed reached 1, approved 6, and resolved 13 cases.

There were 25 cases of natural disasters in NTB during 2022, 1 case being processed, 5 cases approved, and 19 cases of natural disasters being resolved. There are 6 criminal cases reported, of which no cases are currently being processed, 3 cases have been approved, and 3 cases have been resolved or handled. The NTB Regional Police investigated a total of 275 cases with 363 suspects involved in cases of theft (specialists in empty house theft, motor vehicle theft, and theft with violence such as mugging or robbery) and the lowest number of cases related to education, environmental damage and agriculture.

4.2 NTB Community Sentiment Analysis of the NTB Care Application

The results in Fig. 1 are a diagram of the NTB people's sentiment analysis towards the NTB Care Application. Positive sentiment towards the NTB Care application was dominated by 43% and natural sentiment towards the NTB Care application was dominated by 43% having the same number of positive sentiments, while negative sentiment was inversely proportional to the dominance of 14%.

Figure 1 shows sentiment analysis. Positive sentiment towards the Application.

NTB Care, this is obtained from various elements of society who fully support the performance carried out by NTB Care, such as coordinating with relevant agencies in resolving problems that have been reported through NTB Care so that people get direct touch from related offices and NTB Care as a liaison for community reports to the related agencies being able to work together in resolving the problems that have been reported, this was also conveyed because the performance of NTB care was quite good in terms of cases that had been completed and responded to in 2022 reaching 228 cases out of 410 cases reported,

This negative sentiment was conveyed by people who were dissatisfied with NTB Care's performance because the reports they submitted did not receive a response and

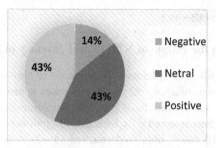

Fig. 1. The dominant sentiment of the people of NTB. Source: Nvivo 12 Plus Sentiment Analysis

tended to take a very long time to be responded to so that not a few people felt that the NTB Care application had not been able to function. be the solution to every problem presented by the people of Nusa. West Southeast, data shows that in 2022 reports that have not been completed or are still in the processing stage reach 82 cases, of which 100 cases have been approved, both those that are being processed and those that have been approved are cases that have not been resolved so far. Resolved by NTB Care out of 410 cases submitted by the NTB Community so,

This neutral sentiment was conveyed by the public who thought that NTB Care was an effective problem-solving medium in conveying problems raised by the NTB community to the government, but they also criticized the NTB Care application for not being able to answer all the problems that had been submitted. by the people of West Nusa Tenggara so that the NTB Care application can be adapted to the wishes of the NTB Care application users. Neutral opinion on the NTB Care application, the public is more likely to provide input or criticism that can build and improve the NTB Care application so that various parties use the NTB Care application as a reporting medium and as a medium that can answer all cases that arise. in West Nusa Tenggara.

From the positive, negative, and neutral sentiments in the NTB Peduli application, it can be seen that NTB Peduli is quite helpful in solving problems reported by the community, but NTB Peduli still has drawbacks because it has not been able to complete all reports. From the NTB Care community so that NTB Care needs a lot of improvement in solving existing problems so that the purpose of the NTB Care application is to become a medium for solving problems in West Nusa Tenggara that can work effectively and efficiently according to the needs of the community.

5   Conclusion

The use of the Peduli NTB application is very helpful for the NTB community in conveying various problems experienced by the NTB community.The results of this study indicate that the sentiment analysis of the NTB community towards the NTB Care application is related to the positive, negative and neutral sentiments of the NTB community. The NTB people's sentiment towards the NTB Cares application, namely positive sentiment reached 43%, negative sentiment reached 14%, and neutral sentiment reached 43%. LimitationsThis study incorporates sentiments from the Peduli NTB application, only looking at the display of the one-way Peduli NTB application without looking at the views of institutions or organizations in West Nusa Tenggara. This research also only looks at the appearance or results that have been carried out by the Peduli NTB application service.

References

1. AHM Nurdin, Towards Open Government (Open Government) Through the Implementation of E Government, J.MP (Government Management), vol. 5, pp. 1–17 (2018)
2. Lestari, D.: WW Winarno, and MP Kurniawan, E-readiness model for measuring readiness management of DIY E-report complaints. Creat. inf. Technol. J. 7(2), 86 (2021). https://doi.org/10.24076/citec.2020v7i2.249
3. Nugraha, J.:E-government and public service (Study of Successful Elements of E-Government development in Sleman Regency Government). J. Commun. Kaji. Media 2(1), 32–42 (2018)
4. Wirawan, V.: Implementation of e-government in welcoming the contemporary industrial revolution 4.0 era in Indonesia. J. Law Enforcement. Justice 1(1), 1–16 (2020). https://doi.org/10.18196/jphk.1101
5. Carter, L., Ubacht, J.: Panel: blockchain applications in government. In: ACM International Conference Proceedings Series (2018). https://doi.org/10.1145/3209281.3209329
6. Manguri, K.H.: Analysis of Twitter sentiments on the COVID-19 outbreak around the world (2020). https://doi.org/10.24017/covid.8
7. Rosdiana, R., Eddy, T., Zawiyah, S., Muhammad, N.: Sentiment analysis on Twitter for Makassar city government services. In: SNTEI Proceedings, no. June 2020, pp. 87–93 (2019)
8. Mitra, A.: Sentiment analysis using machine learning approaches (Lexicon based on movie review dataset), vol. 02, no. 03, pp. 145–152 (2020)
9. Alqaryouti, O., Siyam, N., Monem, A.A.: Aspect-based sentiment analysis using smart government review data analysis (2019). https://doi.org/10.1016/j.aci.2019.11.003
10. Cruz, C.A.: Analyzing public concern responses for formulating ordinances and laws using sentiment analysis through VADER Ap…, https://doi.org/10.25147/ijcsr.2017.001.1.77
11. Wang, K., Shen, W., Yang, Y., Quan, X., Wang, R.: Relational graph attention network for aspect-based sentiment analysis (2019)
12. Ismarmiaty, I., Etmy, D.: Modified UTAUT2 approach model in the analysis of acceptance and use of e-government technology in West Nusa Tenggara. MATRIC J. Manag. Tech. Inf. Comput. Eng. 18(1), 106–114 (2018). https://doi.org/10.30812/matrik.v18i1.347
13. P. 2018. "No. T. . 2018. NTB, PemprovNTB, "No Title, (2018)
14. Nawafleh, S.: Factors affecting the continued use of e-government websites by citizens an exploratory study in the Jordanian (2018). https://doi.org/10.1108/TG-02-2018-0015
15. Yasir, A., Hu, X., Ahmad, M., Rauf, A., Shi, J., Nasir, S.A.: Modeling the impact of word of mouth and E-government on online social presence during the COVID-19 outbreak: a multi-mediation approach. Int. J. Environ. Res. Public Health 17(8) (2020). https://doi.org/10.3390/ijerph17082954
16. Oktavia, L.: Assessment of E-government acceptance in Indonesia. J. Corel T J. Has. Res. Comput. Sci. Technol. Inf. 6(1), 15 (2020). https://doi.org/10.24014/coreit.v6i1.9143
17. Zaliluddin, D., Budiman, B., Rully, A.: Implementation of android-based e-government. JSiI (Inf. Syst. J.) 7(2), 83–88 (2020). https://doi.org/10.30656/jsii.v7i2.2052
18. Incirkuş, L., Cass, A.O.: Quality in e-Government accounting services : a model of relationships between e-service quality dimensions and b … Related papers"
19. Figuccio, M.J.: Examining the efficacy of e-service-learning. Front. educ. 5, 1–6 (2020). https://doi.org/10.3389/feduc.2020.606451

20. Jameel, A.S., Hamdi, S.S., Karem, M.A., Raewf, M.B., Ahmad, A.R.:E-satisfaction based on e-service quality among university students. J. Phys. Conf. Ser. **1804**(1) (2021). https://doi.org/10.1088/1742-6596/1804/1/012039

21. Ginting, E.A., Ginting, S.: Communication strategy for the simpang empat district office in promoting the e-report program! to the community in simpang district. J. Soc. Opin. J. Ilm. Communal Sci. **5**(2) (2020)

22. E. -L. (SPAN), No Titles, https://pesisirbaratkab.go.id/. (2018)

Cybersecurity Compliance in the Public Sector: Are the Best Security Practices Properly Addressed?

Lars Magnusson[⊠], Fisnik Dalipi, and Patrik Elm

Department of Informatics, Linnaeus University, Kalmar, Sweden
{lars.magnusson,fisnik.dalipi,patrik.elm}@lnu.se

Abstract. Improving and strengthening cybersecurity in the public sector should represent a top priority for government agencies, including municipalities and regions. To be resilient against cyberattack surges, organizations should consider establishing a cybersecurity program based on international standards and best practices. In this paper we explore the cybersecurity compliance in the Swedish public sector in relation to the best practices and guidelines highlighted in the ISO/IEC 27001A framework. Our findings indicate that the overall security status among the municipalities and regions contained many flaws, with substantial holes and critical issues. ISO/IEC 27001A creates a standardized base, but it is somewhat theoretical and starts with a policy, not providing insights on how to govern information security. Also, most of these "ISO/IEC"-related gaps were found to have been compiled into a single "Technology" domain. Though compliance with standards, best practices, and regulatory requirements can help reduce cyber risks, it does not guarantee that an organization will have strong cybersecurity. To address this issue and assess how well organizations can protect, discern, react, and recover from cyberattacks, an effective method for measuring security performance must be developed.

Keywords: ISO/IEC 27001 · cybersecurity · risks · flawed governance · compliance · public sector

1 Introduction

Digital technology and innovation have become critical to enhancing the overall quality of life and the convenience of doing business. However, integrating cybersecurity mechanisms while implementing new technologies is a necessary step for achieving sustainable societal and economic development. In this direction, several scholars have stated that cybersecurity is the key and necessary contribution to long-term economic, social, and environmental progress [1–3]. Despite the continued research efforts in the field, it is still challenging for cybersecurity to be properly managed to a level to keep the intruders out and prevent all the "megahacks".

Security post-mortem analyses after events like the Equifax, Capital One, and Solarwinds hacks [4–6] clearly pointed out that flawed governance was the primary reason for

© The Author(s), under exclusive license to Springer Nature Switzerland AG 2023
C. Stephanidis et al. (Eds.): HCII 2023, CCIS 1835, pp. 219–226, 2023.
https://doi.org/10.1007/978-3-031-36001-5_28

incurred data theft. Moreover, during the COVID-19 outbreak, the situation has worsened, where FBI reported a 400% increase in cyberattack cases compared to before the outbreak of the pandemic [7]. Available audit results dealing with Swedish municipalities and regions collected by the prominent auditing firms KPMG, EY, Deloitte, PwC, and Norwegian DSO [8] identify systematic flaws within cybersecurity governance.

To be resilient against cyberattack surges, organizations should consider establishing a cybersecurity program based on international standards and best practices [9]. Some standards, such as ISO/IEC 27001 [10], set requirements for certification via independent third-party audit, and others, such as NIST Cybersecurity Framework (CFS) [11] or ISACA's COBIT [9], serve as a framework or guideline for managing cybersecurity risk. Nevertheless, standards like NIST CFS or COBIT are geared toward resource-able large-scale organizations, not toward Small-Medium Enterprise (SME) organizations [12].

In this paper, we investigate cybersecurity compliance in the Swedish public sector (municipalities and regions) against the best practices and guidelines highlighted in the ISO/IEC 27001 security framework [10]. We analyzed gathered data from 62 municipalities and 10 regions. The rest of the paper is structured as follows: Sect. 2 presents some preliminaries and related work, whereas Sect. 3 highlights the main findings. The paper concludes with Sect. 4, where some conclusions are drawn and recommendations are provided.

2   Background and Related Work

Information security has been studied intensely since the late 1980s, though some of the first cases were in the 1970s when John Draper demonstrated his Phreaking technology to access free phone calls [13]. However, the Morris Worm [14] event gave hacking and information security a public face in 1988. Since then, security crimes have evolved out of the nursery, particularly regarding net-based security. Some key examples are the aftermath of the US firms' Target [15] and Equifax data breaches [16] in the early 2010s or the Capital One breach [17] in 2019. A critical aspect and a valid RQ are why we have these mega-size security breaches, discussed by practitioners [18] and researchers [19]. For one of us, this has been a critical topic for over 30 years as a practitioner, with management and governance issues often identified as critical aspects, not technology. An aspect also voiced by other researchers [9, 20, 21]. We, therefore, defined a survey to study the governance role as a root cause of information security incidents.

After being involved in audits, two of the authors have experienced that access to real-life information security data is hard. Often revealing uncomfortable internal issues affecting the described organization if made public [22]. Information that can become diametrical, reducing the organization's value, bringing disreputation, and, not least, being used for malicious access. Consequently, most organizations will restrict this type of information, limiting researchers' access to viable data to analyze.

However, the first author found that several Swedish municipalities and counties/regions had published such data under Sweden's Publicity and Privacy Act of 2009 [23]. A law that gives access to public sector information more openly than most other countries. A governmental body can limit access to information but must define why it is limited. After investigating similar material in the other Nordic countries, having a related legal framework, only two corresponding public audits were found in Norway, such as [24], which indicates limitations in other countries. Most Swedish government bodies do so regarding their information security status data, but nearly 100 public organizations posted such documents, found via a simplified Google search covering 2013 to 2022. Some 62 information security audits out of the 290 Swedish municipalities and 10 of the 21 counties/regions [8].

The found data must be regarded as secondary data; however, the used audit reports have been performed by certified auditors, verifying the authenticity of the identified reports. Unfortunately, all audits were not equal; in reality, while the auditors used similar complaint groups, most audits dropped one or several of these complaint groups. Therefore, the complaint groups identified over the 72 audits have been grouped into 10 functional "*security domains*", beginning with a management definition and nine related complaint groups, which in total represented 720 possible objects. Of these, 209 objects in total were lacking, spread over the 72 audits, thus creating a knowledge gap. The reason for these gaps can only be guessed but is likely related to defined audit time or cost constraints. The studied organizations perform yearly audits covering all their operational territory, making individual audit topics scarce, thus likely resulting in an uneven audit pattern.

The Swedish Association of Local Authorities and Regions' [SKR.se] primary recommendation, based on the national strategy [25], is that their members use the ISO/IEC 27001A security framework, with its inherent 14 security domains as a base for the security work. SKR has designed a "Klassa" tool [26] to support the use of the ISO/IEC framework. Not being a mandatory SKR recommendation, many organizations also declared using a project management maturity framework, primarily the international "PM3" framework [27]. One critical observation was; the 10 identified audit domains, though loosely tied to ISO/IEC 27001A's declared 14 security domains, are not a perfect match.

3   Findings and Analysis

As already explained, with an included comment distribution from only 4–5 per audit up to all 10 domains to be addressed, this has given observed data gaps. Most of these "ISO/IEC"-related gaps were found to have been compiled into a single "Technology" domain. In total, as shown in Table 1, the following 10 security comments or domains were recognized across the audit reports. Also, two of the auditors, performing 60% of the audits, used a "traffic light" report model for convenience, with green referring to Approved, yellow to Partly failed, and red for Failed inspections, mapping all their audits to this model. For the mentioned gaps, we added grey, indicating a lack of data. The remaining audits were coded the same way, based on those auditors' finding status, as presented in Tables 2 and 3.

Table 1. Mapping of found audit control domains vs. related ISO/IEC 27001 control domains

Compiled audit domains	ISO/IEC 27001A domains	Description of audit security domain questions
0. Chosen governance model	A.6	Has the organization chosen a standard gov. model ?
1. Implementation of gov. model	A.6, A.18	How well does the chosen model work in reality?
2. ISP (policy) + GDPR processes	A.5	Policy documents in general, whats there and how well updated?
3. Information classes + Risk evals	A.7	Any matrix for security classes and GRC evaluations in place?
4. Management processes	A.8	How well is defined control and document processes working?
5. Roles and responsibilities	A.7	Is basic access approvals and responsibility allocation working?
6. Access control	A.9	Status of maintenance of accesses and roll allocations?
7. Technical comments etc.	A.10, A.12, A.13, A.14	Status general technical compliance, incl. required ZeroTrust mgnt?
8. Risk areas in addition to previous	A.15, A.16, A.17	Any additional risk factors outside the above bullets (see ISO groups)?
9. Information Security training	A.7	Any focus on topic training observed?

Note that the color in the tables always reflects the auditors' original complaint findings for each object within each security domain, giving a subdivision of the data per domain.

Table 2. Compilation of audit remarks, information security, 62 Swedish municipalities.

	Governance model	Complaint 1 - Governance performance	Complaint 2 - Policy/GDPR etc.	Complaint 3 - Info Class/Risk evals	Complaint 4 - Lack of processes	Complaint 5 - Roles etc.	Complaint 6 - Access control	Complaint 7 - Technology	Complaint 8 - Misc. comments	Complaint 9 - Education	Sum of each status group
Approved	12	4	3	3	2	6	3	2	1	3	39
Partly Fail	19	19	22	21	20	23	21	5	16	7	173
Fully Failed	13	38	20	30	33	20	29	1	17	12	213
Not Disclosed	18	1	17	8	7	13	9	54	28	40	195

Total: 620

	Sum of each eval groups
Approved	39
Partly Fail	173
Fully Failed	213
N/D	195
Total	620

In %-age	% Approved	% Partly Failed	% Fully Failed	% N/D
of total	6	28	34	31
In %-age of done	9	41	5	

Table 3. Compilation of audit remarks, information security, 10 Swedish regions.

	Governance model	Complaint 1 - Governance performance	Complaint 2 - Policy/GDPR etc.	Complaint 3 - Info Class/Risk evals	Complaint 4 - Lack of processes	Complaint 5 - Roles etc.	Complaint 6 - Access control	Complaint 7 - Technology	Complaint 8 - Misc. comments	Complaint 9 - Education	Sum of each status group
Approved	9	3	4	5	2	0	0	3	1	2	29
Partly Fail	1	6	5	2	5	6	7	2	5	5	44
Fully Failed	0	1	1	3	2	2					15
Not Disclosed	0	0	0	0	1	2	2	3	2	2	12

Total 100

	Sum of each status group
Approved	29
Partly Fail	44
Fully Failed	15
N/D	12
Total:	100

In %-age	% Approved	% Partly Failed	% Fully Failed	% N/D
of total	29	44	15	12
In %-age of	33	50	12	

All audits showed significant issues, though the regions performed better, something to be discussed later. The tables show the numerical compilation of findings divided into the 10 identified security domains for the two organization groups. The upper sub-tables within each table show the distribution of the four fulfillment classes per security domain, while the lower sub-tables on the left show summation of the total 720 possible domain objects, respectively, for the two organizational groups. The sub-tables on the right show the compiled percentages, with separation into showing with the *"N/D"* or *"Not disclosed"* values and without. Data were registered in the data repository according to the traffic light evaluation scheme, divided into the four mentioned evaluation classes extracted from the initial audit reports.

Ernst & Young [EY] and PricewaterhouseCoopers [PwC] normally use this method to enhance readability for their customers. Of the others, Deloitte has sometimes used the method, while KPMG, as last of the "BIG4", or the Norwegian firm BDO, has not been seen using this notation in our observed material. Nevertheless, with their audit comments clearly stating if approved, partly failed, fully failed, or data found missing, transforming all audits to an EY/PwC-inspired model simplified our analysis. Appearing not to induce any secondary evaluation of the material, preserving the original auditors' views or lack thereof. Using color coding in the analysis, the data allowed for effective interpretation of the observed status of how well the organizations succeeded managed their information security processes as per the identified domain as well as on the whole. Unfortunately, a detailed analysis of the individual security domains falls outside this article's scope; therefore, a compounded analysis of the four key evaluation groups will finalize the data analysis, as seen in Fig. 1.

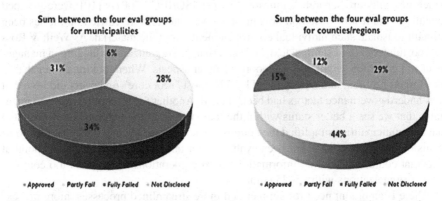

Fig. 1. Compounded percentage per the evaluation groups across municipalities and regions.

This diagram shows that a municipalities' partial/full failure rate was 62% and 59% for the regions, with only 6% of the findings approved for the first group and 12% for the latter. From an information security perspective, the seen result is very unsatisfactory. Additionally, a gap of 31% lack of data from the municipal audits presents a substantial lack of insight into their status. The regions fare a bit better, with only missing 12% of the control objectives. Here, the inclusion of the auditors' comments could have been added to the picture, frequently pointing at *"not yet implemented"* and *"not followed up"* as key causes for the control to fail, but, again, such individual comments are out of the scope of this article.

It is worth mentioning that due to the audits performed between 2013 and 2022, the security focus has shifted during these 10 years, making any direct comparison between the individual audits impossible. One important difference is that the pre-2018 audits all lack any reviews regarding GDPR implementations, though the EU parliament already enforced the regulation in May 2016 [28]. It should also be noted that a few of the audits were follow-up audits, thus only partial in their execution.

4 Discussion and Conclusions

The study, representing 720 possible objects, had data missing for 207 of these objects (labeled "*Not disclosed*"). Primarily because control objects were deliberately excluded from the audits or, for other reasons, were not commented on by the auditors. The majority of the missing objects are mainly found within the security domains "2. Policy/GDPR", "7. Technology", "8. Adjacent comments", as well as "9. Training". In addition, the auditors found that only four of the 22 municipalities adhering to the ISO/IEC model had implemented the model. All the regions were approved, but most not fully implementing the governance framework. One surprising aspect was that, despite the mandatory use of strong authentication with, e.g., SITS security id cards within the domains "5. Roles" and "6. Access", the comments for these domains contained a high percentage of "Partial" and "Not Passed" findings.

Our findings demonstrate that the result is worse than expected. Several audit topics, which normally are separate audit domains per ISO/IEC 27001A [10], were grouped together in the result. Based on how most of these audits were carried out, it has been difficult to isolate such individual control elements from the material. As Weill & Ross [29] postulates in their seminal text, "IT Governance", organizations lagging in management and governance will perform poorly in other aspects. When looking at megahacks like Target, Equifax, and Solarwinds [15–17], most "root core" reviewers did note that substandard governance factors had been at hand. Another factor derived from the material is that we see a better status within the regions than at the municipalities level and that the municipalities simplified their audits to a minimum. Though the individual comments by the auditors have not been evaluated nor tallied, it is noted that they point at facts that could indicate that information security operations have gotten too complex for ICT organizations with 15–25 employees.

There is an urgent need for simpler and more streamlined processes, more process repeatability across the board, and more affordable SIEM (Security Information and Event Management) security surveillance functions to relieve overburdening governance pressure on the personnel. For these organizations, it would be beneficial if SKR enforced a mandatory ISO/IEC 27001A audit domain framework for all to align by [25]. However, today this is not the case. A common audit template for the auditors to use, preferably based on the PwC/EY traffic light model, would enhance knowledge and understanding regarding the current failed governance strategy found within the surveyed group [8]. The studied audits identify a series of factors, particularly auditor-critical "repeat" findings, as noted in each of these audits.

Compliance with standards, best practices, and regulatory requirements can help reduce cyber risks, but it does not guarantee that an organization will have strong cybersecurity. Many ISO 27001-certified organizations, for instance, tend to only focus on achieving certification by applying ISO 27001 minimally within their organizations, as opposed to strengthening security controls throughout their most vital applications, business data, and information systems. This generates inconsistencies in the organization's security controls application, with ISO 27001-certified areas thought to be more secure than other areas. To address this issue and assess how well organizations can protect, discern, react, and recover from cyberattacks, an effective method for measuring security performance must be developed. Because security controls must be dynamic, constantly updated, and upgraded, the measurement method must be quick and cost-effective. Static security controls will ultimately be compromised by an attacker. Therefore, organizations must quickly and frequently conduct measurements to identify existing flaws and enhance their defense planning. They should also avoid oversights by using well-known "Best Practices" that recommend well-designed actions to simplify information security work, processes and to save costs. We observed auditor comments relating to SME organizations, including most of the municipalities, having major resource limitations in performing and operating information security processes and tools.

References

1. Michael, K., Kobran, S., Abbas, R., Hamdoun, S.: Privacy, data rights and cybersecurity: technology for good in the achievement of sustainable development goals. In: 2019 IEEE International Symposium on Technology and Society (ISTAS), pp. 1–13. IEEE, November 2019

2. Andrade, R.O., Yoo, S.G., Tello-Oquendo, L., Ortiz-Garcés, I.: Cybersecurity, sustainability, and resilience capabilities of a smart city. In: Smart Cities and the un SDGs, pp. 181–193. Elsevier (2021)

3. Sadik, S., Ahmed, M., Sikos, L.F., Islam, A.N.: Toward a sustainable cybersecurity ecosystem. Computers 9(3), 74 (2020)

4. Wang, P., Johnson, C.: Cybersecurity incident handling: a case study of the Equifax data breach. Issues in Inf. Syst. 19(3), 150–159 (2018)

5. Khan, S., Kabanov, I., Hua, Y., Madnick, S.: A systematic analysis of the capital one data breach: critical lessons learned. ACM Trans. Privacy Secur. 26(1), 1–29 (2022)

6. Willett, M.: Lessons of the SolarWinds hack. Survival 63(2), 7–26 (2021)

7. Miller, M.: FBI sees spike in cyber crime reports during coronavirus pandemic. The Hill (2020). Accessed 29 Sep 2022. https://thehill.com/pol-%20641%20icy/cybersecurity/493 198-fbi-sees-spike-in-cybercrime-reports-during-coronavirus-pandemic/

8. Vetlanda Council. "Vetlanda municipality - Review regarding IT and information security according to BITS (E&Y)". Vetlanda.se (2013). Accessed 20 June 2022. https://kommun.vet landa.se/download/18.25b13cb915edc34042e2a544/1507290616429/Granskning%20avse ende%20IT-%20och%20informationssäkerhet%20enligt%20BITS.pdf

9. Skrodelis, H.K., Strebko, J., Romanovs, A.: The information system security governance tasks in small and medium enterprises. In: 2020 61st International Scientific Conference on Information Technology and Management Science of Riga Technical University (ITMS, IEEE, pp. 1–4 (2020)

10. Disterer, G.: ISO/IEC 27000, 27001 and 27002 for information security management. J. Inf. Secur. 4(2) (2013)

11. White, G.B., Sjelin, N.: The NIST cybersecurity framework. In: Research An-thology on Business Aspects of Cybersecurity, pp. 39–55. IGI Global (2022)

12. Dent, P.A.: Cybersecurity Failures of Small and Medium-Sized Businesses: Circum-venting Leadership Failure (Doctoral dissertation), Utica College (2021)

13. Nayak, U., Rao, U.H.: The InfoSec Handbook: An Introduction to Information Security, Apress (2014). https://doi.org/10.1007/978-1-4302-6383-8

14. Furnell, S., Spafford, E.H.: The morris worm at 30. ITNOW **61**(1), 32–33 (2019). https://doi.org/10.1093/itnow/bwz013
15. Shu, X., Tian, K., Ciambrone, A., Yao, D.: Breaking the target: an analysis of target data breach and lessons learned (2017)
16. US Gov. "The Equifax Data Breach", Majority Staff Report 115th Congress, US", House of Representatives Committee on Oversight and Government Reform (2018)
17. Khan, S., Kabanov, I., Hua, Y., Madnick, S.: A systematic analysis of the capital one data breach: critical lessons learned. ACM Trans. Priv. Secur. **26**(1), 1–29 (2022)
18. Blackley, J.A., Peltier, T.R., Peltier, J.: Information security fundamentals. Auer-bach Publications (2004)
19. Dlamini, M.T., Eloff, J.H.P., Eloff, M.M.: Information security: the moving target. Comput. Secur. **28**(3), 189–198 (2009). https://doi.org/10.1016/j.cose.2008.11.007
20. Schinagl, S., Shahim, A.: What do we know about information security govern-ance? "From the basement to the boardroom": towards digital security governance. Inf. Comput. Secur. **28**(2), 261–292 (2020). https://doi.org/10.1108/ICS-02-2019-0033
21. Solms, B., Solms, R.: The 10 deadly sins of information security management. Comput. Secur. **23**(5), 371–376 (2004)
22. Gwebu, K.L., Wang, J., Wang, L.: The role of corporate reputation and crisis response strategies in data breach management. J. Manag. Inf. Syst. **35**(2), 683–714 (2018)
23. Sw. Gov., Swedens Public Access To Information and Secrecy Act, Gov., Sweden (2009)
24. Security audit data from Sarpsborg Kommune; https://www.nkrf.no/filarkiv/File/Alle_rapporter_i_pdf/Ostre_Viken_kommunerevisjon_IKS/Sarpsborg_2020_IT_sikkerhet_Delrapport_1.pdf
25. Sw. Gov., A national cyber security strategy, Skr. 2016/17:213, Gov., Sweden (2016). Accessed 15 Feb 2023. https://www.government.se/legal-documents/2017/11/skr.-201617213/
26. SKR, 2016, "About Klassa" (in Swedish), Swedish Association of Local Authorities and Regions, as viewed 19 Dec 2022. https://klassa-info.skr.se/about
27. Remy, R.: Adding focus to improvement efforts with PM3 (1997). https://www.pmi.org/learning/library/adding-focus-improvement-efforts-pm3-5147. Accessed 22 Jan 2023
28. EU., (2016). Regulation (EU) 2016/679 of the European Parliament and of the Council of 27 April 2016 on the protection of natural persons with regard to the processing of personal data and on the free movement of such data, EU, Bruxelles, May 10, 2016
29. Weill, P., Ross, J.W.: IT governance: How top performers manage IT decision rights for superior results. Harvard Business Press (2004)

The Digital Electronic Systems and Business Accounting and Tribute Management During Confinement by Covid 19

Jose Ricardo Mondragon Regalado[1]([✉]) [iD], Alexander Huaman Monteza[1] [iD],
Julio César Montenegro Juárez[1] [iD], Jannier Alberto Montenegro Juárez[1] [iD],
Nazario Aguirre Baique[2] [iD], and Keneth Reategui Del Aguila[2] [iD]

[1] Universidad Nacional de Jaén, Jaén, Perú
`jose.mondragon@unj.edu.pe`
[2] Universidad Nacional Intercultural de La Amazonía, Ucayali, Perú

Abstract. The accounting and tax management of companies requires the incorporation of information and communication technologies through digital electronic systems to better control and collect taxes. For this reason, the objective of this research was: Determine the relationship between digital electronic systems -SED and business accounting and tax management during confinement by Covid 19. In this context, the results of the research allowed us to demonstrate that there is a significant statistical relationship between digital electronic systems and accounting and tax management in companies during confinement; therefore, it is inferred that the SEDs contributed efficiently in the management of the companies that were part of the investigation.

Keywords: Digital electronic systems · accounting management · tax management

1 Introduction

The administrative management of companies and public entities present a constant challenge to incorporate technological means and develop efficient policies in tax control. For this reason, electronic systems played a very important role during the confinement due to the Covid 19 pandemic in accounting and tax management of public and private entities (Rodríguez and Cabell 2021).

Previously, these systems had been implemented globally as a strategic tool by companies and state agencies. For the Economic Commission for Latin America and the Caribbean, electronic systems represent one of the best practices that are currently being implemented in many countries and it is undoubtedly a positive sign that indicates the digitization of the administration for tax control. Likewise, it indicates that the electronic invoice is evidence of the automation of the processes and that it allows having the information in real time (E. González Mata, I. Romero Márquez y R. Padilla Pérez, 2019).

The digital electronic system is an efficient alternative that allows control of taxes without borders to avoid tax evasion, which should be applied as a good practice by

C. Stephanidis et al. (Eds.): HCII 2023, CCIS 1835, pp. 227–231, 2023.
https://doi.org/10.1007/978-3-031-36001-5_29

national and subnational governments. With the aim of obtaining a better control of taxes and tribute, a study presented by the Economic Commission for Latin America and the Caribbean (CEPAL 2019) reports that in Argentina in 2018 implemented the electronic system to provide VAT control services to non-residents or persons with legal domicile in another country. For this reason, the accounting and tax management based on digital electronic systems allows improving tax collection, from the above it is corroborated that some Latin American countries experienced growth in tax collection in terms of GDP, such as Argentina, of 6.4% of collection passed to 7.4%; Ecuador from 4.8% to 6.4% and Uruguay from 8.3% to 9.0% (E. González Mata, I. Romero Márquez y R. Padilla Pérez, 2019).

During the year 2020 and 2021, as a result of the presence of Covid 19, most of the companies and organizations of the State by government provisions in order to prevent contagion, the confinement of the population was decreed and therefore the closure of public entities and private. The companies that managed to maintain the continuity of the provision of their services had to adapt to a new work reality, so the presence of technology became a relevant factor for the management of accounting and tax information. Digital electronic systems have contributed to public health for decision-making by managers based on reliable and quality data in real time (Yazdani et al. 2023).

In addition to promoting public health during confinement, better platforms based on the SED model continued to be implemented, which had a high impact on the accounting and tax management of companies, improving service to users and customers (Tut 2023). Another study reports that private companies and the public sector promoted the use of various electronic means to avoid physical contact and the proliferation of infections (Magdaleno et al. 2023).

In this context, Al Masadeh et al. (2023) argue that technological investment in companies and public entities is essential to guarantee the continuity of activities in the face of possible threats such as epidemics and pandemics. Faced with the advancement of technology and possible threats to public health, small and medium-sized companies have the obligation to implement digital literacy policies in order to improve accounting and financial management based on data processing that ensures efficient control (Phimolsathien 2022).

In the companies that were part of the investigation, it was evidenced that they use digital electronic systems to control their accounting and financial operations. However, it is unknown how these influenced their accounting and tax management during the confinement by Covid 19. Accounting management is broad and complex, so in the present investigation the dimensions were studied: legal formality resources, timely accounting registration process and results of compliance with tax obligations.

In this line of ideas, the following thesis is proposed: What is the relationship between digital electronic systems and business accounting and tax management during the confinement by Covid 19? In order to find an answer to the approach carried out in this investigation, the following general objective was formulated: Determine the relationship between digital electronic systems and business accounting and tax management during the confinement by Covid 19.

Faced with this, the present investigation is important because the results will allow company managers to apply policies that involve the use of Digital Electronic Systems to optimize expenses, efficiently manage time, provide quality customer service, as well as keep track of timely business accounting records and compliance with tax obligations as taxpayers. In addition, it indirectly contributes to the State Control Organizations to take advantage of the use of information technologies to carry out an efficient control of tax collection.

Likewise, the study will benefit managers, accountants, administrators and the personnel that work in the different administrative and accounting areas in the public and private sphere, since the systems will contribute so that the activities are carried out in a safe manner, granting greater reliability in the data. Accounting processes and other activities that are carried out internally and externally.

2 Methodology

The research presents a cross-sectional non-experimental design, correlational descriptive level, with a quantitative approach. The population was made up of 48 companies and micro-enterprises from the Cajamarca region, according to the treatment of the data corresponds to the quantitative research approach, the technique used was the survey.

To select the sample, the non-probabilistic statistical method was applied, the companies that were part of the research study were voluntary prior to informed consent.

The methods applied were inductive and deductive, which have allowed an analysis to be carried out in a general way towards the particular and also from the particular towards the general, thus raising the thesis and objective of the study. In addition, these methods allowed the analysis of the results to determine the general conclusions of the investigation.

3 Results

Table 1 shows the correlation between the digital electronic systems variable and the legal formality resources dimension, the correlation test is 0.348, which represents a moderate correlation with a significance level of $(p = 000)$ less than 5% $(p < 0.05)$. Evidence that there was a moderately significant direct relationship between variable and dimension.

The results indicate that the application of digital electronic systems in companies during the confinement by Covid 19 have allowed to improve business accounting and tax management on the dimension of legal formality resources, which suggests that companies reduce costs in the purchase of physical books, as well as notarial legalization among others; that is, the information is digitally consolidated and sent to State Control agencies.

Likewise, the correlation between the digital electronic systems variable and the timely accounting registration process dimension is evident, the correlation test is 0.748, indicating a very high correlation with a significance level of $(p = 0.000)$ less than 5% $(p < 0.05)$, evidence that there was a significant direct relationship between the variable and the proposed dimension. The results also indicate that the use of digital book systems during confinement by Covid 19 directly affects the timely accounting record dimension; that is to say, the SEDs allow companies to comply with the timely registration of the movements they make according to their business category, they also help them to be carried out in the shortest time and avoid making involuntary errors, among others.

In addition, the correlation between the digital electronic systems variable and the dimension of compliance with tax obligations is presented. The correlation test is 0.857, indicating a very high correlation with a significance level of ($p = 0.000$) less than 5% ($p < 0.05$), shows that there was a significant relationship between the variable and the proposed dimension. The results also allow us to infer that electronic book systems directly influence compliance with tax obligations with respect to filing returns within the periods specified by regulatory bodies, in addition to making timely payment of taxes, tributes and contributions, preventing them from being generated. Unnecessary expenses for fines.

Table 1. Relationship between digital electronic systems and the dimensions: resources for legal formality; timely accounting registration and compliance with tax obligations

Variable/dimention		Legal Formality Resources	Registration with timely table	Compliance with tax obligations
Digital electronic systems	Correlation coefficient	0,348	0,748	0,857
	Sig. (bilateral)	0,000	0,000	0,000

Finally, Table 2 shows that there is a correlation between the variables digital electronic systems and accounting and tax management, the correlation test results in 0.957, indicating a very high correlation with a significance level of ($p = 0.000$). Less than 5% ($p < 0.05$), which shows that there was a significant direct relationship between both variables. The results allowed us to categorically infer that the use of digital electronic systems during confinement by Covid 19 has allowed improving accounting and tax management in companies in the Cajamarca region. The SEDs, apart from contributing to business accounting and tax management, also favor interoperability between companies, public notaries, public registries and tax collection regulatory agencies by the State, which have allowed companies to achieve sustainability in the market during confinement.

Table 2. Relationship between digital electronic systems and accounting and tax management

Variable		Accounting and tax management
Digital electronic systems	Correlation coefficient	0,957
	Sig. (bilateral)	0,000

4   Conclusions

It is concluded that there was a significant direct statistical relationship between digital electronic systems and accounting and tax management in companies in the Cajamarca region during the confinement by Covid 19.

That the dimensions of legal formality resources, timely accounting registration and compliance with tax obligations that correspond to the accounting and tax management variable had a significant direct statistical relationship with the digital electronic systems variable in companies in the Cajamarca region during the confinement by Covid 19.

The digital electronic systems have allowed the interoperability of the institutions of collection and legal formalization of the State. As well as the integration of private companies to achieve sustainability during confinement by Covid 19.

References

Al Masadeh, M., Haimour, F., Haimour, S., Al-Safarini, M., Al Masadeh, F.: The role of information technology to fight the covid-19 pandemic (Jordan is a Model). In: Studies in Systems, Decision and Control, vol. 216, pp. 171–179. Springer, Cham (2023). https://doi.org/10.1007/978-3-031-10212-7_15

Comisión Económica para América Latina y el Caribe (CEPAL). Panorama Fiscal de América Latina y el Caribe Gracias por su interés en esta publicación de la CEPAL ((LC/PUB.20) (2019). https://repositorio.cepal.org/bitstream/handle/11362/44516/1/S1900075_es.pdf

González Mata, E., Romero Márquez, I., Padilla Pérez, R.: Buenas prácticas aplicadas en países de América Latina para reducir la evasión por saldos a favor en el IVA (LC/MEX/TS.2019/21), Ciudad de México, Comisión Económica para América Latina y el Caribe (CEPAL) (2019)

Magdaleno-Palencia, J.S., Marquez, B.Y., Quezada, Á., Orozco-Garibay, J.J.R.: Digital ticketing system for public transport in mexico to avoid cases of contagion using artificial intelligence. In: Arai, K. (eds.) Proceedings of the Future Technologies Conference (FTC) 2022, volume 1. FTC 2022 2022. LNNS, vol. 559, pp. 358–367 (2023). Springer, Cham. https://doi.org/10.1007/978-3-031-18461-1_24

Phimolsathien, T.: Guidelines for driving business sector into digital transactions for business survival: a case study of the impact of covid-19 to smes business in thailand . Polish J. Manag. Stud. 26(2), 293–309 (2022). https://doi.org/10.17512/pjms.2022.26.2.18

Rodríguez, A., Cabell, N.: Importancia de la competencia digital docente en el confinamiento social. Polo del conocimiento 6(1), 1091–1109 (2021)

Tut, D.: FinTech and the COVID-19 pandemic: Evidence from electronic payment systems. Emerg. Mark. Rev. 54 (2023). https://doi.org/10.1016/j.ememar.2023.100999

Yazdani, M., Pamucar, D., Erdmann, A., Toro-Dupouy, L.: Resilient sustainable investment in digital education technology: a stakeholder-centric decision support model under uncertainty. Tech. Forecast. Soc. Change 188 (2023). https://doi.org/10.1016/j.techfore.2022.122282

"Face to Face". Citizen Security Model Based on Information Systems in the Cloud and Artificial Intelligence

Jose Ricardo Mondragon Regalado[1]([⊠]) [ID], Alexander Huaman Monteza[1] [ID],
Julio César Montenegro Juárez[1] [ID], Jannier Alberto Montenegro Juárez[1] [ID],
Abelardo Hurtado Villanueva[1] [ID], Nazario Aguirre Baique[2] [ID],
and Mónica Rosario Yon Delgado[2] [ID]

[1] National University of Jaen, Jaen, Peru
jose.mondragon@unj.edu.pe
[2] National Intercultural University of the Amazon, Ucayali, Peru

Abstract. Bring technology closer to improve services for the population from the public perspective, is one of the most important challenges in national and subnational governments, thus, the main objective of the research was to propose the "face to face" intervention model to optimize citizen security services.at different levels of government basing in information systems on the cloud and artificial intelligence. The purpose of the model called "Face to face" is to optimize and make the public services offered by governments more efficient, since there is currently a wave of citizen insecurity affecting the population as a whole. The "Face to face" model was developed by an interdisciplinary team of professionals based on various pragmatic and theoretical studies as background. It is concluded that the model is adequate to optimize citizen security services through information systems in the cloud with facial biometric recognition supported by artificial intelligence and citizen participation; it is also a model that can be adaptable and replicable at any level of government; it is established that prior to its implementation the legal basis must be regulated as appropriate.

Keywords: Citizen Security · Face to face · Artificial intelligence in the cloud

1 Introduction

Facial recognition is a fundamental aspect to deal with citizen insecurity because it makes it possible to identify or confirm the identity of a person who hascommitted a crime. The development of technology makes it possible to accurately determine a person, this is achieved through the application of a neural network for physiognomic recognition which allows obtaining their characteristics (Imoh et al. 2023).

In research conducted by Jaber et al. (2022) specify that with technological progress it is possible to identify a person through facial recognition, but to achieve this purpose they maintain that said computers must have high precision recognition systems, as well as automatic encoders must be connected to a communication sys-tem for the

C. Stephanidis et al. (Eds.): HCII 2023, CCIS 1835, pp. 232–238, 2023.
https://doi.org/10.1007/978-3-031-36001-5_30

recognition of the individual, so this challenge must be assumed to achieve the success and effectiveness of this method, and thus examine extensive and complex data promptly and accurately.

For Srivastav and Singh (2022), security problems in crowded public places such as squares, airports, shopping and entertainment centers can be guarded with security systems supported by facial recognition. This allows citizens to feel that the State or its authorities protect this public good that implies effectively safeguarding people's rights, especially the right to life.

Crime observatories highlight the high percentage of criminal activity in various countries around the world. Currently, electronic entertainment pages, surveillance and recognition of people who commit criminal acts are proof of the constant development of technology and its various applications. Thus, public and private banking entities have been protected with the innovation of devices that facilitate the identification of the subject and thus activate security alarms to intervene with agility and efficiency and avoid human and material losses (Sowmeya and Karthik 2022).

The human factor in handling or processing data on facial recognition systems is decisive because it may happen that computer operators do not have the capacity to correct system errors and in other circumstances they annul many correct decisions. Reason for which, it is determined that it depends on the supervision carried out by the computerized managers to achieve proper functioning and for the systems to show effectiveness in the processing of results. In addition, in forensic matters, automated facial recognition makes it possible to make the right decisions, which contribute to determining criminal investigations (Carragher and Hancock 2022).

The various techniques allow the indubitable recognition of the people who are targeted in an investigation supported by technology. In this way, physiognomic identification can be achieved using high-performance algorithms with interactivity in the Cloud, which facilitates the respective analysis and comparison with databases based on the images, considering the linking and progression of the images registered (Domínguez and Austria 2019).

Technological innovation makes it easier to store this data in the cloud, which is automatically updated and easily accessible to doctors (Debnath et al. 2023). If information systems based on artificial intelligence in the cloudthey come contributing in the health sector; then it would be feasible to implement them in citizen security.

The incorporation of the quantum approach in research and technology contributes rapidly to the development of research studies and the innovation of mechanical and electronic systems.The new approaches to quantum-supported technologies will revolutionize knowledge and technology, to such an extent that human beings will experience the high-impact effect in their lives when their faculties observe new discoveries in computing, communication, and machine learning quantum, and that the speed of the data and the protection for humanity are developed with high percentiles or efficiency indicators (Fadli and Rawal 2023).

For Verjel and Guerrero (2022) argues that the technologies offered by Smart Cities have advantages by improving their performance and making them more livable and receptive, they feel safe and confident when interacting with the smart technologies that surround them.

In this century (XXI) the digital transformation has changed the lifestyle and way of working of people, this due to the presence of the Internet of Things (IoC), which with cyber-physical systems and integrated computing makes it possible to link with almost everything that man does; In addition, it allows said integration with the required information to be stored in the cloud to be accessed in real time in an instant and from anywhere the person is. Thus, the Internet of Things offers various advantages and opportunities for public and private entities, as well as for people who decide to undertake taking advantage of technology (Rukmony and Gnanamony 2023).

Although it is true, technology through intelligent systems facilitates the processes thatperform humans; however, the risks that these may generate in the programming and configuration of the database must be taken into account,besides in the treatment ofinformation (Su et al. 2023).

From what was stated above, it is considered that technological innovation can be used as a fundamental axis in public management and its application is one of the most important challenges in national and subnational governments because it allows optimizing services for the population from the public perspective. Faced with this, this investigative study arises to contribute to citizen security because the population has to develop in a safe and peaceful coexistence, this issue must be predominant on the agenda of the authorities of the three levels of government in the different countries.

Faced with this context, the following question arises: ¿Does the implementation of the "Face to face" Citizen Security Model based on information systems and artificial intelligence in the cloud contribute to reducing the insecurity rates of the population?

The study is important because it will allow the authorities to have a viable model for its implementation, it also empowers citizen participation in order to exercise better control of citizen security and thus reduce the insecurity rate that currently exists in cities. The incorporation of information systems in the cloud or intelligent systems with facial recognition at the service of citizen security will allow interoperability between the National Police, Serenazgo and the Judiciary will generate a positive impact on the quality of life of the population.

The main objective of the research was to propose the "Face to face" intervention model to optimize citizen security services.at different levels of government basing in information systems on the cloud and artificial intelligence.

2 Methodology

The study is of a propositive descriptive level, of a design notexperimental its purpose was to propose a model based on information systemson the cloud and artificial intelligence that optimizes citizen security services, was addressed with the participation of an interdisciplinary team supported by theoretical and pragmatic background.

3   Modelo "Face to Face"

See (Fig. 1).

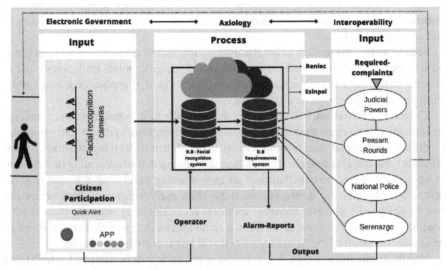

Fig. 1. "Face to face" model scheme citizen security based on information systems in the cloud and artificial intelligence.

4   Model Approach

The model designed when implemented contributes to forming a smart city through the use of information systems in the cloud and artificial intelligence, leaning of the most sophisticated technology in video surveillance cameras in facial recognition and data storage in the cloud; the cooperation of citizen participation will be fundamental and morestill the interoperability of all State agencies in charge of controlling order and administering justice they will play a leading role in the model.

5   Model Intervention Method

In the model there is no mention of brands or models, however for its implementation expert criteria are needed to choose the best technological and human resources to obtain good performance and above all to allow the achievement of the objective of the model. The model has defined two input processes:

First entry, consists of generating registry accesses to the database of the agencies in charge of the control and administration of justice, including the Judiciary, Peasant rounds, National Police and Serenazgo.

In these institutions, the complete registration must be carried out, where the most important would be the facial biometric information, as well as the Biometric registration of Fingerprints, among others. ¿Of who? Well, in this database, information must be cross-referenced and any person who has a requisition or proven complaints for crimes and even for misdemeanors or suspicions of serious crimes must be registered for subsequent intervention. The database has the capacity to support text and numeric data as well as image and video.

Second entry, the system saves the information that is taken in real time in video format from the high-tech cameras installed in the strategic points of the cities and at the same time it is stored in the database that is in the cloud, if applicable it also has the ability to capture images at a certain time.

Citizen Participation, it is considered the main ally of governments to combat citizen insecurity, in this case the model proposes to implement two systems: Early warning, it is the mechanism that must be implemented in agreement with all businessmen, microbusinesses and entrepreneurs in the city, thus demanding that when issuing or renewing the operating license, the installation of an early warning point is an essential requirement to be able to obtain it. In a second stage, these early warning systems or devices must be designed for public transport services. When the early warning point is activated, it will not only activate an alarm in a certain sector, but will also emit a signal to the monitoring point of the technologies that will be properly implemented.

Mobile application (App), A free access application will be designed, which must be activated to give an imminent danger signal of any kind to the central operator in real time, this must capture the coordinates and issue immediate attention signals to the rapid intervention teams such as the National Police, Judicial Power, Serenazgo or peasant rounds. This application must have a traffic light where the red color communicates a criminal act; the color yellow, fires and disasters; the color pink, violence against women; the orange color, traffic accident and the green color, other cases of rapid attention.

6 The Process

First case, the system captures facial recognition data and performs a real-time comparison with the data registered in the requisition database, the comparison will be made by biometric procedures, either by video or by image. This method will be safe as long as the subjects have been previously identified. What will happen to those who have not been previously identified and registered? For this purpose, a second case has been planned which is described below.

Second case, the model is projected for new individuals who join the criminal activity, who are not registered in the database. For this, the early warning or rapid alert points will be used, as well as the App, where once activated, the central processing unit will proceed to carry out a review of the videos already obtained from the cameras in the area and will proceed to take the face of the suspects and will be stored in the required database as unidentified to later cross-reference information with Reniec, it will also serve asantecedent so that the next time it is captured by the cameras, the alert is given for its location and intervention.

7 Output

Once the information is processed, the system will issue alarms to the centrals and institutions in real time, including the geolocation where the incident occurs. These can be: Early alert issued by the citizen from any point of the city when he is a victim of insecurity or also the alert from the mobile device through the App.

In addition, the departures will also be given in real time when the facial recognition systemfind coincidences with the data that have been registered in the database ofrequirements.

The alarms will be reported to the power plants as well as to the Judiciary, peasant rounds, Serenazgo and the National Police, in addition it will issue reportsin between Other data according to the requirements of the pertinent institutions. The alarms will allow authorities to take immediate action to captureIn fraganti to any subject that threatens the peace and tranquility of the citizenry.

As main axis:

Interoperability, consists of maintaining open access to the databases in the cloud, Reniec and Esinpol, likewise it will also be possible to have access to the central database of government requisitions from the central base of peasant rounds, serenazgo,Police National and Judiciary. The information that is shared will be classified data that has the same purpose and objective of the model.

Government Electronic leads to a change in the government paradigm for the control of citizen security, taking advantage of information and communication technologies -ICT that allow efficient management of economic, human and technological resources.Axiology, Those responsible must act under solid principles and values in all areas that are part of the cycle of the new proposed model.

8 Conclusions

It is concluded that the model is adequate to optimize citizen security services through information systems in the cloud with facial biometric recognition supported by artificial intelligence and citizen participation.

The "Face to face" model can be adaptable and replicable at any level of government; it is established that prior to its implementation the legal basis must be regulated as appropriate.

References

Carragher, D., Hancock, P.: Simulated automated facial recognition systems as decision-aids in forensic face matching tasks. J. Exp. Psychol. Gener. (2022). https://doi.org/10.1037/xge000 1310

Debnath, P., Mahmud, A., Hossain, A., Rahman, S.: Design and application of IOT-based real-time patient telemonitoring system using biomedical sensor network. SN Comput. Sci. 4(2) (2023). https://doi.org/10.1007/s42979-022-01516-z

Domínguez, R., Austria,C.: Domínguez-Ramírez, O.A., Austria-Cornejo, A.: Sistema de Reconocimiento de Patrones de Rostros En La Nube 7(13), 54–61 (2019). https://doi.org/10.29057/icbi.v7i13.3540

Fadli, S., Rawal, B.: Quantum bionic advantage on near-term cloud ecosystem. Optik **272** (2023). https://doi.org/10.1016/j.ijleo.2022.170295

Imoh, N., Vajjhala, N., Rakshit, S.: Experimental face recognition using applied deep learning approaches to find missing persons (B. S., K. D.K., M. A.K., P. D., B. D. (eds.); vol. 404, pp. 3–11 (2023). Springer Science and Business Media Deutschland GmbH. https://doi.org/10.1007/978-981-19-0105-8_1

Jaber, A., Muniyandi, R., Usman, O., Singh, H.: A hybrid method of enhancing accuracy of facial recognition system using gabor filter and stacked sparse autoencoders deep neural network. Appl. Sci. (Switzerland) **12**(21) (2022). https://doi.org/10.3390/app122111052

Rukmony, S., Gnanamony, S.: Rough set method-cloud internet of things: a two-degree verification scheme for security in cloud-internet of things. Int. J. Electr. Comput. Eng. **13**(2), 2233–2239 (2023). https://doi.org/10.11591/ijece.v13i2.pp2233-2239

Sowmeya, V., Karthik, R.: Face recognition system for criminal identification using deep metric learning (R. M., K. K., & G. R. (eds.); vol. 2393). American Institute of Physics Inc (2022). https://doi.org/10.1063/5.0074484

Srivastav, G., Singh, R.: Facial recognition based workplace security system using LBPH algorithm (G. M., G. B., K. R., & D. A. (eds.); vol. 2555. American Institute of Physics Inc (2022). https://doi.org/10.1063/5.0124629

Su, X., An, L., Cheng, Z., Weng, Y.: Cloud–edge collaboration-based bi-level optimal scheduling for intelligent healthcare systems. Futur. Gener. Comput. Syst. **141**, 28–39 (2023). https://doi.org/10.1016/j.future.2022.11.005

Verjel, C., Guerrero, B.: Ciudad Inteligente: mejoramiento de la seguridad ciudadana a través del uso de nuevas tecnologías (2022)

Electronic Catalog: Developing Micro Small and Medium Enterprises Through Government Procurement

Heru Nurprismawan[1]([✉]), Achmad Nurmandi[2], Misran[1], and Dimas Subekti[1]

[1] Department of Government Affairs and Administration, Universitas Muhammadiyah Yogyakarta, Yogyakarta, Indonesia
heru.n.psc22@mail.umy.ac.id

[2] Department of Government Affairs and Administration, Jusuf Kalla School of Government, Universitas Muhammadiyah Yogyakarta, Yogyakarta, Indonesia
nurmandi_achmad@umy.ac.id

Abstract. This paper aims to determine the relationship between the use of electronic catalogs on the development of Micro Small and Medium Enterprises (MSMEs), particularly in relation to the procurement of government goods and services. Furthermore, this paper also aims to determine the correlation between the use of electronic catalogs on economic growth. The study in this paper is built with a qualitative approach, using reference data sources from government information media and various mass media and state media news articles on related topics. Based on data analysis various steps have been taken to strengthen efforts to increase the use of domestic products, including digitizing the MSME market and bringing together MSMEs and their beneficiaries, which in this case is the government itself. The digital market was chosen as a transaction space with the consideration that the potential for the digital economy in Indonesia is enormous, competition is more transparent, and will indirectly accelerate the development of digital infrastructure in Indonesia. Procurement of domestic products through electronic catalogs will massively have an impact on the development of MSMEs, starting from increasing transaction values, and expanding markets, as well as increasing capabilities and knowledge of the use of digital media in promotions and transactions. The improvement and development of MSMEs will ultimately have a positive influence on economic growth, which is triggered by an increase in the number of jobs and an increase in the amount of investment both in the region and nationally.

Keywords: electronic catalog · MSMEs · procurement · economic growth

1 Introduction

The Government of the Republic of Indonesia estimates that in 2022 economic growth will reach 5.2% [1]. This figure has increased compared to conditions in 2021 where Indonesia's economic growth reached 5.02% [2]. Efforts to maintain economic stability set for 2022 are linear with the direction of development policies that have been set, namely focusing on efforts to develop human resources and regional equity, which can drive economic growth through investment and exports. To support this, the development implementation strategy is outlined in national development priorities, one of which is strengthening economic resilience for quality and equitable growth. Strategic steps are directed at supporting the recovery of production activities and increasing added value and productivity by optimizing the linkages between the primary, secondary, and tertiary sectors. In this process, implementation is focused on several sectors, one of which is micro, small, and medium enterprises (MSMEs).

The government is trying to answer the urgency of developing the digitization of MSMEs and cooperatives through a series of strategic steps that have been prepared. Various efforts were made to fulfill the target of digitizing MSMEs and cooperatives by the end of 2024, one of which was by initiating the Proudly Made in Indonesia National Movement by placing MSMEs in the government procurement e-catalog [3].

In 2022, efforts to accelerate the use of domestic products and increase the involvement of MSMEs in the procurement of government goods and services are carried out by bringing together the government as consumers and MSMEs as providers of goods/services in a shopping space called an electronic catalog. The government targets that by 2022 there will be a commitment to spend on domestic products through an electronic catalog worth 400 trillion rupiah, which is carried out by the central government, institutions and regions. Based on calculations by the Central Statistics Agency, the impact of purchasing domestic products worth 400 trillion rupiah will spur economic growth up by 1.67–1.71% [4]. In an effort to widen its usefulness, the electronic catalog which was initially developed at the central level was eventually also built in the area of the local government, which is called the local electronic catalog. With the spread of shopping for domestic products available in local electronic catalogs, it is hoped that there will be a massive economic turnaround in the community.

The shift in the role of the government from regulator and facilitator of MSME development to one of the actors directly involved in economic transactions with MSMEs creates a new study space compared to what has been developed so far. While most studies recommend steps and actions that must be taken by the government with the attributes of the power and policies it has to influence the parties in the efforts to develop MSMEs and cooperatives, this paper focuses more on discussing the government's efforts in managing and utilizing its resources, both human resources., finance and information technology directly in transactions with MSMEs. At this point, the discussion is carried out by looking at the implementation of domestic product shopping through MSMEs in the local electronic catalog space.

Placing the target of national economic growth on the one hand, with the expansion of the role of local catalogs in the regions on the other hand, undoubtedly raises several problems that must be studied and answered. First, the use of information technology in the form of a local electronic catalog requires an explanation of how big is the correlation between the use of technology and the increase in the development of MSMEs? Second, departing from the relationship between the use of information technology in the economic cycle of SMEs, it is necessary to study the correlation between the use of information technology, which in this case is the use of electronic catalogs with national economic growth?

2 Literature Review

2.1 Digitalization of MSMEs Through Electronic Catalogs

The development of information technology is recognized as the main driver of economic growth, social change, strengthening a country's competitiveness, encouraging entrepreneurship and innovation, creating jobs, and so on. (Vekic et al., 2020). In the context of MSME development, there are many MSMEs that have begun to adopt the use of information technology that can increase the efficiency and effectiveness of existing processes. On a broader scale, the use of digital technology can increase overall business performance [5] as well as being able to improve the ability of MSMEs in obtaining or conveying information from and for the market [6].

Utilization of digital technology will have an impact on creating opportunities and challenges at the same time [7]. Many opportunities that arise as well as challenges faced depend on the extent to which MSMEs are able to access and use digital devices [8]. In addition, the conditions that are more dominant between opportunities and challenges are influenced by the overall constraints and problems faced, including the ability of the workforce to adapt to business processes that use various applications, and the lack of initiative to improve workforce capabilities. Do not forget that the most important influence is the limited technological infrastructure for MSMEs which is still quite high [9]. Departing from this, the implementation of digitalization originating from MSME innovation requires support from the government and related parties in an effort to realize progress indicators that have not been achieved by the MSMEs themselves [9].

One form of the Indonesian government's efforts in utilizing technology as a medium for developing MSMEs is the use of electronic catalogs in the use of government goods and services. Electronic catalogs as part of the electronic trading process are believed to be able to open up new markets (Hamad et al., 2018). The electronic catalog is one part of the e-marketplace in the process of procuring goods and services, namely an electronic market that is provided to meet the needs of government goods and services. (LKPP, 2018). With diverse market coverage and characteristics, electronic catalogs are distinguished into several types, namely national, sectoral and local electronic catalogs. National electronic catalogs are compiled and managed by the Government Goods/Services Procurement Policy Institute, sectoral electronic catalogs containing information on general goods/services and innovations and managed by ministries/agencies, and local electronic catalogs managed by regional governments.With diverse market coverage and characteristics, electronic catalogs are divided into several types, namely national, sectoral and local electronic catalogs. National electronic catalogs are compiled and managed by the Government Goods/Services Procurement Policy Institute, sectoral electronic catalogs containing information on general goods/services and innovations and managed by ministries/agencies, and local electronic catalogs managed by local governments.

2.2 MSME Development Policy

The challenge of digitizing MSMEs and cooperatives becomes a necessity if we look at the findings of previous studies. Rahmi [10] in a study in West Sumatra explained that mastery of digital technology is one of the external obstacles that must be faced in efforts to develop MSMEs, in addition to other factors such as market conditions after the COVID-19 pandemic and low market absorption. Mastery of information technology will affect business with various kinds of interventions, both in terms of increasing competitive advantage through the development of new products, as stated by Iqbal [11], or through other forms of marketing as the results of a study by Sriyono [12].

MSMEs have an important role in the massive economic development of a country and provide impetus for efforts to reduce poverty [13]. This important role is manifested in the form of increasing productivity, creating job opportunities and reducing inequality in society [14]. In addition to this, the role of MSMEs is also more obvious when one looks at the innovations made and opens up business opportunities for the economic development of a country. (Amoah et al., 2022). These innovations will provide a competitive advantage in doing business, because innovation is a new method, process and technology (Uengpaiboonkit, 2021).

Outside the context of strengthening internally, the development of digitalization of MSMEs also has a close correlation with efforts to establish and expand business networks. Network in this case is a broad concept that describes various types of relationships between two or more businesses that are interconnected, both economically and individually. (Guimarães et al., 2021). The network in this case can be one of the means to overcome the obstacles that are owned by MSMEs, especially related to market availability (Jeong et al., 2019). Networks involve different structures, and therefore can be divided into several classifications (Oparaocha, 2015). The classification includes business networks, social networks and institutional networks. The business network consists of competitors, suppliers and consumers. The social network consists of business partners, workers and family. In the last group, institutional networks include the government, research institutes and other development institutions.

For most opinions, the expansion of international markets is one of the answers for how MSMEs can continue to exist amidst various obstacles (Costa et al., 2017). However, the process should be built on the strength of the domestic market. This is based on the reality that one of the sources of the rapid development of MSMEs today is acknowledged to be the source of the high demand for domestic products (Tshiaba et al., 2021). In this process, the government as part of the MSME business network plays an important role to be involved.

3   Method

This paper was prepared using a qualitative approach, namely a case study on the implementation of the policy of using electronic catalogs in an effort to develop MSMEs and increase domestic products. In the process, this paper examines the existing related variables, namely local catalogs, MSMEs, the use of domestic products and economic growth.

In order to obtain comprehensive data, this paper processes data and information sourced from national media and the government's official website. Several media articles that became the source of discussion were Antara, Kompas, and Liputan.6, which discussed various predetermined variables. To obtain accurate data, the source of the data taken also considers the representation of the relevant parties in the information from the data collected. In the context of this paper, the relevant parties include the government, starting from the President of the Republic of Indonesia, relevant ministries and institutions. Meanwhile, other parties whose information was obtained were about the opinions of the House of Representatives, state-owned enterprises, and the private sector. Through a study of data, information and opinions from related parties, it is hoped that it can support efforts to obtain balanced conclusions and analysis.

Data collection as the first step in the process of reviewing this paper begins with identifying news and information from predetermined news sources, namely news related to the policy of using electronic catalogs in the process of procurement of government goods and services. In addition, other related data collected is about the proud affirmation action policy made by Indonesia, which includes the correlation between local electronic catalogs, empowerment of MSMEs, increasing domestic products and economic growth. In the last series of data analysis processes, in order to obtain answers to research questions, analysis was carried out through data processing software, namely NVivo 12Plus. The analysis is done by doing matrix coding, crosstab and project map analysis.

4 Result and Discussion

The digitization of MSME performance is a process that has developed intensively in recent years. Besides being supported by the rapid development of information technology, the changing character of the market is also one of the reasons for the importance of digitizing the performance of MSMEs. The opportunity to see MSME products freely, knowledge of the prices offered and the ease of transaction processing are the main considerations that consumers pay attention to. With such wide-open potentials and opportunities, the government is ultimately also actively involved, namely by carrying out government procurement of goods and services through an electronic catalog platform. In the process, state and local budgets are spent as much as possible through local catalogs. The value of transparency and efforts to minimize the risk of violating regulations are the spirit of the policy. Electronic recording of transaction processes in this case is believed to be much better than the administrative process carried out when using conventional procurement methods.

By the end of October 2022, 11,619 providers of goods and services had entered the local catalog system developed by the Government Goods/Services Procurement Policy Institute. Providers from the MSME sector dominate the market in electronic catalogs. No less than 77% or 8,915 existing providers come from MSMEs, while the remaining 23% or 2,704 non MSMEs.

The high number of MSMEs that have opened markets in electronic catalogs will certainly provide optimism for the optimal pace of economic growth. Nevertheless, the electronic catalog market still raises a critical note if we look at the data on the number of products produced by MSMEs. A total of 1,448,949 goods/services or 69% of goods/services in the electronic catalog are dominated by goods originating from non-SMEs, and on the contrary, the number of MSMEs in the large electronic catalog is not matched by the number of products they carry, which is only 31% of the total. Items in the electronic catalog.

Although most of the goods come from non-SMEs, it is believed that this does not reduce the potential for national economic movements, especially related to the use of domestic products. The latest data shows that no less than 1,936,414 products, or 92% of the products displayed in the electronic catalog are local products, while the remaining 168,778 products or 8% are imported products.

Currently, of the 2,105,192 products that have been published in the government's electronic catalog, 1,361,548 products have been published in the national catalog, 235,905 products have been displayed in sectoral catalogs and 498,946 others have been displayed in local catalogs.

Medical facilities and infrastructure are the commodities with the highest transaction value, reaching 225 billion rupiah. Physical infrastructure, especially roads, became the commodity with the next largest transaction value, followed by motorized vehicles, office supplies, medicines and various other government needs. These transactions are not only through the national catalog market, but also sectors and local catalogs.

5 Conclusion

The use of electronic catalogs as a medium for transactions between the government and the market, which in this case is MSMEs, is not a policy that only follows the times. This policy is based on a series of thoughts and studies, which are based on the consideration of the extent to which electronic catalog media is able to optimally bring together the government as a consumer and MSMEs as producers. The study includes how big the government's spending potential is, and how prepared MSMEs are in responding to transactions through digital media such as electronic catalogs. In addition, it is also based on the calculation of how large the transaction will be able to trigger economic growth.

Based on the data analysis carried out, the government's high demand for transactions through electronic catalogs was responded to by the high number of MSMEs participating as providers. The high number of MSMEs joining the local electronic catalog provides many alternatives for government agencies to choose MSME providers as shopping partners. The availability of local electronic catalog markets, sectoral electronic catalogs and local electronic catalogs in this case also contributes to the wide variety of markets according to the needs of each government agency. In this process, optimizing spending by government agencies through electronic catalogs is believed to be able to increase market expansion and increase the value of MSME transactions.

Strengthening MSMEs through local electronic catalogs will continue to increase in quality and quantity according to the current flow, however, there are still several critical points to pay attention to in its development. First, the high number of MSME providers is inversely proportional to the low number of MSME products that appear in electronic catalogs. This indicates that most MSMEs tend to act only as sellers of imported goods, instead of being producers of local goods. Although it is believed that this is based on certain business considerations, efforts to produce domestic goods will become a reinforcement for MSMEs when faced with an uncertain global situation. Second, if we pay attention to the types of goods based on the level of domestic components, there are still local goods that do not yet have a calculated value for the level of domestic components. In line with efforts to increase the number of local goods, an increase in the level of domestic components will open up opportunities for expansion of the domestic market which, based on the current policy, continue to be encouraged to choose domestically produced goods.

References

1. Kemenkeu, "Informasi APBN 2022 Melanjutkan Dukungan Pemulihan Ekonomi dan Reformasi Struktural," *Kementeri. Keuang. Direktorat Jenderal Anggar.*, no. 4, pp. 1–55, 2022

2. BPS, "Pertumbuhan Ekonomi Indonesia 2021, www.bps.go.id, no. 13, p. 12 (2022)

3. Kementrian Perekonomian, "Optimalisasi Produktivitas UMKM melalui Go-Digital dan Go-Legal (2022)

4. Sekretariat Kabinet, "Dongkrak Pertumbuhan Ekonomi, Pemerintah Dorong Peningkatan Penggunaan Produk Lokal (2022)

5. Cenamor, J., Parida, V., Wincent, J.: How entrepreneurial SMEs compete through digital platforms: the roles of digital platform capability, network capability and ambidexterity. J. Bus. Res. **100**, 196–206 (2019). https://doi.org/10.1016/j.jbusres.2019.03.035

6. Benitez, J., Castillo, A., Llorens, J., Braojos, J.: IT-enabled knowledge ambidexterity and innovation performance in small U.S. firms: the moderator role of social media capability. Inf. Manag. **55**(1), 131–143 (2018). https://doi.org/10.1016/j.im.2017.09.004

7. Shome, S., Suri, D.: Is India ready for 'digital disruption. IRA-Int. J. Manag. Soc. Sci. **4**(2), 376 (2016). (ISSN 2455–2267). https://doi.org/10.21013/jmss.v3.n2.p9

8. Klein, V.B., Todesco, J.L.: COVID-19 crisis and SMEs responses: the role of digital transformation. Knowl. Process. Manag. **28**(2), 117–133 (2021). https://doi.org/10.1002/kpm.1660

9. Kilay, A.L., Simamora, B.H., Putra, D.P.: The Influence of e-payment and e-commerce services on supply chain performance: implications of open innovation and solutions for the digitalization of micro, small, and medium enterprises (MSMEs) in Indonesia. J. Open Innov. Technol. Mark. Complex. **8**(3), 119 (2022). https://doi.org/10.3390/joitmc8030119

10. Rahmi, E., Yuzaria, D.: The government support model on the development of smes in West Sumatera Province. Indonesia. IOP Conf. Ser. Earth Environ. Sci. **757**(1), 1–9 (2021). https://doi.org/10.1088/1755-1315/757/1/012005

11. Iqbal, M., Suzianti, A.: New product development process design for small and medium enterprises: a systematic literature review from the perspective of open innovation. J. Open Innov. Technol. Mark. Complex. **7**(2) (2021). https://doi.org/10.3390/joitmc7020153

12. Sriyono, S.B., Proyogi, B.: Acceleration of performance recovery and competitiveness through non-banking financing in SMEs based on green economy: impact of Covid-19 pandemic. J. Innov. Entrep. **10**(1) (2021). https://doi.org/10.1186/s13731-021-00166-4

13. Amoah, J., Belas, J., Dziwornu, R., Khan, K.A.: Enhancing SME contribution to economic development: a perspective from an emerging economy. J. Int. Stud. **15**(2), 63–76 (2022). https://doi.org/10.14254/2071-8330.2022/15-2/5

14. Niyi Anifowose, O., Ghasemi, M., Olaleye, B.R.: Total quality management and small and medium-sized enterprises' (SMEs) performance: mediating role of innovation speed. Sustain. **14**(14) (2022). https://doi.org/10.3390/su14148719

Innovation of Government's Policy for Bridging the Digital Divide
(Case Study in Malaysia and India)

Windhi Gita Prabawa[1]([⊠]), Achmad Nurmandi[2], Misran[1], and Dimas Subekti[1]

[1] Department of Government Affairs and Administration, Universitas Muhammadiyah Yogyakarta, Yogyakarta, Indonesia
windhi.gita.psc22@mail.umy.ac.id
[2] Department of Government Affairs and Administration, Jusuf Kalla School of Government, Universitas Muhammadiyah Yogyakarta, Yogyakarta, Indonesia
nurmandi_achmad@umy.ac.id

Abstract. This study aims to analyze the Innovation of Malaysian and Indian government policy for bridging the digital divide. The researcher used a qualitative descriptive approach. Data source from the official websites of Malaysia and India, news, other related documents and processed using the NVivo 12 Plus software. Researchers used Van Dijk's theory of Digital Divide Phase. The indicators are Digital Infrastructure, Digital Skill, Digital Usage. The findings of this study indicate that there are differences in Malaysian and Indian policies in reducing the digital divide. Digital infrastructure policy in Malaysia got the highest percentage reaching 40%. The government has intensified efforts to provide broadband and faster internet. The percentage of Digital Skill and Digital Usage is 30% each, through ICT training, digital literacy curriculum and promoting E-commerce and E-wallet to increase Digital Usage. Indian Government also taking more efforts in improving digital infrastructure with a percentage of 38.89% through the development of broadband and cheaper smartphone costs. India also focuses on Digital Skills with a percentage of 33.33% through training and online learning platforms. The lowest percentage is Digital Used around 27.78% through electronic service policies. Malaysian innovation policy is having an impact on ICT knowledge capabilities and more people used e-government service. While the impact has not been felt significantly in India, many people have not participated in training program and have not used the e-services provided by the government.

Keywords: Innovation policy · Digital divide · Malaysia · India

1 Introduction

Information and communication technology has increased connectivity and become an important part of today's life [1, 2]. The United Nations recognizes ICT as a huge potential for accelerating human progress and achieving sustainable development goals [3]. ICT is widely recognized as a tool to achieve development, especially social development and economic growth [4]. However, at the same time it has contributed to widening the digital divide in developing countries.

C. Stephanidis et al. (Eds.): HCII 2023, CCIS 1835, pp. 246–253, 2023.
https://doi.org/10.1007/978-3-031-36001-5_32

Developing countries such as India experience significant gaps in ensuring all segments of the population have access to ICT. In 2022 India is recorded as the population with the largest population not connected to the internet with more than 751 million people. Interestingly, India is the second largest online market in the world after China but the country's internet penetration is below the world average around 47% [5]. The National Sample Survey conducted between July 2018 and June 2019 showed 44% of households in urban India are connected to the internet compared to 16.9% of households in rural areas [6].

On the other hand, Malaysia which is a developing country like India, but Internet access in Malaysia is much more successful. As stated from the report, Malaysia's internet penetration was 89.6% of total population in early 2022. That internet users in Malaysia increased by 365 thousand (+1.3%) between 2021 and 2022 [7]. Malaysia is also a mobile-first country, with 96.4% of Malaysian internet users using smartphones to access the internet. Considerably this numbers are not critically low when compared to India.

India is left behind compared to Malaysia because India's population is much larger than Malaysia. The Benefits can be got very easily from any policy framework because needs to be done for smaller number of people. The majority of India's population also lives in rural areas, and infrastructure facilities are easily accessible in large cities [8]. Lack of infrastructure in rural areas is a major problem of the digital divide [9].

Seeing that there are still many ICT problems, the United Nations is fully committed to turning the digital divide into an opportunity that can be accessed by everyone [10]. Thus requires all countries make various efforts to bridge the digital divide. Certain countries have made it as a government policy, Including Malaysia and India. The government implements relevant policy innovations according to the conditions of the country [11].

Therefore, this research analyzes how the governments of Malaysia and India bridge the digital divide. There are several reasons why this paper became important. First, with modernization and globalization, infrastructure and technology are important, and with good infrastructure and technology, governments will be able to communicate in an appropriate way. Hence, the governments need to bridging the digital divide. The Indian government can also learn from the policies of the Malaysian government because Malaysia is considered quite successful in bridging the digital divide. Second, this problem is interesting to analyze because the policies taken by the government to bridge the digital divide are very diverse. Most policy makers believe digital divide can be reduced by formulating policies that can expand internet coverage [12]. Mohammad et al. emphasized digital education as the main focus for reducing the digital divide [13]. The proper digital literacy will provide them with better opportunities.

2   Literature Review

2.1   Digital Divide

At the beginning, digital divide only focused on ownership and access to information and communication technology. However, there is a debate that ownership of ICT devices is no longer enough to describe the current reality in describing the digital divide [14]. Van

Dijk explains inequality of ownership as the first stage of the Digital Divide Phase and creates a new concept called the "Digital Divide Phase" [15]. First level digital divide explains the gap in ownership and digital infrastructure facilities. Digital Infrastructure in the form of mobile phones, laptop, computers and other hardware and software. Supporting facilities, such as electricity infrastructure, internet, free wifi coverage. The focus on the digital divide has shifted from the physical access gap to digital skills. This stage is the second level of the digital divide, divided into two aspects. The first aspect involves basic Digital Skills and the second aspect is in terms of Digital Used. Aspects of Digital Used are more focused on Internet of Things (IoT) in various activities. The third level Digital Divide is the effect or outcomes of digital use in various aspects.

2.2 Policy Innovation Challenge

Digital divide policy innovation faces many challenges. Most of the community participates in the implementation of government programs, but there are still community who are not involved [16, 17]. Therefore, collaboration from various stakeholders is needed. Even though the government plays a major role in bridging this gap, based on the UN declaration, the Government, the private sector, the community, development agencies such as the United Nations are responsible for ensuring society has connectivity to ICT. The Other problems, same as the implementation of other policy innovations, all innovations carried out in developing infrastructure, providing programs or ICT Education require a lot of funding.

3   Method

This study uses a qualitative descriptive research method to describe Malaysian and Indian Government policy for bridging the digital divide. Data sources were obtained from the official websites of the two countries namely Malaysia and India, news, other related documents. Data collection techniques used literature studies then analyzed using Q-DAS (Qualitative Data Analysis Software) (Nvivo 12 plus). The data was obtained using the Ncapture feature on Nvivo 12 plus with Web Chrome to capture web content in the form of website, news and other related document The data obtained were then processed with several features namely Croostab, Crosstab Query, and Mind Map Analysis. The Crosstab feature automatically calculates and analysis the variables, The Crosstab Query feature is also used for automatic calculations between all data related to the digital divide policy in two countries. A Mind Map is a diagram for representing words or concepts.

4   Result and Discussion

Malaysian and Indian government has different policies in reducing the digital divide. This difference can be seen from the picture below.

Figure 1 shows that the two countries are taking significant steps in Digital Infrastructure, but there are differences in the Digital Skill and Digital Usage indicators. The

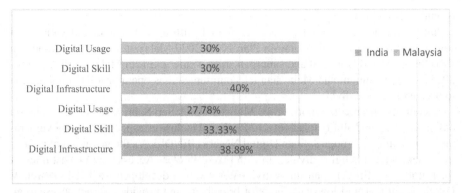

Fig. 1. Comparison Digital Divide Policy. Source: Processed by researchers using Nvivo12plus

Malaysian government has the same percentage in Digital Skills and Digital Usage, which means Malaysia also has a priority on increasing Digital Skills and Increasing Digital Usage. Meanwhile, India focuses more on increasing Digital Skills compared to Digital Usage. This is due to Indian geographic location and many papulation who are not connected to the Internet, Indian government prioritizes infrastructure and skills development [18].

In the discussion below, the differences policies between two countries will be explained further based on Van Dijk's Digital Divide Phase theory, namely Digital Infrastructure, Digital Skills and Digital Usage (Fig. 2).

4.1 Digital Infrastructure

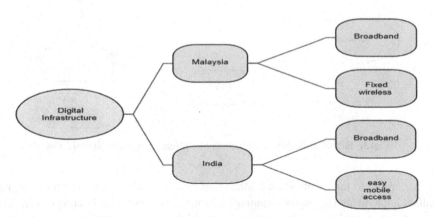

Fig. 2. Digital Infrastructure. Source: Processed by researchers using Nvivo12plus

From the digital infrastructure aspect, Malaysia and Indian Governments has their differences priority. The Malaysian government has allocated 3.7 billion for the National Broadband Initiative. The strategy carried out under the National Broadband Initiative by build a Broadband Community Centre, build 873 new telecommunications towers for cellular coverage expansion and Distribution of 1 million Netbooks to underprivileged students, Through the 11th Malaysia Plan 2016–2020 Malaysia established Suburban Broadband (SUBB) for rural and suburban areas. Under the 12th Malaysia Plan (2021–2025), the government and Malaysian telecommunications operator joint collaboration to bridge the digital divide.

According to a recent report, Prime Minister Datuk Seri Sabri Yaakob said Malaysia has the capacity and ability to achieve 100% digital inclusion, especially among vulnerable communities. Through Jalinan Digital Negara (JENDELA), the government intends to further bridge the digital divide gap with Fixed Wireless Access (FWA). Fast Internet for Rural Area (FIRA) is an innovative FWA solution developed by TM Research & Development that will lower the price of broadband and provide internet access to all spectrums of society in Malaysia.

The Indian government is focusing on broadband and easy mobile access. The Bharat Net project is a government innovation to make it easier for rural areas to have intenet access. The government also launched the "India Ka Smartphone or JioPhone" with a relatively low cost of Rs 1500 or around RP. 288,000. In July 2021, Minister of Education Govind Singh Thakur launched telephone donations namely 'Digital Saathi' to provide under-resourced students with smartphones for remote learning (Fig. 3).

4.2 Digital Skill

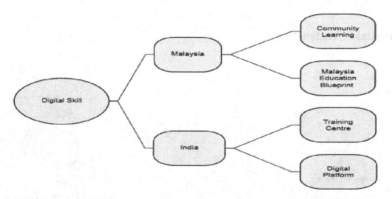

Fig. 3. Digital Skill. Source: Processed by researchers using Nvivo12plus

According to the fig above, the Malaysian government's policy to improve digital skills is implemented through Community Learning in the provided Internet Center. The internet center is a learning program under the Malaysian Communications and Multimedia Commission (MCMC) ICT for rural communities. As of September 2019, a total of 871 Internet centers have been operating nationally in Malaysia and has implications for massive rural communities receiving ICT Training and entrepreneurship empowerment. This training contributes to the ability of the community, especially using social media for online marketing. In addition to focusing on the community, the Malaysia

Education Blueprint Program 2013–2025 aims to close the skills gap among students by providing school-wide ICT training classes. Also, created #mydigitalmaker to teach coding, programming, application development skills to the younger generation.

Meanwhile, the Indian government has established a training center to help rural communities. The community will be introduced to fundamental ICT, after the course, an evaluation test is held to determine whether or not the community can properly use ICT. The National Digital Literacy Mission, and the Pradhan Mantri Gramin Digital Saksharta Abhiyan, were launched to increase digital literacy. The community learns how to use e-mail and even how to use smartphones and computers to access government services. Another major step, the government in collaboration with the Center for Advanced Computing (C-DAC), provides an online library platform. This online library platform offers nearly 1 million free books, including introductory and software development books. These books are open to the public and available in English and Hindi.

Malaysia ranks highly in terms of digital skills as evidenced by the government's efforts to actively integrate digital skills into its curriculum. This highlights that Malaysians are willing, ready and able to embrace the digital economy. Besides that, A Randstad survey found that 70% of Malaysians are actively proactive in learning about technologies [19]. Unlike Malaysians, who believe that digital skills will access up a world of opportunities, community participation in literacy programs in India remains low [20]. The Indian government may require something similar to the Malaysian government in order to integrate digital skills. Most importantly, training is a continuous process that does not end with certification.

4.3 Digital Usage

The Malaysian government's initiatives are focussed toward promoting e-commerce and e wallet. Malaysia has a relatively strong e-commerce sector. Rural communities can use e-commerce to collect and promote agricultural products and other local products, thereby closing the digital divide in technology use. Malaysia's government has also created a national e-commerce strategic roadmap with the goal of improving and expanding e-commerce, developing the e-ecosystem, and strengthening the regulatory environment and policies. The Malaysian government encourages the use of e-wallets by establishing a #MyDigital policy. Community across the country can carry out any official transaction online. Efforts to improve digital financial services and go cashless saw the average Malaysian making 150 e-payment transactions in 2019, compared to just 83 in 2015 [21].

Meanwhile, the Indian government has launched the Digital India program to address the country's lack of digital usage. The Digital India project aims to increase rural communities' participation in using digital devices by making all government information and services available to them. However, the implementation of the Digital India program, which promises universal broadband and e-services, has done little to bridge the digital divide in community, and rural communities are uninterested in government-provided digital services [22]. On the other hand, most Malaysian community use e-government services. As people in Malaysia nowadays have knowledge and skills in IT, they are said to accept and adopt e-government services in their daily lives [23].

5 Conclusions

Malaysian and Indian Policy Innovations in bridging the digital divide has different priorities and different strategy. Malaysia has the highest percentage of 40% in digital infrastructure policies. Steps taken by build broadband throughout the country and fixed wireless. In order to increase Digital Skills and Digital Usage, both of which have a 30% percentage, the government empowers the community through community learning, and offers ICT training classes in accordance with the Malaysia Education Blueprint 2013–2025. To increase Digital Usage are carried out through the use of e-commerce and e-wallets. The impact shows that more Malaysian people know how to use ICT. In contrast, the Indian government is more focused on infrastructure development as seen from the percentage of 38.89%, followed by digital skills and the lowest policy on digital usage. Digital Infrastructure policy focus on developing broadband and launching smartphones at low prices for underprivileged community. India's Digital Skill Policy through training programs and e-literacy Platforms and E-Services to increase Digital Usage among rural communities. However, the results are insignificant; there are still Indian community who do not participate in the program, and even fewer members use the E-Service. As a result, still contributing to inequality and the Digital Divide in India. The Indian government may have to learn from Malaysia's successful implementation. To enable such change, underprivileged groups must be motivated to integrate technology into their daily lives and instilled with digital skills.

References

1. Andrew Perrin, S.A.: 7% of Americans don't use the internet. Who are they? (2021). https://doi.org/10.2991/icosaps-18.2018.45
2. Ashitha: Bridging digital divide through e-literacy programme: the case of Akshaya project in Kerala. Int. J. Res. Anal. Rev. **5**(3), 489–492 (2018)
3. Asrani, C.: Spanning the digital divide in India: Barriers to ICT adoption and usage.J. Public Affairs September **2020** (2021). https://doi.org/10.1002/pa.2598
4. Awalluddin, M.A.: Users Acceptance of E-Government System in Sintok. Applying the UTAUT Model, Malaysia (2020)
5. Ayob, N.H., Aziz, M.A., Ayob, N.A.: Bridging the digital divide: innovation policy and implementation in Malaysia.Int. J. Acad. Res. Bus. Soc. Sci. **12**(8). https://doi.org/10.6007/ijarbss/v12-i8/14554
6. Aziz, A.: Digital inclusion challenges in Bangladesh: the case of the National ICT Policy. Contemp. South Asia **28**, 304–319 (2020). https://doi.org/10.1080/09584935.2020.1793912
7. Dijk, J.A.G.M.: Digital divide: impact of access.Int. Encycl. Media Effect. 1–11 (2017). https://doi.org/10.1002/9781118783764.wbieme004
8. Fang, M.L., Canham, S.L., Battersby, L., Sixsmith, J., Wada, M., Sixsmith, A.: Exploring privilege in the digital divide: implications for theory, policy, and practice. Gerontologist **59**(1), E1–E15 (2019). https://doi.org/10.1093/geront/gny037
9. Gong, R.: Digital inclusion: assessing meaningful internet connectivity in Malaysia. Khazanah Research Institute, Discussion (September), pp. 1–37 (2020).www.KRInstitute.org
10. IASToppers. Bridging digital divide in India (2021)
11. Joju, J., Delhi, N.: Digital Kerala: a study of the ICT initiatives in Kerala State. March (2019)
12. KEMP, S.: DIGITAL 2022: MALAYSIA (2022). https://datareportal.com/reports?author=5576cd58e4b0ba7a870b77fc

13. Lazanyuk, I., Modi, S.: Digitalization and Indian economy: patterns and questions. SHS Web Conf. **114**, 01010 (2021). https://doi.org/10.1051/shsconf/202111401010
14. Literary, P., Shairgojri, A.A.: Digital divide in India: future lies in internet. June (2022)
15. Maiti, D., Castellacci, F., Melchior, A.: Digitalisation and development: issues for India and beyond. In Digitalisation and Development: Issues for India and Beyond. Springer, Singapore (2019).https://doi.org/10.1007/978-981-13-9996-1
16. Malaysian Communication and Multimedia Commission. The National Digital Infrastructure Plan (2020).https://www.mcmc.gov.my/skmmgovmy/media/General/pdf/MCMC-MyConvergence_20.pdf
17. Mohammad, S., Yamani, R., Umar, S., Mohd, M. N., Ariffin, M.I.: COVID-19 pandemic and addressing digital divide in Malaysia. J. Inf. Syst. Digit. Techno. **3**(2), 29–49 (2021)
18. Norman, H., Adnan, N.H., Nordin, N., Ally, M., Tsinakos, A.: The educational digital divide for vulnerable students in the pandemic: towards the New Agenda 2030. Sustainability (Switzerland) **14**(16) (2022). https://doi.org/10.3390/su141610332
19. Quaglione, D., Matteucci, N., Furia, D., Marra, A., Pozzi, C.: Are mobile and fixed broadband substitutes or complements? New empirical evidence from Italy and implications for the digital divide policies. Socio-Econ. Plan. Sci. **71**, 100823 (2020)
20. Road, M.A., Jammu, S., Kashmir, I.: Bridging digital divide in India: way forward & challenges. Int. J. Adv. Res. Dev. **2**, 129–136 (2017). www.advancedjournal.com
21. Simon. (2022). *DIGITAL 2022: INDIA*. Datareportal.Com. https://datareportal.com/reports/digital-2022-india
22. Teo, H.: Closing the Digital Divide in Southeast Asia. In: Centre for East and South-East Asian Studies Public Lecture Series "Focus Asia (2021)
23. Thampi, A.M.: An analysis of India's performance with special reference to digital India initiative. Think India J. Digit. Divide India **49**(39), 49–58 (2019)
24. Zende, S.S.: Digitalization in India prospect and challenges. Int. J. Entrepren. **2**, 29–36 (2021)

Digital Government Management Model for the Modernization of Electronic Services in a Municipality. Peru Case

Luis Eden Rojas Palacios[1] , Carmen Graciela Arbulú Pérez Vargas[1] ,
Moises David Reyes Perez[2] , Danicsa Karina Espino Carrasco[3] ,
Jhoselit Lisset Facho Cornejo[4] , Luis Jhonny Dávila Valdera[5] ,
Madeleine Espino Carrasco[4(✉)] , Ana Maria Alvites Gasco[6] ,
and Jefferson Walter Díaz Lazarte[4]

[1] Cesar Vallejo University, Pimentel, Peru
[2] General Studies Academic Unit, Norbert Wiener University Private S.A, Lima, Peru
mdreyesp@ucvvirtual.edu.pe
[3] Señor de Sipan University, Pimentel, Peru
[4] San Martin de Porres University, Pimentel, Peru
[5] Santo Toribio de Mogrovejo Catholic University, Chiclayo, Peru
[6] Particular de Chiclayo University, Pimentel, Peru

Abstract. For which the general objective is: Propose a digital government management model for the modernization of electronic services in a district municipality of Chiclayo; To achieve this objective, it is necessary to develop the specific objectives a) Identify the level of modernization of electronic services in a district municipality of Chiclayo, through the use of a questionnaire; b) develop the methodological and theoretical foundation that supports the digital government management proposal for the modernization of electronic services in a district municipality of Chiclayo; c) design a digital government management model for the modernization of electronic services in a district municipality of Chiclayo; In such a way that the formulated working hypothesis is: If a digital government management model is designed and implemented, then the electronic services of a district municipality of Chiclayo would be modernized by the year 2022. In the results: The level of modernization of electronic services in a district municipality of Chiclayo was determined, according to the opinion of internal and external users, finding that the majority homogeneously distribute their responses of level of satisfaction in low satisfaction in the first place, followed by medium satisfaction, with a small proportion having a high level of satisfaction.

Keywords: Digital government · modernization of electronic services · digital model

C. Stephanidis et al. (Eds.): HCII 2023, CCIS 1835, pp. 254–261, 2023.
https://doi.org/10.1007/978-3-031-36001-5_33

1 Introduction

1.1 Problematic Reality

Modernization is a forceful phenomenon in recent years where many of the organizations and public entities develop a set of technologies related to the digital world, in order to provide better service and attention to users, constituting a robust model of digital government, where at the same time that development increases, so do the implementation problems that must be converted into opportunities to improve services and products (Allauca 2017).

In the history of digital government in Peru, it is worth mentioning the Supreme Decree No. 060-2001-PCM enacted in 2001, which allows the installation of the portal of the Peruvian state, imposing the concept of "single window" through which various procedures, actions, events, services and campaigns that are executed by various public organizations for the community. The ONGEI, within its actions, has come to build specific organizations for the integration, for example, of the different state systems and platforms on the web, thus coming to consider the proposals and bases that allow an improvement in the development of the Peruvian electronic government (Velasquez 2014).

According to its purpose, this work is framed in applied research to solve a tangible situation of local governance such as the condition of electronic government; in addition to keeping a purpose of expanding and building theoretical knowledge, without intending to apply it in a practical way. Due to its nature, it is prospective since it theoretically describes the characteristics of the phenomenon based on the variables digital government and modernization of electronic services, this according to the nature of the research work, which is quantitative, since it collects and analyzes variable data, based on numerical measurement supported by the statistical treatment of the results obtained and the subsequent implementation of conclusions (Carrasco 2007).

Regarding the district municipality under study belonging to the Lambayeque region where the researcher develops the line of work focused on assessing the government and diagnosing it in the digital framework for effectiveness; supporting the implementation of a relevant model of this digital government, as a basis for the change of a public administration to adapt it to current needs.

It is in this sense that the formulated problem is: What would a digital government management model look like for the modernization of electronic services in a district municipality of Chiclayo?

1.2 Literature Review

Electronic Government. E-government is that there is an improvement in ICTs that allow strengthening government services to meet the needs of users, as in this case of the municipal authority, in such a way that trust in the state apparatus is consolidated, which generates a positive perception towards this (Gutiérrez 2020) these improvements have a long-term impact, allowing an adaptation of strategies and procedures on the important attention service in a local government, in a virtual context developing more robust and controlled processes with a prominent commitment to obtain more power-ful results (Sánchez 2009). Electronic management groups a series of actions such as planning, coordinating, monitoring, directing, controlling and obtaining re-sources to execute activities at the administrative level in the virtual modality, with the objective of achieving strategic goals of an Entity.

Based on the theoretical foundations of our proposed theoretical model, it seeks to develop the potential of digital government in an effective and collaborative manner with municipal workers. In this sense, the theoretical approaches regarding electronic administration propose the reformulation of public policies and public management designs, which together with the culture of the new modernity involves linked values and stereotypes (Moriconi 2008).

ICT technologies have allowed establishing a much higher level such as the estab-lishment of networks that allowed working in real time and in a web community, dis-persing the benefits of this new model of digital activity, the government used it in its local instances until the of national scope, which has been an essential condition for the generation of new management models and managers with a computerized vision.

In this sense, it is proposed that public management acquires an onto-epistemological status of being "science" because it presents three fundamental attributes: the first is that it has a body of knowledge acquired based on research related to public administration (Jiménez 2010) which focus on the relationship between public administration - state - society as a fundamental triad; not without preliminary considering the impact on the social responsibility of said administration.

This guarantees the epistemological statute of public management that gives the onto-epistemic framework to the present investigation. The epistemological intention of this paper is to try to rationally build a body of content that supports the relationship of digital government management with continuous improvement to modernize electronic services in a district municipality, the paradigmatic path according to authors such as Hernández (2018) is of a quantitative route, which we could also classify as the positivist paradigm of research.

Lizardo (2018) sought to determine the level of development that digital government has in relation to corruption in Latin America. According to this study, it shows us that despite the great progress of digital government, it is interesting that Latin American countries are not related to the current perception of corruption with respect to other citizens, being an oversight on their part not to reduce the key digital gap to eradicate or reduce corruption, re-linking with the telecommunications infrastructure.

Cáceres (2017) in his work, aimed to define the main similarities and differences of the digital government in Chile in relation to the states that are part of the organization for economic cooperation and development, concluding that the country in question obtained a lower intention in the alternation of digital government public policy propos-als, obtaining setbacks and little interest in the subject. Seeing thus reflected the lack of competitiveness on the subject, causing stagnation in the agencies belonging to the country, since the inadequate management is not providing care to the key citizen in the country. In this way, it delays the impact of the change in the modern state regarding the new economic development activities for the improvement of the organization and function of continuous digital procedures in which the event submits the current functionalist dependency to the Chilean government.

Objectives. Propose a digital government management model for the modernization of electronic services in a district municipality of Chiclayo.

Identify the level of modernization of electronic services in a district municipality of Chiclayo.

Method. In accordance with its purpose, this work is framed in theoretical research to resolve a tangible situation of local governance such as the condition of electronic government; in addition to keeping a purpose of expanding and building theoretical knowledge, without trying to apply it in a practical way. Due to its nature, it is prospective since it theoretically describes the characteristics of the phenomenon hardened in the variables digital government and modernization of electronic services, this, according to the nature of the research work, is quantitative, since it collects and analyzes variable information, based on the numerical measurement supported by the statistical treatment of the results obtained, for the design of sustainable conclusions (Carrasco 2007). The variables have not been intentionally manipulated, it has been limited to observing and describing how they are presented through the diagnosis of the baseline, proposing a model that pays tribute to reality by modifying it for the good of the users of the edile entity.

The population was constituted by 1220 external users belonging to the District Municipality that come monthly from José Leonardo Ortiz and by 260 public servants, who were developing activities during the application of this research process.

2 Results

Propose a Digital Government Management Model for the Modernization of Electronic Services in a District Municipality of Chiclayo. The proposal is important because it structurally contributes to the concept of organized digital government for the municipality, it generates the bases to give it a systemic orientation or approach; this will allow future researchers to constitute a new theory that supports digital government, the characteristic that surpasses a simple algorithm of functions, is the true and main support position. In this sense, the aim is to structurally articulate the components of the model that have been empirically evidenced in order to organize the activities and public management of digital government. This proposal is necessary thanks to its usefulness for the planning of processes inherent to the municipal activities that are developed using electronic services to satisfy users under an efficient provision using the technological infrastructure that is available.

The comparative advantage over other proposals such as Deming's continuous improvement or the "window of opportunity" theories is that the model developed is directly based on empirical observation of the public management process in the digital government of the municipality; the one that starting from reality and reorganizing it is one of the most robust effects of the modeling method; the model is therefore very pertinent as a study response to reality; another comparative advantage is the adequate distribution of the dimensions of the model that has been validated by experts in the specialty; this adjustment is due to an intention to improve based on reality; Another advantage is the empowerment of the servers as they participate in their opinion in the development of this proposal and model. (Reyes et al. 2020).

As a pertinent introduction to the model, it can be indicated that this structure is designed to solve the central problem of this doctoral research, which is to design a digital government management model for the modernization of electronic services in a district municipality of Chiclayo; and in this framework it must be taken into account that in order to develop an adequate public management of the digital government of the municipality under study, a dynamic model that is coherent and systematic is necessary; coherent in the sense that the parts that make it up, which are the personal - social - relational - promotional dimensions, are articulated with each other to provide heuristic effectiveness, it is also systemic because it allows the integration of components in a continuous cyclical system whose direct output is the improvement of the digital government of the municipality under study.

This systemic characteristic allows processes that effectively link the dimensions described above, they all have the same weight and therefore have the same importance, both internal and external activities support the structure in terms of components and the relational and promotional ones give the dynamics., since the interactions of the digital government are interactions between platform users and the promotional links the correct interface that is required to optimize processes in time and in the effectiveness-effectiveness-efficiency triad and thus the process becomes an axis correct sustainable and sustainable that supports the digital government and makes it evolve positively, even more so in these post-pandemic times.

It is in this sense where the systemic articulation of this structure based on 4 dimensions is evidenced as the tangible solution to the initial problem, which provides a re-emergence and support to the digital government of the municipality. The onto-epistemic foundations of consider the philosophical bases of this model that in the first instance starts from the logical positivist paradigm since the premise to be able to assess the effective condition of a digital government are the achievement or performance indicators to satisfy the users, it is that is why a baseline was started by means of an instrumental; and then the dimensional structure that according to the observation of the baseline was the most appropriate to function as an instrument to build the model was outlined.

Table 1. Global level of satisfaction on the modernization of electronic services by internal and external users of the digital government of the municipality, year 2022.

Dimensions	Satisfaction level	Internal		External	
		F	%	F	%
Implementation of administrative structures	High	8	10,7	11	8,5
	Half	12	16,0	21	16,2
	Low	55	73,3	98	75,4
Service planning	High	5	6,7	10	7,7
	Half	20	26,7	33	25,4
	Low	50	66,7	87	66,9
Strengthening and improvement of the service	High	8	10,7	14	10,8
	Half	18	24,0	25	19,2
	Low	49	65,3	91	70,0
Inclusion and digital incorporation of processes	High	14	18,7	22	16,9
	Half	16	21,3	30	23,1
	Low	45	60,0	78	60,0
Digital collaborative work	High	10	13,3	16	12,3
	Half	21	28,0	33	25,4
	Low	44	58,7	81	62,3
Overall satisfaction	High	11	14,7	18	13,8
	Half	19	25,3	35	26,9
	Low	45	60,0	77	59,2

Note. Table 1 Level of satisfaction regarding the dimension "Administrative Procedures and Services (Table 2)"

Table 2. Factors that do not allow the modernization of electronic services in a district municipality of Chiclayo.

Lack of commitment from the workforce and its culture	E-services modernization is often seen solely as a matter of changing technology, but changes in technology are sustained only if people accept and embrace them, therefore new systems must be aligned with the culture of the company. Company, beginning with a clear recognition of the new habits that people will need to adopt
Lack of a service mindset	The traditional approach to technology treats systems as assets that a company owns and operates. A modern approach treats technology as a set of services that the municipality can consume and integrate as needed, without necessarily owning the systems at all
Lack of organization by skills	Efforts need to be broken down, prioritized, and sequenced, or they will be too large and complex to manage. Most IT modernization efforts are organized by project; they are short-lived efforts, framed by conventional enterprise software categories, and budgeted for and delivered through development teams that disband when the project is complete. This leads to a short-term focus that can divert efforts from the most important goal: building the capabilities that create value
Falta de agilidad y atención en el usuario	You should break the modernization roadmap into discrete delivery increments, releasing usable features on a frequent release cycle, so it's better to be incomplete and fast than complete and slow, as long as you get feedback from system users with frequently and let those comments guide you in changing your direction

3   Conclusions

1. The level of modernization of electronic services in a district municipality of Chiclayo was determined, according to the opinion of internal and external users, finding that the majority homogeneously distributes their satisfaction level responses in low satisfaction in the first place, followed by satisfaction average being a small proportion that are with a high level of satisfaction.

2. A theoretical and methodological foundation was developed that supports the digital government management proposal for the modernization of electronic services in a district municipality of Chiclayo based on the harmonious development of the internal, external, relational and promotional dimensions.
3. The digital government management model for the modernization of electronic services in a district municipality of Chiclayo was presented, as a graphic synthesis of the dimensional processes articulated to achieve an optimal response.

References

Allauca, J.W.: Electronic government as a tool for transparency in public management of local governments in the Ancash region-2014–2015 (2017). http://repositorio.unfv.edu.pe/handle/UNFV/2017. Accessed 13 Nov 2021

Cáceres, J.: Postmodern public management: comparative approach to electronic Government in Chile from the perspective of organizational virtualization [Master's Thesis, Universidad Alberto Hurtado]. E-File (2017). https://repositorio.uahurtado.cl/bitstream/handle/11242/10605/MGSCaceres.pdf?sequence=1

Carrasco, S.: Metodología de la Investigación científica. Editado por San Marcos. Lima, Perú (2007)

Gutierrez, J.: Electronic government and citizen perception in the Provincial Municipality of Abancay, 2020 [Master's Thesis, Cesar Vallejo University, Lima] (2020).https://repositorio.ucv.edu.pe/handle/20.500.12692/39

Jimenez, H.: The management of interests in the Peruvian public administration (2010). http://cybertesis.uni.edu.pe/handle/uni/213. Accessed 13 Nov 2021

Lizardo, R.: A comparative study on their relationship in Latin American countries [Doctoral Thesis, Complutense University of Madrid] E. Archive (2018). https://eprints.ucm.es/47393/1/T39870

Moriconi, M.: Political rhetoric and public administration reforms in Latin America - Critical and comparative study of the official discourse on administrative reforms in Argentina, Chile and Uruguay (2008). https://gredos.usal.es/jspui/bitstream/10366/18590/1/DDPG_Retorica%20politica%20y%20reformas%20de%20la%20Admimistracion.pdf. Accessed 13 Nov 2021

Reyes, M., Gomez, A., Ramos, E.: (Desafíos de la gestión del talento humano en tiempos de pandemia covid 19. **13**(6), 232–236 (2020)

Sanchez, J.: Public administration in the information society: antecedents of the adoption of electronic government initiatives by citizens (2009). http://e-spacio.uned.es/fez/eserv/tesisuned:CiencEcoEmpJcsanchez/Documento.pdf. Accessed 13 Nov 2021

Velasquez, J.: Strategic plan for electronic government and public administration in the municipal management of the district of Independencia, 2014 [Master's thesis, César Vallejo University] E. File (2014). http://repositorio.ucv.edu.pe

Analysis of Human Resources in Sorong City Regional Equipment Organization in Supporting Electronic-Based Public Services

Fauziah Saragih[1]($\boxtimes$), Achmad Nurmandi[2], Misran[1], and Dimas Subekti[1]

[1] Department of Government Affairs and Administration, Universitas Muhammadiyah Yogyakarta, Yogyakarta, Indonesia
`f.saragih.psc22@mail.umy.ac.id`

[2] Department of Government Affairs and Administration, Jusuf Kalla School of Government, Universitas Muhammadiyah Yogyakarta, Yogyakarta, Indonesia
`nurmandi_achmad@umy.ac.id`

Abstract. This study compares the analysis of human resources in Sorong City and regional apparatus organizations in supporting electronic-based public services. In the current era of digitalization, all sectors have developed rapidly, and in their application, they take advantage of technological advances to run more effectively, efficiently, and accountably, one of which is the process of providing public services. The administration of public services is one way for the government to fulfill citizens' rights. Therefore, the quality of human resources is one element that plays an important role in achieving the success of a system implemented by central and regional government agencies. This study uses a qualitative descriptive approach with data analysis using the Nvivo 12 Plus application by taking samples on the DPMPTSP website, the BKPSDM website, and the Sorong City DISKOMINFO website. The results of the study show that the analysis of human resources in Sorong City regional apparatus organizations in supporting electronic-based public services using the E-Government theory from Dwievdi (2017) has four indicators: (1) leadership; (2) human resources; and (3) technology information. On the basis of these three indicators and the author's findings on the analysis of human resources in Sorong City regional apparatus organizations supporting electronic-based public services, the Sorong City Government has been able to implement e-government, as supported by the data analysis contained in Sorong City local government agencies. The main objective of this study is to analyze the human resources in the Sorong City regional apparatus organization supporting electronic-based public services. As a result, strong trust is required, and additional assistance is provided in relation to the development of HR human resources in areas of interest, first from decision makers, so that it can be implemented in a real and optimal manner.

Keywords: Human Resources · Electronic-Based Public Services · E-Government

C. Stephanidis et al. (Eds.): HCII 2023, CCIS 1835, pp. 262–269, 2023.
https://doi.org/10.1007/978-3-031-36001-5_34

1 Introduction

The presence of information and communication technology (ICT) has changed this pattern to be more open, non-hierarchical, non-linear, and open for two-way communication. People can freely access information on the internet whenever they want thanks to its non-hierarchical structure. In addition, the two-way communication pattern allows the public to interact with the government and allows them to better serve the community. Basically, e-government is a public service internet network designed to connect the government and community service providers for the benefit of customers [1]. Therefore, the readiness of human resources, regulations, financial allocations, facilities, and infrastructure are absolute things that must be provided in implementing e-government [2]. According to [3], in the concept of e-government, there are four types of relations, namely: G-to-C, G-to-B, G-to-G, and G-to-E. (1) From the Government to the People: The government develops an information technology portfolio system with the aim of improving relations with the public, making this kind of relationship the most common (2) (Government to Business). It is explained in this sense that, from the point of view of the government's ecosystem, one of the main tasks of the government is to create an ecosystem in a stable business climate so that the wheels of the economy are stable (3). In this type, the relationship structure tends to be focused on developing traffic needs for departmental or governmental contacts (4), Government to Employees, Aspects of internal contact between workers and organizations related to employee performance management, such as career development systems, health and employment insurance systems, and employee performance management systems, are also covered in e-government applications.

Continuous use of this technology is expected to not only bring about positive changes in the processes and procedures for formulating public policies but also to increase accountability and transparency in all government institutions, as well as increase the amount of cost savings in government administration activities. In other words [4], the implementation of e-government is basically an innovative activity for the delivery of public services that can increase public satisfaction and trust in the government. Therefore, human resources need to be continuously improved, for example, through education, training, apprenticeships, courses, and others [5]. Increased human resources (HR) are added to the workforce to increase employee satisfaction, improve quality of performance, overcome deficiencies, and improve the quality of work.There are several crucial factors that can be of particular concern to the government besides the use of ICT in e-government so that the applications released can function efficiently [6] such as: (1), adequate human resources (HR). ICT human resources must be developed to influence people's attitudes toward the use of ICT and enable them to make full use of local government applications. This is due to the fact that poorly qualified ICT personnel will cause existing applications to underperform. (2) Adequate Infrastructure The government must be able to support all ICT needs, both financially and in other infrastructure, such as the availability of computers that can support operational application systems and can improve software standardization implemented by the government (3). External environment. Internal and external pressures can be used to convince people to use the system and encourage them to properly deploy e-government applications. In addition, the following factors support HR development: (1) Internal factors cover the entire life of the organization and can be controlled by both the leadership and members of the organization; (2) External factors Organizations cannot be separated from the influence of the environment in which they live. In order for an organization to carry out its mission and goals, it must pay attention to the environment, or external factors outside the organization itself.

Several studies have been conducted on e-government studies, which are generally divided into several major themes. The first relates to organizational transformation, where the presence of ICT has an impact on changes in organizations internally as well as patterns of interaction between individuals within them as well as by providing services to the public [7]. Found that service development through e-government occurs through the following: provision of public access facilities (infrastructure), formulation of policies, determining vision and mission, preparation of priority scales or master plans, education and training of human resources, the existence of public service contracts through e-government, and socialization of the implementing bureaucracy and the community. The lack of outreach and service information updates is an obstacle to service implementation.

2 Literature Review

2.1 Human Resources

Human resources are the most important element of an organization because they use the resources owned by individuals, such as knowledge, expertise, and skills [8]. Even though it is supported by facilities and infrastructure as well as additional resources, organizational activities will not develop without the support of reliable human resources [9]. Development of the capacity of human resources, especially government apparatus, is carried out by continuously increasing the capabilities of government apparatus [10]. As a result, it is necessary to increase human resource capacity and organize their utilization with careful and comprehensive planning based on needs, with implementation carried out in stages and continuously [11]. Government officials play a role in determining and even being the key to the effective spread and development of electronic government (e-government) as developers, managers, and users of the system (e-government). As a result, it is necessary to increase human resource capacity and organize their utilization with careful and mature planning based on needs, with implementation carried out in stages and continuously. This can be achieved by establishing the competency requirements necessary for the creation and implementation of electronic governance through formal and informal education (e-Gov) channels.

2.2 Electronic-Based Public Services

Basically, the conceptual formulation of the notion of public service can be seen in the Public Service Act 25 of 2009, which states that public service is an activity related to fulfilling service needs according to statutory regulations for every citizen and resident of a country [12]. The public service paradigm continues to develop with a focus on customer satisfaction management (government customer-oriented); this is consistent with the development of domestic state administration to provide excellent service and quality [13]. As required by Law Number 14 of 2008 concerning public information disclosure, excellent public services based on information and communication technology (e-government) can encourage information disclosure and the development of good governance (Public Information Openness Law) [14]. Therefore, information technology must be utilized to create a judiciary that is accountable, transparent, and has high credibility in society.

2.3 E-Government

E-government is a complex and overlapping phenomenon with different dimensions such as e-information, e-events, and e-participation [15]. E-government aims to increase the use of information technology in the relationship between the government and the community and other stakeholders [16]. ([17]) There are five classifications of e-government use in government agencies, which are as follows: (1) Service use: using transactional services (2) Use of general information: seeking general information (3) Policy research: seeking information related to government policies (4) Participation: participating in decision-making processes and discussions (5) Co-creation: creating policies, information, and services together with governments and other citizens Government is a government system process that utilizes ICT (information, communication, and technology) as a tool to provide easy communication and transaction processes to citizens, business organizations, and between government agencies and their staff [18].

3 Method

This study uses a qualitative research method with a descriptive approach to outline the extent of the use of E-Government as an electronic-based internet media (E-Gov) in public services in the City of Sorong. Sources of data for this research include the official websites of the Sorong City DPMPTSP, Sorong City BKD, and Sorong City DISKOMINFO. Data collection techniques using literature studies This research analysis uses Q-DAS (qualitative data analysis software) in Nvivo 12 Plus to collect, manage, and analyze data effectively, efficiently, and validly (Table 1).

Data was obtained by capturing web content in the form of websites using the Nvivo 12 plus Nvivo 12 plus Web Chrome feature. The Nvivo 12 Plus visualization in this study uses several features, namely the crosstab query feature and the mind map feature.

4 Result and Discussion

This section is a discussion of the findings and analysis of human resources in the regional apparatus organizations of the City of Sorong in supporting electronic-based public services. In E-Government theory, according to Dwivedi (2017 there are three indicators to measure the extent to which E-Government is used as an electronic-based internet media (E-Gov) in public services in Sorong City, namely as follows:

Table 1. Sorong City Regional Apparatus Organization (OPD) website

		Amount of Data
Sorong City One Stop Investment and Licensing Service (DPMPTSP)	https://dpmptsp.sorongkota.go.id/	6
Sorong City Regional Civil Service Agency (BKD)	http://badan-kepegawaian-daerah-bkd-kota-sorong/	4
Sorong City Communication and Informatics Office (DISKOMINFO)	https://diskominfo.sorongkota.go.id	22

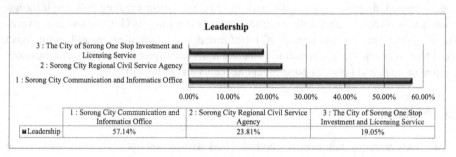

Fig. 1. Leadership. Source: Nvivo 12 Plus was used to process the data.

4.1 Leadership

In terms of leadership indicators, there are three government agencies in Sorong City, which the author describes as follows (Fig. 1):

Based on the data above, it shows that the percentage of leadership in the Sorong City Communication and Information Service (DISKOMINFO) is 57.14%, the Sorong City Regional Personnel Agency (BKD) is 23.81%, and the Sorong City Investment and Licensing Service (DPMPTSP) is 19.05%. Based on the three Sorong City government agencies listed above, the one that obtained the highest data was the Sorong City Communication and Information Service (DISKOMINFO), at 57.14% above average. This is because in the current era of regional autonomy, it is necessary to realize good governance by using information and communication technology, commonly called "e-government".

4.2 Human Resources

In terms of human resource indicators, there are three government agencies in Sorong City, which the authors describe as follows (Fig. 2):

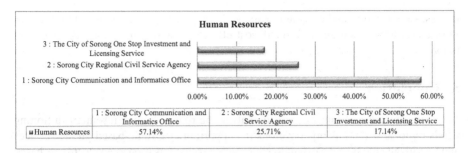

Fig. 2. Human Resources. Source: Nvivo 12 Plus was used to process the data.

Based on the data above, it shows that the percentage of human resources at the Sorong City Communication and Information Service (DISKOMINFO) is 57.14%, the Sorong City Regional Personnel Agency (BKD) is 25.71%, and the One-Stop Integrated Investment and Licensing Service (DPMPTSP) for the City of Sorong is 17.14%. Based on the three Sorong City government agencies listed above, the one that obtained the highest data was the Sorong City Communication and Information Service (DISKOM-INFO), at 57.14%. This is because the implementation of electronic-based government needs to have a structured development process and systematic.

4.3 Technology and Information

On technology and information indicators, there are three government agencies in Sorong City, which the author describes as follows (Fig. 3):

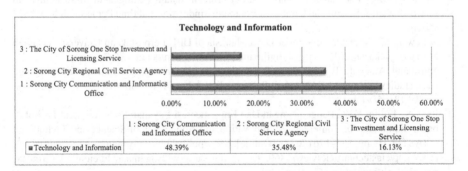

Fig. 3. Technology and Information. Source: Nvivo 12 Plus was used to process the data.

Based on the data above, it shows that the percentage of technology and information at the Sorong City Communication and Information Service (DISKOMINFO) is 48.39%, the Sorong City Regional Civil Service Agency (BKD) is 35.48%, and the One-Stop Integrated Investment and Licensing Service is 16.13%. Based on the three Sorong City government agencies listed above, the one that obtained the highest data was the Sorong City Communication and Information Service (DISKOMINFO), with 48.39% above average. This is because e-government is a form of government service that uses information and communication technology (ICT) to provide public services more conveniently, consumer-oriented, cost-effectively, and overall in a better way than before.

5 Conclusion

The main objective of this study is to analyze the role of human resources in Sorong City's regional apparatus organizations in supporting electronic-based public services and to critically analyze the extent to which e-government is used as an electronic-based internet medium in public services in Sorong City. In public services, considering the influence of leadership, human resources, technology, and information to provide innovations in public services, because as a public service provider, strong trust is required, and additional assistance is carried out related to the development of human resources HR in the fields of interest, first and foremost from decision makers, so that it can be implemented in a real and more optimal way.

References

1. Saputro, R.H.: Tantangan Pelayanan Publik Berbasis Sistem Informasi Di Era Revolusi 4.0. J. Adm. Nigeria **9**(1), 89–101 (2021)
2. Musaddad, A., Ahzani, F., Susilowati, M., Arif, L.: Implementasi SIPRAJA sebagai inovasi Pelayanan publik, vol. 1, no. 6, pp. 206–213, 2020
3. Adhyaksa, R.: Analisis Kesiapan Kementerian Ketenagakerjaan dalam Menerapkan Program Satu Data Ketenagakerjaan Diajukan sebagai salah satu syarat memperoleh gelar Sarjana Ilmu Administasi. no. November (2022)
4. Aprianty, D.R.: Penerapan Kebijakan E-Government dalam Peningkatan Mutu Pelayanan Publik di Kantor Kecamatan Sambutan Kota Samarinda. eJournal Ilmu Pemerintah**4**(4), 1593 (2016)
5. Setiawan, M.: Manajemen Sumber Daya Manusia di UPU Perpustakaan Universitas Gadjah Mada Yogyakarta (2012). https://digilib.uns.ac.id/dokumen/detail/28157
6. Nurmandi, A., et al.: To what extent is social media used in city government policy making? Case studies in three ASEAN cities. Public Policy Adm. **17**(4), 600–618 (2018). https://doi.org/10.13165/VPA-18-17-4-08
7. Ibad, S., Lolita, Y.W.: Pengembangan Dan Implementasi Layanan E-Government Di Kabupaten Situbondo. In: Conference on Innovation and Application of Science and Technology (CIASTECH), pp. 167–176 (2020), [Online]. http://publishing-widyagama.ac.id/ejournal-v2/index.php/ciastech/article/view/1860. http://publishing-widyagama.ac.id/ejournal-v2/index.php/ciastech/article/viewFile/1860/1305
8. Harahap, E.S.: Pengaruh Pengembangan Sumber Daya Manusia Terhadap Kinerja Karyawan (Studi Kasus PT. Asuransi Jiwa Prudential cabang Medan) Skripsi (2019)
9. Regency, M.: Sumber Daya Manusia Kabupaten Majene. The influence of human resource development on the performance of public servant in BKPSDM. **4**(2), 85–90 (2022)
10. Alfraita, A.: 0 % Quotes. pp. 0–7 (2021)
11. Isnawan, A.L., Syaputra, D.: Penerapan E-Government Dalam Aplikasi Sistem Informasi Arsip Dinamis (SIMARDI) Terhadap Kinerja Pegawai di Kantor Camat Bukit Bestari, Kota Tanjungpinang. Soc. Issues Q. **1**(1), 222–231 (2022), [Online]. http://ejournal.umrah.ac.id/index.php/siq/article/view/20. http://ejournal.umrah.ac.id/index.php/siq/article/download/20/20

12. Irawan, A.: Sistem Pelayanan Publik Berbasis E-Government Pada Pemerintah Daerah Kabupaten Merauke Oleh: Dosen STIA Karya Dharma Merauke. Soc. J. Ilmu Adm. dan Sos.7(1), 20–37 (2018) [Online]. http://ejournal.unmus.ac.id/index.php/societas
13. Pratama, R.H.: Pelayanan Publik Berbasis Teknologi Informasi Dan Komunikasi (Tik), Elektronik Rukun Tetangga/Rukun WargA (e-RT/RW). J. Adm. Publik 3(12), 2128–2132 (2015)
14. Khoirul Majid, M.E., Ainayyah, N.H., Amrina, N.: Optimalisasi Sistem Layanan Pengadilan Berbasis Elektronik Guna Menjamin Keterbukaan Informasi Menuju Peradilan Yang Modern. Legislatif3(1), 97–115 (2019) [Online]. https://journal.unhas.ac.id/index.php/jhl/article/view/10209
15. Manoharan, A.P., Ingrams, A.: Conceptualizing E-Government from local government perspectives. State Local Gov. Rev. 50(1), 56–66 (2018). https://doi.org/10.1177/0160323x18763964
16. Kelibay, I., Nurmandi, A., Malawani, A.D.: e-Government adoption of human resource management in Sorong City, Indonesia. J. Asian Rev. Public Aff. Policy5(1), 1–20 (2020). [Online]. https://arpap.kku.ac.th/index.php/arpap/article/view/180
17. Nam, T.: Author's personal copy determining the type of e-government use. Governance 31(2), 211–220 (2014)
18. Aminudin, N.: Langkah – Langkah Taktis Pengembangan E-Government Untuk Pemerintahan Daerah (Pemda) Kabupaten Pringsewu. Aisyah J. Informatics Electr. Eng. 1(1), 89–95 (2019). https://doi.org/10.30604/jti.v1i1.13

Using Social Media Tools to Accelerate the Health Public: Analysis of the Jakarta Health Office

Mohamad Sukarno[1]([✉]), Achmad Nurmandi[2], Misran[2], and Dimas Subekti[2]

[1] Department of Government Affairs and Administration, Universitas Muhammadiyah Yogyakarta, Bantul, Indonesia
m.sukarno.psc22@mail.umy.ac.id
[2] Department of Government Affairs and Administration, Jusuf Kalla School Government, Universitas Muhammadiyah Yogyakarta, Bantul, Indonesia

Abstract. This study aims to analyze social media for public information of health services in DKI Jakarta through @dinkesJKT accounts. Through social media accounts, @dinkesJKT all data and information related to health programs are available and accessible to the public. Through social media accounts, @dinkesJKT all data and information related to health programs are available and accessible to the public. The method used in this study is qualitative using Computer Assigned Qualitative Data Software (CAQDS) analysis, namely Nvivo 12plus. Data sources are obtained from secondary data @dinkesJKT which includes mass media data as well as other related documents. The data is displayed in the form of Crosstab analysis, Chart Analysis, and Cluster Analysis. The results showed that the @dinkesJKT account is active in conducting communication and information transactions up to date in each health service. Health information services are also carried out by optimizing every matter of health care and monitoring account postings. Then, @dinkesJKT collaborates with government institutions Regional Apparatus Organizations (OPD), and Non-Governmental Organizations (NGOs). In addition, @dinkesJKT attracts public engagement to participate in health programs.

Keywords: Social Media · Dinkes JKT · Health Public Policy

1 Introduction

The use of social media in the development of e-government and the interaction involving netizens and government institutions through government channels have been proven to encourage internal bureaucratic changes [1]. The participation of netizens in governance has significant implications for social and political life [3]. This is because social media is a medium that has cheap access to voice and at the same time can determine the portion of votes for public policy [4]. Social media has now also become Public Service Media (PSM) which is a digital platform in public communication and aims to shape user interaction and correspondence in public interests [5].

C. Stephanidis et al. (Eds.): HCII 2023, CCIS 1835, pp. 270–278, 2023.
https://doi.org/10.1007/978-3-031-36001-5_35

Social media has an electronic platform that has facilities for communicating and making it easier to interact between users. [6]. Criado and Villodre, (2021) also mentioned in their research that, in public administration, the last few decades have depended on the use of social media. This is considering social media as a platform from the government that is able to improve the system of transparency, a collaboration between actors, and engagement from the community itself. Therefore, in Hancu-Budui's research (2020) also shows that social media has opened up new opportunities in public institutions with the goal to promote services and expand their audience network.

Dias (2019) explains that the web 2.0 technology adopted by government digital services has been proven sequentially to be able to handle more complex services and not just display static information. This is influenced by the information transparency portal factor which correlates directly with social media so that, any information can be accessed [11]. In Indonesia itself, the use of social media as a means of interaction between citizens and the government is regulated in the Regulation of the Ministry of State Apparatus Empowerment and Bureaucratic Reform No. 83 of 2012 [12]. With the existence of social media, the development the concept of Information and Communication Technology (ICT) has become a new medium in information and communication transaction [14].

The use of social media has been widely adopted by local governments to share information with the public [15, 16]. In the results of the United Nations survey (2020) that many local governments have adopted ICT to disseminate information to the public (UN 2020). The main thing that encourages the existence of a digital ICT platform is the existence of communication and consultation facilities. Then another thing is the possibility to do a wider reach on other stakeholders so that citizen interaction and participation in *local governance* can contribute directly to policy making.

The results of the Global Web Index identified an increase in local government public authorities in promoting e-government through social media to reach information. [18]. Silva (2019) revealed that this massive technological change has provided a new era for local government services. The existence of the digital space provides a coherent audience between the government and its citizens in dialogue and dissemination of information content between the two. Then, the adoption of social media in local governments is indicated to be able to realize public information governance in an informative manner [20].

DKI Jakarta is one of the local governments that has adopted social media as a means of flowing information from the government (Syamsul Bahri Abd. Rasyid, 2021; Windarsih, 2021) [22]. One of them is by using twitter social media to build communication and service information in DKI Jakarta [23]. Through one of the Regional Apparatus Organizations (OPD) of the Health Office, all service information transkip is available through the @dinkesJKT account. In @dinkesJKT account, all healthcare information will be presented and displayed at all times as a health promoter strategy [24].

From the explanation above, this study will explain social media tools in local government to disseminate health service information. Through social media accounts@dinkesJKT all service information will be analyzed using The Circular Model of Some For Social Communication [25] among which there are four indicators in it, namely: share (sharing information or messages), optimize (optimization of messages to be conveyed), manage (monitor), and engage (involve users) [26].

2 Literature Review

2.1 Social Media as a Platform

Social media platforms generate and disseminate information and become a place where information is shared by people with others as social relationships take place. [28]. The use of social media has now also become part of the media organization or workplace because it has good value for the organization and its users [29]. This is influenced by the size of the infinite audience so that their expressions and opinions can be connected to the online audience [30].

Ease of access to social media is also supported by factors from the emergence of the internet and technology integrated in the digital space in the work practices of an organization [31]. Due to the high audience on social media explained that individuals can actively participate in the production and dissemination of news under any conditions.

Twitter is a social media that has platform for discussing scientific issues and is a good medium for exchanging information [33]. Therefore, twitter social media has also been proven to be active in tackling misinformation which can then mislead the public [34]. In addition, the Social Network System (SNS) platform on twitter social media is also a medium of communication and information quickly, and accurately, and is supported by 59% of twitter users who are always active [35].

2.2 Social Media Use in Government Organization

The use of social media tools in government organizations is expected to improve public services because the policymaking process allows the public to participate. The implication is that when the government issues policies, the public can become a shield if something goes wrong because of the discursiveness of social media itself. [38]. Therefore, Bretschneider and Parker (2016) also explained that social media which is an organizational technology will accelerate the implementation, diffusion, and function of organizational goals. So that the acceleration of innovation in organizations can be disseminated comprehensively and accepted by the wider community.

The correlation between social media and government communication is very important to answer the challenges of the current government bureaucracy [40]. This can be seen from the challenges of the current information age which requires an acceleration in every public service and data and information accuracy. Then the presence of social media as an online digital platform encourages collective action to integrate and supervise each other without the limitations of time and public space [41].

3 Research Method

This research uses qualitative methods. The data of this study was taken from social media data, namely the twitter account @dinkesJKT. NCapture is used to retrieve data from Chrome Web. After that, the data were analyzed using Nvivo 12plus. It includes data collection, the process of encoding data, its validity and interpretation, as well as the display of data. After that, the data were analyzed using Nvivo 12plus. It includes data collection, the process of encoding data, its validity and interpretation, as well as the display of data. The analysis was used by utilizing Computer Assigned Qualitative Data Software Nvivo 12plus. There are six phases used for data analysis which include data collection, data analysis using Nvivo 12plus, and understanding of models for utilizing social media as a communicative channel.

4   Result and Discussion

Then in the results of analysis on information services, especially in the account share feature, @dinkesJKT actively disseminate information intensely and has a percentage of 54 percent. Information presented in share indicators such as information about health services from the DKI Jakarta Government is spread out in several points. Then @dinkesJKT account is also active in reporting the latest health information data, both in the form of appeals to residents to always make healthy living efforts. In addition, information about health is also covered (conveyed) in the form of impacts (background to the emergence of a disease) and solutions (tips and tricks to overcome it) (Fig. 1).

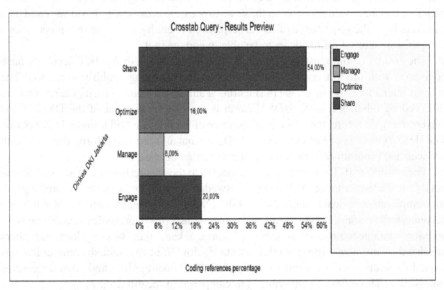

Fig. 1. Crosstab Analysis of Health Information of DKI Jakarta Health Office. Source: Nvivo 12plus (2022)

In the optimize indicator, the @dinkesJKT account reports about its collaboration with other actors, both from Regional Apparatus Organization (OPD) agencies and from Non-Governmental Organizations (NGOs). The results of the analysis showed that the intensity of reporting through @dinkesJKT account reached a percentage of 16 percent. The collaboration carried out is by carrying out health services (medical check-ups or vaccination services) with other agencies. In addition, in collaboration with related agencies of the DKI Jakarta Health Office, it continues to provide public facilities in the form of the nearest puskemas or hospitals.

The manage (management or monitoring) phase of the DKI Jakarta Health Office monitors health services by folding the relevant OPD agencies. Rapid Response Society (CRM) is a feature of complaints that can be addressed by the public if criticism and suggestions. Then in managing health services, @dinkesJKT actively monitor with parties such as the Corruption Eradication Commission (KPK) for budget matters, PKK, National Child Immunization Month, and monitoring visits to health facilities at every puskesmas and hospital in DKI Jakarta.

The last indicator, which is associated with how @dinkesJKT attracts public participation to engage in health care delivered by the account. The percentage intensity is 20% of the total four indicators above. News of public involvement can be seen by the DKI Jakarta Health Office account which continues to campaign for the importance of health and healthy living as well as some tips and tricks in fighting disease. The selection of diction to attracting public participation is done with for example have you protected children with immunizations? How important is immunization for a child? hello healthy buddy! Does anyone already know about the I'm fit app? This example illustrates the form and efforts of the DKI Jakarta Health Office in attracting the attention and participation of its citizens. In addition, in the news process, @dinkesJKT also always add data and facts from the importance of us participating in healthy living, so that it becomes a comparison material for residents to be able to engage in it.

The results of the cluster analysis, it was found that @dinkesJKT accounts have coherence with other accounts as a connection in conveying health information. The biggest interactions occur on @DKIJakarta, @aniesbaswedan, @beritajakarta, and are followed by other accounts. @DKIJakarta is the official account of the DKI Jakarta Government, therefore, the account is in charge of the relevant OPDs under DKI Jakarta. The Health Office is one of the related OPDs, so that all access to information on health services and programs can be monitored and further accessed.

Then @dinkesJKT account is also connected to the @aniesbaswedan account whose notable is the Governor of DKI. @aniesbaswedan became a new media in campaigning for complaints and health services from the DKI Jakarta Health Office. Later the two accounts will be connected to the mentions feature in terms of all health-related needs. In addition, other accounts such as @BeritaJakarta, @kemenkes, @transjakart, and others are also the same steps from the DKI Jakarta Health Office to establish communication-related to health services, I am located in the DKI Jakarta OPD and central agencies (ministries). The ultimate goal remains to campaign for health (Fig. 2).

Dinas Kesehatan Provinsi DKI Jakarta (@dinkesJKT) ~ Twitter - Usernames Clustered by Word similarity

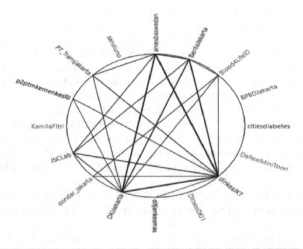

Fig. 2. Word Similarity Analysis. Source: Nvivo 12plus (2022)

5 Conclusion

The DKI Jakarta Health Office is active in spreading news of health service information through social media. Through @dinkesJKT accounts, all health services are available and connected to agencies from the DKI Jakarta Government along with related OPDs and across ministries. In informing health services, the DKI Jakarta Health Office has high activity in sharing service information and healthy living campaigns. Then this is also followed by a collaboration with other agencies in order to make the health program a success and also always monitor the program. In addition, @dinkesJKT account also encourages public engagement to be active in a culture of healthy living and have a high enthusiasm for health facilities and services that have been provided by the DKI Jakarta Health Office.

References

1. Singh, P., Dwivedi, Y.K., Kahlon, K.S., Sawhney, R.S.: Intelligent monitoring and controlling of public policies using social media and cloud computing. In: Elbanna, A., Dwivedi, Y.K., Bunker, D., Wastell, D. (eds.) TDIT 2018. IAICT, vol. 533, pp. 143–154. Springer, Cham (2019). https://doi.org/10.1007/978-3-030-04315-5_11
2. Roengtam, S., Nurmandi, A., Almarez, D.N., Kholid, A.: Does social media transform city government? A case study of three ASEAN cities: Bandung, Indonesia, Iligan, Philippines and Pukhet, Thailand. Transform. Govt. People Process. Policy **11**(3) (2017)
3. Nurmandi, A., et al.: To what extent is social media used in city government policy making? Case studies in three ASEAN cities. Public Policy Adm. **17**(4), 600–618 (2018). https://doi.org/10.13165/VPA-18-17-4-08
4. Kurniawan, D., Sutan, A., Mufandi, I., Supriyanto, E., Rachmawati, M.: Social media used to spread vaccination program: case of Indonesia vaccination Covid-19 Policy. In: ICLSSEE (2021). https://doi.org/10.4108/eai.6-3-2021.2306469

5. van Es, K., Poell, T.: Platform imaginaries and Dutch public service media. Soc. Media Soc. **6**(2), (2020). https://doi.org/10.1177/2056305120933289

6. Demircioglu, M.A.: Examining the effects of social media use on job satisfaction in the australian public service: testing self-determination theory. Public Perform. Manag. Rev. **41**(2), 300–327 (2018). https://doi.org/10.1080/15309576.2017.1400991

7. Criado, J.I., Villodre, J.: Delivering public services through social media in European local governments. an interpretative framework using semantic algorithms. Local Gov. Stud. **47**(2), 253–275 (2021). https://doi.org/10.1080/03003930.2020.1729750

8. Criado, J.I., Sandoval-Almazan, R., Gil-Garcia, J.R.: Government innovation through social media. Gov. Inf. Q. **30**(4), 319–326 (2013). https://doi.org/10.1016/j.giq.2013.10.003

9. Hancu-Budui, A., Zorio-Grima, A., Blanco-Vega, J.: Audit institutions in the European Union: public service promotion, environmental engagement and COVID crisis communication through social media. Sustain. **12**(23), 1–32 (2020). https://doi.org/10.3390/su1223 9816

10. Dias, G.P., Bruzza, M., Tupia, M.: The use of social media by local governments: the case of Manabí's cantons in Ecuador. Epic Ser. Comput. **63**, 170–181 (2019). https://doi.org/10. 29007/sn24

11. Magro, M.J.: A review of social media use in e-government. Adm. Sci. **2**(2), 148–161 (2012). https://doi.org/10.3390/admsci2020148

12. Rahmanto, A.N., Dirgatama, C.H.A.: The implementation of e-government through social media use in local government of Solo Raya. In: 2018 International Conference on Information Communication Technology, ICOIACT 2018 2018–Janua, no. 83, pp. 765–768 (2018). https:// doi.org/10.1109/ICOIACT.2018.8350763

13. Adom, P.K., Amuakwa-Mensah, F., Agradi, M.P., Nsabimana, A.: Energy poverty, development outcomes, and transition to green energy. Renew. Energy **178**, 1337–1352 (2021). https://doi.org/10.1016/j.renene.2021.06.120

14. Anggreani, M.D., Purnomo, E.P., Kasiwi, A.N.: Ruang Publik Virtual Sebagai Pintu Komunikasi Government To Citizen (Studi Perbandingan Media Sosial Pemerintah Kota Yogyakarta dan Surabaya). J. MODERAT**6**(1), 203–220, 2020. https://jurnal.unigal.ac.id/index.php/mod erat/article/view/3165/2919

15. Zhang, C., Fan, C., Yao, W., Hu, X., Mostafavi, A.: Social media for intelligent public information and warning in disasters: an interdisciplinary review. Int. J. Inf. Manage. **49**(April), 190–207 (2019). https://doi.org/10.1016/j.ijinfomgt.2019.04.004

16. Mansoor, M.: Citizens' trust in government as a function of good governance and government agency's provision of quality information on social media during COVID-19. Gov. Inf. Q. **38**(4), 101597 (2021). https://doi.org/10.1016/j.giq.2021.101597

17. United Nations. E-Government Survey 2020. New York (2020)

18. Padeiro, M., Bueno-Larraz, B., Freitas, Â.: Local governments' use of social media during the COVID-19 pandemic: the case of Portugal. Gov. Inf. Q. **38**(4), 101620 (2021). https:// doi.org/10.1016/j.giq.2021.101620

19. Silva, P., Tavares, A.F., Silva, T., Lameiras, M.: The good, the bad and the ugly: three faces of social media usage by local governments. Gov. Inf. Q. **36**(3), 469–479 (2019). https://doi. org/10.1016/j.giq.2019.05.006

20. Satispi, E., DyasTuti, R.W., Fathani, A.T., Kaewhanam, P.: Local government respond to COVID-19 pandemics: a study of South Tangerang City. J. Gov. Public Policy **8**(2), 82–92 (2021). https://doi.org/10.18196/jgpp.v8i2.11439

21. Rasyid, S.B.A., Nurmandi, A., Suswanta, Mutiarin, D., Salahudin.: Public communication of local government leaders: a case study of three major governors in Indonesia. In: Antipova, T. (eds.) Advances in Digital Science. ICADS 2021. Advances in Intelligent Systems and Computing, vol. 1352. Springer, Cham (2021). https://doi.org/10.1007/978-3-030-71782-7_43

22. Windarsih, A.: Public communication conflicts between the central government and the DKI Jakarta Government in handling the Covid-19 Pandemic. In: ICoSPOLHUM 2020, pp. 62–73, Atl. Press 495 (2021). https://doi.org/10.2991/assehr.k.210125.012

23. Jalil, M.J., Nurmandi, A., Muallidin, I., Kurniawan, D., Salahudin.: Quality analysis of local government websites (Study Case DKI Jakarta, Bali, Banten Provinces). In: Stephanidis, C., Antona, M., Ntoa, S. (eds.) HCI International 2021 - Late Breaking Posters. HCII 2021. Communications in Computer and Information Science, vol. 1499, pp. 454–462. Springer, Cham (2021). https://doi.org/10.1007/978-3-030-90179-0_58

24. Hariningsih, A.S., Kurniawan, E.: The utilization of explainer video animation to support the optimalization of health protocol during the Covid-19 outbreak (Case Study: Health Promoters and Cadres in DKI Jakarta). Int. J. Multicult. Multireligious Underst.9(2), 637–643 (2022). https://doi.org/10.18415/ijmmu.v9i2.3579

25. Luttrell, R.: Social Media. Rowman & Littlefield, London (2015)

26. Pakpahan, A.V.B., Djuwita, A.: Penggunaan Circular Model Of SoMe Melalui Instagram @trademark_bdg. e-Proc. Manag. 6(2), 5197–5202. https://openlibrarypublications.telkom university.ac.id/index.php/management/article/view/10571

27. Ren, J., Dong, H., Popovic, A., Sabnis, G., Nickerson, J.: Digital platforms in the news industry: how social media platforms impact traditional media news viewership. Eur. J. Inf. Syst. 00(00), 1–18 (2022). https://doi.org/10.1080/0960085X.2022.2103046

28. Standage, Writing on the Wall: Social Media, First. Bloomsbury: Bloomsbury Publishing USA (2013)

29. Högberg, K.: Multiple social media in practice-investigating emergent work practices. J. Comput. Inf. Syst. 00(00), 1–13 (2022). https://doi.org/10.1080/08874417.2021.2023337

30. Aldous, K.K., An, J., Jansen, J.J.: What really matters?: characterising and predicting user engagement of news postings using multiple platforms, sentiments and topics. Behav. Inf. Technol. 1–24 (2022). https://doi.org/10.1080/0144929X.2022.2030798

31. Asio, S.M., Khorasani, S.T.: Social media: a platform for innovation. IIE Annu. Conf. Expo 2015(July), 1496–1503 (2015)

32. Andreadis, S., et al.: A social media analytics platform visualising the spread of COVID-19 in Italy via exploitation of automatically geotagged tweets. Online Soc. Netw. Media 23, 100134 (2021). https://doi.org/10.1016/j.osnem.2021.100134

33. Pearce, W., Niederer, S., Özkula, S.M., Sánchez Querubín, N.: The social media life of climate change: platforms, publics, and future imaginaries. Wiley Interdiscip. Rev. Clim. Chang.10(2), 1–13 (2019). https://doi.org/10.1002/wcc.569

34. Naseem, U., Razzak, I., Khushi, M., Eklund, P.W., Kim, J.: COVIDSenti: a large-scale benchmark twitter data set for COVID-19 sentiment analysis. IEEE Trans. Comput. Soc. Syst. 8(4), 976–988 (2021). https://doi.org/10.1109/TCSS.2021.3051189

35. Mohammed, A., Ferraris, A.: Factors influencing user participation in social media: evidence from twitter usage during COVID-19 pandemic in Saudi Arabia. Technol. Soc. 66(December 2020). 101651 (2021). https://doi.org/10.1016/j.techsoc.2021.101651

36. A. Chouikh. Supply decisions in emerging social media based services : towards an open and collaborative government. Thesis June, 143 (2016). https://doi.org/10.13140/RG.2.1.1683.9280

37. Song, M., Kim, J.W., Kim, Y., Jung, K.: Does the provision of emergency information on social media facilitate citizen participation during a disaster? Int. J. Emerg. Manag. 11(3), 224–239 (2015). https://doi.org/10.1504/IJEM.2015.071707

38. Hansson, S., Page, R.: Legitimation in government social media communication: the case of the Brexit department. Crit. Discourse Stud. 1–18 (2022). https://doi.org/10.1080/17405904.2022.2058971

39. Bretschneider, S., Parker, M.: Organization formalization, sector and social media: does increased standardization of policy broaden and deepen social media use in organizations? Gov. Inf. Q. **33**(4), 614–628 (2016). https://doi.org/10.1016/j.giq.2016.09.005

40. Torenvlied, R.: Social media and the new organization of government communications: an empirical analysis of twitter usage by the Dutch Police. Am. Rev. Public Adm. **46**(2–3), 143–161 (2014). https://doi.org/10.1177/0275074014551381

41. Linders, D.: From e-government to we-government: defining a typology for citizen coproduction in the age of social media. Gov. Inf. Q. **29**(4), 446–454 (2012). https://doi.org/10.1016/j.giq.2012.06.003

Exploring the Applications, Data and Services Needed for a Cloud-Based Workplace for the Public Sector

Marleen Vanhauer$^{(\boxtimes)}$ [iD], Barbara Haupt, and Stephan Raimer[iD]

University of Applied Sciences for Public Administration and Services, 24161 Altenholz, Germany
team@verwaltungslabor.digital

Abstract. To ensure digital independency, the European program Gaia-X pursues the goal to provide the public sector a secure cloud with open source applications, data and services for a digital workplace [1].Which applications, data and services are needed and useful for a digital sovereign workplace for public employees? This paper presents the preliminary results of the Gaia-X POSSIBLE project and its contextual interviews with public administrative employees conducted in fall 2022, investigating their needs in regard to the Phoenix office suite by Dataport and the digital workplace beyond. Within the Gaia-X POSSIBLE project, according to our knowledge, for the first time public administration employees were involved in user research. To facilitate implementation of the study and within the given scope, in this first round, public administrative employees at state and municipality level in Schleswig-Holstein (Northern Germany) were targeted. These two target groups were supplemented by a third target group, namely students of Public Administration at the University of Applied Sciences for Public Administration and Services. We aimed at 5–20 participants per target group. In total, 32 contextual interviews were conducted. The contextual interviews were evaluated on the basis of a qualitative content analysis according to Mayring [11]. The 5 most essential office applications were e-mail, calendar, word processing, video conferencing and a shared document management system. In addition, an e-file application, telephony and PDF processing were rated as most useful, supplemented by notes, project management and other creativity and collaborative applications. For further studies, we suggest to extend the target group to other federal states, the federal government and other European countries. Quantitative analytics and/or surveys could provide reliable information on user numbers of office, specialist applications and data services. Also, usability studies focused on each single application would deliver more details.

Keywords: Service Design Research · User Studies · Public Administration

1 Introduction

Since 2019, the European Gaia-X project has been pursuing the goal of creating a European next generation data infrastructure that is developed into a digital ecosystem to provide openness, transparency, data sovereignty and trust [4]. Representatives from

© The Author(s), under exclusive license to Springer Nature Switzerland AG 2023
C. Stephanidis et al. (Eds.): HCII 2023, CCIS 1835, pp. 279–285, 2023.
https://doi.org/10.1007/978-3-031-36001-5_36

business, politics and science are asked to collaborate in order to create not another cloud service, but a decentralized architecture and a multitude of individual platforms following a common (Gaia-X) standard [1].

Within the Gaia-X project POSSIBLE funded by the Bundesnetzagentur (Germany's main authority for infrastructure), Phoenix, developed by Dataport, provides web-based open source applications (e.g. Open-Xchange Groupware, Nextcloud, Jitsi Video Conferencing and Matrix/Element Instant Messaging) in a secure cloud for a digital workplace in the public sector [5]. Public administration institutions can select coordinated applications, data and services depending on the individual needs of administrative employees [1].

The main research question which arose, was: Which applications, data and services are needed and useful for a digital sovereign workplace for public employees? Subsequently listed are the sub-research question.

1. Which applications should be part of the Phoenix suite? (Q1)
2. What functionalities (use cases) are useful? (Q2)
3. Which applications and functionalities (use cases) are currently missing? (Q3)
4. Which federal data and services should be integrated into Phoenix? (Q4)

This paper presents the preliminary results of the contextual interviews conducted within the Gaia-X POSSIBLE project with public administrative employees in fall 2022. According to our knowledge, within the POSSIBLE project, public administration employees were involved in user research in one of the earliest cases.

We are aware, that the use of software in the field of public administration sets very specific conditions. Nevertheless, we believe that we can contribute to research in the field of office software, cloud solutions and open source for any public administrations.

2 Related Work

Since 2022, at federal level in Germany [6] and in the state of Schleswig-Holstein [7], similar efforts have been pursued for an alternative digital workplace for public administration, in contrast to commercial cloud solutions like Microsoft Office 365. The characteristic difference is, that it is only with the POSSIBLE project that a European perspective for cloud services is adopted.

From 2021 to 2022, prior to this study, for Phoenix a series of online surveys and a handful of usability interviews with students of Public Administration had been conducted by the authors, which results can be requested from the authors.

3 Method and Procedure

The methodology and approach for this paper investigates use cases and requirements for a cloud workplace based on a case study approach [8] and qualitative research. Furthermore, our research is embedded in design science research [9] with interviews as an empirical research method.

In particular, contextual interviews is a qualitative research method of the service design process following a participant approach [10]. By conducting qualitative interviews with public administration employees, we wanted to reveal their real needs in regard to the web-based Phoenix office suite and the digital workplace beyond. For the contextual interviews, an interview guide with interview questions was created which derived from our research question and sub-research questions.

3.1 Sample Target Groups

To facilitate implementation of the study and within the given scope, in this first round, public administrative employees at state and municipality level in Schleswig-Holstein (Northern Germany) were targeted. These two target groups were supplemented by a third target group, namely students of Public Administration at the University of Applied Sciences for Public Administration and Services.

We aimed to at least interview 20 participants per target group. Participants must be employed at a state authority or at a municipal authority and work within the field of public administration and services and have at least 2 years of work experience, or be a student in Public Administration and be enrolled at least in the 2nd year of study. Moreover, participants should use office applications in their everyday work/studies.

Prospective study participants were invited via e-mail containing a link to participate in a preliminary survey used to screen out interested participants according to the screening criteria. Initially, 40 state authorities, more than 130 municipal authorities and more than 300 students were addressed. We aimed at 5–20 participants per target group.

In total, 32 contextual interviews were conducted: 21 interviews with federal state employees and 10 interviews with municipal employees; the student group resulted in only one interview. 4 out of 21 federal state employees stated to also collaborate with other federal states, the federal government and the EU. The entire group of participants was evenly mixed by executives, project managers, administrative staff, lawyers and IT/tech specialists.

3.2 Implementation of Contextual Interviews

Between September and October 2022 over a period of 6 weeks, 32 qualitative interviews were conducted online and video-recorded, each taking between 30–45 min. The first moderator guided the conversation using the prepared interview guide while simultaneously taking notes. The co-moderator served as additional note-taker, both moderators taking turns (Table 1).

3.3 Qualitative Analysis of Results

The collected results of the interview of each target group were evaluated on the basis of a qualitative content analysis, hence a summary content analysis according to Mayring [11]. The answers to each interview question were summarized and collected in an Excel-spreadsheet by two independent researchers, i.e. the moderators. In a next step, the researchers clustered the collected answers by mutual agreement, transformed these

Table 1. Interview Questions

Code	Interview Question
Q0-1	What does a typical working day look like?
Q0-2	Which technical equipment do you prefer to work with?
Q0-3	What do you prefer: web or native applications?
Q1-1	What applications do you work with?
Q2-1	What are typical tasks and activities you often do with these applications?
Q3-1	Which applications are missing?
Q3-2	Which functionalities are missing?
Q4-1	Which integrations (applications, data or services) should be integrated?
Q5-1	What are your biggest paint points when working with these applications?
Q5-2	What are your wishes and expectations in regard to these applications?
Q5-3	What are your wishes and expectations of a future digital office workplace?

into content themes. Content themes were (A) Everyday work and workplace, (B) Major office applications, (C) Complementary office applications, (D) E-file application, (E) Other specialist applications, (F) Data and services. These resulted in our content structure of sub-chapters of results which provide answers to the previously posed research questions.

4   Results

4.1   Everyday Work and Workplace

The general public stated that they regularly switch between working from home and regular office. Checking e-mails next to recording working hours is often mentioned as the first activity. Common areas of responsibility are (1) Leadership tasks, (2) Communications via e-mail, (3) Meetings in person or via web video, (4) Official file processing, (5) Political and legal tasks, (6) Internal budget and personnel tasks, (7) Organization of business trips and travel expenses, (8) IT tasks, (9) Daily project work, (10) Working with maps and geo-data and (11) Journalistic duties.

More than half of the participants stated to preferably work on a laptop with 1–2 extended monitors. In municipalities, people tend to work with desktop computers, while occasionally working in home office laptops and cameras are borrowed. Almost a third uses additional mobile devices (e.g. a tablet, smartphone or similar) for telephony, e-mails or video meetings (e.g. WebEx). At home office, private devices (e.g. screen, webcam, laptop, smartphone) are in addition used for business purposes (e.g. 2-factor authentication). Some of the state employees wish for a business smartphone with connection to the state network for checking e-mail and calendar. Three more employees (municipalities and state) desire an additional tablet for meetings or a convertible.

At least half of participants have no preference towards either web or installed programs. The other half, especially in municipalities, prefers installed programs over to web programs for a variety of reasons. Two participants mentioned, that in cooperation with other federal states and the EU, often various web applications are used (for video conferences).

4.2 Major Office Applications, Functionalities and Integrations

Applications such as (1) E-mail, (2) Calendar, (3) Word processing and (4) Video conferencing are used by everyone. A (5) Shared document management system is wished for by nearly all participants.

In regard to the most necessary functions, 11 participants stated that they are satisfied with MS Office. 8 participants require compatibility with (older) MS Office versions (in regard to file formats, formatting). 5 participants wish an (6) E-file integration for linking documents to their e-file-application, and (7) an integration to tax procedures (2 participants).

Currently, various document exchange systems are used, basically in form of (8) Local network storages and (9) Diverse cloud services. 4 participants stated, there is major problems when working with cloud storage systems, mostly because of no existing knowledge of such or no possibility to have access to shared documents at all. 100 MB storage space was rated as insufficient for geo survey data by 2 participants. Almost everyone wished for a (10) Universal document management system, so that files can be easily shared between federal, state and local authorities. Moreover, file versioning (3 participants) and external access to documents (1 participant) were also mentioned to be necessary.

MS Outlook is the main means of communication for e-mail, besides RegiSafe in municipalities. For legally compliant communication, DE-Mail is partially available, but not or only occasionally used, beBPo as alternative. 6 participants stated that it should be possible to send e-mails securely and easily (with PDF) across authorities.

A calendar application (e.g. MS Outlook, dReservierung) is used by everyone. 7 participants wished to have access to shared calendars. Also, keeping calendars synchronized between web-, desktop and mobile applications is of high importance.

Almost half of participants stated freely, that between federal states the use of various web-based video-conferencing applications (third-party providers, e.g. WebEx, Zoom) to be problematic due to missing permissions by the state authority. Participants want to make spontaneous video and phone calls (4 participants). An interpretation function or audio-transcription are also necessary (4 participants). Moreover, they wished for additional features such as an integrated chat, breakout rooms, shared document space, mind mapping, whiteboard and note-taking functionalities.

Word processing is used for all official written correspondence (e.g. notices, approvals, speeches, certificates). The most important functions range from creating and working with templates (13 participants), creating official forms, serial letters and PDFs to inserting Excel-tables and table of contents.

4.3 Complementary Office Applications

In addition to the major office programs, (1) Telephony (13 participants) and (2) PDF applications (11 participants) are used most frequently.

One federal state employee stated, that almost all in state authorities use softphone telephony, either via installed software or via softphone device. Municipalities mentioned that there is still no uniform telephony solution; softphone is only partially used. Nevertheless, the standard hard phone is still of relevance for many (9 participants).

Many participants also wished for a PDF editing program in order to create official forms (4 participants) including digital signatures (10 participants), checking their accessibility or archiving PDF/A-documents (3 participants).

Further, (3) Notes (12 participants), (4) Project management tools (7 participants) and (5) Creative apps & collaborative platforms (7 participants) are requested.

4.4 E-File and Other Specialist Applications

Participants answered, that there are numerous specialist applications, mainly from the areas of human resources management, public laws and the e-file, whereas the latter is the most frequently used specialist application.

Some of the various e-file applications in use are (1) VIS, (2) RegiSafe, (3) ePA2 and (4) Optimal. A hybrid (electronic and paper-based) file management was stated to very often be problematic (7 participants) because of multiple media breaks. In particular, assigning an e-file to someone is cumbersome (6 participants) or outside an authority not possible at all. VIS, widely used (22 participants), was criticized by at least 14 participants not to be user-friendly and having an unreliable performance when large data and files. Inside the e-file, text and spreadsheet integrations are essential (4 participants), especially when working with templates – also a PDF export (3 participants) and an e-mail integration (2 participants). Vice versa, an e-file integration for text and spreadsheet applications should make importing and exporting documents to the e-file easy (7 participants).

4.5 Data and Services

In general, a data dashboard was considered to be useful (2 participants). Registers used are (1) Dog ownership register, (2) Marriage register, (3) Data of public gatherings, (4) Competition registry and (5) Registers of organic farms. Furthermore, various external databases were used such as (6) OrganicXlivestock Germany, (7) several GIS/Geo databases, (8) Veterinary-related databases and (9) Directories of agricultural organizations. Further public data of interest were (10) Health data, (11) Traffic data, (14) Environmental energy data, (15) Technical specification data and (16) Metadata from e-files.

5   Conclusions

Based on our research and with the focus set by the Gaia-X project on sovereign open source solutions for the cloud workplace, we can summarize the following findings. Through the evaluation of the qualitative interviews, we can identify 3 key areas that are relevant to employees in public administration with their areas of responsibility: standard office applications, specialized applications for public administration and optional applications for collaboration.

To conclude, for further studies, we suggest to extend the target group to other federal states, the federal government and other European countries. Quantitative analytics and/or surveys could provide reliable information on user numbers of office, specialist applications and data services. Also, usability studies focused on each single application would deliver more details. Moreover, participating students should be offered incentives or other compensations. Finally, a good change management would keep future users constantly in the loop.

The research results will be used in the future within the POSSIBLE project to further prioritize and plan the development of the cloud workplace as well as interfaces of other Gaia-x services.

References

1. Bechtle, A.G.: The POSSIBLE way – Phoenix Open software stack for interoperable engagement in Dataspaces. https://www.possible-gaia-x.eu/index_en.html. Accessed 19 Jan 2023
2. Nielsen, J.: Usefulness, Utility, Usability: 3 Goals of UX Design. https://www.nngroup.com/videos/usefulness-utility-usability/. Accessed 11 May 2023
3. Kun, A.L., et al.: SIGCHI at 40: celebrations and aspirations. Interactions **29**(6) (November–December 2022), 24–29. https://doi.org/10.1145/3564036
4. BMWK - Federal Ministry for Economic Affairs and Climate Action: The Gaia-X Hub Germany. https://www.bmwk.de/Redaktion/EN/Dossier/gaia-x.html. Accessed 19 Jan 2023
5. Dataport: About Project Phoenix. Project Phoenix - for a Digitally Sovereign German State. https://www.dataport.de/about-phoenix/?pk_vid=8bb358ccf7f252df1674140247c109bf. Accessed 19 Jan 2023
6. Bundesministerium des Innern und für Heimat: Souveräner Arbeitsplatz. https://www.cio.bund.de/Webs/CIO/DE/digitale-loesungen/digitale-souveraenitaet/souveraener-arbeitsplatz/souverarner-arbeitsplatz-node.html. Accessed 11 Jan 2023
7. Marita Blank-Babazadeh: Säulen des digital souveränen Open-Source-Arbeitsplatzes. schleswig-holstein.de – Projekte. https://www.schleswig-holstein.de/DE/landesregierung/themen/digitalisierung/linux-plus1/Projekt/projekt_node.html. Accessed 1 May 2023
8. Yin, R.K.: Case Study Research: Design and Methods, 5th edn. SAGE Publications, Los Angeles (2014)
9. Siemon, D.: Methods in Design Science Research. Design Science Research. https://design-science-research.de/en/post/methods-in-dsr/. Accessed 11 Jan 2023
10. Stickdorn et al.: Method Library - This is Service Design Doing. https://www.thisisservicedesigndoing.com/methods. Accessed 11 Jan 2023
11. Mayring, P., Fenzl, T.: Qualitative Inhaltsanalyse. In: Baur, N., Blasius, J. (eds.) Handbuch Methoden der empirischen Sozialforschung, pp. 543–556. Springer, Wiesbaden (2014). https://doi.org/10.1007/978-3-531-18939-0_38

Government Digital Transformation
in Indonesia

Riswan Wagola[1]([⊠]), Achmad Nurmandi[2], Misran[1], and Dimas Subekti[1]

[1] Department of Government Affairs and Administration, Yogyakarta Muhammadiyah
University, Yogyakarta, Indonesia
riswan.wagola.psc22@mail.umy.ac.id
[2] Department of Government Affairs and Administration, Jusuf Kalla School of Government,
Muhammadiyah University Yogyakarta, Yogyakarta, Indonesia
Nurmandi_achmad@umy.ac.id

Abstract. This study aims to analyze the current development of e-government
in Indonesia, the obstacles in its implementation, and how digital government is
transformed. The government's current challenge is to make the most of technology to improve public services and government administration. This study uses
qualitative research with a literature study approach. The data sources in this study
were taken from secondary data via, Focus Group Discussion conducted by the
Ministry of Home Affairs Research and Development in May 2019 to identify
e-government obstacle factors, an e-government survey published by the United
Nations and an E-government Evaluation issued by the Indonesian Ministry of
Apparatus Empowerment and Bureaucratic Reform. The data obtained were analyzed using descriptive analysis techniques. Studies show that the development of
e-government in Indonesia has not been maximized compared to other ASEAN
countries. The E-government index in government institutions is not evenly distributed. There is a gap between the e-government index and the central institution
and a gap between the Provincial and District/City Governments. The inhibiting
factors of e-government are (1) Inadequate regulations to encourage and guide
e-government, (2) Lack of data integration; (3) Gaps in the availability of ICT
infrastructure between regions; (4) Limited competence in the field of ICT and
(5) Bureaucratic culture and leadership. The development of e-government in
Indonesia has not been maximized. The survey, which is published every two
years, ranks the 193 member states of the United Nations (UN). There are three
performance dimensions measured in EGDI, including the Online Service Index
(OSI), Telecommunication Infrastructure Index (TII), and Human Capital Index
(HCI). Indonesia's e-government does not rank low in this index. Indonesia's
EGDI rating has increased from 107 in 2018 to 88 in 2020. Several factors hinder
the implementation of e-government in Indonesia. Explicitly, e-government regulations and policies are considered slow in responding to the dynamics of ICT
development and people's need for digital services. Another crucial problem in
e-government implementation is the lack of data integration; e-government regulations and policies are considered slow in responding to the dynamics of ICT
development and the public's need for digital services. Another crucial problem
in e-government implementation is the lack of data integration; e-government regulations and policies are considered slow in responding to the dynamics of ICT
development and the public's need for digital services.

C. Stephanidis et al. (Eds.): HCII 2023, CCIS 1835, pp. 286–296, 2023.
https://doi.org/10.1007/978-3-031-36001-5_37

Keywords: Indonesia · e-government · digital transformation · obstacle factor

1 Introduction

Rapid technological advances and each industrial revolution bring about extensive structural changes. Technological advances such as the steam engine and electrification and assembly line automation forever changed the way we make, distribute and sell products (Corejova and Roman 2021). The Industrial Revolution 4.0 and Society 5.0 have encouraged the government to utilize technology to improve public services and the quality of government administration. Recently, in the era of the Industrial Revolution 4.0, the world has massively used Internet of Things, Big Data, Artificial Intelligence and Robotic technologies for the industrial and business sectors. Digital innovation is growing rapidly where old ways are being replaced by new technologies (Saksono 2021).

Digital technology is the driving force behind today's industrial revolution. This technology is experiencing rapid development. A well-known example of this is Moore's law, which states that from the 1970s to the present, the number of integrated circuits doubled every two years.(Corejova and Roman 2021) proclaims that the fourth industrial revolution will affect every essence of our human experience. This has disrupted human activities in various fields of life, namely economic, social, political, cultural, and environmental (Schwab 2016).

There are two basic reasons why digital transformation is needed in government, especially in implementing e-government. First, improve public services and governance. Second, building the government's readiness to face a wave of change due to the emergence of Industry 4.0 and Society 5.0. (Koo 2019), it is very important to establish innovative strategies for governments that utilize the Internet of Things, Big Data, Artificial Intelligence, and Robotics. In particular, to keep up with changes in an information-smart society, it is necessary to undertake a significant transformation from today's e-government to digital governance (Saksono 2021).

This study aims to analyze the development of e-government in Indonesia, identify challenges in implementing e-government.

2 Literature Review

2.1 E-government

The era of digitalization has changed governance around the world significantly (Saksono 2020). There are several reasons why governments are transforming and transitioning to e-government. The transition to e-government is part of the current trend to reform the public sector, which has emerged in many countries in recent years, primarily driven by the aspirations of citizens around the world, who are placing new demands on government. Some requests add to the need for efficiency, transparency, and overall better performance, and some are coached by the wave of innovation stemming from the adoption of the internet and web-based services. After witnessing the potential for revolution and administrative feeling (Saksono 2021). The need to reduce the gap that exists between the private and public sectors, more and more governments are adopting e-government as a strategy to support development (Ronchi 2019).

Digitalization in the corporate realm takes place in three phases. In the first phase, the individual activities of the selected processes are automated. In the second phase, related activities are automated and consolidated to eliminate all unnecessary tasks. In the third and most complex phase, business process and information flow systems are integrated into a single enterprise information system, which can be represented by enterprise resource planning software or other digital technologies (Corejova and Roman 2021).

In a previous study, Muñoz and Bolívar (2018) highlighted the importance of implementing e-government in developing countries. In particular, e-government can promote civic engagement by enabling the public to interact with government officials and has the potential to engage citizens in the governance process by engaging them in interactions with policy makers through the policy cycle. Strengthening community involvement contributes to building public trust in the government. It is also associated with a strong commitment to promote transparency and accountability, lead to combating corruption, provide greater access to government information, make government more accountable, reduce crime, and provide citizens with higher quality services (Muñoz and Bolívar 2018)

There is a case in Aceh, Indonesia, where the availability of e-government services provided by several government organizations does not have a positive impact on the economic and social improvement of the community. (Saksono 2021). Instead, it creates a form of exclusivity and creates clear technological gaps that ultimately leave governments to work manually. Governance supports the use of Information and Communication Technology (ICT) systems for each public sector. However, some other public sectors, such as public policy, financial reporting, and organizational planning, do not use it. In addition, ICT is not integrated with each other within the organization (Fazil 2018).

2.2 Digital Transformation

Digital transformation can be understood from the point of view of several experts. Digital transformation can be understood as a strategy for companies to integrate digital and physical elements to change their business models and set new directions for entire industries (Berman and Bell 2011). In the government sector, digital transformation is defined as the use of technology to improve the performance of government agencies (Westerman et al. 2011). The Municipal Government of Austria uses digital transformation as a means of modernizing and updating business processes and business models supported by Information and Technology, so that business processes and business models become the center of attention (Peranzo 2020). It can be concluded that digital transformation in government is a change made by an institution through the development of the internet and digital technology to improve the performance of government agencies. This is important to improve the quality of public services and public administration.

The digital transformation strategy focuses on transforming products, processes and aspects of the organization thanks to new technologies. Their scope is designed to be broader and explicitly include digital activities at the interface with or entirely on the customer side, such as digital technology as part of an end-user product (Matt et al. 2015).

Koo (2019) has stated that the history of digital transformation has experienced three stages of development over time. Phase 1 "Digital Infrastructure Development (1990s)": During this time the Internet was introduced in earnest. The backbone for the internet has been started. Stage 2 "Digital Business Strategy (2000s)": During this period, the Internet became popular and was actively used. In addition, infrastructure providers who have the authority and experience in building infrastructure are the backbone of information. Governments develop many unique functions, such as finance, supply chain and human resources. It is necessary to increase productivity and efficiency via the internet. Stage 3 "Digital Transformation (2010s)": This period is when user access to the internet has expanded and become stronger, and their authority on the internet is strengthened. The mobile revolution and the rise of social media have helped to share information between users easily (Koo 2019).

This study aims to analyze the development of e-government in Indonesia, identify the inhibiting factors, and suggest digital transformation strategies to improve the implementation of e-government in Indonesia. The analysis of barriers to implementation of e-government adapts Muñoz and Bolívar's (2018) concept of some of the limitations of e-government. Furthermore, Serpanos (2018), Gottschalk (2009), Schooley and Horan (2007), and Scholl and Klischewski (2007).

3   Method

This study uses qualitative research with a literature study approach. Characteristics of qualitative research that "qualitative research focuses on the processes that occur and products or results. Researchers are passionate about understanding how things happen (Creswell and Creswell 2018, p. 320).

The research methodology can be grouped into two stages. First, the research phase is based on three sources: (1) an e-government survey published by the United Nations in 2010–2020, to analyze the evolution of the E-Government Development Index (EGDI) which refers to the following elements: Online Services Index (OSI), Telecommunication Infrastructure Index (TII) and Human Capital Index (HCP) and their influence on EGDI composition, from secondary data sets taken from the E-government Survey published by the United Nations (2012–2020). (2) The Digital Competitiveness Survey published by IMD World Digital Competitiveness 2015–2019 consists of 3 elements: knowledge, technology and future readiness.

4 Results and Discussion

4.1 Implementation of e-government in Indonesia

There are three performance dimensions that are measured in EGDI, including the Online Service Index (OSI), the Telecommunication Infrastructure Index (TII), and the Human Capital Index (HCI). Indonesia's e-government does not rank low in this index. Table 1 shows that Indonesia's EGDI ranking has increased from 107th in 2018 to 88th in 2020. However, Indonesia is relatively behind compared to other ASEAN member countries such as Singapore, Malaysia, Brunei, Thailand, the Philippines and Vietnam. In 2020, with the exception of Laos, the e-government ranking of all ASEAN Countries has increased significantly. That is, these countries have maintained and are continuously working to improve their e-government systems (UN 2012, 2014, 2016, 2018, 2020).

Table 1. E-government Development Index and Indonesia's Position in the 2010–2020 ASEAN Country Rankings

No	Country	2010	2012	2014	2016	2018	2020
1	Singapore	11	10	10	4	7	11
2	Malaysia	32	40	59	60	48	47
3	Thailand	76	92	54	77	73	57
4	Brunei	68	54	179	83	59	60
5	Philippines	78	88	51	71	75	77
6	Vietnamese	90	83	65	89	88	86
7	Indonesia	109	97	110	116	107	88
8	Cambodia	140	155	137	158	145	124
10	Timor Leste	162	170	186	160	142	134
9	Myanmar	141	160	172	169	157	146
11	Laos	151	153	137	148	162	167

Source: Compiled from United Nations E-government Survey, 2010–2020

As can be seen in the table above, it shows that in 2014, Indonesia was ranked 110th in the global ranking, and in 2016, Indonesia experienced less than optimal performance, dropping to 116th position. Up more than ten positions every two years, reaching 107th in 2018 and 88 in 2020. In 2020, Indonesia's EGDI ranking rose to position 88 (Table 2).

Table 2. EGDI Index, Its Components and Indonesia's Position in the World

No	Information	2012	2014	2016	2018	2020
1	E-government Development Index (EGDI) Rating	97	106	116	107	88
2	E-government Development Index (EGDI)	0.4949	0.4487	0.4478	0.5258	0.6612
3	Online Services Index (OSI)	0.4967	0.3622	0.3623	0.5694	0.6824
4	Telecommunications Infrastructure Index (TII)	0.1897	0.3054	0.3016	0.3222	0.566
5	Human Capital Index (HCI)	0.7982	0.6786	0.6796	0.6857	0.734

Source: UN E-government Survey, 2012–2020

From the data above it can be seen that in 2012–2020 Indonesia's EGDI ranking also fluctuated. In 2012–2016, the OSITII index and HCI were still below 0.5. Indonesia fared the worst in TII compared to OSI and HCI. The 2018 and 2020 surveys show that EGDI has increased significantly. The performance of the OSI, TII and HCP indexes increased sharply in 2018 and 2020. This resulted in Indonesia's EGDI ranking in 88th position in 2020. Indonesia recorded a fairly good score, OSI score 0.6824, TII score 0.5669., and a score of 0.7342 for HCI. All three components are above the world's average score. However, Indonesia is still below the regional average on the telecommunication infrastructure index score or TII when viewed from the Asian Regional and Southeast Asia Sub-Regional groups.

Table 3. World Digital Competitiveness Index and Indonesia's Position Among ASEAN Countries

No	Country	2015	2016	2017	2018	2019
1	Singapore	1	1	1	2	2
2	Malaysia	21	24	24	27	26
3	Thailand	42	39	41	39	40
4	Philippines	45	46	46	56	55
5	Indonesia	60	60	59	62	56

Source: Compiled from the 2015–2019 WDC IMD Survey

The table above shows that digitalization in Indonesia has not been maximally applied compared to other ASEAN countries. From the World Digital Competitiveness Survey (WDC) published by IMD WDC in 2018, Indonesia is ranked 62 out of 63 countries. This means that Indonesia is ranked second lowest out of 63 countries. From Table 3 it can be seen that in 2015–2018, Indonesia remained in the bottom rank while Singapore was in the top rank, followed by Malaysia and Thailand. In 2019, Indonesia has risen to 56th place. In addition, the readiness for innovation in facing the digital era shown by the Network Readiness Index shows that Indonesia is still ranked 73 out of 139 countries (Table 4).

4.2 E-government Evaluation in Indonesia

Table 4. E-government evaluation Index and its components

Domain and evaluation aspects	Number of indicators	Total score
Domain 1 - Internal E-government Policy	**17**	**17%**
Aspect 1: Internal Governance Policy	7	7%
Aspect 2: Service Internal Policy	10	10%
Domain 2 - E-government Governance	**7**	**28%**
Aspect 3: Institutional	2	8%
Aspect 4: Planning and Strategy	2	8%
Aspect 5: ITC	3	12%
Domain 3 - e-government services	11	55%
Aspect 6: Government Administration Services Based on Electronics	7	35%
Aspect 7: Electronic-Based Public Services	4	20%

Source: Ministry of Administrative Reform and Bureaucratic Reform of the Republic of Indonesia (2019)

Focus Group Discussion (FGD) conducted by the Ministry of Home Affairs Research and Development in May 2019. The FGD aims to understand the inhibiting factors for e-government development and formulate a direction for the transformation of e-government development. FGD participants consisted of individuals from (1) Ministry of Administrative Reform and Bureaucratic Reform (MENPAN), (2) Ministry of Communication and Information (KOMINFO), (3) Ministry of National Development Planning/National Development Planning Agency (Bappenas), (4) Agency for the Assessment and Application of Technology, and (5) State Administrative Institutions (Fig. 1).

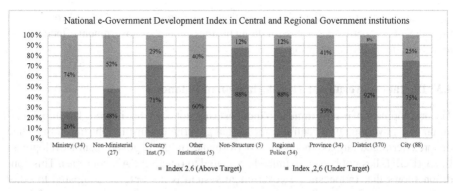

Fig. 1. Central and Regional Government National e-Government Index (Source: Ministry of Administrative Reform and Bureaucratic Reform of the Republic of Indonesia, 2019)

In the Figure above, it can be observed that there are gaps in the development of the e-government index between central and local government agencies. For example, the average index of 34 ministries is 74%, or above the national target (2.88) indicating that e-government systems can be placed in the very good category (2.6–3.5). On the other hand, only 29% of state institutions (MPR, DPR, DPD, Presidential Institution, Constitutional Court, Judicial Commission, and Supreme Audit Agency) have achieved the target. In comparison, the remaining 71% of state institutions have not reached the e-government index target. Disparities also occur in local government. The average index of the 34 provincial governments was 9% above the target, while the district governments (370) were only 8% above the target.

Table 5. Competitiveness Index, Easy Doing Business Index, Corruption Perception Index and Government Index, and Indonesia's Position among ASEAN countries

Country	Global competitiveness index (20 19)		Ease of doing business (2020)		Corruption perception Index 2019 (180 Countries)		Government 2017 effectiveness index	
	Rank	Score	Rank	Score	Rank	Score	Rank	Score
Singapore	1	84.8	2	86.2	4	85	1	100
Malaysia	27	74.6	12	81.5	51	53	51	76.44
Thailand	40	68.1	21	80.1	101	36	71	66.83
Indonesia	50	64.6	73	69,6	85	40	98	54.81
Brunei	58	62.8	66	70.1	35	60		84.13
Vietnamese	67	61.5	70	69.8	96	37	99	52.88
Philippines	64	61.9	95	62.8	113	34	101	51.92

Source: Compiled from World Economic Forum, World Bank, Transparency International

Table 5 shows that Indonesia is not optimal compared to other ASEAN countries in the index of competitiveness, ease of doing business, index of government effectiveness, and ability to control corruption.

4.3 Digital E-government Transformation in Indonesia

The development of e-government in Indonesia has not been maximized. The implementation of e-government in central and regional government institutions has not reached the predetermined targets. Indonesia's performance in the E-government Development Index (EGDI) has not been maximized compared to other ASEAN countries. This condition shows that Indonesia's e-government system is not optimal compared to other ASEAN countries, especially in terms of the competitiveness index, the ease of doing business index, the government effectiveness index, and the ability to control corruption.

Barriers to implementing e-government in Indonesia can be identified as follows: leadership, human resources (ASN), digital divide, lack of coordination, and inadequate regulation. This is in line with the findings (Kumorotomo 2009) which states that the main problems in implementing e-government in Indonesia are infrastructure, leadership, and cultural factors.

The first problem, the lack of availability of ICT infrastructure. The development of e-government in government institutions requires the availability of infrastructure such as satellite technology, electricity networks, internet networks and availability of computers.

The second is the leadership factor. This factor is influenced by the discrepancy between central government policies and local government policies, inadequate regulations, inadequate budget allocations and unclear system standardization, all of which are determined by the commitment of leaders or officials to the implementation of e-government.

Third, cultural factors, e-government often collides with unsupportive work culture factors. This work culture factor among bureaucrats in government institutions often results in a lack of awareness and appreciation of the importance of e-government. What often arises is excessive fear or worry that e-government applications will threaten existing official positions. Integration between state agencies, departmental and non-departmental institutions is always constrained because they do not want to share data and information.

5 Conclusion

From the explanation above it can be concluded that the government's efforts in implementing e-government are quite good, although there are several factors that hinder the implementation of e-government in Indonesia. Explicitly, e-government regulations and policies are considered not optimal in responding to the dynamics of ICT development and the public's need for digital services. Another crucial problem in e-government implementation is the lack of data integration; the application of e-government in public services and government administration is minimal; the use of old technology is not in accordance with the progress of ICT in the industrial era; lack of collaboration between stakeholders, lack of digital leadership vision, and gaps in the availability of ICT infrastructure, especially in remote areas.

Therefore, digital transformation is needed in the performance of e-government in Indonesia, which includes the following elements: legal and policy arrangements that can guide the implementation of e-government; improving digital systems, namely data centers, intra-government networks and applications that are more integrated and straightforward; bureaucratic restructuring; improve bureaucratic ICT competency; changes in work culture that encourage officials to work digitally; developing leadership with a digital vision, increasing sector collaboration and fostering collaboration between the government and the private sector as well as providing ICT infrastructure, especially equal distribution of internet access to remote areas.

This study recommends a strategy to accelerate digital transformation in e-government implementation. First, strengthening the e-government based government system; (1) strengthening policies by developing guidelines for risk management, guidelines for service management, and guidelines for ICT audit management. (2) Effective e-government collaboration by coordinating teams involving relevant agencies (3) Making effective use of e-government architecture and roadmaps. Second, preparing digital infrastructure technology, in particular by building e-government infrastructure together, utilizing broadband networks for accessibility, utilizing cloud-based applications, developing technology-based services 4.0 (cloud computing, artificial intelligence, big data, and internet of things).

References

Aminah, S., Wardani, D.K.: Analysis of regional innovation implementation readiness. Bina Praja J. **10**(1), 13–26 (2018)

Berman, S., Bell, R.: Digital transformation: Creating a new business model where digital meets physical. In: IBM Institute for Business Value (Ed.), IBM Global Business Services: Strategy and Transformation [Executive report]. IBM Global Business Services (2011)

Fazil, M.: Characteristics of Information and Communication Technology (ICT) Innovations and Their Application (Descriptive Study in Lhokseumawe City). J. Commun. Malaysia **34**(3), 379–391 (2018)

Gottschalk, P.: Maturity level for interoperability in digital government. Gov. Inf. Q. **26**(1), 75–81 (2009)

Harayama, Y.: Society 5.0: aiming for a new human-centered society - Japan's science and technology policy to address global social challenges. Cover Story Creating Collaboration through Global R&D TRENDS in Overview Hitachi **66**(6), 553–559 (2017)

Ministry of Communication and Information of the Republic of Indonesia. 2019a report of the Ministry of Communication and Information of the Republic of Indonesia. KOMINFO Indonesia (2019a)

Ministry of Administrative Reform of the Republic of Indonesia. Policy and evaluation of electronic-based government systems (Presentation material delivered at the Focus Group Discussion, at the Research and Development Agency, Ministry of Home Affairs, 8 May 2019)

Ministry of State Apparatus Empowerment and Bureaucratic Reform of the Republic of Indonesia. System government basedelectronic (SPBE) (2019b)

Koo, E.: Government digital transformation: from E-Government to smart E-Government [Master's thesis]. Massachusetts Institute of Technology (2019)

Matt, C., Hess, T., Benlian, A.: Digital transformation strategy. Bus. Inf. Syst. Eng. **57**, 339–343 (2015)

Muñoz, L.A., Bolívar, M.P.R.: Experience of implementing e-government development in developing countries: challenges and solutions. In: International e-government Development: Policy, Implementation, and Best Practice, pp. 3–18. Jumper (2018)

Novita, D.: Factors inhibiting the development of e-government: a case study of the government of Palembang City South Sumatra. J. Inform. Explora **4**(1), 43–52 (2014)

Peranzo, P.: What is digital transformation & why is it important for business. imaginovation.net [blog] (2020, March 4)

Ronchi, A.M.: e-Government: background, today's implementation and future trends In, e-Democracy: towards a new model of (inter)active society (Chapter 5, pp. 93–196) (2019)

Saksono, H.: The new face of regional autonomy: status of performance versus realistic conditions in the province of South Kalimantan. J. Dev. Policy **11**, 63–75 (2016)

Saksono, H.: Center for innovation: Collaborative media towards innovative local government. Nahkoda: J. Govern. Sci. **19**(1), 1–16 (2020)

Salgues, B.: Society 5.0: Future Industries, Technologies, Methods And Tools (Vol. 1). Wiley (2018)

Application of SP4N-LAPOR to Improve the Quality of Public Services and Information (Case Study in Indonesia)

Annisa Millania Wildhani[1]([📧]), Achmad Nurmandi[2], Misran[1], and Dimas Subekti[1]

[1] Department of Government Affairs and Administration, Muhammadiyah University of Yogyakarta, Yogyakarta, Indonesia
`a.millania.psc22@mail.umy.ac.id`

[2] Department of Government Affairs and Administration, Jusuf Kalla School of Government, Muhammadiyah University Yogyakarta, Yogyakarta, Indonesia
`nurmandi_achmad@umy.ac.id`

Abstract. This study aims to analyze the quality of the SP4N-LAPOR E-Government-Based Public Service Application. Researchers use a qualitative descriptive approach. Researchers used the E-GovQual indicator. There are several indicators namely Ease of Use, Trust, Reliability, content and display of information, and citizen support. Data sources from the Website, SP4N-LAPOR Application, and News, the data obtained is processed using Nvivo 12plus software. The data displayed in the form of crosstab analysis and wordcloud analysis are then presented descriptively as a result of SP4N-LAPOR quality observations. The finding of this study is that SP4N-LAPOR has been able to improve the quality of public services in the field of information and complaint reports. This is shown by the ease of use of SP4N-LAPOR received a positive response to ease of use of 78.25%, quick response of 72.79%, and transparency of 71.7%, the number of positive comments was more than negative comments. Trust in SP4N-LAPOR has increased over the past 4 years. In 2017 the number of users was 661,905, in 2018 it was 766,237, in 2019 it was 953,921 users and in 2020 it was 1,145,944 users. Third, the reliability of SP4N-LAPOR is accurate from the managing admin in serving and responding to complaint reports. Content and display make it easier for the public to choose the type of report to create. Finally, citizen support. SP4N-LAPOR provides useful features to protect user confidentiality and personal information when reviewing the reporting process. The features provided are anonymous, secret, and tracking ID features.

Keywords: E-Government · SP4N-LAPOR · Public Service

1 Introduction

In the era of industrial revolution 4.0, almost all sectors of life are undergoing digitalization, one example is the public service sector. In government, the services provided not only meet the needs of the people but also manage complaints about public services

© The Author(s), under exclusive license to Springer Nature Switzerland AG 2023
C. Stephanidis et al. (Eds.): HCII 2023, CCIS 1835, pp. 297–305, 2023.
https://doi.org/10.1007/978-3-031-36001-5_38

[1]. The Indonesian government is also committed to supporting innovation in the civil service, which includes innovations in governance structures and public service delivery [2]. ICT plays an important role in people's lives, including technology solutions and effective applications in E-Service processes. Indonesian public service that uses electronic media is SP4N-LAPOR as a place for public complaints [3]. SP4N-LAPOR is an integrated national service to convey all desires and complaints of the community. Previously, many Indonesians were misplaced to make complaints which resulted in many reports or complaints that were not resolved. SP4N-LAPOR is a system formed to promote the concept of a "No Wrong Door Policy". This complaint management system is a means of collecting social media-based community aspirations [4]. SP4N-LAPOR aims to: 1) Organizers can handle public complaints in a simple, fast, accurate, complete, and well-coordinated manner, 2) Regulators provide rights access to public participation in complaint filing and 3) Improve the quality of public service. SP4N-LAPOR has been connected with 657 Agencies, with the following classifications, 34 Ministries, 100 Institutions, 34 Provincial Governments, 395 District Governments, and 94 Municipalities [5]. According to SP4N-LAPOR annual report data, throughout 2019 there were 196,437 reports received [6] and in 2020, 195,438 reports were coming in [5]. It is hoped that the public will be more confident that the complaints services provided by the government can resolve their complaints with simple and targeted processes and procedures [7]. The presence of public information services functioned as a free space for the public to access the widest possible information, to achieve good governance based on transparency [8].

The previous research was carried out by Laurensia Nindyta Angelina Haspo [3]. Public dissatisfaction with a service provided by the government will lead to complaints because the results received are different from what is expected [9]. The government can create good public services and improve services by conveying aspirations from the public, complaints, and information about conditions being felt [10]. This program is an online service to convey all aspirations and complaints from the community which is integrated nationally with 4 pages of website access, SMS 1708, Twitter @lapor1708, and a mobile application.

This study aims to analyze the quality of the SP4N LAPOR application, to see how administrators can easily and quickly manage community complaints and provide access to the public to convey their aspirations and complaints about government performance as well as efforts to improve the quality of public services.

2   Literature Review

2.1   E-Government

Based on Indrajit's research, e-government is a government that is run through information technology that allows the government to connect with the community quickly [11]. The World Bank defines e-government as providing transparent services to the public, easy access to information, and effective and efficient accountability [12]. The government is run through information technology that can carry out transaction processes and communications between departments, organizations, and individuals. to create good governance [13]. E-GovQual indicators are, 1) Ease of use, 2) Trust, 3) Reliability, 4)

Content and appearance information, and 5) Citizen support (support) [14]. Three main components are service, receiver, and service channel (technology). For example, in public E-Service, the government is the service provider, and citizens and businesses are the recipients of the service.

2.2 E-Service

E-service is an application that needs information and communication technology (ICT) [15]. According to Rowley, the main components are services, service receivers, and service channels (technologies) [16]. For example, electronic services consist of 3 components, the first is the government as a service provider, the second are citizens and service recipients, and the third is the service channels of E-Service. Quality e-service is the way to create long-term success and excellence and be a competitive advantage [17]. The quality of E-Service is good, it will create customer satisfaction. High-quality e-Service, based on a thorough analysis and understanding of the needs, behaviors, and attitudes of citizens can be a way to achieve those goals [18]. In an attractive value position for E-Service, the public can contribute to more citizens choosing online services, rather than calling or making private visits. Quality E-Service is a service provided to consumers using the Internet [19]. People's satisfaction as consumers is paramount for the government.

3   Research Methods

This research uses a qualitative descriptive method using the E-GovQual theory. In this study, researchers took research data obtained from the Website, SP4N-LAPOR Mobile Application, and Mass Media. Data collection techniques through the Literature Study approach and then the data obtained will be processed using Computer Assigned Qualitative Data Software (CAQDS) analysis, namely Nvivo 12plus. The data is displayed in the form of Crosstab visualizations and WordCloud Analysis.

4   Results and Discussion

4.1   Ease of Use

To realize a "No Wrong Door Policy" that guarantees the right of the public to complaints from anywhere. E-government is a solution to realize easy service for the community based on applications. The ease of using SP4N-LAPOR, three indicators to see how users respond to the SP4N-LAPOR application 1. Access 2. Response 3. Transparency (Fig. 1).

Based on the diagram above, the user convenience of the SP4N LAPOR application shows two different responses, 1). Positive Comments 2). Negative Comments are viewed using the Access, Response, and Transparency Indicators. The chart above shows the 78.25% Ease of Access rate getting a good response from the community while 21.75% got negative feedback. Furthermore, regarding the response to get a percentage of 72.79 for positive comments while negative comments of 72.21%, it can be concluded that

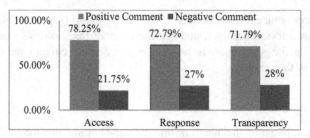

Fig. 1. Community Response in the case of SP4N-LAPOR. Source: Processed by researchers using Nvivo12plus.

positive comments from the public are more dominant on this indicator. Then the last indicator is Transparency, which a percentage of positive comments of 71.79% while the percentage of negative comments is 28.03%. The conclusion is that the SP4N- LAPOR application has been able to provide convenience for the public in terms of ease of users in accessing the application, as well as good responsiveness and transparency.

4.2 Trust

The development of the SP4N-LAPOR Application has progressed very significantly, it has been developed in such a way that it can be utilized easily and optimally by all Indonesian people. However, before this application can be utilized properly and optimally by the community, the first step the government must take is to first convince the public to want to access and use the SP4N-LAPOR to gain the trust and support of the community. Because trust from the community is the first thing that will affect the usability of the SP4N-LAPOR application so that it is efficient and achieves its targets (Fig. 2).

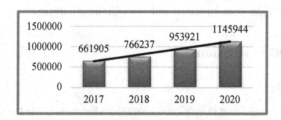

Fig. 2. The number of SP4N-LAPOR Users. Source: SP4N-LAPOR Annual Report 2020.

Based on the diagram above, SP4N-LAPOR users based on complaints, submission of aspirations, and aspirational requests from 4 years, in 2017 the number of users was 661,905 users, in 2018 the number of users was 766,237 users, in 2019 the number of users was 953,921 users and in 2020 the number of users was 1,145,944 users. This shows that the level of public trust in SP4N-LAPOR is increasing from year to year. The increasing number of users shows the trust of the Indonesian people in implementing Electronic-based Public Services or E-Services, in reporting, conveying aspirations, and requesting data. Public trust in using the application can also be seen from the number of reports that come in, including the 5 most popular report categories (Table 1).

Table 1. Most Popular Report SP4N-REPORT!

No.	Report name	Number of reports
1	Staff	22008
2	Population Administration	17272
3	Infrastructure	16906
4	Social Health Insurance Administration Agency	15918
5	Community Temporary Direct Assistance (BLSM)	15182

Source: SP4N-LAPOR Application

The table above shows the 5 most popular reports in reporting, submission of aspirations, and requests for information in SP4N-LAPOR, the Population Service is at the top with a total of 22,008 reports, the Population Administration 17,272 reports, Infrastructure 16,906 reports, BPJS Kesehatan 15,918 reports, and the Community Temporary Direct Assistance (BLSM) 15,182 reports. Of the many complaints that come in, the following will show the status of the report that is being completed, followed up and the report is being processed in the diagram below (Fig. 3).

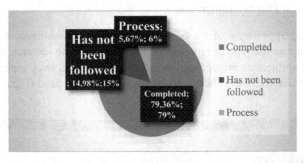

Fig. 3. Status Report for 2020

The report completion rate is one of the benchmarks for E-Service success, the 2020 status report on SP4N-LAPOR for reports, aspiration submissions, and data requests has been completed or completed by 79.36%, 14.98% has not been followed up, and 5.67% is still in the process stage (Fig. 4).

4.3 Reliability

SP4N-LAPOR Application Position self as a facilitator of provision E-Service, SP4N LAPOR provides various conveniences in the service. Reliability is seen from the accuracy of the managing admin in serving and responding to complaint reports that come in on the application and website.

Fig. 4. Reliability of SP4N-LAPOR. Source: Processed by researchers using Nvivo12plus

From the data presented, Reability of SP4N-LAPOR Applications, WordCloud results show that the dominant words that come out are Access, Response, and Transparency. Understandably, many SP4N-LAPOR users comment on access rights, transparent feedback, and validation. This shows the reliability of this application to help people easily access online services, the SP4N-LAPOR application also provides features that can meet people's service needs. Based on the 2021 user satisfaction survey, out of 1,329 respondents, 75.7% said they were satisfied with the complaint service. There are also some complaints. Several indicators need to be improved, including the accuracy of admins in determining agencies/management units, the speed of response from relevant agencies, and the speed of complaint resolution [20].

4.4 Content and Display Information

The content and appearance of the SP4N LAPOR application make it very easy for the public to choose the type of report to be made because the features available in the SP4N-LAPOR application are optional to make complaints, convey aspirations and ask for information that users can choose according to what they need (Fig. 5).

Fig. 5. Display of contents and information of the SP4N-LAPOR Mobile Application. Source SP4N-LAPOR Mobile Application

The figure above shows that Content and Display Information is a structured information design displayed on the SP4N-LAPOR Application. In the Home view, it contains all the incoming reports that have been verified, then processed and the report complete. Then the search feature can be used to make it easier to see incoming news displayed according to the report category. Such as the categories of Education, Health, Environment, Corruption, and others. Furthermore, how to make a report is presented easily, just by writing a problem report and choosing the date of the incident, location, and intended agency. Then the second step is to select the report category, the last step is to review to see the status or process of the report. Content and appearance that is structured and can be understood easily and clearly to produce quality complaint information, namely Accuracy, (Relevance), Completeness, and Updates [21].

4.5 Citizen Support

This aspect explains that community support is assured when needed, related to the interaction between the community and customer service or features to support complaints from the community if the community has problems, difficult difficulties in the process of using the e-government site [22]. In providing optimal and efficient services to the public through digital-based services, the SPN4-LAPOR application provides useful features to protect the confidentiality and personal information, of users, and ease of reviewing the reporting process. Features provided for citizen support in SP4N-LAPOR: 1) Anonymous: A feature that can be selected by the whistleblower that will make the identity of the whistleblower unknown to the reported person and the general public; 2) Confidential: The entire contents of the report are not visible to the public; 3) Tracking id: A unique number useful for reviewing the follow-up process of reports submitted by the public. Using this complaint service, user data will be provided to agencies related to complaints and/or aspirations submitted by users.

5 Conclusion

The conclusion of this study shows that the application of SP4N- LAPOR has been able to improve the quality of public services in the field of information and complaint reports. This is demonstrated by the ease of use of the SP4N LAPOR application which received a positive response to ease of access by 78.25%, fast response of 72.79%, and transparency of 71.79%, where the number of positive comments was more than negative comments. Second, trust, based on complaints, the submission of aspirations, and requests for aspirations have always increased over the last 4 years. Namely, in 2017 the number of users was 661,905, in 2018 was 766,237, in 2019 was 953,921, and in 2020 were 1,145,944 users. This shows that the level of public trust in SP4N-LAPOR has increased from year to year. Third, the reliability of the SP4N LAPOR Application can be seen from the accuracy of the managing admin in serving and responding to incoming complaint reports on the application and website, the Word Cloud results show that the dominant words that appear are Access, Response, and Transparency and confirm. Plus, the content and appearance make it easy for people to choose the type of report to create.

References

1. Yulianto, M.: Efektivitas Aplikasi Sp4n Lapor (Sistem Pengelolaan Pengaduan Pelayanan Publik Nasional) Dalam Pengelolaan Pengaduan Masyarakat Di Dinas Komunikasi Dan Informatika Kabupaten Tangerang Provinsi Banten, pp. 1–14 (2022)
2. Pratama, A.B.: The landscape of public service innovation in Indonesia: a comprehensive analysis of its characteristic and trend. Innov. Manag. Rev. 17(1), 25–40 (2020). https://doi.org/10.1108/INMR-11-2018-0080
3. Haspo, L.N.A., Frinaldi, A.: Penerapan Aplikasi Sp4N-Lapor Dalam Manajemen Pengaduan Masyarakat Di Kota Solok. J. Manaj. dan Ilmu Adm. Publik 2(2), 26–33 (2020). https://doi.org/10.24036/jmiap.v2i2.122
4. Yahya, A.S., Setiyono: Efektivitas Pelayanan Publik Melalui Sistem Pengelolaan Pengaduan Aplikasi SP4N-LAPOR Pendayagunaan Aparatur Negara Dan Reformasi Birokrasi Nomor 3 Tahun 2015 Tentang Road Map Pengembangan Sistem Pengelolaan Pengaduan Pelayanan Publik Nasional (2015). K. J. Media Birokrasi 4, 1–22 (2022)
5. KEMENPAN-RB. Laporan Tahunan Pengelolaan SP4N-LAPOR (2020)
6. KEMENPAN-RB. Laporan Tahunan Pengelolaan SP4N-LAPOR (2019)
7. Sri Zulaikah, R., et al.: Analisis Sp4N Lapor Di Kantor Bagian Organisasi Sekretariat Daerah Kabupaten Karimun Analysis of Sp4N Lapor in the Office of the Organizational Secretariat of the Regional Secretariat of Karimun Regency", [Online]. https://doi.org/10.46730/jiana.v20i2
8. Arsyiah, W.O., Ramadhan, S.: Implementation of Open government partnership in public information services in Baubau City. Ann. Rom. Soc. 25(2), 2311–2316 (2021). http://annalsofrscb.ro/index.php/journal/article/view/1180
9. Chinedu, A.H., Haron, S.A., Osman, S.: Predictors of complain behaviour among mobile telecommunication network consumers. Int. J. Mark. Stud. 9(1), 119 (2017). https://doi.org/10.5539/ijms.v9n1p119
10. Hamjen, H., Nikmah, R.A.: Keragaman Pengaduan Layanan Publik Di Kalimatan Selatan Melalui Aplikasi Sp4N Lapor! Metacommun. J. Commun. Stud. 5(1), 66 (2020). https://doi.org/10.20527/mc.v5i1.7502
11. Indrajit, R., Prastowo, B., Abdullah, H.: Membangun aplikasi e-Government. Jakarta: Elex Media Komputindo (2002)
12. Bank, T. W.: e-Government. 2015. https://www.worldbank.org/en/topic/digitaldevelopment/brief/e-government. Accessed 25 Nov 2022
13. Putra, D.A.D., et al.: Tactical steps for e-government development. Int. J. Pure Appl. Math. 119(15), 2251–2258 (2018)
14. Maulani, W.: Penerapan Electronic Government Dalam Peningkatan Kualitas Pelayanan Publik (Studi Kasus Program E-Health Di Kota Surabaya). AS-SIYASAH J. Ilmu. Sos. Dan. Ilmu. Polit.5(2), 44–54, 2020 [Online]. https://ojs.uniska-bjm.ac.id/index.php/Asy/article/view/3248
15. Buchari, R.A.: Implementasi E-Service Pada Organisasi Publik Di Bidang Pelayanan Publik Di Kelurahan Cibangkong Kecamatan Batununggal Kota Bandung. Sosiohumaniora 18(3), 225 (2016). https://doi.org/10.24198/sosiohumaniora.v18i3.8762
16. Rowley, J.: An analysis of the e-service literature: towards a research agenda. Internet Res. 16(3), 339–359 (2006). https://doi.org/10.1108/10662240610673736
17. Naqibah, L.S., Cikusin, Y., Abidin, A.Z.: Implementasi Kebijakan Pelayanan Administrasi Kependudukan Berbasis E-Service (Studi Kasus Pelayanan E-Ktp Di Dinas Kependudukan Dan Pencatatan Sipil Kabupaten Rembang). J. Respon Publik 15(9), 22–30 (2021)
18. Candra, S., Valtin, E.I., Agustine, R.T.: E-Service quality of online transportation in Indonesia: a preliminary finding. In: 2019 7th International Conference on Cyber and IT Service Management (CITSM) (2019). https://doi.org/10.1109/CITSM47753.2019.8965343

19. Wallstrom, A., Engstrom, A., Sangari, E.S., Styven, M.E.: Public E-services from the citizens' perspective. Int. J. **2**, 123–134 (2009)
20. Juwaini, A., et al.: The role of customer e-trust, customer e-service quality and customer e-satisfaction on customer e-loyalty. Int. J. Data Netw. Sci. **6**(2), 477–486 (2022). https://doi.org/10.5267/j.ijdns.2021.12.006
21. KOMINFO. Penggunaan SP4N-LAPOR! Tingkatkan Pelayanan Publik Berkualitas. p. 2022, 2021 [Online]. https://aptika.kominfo.go.id/2021/11/Penggunaan-Sp4N-Lapor-Tingkatkan-Pelayanan-Publik-Berkualitas/
22. Wiranata, L.M.: Kualitas Aplikasi Lapor Mataram Dalam Layanan Pengaduan Masyarakat Di Kota Mataram Nusa Tenggara Barat **4**(1), 88–100 (2022)

Analysis of Service Quality Mobile Government on the PeduliLindungi

Lisa Sophia Yuliantini[1(✉)], Achmad Nurmandi[2], Misran[1], and Dimas Subekti[1]

[1] Departement of Government Affair and Administration, Universitas Muhammadiyah Yogyakarta, Yogyakarta, Indonesia
lisa.sophia.psc22@mail.umy.ac.id

[2] Departement of Government Affair and Administration, Jusuf Kalla School of Government, Universitas Muhammadiyah Yogyakarta, Yogyakarta, Indonesia
nurmandi_achmad@umy.ac.id

Abstract. This study aims to analyze the quality of mobile Government services on the PeduliLindungi application to combat the COVID-19 pandemic in Indonesia. The PeduliLindungi application is a mobile-based Government service in Indonesia that provides health services in combating the COVID-19 pandemic. The research method used in this study is descriptive qualitative by utilizing the N-Vivo 12plus in processing research data. The data sources of this study were obtained from the journal literature studies, the PeduliLindungi application, the website PeduliLindungi, online media, and the play store. This study uses four indicators of Service Quality for Mobile Government (SQ mGov) in analyzing the quality of mobile Government services based on indicators of Connectivity, Interactivity, Authenticity, and Understandability. The results that the quality of mobile Government services on the PeduliLindungi Applications is not yet optimal. This is based on the results of the analysis of the four Service Quality for Mobile Government (SQ mGov) indicators. The results of data processing from the connectivity indicator, the PeduliLindungi application, received 11%, the interactivity indicator received 12%, the authenticity indicator received 54% and understandability received 21%. The PeduliLindungi application is a form of mobile-based Government service that aims to make it easier for the community to get health services in handling the COVID-19 pandemic in Indonesia. However, in implementing these services, the Government needs to pay attention to the quality of services of the PeduliLindungi application so that the objectives of implementing mobile Government are achieved, and the benefits can be felt maximally by the community of Indonesia.

Keywords: Mobile Government · Service Quality · The PeduliLindungi App

1 Introduction

The spread of Corona Virus Disease – 19 or COVID -19 which first spread in Wuhan City, China has been announced as a global pandemic by the World Health Organization (WHO) on March 11, 2020 [1]. The spread of COVID-19 is very fast and uncontrolled throughout the world. The Covid-19 pandemic has been one of the toughest periods for all countries experiencing it, including Indonesia [2].

The COVID-19 pandemic not only has a direct impact on health aspects but also other aspects of life, such as economic and social aspects. The policy of social restrictions and regional quarantine has the potential to limit the community in carrying out economic activities so that the circulation of goods and services will be hampered and social [3].

In one of the government's efforts to maintain the stability of the health, economic, and social aspects of the community, the Indonesian government created an application PeduliLindungi [4]. The PeduliLindungi application is designed to help people take care of each other and protect each other so that the transmission of Covid-19 can be stopped [5].

A previous study that discussed the E-Service Quality Analysis in PeduliLindungi Applications During the COVID-19 Pandemic in DKI Jakarta indicates that the quality of e-service in the PeduliLindung application is in a good category [6]. Then another study showed that the PeduliLindungi application provided convenience to users through the features in the applications offered. The government also has a good strategy for convincing the public to use the PeduliLindung application by making rules that explain the obligation to use the PeduliLindung application in daily life during the COVID-19 pandemic [7].

The contribution of this research that distinguishes it from previous research is that this research will focus on analyzing the quality of mobile Government services on the Cares for Protection Application by using 4 (four) measurement indicators from Service Quality for Mobile Government (SQ mGov) [8].

This study aims to enrich scientific treasures in the quality of public services and the results of this study will assist the government in mapping aspects that are weak points in the quality of public services based on mobile applications organized by the government (m-Government). The results of this study are expected to be able to improve the quality of public services, especially in the application of m-Government in service delivery, both during the COVID-19 pandemic and the implementation of mobile application-based public services in the future.

2 Literature Review

2.1 Mobile Government

Mobile Government is a government service by utilizing the sophistication of mobile phone devices [9]. The background of the application of mobile government is the large number of people who use mobile devices, so this encourages the government to utilize mobile applications in providing services to the community with the aim that people can get government services more effectively and efficiently [10]. The use of mobile devices in government services is considered a pretty good service innovation, this is because by utilizing mobile devices, people can access government services anytime and anywhere [11].

Mobile Government is the development of e-Government implementation. This is because m-Government is a service replication of e-Government on a mobile platform [12]. Mobile Government based services can improve service quality in many fields. This is because services that were initially carried out face-to-face can be carried out online by simply utilizing the sophistication of mobile phone devices [13]. In addition, m-Government-based government services can increase community participation in development and are also able to reduce the digital divide, making government services much more transparent and reducing levels of corruption [14].

2.2 Service Quality of Mobile Government

Measuring service quality in the implementation of mobile government is very necessary for ensuring community satisfaction as recipients of services from mobile government. This is because the quality of service in implementing mobile government determines the continuation of society in using mobile government-based services [15]. In improving the quality of mobile government implementation, it is necessary to pay attention to the quality of information communication technology (ICT) implementation [16]. Measuring the quality of government services based on mobile government will assist the government in placing the necessary positions and priorities in providing services and can measure the level of success of implementing mobile government in a government service [17].

Furthermore, in looking at the success of service quality in the implementation of mobile government in Shareef and Mahmud Akhter (2014) it is stated that in measuring the quality of mobile government services it is measured based on indicators of connectivity, interactivity, authentication, and understandability, which is then called Service Quality Mobile Government (SQ mGov). The connectivity indicator measures the extent to which application services are available and can be accessed anywhere, any-time with a reasonable connection speed via the user's mobile device or mobile device. The interactivity indicator in the SQ mGov measures the extent to which the Government mobile application is easy to find and has easy steps in providing services as well as seeing the extent to which the interaction of services. The authentication indicator in SQ mGov measures how far the Government's responsible for any discrepancies during the processing of services of mobile Government and the understandability indicator measures how far service processing instructions and application service results are easily understood by users' mobile devices [8].

3 Method

The research method used in this study is descriptive qualitative by utilizing the N-Vivo 12plus in processing research data. The data sources of this study were obtained from the relevant journal literature studies, the PeduliLindungi application, the website PeduliLindungi, online media, and the play store. The mass media data used are from Antaranews, CNN Indonesia, Detik.com, and Kompas.com. This study uses four indicators of Service Quality for Mobile Government (SQ mGov) in analyzing the quality of mobile Government services based on indicators of Connectivity, Interactivity, Authenticity, and Understandability. Data analysis using Nvivo 12plus software with crosstab and world cloud analysis visualization. Data processing is carried out by capturing mass media and play store PeduliLindungi and then processing and coding manually. The flow of research methods in this study is as shown in the following figure (Fig. 1):

Fig. 1. The Stage of data processing research methods

4 Result and Discussion

The results of data processing using the nvivo 12plus application crosstab query in this study resulted in data processing analysis as follows:

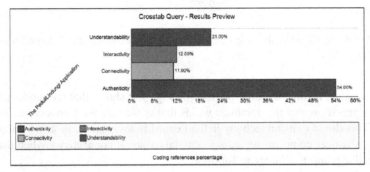

Fig. 2. The Crosstab Query analysis of SQ mGov of The PeduliLindungi Application. Using Nvivo 12plus 2022

Based on the results of the Crosstab Query on the quality analysis of the PeduliLindungi application, it shows that the lowest intensity is the connectivity indicator, with an intensity of 11%, then the interactivity indicator with an intensity of 12%, the authenticity indicator with 54%, then the understandability indicator, with an intensity value of 21%. Furthermore, an explanation of the four SQ mGov indicators in measuring the service quality of the PeduliLindungi application is explained as follows:

4.1 Connectivity

The connectivity indicator measures the extent to which the PeduliLindungi application service is available and can be accessed anywhere, anytime with a reasonable connection speed via the user's mobile device or mobile device. Based on the results of the crosstab query analysis in Fig. 2, it shows that the connectivity indicator in the PeduliLindungi application gets the lowest intensity value, namely 11%. This is because there are many complaints from users of the PeduliLindungi application in terms of connectivity. Many users of the PeduliLindungi application complain that when using the PeduliLindungi application they often experience connection problems, so users cannot access the PeduliLindungi application even though the network is stable. Connectivity problems in the PeduliLindungi application are very troubling to the community. This is because the

PeduliLindungi application is an application that is required by the government to be used by the public when entering public spaces and public transportation facilities. So connectivity problems in the PeduliLindungi application hinder people's daily activities. The following data will show the connectivity of The PeduliLindungi application:

Fig. 3. The World Cloud analysis of Connectivity of The PeduliLindungi Application. Using Nvivo 12plus 2022.

Based on the results of data processing in Fig. 3, it shows that the results of world cloud analysis show that the dominant words that appear are the words connection and trouble. This shows that connectivity in the PeduliLindungi application is a community problem. The user comment regarding complaints about connectivity when using the PeduliLindungi application are as follows:

> "Sorry... This app tests my patience. The information is not up to date, the network is smooth, loading all the time, and has a white screen when checking the certificate. Please handle it right away, because a certificate is needed when you want to travel" – User of PeduliLindungi

Based on this, it shows that the quality of mobile government services in terms of connectivity indicators needs to be a concern of the government in improving its quality so that people can use health services easily and do not experience problems.

4.2 Interactivity

Interactivity indicators in SQ mGov measure the extent to which the PeduliLindungi application is easy to find and has easy steps in providing services and sees the extent to which the interaction of services from the Government to the community has been successfully carried out using the PeduliLindungi application. Based on the results of crosstab query data processing in Fig. 2, showing interactivity indicators, the PeduliLindungi application gets an intensity of 12%. The appearance of the PenduliLindungi application on the play store shows the ease of searching for the PeduliLindungi application by users so that the PeduliLindungi application has become the second most popular application in the medical field in the play store with data of 1 million reviews and 50 million downloads and 3+ review ratings from PeduliLindungi application users. In addition, the PeduliLindungi application provides many means of communication to the public so that good interaction can be established between health services in the PeduliLindungi application and the community as users of the PeduliLindungi application. The community who uses the PeduliLindungi application can submit complaints and messages regarding the PeduliLindungi application through the official WhatsApp application of the Ministry of Health of the Republic of Indonesia at +6281110500567 and also via email at carelin-dungi@kemkes.go.id. Based on this, it shows that the government, especially the Ministry of Health of the Republic of Indonesia, always strives to improve the quality of mobile government services in the PeduliLindungi application.

4.3 Authenticity

The authentication indicator in SQ mGov's measurement measures how far the Government's responsibility is for non-compliance during service processing in the PeduliLindungi application and looks at service policies carried out via the user's mobile device sufficiently to protect users from problems that threaten data security using the PeduliLindungi Application. Based on the results of processing the crosstab query data in Fig. 2, the indicator for the authenticity of the PeduliLindungi application has an intensity of 54%. This is based on research data that explains that the PeduliLindungi application seeks to handle complaints from users of the PeduliLindungi application when experiencing problems and government efforts to resolve them. In addition, the high authenticity indicator is also based on data in the mass media which explains that the authenticity of the PeduliLindungi application starts from the process, and the results of the transaction are guaranteed security and are legally accountable by the Government. The data security of PeduliLindungi application users is guaranteed by the Government and overseen by the Indonesian National Cyber and Crypto Agency (BSSN). In this case, PeduliLindungi application users can access the official PeduliLindung website in the data privacy policy section (https://www.pedulilindungi.id/kebijakan-privasi-data). On the website, there is an explanation regarding data security, terms, and conditions as well as the confidentiality policy of the PeduliLindungi application.

4.4 Understandability

The understandability indicator measures how far service processing instructions and application service results are easily understood by the user's mobile devices and measures how far the PeduliLindungi application provides relevant information needed and fulfills user needs when accessing the PeduliLindungi application. Based on the results of the crosstab query analysis in Fig. 2 shows the understandability indicator on the PeduliLindungi application gets an intensity of 21%. This is because the PeduliLindungi application has features and explanations on how to use the application that is easy for users to understand. In addition, the understanding of the public using the PeduliLindungi application was also influenced by the socialization efforts carried out by the Ministry of Health of the Republic of Indonesia in socializing the use of the PeduliLindungi application. The socialization effort was carried out through the official PeduliLindungi website (https://www.pedulilindungi.id/#cara-kerja) and the official PeduliLindungi social media, namely the official Instagram of the PeduliLindungi application with 196 thousand, the official Twitter account of the PeduliLindungi application with followers, 28.2 thousand followers and the official PeduliLindungi YouTube Channel account with 2.94 thousand subscribers. Through the official website and official social media of the PeduliLindungi application, the government provides socialization to increase public understanding regarding the use of the PeduliLindungi application. Based on the high number of followers on the official PeduliLindungi social media, shows that the public understands the purpose and use of the PeduliLindungi application. This also shows that the government, in this case, the Ministry of Health of the Republic of Indonesia, is trying to improve the quality of mobile government-based services in the PeduliLindungi application.

5 Conclusion

Based on the results of this study, it was concluded that the quality of mobile government-based services in the PeduliLindungi application has not been implemented optimally. This is because in practice many people as users complain about connectivity problems when using the PeduliLindungi application. Based on the results of the Crosstab Query on the quality analysis of the PeduliLindungi application, it shows that the highest indicator is the Authenticity indicator, with an intensity of 54%, then the understandability indicator with an intensity of 21%, the interactivity indicator with 12% then the indicator with the lowest intensity value, namely the authentication indicator, with an intensity value of 11%. This shows that the service quality of the PeduliLidungi application in terms of authentication is high, but in terms of connectivity, quality is low. However, in implementing these services, the Government needs to pay attention to the connectivity quality of services of the PeduliLindungi application so that the objectives of implementing mobile Government are achieved, and the benefits can be felt maximally by the community of Indonesia.

References

1. Agung, I.M.: Memahami Pandemi Covid-19 Dalam Perspektif Psikologi Sosial. PsikobuletinBuletin Ilm. Psikol. 1(2), 68 (2020). https://doi.org/10.24014/pib.v1i2.9616
2. Aeni, N.: Pandemi COVID-19: Dampak Kesehatan, Ekonomi, & Sosial. J. Litbang Media Inf. Penelitian, Pengemb. dan IPTEK 17(1), 17–34 (2021). https://doi.org/10.33658/jl.v17i1.249
3. Rupani, P.F., Nilashi, M., Abumalloh, R.A., Asadi, S., Samad, S., Wang, S.: Coronavirus pandemic (COVID-19) and its natural environmental impacts. Int. J. Environ. Sci. Technol. 17(11), 4655–4666 (2020). https://doi.org/10.1007/s13762-020-02910-x
4. Rachmawati, R., Mei, E.T.W., Nurani, I.W., Ghiffari, R.A., Rohmah, A.A., Sejati, M.A.: Innovation in coping with the covid-19 pandemic: the best practices from five smart cities in Indonesia. Sustain. 13(21), 1–30 (2021). https://doi.org/10.3390/su132112072
5. Whitelaw, S., Mamas, M.A., Topol, E., Van Spall, H.G.C.: Applications of digital technology in COVID-19 pandemic planning and response. Lancet Digit. Heal. 2(8), e435–e440 (2020). https://doi.org/10.1016/S2589-7500(20)30142-4
6. Sherissa, L., Anza, F.A.: Analisis e-service quality pada aplikasi PeduliLindungi selama masa pandemi Covid-19 di DKI Jakarta. Publisia J. Ilmu Adm. Publik 7(1), 26–36 (2022). https://doi.org/10.26905/pjiap.v7i1.7494

7. Istiqoh, A.E., Nurmandi, A., Muallidin, I., Loilatu, M.J., Kurniawan, D.: The successful use of the PeduliLindungi application in handling COVID-19 (Indonesian Case Study). In: Yang, X.S., Sherratt, S., Dey, N., Joshi, A. (eds.) Proceedings of Seventh International Congress on Information and Communication Technology, LNNS, vol. 464, pp. 353–363. Springer, Singapore (2023). https://doi.org/10.1007/978-981-19-2394-4_33

8. Shareef, M.A.: SQ mGov : a comprehensive service quality paradigm for mobile Government (mGov). Inf. Syst. Manag. **31**, 126–142 (2014), [Online]. http://cronfa.swan.ac.uk/Record/cronfa17916

9. Cahyono, T.A., Susanto, T.D.: Acceptance factors and user design of mobile e-government website (Study case e-government website in Indonesia). Procedia Comput. Sci. **161**, 90–98 (2019). https://doi.org/10.1016/j.procs.2019.11.103

10. Jaafar Mohamed, A., Khalit Bin Othman, M., Binti Hamid, S., Hussein Zolait, A., Ahmad Kassim, N.B.: Exploring interaction's quality attributes at Mobile Government services. J. Phys. Conf. Ser.**1339**(1) (2019). https://doi.org/10.1088/1742-6596/1339/1/012094

11. Nafi'ah, B.A., Mustikasari, R.P., Bataha, K.: Analysis of local government mobile government application mapping in East Java Province. DiA J. Adm. Publik**19**(2), 345–357 (2021)

12. Eibl, G., Lampoltshammer, T., Temple, L.: Towards identifying factors influencing mobile government adoption: an exploratory literature review. JeDEM - eJournal eDemocracy Open Gov. **14**(1), 1–18 (2022). https://doi.org/10.29379/jedem.v14i1.693

13. Hussein, D., Alharbi, A., Alotaibi, M.F., Ibrahim, D. M.: Comparative study between emergency response mobile applications. J. Comput. Sci. IJCSIS**17**(2), 5 (2019). [Online]. https://sites.google.com/site/ijcsis/

14. Xiong, L., Wang, H., Wang, C.: Predicting mobile government service continuance: a two-stage structural equation modeling-artificial neural network approach. Gov. Inf. Q. **39**(1) (2022). https://doi.org/10.1016/j.giq.2021.101654

15. Desmal, A.J., Khalit Othman, M., Hamid, S.: The uniqueness of mobile government service quality: a review on quality drivers. In: 2021 International Conference on Computer Science and Engineering (IC2SE), November 2021, pp. 1–6. https://doi.org/10.1109/IC2SE52832.2021.9791955

16. Alsaadi, M.R., Ahmad, S.Z., Hussain, M.: A quality function deployment strategy for improving mobile-government service quality in the Gulf cooperation council countries. Benchmarking **25**(8), 3276–3295 (2018). https://doi.org/10.1108/BIJ-12-2017-0333

17. Chanana, L., Argawal, R., Punia, D.K.: Service quality parameters for mobile government services in India. SAGE J.**17**(1),136–146 (2016). https://doi.org/10.1177/09721509156107

Research on the Influence Mechanism of Digital Service Quality on the Credibility of Local Government

Xinyi Zheng and Cong Cao[✉] [iD]

Zhejiang University of Technology, Hangzhou 310023, China
congcao@zjut.edu.cn

Abstract. This paper explores the relationship between the quality of digital services and the credibility of the government, summarizes the influencing mechanisms involved, and establishes a more complete set of influencing factor models. Based on stimulus-response theory (SOR), the model comprehensively summarizes the factors determining the quality of digital services in four aspects: service efficiency, personalized demand, social interaction, and service transparency. This study will explore the influencing factors of digital service quality and the relationship between public satisfaction with digital services and government credibility. The model is well adapted to support subjects providing digital services to access the real needs of the public through big data technology and further optimize digital services.

Keywords: Digital Services · Government Credibility · Government Trust · Government Satisfaction

1 Introduction

Local governments, as the helmsmen of city building and leading the way, have a keen foresight and are always at the forefront of digital reform. While many regions have come to a standstill in just three years under the impact of the epidemic, only cyberspace remains active, and major digital government platforms are developing rapidly. Digital technology has widely penetrated all aspects of public life, including transport, education, healthcare, employment, and many other areas. Governments are increasingly focused on interacting with the public and are committed to providing better digital services to the public. A large number of local governments have established platforms to provide digital services, using emerging technologies to build digital service platforms. Local e-government is mainly about providing information and services online, followed by a small number of transactions and limited interaction [1]. In Zhejiang Province, for example, the government has used "Zhejiang Office" and "Zhejiang Government nail" to build a platform for the public to access policy information, achieve mutual assistance in the neighbourhood, and conduct various businesses, while on the other hand, local governments have also used big data technology to access the real needs of the public and On the other hand, local governments are also using big data technology to obtain the real needs of the public and further optimize their digital services.

2 Literature Review

Studies have focused on the reasons for the success or failure of digital government, and have analyzed them in terms of government initiatives and public behaviour [2]. It has been argued that the high level of public trust in government is attributed to the Chinese government's success in economic development, and that respect for traditional authority may undermine the impact of good economic performance on government trust [3]. Digital transformation has become an inevitable trend in a government building in the digital economy, and scholars at home and abroad have conducted a series of studies in this direction. The field of Digital Government Research (DGR) emerged in the late 1990s as an intersection of several traditional disciplines such as information systems research and business administration [4]. Trust in government is often considered to be related to the quality of government [5]. Citizens' attitudes towards government, including trust, are a central issue in democratic governance and public administration [6]. Studies have proposed that the functional value of digital services focuses on three dimensions of service efficiency, personalisation and social interaction [7]. Digital services have become a way to increase citizens' trust in the government and to improve their evaluation of the government.

3 Theoretical Development

This paper aims to develop a model of the influence mechanism that reveals the factors influencing the quality of digital services and the mechanism by which the quality of digital services affects the credibility of the government. Therefore, through the analysis and comparison of different behavioural theories, it was finally decided to adopt the stimulus-response (SOR) theory as the theoretical basis of the model.

Various theories have been developed in the field of user perception, and Zaithaml has proposed the Customer Perceived Value (CPV) theory from the customer's perspective. She defines customer-perceived value as the overall evaluation of the utility of a product or service after weighing the benefits that customers can perceive against the costs they pay in acquiring the product or service [8]. Parasuraman and Grewal [9] proposed the Service Quality Model (SQM). Expectation Confirmation Theory (ECT) integrates the perceived usefulness of technology acceptance models and user satisfaction to predict the ongoing intentions of IS [10].

Each theory has its limitations. The SOR theory model reveals the basic laws of social organization activities, the social organization process consisting of three stages: social structure, social perception, and social action, and reveals the interconnection and interaction of the three stages. The SOR theory is more compatible with the government's behaviour in providing digital services and provides ideas and tools for this study.

4 The Proposed Model

Based on SOR theory, this paper constructs a model of the mechanism of the impact of the quality of digital services on the credibility of local governments. The model measures the quality of digital services in four aspects: service efficiency, personalized demand, social interaction and service transparency, and explores its impact on the satisfaction of digital services. At the same time, this paper will study the mechanism of the influence of digital service satisfaction on the overall satisfaction of the government and the credibility of the government. As shown in Fig. 1.

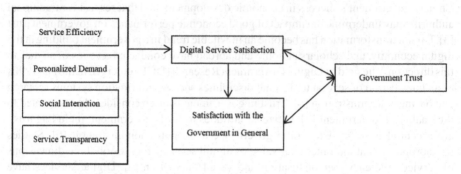

Fig. 1. Quality of digital services affects government trust model

4.1 Digital Service Satisfaction

In this model, digital service satisfaction is the judgement made by citizens on the digital services provided by the government. Access to and interaction with digital services is a new window for the public to participate in government governance, where the public is brought closer to government and government behaviour is gradually made transparent. Digital technologies affect government functions by influencing applications, processes, culture, structures and other factors [11]. The government has been expanding its operations in the area of digital services, but the level of service has not yet reached the level expected by citizens. The model measures citizens' satisfaction with digital services in four areas.

4.2 Satisfaction with the Government in General

With the advent of the information age, the public's awareness of political participation, monitoring and rights has increased. Traditional digital services can no longer meet the public's needs. The government uses new-generation information technology such as the Internet of Things and cloud computing to provide the public with a modern and intelligent platform that is safe, comfortable and convenient. The public's overall satisfaction with the government is made up of various aspects, and the public's sense of experience and satisfaction in the area of digital services largely influences the public's judgement of the government.

4.3 Trust in Government

Trust in government mainly refers to citizens' perceptions of the extent to which government policies or actions meet their psychological expectations [12]. Government trust is the cornerstone of ensuring residents' participation in government activities and plays a decisive role in residents' participation [13]. Residents in communities with stronger trust have a greater positive impact on policy support than residents in communities with weaker trust in government [14].

5 Full Cycle Support

Public satisfaction with the government varies at different stages of e-government development. The government's optimization solutions for digital services are also different. The digital service and government trust model proposed in this paper can not only be used to analyse the criteria for determining public satisfaction with the quality of digital services but also to provide the government with digital improvement suggestions.

The key to the model is to measure the quality of digital services from four aspects, which ultimately promote public trust in government. In the trust-building phase, the government needs to continuously improve the efficiency of the digital service platform, meet the personalized needs of users, enhance social interaction between the government and the public, and improve service transparency. After continuous improvement of the digital service platform, the public's satisfaction and trust in the government will increase. With the further development of the trust relationship, the government can better implement government decisions and promote urban construction and development.

The above steps all rise in a continuous cycle. However, once a loss of trust is caused, the government should first control the spread of the adverse effects of public opinion and re-improve its digital services to rebuild trust. In summary, the model of digital service quality affecting government trust proposed in this paper provides a comprehensive cycle of support for government digital construction decisions.

6 Conclusion

Through literature review and research, a model of the impact mechanism of digital service quality on service provider trust based on SOR theory is proposed. The model includes four influencing factors for digital service quality in the digital service domain, namely service efficiency, personalized demand, social interaction and service transparency. At the same time, the model also describes the mechanism of influence of digital service quality on government credibility.

The study has multiple theoretical and practical implications. At the theoretical level, by studying the relationship between the quality of digital services and government credibility, summarizing the influence mechanisms involved and establishing a more complete set of influence factor models, it fills a gap in the relevant field and provides a theoretical reference for related research. At the practical level, with China being in a stage of rapid development, the lack of government credibility can seriously affect policy implementation. This study helps explore the direction of improvement in the provision of digital services by local governments, innovate service methods, strengthen service effectiveness and enhance communication and cooperation between the public and the government.

At the same time, credit is the foundation and soul of digital governance. Introducing credit policies and measures helps to alleviate the problem of information asymmetry, make up for the shortcomings of the market economy itself, and enhance the credibility of the government to help resolve various social conflicts and promote social harmony and stability. It also helps to promote the advancement of digital services, accelerate the modernization of the national governance system and governance capacity, and build a service-oriented government that satisfies the people. In the following research, this paper will focus on collecting relevant data and conducting analysis to validate and modify the model, to provide better decision-making support for the digital construction of the government.

Acknowledgments. The work described in this paper was supported by grants from the Humanities and Social Sciences Research Project of Zhejiang Provincial Department of Education, grant number Y202248811; the Zhejiang Provincial Federation of Social Sciences, grant number 2023N009; and China's National Undergraduate Innovation and Entrepreneurship Training Program, grant number 202210337052.

References

1. Norris, D.F., Reddick, C.G.: Local E-government in the united states: transformation or incremental change? Public Adm. Rev. **73**(1), 165–175 (2013)
2. Gil-Garcia, J.R., Flores-Zúñiga, M.Á.: Towards a comprehensive understanding of digital government success: integrating implementation and adoption factors. Gov. Inf. Q. **37**(4), 101518 (2020)
3. Yang, J., Dong, C., Chen, Y.: Government's economic performance fosters trust in government in China: assessing the moderating effect of respect for authority. Soc. Indic. Res. **154**(2), 545–558 (2021). https://doi.org/10.1007/s11205-020-02553-y
4. Scholl, H.J.: The Digital Government Reference Library (DGRL) and its potential formative impact on Digital Government Research (DGR). Gov. Inf. Q. **38**(4), 101613 (2021)
5. Horsburgh, S., Goldfinch, S., Gauld, R.: Is public trust in government associated with trust in e-government. Soc. Sci. Comput. Rev. **29**(2), 232–241 (2011)
6. Lim, K.H., Sia, C.L., Lee, M.K., Benbasat, I.: Do I trust you online, and if so, will I buy? An empirical study of two trust-building strategies. J. Manag. Inf. Syst. **23**(2), 233–266 (2006)
7. Vu, V.T.: Public trust in government and compliance with policy during COVID-19 pandemic: empirical evidence from Vietnam. Public Organ. Rev. **21**(4), 779–796 (2021)
8. Grunert, K.G., Grunert, S.C.: Measuring subjective meaning structures by the laddering method: theoretical considerations and methodological problems. Int. J. Res. Mark. **12**(3), 209–225 (1995)
9. Parasuraman, A., Grewal, D.: The impact of technology on the quality-value-loyalty chain: a research agenda. J. Acad. Mark. Sci. **28**(1), 168–174 (2000)
10. Bhattacherjee, A.: Understanding information systems continuance: an expectation-confirmation model. MIS Q. **25**(3), 351-370 (2001)
11. Luca, T., Marijn, J., Michele, B., Giuliano, N.: Digital government transformation: a structural equation modelling analysis of driving and impeding factors. Int. J. Inf. Manage. **60** (2021)
12. Miller, A.H., Listhaug, O.: Political parties and confidence in government: a comparison of Norway, Sweden and the United States. Br. J. Polit. Sci. **20**(3), 357–386 (1990)

13. Teye, V., Sirakaya, E., Sönmez, S.F.: Residents' attitudes toward tourism development. Ann. Tour. Res. **29**(3), 668–688 (2002)
14. Yajun, J., Yu, G., Huiling, Z.: Residents' Perception of tourism impact, participation and support in destinations under the COVID-19 pandemic: the intermediary role of government trust. Sustainability. **15**(3), 2513 (2023)

eCommerce, Mobile Commerce and Digital Marketing: Design and Customer Behavior

Digital Marketing Strategies for Consumer Websites on the Ecuador/Colombia Border

Hugo Arias-Flores[1]([envelope]) [iD] and Marcos Chacon-Castro[2] [iD]

[1] Centro de Investigación en Mecatrónica y Sistemas Interactivos - MIST, Universidad Indoamérica, 170103 Quito, Ecuador
hugoarias@uti.edu.ec

[2] Grupo de Investigación GIECI, Fundación Universitaria Internacional de La Rioja, Bogotá, Colombia

Abstract. The use of web pages as a means of communication with customers has transformed online consumer interaction. The opportunities offered by technology and the challenges it brings to the marketplace are different for online consumers, as strategies to meet their needs must be identified based on their behavior on the website. In this context, the study seeks to determine if the websites of two financial institutions located on the border of Ecuador and Colombia present significant differences for clients, both in their presentation and in their ease of access. Through a survey (N = 96) the digital marketing strategies used were evaluated. The results show that a higher percentage (68.8%) accesses the websites through mobile devices and the age range is concentrated in the 25 to 34-year-old segment. However, the statistical tests show that there are no significant differences in the two websites analyzed, this shows that customers do not find a difference between the two institutions, which could reduce the perceived value and customer satisfaction.

Keywords: online consumer · web · digital marketing

1 Introduction

The success of a website depends on the quality of its system and the quantity of motivating values for the consumer [1, 2]. Indeed, quality has a positive relationship with perceived value, satisfaction and loyalty. On the other hand, it has a negative relationship with perceived risk. Website ease of use, design, responsiveness and security lead to higher levels of perceived value; while ease of use, responsiveness and personalization lead to an increase in overall consumer satisfaction. Likewise, satisfaction and perceived value by the consumer based on the quality level of the system, mitigates the perceived risk and has a positive impact on the adoption of desirable consumption behaviors that are reflected in customer loyalty [3] and repurchase intentions [4].

Perceived risk could be classified into four categories: product risk, financial risk, security risk, and privacy risk. Therefore, perceived product risk and privacy risk have a negative effect on consumers' satisfaction and purchase intent; while financial risk and information security risks, are related to secure shopping and security of personal information, which reduces purchase intentions in the consumer [5].

In this sense, websites must strengthen the security of their transactions, improve the online shopping experience and desires of consumers, updating the contents with the latest trends in electronic commerce, especially in the quality, design and accessibility of the website [6]. Understanding the consumer's perceptual process, from exposure to sensory design stimuli to their loyalty, will allow the offer to be adapted to the specific characteristics of consumers [7].

In the face of increasing digitalization [8], consumer behavior in the use of banking services is changing, as customer-bank interactions provide opportunities for both parties. This makes the digital presence of financial institutions a priority, since the benefits can promote competition among banks, given the predilection of customers [9]. In this context, the city of Tulcán is located on the border with Colombia, and its currency exchange transactions are carried out informally in the central park of the city between the money changer and the client; This traditional activity allows customers to handle their transactions without a financial institution. Given this border scenario, this study sought to determine whether the websites of two financial institutions located in the border city with Colombia present significant differences for customers, both in their presentation and in their ease of access.

2 Method

This research used a survey targeting customers of the two financial institutions to identify whether there are significant differences on the two institutions' website from the point of view of customers. For the study, customers who used the website (n = 96) were considered. Consideration was given to codifying institutions as F1 and F2. In F1 men (n = 24) represent 48% and 52% are women (n = 26), while in F2 men (n = 24) represent 52% and 48% are women. The age range of highest participation is 25 to 34 years in F1 (42%) and for F2 the age range of highest participation is 15 to 24 years (30%). Considering the total number of participants, the age range of highest participation is 25 to 34 years (34%).

Participation for the research was voluntary and the people who collaborated were informed of the objective of the research. The survey was taken from clients of the participating institutions, it was clarified that the information is anonymous and exclusively for research.

The analysis of the information was carried out with the IBM SPSS software, which was fed with the data collected from the survey carried out with the clients of the two institutions participating in the study. This questionnaire featured 16 questions on a Likert scale, ranging from Strongly Disagree to Strongly Agree.

3   Results

The authors conducted the analysis of the survey, in which 68.8% of respondents enter the website through the cell phone, of these 58% are women. On the other hand, 31.2% enter the website through a computer, here the majority are men (67%), showing that according to gender the device has preferences for entering the website.

On the other hand, in Table 1, the results are presented according to the questions posed and grouped for a better analysis.

Table 1. Survey results

Institution	F1	F2	Total
Flow			
Enter the page on the first attempt	41.67%	35.42%	77.08%
The page shows all the information I'm looking for	41.67%	37.50%	79.17%
The information is organized within the page and the search is easy	37.50%	35.42%	72.92%
The design of the website is attractive to navigate	39.58%	32.29%	71.88%
Functionality			
When you search for the institution in the browser, it appears first	37.50%	40.63%	78.13%
The page features high-quality multimedia elements	31.25%	33.33%	64.58%
The text on the website is clear and consistent	43.75%	35.42%	79.17%
The information on the website is reliable	42.71%	36.46%	79.17%
Feedback			
The colors of the website are striking	42.71%	37.50%	80.21%
The structure of the Web page is sorted by categories	42.71%	38.54%	81.25%
The content is organized to understand it at a glance	40.63%	37.50%	78.13%
The links on the page work correctly	38.54%	32.29%	70.83%
Loyalty			
It would be part of interaction groups on the Web page	31.25%	30.21%	61.46%
I would visit the website again	44.79%	42.71%	87.50%
I would recommend visiting the website	46.88%	36.46%	83.33%
I participate in what the website offers	32.29%	32.29%	64.58%

According to the averages of the two institutions, it can be seen that there is almost no difference in the score, as can be seen in Table 2.

To confirm the equality of means, we proceeded to calculate the student's t-test. From this statistic it can be seen in Table 3, that the value of gis (significance) is greater than 0.05.

Table 2. Statistical variable by membership group

	Institution	N	Stocking	Desv. Deviation	Desv. Average error
Flow	F1	46	16,9348	3,58021	,52787
	F2	50	16,6600	3,02108	,42725
Functionality	F1	46	16,9348	3,50493	,51677
	F2	50	16,8000	2,71052	,38333
Feedback	F1	46	17,0000	2,89828	,42733
	F2	50	16,9400	2,50233	,35388
Loyalty	F1	46	16,4565	3,20213	,47213
	F2	50	16,3800	3,39201	,47970

Table 3. Comparison of variables by institution

	T-test for equality of means						
	t	Gl	Sig. (bilateral)	Mean difference	Standard error difference	95% confidence interval difference	
						Inferior	Superior
Flow	,407	94	,685	,27478	,67432	−1,06409	1,61365
Functionality	,212	94	,833	,13478	,63664	−1,12929	1,39885
Feedback	,109	94	,914	,06000	,55144	−1,03489	1,15489
Loyalty	,113	94	,910	,07652	,67470	−1,26311	1,41615

4   Discussion and Conclusions

From the research carried out, it can be established that the average of the two institutions do not present significant differences in the components evaluated by the clients, this was verified with the student's t test, yielding a level of significance greater than 0.05. In addition, it can be established that the design of the website is not attractive for customers, since the valuation is less than 40%. It must be remembered that the quality of the services presented on the websites have a positive and statistically significant relationship with the perceived value, satisfaction and loyalty of the client [3]. In this sense, institutions can increase customer loyalty directly by improving the ease of use, attractiveness and security of their website [10, 11].

In this line, customers show that they are not motivated to be part of the interaction activities of the website (<35%) and it is also appreciated that visiting the website again (<43%), along with recommending it (<41%), are problems of the brand, appearance and functionality of the site, as well as your own personal environment, such as geographic location and previous experiences with the financial institution. Thus, the user experience is key in the immediate and future relationship between the client and the institution, this can be achieved by understanding the wishes and needs of the client, seeking a greater commitment from the client and influencing, either consciously or unconsciously, in their decision when interacting with the institution [12].

As for the limitations, we can point out that the sample is very small and the results cannot be generalized, since there may be other types of customers that impact on the probability of generalization. On the other hand, in the future you should work on customer interaction on the website, especially analyze the opinions of your interaction experience.

Acknowledgment. The authors would like to thank the Corporación Ecuatoriana para el Desarrollo de la Investigación y Academia-CEDIA for their contribution in innovation, through the "FONDO I+D+i" projects, especially the project I+D+I-XVII-2022-61, "Análisis y aplicación de formas de Interacción Humano – Computador (HCI) en una herramienta tecnológica de Comunicación Aumentativa y Alternativa (CAA) basada en pictogramas, que ayude a las personas adultas mayores a comunicarse con su entorno"; also the Universidad Tecnológica Indoamérica, Universidad de Cuenca, Universidad de las Fuerzas Armadas and Universidad del Azuay for the support for the development of this work.

References

1. Ahn, T., Ryu, S., Han, I.: The impact of Web quality and playfulness on user acceptance of online retailing. Inf. Manag. **44**(3), 263–275 (2007)
2. Stoian Bobalca, C., Țugulea, O., Ifrim, M., Maha, L.-G.: Analysing the predictors of the young buyers' satisfaction in the e-retailing apparel sector. Int. J. Retail Distrib. Manag. **49**(12), 1597–1620 (2021)
3. Tzavlopoulos, I, Gotzamani, K., Andronikidis, A., Vassiliadis, C.: Determining the impact of e-commerce quality on customers' perceived risk, satisfaction, value and loyalty. Int. J. Qual. Serv. Sci. **11**(4), 576–587 (2019)
4. Hassan, M., Kazmi, S., Rehman, M.A., Amaad, H., Padlee, S.F.: The online shoppers' behavioral intentions, e-satisfaction, the pathway to repurchase behavior: a quantitative analysis. Estudios de Economía Aplicada **39**(4) (2021)
5. Tran, V.D.: The relationship among product risk, perceived satisfaction and purchase intentions for online shopping. J. Asian Finance Econ. Bus. **7**(6), 221–231 (2020)
6. Pradeep, E., Arivazhagan, R.: A study on attributes of websites with specific reference to online purchase intentions of baby products in Chennai. In: Sharma, S.K., Dwivedi, Y.K., Metri, B., Rana, N.P. (eds.) TDIT 2020. IAICT, vol. 617, pp. 484–492. Springer, Cham (2020). https://doi.org/10.1007/978-3-030-64849-7_43
7. Paștiu, C.A., Oncioiu, I., Gârdan, D.A., Maican, S.Ș., Gârdan, I.P., Muntean, A.C.: The perspective of E-business sustainability and website accessibility of online stores. Sustainability **12**(22), 9780 (2020)
8. Herhausen, D., Emrich, O., Grewal, D., Kipfelsberger, P., Schoegel, M.: Face forward: how employees' digital presence on service websites affects customer perceptions of website and employee service quality. J. Mark. Res. **57**(5), 917–936 (2020)
9. Son, Y., Kwon, E., Tayi, G.K., Oh, W.: Impact of customers' digital banking adoption on hidden defection: a combined analytical–empirical approach. J. Oper. Manag. **66**(4), 418–440 (2020)

10. Kassim, N., Asiah Abdullah, N.: The effect of perceived service quality dimensions on customer satisfaction, trust, and loyalty in e-commerce settings: a cross cultural analysis. Asia Pacific J. Mark. Logist. **22**(3), 351–371 (2010)
11. Cui, L., He, S., Deng, H., Wang, X.: Sustaining customer loyalty of fresh food e-tailers: an empirical study in China. Asia Pac. J. Mark. Logist. **35**(3), 669–686 (2023)
12. González-Mena, G., Del-Valle-Soto, C., Corona, V., Rodríguez, J.: Neuromarketing in the digital age: the direct relation between facial expressions and website design. Appl. Sci. **12**(16), 8186 (2020)

A Comparative Between S-Commerce and M-Commerce

Franklin Castillo-Ledesma[1](✉), José Varela-Aldás[1,2], José Oleas-Orozco[3], and Juan Soberón-López[1]

[1] SISAu Research Group, Facultad de Ingeniería, Industria y Producción, Universidad Indoamérica, Ambato 180103, Ecuador
{franklincastillo,josevarela}@uti.edu.ec
[2] Centro de Investigaciones de Ciencias Humanas y de La Educación - CICHE, Universidad Indoamérica, Ambato 180103, Ecuador
[3] Facultad de Arquitectura y Construcción, Universidad Indoamérica, Ambato 180103, Ecuador
joseoleas@indoamerica.edu.ec

Abstract. The internet has contributed with the development of various economic sectors, one of the most important is the sale of products and services. This research aims to present two types of sales, that can be done online and through the use of social media, which can favor businesses in their growth. The objective of this work is to carry out an analysis of the sales that are made through social media and those made through a mobile application. The development of the mobile application was produced using Android Studio with its Kotlin language in conjunction with the MySql database manager. The methodology has been of a qualitative type, with data obtained through surveys carried out with the clients of the business that were the object of the initial study. Considerable results could be obtained in social media, since its development is easier and less expensive than developing your own mobile application for the business. Finally, surveys were carried out on the participating people to measure the level of acceptance of the tools used in the commercialization of the products, in results a summary of the acceptance per question is shown, with an average acceptance of 3.16/ 5 for the mobile application and 4.5/5 for the social network used to sell the products.

Keywords: s-commerce · m-commerce · social media · mobile application · kotlin

1 Introduction

Currently, information technologies are accessible to almost the entire population. The use of the internet has been changing and evolving to not only obtain information, but it has also become a space to market products that previously could only be obtained by buying in physical stores [1]. Mobile applications have become popular, with the decrease in the cost of smartphones, which has caused the continuous use of these devices [2], and their use as support to the commercial processes of existing businesses. The health

© The Author(s), under exclusive license to Springer Nature Switzerland AG 2023
C. Stephanidis et al. (Eds.): HCII 2023, CCIS 1835, pp. 329–336, 2023.
https://doi.org/10.1007/978-3-031-36001-5_42

emergency in developing countries has caused the growth of electronic commerce (E-commerce), allowing the supply of products online [3]. It is important to highlight that purchases using these means are very frequent [4].

Large companies such as Apple, IBM or Lenovo, which have sold their products online, as well as in physical stores such as Best Buy and Circuit City, taking this as an example can serve as a basis to apply it in different types of businesses or services, even if they are small or medium-sized companies. E-commerce gives business owners the flexibility to operate an online branch through a platform in addition to their existing physical stores [5].

There is also social commerce, which is different from traditional e-commerce since here people buy products through search by initiative or recommendations from the platform, it transforms a social community into an inclusive place to do business. By allowing people to share products with their friends, one of the most important factors in social commerce is word of mouth, which is nothing more than a person talking about a business, this type of information transmission is generally done through social networks which are currently widely used [6]. Therefore, social networks are an important factor in commerce since they positively affect marketing activities and the value that the brand acquires with its use [7].

A study carried out reveals that the intention to buy through a social network is closely related to the dependence that people have on the use of these platforms, saying that the popularity of the platform directly influences the sales that a company has that uses this method [8].

The present investigation proposes to develop a software for the sale of articles through the internet, to be able to analyze the data of the sales that are made through the mobile application and two other means that are physically in the premises and the sales that are done with the help of social media. The IMRD methodology (Introduction, Methods, Results, and Discussion) will be used to prepare the article.

2 Methodology

For the development of this proposal, certain steps must be followed, which are part of the Introduction, Materials and Methods, Results and Discussion (IMRD) methodology. Figure 1 presents the proposal's schema. Requirements are collected directly from those who traditionally sell the products, in this case, the company owners. A user interface design is created that serves as a means of communication between the user and the database that stores the necessary commercial activity information. With the help of development software, the mobile application that connects and manipulates the information stored in the database is built. In the next step, the application is implemented with all its functionalities in the company so that the data can be obtained through a survey. Finally, it is necessary to analyze the data collected during the relevant time period.

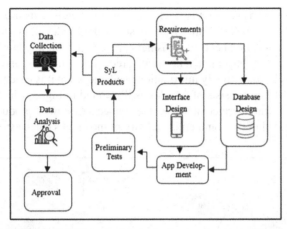

Fig. 1. Steps to follow in the IMRD methodology for the development of the proposal and analysis of results are as follows.

2.1 Graphic Interface Design

For the design of the interfaces, it is important to consider the different functionalities of the application. For this purpose, three interfaces are considered, which are shown in Fig. 2. The first interface is used for accessing the application through a login system validated by email and password registered in the system. The second interface contains information about the products used in the commercialization process, along with their respective images. Finally, a third interface is designed for user registration for those who do not have an active account and cannot use the application. All of the above will be developed in the Android Studio tool using the Kotlin programming language.

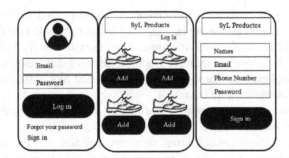

Fig. 2. Application Interfaces for Interacting with Customers in Product Commercialization

2.2 Database Design

MySQL is a well-known database management system due to its simplicity and reliability, with excellent performance. The minimum requirements for installation and optimal functioning are very basic, and it is freely distributed, therefore its use and implementation are free of cost [9]. The Entity Relationship (ER) Model allows for the graphical representation of the components of a business process and the way in which data interrelates, in order to store information in a structured manner that responds to the logic of the business, thus keeping timely information available when it is needed. The database implemented in MySql consists of 4 tables as illustrated in Fig. 3, which are the users, products, sales, and an intermediate table that connects sales with products, in this way, different data needed in the commercial activity of the clients can be stored.

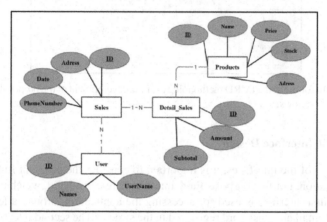

Fig. 3. Entity-Relationship diagram, indicating the data to be stored for the system users with their respective interrelationships.

2.3 Application Development

To develop the mobile application, three computer tools are needed, which are:

Kotlin, which is a programming language for Android. It makes the development of applications easier and faster by solving some of the errors that Java had when developing for this platform. It provides an intuitive graphical interface that facilitates the construction of mobile applications. Through the aforementioned tool, different interfaces are built that allow interaction with the user.

MySQL as a management system for storing data resulting from the activities carried out by the user in the application.

PHP (Hypertext Preprocessor), a free interpreted language used for server-side applications. This language serves as a connection between the two aforementioned tools, using web services integrated into Android operating systems.

2.4 Data

The way in which data will be analyzed is through tables that compare the sales made during a week. These sales are divided into those made by customers in person at the physical location, those made using some social network, and finally those that were registered online thanks to the use of the mobile application developed for this research.

2.5 Participants

The people who will participate in the research are those indicated in Table 1. They will use the mobile application for an average of 1 h per day and Facebook social network for 1 h per day.

Table 1. Participants who will manipulate the application.

Position	Gender	Age
Co-Owner	Male	32
Co-Owner	Female	29

2.6 Acceptance Survey

For the development of the survey, certain factors were taken into consideration that are important in software design. Table 2 shows the questions that were taken from the available resource of a survey based on the UTAUT model (Unified Theory of Acceptance and Use of Technology) for mobile technology acceptance among students and teachers [10], which will be administered to the research participants after one week of using the application and will be rated on a scale of 1 to 5 where 1 is very low and 5 is very high.

3 Results

The waterfall methodology was used for the development of the mobile application, which has the following phases: User Requirements Analysis, Application Design, Implementation, Testing, and Maintenance. As a result of this process, the MySQL database and 3 interfaces were obtained, which allow entering or manipulating the information of the database. Finally, users were able to use the mobile application in the business for a week.

3.1 Data Collected

The data obtained during the week of using the mobile application in product marketing were divided into 4 diagrams shown in Fig. 4. The percentages of each sales method, either via online or direct sales in the physical store with the presence of customers, were observed. For women's footwear, it was found that 75% of sales were made in the physical store and the remaining sales were through a social network. In men's footwear, 66.66% of sales were made in the physical store while 16.66% were made through social networks and the other 16.66% were made through the mobile application. For children's footwear, a total of 6 shoes were sold, of which 16.66% were sold through the mobile application and the rest in the physical store. The last item offered by the store is jackets, of which only 1 was sold in the physical store and none through digital means.

Table 2. Questions that make up the survey applied to research participants

Number	Questions
1	I find the mobile device easy to use
2	Learning to use the mobile device is easy for me
3	I have the necessary resources to use the mobile device
4	The mobile device increases my productivity
5	I can complete a task or work using the mobile device even if there is no one around to help me
6	I would recommend using apps to a colleague
7	I hesitate to use the app in case I make a mistake that I cannot correct later
8	The use of Apps somehow intimidates me
9	I consider a quality certificate for applications necessary to increase confidence when downloading an App

Fig. 4. Sales Diagram, presents a summary of sales by product and by the medium where the sale was made

3.2 Acceptance

The result of the surveys carried out is evidenced in Fig. 5, where the average score of the first 6 questions on the Facebook social network is 4.5, while the average score for the mobile application is 3.16. There is uncertainty about question 7 after making a mistake in the mobile application, while this is not the case for Facebook. As for the last 2 questions, participants reported no impediment for using either the mobile application or Facebook.

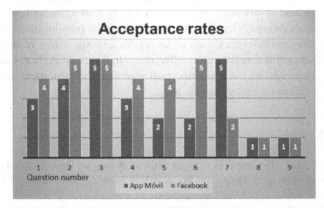

Fig. 5. Acceptance percentages for different product marketing channels

4   Discussion

In the collected data, we can observe that the sales percentage of the different products offered by the company is similar. The result shows that sales in physical stores are predominant over internet sales, whether they were made through social networks or mobile applications. This is due to the short time that the products have been offered online. The study conducted by C. Bianchi et al. [11] confirms that it is essential for the business to be more present on social media to increase sales through these modern channels. Social media handles a lot of information, and good management of social media is crucial for brand recognition and the success of social commerce. One crucial aspect to consider is that social media platforms allow us to have well-developed software, which usually has no connectivity or design errors and is either free or low-cost. This makes the implementation of social media channels in business simple and useful.

A crucial part of software development and application deployment is the user acceptance. The survey showed an acceptable average score of 3.16/5, indicating that there were technical issues with the application that negatively affected its productivity. The study of app store reviews [13] confirms that many negative user reviews are due to poor connectivity or lack of effectiveness in searches, all caused by technical errors that may occur in a mobile application.

5   Conclusion

In small businesses, traditional sales methods are predominant, meaning that people enter the store and buy something that catches their attention or that they need. However, due to the economic and social crisis of recent years, it is important to consider more innovative methods such as social or electronic commerce. These two methods, although not as efficient in small businesses or startups, can provide an extra boost for the business to thrive. However, patience is also necessary for the business to become more recognized and for the economic part to grow. Developing and implementing a mobile application is more difficult and costly than simply using social media. Nevertheless, it had an average acceptance rating of 3.16/5, which opens up many possibilities for its potential use. Limited time and resources such as servers or existing errors in the application prevented us from collecting data more effectively. In future work, better digital media socialization can be carried out to commercialize products to customers and expand the use of the application for better data analysis.

References

1. Suleman, D., et al.: The impact of changes in the marketing era through digital marketing on purchase decisions. Int. J. Data Netw. Sci. **6**, 805–812 (2022). https://doi.org/10.5267/j.ijdns. 2022.3.001
2. Castillo, F., Guangasi, L., Palacios-Navarro, G., Varela-Aldás, J.: Smart armband for tracking children using a mobile application. In: Stephanidis, C., Antona, M., Ntoa, S. (eds.) HCII 2022. CCIS, vol. 1581, pp. 325–331. Springer, Cham (2022). https://doi.org/10.1007/978-3-031-06388-6_43
3. Alam, S., Rahman, M.: COVID-19 impact on facebook-based social commerce in Bangladesh. Int. J. Electr. Comput. Eng. **12**, 1636–1649 (2022). https://doi.org/10.11591/ijece.v12i2.pp1 636-1649
4. Petrova, K., Datta, S.: Value and sustainability of emerging social commerce professions: an exploratory study. Information **13**, 178 (2022). https://doi.org/10.3390/info13040178
5. Fu, F., Chen, S., Yan, W.: The implications of supplier encroachment via an online platform. RAIRO Oper. Res. **56**, 529–564 (2022). https://doi.org/10.1051/ro/2022003
6. Gao, C., et al.: Item recommendation for word-of-mouth scenario in social e-commerce. IEEE Trans. Knowl. Data Eng. **34**, 2798–2809 (2022). https://doi.org/10.1109/TKDE.2020. 3017509
7. Maskuroh, N., Fahlevi, M., Irma, D., Rita, R., et al.: Social media as a bridge to e-commerce adoption in Indonesia: a research framework for repurchase intention. Int. J. Data Netw. Sci. **6**, 107–114 (2022). https://doi.org/10.5267/J.IJDNS.2021.9.017
8. Bianchi, C., Andrews, L., Wiese, M., Fazal-E-Hasan, S.: Consumer intentions to engage in s-commerce: a cross-national study. J. Mark. Manag. **33**, 464–494 (2017). https://doi.org/10. 1080/0267257X.2017.1319406
9. Huillcen Baca, H.A., Palomino Valdivia, F. de L., Soria Solís, I.: Introducción a las Bases de Datos con MySQL. 180 (2022)
10. Briz-Ponce, L., Juanes-Méndez, J.., García-Peñalvo, F.: Recurso disponible de una encuesta basada en modelo UTAUT para aceptación de tecnologías móviles entre estudiantes y profesores. 1–7 (2016)

Shopping Profiles of Supermarket Customers

How the Composition of Needs Effects the Decision to Use Assistance Robot

Vera Fink[1]([⊠]), Marc Ritter[1], and Maximilian Eibl[2]

[1] University of Applied Sciences, Technikumsplatz 17, 09648 Mittweida, Germany
{vera.fink,marc.ritter}@hs-mittweida.de
[2] University of Technology Chemnitz, Straße Der Nationen 62, 09110 Chemnitz, Germany
maximilian.eibl@informatik.tu-chemnitz.de

Abstract. The results from the study show that it is the combination of the needs of an individual that determines WHETHER and HOW the product is used in the supermarket context. Because if the product is great, people with the need for connectedness & sense of community (high subjective prioritization) would be more likely to refrain from using the device (tablet while shopping) because it has an isolating effect on them to maintain contact with the people around, knowing that there are features on the tablet that would help you shop. Users with high subjective prioritization of needs such as stimulation and or competence, are more inclined to be stimulated by offers and recipes and keep track of the supermarket through the device and thus are more likely to enjoy using it and exploring the menu navigation.

We have created the profiles of the customers on this basis in order to work precisely with the customer needs. Thus, the target group of users can be better enclosed in the aforementioned context, and the aspect of acceptance of the application is increased by the profiles and its understanding of customer needs.

Keywords: positive user experience · psychological needs · hci

1 Introduction

All the listed workshops [1], exercises, studies, and experiments [2] were developed within a project called "I-RobEka". In the increasingly aging society, scientists and experts studied robotic shopping assistance for supermarkets from 2017–2021. The goal is to develop autonomous and mobile shopping assistance with a human-robot interaction that contributes to the solution of dynamic and complex situations in the supermarket. In this context, interaction concepts are to be developed, designed, and tested, which are adaptable to the situation. The interactions of the inputs and outputs for the users happen via the mobile end device (tablet), which is located on the robot.

In addition to the results (which we write about in the poster) of the tested digital prototype in the context of shopping assistance, we were able to establish profiles of

C. Stephanidis et al. (Eds.): HCII 2023, CCIS 1835, pp. 337–343, 2023.
https://doi.org/10.1007/978-3-031-36001-5_43

the clientele that we believe are important for the HCI community to consider when developing shopping applications.

2 Description of Study

As could be expected, we found that a developed application based on the needs we found out (we also present these in the paper) was happily used and received positive feedback for it. However, the interesting thing was that as soon as the priority of the needs changed, we are talking, for example, about autonomy, the willingness of the clientele to use a shopping assistance is rather low, which we did not expect. These results lead us to present different profiles in the poster based on the study.

2.1 Baseline

Before the demo application could be designed according to the psy. Needs of the customers, an extensive experimental setting was carried out with the help of the students. In the context of the Human-Computer Interaction lecture, the students had the task to apply the contents from the lecture based on their own group project (I-RobEka). With the addition of working into the design process with the psychological needs. In the three years 2019, 2021, and 2022, a total of 229 students successfully participated in the exercise and surveyed more than 540 customers about their shopping behaviors and experiences. Figure 1 below shows the generalized and prioritized needs that came out. We do not plead for completeness, as the qualitative study is limited to only 30 subjects, but there are some clues to further expand the profiles and apply them in research in general.

The results were quantitatively proven psychological needs that are important for the shopping experience [3]. From this publication, it emerged that the needs for comfort, stimulation, competence, autonomy, and security in order, proved to be the most important general needs from the 13 fundamental needs according to Desmet [4], in the shopping scenario. In this context, needs such as community, impact, recognition, fitness, and beauty were also important but not as crucial as the needs mentioned above. Based on the identified needs, a demo application was developed and tested in the supermarket in the study.

2.2 Study Procedure

A total of 31 supermarket customers participated in the qualitative study. Audio recordings as well as screencast recordings of a total of 14 h and 31 min were evaluated. The demo prototype was built in a Wizzard-of-Ozz approach. We built a prototype framework, which was operated remotely by the other study participant. That is, there were interaction functions for the customer, such as product search, and item scanning. And there were "system" functions that went back to the customer in the background as feedback.

First, we attached the tablet to the shopping cart. During the shopping process, we asked questions about the process. Second, we conducted an interview about the

Comfort	Having an easy, simple, relaxing life, rather than experiencing strain, difficulty or overstimulation.	- Peace of mind - Convenience - Simplicity - Overview and structure
Stimulation	Being mentally and physically stimulated by novel, varied, and relevant impulses and stimuli, rather than feeling bored, indifferent or apathetic.	- Novelty - Variation - Play - Bodily pleasure
Competence	Having control over your environment and being able to exercise your skills to master challenges, rather than feeling that you are incompetent or ineffective.	- Knowledge and understanding - Challenge - Environmental control - Skill progression
Autonomy	Being the cause of your actions and feeling that you can do things your own way, rather than feeling as though external conditions and other people determine your actions.	- Freedom of decision - Individuality - Creative expression - Self-reliance
Security	Feeling that your conditions and environment keep you safe from harm and threats, rather than feeling that the world is dangerous, risky or a place of uncertainty.	- Physical safety - Financial security - Social stability - Conservation

Fig. 1. Excerpt about the main generalized needs found in the supermarket shopping scenario [4]

functions of the tablet. We did not have a strict schedule for this but wanted to talk about the tablet functions as naturally as possible. Many participants registered in advance by email to take part in the study, and some we asked spontaneously on-site. Since the group of respondents was randomly selected, the age range was between 20–70 years. Study participants included couples, single people, and mothers. The guideline consisted of the following question areas (Fig. 2):

- Questions about the use of a recipe function in the market
- Shopping with or without a shopping list
- Online payment or at the checkout
- Self-searching, using a tablet function, or asking employees
- Viewing offers
- Suggest alternatives to products
- Create a quick route through the market
- Filter by eating habits

Finally, questionnaires were filled out about the tablet and its interaction with AttrakDiff, PANEM, and participants were rewarded with a shopping voucher for 20 euros. The shopping process took 20–40 min to complete.

3 Profiles

We found that the above needs are valuable for creating an assistant application in the supermarket, but during testing, the actual more detailed usage scenarios emerged.

Fig. 2. To simplify handling, the tablet was attached to the shopping basket, as there was no release for testing the robot yet.

After the study, we noticed that the needs can be mapped in individual combinations and thus a better statement can be made about who would use a shopping assistant and why, and on the basis of which needs the customers to decide not to use it if necessary. We have examined individual statements according to experience categories and classified them according to the definition of Desmet [4].

Need for comfort, all respondents from the study placed a high value on the. This was not up for discussion. All of them aspired to more Comfort, in that the application accommodates the information, such as an overview of time and money, and product location. Of course, under the fundamental 13 needs, more is meant than just a quick route or a product search function. But if we take out the single statements and analyze them, e.g. by valence method [5], it makes the needs accessible and touchable for everyone. We can work with it and learn more about the needs.

Profile Autonomy-Competence
Customers who have particularly pronounced needs in the direction of autonomy and competence. They are self-determining and consciously choose what they want to buy when they look at offers. They are not distracted by advertising, suggestions of recipes, and offers and do not look very closely at the price. They still like to give their data and would rather buy anonymously and quickly. If given the opportunity, these customers would rather have home delivery than go shopping themselves. Shop for products they already know. Have a plan in mind and would prefer to search for products themselves rather than ask something or someone. A shopping assistant would hinder rather than assist them in the pace of shopping. Statements have fallen, such as "Only when I have time and desire, I stroll in the market", "I do not want to get information from the tablet, I want to look at myself when I need it", and "I know what I need and buy already known products". Are rather opponents to the need for stimulation (Table 1).

Profile Competence-Stimulation
For customers with a pronounced need for competence and stimulation it is important to

Table 1. Profile description for Autonomy-Competence

Attributes	Description
General	name, age, gender, place of living, technology usage behavior, wishes, motivation
Needs	Autonomy, Competence
Shopping Behavior	- self-determining - consciously choose what they want - not distracted - not look at price - buy anonymously and quickly - prefer home delivery - shop products they already know - searching by themselves

plan everything in advance, thereby can be supported by intelligent decision processes for example; "If I know how much the purchase costs in time, by the default of the shopping list, then I can decide whether I still manage to buy before the work or rather after the work.". He looks closely at how long the wait is at the lines. Takes a rather pragmatic approach. Likes to face challenges and during the study explores through the application. He is curious and likes to have the application display important information, such as certain recalls, or quickly browse through offers directly in the store. The user would interact with the tablet on the spot. The cost overview for the purchase lets him decide whether he can pay for the purchase in cash or with a card. He would also disclose data about himself if it supported the planning of the purchase even better (Table 2).

Table 2. Profile description for Competence-Stimulation

Attributes	Description
General	name, age, gender, place of living, technology usage behavior, wishes, motivation
Needs	Competence, Stimulation
Shopping Behavior	- plan everything in advance - makes decisions based on time - pragmatic approach - explore application - likes to face challenges - likes display important information - cost overview

Profile Competence-Security
People with proficiency Competence and Security make sure that they buy products

that they already know. As a strategy for finding products, they take their time and look for them. Have their recipes in mind and do not want to try novelties only on the recommendation of others. They trust in the signet and judgments about the quality of the products from others not to check again what ingredients are included. They also plan ahead. Walk only the shelves they already know. Stimulation is not important, only if they happen to discover something. Overview of the store and shelf labeling helps them shop a lot. Statements such as "It's on sale, but do I need it?" or "Looking for recipes in the store is too stressful for me, I don't know what I want to eat in a few days" are representative of this user group (Table 3).

Table 3. Profile description for Competence-Security

Attributes	Description
General	name, age, gender, place of living, technology usage behavior, wishes, motivation
Needs	Competence, Security
Shopping Behavior	- buy products they already know - take time and search for products - recipes in mind - not try novelties - trust in signet and judgements from others - plan ahead - overview of the store

4   Conclusion

Since we conducted the study in a project "I-RobEka" about robotic shopping assistance in supermarkets, these results make their contribution to all assistance systems and assistance applications. The knowledge about the profiles of people structured according to the priority of their needs, from the information of our study, opens new perspectives to see the end users with broader view. Even the preparatory studies, pretests or user interviews can be formulated much more precisely and other, many better questions can be asked, focusing on the core of the projects. In the further course of the projects, the presented profiles will support the process of keeping the focus until the end. We do not plead for completeness, as the qualitative study is limited to only 30 subjects, but there are some clues to further expand the profiles and apply them in research in general.

References

1. Fink, V., Börner, A., Eibl, M.: Living-lab and experimental workshops for design of I-RobEka assistive shopping robot: ELSI aspects with MEESTAR. In: 2020 29th IEEE International Conference on Robot and Human Interactive Communication (RO-MAN), pp. 839–844 (2020)

2. Fink, V., Langner, H., Burmester, M., Ritter, M., Eibl, M.: Positive user experience: novices can assess psychological needs: psychological needs in context of robot shoppingassistant. In: 2022 IEEE 9th International Conference on Computational Intelligence and Virtual Environments for Measurement Systems and Applications (CIVEMSA), pp. 1–6 (2022)
3. Fink, V., Zeiner, K.M., Ritter, M., Burmester, M., Eibl, M.: Design for positive UX: from experience categories to psychological needs. In: Stephanidis, C., Antona, M., Ntoa, S., Salvendy, G. (eds.) HCII 2022. CCIS, vol. 1654, pp. 148–155. Springer, Cham (2022). https://doi.org/10.1007/978-3-031-19679-9_19
4. Desmet, P., Fokkinga, S.: Beyond Maslow's pyramid: introducing a typology of thirteen fundamental needs for human-cendered design. In: Multimodal Technologies and Interaction (2020). https://doi.org/10.3390/mti4030038
5. Zeiner, K.M., Laib, M., Schippert, K., Burmester, M.: Identifying experience categories to design for positive experiences with technology at work. In: Proceedings of the 2016 CHI Conference Extended Abstracts on Human Factors in Computing Systems, pp. 3013–3020 (2016)

Personal Branding and Its Impact on Users' Engagement: A Case of Health/Fitness Creators on TikTok

Lina Gomez-Vasquez[✉] [iD] and Isabella Dias

The University of Tampa, Tampa, FL 33606, USA
lgomezvasquez@ut.edu

Abstract. This paper examines how health and fitness content creators use personal branding factors when planning short-form video content to engage and strengthen relationships with followers on TikTok. The study was conducted using a quantitative content analysis technique to analyze aspects that form a creator's brand awareness, including technical aspects of the video, authenticity traits, content themes, and message strategies. Authors were also interested in examining how personal branding factors impact engagement (e.g., views, likes, comments, and shares). One hundred eighty videos from six TikTok content creators (three accounts about Fitness and three in Wellness/Nutrition) posted in 2021 were examined. Results showed personal brand awareness aspects like text/captions and hashtags were widely used when planning technical aspects of the video that reinforce brand communication. Music and text speech were also used frequently. Other elements, such as authentic traits of communication, were vital to employ. For instance, when a content creator was making an action on the video (like showing their fitness routine), music and captions were also included, promoting relatable content among their followers. Personal brand awareness also includes carefully selecting topics/themes for communication. The most common video topic among health and fitness creators was assisting/advising their followers, such as, how to use a product or service or providing emotional support. Lastly, the most used message strategies that helped to reinforce the topic were building connections and relationships.

Keywords: Personal Branding · TikTok · Content Creators

1 Background

1.1 Importance of the Study

TikTok is one of the fastest-growing social media platforms, with over 1 billion monthly active users [1], allowing creators to build their personal brands and interact with their audience. Diverse niches and industries can be found on TikTok, being among the most popular: health and fitness; and wellness and nutrition, commonly known as "FitTok", which is composed of fitness, nutrition, and wellness content. FitTok is one of the most

C. Stephanidis et al. (Eds.): HCII 2023, CCIS 1835, pp. 344–349, 2023.
https://doi.org/10.1007/978-3-031-36001-5_44

popular genres on TikTok, to inspire others through motivational content (e.g., workouts, fitness challenges, recipes, and nutritional advice), encouraging an active life more accessible [2]. However, research around authenticity and personal branding on TikTok is still scarce, especially for FiTok creators. Research is needed to analyze aspects that form a creator's brand awareness, including technical aspects of the video, authenticity traits, content themes, and message strategies and how they impact on building engagement and relationships.

1.2 Personal Branding and Authenticity on TikTok

Personal branding involves human branding, self-promotion, impression management, image, reputation, and fame through the use of self-made work artifacts (videos, audio, blog posts, links, and other media) [3]. In order to develop a personal brand online, creators share these artifacts with their followers or potential audiences [4]. Self-presentation on social media often involves presenting oneself in a positive light, where positive content is more common and receives more interaction [5, 6]. Through personal branding and the creation of relatable and authentic content, people will follow creators and a unified community could be born based on these interactions. Through the development of communities, content creators can help their followers with similar interests and values, becoming communities of "shared relevance" [7], especially young generations who want to connect with influencers that work towards change and provide value to them [7].

Authenticity is born through the interactions between self-awareness, behaviors, and one's experience [8, 9]. When there is an agreement across those dimensions, there is a likelihood to increase feelings of authenticity with the content shared [10]. Authenticity refers to what is genuine, real, and/or true [11]. In social media, user-generated content is usually viewed as more authentic, transparent, and trustworthy than branded content [11]. Particularly on TikTok, authenticity is a unique aspect of the TikTok community compared to other social media platforms [12]. According to a study by TikTok and Nielsen [12], 64% of TikTok users say they can be their true selves on TikTok. TikTok content is seen as authentic, genuine, unfiltered, and trendsetting. TikTok promotes social acceptance and the adoption of a "just be you" attitude that contributes to support authenticity through unfiltered content that shows a selective presentation of a partial but still authentic self [10].

Authenticity can impact engagement, which is key to developing genuine relationships with followers. TikTok is the most engaging social media platform across platforms, with an engagement rate of 4.25% [12]. Producing content with enthusiasm and energy increases emotions, encouraging engagement [13]. For instance, athletes' videos on TikTok are focused on playfulness and authentic content. This provides athletes creators to foster exciting fan relationships and appeal to new target audiences [14]. Content on TikTok can feel more personal regardless of connection to the creator (seeing it on For You Page) [10]. Content personalization helps to increase perceived authenticity among followers [15]. Creativity also plays a crucial role in developing authenticity [15]. In fact, personalized videos on the "For You page" may increase the perceived creativity and authenticity of TikTok videos [16]. This paper contributes to understanding how personal branding elements, including content authenticity helps to impact users' engagement with FitTok creators.

2 Methods

A quantitative content analysis technique was done to analyze personal branding elements on TikTok. One hundred eighty videos from six TikTok content creators posted between July – August 2021 were examined. Three of these accounts were included in the fitness niche, and the other three in the Wellness/Nutrition niche (30 videos were analyzed per account). Diverse creators based on their follower count and content type were selected. A codebook was developed using inductive and deductive reasoning involving expert consensus. Each TikTok video was analyzed to identify: 1. Technical aspects of the video (e.g., captions, hashtags, filters/emoji/gif, music/duet/text to speech, etc.). 2. Authenticity traits (e.g., voice-over or person talking directly to the camera, and the person doing an action not directly talking to the camera, etc.). 3. Content topics/themes (e.g., playfulness, assistance/advice, challenges, inspiration, trends, etc.), and 4. Message strategies (information/education, dialogue/engagement, mobilization/action, etc.).

To determine intercoder reliability, about 25% of the videos were randomly selected and independently coded by each author. The inter-coder reliability tests performed on each variable indicated scores ranging from 0.77–0.99 agreement (Cohen's Kappa), indicating an adequate level of inter-coder reliability. The remaining videos were split and independently coded by the two authors.

3 Results

Descriptive results showed that most of the TikTok videos were focused on promoting dialogue, engagement, or mentions. TikTok videos were also common to have text/captions on them, hashtags, and music, duet, or text-to-speech. To identify authenticity traits, the most used one was when a person was doing an action in the video, not directly talking to the camera (like showing their fitness routine) with captions on the video. The strategy found most in the TikTok videos was assistance/advice. This means content creators were asking followers a piece of advice or giving assistance or suggestions to them. On TikTok people want to learn from others and share experiences. This is key when building communities, in other words, identifying and defining an essential purpose or strategy that resonates with the community, like learning something, growing and becoming healthier, or just because followers want to belong to something with the creator because they believe in them [7].

Table 1 shows crosstabs among the variables analyzed and the different personal branding elements depending on the strategy employed.

For promoting authenticity, 63 videos included text captions when there was a voiceover or a person talking directly to the camera, 118 were found when a person was doing an action (not talking directly to the camera), and captions appeared on the video. Fifty-two videos had hashtags when there was a voice-over or a person talking, and 110 videos were found when a person was doing an action and captions appeared on the video. Stickers, gif, filters, emojis, polls, music, and duets were not popular to include unless

Table 1. Crosstabs among variables.

Message strategy	Text/captions and hashtags	Hashtags	Music/duet/text-to-speech	Stickers/filters/gif/emoji/poll
Dialogue/engagement/mentions	84 videos	76 videos	69 videos	43 videos
Informational	66 videos	61 videos	48 videos	34 videos
Mobilization	58 videos	55 videos	45 videos	30 videos

a person doing an action (not talking directly to the camera) with captions in the video (107 videos had music/duet/text to speech, and 71 had gif/stickers/filters/emojis/polls). Authenticity traits were most likely to be found in dialogue and engagement videos, and assistance/advice videos which is expected.

A chi-square test of independence was performed to examine the relationship between all variables. The relation between authenticity variables and technical aspects of the video was significant: a person doing an action/with captions and hashtags χ^2 (1, N = 180) = 4.476, p < 0.03, voice-over/person talking with hashtags χ^2 (1, N = 180) = 3.956, p < 0.04, person doing an action/with captions and music/duet/text to speech χ^2 (1, N = 180) = 23.579, p < 0.01, voice-over/person talking and music/duet/text to speech χ^2 (1, N = 180) = 43.471, p < 0.01. In addition, themes that revolved with asking questions with adding stickers/gifs/filters/emojis/polls were significant, χ^2 (1, N = 180) = 5.389, p < 0.02. Informational strategies were statistically significant when a person was doing a voice-over or talking directly to the camera, χ^2 (1, N = 180) = 5.007, p < 0.02, and doing an activity (not talking directly to the camera) with captions, χ^2 (1, N = 180) = 9.368, p < 0.002.

To impact engagement in terms of likes, shares, and comments, videos should include minimum text or captions and hashtags. It will increase more chances of getting likes, shares, and comments if stickers/gifs/filters/emojis, or polls are included and music/duets or text-to-speech. Most of the videos analyzed had more than 100 K likes, 1000 comments, and shares, and had at least four technical aspects of the video. Those popular videos showed authenticity by having a creator doing an activity that relates to the audience with captions on it, focused on engagement and informational strategies addressing topics related to assistance/advice and being playful.

4 Discussion and Conclusion

This paper analyzed personal branding elements used by health and fitness content creators on TikTok. TikTok has gained immense popularity among younger generations, especially Gen Zs. Although TikTok is mainly used for entertainment purposes, it has also become an essential tool for personal branding due to its unique features like short-form nature and how it rapidly disseminates with a global audience [17]. Findings indicate that content in the platform must include a high level of creativity through the use of technical aspects of the video to make the content resonate with audiences and promote engagement. The short-form nature of TikTok videos requires a high degree of creativity, humor, and self-expression from creators to showcase their true selves in unique and creative ways [18]. If a video is authentic, creative, and engaging, it has a high chance of going viral and reaching a wider audience. This can help individuals build a following, grow their personal brand, and increase their visibility [19]. Content on TikTok will always favor authenticity and engagement regardless of production quality [19].

This study has some limitations that suggest avenues for further studies. For instance, further research can provide a more in-depth analysis to understand personal branding traits that impact community resonance in other industries (not health/fitness-related accounts). Furthermore, the rise of TikTok influencers and the platform's monetization has led to questions about the authenticity of sponsored content [20]. Future research can study the impact of sponsored content on authenticity. In conclusion, TikTok is an essential tool for personal branding in today's digital age. Its unique features, such as short-form videos and engaging algorithms, make it an ideal platform for showcasing authenticity, creativity and building a community. As such, individuals looking to establish a solid personal brand should consider leveraging TikTok's potential to offer audiences an experience, so a community is formed and connections are then formed through a relevant purpose [7]. Our paper contributes to the literature of social media and influencer marketing by understanding the personal branding traits commonly used by FiTok creators to connect with audiences.

References

1. Sprout Social. https://sproutsocial.com/insights/tiktok-stats/. Accessed 8 Mar 2023
2. Action Group. https://action-group.co.uk/why-fitness-brands-should-use-tiktok/. Accessed 8 Mar 2023
3. Gorbatov, S., Khapova, S.N., Lysova, E.I.: Personal branding: Interdisciplinary systematic review and research agenda. Front. Psychol. e2238 (2018)
4. Labrecque, L.I., Markos, E., Milne, G.R.: Online personal branding: processes, challenges, and implications. J. Interact. Mark. **25**(1), 37–50 (2011)
5. Forest, A., Wood, J.V.: When social networking is not working: individuals with low self-esteem recognize but do not reap the benefits of self-disclosure on Facebook. Psychol. Sci. **23**(3), 295–302 (2012)
6. Reinecke, L., Trepte, S.: Authenticity and well-being on social network sites: a two-wave longitudinal study on the effects of online authenticity and the positivity bias in SNS communication. Comput. Hum. Behav. **30**, 95–102 (2014)
7. Schaefer, M.: Belonging to the brand. Why community is the last great marketing strategy. Schaefer Marketing Solutions (2022)
8. Godfrey, T., Barrett, L.: Carl Rogers' Helping System: Journey and Substance. Sage, London (1998)
9. Wood, A., Linley, A., Maltby, J., Baliousis, M., Joseph, S.: The authentic personality: a theoretical and empirical conceptualization and the development of the authenticity scale. J. Couns. Psychol. **55**(3), 385–399 (2008)
10. Barta, K., Andalibi, N.: Constructing authenticity on TikTok: social norms and social support on the "fun" platform. PACM Hum.-Comput. Interact. **5**(2) (2021)
11. Dekavalla, M.: Gaining trust: the articulation of transparency by YouTube fashion and beauty content creators. Media Cult. Soc. **42**(1), 75–92 (2020)
12. TikTok For Business. https://www.tiktok.com/business/en-US/blog/nielsen-study-tiktok-discovery-content-authentic. Accessed 8 Mar 2023

13. The Drum. https://www.thedrum.com/news/2021/11/15/be-more-you-how-brands-can-con nect-authentically-tiktok. Accessed 8 Mar 2023

14. Su, Y., Baker, B.J., Doyle, J.P.: Fan engagement in 15 seconds: athlete's relationship marketing during a pandemic via TikTok. Int. J. Sport Commun. **13**, 436–446 (2020)

15. Avtex. https://avtex.com/articles/personalization-and-its-impact-on-loyalty-and-profitabi lity. Accessed 8 Mar 2023

16. Chu, S-C., Deng, T., Mundel, J.: The impact of personalization on viral behavior intentions on TikTok: the role of perceived creativity, authenticity, and need for uniqueness. J. Mark. Commun. (2022)

17. The Verge. https://www.theverge.com/21289405/tiktok-what-is-how-to-use-video-app-music-memes-trends. Accessed 8 Mar 2023

18. Hootsuite. https://blog.hootsuite.com/creativity-on-tiktok/. Accessed 8 Mar 2023

19. HubSpot. https://blog.hubspot.com/marketing/tiktok-algorithm. Accessed 8 Mar 2023

20. BBC News. https://www.bbc.com/news/business-56179684. Accessed 8 Mar 2023

The Influence of Electronic Word of Mouth, Quality Perception and Price Perception on Purchase Interest Through Brand Image

Soffi Hayanti and Nuryakin[✉]

Management Department, Universitas Muhammadiyah Yogyakarta, Kasihan, Indonesia
nuryakin@umy.ac.id

Abstract. This study analyzes the effect of Electronic Word of Mouth, Perceived Quality, and Perceived Price on Purchase Intention through Brand Image on Roughneck 1991 products in Yogyakarta. The subjects in this study were consumers or customers of local fashion products who live in Yogyakarta. In this study, 232 respondents became samples and were collected using a non-probability sampling method with a purposive sampling technique. The analysis tool used was SEM analysis with AMOS software. Based on the analysis, the results showed that Electronic Word of Mouth had a positive and significant effect on Brand Image, Perceived Quality had a positive and significant effect on Brand Image, Perceived Price had a positive and significant effect on Brand Image, Electronic Word of Mouth had a positive and significant effect on Purchase Intention, Perceived Quality had a positive and significant effect on Purchase Intention, Price Perception had a positive and significant effect on Purchase Intention, Brand Image had a positive and significant effect on Purchase Intention, Electronic Word of Mouth had an indirect effect on Purchase Intention which was mediated by Brand Image, Perceived Quality had an indirect effect on Purchase Intention which was mediated by Brand Image. Perceived price indirectly affected Purchase Intention, which was mediated by Brand Image.

Keywords: Electronic Word of Mouth · Perception of Quality · Price Perception · Brand Image · Purchase Intention

1 Introduction

The rapid development of the internet has an impact on expanding information for its users. Internet user data in Indonesia in 2021 increased by 11% from the previous year, from 175.4 million to 202.6 million users (https://aptika.kominfo.go.id/). Various platforms have now been widely used for exchanging information and communication markets for consumers where eWOM activities are affected too. For businesspeople, eWOM supports business development through customer reviews of online shops.

This study begins with a gap in previous studies about the influence of brand image on eWOM. [1] found that brand image could significantly mediate the eWOM variable

C. Stephanidis et al. (Eds.): HCII 2023, CCIS 1835, pp. 350–359, 2023.
https://doi.org/10.1007/978-3-031-36001-5_45

on the intention to buy a smartphone. However, [2] and [3], who tested the relationship between eWOM and purchase intention, showed different results from previous researchers. [4] revealed a negative or positive influence from actual consumers, potential customers of products or services from a company where the information is available to others or through internet social media. eWOM is part of viral marketing that encourages consumers to talk about a company's products or services accompanied by the value consumers feel. This study analyzed the effect of electronic word of mouth, perceived quality, and perceived price on purchase intention. This study also examined the important mediating role between brand image and purchase intention. The subjects in this study were consumers or customers of local fashion products who live in Yogyakarta.

2 Hypothesis Development

2.1 The Influence of Electronic Word of Mouth on Brand Image

Positive ratings will affect the brand image of the product. Jalilvand and Samiei (2012) stated that eWOM would increase the company's brand image in the eyes of consumers, which will have an impact on reducing promotional costs by companies. [3] tested several research variables such as brand image, eWOM, purchase intention and trust. They found that eWOM was a positive and significant predictor of brand image variables. [2] revealed that eWOM positively and significantly influenced brand image. The researchers stated the following hypothesis based on the theory and previous research.

H₁: **Electronic Word of Mouth Positively And Significantly Affects Brand Image.**

2.2 The Influence of Perceived Quality on Brand Image

The more consumers think or have a good quality perception of a product or service, the more the brand image is improved. This situation can be influenced by various factors, one of which is perceived quality from consumers. After the consumers receive the quality they deserve, the brand image will gain popularity.

H₂: **Perceived quality positively and significantly affects brand image.**

2.3 The Influence of Price Perceptions on Brand Image

[5] stated that perceptions or assumptions about price are related to how a price can be meaningful to consumers. Only some people with high or expensive prices have a good brand image, and vice versa. The brand image can be good even though a product or service offers a low or cheap price. [6] stated that country of origin, perceived quality and price directly could affect brand image variables. [7] mentioned that price positively and significantly affected brand image. The researchers stated the following hypothesis based on the theory and previous research.

H₃: **The perceived price positively and significantly affects brand image.**

2.4 The Influence of Electronic Word of Mouth on Purchase Intention

When a business account has many followers, an official sales account can convince consumers. An online assessment or review of something about a product or service will certainly greatly influence buying interest, supported by ratings or reviews given by other consumers, recommendations from other people, or all exchanges of information via social media regarding products or services that refer to recommending or simply sharing personal experiences after purchasing the product. [8] found that electronic word of mouth positively and significantly affected the intention to buy Naava Green skincare products at the Yogyakarta Branch. Similarly, [9] revealed that eWOM positively influenced Innisfree customers' buying interest in Jakarta. The researchers stated the following hypothesis based on the theory and previous research.

H_4: **Electronic word of mouth positively and significantly affects purchase intention.**

2.5 The Influence of Perceived Quality on Purchase Intention

A consumer will be interested in buying if his needs are fulfilled, so consumer quality can also affect his buying interest. [10] showed a positive influence between product quality and purchase intention. [11] raised several independent variables, such as perceived product quality, brand awareness and celebrity endorsers, with purchase intention as the dependent variable. Perceived product quality had a positive and significant effect on purchase intention. [12] also revealed that perceived quality had a dominant, significant and positive effect on purchase intention. The researchers stated the following hypothesis based on the theory and previous research.

H_5: **Perceived quality positively and significantly affects purchase intention.**

2.6 The Influence of Perceived Price on Purchase Intention

Price is what consumers consider before making a purchase process. Sometimes consumers also compare prices offered for the same product, so a perception of price begins to form. Hence, the price also determines purchase intention [13] found a positive influence between the price perception and purchase intention variables. [14] also showed that perceived price and design variables positively and partially influenced the intention to buy Xiaomi smartphones in Pangkal Pinang City. However, [15] revealed different findings. They tested the hypothesis that price influenced buying interest positively and significantly, proving that this hypothesis was rejected. The researchers stated the following hypothesis based on the theory and previous research.

H_6: **The perceived price positively and significantly affects purchase intention.**

2.7 The Influence of Brand Image on Purchase Intention

Brand image will greatly influence consumer buying interest because various perceptions will emerge from consumers and then influence buying behavior. Consumers must have a choice of brand in their minds. They may be influenced because the quantity used, or the quality obtained makes the brand well embedded in their minds. Several studies, such as those from [1] found a positive and significant influence between brand image and intention to buy Xiaomi smartphones. [16] also stated that brand image positively and significantly affects purchase intention. The researchers stated the following hypothesis based on the theory and previous research.

H_7: **Brand image positively and significantly affects purchase intention.**

2.8 The Influence of Electronic Word of Mouth on Buying Interest Mediated by Brand Image

Ratings or reviews given on social media by consumers will have a certain impact. The reviews can be positive or negative, influencing other consumers' decisions. Now, most e-commerce implements this review system. It is also expected to build its brand image through the experiences they get written in these reviews and influence the buying interest of other potential customers. [17] stated in their research on the electronic word-of-mouth variable on buying interest that a significant value was obtained and had a positive effect through brand image. The researchers stated the following hypothesis based on the theory and previous research.

H_8: **Electronic word of mouth positively and significantly affects purchase intention, mediated by brand image.**

2.9 The Influence of Perceived Quality on Purchase Intention, Which is Mediated by Brand Image.

Suppose the perceived quality of a product increases. In that case, the product's brand image also increases, followed by an increase in consumer buying interest in the product because there are many positive assumptions or judgments, which can make potential consumers more confident in choosing products or services. [6] stated that country of origin, perceived quality and price indirectly affected the purchase intention through brand image as a mediating variable. The researchers stated the following hypothesis based on the theory and previous research.

H_9: **Perceived quality influences purchase intention, which is mediated by brand image.**

2.10 The Influence of Price Perceptions on Purchase Intention Mediated by Brand Image

Every product or service company must have its target and market segment, so if there is an expensive product or service price, the brand image will be low, and the buying interest will decrease or vice versa. The better the product's perceived quality, the better the brand image influences purchase intention. [6] showed that the variables of the perceived country of origin, perceived quality, and perceived price as independent variables indirectly influence purchase intention as the dependent variable, mediated by brand image. The researchers stated the following hypothesis based on the theory and previous research.

H_{10}: **Perceived price influences purchase intention, which is mediated by brand image.**

3   Research Model

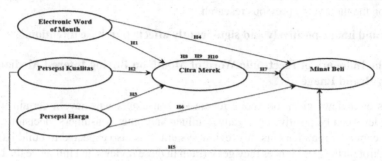

Fig. 1. Research Model

This research makes Roughneck 1991 products the object of research, and the subjects in this study are consumers/customers of local fashion products who live in Yogyakarta. This study used primary data, where the source came from questionnaires through Google forms distributed to consumers/customers of local fashion products who live in Yogyakarta-using sampling technique and a non-probability sampling method with a purposive sampling technique, with sample criteria such as having visited an official store on e-commerce or Roughneck 1991 social media, having an interest in Roughneck 1991 products and being ≥ 17 years old. With 232 samples, this study used SEM analysis or the Goodness of fit test assisted by the AMOS (Analysis of Structural Moment) statistical application program. Validity test using Confirmatory Factor Analysis (CFA), and reliability testing in this study using Construct Reliability (CR) (Fig. 1).

4   Result and Discussion

4.1   Validity Test and Reliability Test

This test states the results of this study's overall hypothesis testing, specifically the Confirmatory Factor Analysis and Construct Reliability tests. From this hypothesis's comprehensive testing, all indicators must meet valid and reliable criteria for further analysis (Table 1).

4.2   The Goodness of Fit Test

Next is to test the fit test of the SEM model to find out whether the model created is based on observational data under the theoretical model or not and find out how far the hypothesized model is said to "Fit" by looking at the measurement results adjusted for the cut-off value or limits on each index on SEM analysis. The results of the Goodness of fit are presented in the table below (Table 2).

Table 1. Confirmatory Factor Analysis Test Results and Construct Reliability Test

Constructions & Indikators	Standardized Loading Factor	Standard Loading2	Measurement error	AVE
Electronic Word of Mouth (CR = 0,877)				
I read online reviews of 1991 Roughneck products from other consumers (EWOM1)	0,811	0,685	0,342	
I gathered information about the 1991 Roughneck product from consumer reviews via the internet (EWOM2)	0,785	0,616	0,384	
I asked other people about Roughneck 1991 products online (EWOM3)	0,718	0,516	0,484	0,589
I am worried about purchasing without reading online reviews for Roughneck 1991 (EWOM4) products	0,785	0,616	0,384	
I feel more confident about purchasing after reading online reviews for Roughneck 1991 (EWOM5) products	0,733	0,537	0,463	
Perceived Quality (C.R = 0.904)				
Roughneck 1991 product has the quality according to my expectations (PK1)	0,789	0,632	0,337	
Roughneck 1991 products offer prices according to their quality (PK2)	0,808	0,653	0,347	
Roughneck brand 1991 is a popular brand (PK3)	0,787	0,619	0,381	0,609
Roughneck product 1991 is comfortable when used (PK4)	0,785	0,616	0,384	
1991 Roughneck product easy to get (PK5)	0,783	0,613	0,387	
Roughneck products are reliable fashion products (PK6)	0,730	0,533	0,467	
Price Perception (C.R = 0.883)				
Roughneck 1991 product quality according to the price offered (PH1)	0,800	0,640	0,360	
Roughneck 1991 products have very competitive prices (PH2)	0,843	0,711	0,289	0,653
Affordable 1991 Roughneck Products (PH3)	0,840	0,706	0,294	
Roughneck product 1991 useful (PH4)	0,746	0,557	0,443	
Brand Image (C.R = 0.900)				
The Roughneck 1991 brand is a local product brand that is dominant compared to other local brands (CM1)	0,768	0,590	0,410	
The Roughneck 1991 brand is a well-known local product brand (CM2)	0,869	0,755	0,245	0,694
Roughneck brand 1991 is a brand known to many (CM3)	0,844	0,712	0,288	
Roughneck 1991 brand is a trusted local product brand (CM4)	0,847	0,717	0,283	
Buying Interest (C.R = 0.889)				
I often look for information about the product Roughneck 1991 (MB1)	0,826	0,682	0,318	
I've recommended Roughneck 1991 products to others (MB2)	0,825	0,682	0,319	0,666
I am interested in buying a 1991 Roughneck product after receiving information regarding the product (MB3)	0,816	0,666	0,334	
Roughneck 1991 product is the product that I prioritize buying (MB4)	0,798	0,637	0,363	

Table 2. The Goodness of Fit Test Result

The goodness of the fit index	Cut-off Value	Measurement results	Model
Chi-Square	Expected small	381.139	Not
Significant Probability	≥ 0.05	0.000	Not
RMSEA	≤ 0.08	0.056	Fit
GFI	≥ 0.90	0.881	Marginal
AGFI	≥ 0.90	0.851	Marginal
CMIN/DF	≤ 2.0	1.732	Fit
TLI	≥ 0.90	0.949	Fit
CFI	≥ 0.90	0.947	Fit
NFI	≥ 0.90	0.903	Fit
PNFI	0,60-0,90	0,785	Fit
PGFI	≥ 0,90	0,703	Tidak Fit

4.3 Hypothesis Test

Hypothesis data analysis can be seen from the standardized regression weight value, which shows the coefficient of influence between variables. This test answers the research problem formulation and analyzes the structural model relationship. The following are the results of the relationship between variables (Table 3).

H1: The Influence of Electronic Word of Mouth on Brand Image

Table 4.19 shows a regression weight coefficient of 0.320 and a CR of 4.327, and a P value of 0.000 so that it meets the criteria of a value ($p < 0.05$). The relationship between electronic word of mouth and brand image is positive because the better word of mouth,

Table 3. Results between variables

			Estimate	SE.	CR.	P	Hypothesis
Electronic word of mouth	→	Brand Image	.320	.074	4.327	***	Significant Positive
Perceived Quality	→	Brand Image	.351	.086	4.083	***	Significant Positive
Price Perception	→	Brand Image	.341	.093	3.666	***	Significant Positive
Electronic word of mouth	→	Purchase Interest	.149	.075	1.983	.047	Significant Positive
Perceived Quality	→	Purchase Interest	.183	.086	2.120	.034	Significant Positive
Price Perception	→	Purchase Interest	.188	.093	2.016	.044	Significant Positive
Brand Image	→	Purchase Interest	.604	.099	6.094	***	Significant Positive

the better the brand image. Thus, electronic word of mouth positively and significantly affects brand image.

H2: The Influence of Perceived Quality on Brand Image

Table 4.19 illustrates a regression weight coefficient of 0.351 and a CR of 4.083, and a P value of 0.000 so that it meets the criteria of a value ($p < 0.05$). The relationship between perceived quality and brand image is positive because the better the perceived quality, the better the brand image. Thus, perceived quality has a positive and significant effect on brand image.

H3: The Influence of Perceived Price on Brand Image

Table 4.19 illustrates a regression weight coefficient of 0.341 and a CR of 3.666, and a P value of 0.000 so that it meets the criteria of a value ($p < 0.05$). The relationship between price perception and brand image is positive because the better the price perception, the brand image will improve. Thus, price perception positively and significantly affects brand image.

H4: The Influence of Electronic Word of Mouth on Purchase Intention

Based on Table 4.19, the regression weight coefficient is 0.149. The CR is 1.983 and has a P value of 0.047, so it meets the value criteria ($p < 0.05$). So this states that the relationship between electronic word of mouth and purchase intention is positive because the better the electronic word of mouth, the higher the purchase intention. Thus, electronic word of mouth positively and significantly affects purchase intention.

H5: The Influence of Perceived Quality on Purchase Intention

Table 4.19 illustrates a regression weight coefficient of 0.183 and a CR of 2.120, and a P value of 0.034 so that it meets the criteria of a value ($p < 0.05$). The relationship between perceived quality and purchase intention is positive because the better the quality perception, the higher the purchase intention. Thus, perceived quality positively and significantly affects purchase intention.

H6: The Influence of Perceived Price on Purchase Intention

Based on Table 4.19, a regression weight coefficient is 0.188, a CR of 2.016 and a P value of 0.044, so it meets the criteria of a value ($p < 0.05$). The relationship between price perception and purchase intention is positive because the better the price perception, the higher the purchase intention. Thus, price perception positively and significantly affects purchase intention.

H7: The Influence of Brand Image on Purchase Intention

Table 4.19 shows that the regression weight coefficient is 0.604 and the CR is 6.094, with a P value of 0.000 to meet the criteria of a value (p < 0.05). The relationship between brand image and purchase intention is positive because the better the brand image, the higher the purchase intention. Thus, brand image positively and significantly affects purchase intention.

H8: The Influence of Electronic Word of Mouth on Purchase Intention Mediated by Brand Image

In this study, to find out how the effect of electronic word of mouth on purchase intention mediated by brand image is by comparing the direct effect value of 0.131 with the indirect effect value of 0.171, where in this study, electronic word of mouth positively and significantly affects purchase intention through brand image. Based on the results showing the value of the direct effect < indirect effect, there is an indirect effect between the electronic word of mouth on buying interest.

H9: The Influence of Perceived Quality on Purchase Intention Mediated by Brand Image

This study aims to find out how the influence of perceived quality on purchase intention is mediated by brand image by comparing the direct effect value of 0.152 with the indirect effect value of 0.177. In this study, perceived quality positively and significantly affects purchase intention through brand image. Based on the results showing the value of the direct effect < indirect effect, there is an indirect effect between perceived quality and purchase intention.

H10: The Influence of Perceived Price on Purchase Intention Mediated by Brand Image

This study aims to find out how the influence of price perceptions on purchase intention is mediated by brand image by comparing the direct effect value of 0.154 with the indirect effect value of 0.170, where in this study, price perception positively and significantly affects purchase intention through brand image. Based on the results showing the value of the direct effect < indirect effect, there is an indirect effect between perceived price and purchase intention.

5   Conclusions

Based on data analysis and hypothesis testing carried out using Structural Equation Modeling (SEM) modeling with the Amos program regarding the influence of electronic word of mouth, perceived quality and perceived price on buying interest mediated by brand image, electronic word of mouth had an effect positive and significant impact on Brand Image on Roughneck 1991 products, Perceived quality had a positive and significant effect on Brand Image on Roughneck 1991 products, the perceived price had a positive and significant effect on Brand Image on Roughneck 1991 products, Electronic word of mouth had a positive and significant effect on Purchase Intention on Roughneck 1991 products. Perceived quality positively and significantly affected the purchase intention of Roughneck 1991 products. Price perception positively and significantly affected purchase intentions on Roughneck products in 1991, and brand image positively and significantly affected interest. Buying interest in Roughneck 1991 products, electronic word of mouth indirectly affected Buying Interest in Roughneck 1991 products mediated by Brand Image. Perceived quality indirectly affected Buying Interest in Roughneck 1991 products mediated by Brand Image. Perceived price had an indirect effect directly to Buying Interest in Roughneck 1991 products mediated by Brand Image.

References

1. Yohana, N.K.Y., Dewi, K.A.P., Giantari, I.: The role of brand image mediates the effect of electronic word of mouth (E-WOM) on purchase intention. Am. J. Humanit. Soc. Sci. Res. **4**(1), 215–220 (2020)
2. Firdaus, R., Sharif, O.O.: Analisis Pengaruh Electronic Word Of Mouth (E-Wom) Pada Brand Image Dan Purchase Intention Terhadap Produk Sepatu Nike (Studi Pada Konsumen Di Kota Bandung). J. Mitra Manaj. **4**(6), 900–914 (2020)
3. Hendro, H., Keni, K.: Ewom dan trust sebagai prediktor terhadap purchase intention: Brand image sebagai variabel mediasi. J. Komun. **12**(2), 298–310 (2020)
4. Reza Jalilvand, M., Samiei, N.: The effect of electronic word of mouth on brand image and purchase intention: an empirical study in the automobile industry in Iran. Mark. Intell. Plan. **30**(4), 460–476 (2012)
5. Peter, J.P., Olson, J.C.: Perilaku konsumen & strategi pemasaran. Salemba Empat, Jakarta (2014)
6. Rachma, N., Slamet, A.R.: Pengaruh country of origin, perceived quality dan price terhadap purchase intention dengan brand image sebagai variabel intervening (Studi kasus pada pengguna Oli Castrol di Bengkel Castrol Active Sawojajar Kota Malang). J. Ilm. Ris. Manaj. **8**(12) (2019)
7. Febriani, R., Khairusy, M.A.: Analisis Pengaruh Celebrity Endorser/Brand Ambasador, Harga Dan Desain Produk Yang Dimediasi Oleh Citra Merek Terhadap Keputusan Pembelian Di Online Shop Shopee. Prog. J. Pendidikan Akunt. dan Keuang. **3**(1), 91–109 (2020)
8. Jayanti, D.D., Welsa, H., Cahyani, P.D.: Pengaruh electronic word of mouth dan celebrity endorsment terhadap purchase intention dengan brand image sebagai variabel intervening. J. Ilm. MEA (Manajemen, Ekon. Akuntansi) **4**(2), 686–703 (2020)
9. Yonita, T., Budiono, H.: Pengaruh Ewom Terhadap Brand Image dan Purchase Intention Produk Innisfree di Jakarta. J. Manajerial Dan Kewirausahaan **2**(1), 152–161 (2020)
10. Prawira, Y.: Pengaruh Citra Merek, Persepsi Harga dan Kualitas Produk Terhadap Minat Beli Pelanggan. J. Manaj. Bisnis dan Kewirausahaan **3**(6), 71–76 (2019)
11. Pratiwi, A.I., Mursito, B., Kustiyah, E.: Persepsi Kualitas Produk, Brand Awareness Dan Celebrity Endorsement Terhadap Minat Beli Oppo Smartphone Pada Mahasiswa Fakultas Ekonomi Uniba Surakarta. J. Ilm. Edunomika **4**(2) (2020)
12. Sihombing, M.A.T., Johannes, J., Ekasari, N.: Pengaruh persepsi harga, persepsi kualitas, dan persepsi merk terhadap minat pembelian mobil merk Wuling di Kota Jambi. J. Din. Manaj. **9**(3), 149–162 (2021)

13. Rizky, D., Firdausy, C.M.: Pengaruh Citra Merek, Persepsi Harga dan Kualitas Produk Honda Brio Satya Terhadap Minat Beli Pelanggan di Jakarta. J. Manaj. Bisnis dan Kewirausahaan **4**(4), 156–161 (2020)
14. Lestari, D.S.: Pengaruh Persepsi Harga, Citra Merek, Fitur dan Desain Terhadap Minat Beli Produk Smartphone Xiaomi di Kota Pangkalpinang. J. Progresif Manaj. Bisnis **8**(1), 17–24 (2021)
15. Wardani, R., Oktavia, F., Ali, S.A., Suhud, U.: Analisis Pengaruh Trust, Price, Brand Image, Service Quality, dan Customer Satisfaction terhadap Purchase Intention Pelanggan Kedai Minuman Boba. Communications **4**(1), 41–76 (2022)
16. Ellen, E., Tunjungsari, H.K.K.: Pengaruh Electronic Word Of Mouth (e-Wom) Dan Country Of Origin (Coo) Terhadap Purchase Intnsion; Melalui Mediasi Brand Image Terhadap Produk Nature Republic Di Universitas Tarumanagara. J. Manajerial Dan Kewirausahaan **1**(3), 411–419 (2019)
17. Sitinjak, T., Pramudita, E.: The Effect Of Social Media Marketing And Electronic Word Of Mouth On Purchase Intention Through Brand Image On Tokopedia, Shopee, And Bukalapak Users In Jakarta. J. Manaj. **10**(2), 1–10 (2021)

Influence Factors of Green Packaging on Consumers' Willingness to Accept Festive Gifts

Ouyang Li[1]([✉]) [iD], Xiansi Zeng[1] [iD], and Jie Ling[2] [iD]

[1] Guangzhou Academy of Fine Arts, Guangzhou, Guangdong, China
935256396@qq.com
[2] Zhongkai University of Agriculture and Engineering, Guangzhou, Guangdong, China

Abstract. As people pay more attention to gift packaging, excessive packaging of festival gifts causes environmental pollution and waste of resources. Green packaging is very beneficial to environmental protection and sustainable development, and it is of great significance to increase consumers' willingness to accept green packaging. Therefore, exploring how to make consumers more willing to accept green packaging in festival gifts is important. Based on the investigation of green packaging in festival gifts, the article summarizes and analyzes the factors that affect consumers' willingness to accept, establishes a model of factors affecting the willingness to accept green packaging, and uses PLS3.0 software to verify. The study's results found that the ease of use and usefulness of green packaging positively impact consumers' willingness to accept, and consumers' ecological values will indirectly affect their willingness to accept green festival gift packaging. Consumers strongly perceive the usefulness and ease of use of gift packaging, and their ecological values play an essential role in their acceptance of green packaging. Therefore, making consumers aware of the environmental problems caused by festival gift packaging and making green packaging more convenient to use can better promote the development of green packaging in festival gifts.

Keywords: Festive gifts · Gift packaging · Green packaging · Sustainable development · Willingness to accept

1 Introduction

Green consumption has attracted more and more attention worldwide, and green design has also become an important way for design to shape consumption values. In 1987, the United Nations put forward the concept of environmentally friendly packaging in "To Our Common Future", but the construction of environmentally friendly packaging has been slow for many years, and excessive packaging and waste of resources are still emerging1. As one of the crucial ways to solve the waste of packaging resources, design has not only failed to solve the problem of excessive packaging in festive gifts but has aggravated the phenomenon of excessive packaging.

C. Stephanidis et al. (Eds.): HCII 2023, CCIS 1835, pp. 360–368, 2023.
https://doi.org/10.1007/978-3-031-36001-5_46

Festive gift wrap is an integral part of gift packaging. Because gift packaging is a gift-giving product, it is easy to cause excessive packaging. In recent years, China and the world have advocated green consumption and packaging, which has led to a bottleneck in festival gift packaging. Merchants have also begun to try green designs of festive gift packaging, mainly starting from the packaging materials and structure, and the breadth and depth involved have yet to be studied. Therefore, this study conducts research from the perspective of consumers, explores the influencing factors of consumers' acceptance of green packaging in festival gifts, and aims to provide feasible design strategies and solutions for the packaging market and designers.

2 Theoretical Basis and Literature Review

2.1 Green Packaging and Circular Economy

The circular economy is a sustainable economic development model in which the 3R principle mentioned is the economic principle of resource reduction, reuse, and recycling2. However, China's packaging industry has always had a "mass production, loss, and waste" situation. Green packaging has always been the direction of exploration and research in China's packaging industry, and implementing the 3R principle in the packaging industry is particularly important for developing green packaging. Today, when people's desires are getting stronger and stronger, the packaging industry's circular development needs to consider people's needs rather than blindly satisfying people's desires. As Victor Papanek said: "Design for people's needs, not for people's desires or human-designed desires"3. As far as green packaging and green consumption are concerned, there have been some studies. The author analyzes the relationship between people's consumption behavior and various factors and provides feasible suggestions for enterprises and society.

However, in the research on green packaging and behavior, few studies link these influencing factors with festive gift packaging. For example, Wang Guomeng's (2010) research confirmed the relationship between environmental values and green purchasing behavior4. The public's perception of environmental protection will guide him to make green behaviors. Pan Chi (2019) verified that the ease of use and usefulness of green packaging and consumers' awareness of environmental consequences would have a certain impact on consumers' willingness to accept green packaging5. The ease of use and usefulness of green packaging has a certain effect on consumers' acceptance of green packaging; consumers' awareness of environmental consequences will also affect consumers' willingness to accept green packaging. Dai Xuehong (2022) suggested sustainable packaging development to promote green packaging consumption, implement a multi-purpose packaging model, and share packaging6. Green packaging can improve the sustainability of packaging the perspectives of consumer, external, and material factors. For festive gifts, their packaging needs to be acceptable to consumers while reflecting environmental protection. Therefore, this study will explore from the perspective of consumers and study the factors that affect consumers' willingness to use green packaging in festive gifts.

2.2   Current Status of Research on the Green Design of Festival Gift Packaging

Common gift packaging styles will be more diverse, while festive gift packaging will be influenced by festival culture and regulated by festival customs. Therefore, the research on green packaging in festive gifts will be more restricted, but many researchers have explored and practiced green packaging in festive gifts.

In the study of festival gift packaging, Wang Guolun (2003) believed that festival gift packaging should be made by yourself, emphasizing the cultural taste and festive atmosphere of packaging rather than excessive packaging7. From the perspective of green packaging, scholars in the 1990s proposed that gift packaging should not be too luxurious and then proposed various green design methods. Yin Dan (2013) proposed that gift packaging should express feelings, embody gift culture, and contribute to green environmental protection8. Zhang Yu (2017) summarized the characteristics of gift packaging based on the concept of ecology and proposed the methods and principles of gift packaging design9. He believes that improving the sustainability of green packaging can be considered from consumer, external, and material factors perspectives. There needs to be more research on green packaging in festive gifts, and the research angle needs to be improved.

3   Theoretical Model and Research Hypothesis

3.1   Research Model

Ajzen (1977) conducted various studies on the relationship between consumer attitudes, subjective norms, and behaviors and constructed a theoretical model of planned behavior10. This model is widely used to measure consumers' behavioral intentions in different consumption situations. In this study, behavioral attitudes refer to consumers' attitudes towards green packaging when purchasing festival gifts; subjective norms refer to the intensity of consumers' perceptions of people around them that they should pay attention to green packaging when purchasing festival gifts.

Davis constructed a technology acceptance model in 1989 to study which key elements affect consumers' acceptance and use of new technologies11. Green packaging is a new form of ordinary packaging after environmental protection design and new technology. In consuming festive gifts, the ease of use and usefulness of green packaging still needs to be improved and improved. In this study, perceived usefulness refers to the value consumers perceive green packaging in festive gifts; perceived ease of use refers to whether consumers perceive green packaging as convenient to use in festive gifts.

Consumer behavioral attitudes, subjective norms, and purchase intentions are correlated and vary according to different products and purchase situations12. If green packaging is more valuable and convenient, consumers are more willing to accept green packaging. Therefore, this study will combine the theory of planned behavior and technology acceptance theory with building a model (Fig. 1) to analyze the impact of these factors on consumers' willingness to accept.

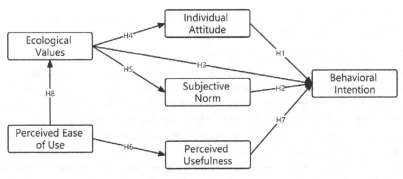

Fig. 1. Research model

3.2 Research Hypothesis

When purchasing festive gifts, the additional consumption of green packaging is also a consumption behavior. According to the theory of planned behavior, the stronger the consumption attitude of consumers towards green packaging when purchasing festival gifts, the stronger their willingness to accept green packaging. The stronger the impact of subjective norms on consumers' purchase of festival gifts, the stronger their acceptance of green packaging. Therefore, put forward hypotheses H1 and H2.

H1: Consumers' individual attitudes will positively affect their willingness to accept green packaging.
H2: Consumers' subjective norms will positively affect their willingness to accept green packaging.

Attitude change depends on individual factors, situational factors, and marketing activities13. Situational factors include environmental influences and surrounding situations. Sheng Guanghua's research believes that when consumers make purchase decisions, they will consider the environmental impact, including consumers' ecological values14. Consumers' environmental awareness primarily affects their acceptance of green packaging. Therefore, put forward hypotheses H3, H4, and H5.

H3: Consumers' ecological values will positively affect their willingness to accept green packaging.
H4: Consumers' ecological values will positively affect their attitudes toward green packaging.
H5: Consumers' ecological values will positively affect their subjective norms for green packaging.

The technology acceptance model has a certain basis in the application research of green packaging. Pan Chi (2019) confirmed that consumers are more willing to accept green packaging that is convenient to use and has economic benefits5. In festive gifts, the ease of use and usefulness of green packaging are closely related. Therefore, put forward hypotheses H6 and H7.

H6: Consumers' perceived ease of use of green packaging will positively affect their perceived usefulness.

H7: Consumers' perception of the usefulness of green packaging will positively affect their willingness to accept green packaging.

Psychologist Schwartz (1977) believes that when people realize their behavior has adversely affected the external environment, it will further affect individual behavior15. Conversely, the higher the social benefits of green packaging, the more it can cater to consumers' behavioral intentions. Consumers' awareness of the adverse effects of their actions can be seen as ecological values. The easier the green packaging is to use, the more likely consumers are to become aware of the consequences for the environment. Therefore, put forward hypothesis H8.

H8: Consumers' perception of the ease of use of green packaging will positively affect their ecological values.

4   Study Design

4.1   Questionnaire Design and Data Collection

Based on the designed theoretical model, this study conducts questionnaire design and investigation. The questionnaire consists of three parts: the first part is to measure consumers' essential attitude and understanding of green packaging in festive gifts; the second part is to measure the specific influencing factors of consumers' acceptance of green packaging in festive gifts; the third part of it is to measure the basic situation of the respondents. The measurement method of each variable in the second part adopts a 5-level Likert scale and designs 3 to 5 questions for each core variable in the model.

4.2   Data Processing

Before the formal research, the author collected 56 samples for testing and adjusted the questionnaire according to the sample data. The formal survey adopts the method of distributing questionnaires online, and 265 questionnaires were collected. Spss was used to clean up and screen the data, delete invalid questionnaires, recover 258 valid questionnaires, and describe the characteristics of the samples (Table 1).

4.3   Reliability and Validity Analysis

The author used PLS3.0 software to evaluate the model parameters. The Cronbach's Alpha reliability coefficient, index reliability value, combined reliability value, and AVE value are mainly measured to test the reliability and validity of each potential variable. If the data meets the following standards, it proves that the questionnaire has reliability and validity: Cronbach's Alpha coefficient should be greater than 0.5; index reliability, that is, the value of factor loading should be greater than 0.7; the value of combination reliability should be greater than 0.7; the value of AVE represents Convergent validity should be greater than 0.5.

The calculated Cronbach's Alpha of each variable is greater than 0.5, the value of index reliability is greater than 0.7, the value of combination reliability is greater than 0.7, and the value of AVE is greater than 0.5. The data show that all indicators meet the requirements, indicating the scale's reliability and validity.

Table 1. Characterization of the sample.

	Sample characterization	Frequency	Percentage (%)
Gender	Male	82	31.78
	Female	176	68.22
Age	under 18 years old	2	0.78
	18–25 years old	163	63.18
	26–30 years old	55	21.32
	31–40 years old	23	8.91
	Above 41 years old	15	5.81
Festive gift consumption budget	Below RM5,00	115	44.57
	RM5,00- RM2,000	89	34.5
	RM2,000- RM5,000	40	15.5
	RM5,000- RM1,0000	13	5.04
	Above RM1,0000	1	0.39

4.4 Structural Model Path Relationship Inspection

According to the model of factors influencing the willingness to accept green packaging in festive gifts, the path coefficient and P value between related variables are calculated. The results are shown in Table 2. Hypothesis H3 does not hold; ecological values will not directly affect behavioral intentions.

4.5 Results and Analysis

Consumers' attitudes and subjective norms towards green packaging in festival gifts can positively affect their acceptance of green festival gift packaging; consumers' ecological values also affect their attitudes and subjective norms towards green packaging. Therefore, consumers' willingness to accept green packaging in festival gifts will be indirectly affected by their ecological values. When consumers have better environmental awareness, this environmental awareness affects their attitudes and subjective norms toward green packaging, enhancing their willingness to accept green packaging.

Consumers' subjective norms have a more significant coefficient on their behavioral intentions than individual attitudes. Due to the socially symbolic nature of gifts, gift givers will pay more attention to other people's ideas when purchasing gifts, hoping that gift recipients will be recognized and satisfied. Therefore, if subjective norms more strongly influence consumers, their willingness to accept green packaging in festive gifts will be stronger.

Consumers' willingness to accept green packaging in festive gifts will be affected by the packaging's ease of use and usefulness. Therefore, the stronger the convenience and practicality of green packaging, the higher the consumers' acceptance.

Consumers' perceived ease of use of green packaging affects their ecological values. The stronger the ease of use of green packaging, the higher the social benefits consumers

Table 2. Model path coefficients and hypothesis verification

Hypothetical path	Normalized path coefficients	P	Conclusion
H1: Individual attitude → Behavioral intention	0.273	***	Support
H2: Subjective norm → Behavioral intention	0.400	***	Support
H3: Ecological values → Behavioral intention	0.092	0.173	Not supported
H4: Ecological values → Individual attitude	0.550	***	Support
H5: Ecological values → Subjective norm	0.485	***	Support
H6: Perceived ease of use → Perceived usefulness	0.666	***	Support
H7: Perceived usefulness → Behavioral intention	0.173	***	Support
H8: Perceived ease of use → Ecological Values	0.622	***	Support

Note: *** $p < 0.05$

perceive. However, a certain relationship exists between consumers' ecological values and the social benefits of green packaging. Therefore, the stronger the ease of use of green packaging, the stronger the ecological value of consumers on it.

Consumers' ecological values cannot directly affect their behavioral intentions. However, consumers' ecological values can indirectly affect their behavioral intentions through subjective norms and individual attitudes.

5　Research Conclusions and Limitations

5.1　Research Conclusions

This study mainly explores the influencing factors of consumers' willingness to accept green packaging in festival gifts and verifies the feasibility of the model and the correlation among variables. The research on the factors influencing consumers' willingness to accept green packaging in festive gifts enriches the research content of green packaging. It refines the research on green packaging to the field of festive gifts.

This study confirms that consumers' ecological values and the ease and usefulness of green packaging can affect consumers' willingness to accept. Explore targeted solutions based on research findings.

From a theoretical point of view, enhancing consumers' ecological values and improving the ease of use and usefulness of green packaging have a specific effect on increasing consumers' willingness to accept. Only when consumers are aware of the environmental problems brought about by festive gift packaging can consumers have a higher degree of recognition of green packaging. The improvement of green packaging in its usability and usefulness will also make consumers more willing to accept green packaging.

Consider the issue of festive gift packaging from an application perspective. First of all, festive gifts should clearly show the green characteristics of packaging so that consumers can fully perceive the environmental protection advantages of festive gift packaging so that consumers can establish good ecological values. Secondly, it is necessary to be innovation-oriented to improve the usability and usefulness of green packaging. On the premise of improving the environmental protection of festival gift packaging, it can be convenient for consumers to use and carry. Third, it is necessary to make the green value of festival gift packaging resonate with the use value of consumers so that consumers can identify with the green packaging of festival gifts.

5.2 Limitations

This study also has certain research limitations. First, this study only explores the two perspectives of ecological values and perceived ease of use, and follow-up research can continue to explore the influence of other perspectives. Second, it can take into account traditional culture to How the change in consumer culture affects packaging design needs to be further studied in festival gift packaging. Thirdly, in the follow-up research, groups of people can be selected for detailed research.

Acknowledgments. We want to thank the Guangzhou Academy of Fine Arts academic promotion project "Research on Innovative Design of Traditional Festival Products in the Greater Bay Area" (20XSB07) and the Guangdong Provincial Department of Education's "Green Gift Packaging Design Based on Lingnan Festival Culture" project (22ZX027) for their support for this research.

References

United Nations: Report of the world commission on environment and development: our common future. UN (1987)

Zhang, M.: "No Waste": packaging design's nature and future. Decoration **2**, 37–41 (2018)

Papanek, V.: Design for the Real World. CITIC Press, Beijing (2013)

Wang, G., Li, J., Liao, S., et al.: Study of the relationship between environmental values and green purchasing behavior: the mediating effect of environmental attitude. J. Dalian Univ. Technol. (Soc. Sci.) **31**(4), 37–42 (2010)

Pan, C., Guo, Z.: Influencing mechanism of public willingness on green packaging. Packag. Eng. **40**(3), 136–142 (2019)

Dai, X., Ai, M.: Sustainable development path of shared packaging under the background of internet plus. Packag. Eng. **43**(8), 340–347 (2022)

Wang, G.: Holiday gift packaging design. Art Obs. **2**, 12 (2003)

Yin, D.: Research on the green design of gift packaging. Popular Lit. Art **13**, 115–118 (2013)

Zhang, Y.: Research on gift packaging design based on ecological concepts. Xi'an Polytechnic University (2017)

Ajzen, I., Fishbein, M.: Attitude-behavior relations: a theoretical analysis and review of empirical research. Psychol. Bull. **84**(5), 888–918 (1977)

Bian, P.: Review of technology acceptance model research. Libr. Sci. Res. **1**, 2–6 (2012)

Chen, W., Zhou, Y., Lv, W.: A study on the impact of gift dual-dimensionality attributes on purchase intention of gift—based on Fishbein's reasoned action model. Ind. Eng. Manag. **18**(1), 62–70 (2013)

Mothersbaugh, D.L., Hawkins, D.I.: Consumer Behavior: Building Marketing Strategy, 13th edn. Machinery Industry Press, Beijing (2018)

Sheng, G., Gong, S., Xie, F.: Theoretical basis and empirical test of Chinese consumers' green purchasing intention: TPB expansion model based on ecological values and personal perception correlation. Jilin Univ. J. Soc. Sci. Ed. **59**(1), 140–151 (2019)

Schwartz, S.H.: Normative Influences on Altruism. Academic Press (1977)

Research on Demand Evaluation of Live Broadcast Interface of Agricultural Product Based on Factor Analysis and CRITIC Method

Dashuai Liu[✉], Jie Zhang, Chenglin He, Chenlu Wang, Yue Cui, and Ying Zhang

School of Art Design and Media, East China University of Science and Technology,
Shanghai 200237, China
liudashuaichn@163.com

Abstract. To solve the problems that the existing live broadcast interface of agricultural product (LBIAP) can't meet the diverse needs of users, the demand elements of LBIAP were analyzed from several dimensions, so as to provide reference for the design of LBIAP. Firstly, a questionnaire survey was conducted to collect users' demand elements for the LBIAP. Next, experts determine the importance of each demand element through the 5-level scale. Then, factor analysis (FA) is used to reduce the dimension of the evaluation information of each demand element and construct a hierarchical model of demand evaluation indicators for LBIAP. Furthermore, the weights of extracted factors can also be obtained by FA. Secondly, the objective weights of each demand indicators are obtained by the CRITIC method. Combined with the both weights, the final weights are obtained. Then, the final importance of demand evaluation of the LBIAP is analyzed combining the current situation. Finally the results show that the demand elements of LBIAP are represented by four dimensions: usability, standardization, interaction and communication, and activity attraction. Moreover, the simplicity and standardization of the demand elements of the LBIAP are the basis. And the elements of interactive and communication and activity attraction are the key to improve the LBIAP. The combination of the factor analysis method and the CRITIC method can systematically analyze users' multi-dimensional demands for the LBIAP, providing new design ideas for the LBIAP.

Keywords: Industrial design · FA · CRITIC method · LBIAP · Demand evaluation of live broadcast interface

1 Introduction

With the rapid development of the Internet and the comprehensive coverage of the Internet in rural areas, live broadcast of agricultural products has gradually become a new product of rural revitalization, which can promote the rapid development of rural areas. And that has become a hot topic of current research. In the process of live broadcast of agricultural products, the LBIAP is an important medium for transmitting live broadcast information. However, with the continuous improvement of people's living standards, as well as the continuous improvement of users' cognition and aesthetics, users' demands for LBIAP have also changed greatly. So the existing LBIAP couldn't meet the real needs of the current users. Therefore, this paper carries out a systematic study on the demand evaluation of the LBIAP. And this paper systematically analyzes the importance of users' requirement of LBIAP through a combination of qualitative and quantitative methods, which is an important guide to the design of LBIAP.

2   Literature Review

2.1   A Subsection Sample Review of Integration and Application of the FA and CRITIC Method

Factor Analysis is widely used in index evaluation research. It uses the idea of dimensionality reduction to objectively extract representative common factors from multiple overlapping and complex variables with the help of the relationship between index research data [4]. This can't only ensure the authenticity and comprehensiveness of information, but also avoid the problem of collinearity of various factors. At the same time, an objective and reasonable multi-level index evaluation system can be accurately constructed. Li Hao and others used factor analysis method to objectively and accurately construct a multi-level evaluation system of global design elements of smartphone voice system [5]. Xu Lin and others used the factor analysis method and AHP to structure availability evaluation system of the urban home care services and calculate the weight of the evaluation indicators. And then the key factors that need to improve the availability of urban home care services were analyzed [6]. However, the factor analysis method can only calculate the objective weight of the extracted common factors, but can't calculate the objective weight value of the specific index items.

The CRITIC method is an objective weight weighting method proposed by Diakoulaki in 1995. It can accurately calculate the objective weight value of indicators based on the information provided by the original data [7]. Li Zhiqiang et al. used the CRITIC method to accurately calculate the objective weight of the index elements in the evaluation of the design scheme of switch packaging, which provided support for the optimization process of the packaging scheme [8]. Guan Xinjian et al. determined the objective weight value of the river water quality evaluation index by using the CRITIC method, and objectively analyzed the water quality evaluation results of Qingyihe River through the pollution index weight [9].

In conclusion, the factor analysis method can extract the common factors from multiple indexes through the data information to complete the model construction of the index evaluation layer. The CRITIC method can accurately calculate the objective weight value of each index evaluation, but using the factor analysis method or the CRITIC method alone has some limitations. Moreover, few studies have combined factor analysis with CRITIC method. Therefore, this paper combines the factor analysis method and CRITIC method to study the demand evaluation of live interface of agricultural products. Firstly, the factor analysis method is used to construct the hierarchical structure of the demand evaluation of the LBIAP. Then, the CRITIC method is used to calculate the objective weight of each demand index. Finally, the evaluation results of the importance of the calculation are analyzed by combining with the current situation of the live interface of agricultural products, so as to provide new ideas and references for subsequent designers to carry out the design of the live interface of agricultural products.

2.2 Review of Research on the Requirements of LBIAP

With the rapid development of the global live broadcast shopping, live broadcast shopping is becoming more and more popular with the public. And the live broadcast interface is the key to transmit live broadcast information in the process of live broadcast shopping. So, the design of live broadcast interface has gradually become a hot research topic. Yang Qin and others analyzed the characteristics of Taobao live streaming users and the necessity of live streaming interface design. They researched the design principles, elements and content of Taobao live interface, which provide reference for the design of live interface [10]. Huang Xiangling analyzed the current development trend and existing problems of live broadcast APP, studied the principles of live broadcast interface design, and provided new inspiration for the design of live broadcast interface [11]. Wang Wanqing and others [12] have studied the characteristics and users' needs of the mobile live streaming client interface design, which has improved users' experience of the current live streaming client. However, compared with the demand for live broadcast interface of general products, the demand for the LBIAP is mainly to highlight the characteristics of agricultural products and the real environment, and have good activity attraction and users' experience. At present, the interface advantages and disadvantages of the four most representative agricultural products live broadcasting platforms in China are shown in Table 1.

Table 1. Analysis of the advantages and disadvantages of four types of LBIAP.

Four platform of LBIAP	Advantages of LBIAP	Disadvantages of LBIAP
Pinduoduo	1. The activity content displayed on the interface is more eye-catching 2. The background of interface communication information is prominent	1. Interface interaction information display delay 2. Push purchase products can't be directly displayed
Kwai	1. Interface activity notification is obvious 2. Communication information is prominent and easy to read	Agricultural products display is simple That characteristics aren't obvious
Taobao	1. The interface design is well standardized 2. Agricultural product playback interface is clear	1. Less communication and interaction 2. Communication information isn't easy to read
TikTok	1. The interface design is simple and easy to use 2. Interface push purchase link is clear	1. Environmental characteristics aren't outstanding 2. Reading information is prone to error

Based on the analysis of the advantages and disadvantages of the existing LBIAP, the current LBIAP mainly focuses on meeting the needs of users for simple communication and purchasing agricultural products. It fails to take into account the ease of use and normative of interface information transmission, which brings bad user experience to users. At the same time, the existing LBIAP only focuses on the display of agricultural products, but lacks the interaction between anchors and buyers, as well as the attraction of live broadcast. In addition, there are relatively few studies on the LBIAP, and the existing studies lack the comparative analysis of the requirement importance of LBIAP. As a result, the primary and secondary needs of the existing LBIAP are unclear. Therefore, this paper needs to construct the requirement evaluation system for LBIAP, and analyze them systematically.

3   Construct the Requirement Evaluation System of LBIAP Based on FA-CRITIC Method

3.1   Obtain the Demand Evaluation Index of LBIAP

To obtain needs evaluation index of LBIAP, this paper uses the research method of combining online questionnaires and field interviews to survey the needs of users related to the LBIAP. Next, the original demand information obtained by the survey is sort out. Then, the same and irrelevant demand information is eliminated. The KJ method was used to cluster the original requirements and the *results* are shown in Table 2.

Table 2. Clustering of original descriptions of users' needs for LBIAP.

SN	Demand evaluation index of LBIAP	SN	Demand evaluation index of LBIAP
1	Simplification of interactive actions	9	The relevance of the push content
2	Availability of interactions	10	A sense of affirmation in the communication process
3	Ease of use of the interface navigation	11	The reality of the live broadcast interface environment
4	Standardization of the live broadcast interface	12	The timeliness of communication
5	Accessibility of interface vision	13	The sense of attraction into the interface
6	Readability of the live interface	14	The credibility of anchors
7	Effectiveness of interface feedback	15	The sense of reality of agricultural products on display
8	The immersion of communication and interaction	16	The accessibility of the interface atmosphere

3.2   Construct the Hierarchical Model of the Demand Evaluation Index of LBIAP Using FA

In the process of establishing the hierarchical model of the demand indicators of the LBIAP, various demand indicators may have the problem of multicollinearity. However, the factor analysis method extracts representative factors from many variables according to the linear correlation between research data. So it can reduces the dimension of demand index variables, and then determines the hierarchical structure of demand index [13]. IBM SPSS was used for data processing throughout the calculation of the factor analysis.

Firstly, according to the 16 indicators, a 5-level importance survey questionnaire was designed. The importance evaluation grades are divided into 5 grades: very unimportant, not very important, general, relatively important and very important, which correspond to following scores 1, 2, 3, 4 and 5, respectively. Then, questionnaires were distributed to relevant expert users through the online and on-site survey methods. The expert group is mainly composed of 240 people related to the five categories of live agricultural products. Finally, 240 questionnaires were collected and 221 valid questionnaires were gained. The effective rate of questionnaires reaches 92.08%, which meets the standard of questionnaires. Before the factor analysis, IBM SPSS was used to calculate KMO and Bartlett sphere values on the survey data. Finally, the KMO value of 0.912 is greater than 0.8. And the Sig value of Bartlett test is 0.000. That is less than 0.05. So the results showed that the data is suitable for factor analysis.

According to Table 3, four common factors were extracted. The extracted factors were named respectively, activity attraction factor of the LBIAP (R_1), the interaction and communication factor of the LBIAP (R_2), the simplicity factor of the LBIAP (R_3), and the standard factor of the LBIAP (R_4). The variance explanation rates of the four common factors after rotation were 25.146%, 23.842%, 22.220% and 17.564%, respectively, and the cumulative variance explanation rate after rotation was 88.772%. So that means the extracted four common factors could well represent the original data.

For the weights of the four common factors, the ratio of the amount of information extracted from each factor to the total cumulative information of the factors was used as the objective weights of the factors in this paper [14]. In addition, a multi-level structural model of demand evaluation indicators of the LBIAP is constructed through the loading matrix of the factor analysis. The results are shown in Table 4.

However, by aggregating the original data information through factor analysis method, only the weights of the extracted common factors can be obtained, but not the weights of each specific indicator. Therefore, this paper needs to calculate the objective weights of each demand indicator with the help of CRITIC method, and then multiply the two to construct the final weight system.

3.3 Calculate the Demands Evaluation Index Weight of LBIAP Using CRITIC Method

As an objective weight weighting method, CRITIC method not only considers the influence of indicator variability on the weight, but also considers the conflict between indicators [15]. Among them, the index variability is expressed in the form of its standard deviation. And the larger the standard deviation value, the greater the value difference of each index. The index conflict is represented by the correlation coefficient. When there is a strong positive correlation between the characteristics of two indicators, the conflict between them is low [16]. Calculate the importance of LBIAP by CRITIC method are as follows:

Table 3. Table of eigenvalues and variance contribution of principal components.

Project	Initial eigenvalue variance			Extract squared and loaded square			Rotate and loaded square		
	Eigenvalue	variance interpretation rate	Cumulative interpretation rate	Eigenvalue	variance interpretation rate	Cumulative interpretation rate	Eigenvalue	variance interpretation rate	Cumulative interpretation rate
1	7.801	25.329	25.329	7.912	26.104	26.104	8.297	25.146	25.146
2	5.663	24.372	49.701	6.273	22.734	48.838	5.882	23.842	48.988
3	4.524	21.019	70.72	4.504	21.978	70.816	4.566	22.220	71.208
4	1.211	17.127	87.847	2.002	17.163	87.979	1.285	17.564	88.772
5	0.517	6.085	93.932						
6	0.137	1.581	95.513						
...	...	...	...						
16	0.000	0.001	100.00						

Table 4. A multi-level structure of indicators for evaluating the demand of LBIAP.

Target	Standard layer	Index layer
Demand evaluation index system of LBIAP (R)	R_1 (0.2833)	The sense of attraction into the interface (R_{11})
		The credibility of anchors (R_{12})
		The sense of reality of agricultural products on display (R_{13})
		The accessibility of the interface atmosphere (R_{14})
		The reality of the live broadcast interface environment (R_{15})
	R_2 (0.2686)	The immersion of communication and interaction (R_{21})
		The relevance of the push content (R_{22})
		A sense of affirmation in the communication process (R_{23})
		The timeliness of communication (R_{24})
	R_3 (0.2503)	Simplification of interactive actions (R_{31})
		Availability of interactions (R_{32})
		Ease of use of the interface navigation (R_{33})
	R_4 (0.1979)	Standardization of the live broadcast interface (R_{41})
		Accessibility of interface vision (R_{42})
		Readability of the live interface (R_{43})
		Effectiveness of interface feedback (R_{44})

Step 1: Dimensionless processing of expert evaluation of each demand index data;

$$Xij = \frac{xj - x\min}{x\max - x\min} \tag{1}$$

Step 2: Determine the variability of each indicator, that is, calculate the standard deviation of each indicator;

$$\sigma j = \sqrt{\frac{1}{m-1} \sum\nolimits_{i=1}^{m} \left(Xij - \overline{X}j\right)^2}; \quad \overline{X}j = \frac{1}{m} \sum\nolimits_{i=1}^{m} Xij \tag{2}$$

where, $\overline{X}j$—average value of m indicators in expert evaluation;

Step 3: Determine the conflict of each indicator, calculate the correlation coefficient between each indicator and construct the correlation coefficient matrix rij;

$$rij = \frac{\sum_{i=1}^{n}(Xi - \overline{X}i)(Xj - \overline{X}j)}{\sqrt{\sum_{i=1}^{n}(Xi - \overline{X}i)^2 \sum_{i=1}^{n}(Xj - \overline{X}j)^2}} (i = 1, 2, \cdots, n; j = 1, 2, \cdots, m) \quad (3)$$

where, $\overline{X}i$—average value of all expert evaluations of the index Xi;

$\overline{X}j$—average value of all expert evaluations of the indicator Xj;

rij—Correlation coefficient between indicators Xi and indicators Xj.

Step 4: Calculate the amount of information contained in each indicator.

$$Cj = \sigma j \sum_{i=1}^{n}(1 - rij)(j = 1, 2, \cdots, m) \quad (4)$$

Step 5: Calculate the objective weight value of each indicator.

$$Wj = \frac{Cj}{\sum_{j=1}^{n} Cj}(j = 1, 2, \cdots, m) \quad (5)$$

According to the questionnaire data, the variability, conflict and information quantity results of the demand evaluation index of LBIAP are calculated through Eq. 1–4. Then, the objective weight value of each index is calculated by using Eq. 5. Finally, based on the results, the weight of criterion layer and index layer in the above index system are multiplied to obtain the relative weight values of each index. The results are shown in Table 5.

4 Results and Analysis

4.1 Analyze the Weight of Evaluation Index

According to the results of Table 5, the weight values of factor R_1 and factor R_2 are larger, 0.2833 and 0.2686, respectively. Therefore, in the context of limited resources, more attention needs to be paid to the two demand elements mentioned above. In the indicator layer, the specific demand indicators are ranked as $R_{11} > R_{13} > R_{21} > R_{14} > R_{15} > R_{31} > R_{24} > R_{12} > R_{22} > R_{33} > R_{23} > R_{32} > R_{44} > R_{41} > R_{43} > R_{42}$.

Among them, within the R_1, R_2, R_3 and R_4, the largest weights are R_{11}, R_{21}, R_{31} and R_{44}, respectively. Their weights are 2.555%, 2.108%, 1.730% and 1.124%, respectively. Because they are the most important indicators under their respective criteria layers, more attention needs to be paid to them. In addition, the weights of R_{13}, R_{14} and R_{15} in the R_1 are relatively large, with 2.272%, 1.779% and 1.765%, respectively. Therefore, they also need to be considered in the design process of the LBIAP.

Table 5. Multi-level demand indicators of LBIAP and their weights and ranking.

Target	Standard layer	Weight	Index layer	Weight	Total index weight (%)	Rank
R	R_1	0.2833	R_{11}	0.0902	2.555%	1
			R_{12}	0.058	1.643%	8
			R_{13}	0.0802	2.272%	2
			R_{14}	0.0628	1.779%	4
			R_{15}	0.0623	1.765%	5
	R_2	0.2686	R_{21}	0.0785	2.108%	3
			R_{22}	0.0594	1.595%	9
			R_{23}	0.0543	1.458%	11
			R_{24}	0.0627	1.684%	7
	R_3	0.2503	R_{31}	0.0691	1.730%	6
			R_{32}	0.0518	1.297%	12
			R_{33}	0.0587	1.469%	10
	R_4	0.1979	R_{41}	0.0568	1.124%	14
			R_{42}	0.0441	0.873%	16
			R_{43}	0.0513	1.015%	15
			R_{44}	0.0600	1.187%	13

4.2 Weight Classification of Each Evaluation Index Relative to the Overall Objective

According to the total weight value of the evaluation index to the total target, it is divided into three categories: key indicators (1.7%), important indicators (1.15%–1.7%) and general indicators (1.15%) (see Fig. 1). Among them, there are 6 key indicators, namely R_{11}, R_{13}, R_{14}, R_{15}, R_{21} and R_{31}, with the total weight of 47.78%. There are 7 important indicators, namely R_{12}, R_{22}, R_{23}, R_{24}, R_{32}, R_{33} and R_{44}, with the total weight of 40.44%. There are 3 general indicators, namely R_{41}, R_{42} and R_{43}, with a total weight of 11.78%.

Specifically, in the R_1, R_{11}, R_{13}, R_{14} and R_{15} are the key indicators. And R_{12} is the important indicator. Therefore, the results show that the LBIAP needs to create a real, accessible and attractive live broadcast atmosphere. Finally, in the future design work of LBIAP, we should focus on the activities' attraction demand.

In the R_2, R_{21} is the key indicator, and R_{24}, R_{22}, and R_{23} are the important indicators. The results show that people focus on immersive experiences in the communication and interaction of the live produce interface, requiring the platform or anchor to push relevant content timely during the live communication process.

In the R_3, R_{31} is the key indicator, and R_{33} and R_{32} are the important indicators. The results show that the simplicity of LBIAP is based on the simplification of interface

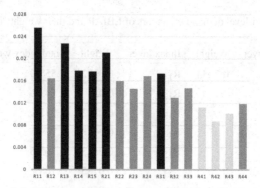

Fig. 1. Weights and classification of demand evaluation index of LBIAP to the total target.

interaction. The ease of use of interface navigation and the availability of interaction are designed to facilitate the simplification of interface interaction operation.

In the R_4, R_{44} is an important indicator. And R_{41}, R_{43}, and R_{42} are the ordinary indicators. The results show that people are more concerned about the effectiveness of interactive feedback. With the popularization of live broadcasting, people become more comfortable with live interfaces, neglecting the interface needs of standardization and accessibility.

5   Conclusions

In this paper, the demand elements of the LBIAP were obtained by questionnaire survey. And then the demand evaluation index system of the LBIAP was constructed by using factor analysis method, which included 4 factor indexes in the criterion layer and 16 specific demand evaluation indexes. Secondly this paper uses CRITIC method to calculate the objective weight value of the demand index of LBIAP. Finally, this paper makes a research exploration on the multi-level and importance evaluation of the need of LBIAP, which provides a new design idea and reference for the design direction of LBIAP.

The subsequent related research can be based on the demand index system of LBIAP constructed in this paper. And according to the weight value ranking of the indicators, the main needs and secondary needs of LBIAP can be quickly identified. That can shorten the design cycle of LBIAP, improve the design quality, and greatly improve users' satisfaction and experience.

References

1. Fu, Z.: Research on bringing goods of agricultural products by e-commerce live broadcast under the background of digital economy. Agric. Econ. (01), 137–139 (2021)
2. Zan, M., Wang, Z.: Live broadcast of agricultural products by e-commerce: a new model of poverty alleviation by e-commerce. Agric. Econ. Issues (11), 77–86 (2020)
3. Zhao, B.: Research on Interactive Design of Social Sharing in Pan-entertainment Mobile Live Broadcasting. Jiangnan University (2018)

4. Zhao, L., Lu, J.: Environmental assessment method of virtual reality based on factor analysis. Comput. Appl. **39**(S1), 159–163 (2019)
5. Li, H., Hou, W., Chen, X.: Evaluation system of smart phone voice system design based on factor analysis. Packag. Eng. **39**(16), 42–49 (2018)
6. Xu, L., Zhao, M.: Evaluation system of availability of urban home care services-based on factor analysis and analytic hierarchy process. J. Northwest Univ. (Philos. Soc. Sci. Ed.) **47**(06), 63–71 (2017)
7. Diakoulaki, D., Mavrotas, G., Papayannakis, L.: Determining objective weights in multiple criteria problems: the critic method. Comput. Oper. Res. **22**(7), 763–770 (1995)
8. Li, Z., Li, L., Zhang, S., et al.: Comprehensive evaluation of packaging schemes based on CRITIC _ G1 method. Packag. Eng. **42**(13), 180–185 (2021)
9. Guan, X., Liu, W., Hu, D.: Application of pollution index method based on CRITIC weight in water quality evaluation of Qingfei River. Hydropower Energy Sci. **35**(08), 49–52 (2017)
10. Yang, Q., Liu, R.: Research on the design of Taobao live broadcast interface based on user characteristics. Packag. Eng. **41**(08), 219–222 (2020)
11. Huang, X.: Talking about the interface design of the current live APP. Art Tasting (01), 63 (2017)
12. Wang, W., Yin, J.: Research on mobile live client interface design based on cognitive psychology. Public Art (06), 49–50 (2018)
13. Li, S., Zhang, Y., Dou, R.: Construction of perceptual image space in yacht design. Packag. Eng. **41**(14), 135–142 (2020)
14. Wang, L., Zhang, J., Yang, L., Zhang, M.: A survey of tourist satisfaction in Hangzhou Chaoshan Plum Blossom Festival based on factor analysis. J. Shandong Agric. Univ. (Nat. Sci. Ed.) **51**(04), 774–781 (2020)
15. Wang, S., Huang, T., Chen, H., Liu, M., Xue, H.: Application of fuzzy comprehensive evaluation model based on CRITIC weight in water quality evaluation. Hydropower Energy Sci. **36**(06), 48–51 (2018)
16. Liu, X., Yang, W., Zhang, X.: Multidimensional cloud model rockburst prediction based on improved hierarchy method and CRITIC method. J. Hunan Univ. (Nat. Sci. Ed.) **48**(02), 118–124 (2021)

The Influence of Electronic Word of Mouth on Purchase Intention Through Brand Image as Variable Intervening

Uci Mariantika and Nuryakin[✉]

Universitas Muhammadiyah Yogyakarta, Kasihan, Indonesia
nuryakin@umy.ac.id

Abstract. This study analyzes the influence of electronic word of mouth on purchase intention through brand image as a mediator. The sample and respondents in this study were 151 Bukalapak.com consumers. Sampling was done by purposive sampling technique. Data analysis was performed using Structural Equation Modeling (SEM) analysis with the AMOS program. Based on analysis: 1) Electronic word of mouth had a significant effect on purchase intention at Bukalapak.com, 2) Electronic word of mouth had a significant effect on brand image on Bukalapak.com, 3) Brand image had a significant effect on purchase intention at Bukalapak.com, 4) Brand image did not act as a mediating effect of electronic word of mouth on purchase intention at Bukalapak.com.

Keywords: Electronic word of mouth · brand image · purchase intention

1 Introduction

Online shop users are experiencing rapid development through virtual media [1]. Many conveniences in shopping and goods or services available encourage consumers to implement online shopping as one of the current choices [2]. This condition triggers many online shop owners to compete in offering their products to attract consumers' attention. They take advantage of the situation where the public is currently targeting online shopping.

Business growth through internet media has increased daily, accompanied by increasing internet users worldwide compared to direct shopping [3]. Currently, the internet is one of the media in promoting products because of promising opportunities. The role of internet media can reach customers widely. Internet users in Indonesia have experienced a significant increase every year. Marketers and e-commerce service providers compete to attract consumers to shop on their sites. It is important for marketers and e-commerce service providers to continuously study consumer behavior so that marketing strategies are carried out on target through digital technology [4]. E-commerce or electronic commerce can increase market share because online transactions allow everyone worldwide to order and buy their products [5]. This study aims to analyze the effect of electronic word of mouth on purchase intention and explore the mediating role of brand image in the relationship between electronic expression of mouth and purchase intention.

C. Stephanidis et al. (Eds.): HCII 2023, CCIS 1835, pp. 380–385, 2023.
https://doi.org/10.1007/978-3-031-36001-5_48

2   Theoretical Review

2.1   Purchase Intention

Purchase Intention is a plan in certain situations where someone behaves in a certain way. Someone may or may not do it. There are four elements of interest: behavior, objects, the place where the behavior is shown, the conditions when it is carried out, and when it is carried out [6]. Purchase intention, according to [7], is the desire that exists within the consumer for the product to be consumed. It occurs due to consumer observation of the product. *Purchase intention* is the desire to get a product and will arise when a consumer is interested in product quality and all product-related information. The consideration could be price or comparing product quality with similar products.

Electronic Word of Mouth. Word-of-mouth communication is the process of conveying messages both orally, in writing, and electronically between people related to the superiority or experience of making a purchase or when consuming an item or service [8]. According to Lovelock [9], Word of Mouth includes comments or recommendations disseminated by customers based on their experiences, strongly influencing decision-making by other parties. In addition, [10] argued that eWOM is communication through internet media where website visitors send and receive information about products online.

Brand image is when someone thinks about a brand [11]. Brand image can be interpreted as a perception of a brand reflected by brand associations held in consumer memory. According to [12], brand image is a set of brand associations formed in consumers' minds. Consumers accustomed to using a particular brand tend to have consistency with that brand. According to [13], brand image is the perception of a brand as reflected by brand associations in the minds of consumers. [8] described the brand image as a series of ideas, beliefs, and impressions within an individual toward a brand. Hence, consumers' attitudes and behavior toward a brand are based on the brand's image. Deeper Kotler added the brand image as a factor to strengthen a brand.

The Influence of Electronic Word of Mouth on Purchase Intention. Electronic Word of Mouth provides information to someone explaining a product or service so that consumers can understand and believe in the product or service. Before consumers are interested in buying a product or service, consumers will usually see reviews and comments from consumers on a product or service.

[14] showed that electronic word of mouth significantly influenced purchase intention. Furthermore, it is strengthened by the research results of [15], showing that electronic word of mouth has a significant influence on purchase intention. [16] revealed that electronic word of mouth significantly influenced purchase intention. The more positive the electronic word of mouth, the greater the effect on purchase intention.

H_1: Electronic word of mouth has a positive effect on purchase intention.

2.2 The Influence of Electronic Word of Mouth on Brand Image

Electronic word of mouth is a non-formal communication that is often done by consumers all over the world. Electronic word of mouth is another factor consumers consider to evaluate a brand. The brand will be perceived as good or positive if more and more consumers give positive impressions or testimonials, both in print and in the mass media.

[17] showed that electronic word of mouth significantly influences brand image. Subsequent research conducted by [18], the results of the study show that electronic word of mouth has a significant influence on brand image. [19] revealed that electronic word of mouth significantly influences brand image. The more positive electronic word of mouth is, the more positive consumer perceptions of the brand image will be.

H_2: Electronic word of mouth has a positive effect on brand image.

2.3 The Influence of Brand Image on Purchase Intention

Brand image is an association active in memory when someone thinks about a brand [11]. Companies and consumers must pay close attention to this vital factor. A positive brand image will be easier to stimulate and, at the same time, convince consumers of a product or service.

[20] proved that brand image significantly influenced purchase intention. [21] found that brand image significantly influenced purchase intention. The better the consumer's perception of the brand image, the greater the influence on purchase intention.

H_3: Brand image has a positive effect on purchase intention.

2.4 The Influence of Brand Image as a Mediator for the Effect of Electronic Word of Mouth on Purchase Intention

[22] revealed that brand image mediated electronic word of mouth and purchase intention. [18] brand image mediated electronic word of mouth and purchase intention. The more attractive the positive electronic word of mouth from other consumers is, the more positive the brand image will be. The influence on purchase intention will be greater if the consumer perceives the brand image well.

H_4: Brand Image acts as a mediator between the effect of Electronic Word of Mouth on Purchase Intention.

3 Methods

The model in this study is used to see each research variable's direct and indirect effects. The models in this study are as follows (Fig. 1).

The sample used in this research was Bukalapak.com users. The data collection process used a survey model and purposive sampling as a sampling technique, while the data analysis stage implemented SEM with the AMOS method.

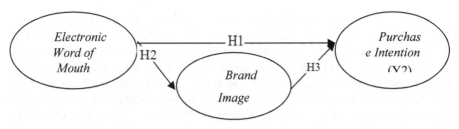

Fig. 1. Research Model

4 Discussion

In the structural model fit test, the Goodness of Fit test results met four good fit criteria, including CFI = 0.930, TLI = 0.919, IFI = 0.931, RMSEA = 0.068, and 3 criteria were at the limit of marginal fit, including GFI = 0.863, AGFI = 0.823, NFI = 0.847. The results of hypothesis testing to test the effect of endogenous variables on exogenous variables can be seen in Table 1.

Table 1. Hypothesis Test Results

	Estimate	S.E	C.R	P	Description
Purchase Intention <— Electronic Word of Mouth	0,916	0,122	7,487	***	**Significant**
Brand Image <— Electronic Word of Mouth	0,417	0,145	2,880	0,004	**Significant**
Purchase Intention <— Brand Image	0,415	0,153	2,723	0,006	**Significant**

Table 2. Standardized Direct Effect Test Results

Variable	EW	BI	PI
Brand Image	0,884	0,000	0,000
Purchase Intention	0,495	0,501	0,000

Table 3. Standardized Indirect Effect Test Results

Variable	EW	BI	PI
Brand Image	0,000	0,000	0,000
Purchase Intention	4,449	0,000	0,000

Based on Table 1, the three hypotheses are accepted. Electronic word of mouth had a positive effect on purchase intention. Electronic word of mouth positively affected the brand image, and brand image positively affected purchase intention.

Meanwhile, the fourth hypothesis is rejected based on Tables 2 and 3. The brand image did not as a mediating effect of electronic word of mouth on purchase intention. Electronic word of mouth had a significant effect on purchase intention at Bukalapak.com. In this case, the factor that causes the electronic word of mouth to affect purchase intention significantly is that consumers become more confident and trust after seeing testimonials from previous buyers. Testimonials play a big role in building consumer trust, from disbelief in a product to becoming more convinced after seeing testimonials from previous buyers.

Electronic word of mouth positively and significantly affected the brand image at Bukalapak.com. Electronic word of mouth aims to convince consumers to want to buy a product. Consumer confidence will grow if consumers see or know how testimonials from previous buyers about a product. If the testimonials from previous buyers are positive, consumers will be more confident in buying the product, and vice versa.

The brand image positively and significantly affected purchase intention at Bukalapak.com. Brand image can add value to the product/service and is a critical factor for the company. With a good brand image, consumers trust and easily accept products, even from new companies. The better the brand image of a brand, the greater the influence on purchase intention.

However, the brand image did not act as a mediating effect of electronic word of mouth on purchase intention at Bukalapak.com. Based on the results, the factor causing brand image not to act as a mediator for the effect of electronic word of mouth on purchase intention is that Bukalapak.com still needs to improve its brand image. A weak brand image will not easily convince consumers to believe in the brand. They will look for other factors by using electronic word of mouth to avoid the risk of uncertainty about the brand image.

5   Conclusion

Based on the results, electronic word of mouth had a significant effect on purchase intention at Bukalapak.com, electronic word of mouth had a significant effect on brand image on Bukalapak.com, the brand image had a significant effect on purchase intention, and brand image did not act as a mediating effect of electronic word of mouth on purchase intention at Bukalapak.com.

For further research is expected to develop research variables to obtain better results. The research variables include lifestyle, reference groups, price perceptions, and other variables related to consumer buying interest. Future research should increase the number of research samples and representation in the research area to better and more comprehensively explain the phenomenon under study.

References

1. Zhou, L., Dai, L., Zhang, D.: Online shopping acceptance model-a critical survey of consumer factors in online shopping. J. Electron. Commer. Res. 8(1) (2007)
2. Farida, N.: Effects of convenience online shopping and satisfaction on repeat-purchase intention among students of higher institutions in Indonesia. J. Internet Bank. Commer. 21(2), 1 (2016)

3. Al-Hawari, M.: The effect of automated service quality on bank financial performance and the mediating role of customer retention. J. Financ. Serv. Mark. **10**(3), 228–243 (2006)
4. Singh, S., Srivastava, S.: Engaging consumers in multichannel online retail environment: a moderation study of platform type on interaction of e-commerce and m-commerce. J. Model. Manag. **14**(1), 49–76 (2019)
5. Yen, Y.-S.: The interaction effect on customer purchase intention in e-commerce: a comparison between substitute and complement. Asia Pacific J. Mark. Logist. **26**(3), 472–493 (2014)
6. Peña-García, N., Gil-Saura, I., Rodríguez-Orejuela, A., Siqueira-Junior, J.R.: Purchase intention and purchase behavior online: a cross-cultural approach. Heliyon **6**(6), e04284 (2020)
7. Durianto, D., Sugiarto, T.S.: Strategi menaklukkan pasar melalui riset ekuitas dan perilaku merek. Gramedia Pustaka Utama, Jakarta (2001)
8. Kottler, P., Keller, K.L.: Marketing management. Erlangga, Jakarta (2009)
9. Yoga, S.I., Gde, S.I.: The effect of service quality on customers' satisfaction and word of mouth. Russ. J. Agric. Socio-Economic Sci. **98**(2), 67–75 (2020)
10. Goldsmith, R.E., Lafferty, B.A., Newell, S.J.: The impact of corporate credibility and celebrity credibility on consumer reaction to advertisements and brands. J. Advert. **29**(3), 43–54 (2000)
11. Shimp, T.A.: Integrated Marketing Communication in Advertising and Promotion/por Terence A Shimp., no. 658.8 S45 (2010)
12. Rangkuti, F.: Strategi promosi yang kreatif dan analisis kasus. Gramedia Pustaka Utama (2013)
13. Lee, J.L., James, J.D., Kim, Y.K.: A reconceptualization of brand image. Int. J. Bus. Adm. **5**(4), 1 (2014)
14. Jalilvand, M.R., Esfahani, S.S., Samiei, N.: Electronic word-of-mouth: challenges and opportunities. Procedia Comput. Sci. **3**, 42–46 (2011)
15. Kajtazi, K., Zeqiri, J.: The effect of e-WOM and content marketing on customers' purchase intention. Int. J. Islam. Mark. Brand. **5**(2), 114–131 (2020)
16. Jalilvand, R.M., Samiei, N.: The effect of eWOM on brand image and purchase intention: an empirical study in the automobile industry in Iran. Mark. Intell. Plan. **30**(4), 406–476 (2012)
17. Arslan, M., Zaman, R.: Impact of Brand Image and Service Quality on Consumer Purchase Intentions. A Study of Retail Stores in Pakistan. GRIN Verlag (2015)
18. Luong, D.B., Vo, T.H.G., Le, K.H.: The impact of electronic word of mouth on brand image and buying decision: an empirical study in Vietnam tourism. Int. J. Res. Stud. Manag. **6**(1), 53–63 (2017)
19. Pham, T.M.L., Ngo, T.T.: The effect of electronic word-of mouth on brand image, perceived value and purchase intention of the smartphone's consumer. In: 11th International Days of Statistics and Economics, pp. 1192–1205 (2017)
20. Fakharmanesh, S., Ghanbarzade Miyandehi, R.: The purchase of foreign products: the role of brand image, ethnocentrism and animosity: Iran market evidence. Iran. J. Manag. Stud. **6**(1), 145–160 (2013)
21. Chao, R.-F., Liao, P.-C.: "The impact of brand image and discounted price on purchase intention in outlet mall: consumer attitude as mediator", source. J. Glob. Bus. Manag. **12**(2), 119–128 (2016)
22. Kazmi, A., Mehmood, Q.: The effect of electronic word of mouth communication and brand image on purchase intention: a case of consumer electronics in Haripur, Pakistan. Manag. Sci. Lett. **6**(7), 499–508 (2016)

Post-COVID-19 Pandemic: Recovery of the Indonesian Tourism Sector Through Promotion on Twitter

Alfira Nurfitriana[✉], Budi Dwi Arifianto, Filosa Gita Sukmono,
and Zein Mufarrih Muktaf

Department of Communication Studies, Universitas Muhammadiyah Yogyakarta, Yogyakarta,
Indonesia
alfira.n.isip19@mail.umy.ac.id

Abstract. This study aims to explain the Indonesian Government's use of Twitter social media in promoting Tourism After the COVID-19 Pandemic. This research uses qualitative methods. This study used NVIVO 12 Plus to analyze data. The findings of this study Twitter, one of the technological facilities used by the Indonesian Government to promote tourism after the COVID-19 pandemic, is running effectively. However, the @pesonaindonesia account is more dominant in spreading Indonesian tourism promotional content than the @wonderfulid accounts. The tourism promotion narrative spread by the two versions is related to Indonesia's readiness to receive domestic and foreign tourists. Then, the @pesonaindonesia account has a high intensity in promoting on Twitter social media compared to @wonderfulid. Government figures dominate actors in promoting Indonesian tourism on the @pesonaindonesia Twitter account. Meanwhile, the Twitter account @wonderfulid is dominated by international tourism zorganization accounts.

Keywords: Twitter · Tourism Promotion · Social Media · Post Pandemic · Indonesia

1 Introduction

COVID-19 became a global pandemic in 2019, a fatal virus (COVID-19). The effects of various activities and the mobility of the global community are limited. The pandemic has become an essential concern for both society and tourism. In addition to the community, the mobility of numerous agencies was impacted. Due to this pandemic, the public and government agencies are utilizing social media more frequently. The Indonesian Government prioritized the tourism industry, which was believed at the time to have the potential to stimulate economic growth. The tourism sector's development demonstrates this through various programs designed to make Indonesian tourism more advanced and well-known internationally [1].

The pandemic has had a different effect than other natural disasters that have triggered multiple crises in diverse industries, including tourism [2]. The World Tourism Organization United Nations (UNWTO) is an international organization promoting world

C. Stephanidis et al. (Eds.): HCII 2023, CCIS 1835, pp. 386–393, 2023.
https://doi.org/10.1007/978-3-031-36001-5_49

tourism. UNWTO estimates that there will be a significant decline in national and international tourism. The decline in the number of tourists was due to the spread of COVID-19, which at that time was so massive. International travellers dropped from 58%–78% in 2020 compared to 2019 [3]. All tourism agencies must cut back according to the Government's social restriction program. Thus, several tourist attractions cannot operate normally, affecting government tourism industry advertisements. Indonesia began allowing domestic and foreign tourists in 2022. After the COVID-19 outbreak, Indonesian tourism will alter.

The Government continues to increase its use of technology and the internet. Digital usage always leaves a trace after use, which only accumulates and becomes invisible; interactions between people will continue to be stored, just as the expression "the internet never forgets" suggests [4]. Social media used by the has an essential role in social information and can be used as a way for people to interact with the government or e-government [5]. Twitter helps agencies and institutions connect with the community. After the COVID-19 pandemic, the Government is heavily promoting tourism on Twitter.

Research by Folrencio [6] shows how sustainable tourism development can help the tourism industry's sustainability. This research assumes that the practice of Sustainable Tourism is the potential to stimulate the movement of tourists. It differs from the research conducted by those who explain the perspective of the importance of tourism development, which requires unique and fast attention from the Government [7]. Research conducted by discussing the recovery of the tourism sector during the COVID-19 pandemic said that the Government had designed long- and short-term programs to restore tourism in 2020, which will be implemented in 2021 [8].

It is more about how the restores the tourism sector's condition by implementing a sustainable program, according to previous research. The use of social media as a tool to recover the tourism industry from the effects of the COVID-19 pandemic has not been adequately explored. This study focuses on how the Indonesian Government uses Twitter to promote tourism. This study's objective is to explain how the Indonesian Government utilized Twitter to promote tourism after the COVID-19 pandemic.

2   Overview of Literature

2.1   Use of Social Media by Government Institutions

The influence of social media today is huge on life in society. Communication on social media can be an advanced method involving part of the Government and participation in interaction with the public. Information quickly spreads and reaches many users if the information is spread through social media [9]. Social media can have a maladaptive effect on its users, so the Government needs to wisely use it to disseminate information to the broader community during the COVID-19 pandemic [10].

Governments must strategically manage citizens' expectations. The internet meets these needs. Social media-representative governments harness the internet's cultural wave to meet rising demands. Government social media use can solve citizen information challenges. Classifies several pieces of information that are effective for the Government to educate the public, for example, information about government policies, public services, health, natural disasters, and socio-culture. Social media interacts more often and likes posts on government social media pages in the U.S. area in the form of symbolic and image-based content than others. This proves that social media's role is very influential in Government [11].

2.2 Tourism Promotion on Twitter

Tourism is primarily responsible for the spread of the novel coronavirus and the COVID-19 outbreak. Due to this pandemic, almost all tourism-related activities have been temporarily suspended. The pandemic has severely impacted the global tourism industry [14]. The expansion of tourism in a country's region is proceeding well. The protocol regarding the desire to visit is adhered to correctly. Twitter significantly impacts the dissemination of information about the state of tourism during the COVID-19 pandemic. Twitter helps share travel information during the COVID-19 pandemic [13]. How to use Electronic word-of-mouth (e-WOM) is increasingly used by tourism players to increase engagement [14]. Factors that influence tourist decision-making show that social media is not a factor that significantly influences tourist decision-making if, on social media, there is no relevant information related to the current tourism situation and conditions [15]. Social media is one of the best ways to educate the public about COVID-19 and reduce information uncertainty [16].

3   Research Method

This research employed a descriptive qualitative methodology to research, in the post-COVID-19 era, how the Indonesian Government can restore tourism through the promotion of Twitter. This study utilized the NVIVO 12 Plus graph analysis and word frequency features. This research information comes from the @pesonaindonesia and @wonderfulid Twitter accounts of the Indonesian Ministry of Tourism and Creative Economy. It is then supplemented with additional information from credible online news sources such as kompas.com, CNN Indonesia, Tempo.co, and Detiknews.com, as well as pertinent journal articles. From January 2021 until September 2022, Twitter data will be recovered. During this era, Indonesia will be in the post-COVID-19 pandemic phase and have started relaxing tourism policies for both domestic and international tourists. This study will assess the Government's efforts to restore Indonesia's tourism industry following the COVID-19 pandemic by comparing the two accounts and evaluating the Government's efforts to restore the two accounts.

4   Result and Discussion

4.1 Tourism Promotion Intensity Analysis on Twitter

Figure 1 displays NVIVO 12 Plus' analysis of the promotion intensity of the two Twitter accounts.

Figure 1 shows that tourism promotion reached the highest level between July and September 2022. The two narratives have monthly widely different intensities for a year.

Fig. 1. Tourism Promotion Intensity

July and September 2022, however, have more significanthigher rising costs than previous months. According to Twitter @pesonaindonesia content observations, the Ministry of Tourism and Creative Economy in Indonesia is preparing for major events such as the G20 Indonesia Summit, Jakarta Fair, and World Superbike from July to September 2022. By 2022, the average will increase [17]. These events involve the role of the Ministry of Tourism and Creative Economy. The Ministry of Tourism and Creative Economy's efforts are promoting 9 upcoming events through the Twitter accounts. The task of the Ministry of Tourism and Creative Economy is to organize government affairs in the tourism and creative economy sector to assist the President in administering state government. Therefore the involvement of these two accounts with events organized by the Indonesian state government is significant, because these two accounts are responsible for disseminating information for promotional needs about the country of Indonesia.

4.2 Analysis of Actors in Tourism Promotion on Twitter

Social media as a promotional tool in Government has benefits for the wider community to disseminate information efficiently and effectively [12]. Social media is a very suitable medium for disseminating information to audiences. The role of an actor on social media is crucial for the continuity of information dissemination and effectiveness in gathering information. The impact of social media is that it can influence and change the attitudes and behaviour of its users (Fig. 2).

Fig. 2. Actors involved in tourism promotion.

The @pesonaindonesia Twitter account references @sandiuno and @jokowi the most frequently. Since @sandiuno is the official account of Sandiaga Salahuddin Uno, the @pesonaindonesia and @sandiuno accounts are quite influential. Indonesian Tourism and Creative Economy Minister. He led the Tourism and Creative Economy Agency in the Advanced Indonesia Cabinet since 2020.

The correlation between @wonderfulid and @g20org is that because @wonderfulid focuses on an international audience, the actors mentioned on @g20org must be relevant to their intended audience. The G20 is one of the international organizations that Indonesia recently hosted. Analysis of emerging actor data reveals that @pesonaindonesia's tourism promotion activities involve the highest head of Government for every promotion. Unlike @wonderfulid accounts, @wonderfulid accounts mention more organization-owned Twitter accounts than government-owned personal accounts, such as @pesonaindonesia. The participants in the two accounts are distinct. It is evident from the preceding discussion that the @pesonaindonesia account is primarily concerned with promoting the domestic community and transforming some government officials into actors. Using the accounts of multiple international organizations, the @wonderfulid Twitter account focuses on promoting tourism for the international community.

4.3 Tourism Promotion Content Analysis

The analysis conducted on Twitter @pesonaindonesia and @wonderfulid showed a very significant difference in the tourism promotion content they produced. Several discussion indicators on both versions include tourist destination indicators, influencer artists, tourists, and tourism events.

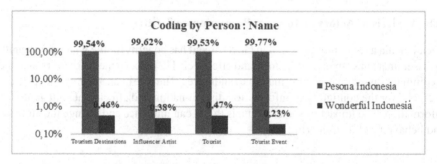

Fig. 3. Tourism promotion content

Figure 3 describe the comparison the intensity of two accounts. There are several differences between the two accounts. The highest intensity is an indicator of tourism activities. Indonesia's tourism industry improved after COVID-19 cases were reduced and Community Activities Restrictions Enforcement (CARE) was lifted [3]. Thus, the Ministry of Tourism and Creative Economy metrics market destinations. Research shows @pesonaindonesia posts more tourism destination content than @wonderfulid. Government-sponsored tourism. The second indicates influential artists and tourist destinations. The Government is collaborating with influencer artists to re-promote post-pandemic tourism [18]. The Government supports Indonesian tourism by working with celebrities, brand ambassadors, and local brands to rebuild the tourism industry. Indonesia promotes tourism events. The Moto GP Mandalika may be the Government's attempt to attract overseas tourists. Indonesia rebranded tourism with Super Priority Destinations after COVID-19 [17].

4.4   Tourism Promotion Narrative Analysis

Promotion is one of the primary needof information dissemination, especially in the government sector. Promotion through social media is an effective solution in this all-digital era, especially during the post-pandemic period. Tourism is one industry that spreads COVID-19 worldwide. Thus, social media helps the community get information. Analyzing social media narratives can show how much knowledge it spreads. The @pesonaindonesia and @wonderfulid accounts use narrative analysis to spread information.

Fig. 4. Tourism promotion narratives

   Figure 4 illustrates the Word Cloud of both Twitter accounts @pesonaindonesia and @wonderfulid, with #diindonesiaaja (#justinindonesia) and #fromindonesiawithlove being the most often used hashtags #diindonesiaaja (#justinindonesia) invite travellers to Indonesia. Due to COVID-19, #fromindonesiawithlove invites local and global travellers to visit Indonesia. Since 2020, Indonesia's tourism promotion ads have used this hashtag to prove that the country can recover from the COVID-19 pandemic [19].

5   Conclusion

After the COVID-19 pandemic, Indonesia has effectively promoted tourism. @pesonaindonesia accounts are more effective than @wonderfulid accounts at promoting Indonesian tourism. Both accounts highlight Indonesia's readiness to welcome both domestic and international tourists. @pesonaindonesia is more promotional than @wonderfulid. On @pesonaindonesia, government officials promote Indonesian tourism. International tourism organizations predominate on @wonderfulid. This study suggests that the structured use of Twitter by the government improves performance support. Twitter can enhance the reputation of a country's tourism industry. Twitter is the only data source utilized for this study. Therefore, future research may utilize Facebook and other social media platforms to collect additional data.

References

1. Subekti, D.: Tourism campaign in the new normal Era : social media analysis Indonesia Goverment. Profetik J. Komun. **15**(1), 101 (2022). https://doi.org/10.14421/pjk.v15i1.2188
2. Hall, C.M., Scott, D., Gössling, S.: Pandemics, transformations and tourism: be careful what you wish for. Tour. Geogr. **22**(3), 577–598 (2020). https://doi.org/10.1080/14616688.2020. 1759131
3. Mutiarin, D., Utami, S., Damanik, J.: New normal policy: promosi kebijakan pariwisata dalam rangka percepatan penanganan dampak Covid-19. J. Kepariwisataan Destin. Hosp. dan Perjalanan **5**(1), 20–33 (2021). https://doi.org/10.34013/jk.v5i1.277
4. Amalia, A., Sudiwijaya, E.: Yogyakarta tourism promotion using user-generated-content feature. Komunikator **12**(2), 136–145 (2020) https://doi.org/10.18196/jkm.122042
5. Weng, S., Schwarz, G., Schwarz, S., Hardy, B.: A framework for Government response to social media participation in public policy making: evidence from China. Int. J. Publ. Adm. **44**(16), 1424–1434 (2021). https://doi.org/10.1080/01900692.2020.1852569
6. Palacios-Florencio, B., Santos-Roldán, L., Berbel-Pineda, J.M., Castillo-Canalejo, A.M.: Sustainable tourism as a driving force of the tourism industry in a post-covid-19 scenario. Soc. Indic. Res. **158**(3), 991–1011 (2021). https://doi.org/10.1007/s11205-021-02735-2
7. Jamal, T., Budke, C.: Tourism in a world with pandemics: local-global responsibility and action. J. Tour. Futur. **6**(2), 181–188 (2020). https://doi.org/10.1108/JTF-02-2020-0014
8. Hermawan, E.: Strategi Pemulihan Sektor Pariwisata Dan Ekonomi Kreatif Masa Pandemi Covid-19. JPEK (Jurnal Pendidikan Ekonomi dan Kewirausahaan), **5**(2), 230–244 (2021). https://doi.org/10.29408/jpek.v5i2.4462
9. Solihin, F., Awaliyah, S., Muid, A., Shofa, A.: Pemanfaatan Twitter sebagai media penyebaran informasi oleh dinas komunikasi dan informatika. J. Pendidik. Ilmu Pengetah. Sos. 1(13), 52–58 (2021). http://e-journal.upr.ac.id/index.php/JP-IPS
10. Shao, R., Shi, Z., Zhang, D.: Social media and emotional burnout regulation during the COVID-19 Pandemic: multilevel approach. J. Med. Internet Res. **23**(3), e27015 (2021). https://doi.org/10.2196/27015
11. DePaula, N., Dincelli, E.: Information strategies and affective reactions: how citizens interact with government social media content. First Monday **23**(4), (2018). https://doi.org/10.5210/ fm.v23i4.8414
12. Suminto, A., Al Farizi, A.: Analisis pemanfaatan media sosial twitter oleh ganjar pranowo dan ridwan kamil. J. Islamic Commun. **2**(2), 191–206 (2020). https://doi.org/10.21111/sjic. v2i2.nomor.4394
13. Kurniawan, D., Wahyuni, H., Sutan, A.J.: Analysis of tourism promotion strategies through Twitter social media: a case study in Yogyakarta. J. Local Gov. Issues **4**(1), 76–89 (2021). https://doi.org/10.22219/logos.v4i1.14732
14. Sotiriadis, M.D., van Zyl, C.: Electronic word-of-mouth and online reviews in tourism services: the use of twitter by tourists. Electron. Commer. Res. **13**(1), 103–124 (2013). https:// doi.org/10.1007/s10660-013-9108-1
15. Malawani, A.D., Nurmandi, A., Purnomo, E.P., Rahman, T.: Social media in aid of post disaster management. Trans. Gov.: People Process Policy **14**(2), 237–260 (2020). https://doi. org/10.1108/TG-09-2019-0088
16. Rosemary, R., Rochimah, T.H.N., Susilawati, N.: Efficacy information in Government's initial responses to Covid-19 pandemic: a content analysis of the media coverage in Indonesia. Int. J. Disaster Risk Reduction **77**, 103076 (2022). https://doi.org/10.1016/j.ijdrr.2022.103076

17. Arieza, U.: 10 Event Besar Pariwisata Sepanjang 2022, Ada Tingkat Internasional. Kompas.com (2022).https://travel.kompas.com/read/2022/12/27/204500827/10-event-besar-pariwisata-sepanjang-2022-ada-tingkat-internasional-?page=all. Accessed 18 Jan 2023

18. Glover, P.: Celebrity endorsement in tourism advertising: effects on destination image. J. Hosp. Tour. Manag. **16**(1), 16–23 (2009). https://doi.org/10.1375/jhtm.16.1.16

19. Bagastiwi, I.R., Nuur Rasyid, H.A., Junaedi, F.: Virtual services during Covid-19 using social media of minister of public health. In: Stephanidis, C., Antona, M., Ntoa, S., Salvendy, G. (eds.) HCI International 2022 – Late Breaking Posters, HCII 2022, vol. 1655, pp. 3–9. Springer, Cham (2022). https://doi.org/10.1007/978-3-031-19682-9_1

Development of Short Circuits for Agroecology: Case of the Madre Tierra Solidarity Market in Quito, Ecuador

Lizzie Pazmiño-Guevara[1]([✉]) [iD], Jorge Álvarez-Tello[2,4] [iD],
María Becerra-Sarmiento[1] [iD], and Roberto Guerrero-Vargas[3] [iD]

[1] Facultad de Administración y Negocios, Universidad Indoamérica, Machala y Sabanilla, Quito, Ecuador
{lizziepazminio,mariabecerra}@uti.edu.ec
[2] Escuela Superior de Ingeniería, Tecnología y Diseño, Universidad Internacional de la Rioja (UNIR), Logroño, Spain
[3] Cooperativa de Comercio Justo Sur-Siendo Redes y Sabores, Quito, Ecuador
r.guerrero@alimentosmadretierra.com
[4] Centro de Innovación Social y Desarrollo (CISDE), Quito, Ecuador
jorge.alvarez@cisde-ec.com

Abstract. Introduction: The study evaluates the potential for responsible consumption of agroecological products in Madre Tierra fairs, in the D.M. of Quito-Ecuador, its impact on food security and the recognition of agroecological products in the region. Objective: To evaluate the promotion of responsible consumption and the adoption of business models that integrate technology and digital marketing strategies. Method: A descriptive qualitative-quantitative approach is used, through participatory research that evaluated the profile of the agroecological food consumer. An ecosystem is built with actors that contribute to the strategies and strengthen characteristics of a resilient environment for the improvement of accessibility to agroecological products. Results: The study shows that final consumers, who source their food from agroecological fairs, play a crucial role in their diet. Most consumers are women (62%), are between 31 and 50 years old and spend an average of 20 USD in family units of 4 people. In addition, 60% of the respondents are not aware of toxic-free foods and only 22% consume adequately. The surveys were conducted in four different locations in La Mena. Conclusion: Finally, the Madre Tierra fairs promoted responsible consumption through consumer characterization, training, new business models for associative enterprises and digital marketing strategies. In addition, the integration of stakeholder information and the improvement of responsible consumption through social construction projects were promoted.

Keywords: Short circuits · Agroecology · associative entrepreneurship · digital marketing · solidarity market

C. Stephanidis et al. (Eds.): HCII 2023, CCIS 1835, pp. 394–400, 2023.
https://doi.org/10.1007/978-3-031-36001-5_50

1 Introduction

In recent times, there has been a growing interest in promoting more sustainable and environmentally friendly agricultural practices. One of the strategies that is becoming increasingly common is the implementation of short circuits in the production and sale of food, which can promote agroecology and reduce the ecological footprint of agriculture. The Madre Tierra solidarity market in Quito, Ecuador, is an example of how short circuits can contribute to the promotion of fairer and more sustainable agriculture. Agroecology has become an important trend due to the demand for local and fresh food produced in a sustainable and responsible way; also, agroecology seeks sustainable and fair agricultural systems based on the principles of ecology and biodiversity [1] and originated as a response to the problems of industrialized agriculture [2]. Agroecology is currently focused on the creation of sustainable and fair food systems [3], through short circuits that directly connect the producer to the end consumer [4]. Short circuits offer benefits for health, the local economy, and the environment, reducing transportation costs and boosting employment and the local economy. In the European Union, short food supply chains focus on the relevance of the systems for agroecology and sustainability, improving food security and reducing the carbon footprint [5]. It also discusses the barriers and opportunities of short food supply chains in Andalusia and highlights the importance of a collective and sustainable approach at the local and regional level to promote more sustainable food systems [2]. In Mexico City, small producers play an important role for more sustainable urban food systems, but more resources and support are needed to consolidate their initiatives [6]. In the Andean region, short-circuit marketing projects for organic or agroecological products are being implemented to promote sustainable agricultural practices and establish new forms of solidarity between farmers and consumers [7]. In Bolivia, the EcoTambo Fair is a space for social coexistence that has proven to be a successful model for the production, marketing, and consumption of healthy food at affordable prices, with the potential to expand and generate social awareness at the national level [8]. In Ecuador, agroecology and short marketing circuits can be beneficial for agricultural production in Ecuador, if there is good organization between producers and consumers [9]. Agroecology is considered a sustainable and viable alternative for agricultural production in Ecuador, which promotes food sovereignty and rural development [10]. Although short agroecological food sales circuits are a desirable option, there are obstacles that hinder their implementation, such as the lack of government support and adequate infrastructure, as well as the need to improve the technical and organizational capacity of farmers and the relationship with consumers. On the other hand, the sustainable food supply chain highlights the importance of management to generate impacts in the process, systems, practices, production, and quality, as well as in the environmental, economic, and social dimensions. The main research topics and food supply chain models studied in association with sustainability are identified and gaps and future avenues for research are highlighted [11]. The implementation of certification and labelling systems is important to ensure the quality and traceability of agroecological products and guarantee consumer confidence. Regarding short food supply chains, their advantages, and challenges for the promotion of sustainable agriculture, food security, innovation and rural development are analyzed [12]. The Metropolitan District of Quito is working to improve its food sovereignty and the sustainability of its territories. A diagnosis of the food system was conducted in 2016–2017 and it was found that the system is divided into three rings. Only Ring 1 produces 5% of local food requirements, while Ring 3 produces 2.6 times more food than the population needs [13]. On the other hand, the Sur-Siendo Redes y Sabores project seeks to establish associative ventures between academia, teaching and society to provide access to healthy and affordable food for the low-income population. The Sur-Siendo consumer cooperative is working together with actors from the peasant social movement in various cantons of the country, researchers, academics, and urban and environmental organizations to promote agroecology in Ecuador [14]. Currently, the Sur-Siendo Redes y Sabores project seeks to establish associative ventures between academia, teaching and society in the food system to provide access to healthy and affordable food for the low-income population.

Based on the experiences and contributions of the authors, the importance of agroecological consumption circuits is highlighted, which promote care for the environment, the supply of healthy products, the integration of producers and channels, as well as the possibility of generating public policies that involve various groups through technological platforms for learning, awareness, and marketing. Through which, the following research question is formulated in Ecuador: What is the potential of implementing business models that integrate technology and digital marketing strategies, together with the promotion of responsible consumption of agroecological products and food safety in fairs such as Madre Tierra, to increase the valuation and identification of these products in the region?

2 Method

Through the construction of an ecosystem, this exploratory participatory action research is framed using qualitative and quantitative sources, documentary and field analysis based on observations and surveys on the profile and consumption behaviour of fresh food. The collection of statistical and bibliographic data was complemented with participatory research, capacity building and the adaptation of solutions to local conditions for the improvement of business models and the creation of spaces for commercial interaction of agroecological products (see Fig. 1). It is important to mention that, in determining the consumer profile of agroecological products, feedback is needed from information areas to raise awareness of agroecological marketing. Through the configuration analogous to a neural network, a framework is achieved that has as its main pillar the creation of an ecosystem with stakeholders who collaborate in the process, which facilitates the integration of new business models and the development of technological environments for the improvement of the market (see Fig. 2). In this space, the training of each of the actors reach the sensitization to induce the acceptance of the fairs in each point of Mena 2 south of Quito.

Through the framework, it is possible to observe the participation of stakeholders with the contribution of strategies, especially financing for the transportation of both human resources and the product, which influenced the final price of the product, in addition to the accessibility of the products, eliminating the middleman. From the survey of results, we have a mixed approach (qualitative-quantitative) descriptive to characterize the baseline in the development of the project, which allows to establish the circuits based on the resilience that helps in this initial time of pandemic and that currently helps to develop the replication of the model in other latitudes of the country.

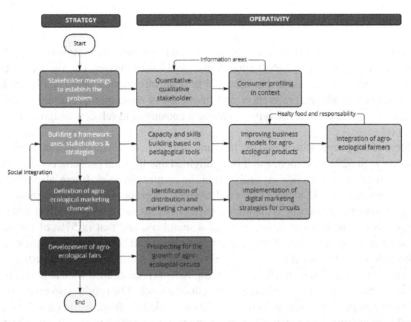

Fig. 1. Method for the development of marketing circuits for agroecological products. Source: prepared by the authors

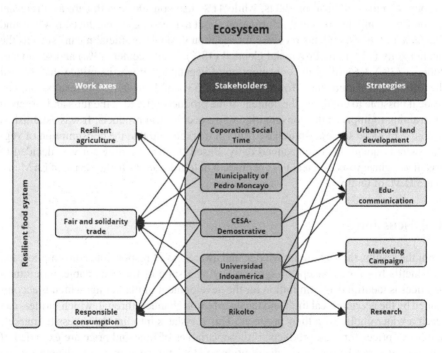

Fig. 2. Framework to guarantee access to the right to healthy food, without exclusion. Source: Cooperativa Sur-Siendo Redes y Sabores, modified by the authors.

3 Results

The manuscript presents results from a survey of a representative sample of 372 people from a finite population of 43680 inhabitants and 12042 families. The survey included six items with five questions that assessed general information about the individual, food practices, food type preferences and frequency of consumption, family social life and knowledge base about the type of products consumed in relation to agroecological products.

Most of the people who attend the fairs and who were surveyed show a strong female presence, with 62% of women, and it is highlighted that the final consumers have a decisive role in their food choice, as reflected in the results obtained. It was also observed that women between 31 and 50 years old are the age group that consumes most agro-organic products. In relation to the people living in the home, it was identified that most households are made up of between 1 and 4 members, and that in 57% of the cases, the father and mother reside in the same house. The head of household contributes to the household in 31% of the cases, while the children contribute 7%. Regarding food consumption, it was found that 90% of the respondents prepare their food at home, while 67% consume food outside the home at least once a week. The results also revealed that 60% of the respondents had no knowledge about toxic-free food, while only 22% consumed agroecological products adequately, in terms of health benefits. It was observed that the expenditure made is uniform, being around 20 USD or more. In addition, it was identified that 53% of the respondents have family economy as the main reason for buying agroecological products, while 41% also consider health care as a relevant factor. Regarding the source of information about agroecological products, it was found that 69% of the respondents received information through unofficial means such as the municipality (11%), the Provincial Council (13%), health centers (3%) and schools or colleges (3%). Regarding the consumption of vegetables, it was identified that 97% of the respondents include these foods in their diet, 53% of them daily. The results obtained made it possible to configure the content of the products offered at the fairs and structure the training to improve the consumption of agroecological products. It was established that 82% of those surveyed purchase fruits in markets and that the consumption of vegetables is frequent, being consumed daily. Based on these findings, it was decided to organize eight agro-ecological fairs per month in four locations in the parish of La Mena, in the D.M. of Quito.

4 Discussion

From the results, the lack of knowledge and awareness of responsible consumption and its benefits from the concept of agroecology as a support for sustainable agricultural practices is identified as a limitation for the development of marketing, which is accompanied by the geographical limit and the distribution channels through which farmers can reach a wider public with their products. This translates into limited access to markets and lower prices for their products, if these variables of time and price are extended, if it is desired to reach other areas, distribution and logistics costs may rise, decreasing the accessibility to healthy products for a fair price.

Similarly, agroecological products can be more expensive compared to conventionally produced products, with pesticides and transgenics to increase production, which in large supermarkets have a lower value but that changes limits the consumption of agroecological products. The lack of certification for consumer confidence in the trade of agro-eco-logical products is an added value that farmers can work on the adoption of better agroecological practices, for production and consumption and family nuclei in which the products are distributed.

On the other hand, the government's limited policies and low budget limit agroecological consumption practices and the promotion of responsible consumption to improve sustainable agriculture. The general discussion highlights the importance of strengthening the coordination and cooperation of actors involved in short agroecological marketing circuits in Ecuador, to promote their consolidation and sustainability [1].

5 Conclusion

The development of short circuits for agroecology is an increasingly popular trend that can have important benefits for health, the local economy, and the environment. Short circuits can promote healthy and sustainable food production, as well as reduce transportation costs and improve quality by directly connecting producers with consumers.

The Sur Siendo Redes y Sabores Cooperative has implemented several strategies and actions to market the "Madre Tierra" agroecological baskets during and after the pandemic. The focus on digital marketing, home delivery and local partnerships has been fundamental to its success in marketing the products. The cooperative has used several tools, such as the optimization of its website, online advertising and social networks, development of quality content for its online followers that has allowed it to create a community of followers committed to its cause and improve marketing. Alliances with local stores and restaurants and participation in fairs and events in the city were also highlighted, reaching a wider audience, and increasing visibility in the city. Education and awareness-raising are key to promoting the transition to more sustainable and equitable food systems. The Sur Siendo Redes y Sabores Cooperative emphasizes the importance of education in promoting agroecology and improving short marketing circuits for agroecological products. By building capacity through education and social participation, the cooperative has succeeded in raising awareness of the importance of agroecological food production and consumption and in fostering the development of sustainable practices in the agrifood sector.

Finally, the products of the region that are best valued for responsible consumption and marketing of agroecological products are identified. It is important to note that this requires a different approach than industrial production. Depending on the type of product, conditions, and factors such as the target audience and market demand influence variables such as direct communication for the transmission of values and knowledge associated with agroecological sustainability and the development of new sustainable agriculture programmes is required. Certification is an important factor that builds consumer confidence towards responsible consumption with a positive environmental and socio-economic impact. Finally, the development of new collaborative networks allows for the integration of more healthy consumption hubs, which in turn allows for the processing of information through technological platforms to provide a different experience and greater accessibility to agroecological products for new entrepreneurial business models.

Acknowledgments. We are grateful for the support of Universidad Indoamérica in the development of the community social construction project, as well as the work done by the Sur-Siendo cooperative through the Madre Tierra Fair to promote collaboration between the rural and urban sectors. We are also grateful for the efforts of the Business Administration students in this project.

References

1. Wezel, A., et al.: Agroecological principles and elements and their implications for transitioning to sustainable food systems. Rev. Agron. Sustain. Dev. **40**, 1–13 (2020)
2. Yacamán, C., et al.: Peri-urban organic agriculture and short food supply chains as drivers for strengthening city/region food systems-Two case studies in Andalucia. Spain. Land **9**(6), 177 (2020)
3. Da Silva Muniz, A., et al.: Contaminação química de alimentos vegetais e a saúde: Agricultura convencional x orgânica. Rev. Sustinere **10**(2), 434–450 (2022)
4. Bonomelli, V., Roudart, L.: Quels effets des circuits courts de commercialisation sur les moyens d'existence des agriculteurs familiaux? Le cas d'une foire paysanne à Quito (Équateur). Économie rurale 95–111 (2019)
5. Kneafsey, M., et al.: Short food supply chains and local food systems in the EU: a state of play of their socio-economic characteristics. JCR Sci. Policy Rep. **123**, 129 (2013)
6. Bertran-Vilà, M., et al.: Food producers in the peri-urban area of mexico city a study on the linkages between social capital and food sustainability. Sustainability **14**(23), 15960 (2022)
7. Girard, M. & Nasser, R.: Circuits courts de commercialisation et transition territoriale dans les Andes. Une réflexion depuis le Pérou et l'Équateur. Cybergeo: Eur. J. Geogr. (2020)
8. Alanes, C., Tapia, N.: Producto 2. Informe con 12 estudios de caso concluidos Estudio de la experiencia sobre producción, comercialización y consumo de productos agroecológicos, EcoTambo, La Paz, Bolivia (2021)
9. Proaño, V., Lacroix, P.: Marketing dynamics for peasant family farming: challenges and alternatives in the Ecuadorian scenario. Agronomists and Veterinarians without Borders (AVSF), Quito, Ecuador (2013)
10. Contreras, J., et al.: Circuitos cortos de comercialización agroecológica en el Ecuador. Ideas **35**(3), 71–80 (2017)
11. Latino, M., et al.: Evaluating the sustainability dimensions in the food supply chain: literature review and research routes. Sustainability **13**(21), 11816 (2021)
12. Velez, L.: Agricultura campesina y Desarrollo Rural. Biotecnología en el sector agrícola y agroindustrial **6**(1), 78–86 (2008)
13. Castillo, A.: Socio-spatial analysis of short circuits of commercialization of agroecological foods in the Metropolitan District of Quito: Case Study Cooperativa Sur-Siendo Redes y Sabores, Flacso, Ecuador (2020)
14. Andino, V., et.al.: Report on the dynamic synthesis and planning of the agri-food system in the city-region of Quito. Food & Agriculture Org (2021)

The Impact of Customer Service Robot's Proactive Behavior on Consumer Purchase Intention in a Pre-sale Consultation Scenario

Zhenyang Shen, Jinyang Zhou, Lewen Wang, and Cong Cao[✉] [iD]

Zhejiang University of Technology, Hangzhou, China
congcao@zjut.edu.cn

Abstract. This paper discusses the mechanism of the role of the active behavior of customer service robots in the pre-sale consultation scenario in the consumer purchase process. Based on SOR theory, this paper constructs a model of the influence of customer service robot active behavior on consumers' purchase intention. The model comprehensively analyzes the influence of customer service robot active behavior in four stages: induced demand, collect information, comparison and selection, and purchase decision. The model provides holistic and systematic support for maximizing the utility of customer service bots' proactive behavior and can help e-commerce platforms to optimize and improve customer service bots.

Keywords: Customer service robot active behavior · SOR theory · E-commerce

1 Introduction

A business is a great service. In past consumption scenarios, shopping guides often provide consumers with shopping advice. However, with the rapid development of online shopping, it is difficult for consumers to communicate with merchants face-to-face when shopping, and human customer service is used to make up for the lack of interpersonal communication attributes of online shopping. But the cost of labor is undoubtedly huge for merchants. AI robots began to play a greater role in all aspects of human life as artificial intelligence developed and combined with e-commerce to compensate for interactive proper-ties and the need to save money on manual customer service, they gradually replaced manual customer service [1].

Early intelligent customer service bots often only answered consumers' questions "passively," and only when they asked questions with specified keywords could they answer them [2]. Under such conditions, consumers often encounter scarce information, and the answer is not the right one. Therefore, how to meet consumers' service needs has become a major concern for e-commerce platforms.

With the development of information technology, some e-commerce platforms have started to adopt customer service robots with active intervention functions to improve service quality [2]. However, no research has been con ducted to analyze the mechanism of the active behavior of customer service bots, so this paper develops a model to

C. Stephanidis et al. (Eds.): HCII 2023, CCIS 1835, pp. 401–408, 2023.
https://doi.org/10.1007/978-3-031-36001-5_51

explain the impact of the active behavior of customer service bots at various stages of the purchase process. This model allows e-commerce platforms to better understand the role of customer service bots in e-commerce and promote and improve customer service bots.

2 Literature Review

Past research on the consumer shopping process has found that positive service behaviors by store associates play a significant role in enhancing consumers' purchase intentions. When offline retailers provide high-quality service, consumers' perception of service quality increases [3]. As in the offline scenario, online customer service also has a facilitative effect on improving service quality [4].

Consumers' service perceptions further influence their willingness to shop; Qin et al. Study results indicate that positive perceived service quality has a positive effect on facilitating consumers' purchase behavior [4]. Observed that the stronger the perceived pleasure, the greater the likelihood that consumers will make more purchases [5].

In the field of e-commerce, only a small number of e-commerce platforms have started experimenting with customer service bots with proactive intervention capabilities. No scholars have also explored the mechanism of action of customer service bots' proactive behavior. However, previous studies have found that the presence of customer service bots plays a significant role in e-commerce [6].Customer service bots help to eliminate differences and disputes between buyers and sellers and make the shopping process more efficient and smoother [7]. And it can also have a catalytic effect on improving service quality [4]. The importance of customer service bots is thus self-evident, and with the development of artificial intelligence technology, customer service bots have gradually been upgraded to have active intervention functions. This undoubtedly makes customer service robots closer to human customer service, which is a substantial benefit for improving service quality and promoting purchase intention.

3 Theory Development

The purpose of this paper is to develop a model that reveals the mechanism of the role of customer service robots' proactive behavior in influencing consumers' purchase intentions. Therefore, the stimulus-organism-response theory (SOR) is chosen as the theoretical basis of this model. SOR theory can explain the influence of environmental features on individual emotional responses and subsequent behaviors and can be effectively applied to the study of consumer emotions and behaviors.

It is generally believed that the consumer's purchase process is divided into five stages: Inducing demand, collecting information, comparing and selecting, purchasing decision, and after-sales service. This paper focuses on the influence of customer service robots' active behavior on consumers' purchase intention, so this paper selects four stages in the pre-sale consultation scenario: induced demand, collect information, comparison and selection, and purchase decision, for analysis. The customer service robot's active behavior is the stimulus for this model. This model also illustrates the specific performance of the customer service robot's active behavior at each stage. Service perception is the organism factor in this model. This paper draws on scholars' research on service perception, proposing that perceived usefulness and perceived pleasure are the key variables. Additionally, satisfaction plays a core role in both. This model ultimately points to the purchase factor as the response factor. In this paper, we propose the research model illustrated in Fig. 1.

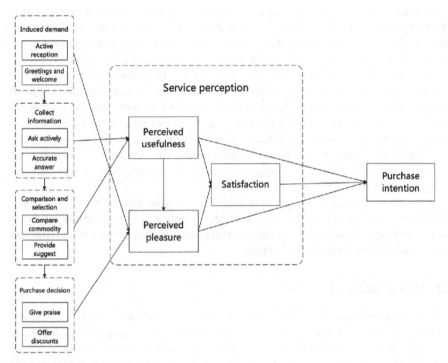

Fig. 1. A model of the influence of customer service robot's active behavior on consumers' purchase intention

4   The Proposed Model

Using SOR theory, this paper develops a model. The model explores the role of customer service robots' proactive behavior on consumers' purchase intention at different stages of the purchase process, starting with the four stages of the purchase process: induced demand, collect information, comparison and selection, and purchase decision.

4.1   Induced Demand

Induced demand is the beginning of the purchase process and is an essential prerequisite for the consumer to reach a purchase decision. The subsequent stages of the purchase process take place when the consumer is stimulated by stimuli that create a demand for a product. Without this prerequisite, consumers will not be able to make a purchase decision. Therefore, both offline and online businesses should focus on accurately grasping the market demand related to their products and understanding the stimulus of this demand.

In the traditional offline consumer scenario, person-to-person marketing plays the most effective role because it involves direct interaction between merchants and consumers, and merchants can make timely and rapid adjustments to their promotions by observing consumers. The Virtual Platform Barrier, however, prevents merchants from directly observing consumers in the online consumer scenario, which is a major part of the online shopping platform. This leads to the loss of personal sales. However, with the development of information technology, customer service robots with active intervention functions can effectively simulate offline merchants' customer meeting methods. For example, customer service bots can send "invitation stickers" and "welcome messages" to consumers on shopping platform pages to encourage them to enter the store pages for browsing; and analyze consumers' browsing trajectories on the shopping platform through big data to infer their shopping needs. The company also uses big data to analyze consumers' browsing trajectories on the shop-ping platform to predict their shopping needs.

For offline stores, positive greeting behaviors by store associates help to enhance consumers' pleasure [8]. To this end, this paper hypothesizes that active interventions such as greeting and welcoming by customer service robots can also improve consumers' overall satisfaction with online shopping.

4.2 Collect Information

Collecting information is the second stage of the consumer buying process. Consumers primarily obtain information about products through the commercial channel. Since consumers do not have direct contact with the actual product in online shopping, the description of the product by the merchant becomes dependent on the consumer. This provides an opportunity for merchants to show the advantages of their products to attract consumers. In addition, merchants provide consumers with information about their products and answer their questions, which helps to improve their perceived usefulness.

According to the above description, customer service bots should continuously provide product information to meet the needs of consumers during the information-gathering phase. Customer service bots must take the initiative to ask consumers questions and discover their doubts about products before they leave the store. Furthermore, customer service robots should provide accurate answers to consumers' questions so that their doubts about products can be dispelled. This is so that consumers can get the most complete information possible about products.

4.3 Comparison and Selection

Comparison and selection are the third stage of the purchase process and is an essential part of it. Based on the information collected, consumers will compare, analyze and study the characteristics and performance of the products, and then choose the one that best meets their needs.

Before online shopping, consumers had to switch between different products by browsing different product interfaces repeatedly. In addition to being time-consuming, this approach increases the risk of memory confusion. However, customer service bots can integrate the information of different products based on their technical character-istics and provide consumers with visual cross-comparison services to facilitate their comparison of different products. In addition, customer service robots can match con-sumer buying needs with product information. This will provide consumers with the most appropriate recommended purchase solution, avoiding difficulties in choosing due to lack of expertise. Customers can benefit from technological advances and im-prove their shopping experience through the use of customer service robots that analyze data.

4.4 Purchase Decision

The purchase decision is the final stage of the buying process, and when a consumer proceeds to this stage, he is much more likely to buy. However, the consumer may still abandon the purchase due to other factors. So, merchants still need to pay attention to this stage and promote the consumer's purchase utilizing appropriate stimuli.

Faced with such a critical opportunity, customer service robots can use some surprise rewards to stop consumers' hesitant thinking. When they are hesitant to purchase, this will boost their positive emotions. Customers can be complemented by customer service bots. For example, skincare brands usually tell consumers that their skin looks better after using skin care products. As a promotional tool, price discounts positively influence purchase decisions [9]. Combining the above arguments, this paper argues that the active behavior of customer service robots in the purchase decision stage affects consumers' perceived pleasure.

4.5 Service Perception

By analyzing the above four stages of the purchase process, this paper argues that the proactive behaviors of customer service robots in the demand elicitation and purchase decision stages have an impact on consumers' awareness of pleasure, and the proactive behaviors in the information gathering and comparison selection stages have an impact on consumers' awareness of usefulness. To better understand the internal mechanism of action of the proactive behavior of customer service robots, we further analyzed consumers' service awareness. Research on technology acceptance has shown that con-scious usefulness and perceived pleasure together influence user acceptance [10]. Fur-ther, perceived usefulness can affect satisfaction indirectly through conscious pleasure realization [11], as well as directly [12]. In addition, conscious pleasure plays a crucial role in enhancing satisfaction [13].

The proposed model relies on conscious usefulness and conscious pleasure as key variables. A comprehensive analysis of consumers' awareness of service is conducted using satisfaction as the core variable.

5 Systematic Supports

At different stages of the purchase process, the specific manifestations of customer service bots' proactive behaviors differ, and so do the impacts. The proposed model of the impact of customer service robots' active behavior on consumers' purchase intention is not only applicable to the analysis of specific stages. It also provides systematic support for the overall purchase process. This model focuses on strengthening consumers' perceptions of service through four stages and ultimately enhancing their purchase intentions.

In the demand elicitation stage, the customer service robot's proactive behavior focuses on actively receiving consumers. The customer service bot needs to do this by ushering the consumer into the store and staying in the store. It is only after consumers begin browsing the store that subsequent stages occur. In the store, consumers evaluate the value of their products through the two stages of collecting information and comparing and selecting. Customer service robots need to provide consumers with abundant product information and make reasonable recommendations to match supply and demand and meet consumers' expectations. Once the customer service robot has established the affirmation of the goods, the customer service robot can promote the consumer's purchase decision by offering incentives such as compliments and discounts.

Each of the above stages is dependent on the previous stage for its existence. Therefore, if the consumer terminates his purchase at some stage, the customer service bot first needs to try to attract the consumer again. If attraction fails, the customer service bot can solicit the consumer's evaluation of the service and use that sample data for machine learning to enhance its functionality.

In summary, the model proposed in this paper provides systematic support to promote the maximum utility of the customer service bot's proactive behavior.

6 Conclusion

Based on the existing theories about e-commerce and the consumer purchase process and the current development of customer service robots, this paper constructs a model of the influence of customer service robots' active behavior on consumer purchase intention based on SOR theory. The model includes four stages of the consumer purchase process in the context of e-commerce, i.e., inducing demand, collecting information, comparing and selecting, and purchasing decision. It also illustrates the specific performance of customer service robots in each stage of the process. At different stages, the impact of the proactive behavior of customer service bots is different. Through an analysis of these influence paths, this paper explains the role of customer service bots' proactive behavior in influencing consumers' purchase intentions.

Little existing research on e-commerce has addressed the consumer purchase process, and no research has yet focused on the proactive behavior of customer service bots. Therefore, the model proposed in this paper provides a new opportunity to better understand the role of customer service bots' proactive behavior in enhancing consumers' purchase intentions. It helps e-commerce companies to improve the design of customer service bots to compensate for the lack of human sales on current e-commerce platforms.

This paper's model does not focus solely on analyzing the role of customer service bots' proactive behavior during specific stages of the purchase process. Instead, it provides support during all stages. Customer service bots can be fully utilized by e-commerce platforms by integrating the four stages of the purchase process.

Currently, there is little academic research on the consumer purchase process and the active behavior of customer service bots in e-commerce. Based on SOR theory, this study constructs a model to understand the mechanism of customer service bots' proactive behavior. The model extends the application scenarios of SOR theory in e-commerce and provides directional suggestions for subsequent research to guide scholars' attention to the proactive intervention of customer service bots.

The objective of this paper is to provide theoretical support and practical guidance to improve the quality of human life through the use of active behavior of customer service robots. In the field of e-commerce, customer service robots can not only increase the sales volume of e-commerce platforms and improve the shopping quality of consumers at the micro level but also promote a better match between the supply of e-commerce platforms and the demand of consumers at the macro level to achieve optimal allocation and thus enhance the quality and quantity of social and economic growth. The construction of a barrier-free society is a broader use of customer service robots, which can analyze users' operation trajectories to infer their needs, provide process guidance, help functionally limited groups with behavioral or cognitive impairments to handle their affairs more conveniently and enjoy the convenience brought by technological progress.

Based on existing research, this paper proposes a theoretical model based on SOR using an experimental research method. It will be the responsibility of this paper to collect and analyze relevant data to assess the hypothesis and to validate and modify the model depending on the findings. This will provide better decision support for leveraging the proactive behaviors of customer service robots to improve human lives in the future.

Acknowledgments. The work described in this paper was supported by grants from the Zhejiang Province University Students Science and Technology Innovation Activity Program (Xinmiao Talent Program); the Zhejiang Provincial Federation of Social Sciences, grant number 2023N009; the Humanities and Social Sciences Research Project of Zhejiang Provincial Department of Education, grant number Y202248811; and the Zhejiang Province Undergraduate Innovation and Entrepreneurship Training Program, S202210337008.

References

1. Adam, M., Wessel, M., Benlian, A.: AI-based chatbots in customer service and their effects on user compliance. Electron. Mark. **31**(2), 427–445 (2020). https://doi.org/10.1007/s12525-020-00414-7
2. Zhong, S.H., Peng, J., Liu, P.: Question generation based on chat-response conversion. Concurrency Comput.: Pract. Exp. **33**(15), e5584 (2021). https://doi.org/10.1002/cpe.5584
3. Huang, M.H.: Using service quality to enhance the perceived quality of store brands. Total Qual. Manag. **20**(2), 241–252 (2009). https://doi.org/10.1080/14783360802623100
4. Qin, M., Zhu, W., Zhao, S., Zhao, Y.: Is artificial intelligence better than manpower? the effects of different types of online customer services on customer purchase intentions. Sustainability **14**(7), 3974 (2022). https://doi.org/10.3390/su14073974

5. Menon, S., Kahn, B.: Cross-category effects of induced arousal and pleasure on the Internet shopping experience. J. Retail. **78**(1), 31–40 (2002). https://doi.org/10.1016/s0022-435 9(01)00064-1

6. Yuyao, S.: Multi-round tag recommendation algorithm for shopping guide robots. In: 4th International Conference on Industrial and Business Engineering (ICIBE), Univ Macau, Zhuhai, 24–26 Oct 2018, pp. 191–196. Association Computing Machinery, New York (2018). https://doi.org/10.1145/3288155.3288188.WOS:000471064700034

7. Zhu, Y., Gan, Z.C., Huang, Y.: The virtual sales assistant in SaaS. In: 2010 3rd International Conference on Advanced Computer Theory and Engineering (ICACTE 2010), pp. 238–241 (2010). https://doi.org/10.1109/icacte.2010.5579806

8. Kuo, C.M.: The managerial implications of an analysis of tourist profiles and international hotel employee service attitude. Int. J. Hospitality Manag. **28**(3), 302–309 (2009). https://doi.org/10.1016/j.ijhm.2008.10.003

9. Jee, T.W.: The perception of discount sales promotions–A utilitarian and hedonic perspective. J. Retail. Consum. Serv. **63**, 102745 (2021). https://doi.org/10.1016/j.jretconser.2021.102745

10. Igbaria, M., Schiffman, S.J., Wieckowski, T.J.: The respective roles of perceived usefulness and perceived fun in the acceptance of microcomputer technology. Behav. Inf. Technol. **13**(6), 349–361 (1994). https://doi.org/10.1080/01449299408914616

11. Konradt, U., Held, G., Christophersen, T., Nerdinger, F.W.: The role of usability in E-Commerce services. Int. J. E-Bus. Res. (IJEBR) **8**(4), 57–76 (2012). https://doi.org/10.4018/jebr.2012100104

12. Joo, Y.J., Kim, N., Kim, N.H.: Factors predicting online university students' use of a mobile learning management system (m-LMS). Educ. Tech. Res. Dev. **64**(4), 611–630 (2016). https://doi.org/10.1007/s11423-016-9436-7

13. Hassenzahl, M.: The effect of perceived hedonic quality on product appealingness. Int. J. Hum.-Comput. Interact. **13**(4), 481–499 (2001). https://doi.org/10.1207/s15327590ijhc13 04_07

Understanding Bidding Strategy of Service Providers in Crowdsourcing Marketplace: The Influence of Buyer's Preference Disclosure

Zhihao Sun[1], Xiaolun Wang[1]([✉]), Zhijuan Hong[2], and Qian Yao[1]

[1] College of Economics and Management, Nanjing University of Aeronautics and Astronautics, Nanjing, China
w_xl@nuaa.edu.cn
[2] School of Management Science and Engineering, Shandong University of Finance and Economics, Jinan, China

Abstract. Crowdsourcing platforms are Internet-enabled systems that bring together service providers and buyers to source ideas from the crowd. Service providers compete in bidding price and bidding duration to stand out from numerous competitors to win the chance to fulfill buyer's tasks. Therefore, it is vital for service providers to understand buyer's preferences from limited task description, in order to adopt the optimal bidding strategy to match buyer's needs in the hyper-competitive crowdsourcing marketplace. Based on vertical preference theory from the auction field, this study attempts to explore how buyer's hidden preference disclosure affects bidding strategy of service providers. A large-scale empirical dataset was collected from epwk.com, containing a total of 9685 tasks and 52791 bids. Using BERT to extract buyer's preferences from task descriptions and OLS regression to perform data analysis, the results show that: (1) Buyer's price preference significantly reduces service providers' bidding price but not bidding duration; (2) Buyer's duration preference has a significant positive impact on bidding price and a significant negative impact on bidding duration. This study offers a new perspective for the research in the field of crowdsourcing, as well as provides profound practical implications for buyers, service providers, and crowdsourcing marketplace.

Keywords: Crowdsourcing · Information Disclosure · Bidding Strategy · Preference Signaling

1 Introduction

Crowdsourcing, the marketplace that brings together service providers and buyers to source ideas from crowd, is an emerging new business model in the sharing-economy age [1]. On crowdsourcing marketplace, after reading task descriptions posted by buyers, service providers compete in bidding price and bidding duration to stand out from numerous competitors to win the bid. Therefore, the information carried in task description is of great significance for service providers in the hyper-competitive crowdsourcing

© The Author(s), under exclusive license to Springer Nature Switzerland AG 2023
C. Stephanidis et al. (Eds.): HCII 2023, CCIS 1835, pp. 409–415, 2023.
https://doi.org/10.1007/978-3-031-36001-5_52

marketplace. Previous literature has mainly investigated the impact of text length and sentiment on service providers' bidding actions. However, other latent information, such as buyer's preferences, has been largely neglected. In this study, we attempt to answer the following two research questions: (1) How can we extract buyer's preference information (price preference and duration preference) from their task description text? (2) How do buyer's task preferences affect service provider's bidding strategies (bidding price and bidding duration)?

2 Literature Review

2.1 Crowdsourcing Platform: Concept and Transaction Mode

Proposed by Jeff Howe in 2006, crowdsourcing is a new business model that combines the words "crowd" and "outsourcing," indicating a way to use the public to complete tasks [2]. Crowdsourcing platforms are online service markets where service providers sell solutions to companies or individuals acting as buyers [3].

The mainstream transaction mode in crowdsourcing platform is bidding-based tasks, whose typical business process is as follows: (1) buyer posts a bidding task; (2) interested service providers submit bids with multiple attributes (i.e., price, duration); (3) buyer selects a satisfactory service provider and enters into a contract [4]. In this study, we focus on the interaction between buyers and service providers in the bidding-based tasks.

2.2 Antecedents of Service Provider's Bidding Strategy in Crowdsourcing Platforms

Service provider's bidding strategy refers to the price and duration committed in their bid, which reflects how much and how long it will take to complete the task. As the quality of service provider's bid determines whether they can win the bid, prior research has extensively explored the factors that impact service providers' bidding strategies.

To sum up, antecedents of service provider's bidding strategy include task-related factors (reward, task difficulty, deadline, etc.), service provider-related factors (competition, service quality, etc.), and buyer-related factors (credit, type, etc.). Wang and Yu (2020) have noted that task reward has a significant impact on service provider's participation [5]. Li et al. (2021) found that task deadline serves as a gauge of task difficulty and affects the resources service providers allocate [6]. As a specific manifestation of service providers' abilities, service quality levels can motivate them to participate in tasks [7].

However, past research has only examined existing factors while neglected the in-depth analysis of buyer's task descriptions. In fact, these texts may disclose detailed information about buyer's preferences, which could potentially function as the signal mechanism to alter service providers' bidding strategies. This study is among the first to investigate the impact of preference information on bidding strategies.

2.3 Vertical Preference Theory

In traditional auctions for tangible goods, the intermediary agent typically discloses clear scoring rules in advance, which reveal buyer's preferences and trade-offs among various attributes [8]. Applied to the online crowdsourcing marketplace, buyers also have multi-attribute criterion (price and duration) when selecting among lots of service providers. The priority of different attributes differs among buyers, reflecting their different "vertical preferences".

Horton and Johari (2018) argued that when buyers disclose vertical preference information, the signal will be perceived by sellers and lead to a significant sorting effect [9]. In our research context, the sorting effect means that buyers who prefer lower prices will attract more bids with lower prices, and buyers who value more on speed will attract more bids with shorter durations. Based on the theory, this study attempts to unearth buyer's vertical preferences, and explore their sorting effects on service providers.

3 Research Model and Hypotheses

3.1 Research Model

Figure 1 depicts the research model of this study. Based on the theory of vertical preference signaling from auction field, we attempted to explore the impact of buyer's price and duration preferences disclosure on service providers' bidding strategies (bidding price and bidding duration) on crowdsourcing platforms.

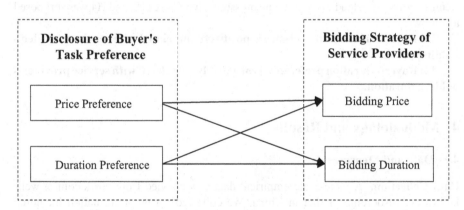

Fig. 1. Research model

3.2 Impact of Buyer's Price Preferences on Service Provider's Bidding Strategies

Buyer's preferences reflect the attribute they value most when choosing service providers. When a buyer discloses his or her preference for a lower price in the task description texts, a significant sorting effect will occur. That is, only service providers who are willing or able to accept lower prices will compete in the bid, who intendedly offer lower prices to meet buyer's expectation and increase their chances of winning. Hence, we propose hypothesis H1.

Meanwhile, based on cost-benefit analysis, service providers tend to find a balance between price and duration as a rational-economic man. In other words, to make up for the loss in monetary rewards, service providers will leave themselves adequate time in completing the task, thereby reducing the task's urgency and difficulty. Therefore, we propose hypothesis H2.

H1: Buyer's price preference is negatively correlated with service provider's bidding price.

H2: Buyer's price preference is positively correlated with service provider's bidding duration.

3.3 Impact of Buyer's Duration Preferences on Service Provider's Bidding Strategies

With regard to buyers' duration preferences, some tasks are urgent and others are non-urgent. Based on vertical preference theory, the "urgent" duration preferences may function as a signal to screen out those service providers who cannot hand in a satisfactory work in time. In other words, if the buyer requires strict time limits, service providers who participate have to expedite the work schedule while maintaining task quality. The dilemma markedly influences service provider's bidding strategy. On one hand, as the foremost requirement of the buyer, a bidding with a shorter duration is necessary. On the other hand, service providers tend to charge a higher price due to the potential cost stemming from overload work and time pressure. Hypotheses H3 and H4 were proposed as follows:

H3: Buyer's duration preference is positively correlated with service provider's bidding price.

H4: Buyer's duration preference is negatively correlated with service provider's bidding duration.

4   Methodology and Results

4.1   Data and Measures

Data Collection. A large-scale empirical data was crawled from epwk.com, a well-known crowdsourcing market in China. We collected various information including task characteristics (i.e., task type, task name, task description, task budget, number of service providers in each task), service provider's characteristics (i.e., capability score), and bid characteristics (i.e., bidding price, bidding duration). After removing samples with missing and outlier values, the final data set included a total of 9685 tasks and 52791 bids.

Independent Variables. We utilized the BERT (Bidirectional Encoder Representations from Transformers) model to identify buyer's price and duration preferences disclosed in task descriptions. In practice, when the buyers prefer a lower price, phrases such as "limited budget", "cost-effective", and "price-sensitive" are typically appeared in the texts. Similarly, the buyers convey their preferences for a shorter duration using phrases like "tight deadline", "urgent", and "the faster, the better". Based on this, we first manually annotated 2500 task description contents randomly selected from the dataset. Next, we split the annotated sample into a training set and a test set at the ratio of 7:3. Finally, we used the BERT model to annotate the price and duration preferences for all the task descriptions in the dataset.

Dependent and Control Variables. Service provider's bidding strategy determines whether they can win the bid, which is combined by two dependent variables: bidding price and bidding duration. To ensure the robustness, a number of task characteristics and service provider's characteristics that might affect bidding strategy were also controlled. Table 1 illustrates the main variables and definitions in this study.

Table 1. Main variables and definitions

Variable Name (Abbreviation)		Description
Dependent Variables	Service provider's bidding price (BidPrice)	The bidding price of each service provider in each task
	Service provider's bidding duration (BidDuration)	The bidding duration of each service provider in each task
Independent Variables	Buyer's price preference (PrefInfo_price)	A dummy variable representing whether the buyer discloses his price preference (1) or not (0)
	Buyer's duration preference (PrefInfo_duration)	A dummy variable representing whether the buyer discloses his duration preference (1) or not (0)
Control Variables	Task budget (TaskBudget)	The maximum value of budget range specified by the buyer
	Number of service providers in each task (BidNum)	The total number of service providers participating in the bidding process for a task
	Service provider's capability score (Capability)	The service provider's capability score evaluated by the crowdsourcing platform

4.2 Model Specification and Analysis

Based on the hypotheses, we developed the following econometric model and conducted data analysis using ordinary least squares (OLS) regression:

$$Bid_{i,j,u} = \beta_0 + \beta_1 \times PrefInfo\_price_{i,u} + \beta_2 \times PrefInfo\_duration_{i,u} + \beta_3 \times TaskBudget_{i,u} + \beta_4 BidNum_i + \beta_5 \times Capability_{i,j} + \varepsilon_{i,j,u} \tag{1}$$

where i is the index of each task, j is the index of each service provider, and u is the index of each buyer. $Bid_{i,j,u}$ indicates two dependent variables: $BidPrice_{i,j,u}$ and $BidDuration_{i,j,u}$.

We analyze how buyer's task preference information disclosure impacts service provider's bidding strategies, with the results shown in Table 2. Columns 1 and 2 examine the effects of buyer's price and duration preference on service provider's bidding prices, whereas columns 3 and 4 investigate the effects on service provider's bidding duration.

Table 2. Regression results of the influence of buyer's task preference on service provider's bidding strategy

Dependent Variables	BidPrice		BidDuration	
	1	2	3	4
Independent variables				
PrefInfo_price		−0.086***		0.174
		(0.000)		(0.892)
PrefInfo_duration		0.030***		−2.215**
		(0.000)		(0.029)
Control variables				
BidNum	0.000*	−8.571E-5	0.074***	0.074***
	(0.087)	(0.191)	(0.000)	(0.000)
TaskBudget	1.146***	1.145***	15.444***	15.485***
	(0.000)	(0.000)	(0.000)	(0.000)
Capability	0.014***	0.014***	−0.239***	−0.239***
	(0.000)	(0.000)	(0.000)	(0.000)
Constants				
β_0	−0.736***	−0.733***	−41.026***	−41.099***
	(0.000)	(0.000)	(0.000)	(0.000)
R-square	0.713	0.714	0.025	0.025

Notes. *** $p < 0.01$, ** $p < 0.05$, * $p < 0.1$; Numbers in parentheses are p-values.

As shown in Table 2, buyer's price preference has a significant negative impact on service provider's bidding price ($\beta = -0.086$, $p < 0.01$). This suggests that when a buyer discloses the preference for a lower price in the task description, service providers tend to offer a lower price to meet the buyer's expectation, so as to increase their chances of winning the bid. Therefore, hypothesis H1 was supported. However, the results show that buyer's price preference does not have a significant effect on service provider's bidding duration, we failed to support hypothesis H2. The possible reason lies in that service providers may either want to finish the cheap task as soon as possible or put it to the lowest priority by using only spare time to complete it. Besides, service providers tend to believe that buyers with the preference for a lower price will pay less attention to the bidding duration.

Regarding the impact of the buyer's duration preference on service provider's bidding strategy, hypotheses H3 and H4 were both supported. Specifically, buyer's duration preference has a significant positive effect on service provider's bidding price ($\beta = 0.030, p < 0.01$) and a significant negative effect on service provider's bidding duration ($\beta = -2.215, p < 0.05$). This implies that service providers are able to cut down the task duration when buyers require them to do so, but meanwhile, the acceleration of work progress increases their costs, resulting in a higher bidding price to ensure their benefits.

5   Discussion and Implications

Based on vertical preference theory, this study explores how buyer's hidden preference disclosure affects service provider's bidding strategy. The profound theoretical and practical contributions are as follows: First, using the BERT model, we are among the first to explore buyer's task description texts from the "preference disclosure" perspective. Besides, different from prior literature that focuses on existing information in crowdsourcing platform, this study illustrates the significant impact of buyer's "latent" preference information on service provider's bidding strategy. Last, our results also offer practical guidance for buyers when releasing tasks, for service providers when bidding for tasks, as well as for crowdsourcing marketplace to achieve the best fit in tasks.

However, this study has certain limitations which need to be improved in the future. First, some buyers only prioritize the quality of task, whose impact on service provider's bidding strategy is unclear. Second, task description text may also disclose other important information to be further analyzed.

Acknowledgement. This work was supported by National Science Foundation of China (#71802108) and Research Start-up Funds from NUAA.

References

1. Hong, Y., Pavlou, P.A.: On buyer selection of service providers in online outsourcing platforms for IT services. Inf. Syst. Res. **28**(3), 547–562 (2017)
2. Howe, J.: The rise of crowdsourcing. Wired. Mag. **14**(6), 1–4 (2006)
3. Zheng, H., Xu, B., Lin, Z.: Seller's creditworthiness in the online service market: a study from the control perspective. Decis. Support. Syst. **127**, 113118 (2019)
4. Hong, Z., Wu, R., Sun, Y., Dong, K.: Buyer preferences for auction pricing rules in online outsourcing markets: Fixed price vs. open price. Electron. Mark. 30, 163–179 (2020)
5. Wang, G., Yu, L.: Analysis of enterprise sustainable crowdsourcing incentive mechanism based on principal-agent model. Sustainability. **12**(8), 3238 (2020)
6. Li, J., Wang, Y., Yu, D., Liu, C.: Solvers' committed resources in crowdsourcing marketplace: do task design characteristics matter? Behav. Inf. Technol. **41**(8), 1689–1708 (2022)
7. Feng, Y., Ye, H.J., Yu, Y., Yang, C., Cui, T.: Gamification artifacts and crowdsourcing participation: Examining the mediating role of intrinsic motivations. Comput. Hum. Behav. **81**, 124–136 (2018)
8. Asker, J., Cantillon, E.: Properties of scoring auctions. Rand. J. Econ. **39**(1), 69–85 (2008)
9. Horton, J.J., Johari, R.: Buyer signaling improves matching: Evidence from a field experiment. https://papers.ssrn.com/sol3/papers.cfm?abstract_id=3245704. Accessed 15 Mar 2023

Mechanisms of Green Product Advertisements on Xiaohongshu that Influence Consumers' Purchase: Exploring Green Product Strategies

Jingwen Wang and Cong Cao[✉] [iD]

Zhejiang University of Technology, Hangzhou 310023, China
congcao@zjut.edu.cn

Abstract. This research focuses on the Xiaohongshu platform and explores which green product advertising can have a greater impact on consumers' green purchasing behaviour, to explore optimized green advertising strategies. Based on the theoretical foundations of constrained behaviour theory (CLT), signal transduction theory, the theory of consumption values, and other theoretical foundations, the model uses relevant mediating factors to connect the path between green product advertising strategy and green purchase intention. This model provides new theoretical support for the antecedent path of consumers' green purchasing behaviour, and at the same time provides reference significance for the promotion of green products on the green emerging social e-commerce platform taking Xiaohongshu as an example.

Keywords: Green Purchasing · Social Media · Advertisement · Xiaohongshu

1 Introduction

The contradiction between economic development and environmental problems has become increasingly obvious, and in recent years, the world has paid more and more attention to the deterioration of the ecological environment. Since the new crown pneumonia epidemic, people's attention to ecological environmental protection has reached a new height. A green product is a recyclable and remanufactured product that minimizes environmental pollution and mitigates the crisis caused by environmental problems [1]. In this case, the promotion and use of green products and people's desire to buy green products are increasing. There will be a huge market for green consumption in the future. Green marketing is currently an important research area. Green marketing is a marketing method that aims at sustainable development to achieve the economic benefits of production enterprises, meet consumer needs, and unify the interests of environmental protection [2]. As an important means of green marketing, social media plays a vital role in green promotion. Xiaohongshu is a sharing social consumption software operating in the UGC model. With the maturity of development, Xiaohongshu has become the "leader" of China's social software and is the representative of the social and e-commerce platform, which can have a huge impact on consumers. How to optimize the advertising of the Xiaohongshu platform to increase users' attention to green products, to further improve purchase intention, and even generate sustainable purchase intention, has great research prospects. At the same time, it can also draw reference significance for the green development of the social and e-commerce model platform taken as an example of Xiaohongshu.

2 Literature Review

Studies have shown that young consumers have a high degree of willingness to purchase green products [3], a group that fits the user profile of Xiaohongshu. In the field of green marketing, scholars have put forward new theories on how to optimize social advertising strategies to increase user engagement with green information, providing more direct guidelines for social media, advertisers, and green product enterprises. For example, Kim, et al. [4] uses the construal level theory (CLT) to explore the impact of the interest appeal of advertising content and the specificity of information statements on green message participation. In addition, consumer awareness of green products [5], and the sense of crisis about the pandemic [6] have all been shown to influence consumers' purchase intentions. In Sun, et al. [6]'s research, it was also pointed out that social media marketing, product knowledge, and crisis awareness all have direct or indirect positive effects on purchase intention. The existing literature has made a detailed analysis of consumers' purchase intention and the influencing factors of purchase behaviour, but there are still many problems. (1) The existing models can often only stay in the study of influencing factors, and the path cannot penetrate to the end of the execution strategy. (2) The existing model has not been studied using emerging social e-commerce platforms as an example. So what kind of green advertising appeal on the social e-commerce platform can affect the effect and thus have a positive impact on consumer purchase behaviour is the main research content of this paper.

3 Theoretical Development

Different theories, such as stimulus-organism-response model (S-O-R) [7], rational behaviour theory (TRA) [8], construal level theory (CLT) [9], the theory of consumption values [10], and planned behaviour theory (TPB) [11] have been used by various scholars as tools to assess consumers' green purchase intentions. The constraint-level theory originally explained the problem of temporal distance but has since been extended by many scholars to the study of social distancing. This theoretical view holds that an individual's mental representation of an object is more acceptable when the relationship between social distance (i.e., proximal vs. distal) and the consumer's internal state of mind (concrete vs abstract) is optimal or matched [12, 13]. Therefore, this theory can be used to study the impact of advertising appeal content on consumer behaviour. Icek Ajzen proposed the TPB by pointing out that the purpose of the behaviour is influenced by behavioural attitudes, subjective criteria, and perceptual behavioural control, which in turn affects actual behaviour [11]. Today, the TPB model has been used by many scholars to study green purchasing behaviour. The theory of consumption values, which states that consumers make informed purchasing decisions based on multiple value dimensions such as enjoyment, quality, society, monetary value, and their trade-offs [14], has been used in many studies and is successful in explaining a wide range of consumer choice behaviours. However, these theoretical models have certain limitations when used alone, so this study will comprehensively use CLT, TPB, and the theory of consumption values to explore a more complete and reliable green purchase intention model (Fig. 1).

4   The Proposed Model

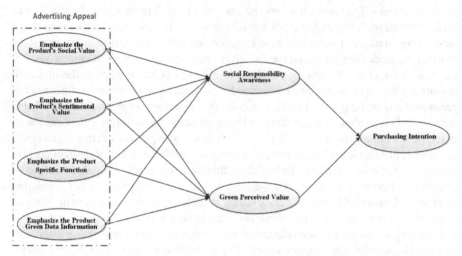

Fig. 1. A model of the influence of advertising appeal on consumers' purchasing intention

This paper comprehensively uses the construal level theory (CLT), planning behaviour theory (TPB) and the theory of consumption values to construct a model of consumers' green purchase intention based on the advertising appeal of the Xiaohongshu platform. Starting from four advertising appeal focuses, this model discusses the impact and mechanism of advertising appeal with different focuses on purchase intention. Explore models that are conducive to promoting consumers' willingness to buy green, to promote the development of green undertakings.

4.1   Product Social Value

In this model, content emphasizes the social value of products as one of the focuses of advertising strategy. In the era of the epidemic, the concept of green environmental protection has gradually taken root in the hearts of the people, people's acceptance of green products is getting higher and higher, and the voice of society is also increasing. When emphasizing the social value of green products, consumers will recognize and feel the social benefits brought by the products. And feel the value of their purchasing behaviour from this social benefit, and obtain the realization of self-worth. The social value of the product improves the green perceived value of consumers, and at the same time promotes the realization of social responsibility awareness, so the willingness to buy green products also increases.

4.2 Product Emotional Value

Content that emphasizes the emotional value of the product is another focus of advertising strategy. Affective value is the perceived utility obtained from the ability to evoke an emotion or affective state from another option [10]. For example, corporate green behaviour evokes positive emotions of consumer gratitude, which in turn influence the positive behaviour of consumers [15]. In other words, when you add emotional factors to your advertising appeal, consumers will be moved by your sincerity and have psychological resonance, which will affect consumers' willingness to pay a green premium.

4.3 Product-Specific Function Information

Emphasizing product-specific feature information is also one of the focuses of advertising strategy. Today's consumers have strong access to information and capabilities, focusing on obtaining the highest possible benefits at the lowest possible cost. Therefore, the function of the product itself is a key part of the perceived value of the consumer. When consumers perceive stronger functional effects, the more functions that can meet the needs of consumers, the higher the perceived value of consumers' green, and they are more willing to buy green products.

4.4 Product Green Data Information

According to the construal level theory, when the target stimulus is psychologically close to the individual, a low-level explanation is formed, resulting in concrete thinking. That is to say, when consumers are interested in the characteristics of "green", the more specific the advertising appeal, the more persuasive it can be to consumers. Therefore, product-specific green data is presented, such as how much carbon emissions can be reduced by the world every time a shared bicycle is used. Detailed and specific advertising content can often bring a stronger and more direct impact, thereby increasing consumers' value perception.

4.5 Perceived Green Value and Social Responsibility Awareness

Divide the mediating factors of consumers' green purchase intentions into themselves and others. The green perceived value represents consumers' subjective awareness, while social responsibility awareness represents the impact of the social environment and social pressure. With these two changes, consumers' purchase intentions will also change. Green advertising content affects the above two aspects through different focuses, and when the impact on a certain factor reaches a certain level, it can have an impact on consumers' purchase intentions.

5 Discussion

This study has rich theoretical and practical significance. At the theoretical level, this study provides new theoretical support for the antecedent path of consumers' green purchase intention and fills the theoretical gap in which green marketing advertising strategies can affect consumers' green purchase intention. The theoretical model of the influence mechanism on continuous purchasing behaviour provides theoretical support for enterprises to stabilize customer sources and increase market share. At the practical level, this study innovates the case study of green marketing on emerging social platforms, and the optimized advertising strategies obtained have a practical guiding role for Xiaohongshu and other similar social e-commerce platforms to formulate marketing strategies and enterprises to increase their market share of green products. Communities and governments can also use this advertising and marketing strategy to promote green concepts on social platforms, enhance public awareness of green consumption, and create a green community and green society.

6 Conclusion

This study focuses on the Xiaohongshu platform and uses existing models to find the influence mechanism of green purchase intention. Constrained behaviour theory (CLT), planning behaviour theory (TPB), the theory of consumption values and other theoretical foundations, the study of which green advertising can have a greater impact on these factors, and explore optimized green advertising strategies. The existing research does not specifically focus on the green marketing of social media to improve users' purchase intention, but also on the optimization of advertising strategy. Moreover, most of the current research on green marketing takes popular foreign social platforms as examples, and how emerging social media e-commerce platforms with Chinese characteristics such as Xiaohongshu can use comprehensive advertising methods such as pictures + text and short videos to carry out social media marketing to influence users' green consumption intentions. Therefore, this comprehensive model can play a better-guiding role in the green marketing of social e-commerce platforms. It will connect the path between green product advertising strategy and sustainable green purchase intention and find mediating factors. In the following research, this paper will focus on collecting relevant data and analyzing it, verifying and modifying the model, and contributing to the development of green causes.

Acknowledgments. The work described in this paper was supported by grants from the Zhejiang Provincial Federation of Social Sciences, grant number 2023N009; the Humanities and Social Sciences Research Project of Zhejiang Provincial Department of Education, grant number Y202248811; and the Zhejiang Province Undergraduate Innovation and Entrepreneurship Training Program, S202210337052.

References

1. Kamalanon, P., Chen, J.S., Le, T.T.Y.: "Why do we buy green products?" an extended theory of the planned behavior model for green product purchase behavior. Sustainability. **14**(2), 689 (2022)

2. Fuller, D.A.: Sustainable Marketing : Managerial-Ecological Issues (1999)
3. Yadav, R., Pathak, G.S.: Determinants of consumers' green purchase behavior in a developing nation: applying and extending the theory of planned behavior. Ecol. Econ. **134**, 114–122 (2017)
4. Kim, Y.K., Yim, M.Y.C., Kim, E., Reeves, W.: Exploring the optimized social advertising strategy that can generate consumer engagement with green messages on social media. J. Res. Interact. Mark. **15**(1), 30–48 (2021)
5. Tsai, P.H., Lin, G.Y., Zheng, Y.L., Chen, Y.C., Chen, P.Z., Su, Z.C.: Exploring the effect of Starbucks' green marketing on consumers' purchase decisions from consumers' perspective. J. Retail. Consum. Serv. **56**, 102162 (2020)
6. Sun, Y., Leng, K., Xiong, H.T.: Research on the influencing factors of consumers? green purchase behavior in the post-pandemic era. J. Retail. Consum. Serv. **69**, 103118 (2022)
7. D.E., B.: xii + 266 Pp. $12.50. Mehrabian A., Russell J.A., An Approach to Environmental Psychology, MIT Press, Cambridge, MA (1974). Behavior Therapy **7**(1), (1976)
8. Fishbein, M., Ajzen, I.: Predicting and understanding consumer behavior: attitude-behavior correspondence. Understand. Attitudes Predicting Soc. Behav. **1**(1), 148–172 (1980)
9. Dhar, R., Kim, E.Y.: Seeing the forest or the trees: implications of construal level theory for consumer choice. J. Consum. Psychol. **17**(2), 96–100 (2007)
10. Sheth, J.N., Newman, B.I., Gross, B.L.: Why we buy what we buy: a theory of consumption values. J. Bus. Res. **22**(2), 159–170 (1991)
11. Icek, A.: The theory of planned behavior. Organ. Behav. Hum. Decis. Process. **50**(2), 179–211 (1991)
12. Higgins, E.T.: Making a good decision: value from fit. Am. Psychol. **55**(11), 1217–1230 (2000)
13. Steinhart, Y., Carmon, Z., Trope, Y.: Warnings of adverse side effects can backfire over time. Psychol. Sci. **24**(9), 1842–1847 (2013)
14. Turel, O., Serenko, A., Bontis, N.: User acceptance of hedonic digital artifacts: a theory of consumption values perspective. Inf. Manag. **47**(1), 53–59 (2010)
15. Xie, C., Bagozzi, R.P., Grønhaug, K.: The role of moral emotions and individual differences in consumer responses to corporate green and non-green actions. J. Acad. Mark. Sci. **43**(3), 333–356 (2014). https://doi.org/10.1007/s11747-014-0394-5

The Influence of Perceptions of Convenience and Service Quality on Trust and Repurchase Interest (A Study on Shopee Users)

P. A. Retno Widowati[✉] and Rifan Dhika Ananda

Universitas Muhammadiyah Yogyakarta, Yogyakarta, Indonesia
retno.widowati@umy.ac.id

Abstract. This study aims to analyze and determine the effect of perceived convenience and service quality on trust and repurchase intention. The object of this research is Shopee e-commerce, while the subject is Shopee users in Bantul. This data collection technique used purposive and non-probability sampling with a total sample of 184 respondents. Data were obtained through questionnaires distributed directly to respondents using Google Forms. The data analysis technique used SEM with the AMOS application version 21.00. Based on the analysis, perceived convenience had no effect on trust, perceived service quality had a positive and significant impact on trust, trust had no effect on repurchase intention, perceived convenience had a positive and significant effect on repurchase intention, perceived service quality had a positive effect and significant to repurchase intention, trust could not mediate the effect of perceived convenience on consumer repurchase intention, trust could not mediate the effect of perceived service quality on consumer repurchase intention.

Keywords: Perceived Convenience · Perceived Service Quality · Trust · Repurchase Intention · Shopee

1 Introduction

The development of technology and science is currently rapid. Technological developments encourage people to do everything efficiently. This development also helps the economy, politics, tourism, and transportation. Current technological developments have changed everything to be practical. Almost all the elements humans need can be obtained digitally, not to mention the economic field, marked by the Industrial Revolution 5.0. Industry 5.0 can be seen in renewable technology by utilizing the internet, which affects human life. Even graphically, internet users in the world are increasing rapidly. Indonesian internet users have increased from year to year. In 2020, internet users in Indonesia reached more than 170 million, and 200 million users in 2021.

The internet has opened a massive business opportunity for business people. One growing business in Indonesia is e-commerce. This business directly changes the classic business system to a new one, where all needs are available online. E-commerce also makes time and energy more efficient in conducting business activities.

© The Author(s), under exclusive license to Springer Nature Switzerland AG 2023
C. Stephanidis et al. (Eds.): HCII 2023, CCIS 1835, pp. 422–430, 2023.
https://doi.org/10.1007/978-3-031-36001-5_54

The development of e-commerce in Indonesia is rapid. Based on data sourced from databoks.katadata.co.id, Indonesia is the country with the highest level of e-commerce transactions in the Southeast Asian region. Shopee is one of many e-commerce sites originating from Singapore. Based on data from iprice.co.id, Shopee is one of the consumers' most frequently visited e-commerce sites, competing with Tokopedia (Fig. 1).

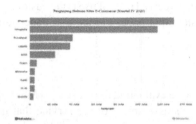

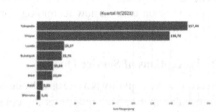

Fig. 1. Monthly e-commerce visitors in Indonesia in the fourth quarter of 2020

Fig. 2. Monthly e-commerce visitors in Indonesia in the fourth quarter of 2021

Based on Figs. 2 and 3, Shopee can become the market leader in the fourth quarter of 2020, even though it fell to second place in the fourth quarter of 2021. Shopee continues to compete with Tokopedia. This success is inseparable from the strategies used by Shopee so that consumers are willing to make repeat purchases. Due to the success of an e-commerce company, repurchase intention is an important aspect that can determine the success of a company, as explained by [1] that bank consumers in India will continue to use services from banks that as long as the quality of services delivered goes well.

Repurchase intention is important for companies because consumers willing to buy back from the company are an important asset—the ease-of-use influences repurchase intention. Besides perceived convenience, there is a perception of service quality which is also an important factor that can influence repurchase intention. Wilson & Keni (2018) revealed that service quality positively affected repurchase intention [1]. Companies can also build trust through perceived ease of use and perceived quality of services provided by e-commerce. Deborah Wiendy & Keni found that perceived ease of shopping significantly affected trust [2]. Meanwhile, Wilson & Keni suggested that the service quality variable significantly influenced the trust variable [1].

Wilson & Keni who in their research found that quality of service has more influence on repurchase intentions through trust as mediation or directly [3]. Likewise, Wilson (2019) found that perceived ease of use played a greater role in determining or influencing consumer repurchase intentions than perceived benefits. Based on the background and results of previous research, this study has entitled *The Influence of Perceived Convenience and Service Quality on Trust and Repurchase Intention (Study on Shopee Users).*

2 Literature Review

2.1 Perceived Ease of Use

Perceived ease of use is a customer's assessment of the effort customers have to learn and use a new technology or system. Then, according to Deborah Wiendy & Keni (2019), convenience is defined as the degree to which a person believes that using technology will make a person free from effort [2]. Therefore, perceived ease of use is the customer's point of view on using a new technology or system that is easy to use and understand without much effort.

2.2 Perceptions of Service Quality

Perceived service quality is a cue used by customers in evaluating the service [4] Munhurrun revealed that service quality is the consumer's assessment of the service that the consumer receives or feels. Good service quality measurements are needed to identify service aspects that require performance improvement, assess how much improvement is needed in each aspect, and evaluate the impact of improvement efforts [5]. Therefore, service quality is the customer's perceived satisfaction with the services provided.

2.3 Trust

Trust can be defined as customer confidence to transact with a company based on the credibility and reliability of that company [1]Then according to Deborah Wiendy & Keni (2019), trust can be interpreted as a person's desire to be sensitive to other people's actions based on the hope that others will take certain steps toward people they trust without depending on their ability to supervise and control them. Trust can be interpreted as a customer's perception of the extent of risk that may occur during transactional activities between two or more parties [2]. Hence, trust is the knowledge and psychological outcome of a relationship between parties regarding interaction and transaction processes.

2.4 Repurchase Intention

Repurchase intention results from a positive buying experience that increases the likelihood of repurchasing at the same store [6]. Furthermore Saidani Basrah et al. defined repeat purchase as a motivational level of a consumer to repeat purchasing behavior for a product [7]. From this statement, it can be concluded that repurchase intention is a person's planned decision to repurchase a product, considering the situation/experience that occurs after shopping and the satisfaction received from a product.

3 Hypothesis Development

3.1 The Effect of Perceived Convenience on Trust

Wilson found that perceived ease of shopping significantly affected trust. Furthermore, Deborah Wiendy & Keni also showed that perceived ease of shopping significantly affected trust. The following hypothesis is proposed based on the theory and results of previous research.

H1: Perceived convenience has a positive and significant effect on trust.

3.2 The Effect of Perceived Service Quality on Trust

Nurfath et al. showed that perceived service quality significantly affected trust in sales-people [8]. Then, Wilson & Keni (2018) also suggested that the service quality variable significantly influenced the trust variable. The following hypothesis is proposed based on the theory and results of previous research.

H2: Perceived service quality has a positive and significant effect on trust.

3.3 The Effect of Trust on Consumer Repurchase Intention

Wilson & Keni (2018) found that trust positively influenced consumer repurchase intention. Nurfath et al. (2017) also showed that trust in salespeople significantly affected repurchasing intention [8]. The following hypothesis is proposed based on the theory and results of previous research.

H3: Trust has a positive and significant effect on consumer repurchase intention.

3.4 The Effect of Perceived Convenience on Repurchases Intention

Basyar et al. (2016) found that perceived convenience had a positive relationship and significant influence on online repurchase intention, meaning that the better the perceived benefit, the higher the online repurchase intention [9]. Then, Puteri Woro Subagio & Hadiwidjojo also proved that the perceived ease of use felt by Go-Jek consumers in Malang City significantly affected repurchase intention. The following hypothesis is proposed based on the theory and results of previous research.

H4: Perceived convenience positively and significantly affects consumer repurchase intention.

3.5 The Effect of Perceived Service Quality on Repurchases Intention

Ramadhan & Santosa (2017) stated that service quality is a function of what is received by the customer directly (technical quality) and how the service is performed (functional quality) [10]. Then, Wilson & Keni (2018) showed that service quality positively affected repurchase intention.

H5: Perceived service quality positively and significantly affects consumer repurchase intention.

3.6 The Effect of Perceived Convenience on Consumer Repurchase Intention with Trust as a Mediator

According to Wilson's research (2019), perceived ease of use positively affected consumer repurchase intentions directly and through trust as mediation. The following hypothesis is proposed based on the theory and results of previous research.

H6: Perceived convenience influences consumer repurchase intention with trust as a mediator.

3.7 The Effect of Perceived Service Quality on Consumer Repurchase Intention with Trust as a Mediator

Nurfath et al. (2017) proved that trust in salespeople mediates partially (partial mediation) the effect of perceived service quality on repurchase intentions. Wilson & Keni (2018) showed that service quality positively affected repurchase intention through trust. The following hypothesis is proposed based on the theory and results of previous research.

H7: Perceived service quality influences consumer repurchase intention with trust as a mediator.

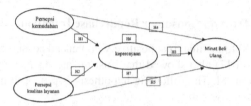

Fig. 3. Research Model

4 Research Method

In this study, the object used was Shopee e-commerce, while the research subjects were Shopee e-commerce consumers. The sample used in this research was 184 respondents with data collection techniques using purposive sampling with non-probability sampling method with criteria 1) 17–25 years old and domiciled in Bantul, 2) Already did a purchase or transaction on e-commerce Shopee, and 3) Making purchases or transactions on Shopee e-commerce for at least the last 4 months. Data were obtained through questionnaires distributed directly to respondents using the Google form application. The data analysis technique used SEM with the AMOS application version 21.0.

5 Result

Testing of the instrument used Confirmatory Factor Analysis (CFA) to test the validity and Composite Reliability (CR) to test reliability. In this study, the CFA obtained from each question item has a loading factor value of > 0.5. So that all statements regarding perceived convenience, perceived service quality, trust, and repurchase intention submitted to respondents are valid. As for the reliability test, if the construct reliability value meets the requirements, it has a value of > 0.7 and VE > 0.5. Based on the study's results, all variables have CR values > 0.7 and VE > 0.5, so the variables of perceived convenience, perceived service, trust, and repurchase intention proposed for respondents are reliable. The following is the Structural Equation Modeling (SEM) (Fig. 4).

The structural model feasibility test looked at several criteria of goodness of fit models such as Chi-Square value, probability, df, GFI, AGFI, TLI, CFI RMSEA, and RMR. The following is the modified goodness of fit model.

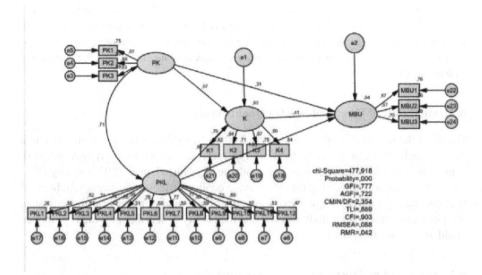

Fig. 4. Model Structural Equation Modelling (SEM)

Table 1. Goodness-of-Fit Criteria

No	Criteria	Recommendation Value	Model Results	Description
1	Chi-Square	Expected low	477,918	Not fit
2	Significant Probability	$\geq 0{,}05$	0,000	Not fit
3	GFI	$\geq 0{,}90$	0,777	Not fit
4	RMSEA	$\leq 0{,}08$	0,088	Marginal Fit
5	AGFI	$\geq 0{,}90$	0,722	Not fit
6	TLI	> 0.90	0,889	Marginal Fit
7	CMIN/DF	< 2.00	2,354	Not fit
8	CFI	$\geq 0{,}90$	0,903	Fit

Based on the Goodness of Fit criteria in Table 1, some requirements are declared fit. The results of the structural equation model testing are accepted, and further analysis can be carried out.

6   Discussion

6.1   The Effect of Perceived Convenience on Trust

Based on the results of hypothesis 1 testing, perceived ease of use had no positive and significant effect on trust, or hypothesis 1 (H1) in this study was rejected. This study's results differ from the results of research conducted by Wilson (2019), Deborah

Wiendy & Keni (2019), showing that perceived ease of shopping had a significant effect on trust. The high or low perceived convenience does not affect consumer trust in Shopee. Consumer trust will arise from what Shopee has provided to consumers. Based on the results of this study, the ease of use of Shopee e-commerce needs to convince consumers to trust Shopee.

6.2 The Effect of Perceived Service Quality on Trust

Based on the results of hypothesis testing 2 states that perceived service quality had a positive and significant effect on trust, so hypothesis 2 (H2) in this study was accepted. This study's results align with research conducted by Nurfath et al. (2017) and by (Wilson & Keni, 2018), suggesting that the service quality variable significantly influenced the trust variable. High or low perceptions of service quality affect consumer trust in Shopee e-commerce. This study showed that the quality of services provided by Shopee could affect consumer trust.

6.3 The Effect of Trust on Repurchases Intention

Based on hypothesis testing 3, trust negatively and significantly affected repurchase intention. For this reason, hypothesis 3 (H3) in this study was rejected. This hypothesis test does not align with the research conducted by Wilson & Keni (2018), finding that trust positively influenced consumer repurchase intention. Further investigation by Saidani Basrah et al. (2019) showed that trust influenced the repurchase intention being accepted. However, this study is consistent with the results of researchLuqman Dzaki & Amanda Zuliestiana (2022), proving that the trust variable did not have a significant effect on the repurchase intention of users of the JD e-Commerce site.id. This study proved that trust could not influence consumer repurchase intention. Thus, high and low levels of Shopee consumer trust could not affect consumer repurchase interest.

6.4 The Effect of Perceived Convenience on Repurchases Intention

Hypothesis 4 testing revealed that perceived convenience had a positive and significant effect on repurchase intention, or hypothesis 4 (H4) in this study was accepted. The results of the hypothesis test follow the results of research by Basyar et al. showing that perceived convenience had a positive relationship and a significant influence on online repurchase intention, meaning that the better the perceived benefit, the better online repurchase intention. High or low perceived convenience can affect consumer repurchase intention. This study showed that a higher perception of convenience in e-commerce Shopee could increase consumer repurchase interest in e-commerce Shopee.

6.5 The Effect of Perceived Service Quality on Repurchases Intention

The results of testing hypothesis 5 in this study indicated that perceived service quality had a positive and significant effect on repurchase intention. Hence, hypothesis 5 (H5) in this study was accepted. This test's results align with the research by Wilson &

Keni showing that service quality positively affected repurchase intention. Based on the hypothesis test results, the perception of service quality in Shopee could affect the level of consumer repurchase interest.

6.6 The Effect of Perceived Convenience on Repurchase Intention with Trust as a Mediator

Based on hypothesis 6 testing conducted in this study, the results of perceived ease of use did not affect repurchase intention with trust as a mediator, or hypothesis 6 (H6) was rejected. These results do not align with Wilson's research, showing that perceived ease of use positively affected consumer repurchase intentions directly and through trust as mediation. However, Enisia Laora proved that consumer trust could not mediate the effect of perceived convenience on repurchase intention. Trust could not mediate perceived ease of repurchase intention. In this study, consumer trust cannot influence the effect of perceived convenience on the purchase intentions of Shopee consumers. The results of this study on hypothesis 4 showed a direct effect. Perceived convenience had a positive and significant effect on repurchase intention. The relationship between perceived convenience and repurchase intention is better directly than having to be mediated by trust. The higher the consumer's perception of convenience in Shopee, the higher the consumer's repurchase intention.The Effect of Perceived Convenience on Repurchase Intention With Trust As A Mediator.

The results of hypothesis 7 testing showed that perceived service quality did not affect repurchase intention, with trust as a mediator. Hence, hypothesis 7 (H7) in this study was rejected. This result is not in line with Nurfath et al. showing that trust in salespeople mediates partially (partial mediation) the effect of perceived service quality on repurchase intentions. Then, Wilson & Keni (2018) proved that service quality positively affected repurchase intention through trust. In this study, trust could not mediate perceived service quality's effect on customer repurchase intention on Shopee. Consumer trust in the perceived quality of services provided by Shopee could not influence consumer repurchase interest in Shopee e-commerce. The results of hypothesis 5 testing showed a direct effect. Perceived service quality had a positive and significant effect on repurchase intention, meaning that the relationship between the variable perceived service quality on repurchase intention is better directly than having to be mediated by trust. The higher the consumer's perception of the quality of Shopee's e-commerce services, the higher the consumer's repurchase intention.

7 Conclusion

Based on data analysis and results of hypothesis testing regarding the effect of perceived convenience and perceived service quality on trust and repurchase intention of Shopee users in Bantul using Structural Equation Modeling (SEM) modeling run with AMOS software version 21.0, the conclusions are as follows: 1) Perceived convenience did not affect consumer confidence in Shopee e-commerce; 2) Perceived service quality had a positive and significant effect on consumer confidence in Shopee; 3) Trust did not affect consumer repurchase interest in Shopee; 4) Perceived convenience had a positive and significant effect on consumer repurchase intention on Shopee; 5) Perceived service quality had a positive and significant impact on consumer repurchase intention on Shopee; 6) Trust could not mediate the effect of perceived convenience on consumer repurchase intention in e-commerce Shopee; and 7) Trust could not mediate the impact of perceived service quality on consumer repurchase intention on Shopee.

References

1. Wilson, N., Keni, K.: Pengaruh website design quality dan kualitas jasa terhadap repurchase intention : variabel trust sebagai variabel mediasi. J. Manaj. dan Pemasar. Jasa 11(2), 291–310 (2018). https://doi.org/10.25105/jmpj.v11i2.3006
2. Keni, W.D.D.: Pengaruh persepsi kemudahan berbelanja, reputasi website, dan kualitas website terhadap minat beli online: kepercayaan sebagai variabel mediasi. J. Manaj. Bisnis dan Kewirausahaan 3(1), 102–109 (2019). https://doi.org/10.24912/jmbk.v3i1.4933
3. Wilson, N.: the impact of perceived usefulness and perceived ease-of-use toward repurchase intention in the Indonesian e-commerce industry. J. Manaj. Indones. 19(3), 241 (2019). https://doi.org/10.25124/jmi.v19i3.2412
4. Tjiptono, F.: Service, quality dan satisfaction. Andi Offset, Yogyakarta (2016)
5. Zeithaml, V.A., Bitner, M.J., Gremler, D.D.: Services Marketing: Integrating Customer Focus Across The Firm. McGraw-Hill Education, New York (2006)
6. Peter, J.P., Olson, J.C.: Perilaku Konsumen & Strategi Pemasaran. Salemba Empat (2016)
7. Saidani, B., Lusiana, L.M., Aditya, S.: Analisis pengaruh kualitas website dan kepercayaan terhadap kepuasan pelanggan dalam membentuk minat pembelian ulang pada pelanggan shopee. JRMSI-Jurnal Ris. Manaj. Sains Indones. 10(2), 425–444 (2019)
8. Nurfath, D., Utami, S.: Pengaruh persepsi kualitas pelayanan terhadap niat membeli ulang yang dimediasi oleh kepercayaan pada tenaga penjual di toko ritel lyradyba kota banda aceh. J. Ilm. Mhs. Ekon. Manaj. 2(1), 67–84 (2017)
9. Basyar, K., Sanaji, S.: Pengaruh persepsi kemudahan dan persepsi manfaat terhadap niat beli ulang secara online dengan kepuasan sebagai variabel intervening. BISMA (Bisnis dan Manajemen) 8(2), 204–217 (2016)
10. Ramadhan, A.G., Santosa, S.B.: Analisis pengaruh kualitas produk, kualitas pelayanan, dan citra merek terhadap minat beli ulang pada sepatu nike running di semarang melalui kepuasan pelanggan sebagai variabel intervening. Diponegoro J. Manag. 6(1), 59–70 (2017). http://ejournal-s1.undip.ac.id/index.php/management
11. Dzaki, A.L., Zuliestiana, D.A.: Analisis pengaruh kepercayaan dan kepuasan terhadap minat beli ulang pada pengguna situs e-commerce jd ld. e-Proc. Manag. 9(2), 125–139 (2022)

A Model of Factors Influencing Anthropomorphic Intelligent Customer Service on Angry Consumer Satisfaction

Quan Zhou[1], Huangyi Dai[1], Jinhua Xiao[2], and Cong Cao[1](✉) iD

[1] Zhejiang University of Technology, Hangzhou 310023, China
congcao@zjut.edu.cn
[2] China United Zhujing Architecture Design Co., Ltd., Hangzhou 310023, China

Abstract. Labor costs continue to rise, and many companies are unwilling to hire too many human customer service personnel. Driven by market demand, intelligent customer service robots emerged as the times require. Intelligent customer service robots can help companies reduce employment costs and improve user efficiency. However, compared with intelligent customer service robots, more users still prefer to communicate with human customer service. Intelligent customer service robots are beginning to become anthropomorphic, adding a touch of humanity, but at the same time may lead to increased user anger. Items that don't meet expectations are a common occurrence in online shopping, and they often lead to angry consumers. In the above scenario, based on the Technology Acceptance Model combined with existing theoretical literature, this paper constructs a consumer satisfaction model with perceived usefulness, perceived ease of use, and perceived social presence as dependent variables and perceived value as an intermediary variable. Influencing factor model. This model explores the impact of anthropomorphic intelligent customer service on the satisfaction of angry consumers in the above scenarios. At the same time, we also propose strategies for enterprises to improve consumer satisfaction.

Keywords: Anthropomorphic Intelligent · Customer Service · TAM Model · User Satisfaction

1 Introduction

Online shopping has long been a mainstream method, and with it comes a huge demand for online customer service. Due to rising labour costs, companies are gradually becoming reluctant to hire too many human customer service agents. Intelligent customer service bots have emerged. On the one hand, intelligent customer service bots can help enterprises reduce labour costs and increase profits; on the other hand, intelligent customer service can help realize round-the-clock service, improve communication accuracy and enrich user service experience [1]. More and more enterprises are applying intelligent customer service. China's intelligent customer service market is expected to exceed 13 billion.

© The Author(s), under exclusive license to Springer Nature Switzerland AG 2023
C. Stephanidis et al. (Eds.): HCII 2023, CCIS 1835, pp. 431–437, 2023.
https://doi.org/10.1007/978-3-031-36001-5_55

Nevertheless, users still prefer to communicate with human customer service [2]. This is because communication with intelligent customer service is considered less human than communication with an actual human [3]. Driven by natural language processing technology and market demand, intelligent customer service is beginning to trend toward anthropomorphism. Many scholars have researched the association between anthropomorphic intelligent customer service and consumer experience, but few have focused on the impact of emotions on consumer perception and satisfaction.

For online shopping, it is common for consumers to become angry due to the discrepancy between the actual product and their expectations. The inappropriate communication between intelligent customer service and consumers also often enhances consumers' anger. This paper develops a model of factors influencing consumer satisfaction based on the TAM model. The model explains the factors influencing angry consumers' increased anger and decreased satisfaction after anthropomorphic intelligent customer service communication. Through this model, merchants can further understand the factors that affect consumer emotions and satisfaction. It further helps merchants and improves consumer satisfaction.

2   Literature

Anthropomorphism is defined as making non-human agents with human physical and psychological characteristics [4]. Visual, identity, and conversational cues are believed to enable non-human agents to converge towards anthropomorphism [2].

Pelau, et al. [5] demonstrated that anthropomorphism could enhance consumers' perceived empathy and interaction quality. At the same time, Chiang, et al. [4] also noted that anthropomorphism could enhance the intimacy between consumers and customer service robots and their service quality. Through the above emotional enhancement effects, anthropomorphism promotes consumer acceptance. Furthermore, Min Chung [6] pointed out that anthropomorphism indirectly promotes consumer purchase intentions by enhancing perceived social presence and enjoyment. Despite the positive effects, many scholars soon found that anthropomorphic features also have several negative effects. According to the Valley of Terror effect, when the anthropomorphization of intelligent customer service is enhanced, it can cause discomfort and lead to negative emotions among consumers. Yang, et al. [7] found that with low perceived control, users feel threatened by anthropomorphic intelligent customer service and thus prefer non-anthropomorphic customer service bots. Cheng [8]. Pointed out that in the case of service failure, high anthropomorphism leads to enhanced user dissatisfaction with intelligent customer service.

In addition, other scholars have linked anthropomorphic features to user emotions. Gursoy, et al. [9] and other scholars confirmed that emotions impact users' intention to use smart customer service. Crolic, et al. [10] scholars explored consumers by placing them under the emotion of anger. Ultimately, it was found that expectations of bots, exaggerated by anthropomorphic features, negatively affect satisfaction, merchant evaluation, and purchase intention by angry users.

Through an analysis of the existing literature, I found that scholars have conducted many studies on the positive and negative effects of anthropomorphic intelligent customer service, and numerous valuable conclusions have been drawn. Unfortunately, although scholars have linked user emotions to the use of anthropomorphic intelligent customer service, few scholars have been able to explain the process of the impact of anthropomorphic intelligent customer service on user experience under specific emotions.

3   Theoretical Foundation

Technology Acceptance Model The Technology Acceptance Model (TAM), proposed by Davis [11], uses perceived usefulness (PU) and perceived ease of use (PEOU) as core variables to explain the model that affects users' technology acceptance. (Numerous studies have confirmed that the TAM with high reliability, and can be used effectively in relevant studies [12]. Since its introduction, TAM has been widely used in various fields, including online education [13], telemedicine [14] and online shopping [15]. Smart technology with anthropomorphic features Given that intelligent customer service with anthropomorphic technology features is different from information systems in the traditional sense, not only influenced by perceived ease of use and perceived usefulness, but a model also influencing consumer satisfaction is constructed based on the TAM model combined with theoretical literature on perceived value and perceived social presence.

4   The Proposed Model

In this paper, we construct an influence factor model based on the TAM model with a perceived social presence, perceived usefulness, perceived ease of use, and perceived value as perceptual variables and user satisfaction as outcome variables. We investigate how consumers who are angry about product expectations become angrier and less satisfied after communicating with anthropomorphic intelligent customer service and suggest strategies for companies to improve user satisfaction (Fig. 1).

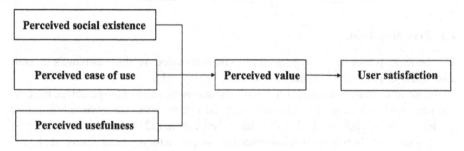

Fig. 1. Influence model of consumer satisfaction

4.1 Perceived Usefulness and Perceived Ease of Use

Perceived usefulness is defined as the extent to which a person believes that using a particular system will improve his or her job performance and directly affects user acceptance of IT and perceived ease of use is the extent to which a person believes that using a featured system will require no effort, indirectly influencing user acceptance of IT [11].

Perceived usefulness and perceived ease of use in this model refer to the extent to which consumers perceive anthropomorphic intelligent customer service to be able to meet their needs and easy to use in the presence of anger. Numerous studies have found that perceived usefulness and ease of use positively affect the satisfaction level of information systems [16, 17]. Also, perceived usefulness and perceived ease of use have a significant positive impact on perceived value [18]. However, it has also been noted that when perceived ease of use decreases information system usage is reduced [19].

Based on the above studies, we believe that anger may negatively affect the perceived usefulness and ease of use of anthropomorphic intelligent customer service to some extent, leading to a decrease in user satisfaction.

4.2 Perceived Social Presence

Social presence is the degree to which a person is perceived as real in mediated communication [20]. In this model, social presence is the extent to which consumers perceive anthropomorphic intelligent customer service as a human being. The technical features of anthropomorphism enhance consumers' perceived social presence of intelligent customer service. The high level of perceived social presence, in turn, positively influences users' expectations of intelligent customer service to a certain extent. However, limited by current technology, smart customer service will likely fail to meet users' performance expectations, and may negatively affect users' perceived value. Scholars such as Crolic, et al. [10] point out anger further enhances this negative impact. The negative impact of perceived social presence on perceived value stems from consumers' incorrect expectations of anthropomorphic intelligent customer service.

4.3 Perceived Value

The benefits perspective suggests that perceived value is the customer's overall assessment of perceived benefits and sacrificial utility [21].

In this model, we understand it as the user's total assessment of the perceived benefits and perceived sacrifices of replacing human customer service with virtual customer service. Scholars such as Meidute-Kavaliauskiene, et al. [22] found that the perceived value of service robots positively influenced the intention to use them. Zhang, et al. [23] based on the PLS-SEM model confirmed that passengers' perceived value is a positive factor significantly affecting passenger satisfaction.

Perceived social presence, perceived usefulness and ease of use affect user satisfaction with perceived value as a mediating variable. Angry users in communicating with anthropomorphic intelligent customer service may lead to a decrease in perceived value and thus user satisfaction.

5   Innovation and Limitations

Users' perceptions of anthropomorphic intelligent customer service are different under anger than non-angry emotions.

In this paper, we take anger emotion as the background condition and combine the TAM model with perceived social presence and perceived value to explore the influence of influencing consumers on anthropomorphic intelligent customer service. Anger may lead to a decrease in consumers' perceived usefulness, perceived ease of use, and consequently, a decrease in perceived value leading to a decrease in user satisfaction. On the other hand, anger enhances the negative impact of perceived social presence on perceived value.

Although this paper has extended the TAM model with the expectation of exploring more comprehensively the factors that influence consumer satisfaction with smart customer service, it should still be acknowledged that this study has limitations. First, this paper only explores users' perceived usefulness and perceived ease of use and their impact on user satisfaction. However, user satisfaction is not only influenced by these factors but may also be influenced by perceived risk and other environmental variables. Secondly, this paper was conducted only through literature analysis, which may result in the conclusions of the paper not being accurately confirmed.

6   Conclusion and Contribution

Based on the existing literature, this study explored the factors affecting anthropomorphic intelligent customer service user satisfaction under anger emotions by extending the TAM model with three aspects of perceived usefulness, perceived ease of use, and perceived social presence, and using perceived value as a mediating variable. Our study found that perceived usefulness, ease of use, and social presence negatively affect user satisfaction through perceived value in the presence of anger. In addition, we offer some suggestions for companies to improve user satisfaction. First, improving users' perceived ease of use and usefulness through technology upgrades to meet users' performance expectations is the best solution to improve user satisfaction. Second, given technical limitations, businesses can lower consumer expectations by prompting users, for example, by informing them of the range of capabilities of intelligent customer service, thereby avoiding the negative impact of excessive consumer expectations. Finally, merchants can minimize losses by detecting user sentiment and replacing human customer service on time.

Despite the limitations of this study, it still contributes to existing research. First, this study extends the TAM model by incorporating perceived social presence and perceived value into the existing model. Second, this study suggests how companies can improve angry consumers' satisfaction with anthropomorphic intelligent customer service. Third, this study, using specific emotions as the context of the study, provides some new ideas for future research.

In future research, we will improve the model and collect data for empirical studies to reduce the experiment's limitations as much as possible.

Acknowledgments. The work described in this paper was supported by grants from the Zhejiang Provincial Federation of Social Sciences, grant number 2023N009; the Humanities and Social Sciences Research Project of Zhejiang Provincial Department of Education, grant number Y202248811; the Zhejiang Province University Students Science and Technology Innovation Activity Program (Xinmiao Talent Program); and the Zhejiang Province Undergraduate Innovation and Entrepreneurship Training Program, S202210337022.

References

1. Chung, M., Ko, E., Joung, H., Kim, S.J.: Chatbot e-service and customer satisfaction regarding luxury brands. J. Bus. Res. **117**, 587–595 (2020)
2. Roy, R., Naidoo, V.: Enhancing chatbot effectiveness: the role of anthropomorphic conversational styles and time orientation. J. Bus. Res. **126**, 23–34 (2021)
3. Van Pinxteren, M.M.E., Pluymaekers, M., Lemmink, J.G.A.M.: Human-like communication in conversational agents: a literature review and research agenda. J. Serv. Manag. **31**(2), 203–225 (2020)
4. Chiang, A.-H., Trimi, S., Lo, Y.-J.: Emotion and service quality of anthropomorphic robots. Technol. Forecast. Soc. Chang. **177** (2022)
5. Pelau, C., Dabija, D.C., Ene, I.: What makes an AI device human-like? The role of interaction quality, empathy and perceived psychological anthropomorphic characteristics in the acceptance of artificial intelligence in the service industry. Comput. Hum. Behav. **122** (2021)
6. Min Chung, H.: The impact of anthropomorphism on consumers' purchase decision in Chatbot commerce. J. Internet Commer. **20**(1), 46–65 (2021)
7. Yang, Y., Liu, Y., Lv, X., Ai, J., Li, Y.: Anthropomorphism and customers' willingness to use artificial intelligence service agents. J. Hosp. Market. Manag. **31**(1), 1–23 (2022)
8. Cheng, L.-K.: Effects of service robots' anthropomorphism on consumers' attribution toward and forgiveness of service failure. J. Consum. Behav. **22**(1), 67–81 (2023)
9. Gursoy, D., Chi, O.H., Lu, L., Nunkoo, R.: Consumers acceptance of artificially intelligent (AI) device use in service delivery. Int. J. Inf. Manage. **49**, 157–169 (2019)
10. Crolic, C., Thomaz, F., Hadi, R., Stephen, A.T.: Blame the bot: anthropomorphism and anger in customer-Chatbot interactions. J. Mark. **86**(1), 132–148 (2022)
11. Davis, F.D.: Perceived usefulness, perceived ease of use, and user acceptance of information technology. MIS Q.: Manage. Inf. Syst. **13**(3), 319–339 (1989)
12. Yousafzai, S.Y., Foxall, G.R., Pallister, J.G.: Technology acceptance: a meta-analysis of the TAM: part 1. J. Model. Manag. **2**(3), 251–280 (2007)
13. Granic, A., Marangunic, N.: Technology acceptance model in educational context: a systematic literature review. Br. J. Edu. Technol. **50**(5), 2572–2593 (2019)
14. Kamal, S.A., Shafiq, M., Kakria, P.: Investigating acceptance of telemedicine services through an extended technology acceptance model (TAM). Technol. Soc. **60** (2020)
15. Wu, J., Song, S.: Older adults' online shopping continuance intentions: applying the technology acceptance model and the theory of planned behavior. Int. J. Hum.-Comput. Interact. **37**(10), 938–948 (2021)
16. Tsai, H.-T., Chien, J.-L., Tsai, M.-T.: The influences of system usability and user satisfaction on continued Internet banking services usage intention: empirical evidence from Taiwan. Electron. Commer. Res. **14**(2), 137–169 (2014). https://doi.org/10.1007/s10660-014-9136-5
17. Ma, L., Feng, J., Feng, Z., Wang, L.: Research on user loyalty of short video app based on perceived value - take Tik Tok as an example. In: 2019 16TH International Conference on Service Systems and Service Management (ICSSSM2019).IEEE (2019)

18. Al Khasawneh, M.H., Haddad, N.: Analysis of the effects of ease of use, enjoyment, perceived risk on perceived value and subsequent satisfaction created in the context of C2C online exchanges. Int. J. Electron. Mark. Retail. **11**(3), 217–238 (2020)
19. Hyo-Jeong, K., Mannino, M., Nieschwietz, R.J.: Information technology acceptance in the internal audit profession: Impact of technology features and complexity. Int. J. Account. Inf. Syst. **10**(4), 214–228 (2009)
20. Gunawardena, C.N., Zittle, F.J.: Social presence as a predictor of satisfaction within a computer–mediated conferencing environment. Int. J. Phytorem. **21**(1), 8–26 (1997)
21. Kuo, Y.-F., Wu, C.-M., Deng, W.-J.: The relationships among service quality, perceived value, customer satisfaction, and post-purchase intention in mobile value-added services. Comput. Hum. Behav. **25**(4), 887–896 (2009)
22. Meidute-Kavaliauskiene, I., Cigdem, S., Yildiz, B., Davidavicius, S.: The effect of perceptions on service robot usage intention: a survey study in the service sector. Sustainability **13**(17) (2021)
23. Zhang, C., Liu, Y., Lu, W., Xiao, G.: Evaluating passenger satisfaction index based on PLS-SEM model: evidence from Chinese public transport service. Transp. Res. Part A-Policy Pract. **120**, 149–164 (2019)

Designing and Developing Intelligent Green Environments

Remote Sensing Applied for Land Use Change Assessment and Governance in Riau-Indonesia

Agustiyara Agustiyara[1,3]([✉]) [iD], Balázs Székely[1,2] [iD], Achmad Nurmandi[3] [iD], and Peter K. Musyimi[2,4] [iD]

[1] Department of Geophysics and Space Science, Doctoral School of Environmental Sciences, Eötvös Loránd University, Budapest, Hungary
agustiyara@student.elte.hu, balazs.szekely@ttk.elte.hu
[2] Institute of Geography and Earth Sciences, Department of Geophysics and Space Science, Doctoral School of Earth Science, Eötvös Loránd University, Budapest, Hungary
musyimipeter@student.elte.hu
[3] Department of Government Affairs and Administration, Jusuf Kalla School of Government, Universitas Muhammadiyah Yogyakarta, Yogyakarta, Indonesia
nurmandi_achmad@umy.ac.id
[4] Department of Humanities and Languages, Karatina University, P.O BOX 1957-10101, Karatina, Kenya

Abstract. Remote sensing offers the potential to provide up-to-date information on changes in forestry areas over large areas. Its application makes it possible to make assessments related to land use change. This research aims to assess whether land change using remote sensing can provide an efficient alternative, both in terms of cost and time, including improving forest governance policy support. Remote sensing and forest governance are state-of-the-art in this research for the development of knowledge from in-depth data analysis. This study was conducted in Bengkalis-Riau Province, Indonesia because, the regency has become the most vulnerable region for forest fires since 2013 and the province has experienced growing pressure from an expanding palm oil industry. It has the largest tropical peatland area and palm oil plantation in Indonesia. The use of remote sensing data methods improved the sensitivity of detecting classified forest cover, providing a better understanding of changes that are usually difficult to map, including fires, smallholders and industrial scale of agricultural areas, peatland cover, wetlands, and barren forest land. Both smallholder and industrial agricultural areas are also better detected. The result from Sentinel data indicate forest, and land cover changes after evaluation, which focuses on the spatial, spectral, and temporal resolution of the imagery. The cover of land use change generated by remote sensing data shows the classification of land conditions in the study area, ranging from cultivated land, bare soil, forestry, oil palm plantations, and peatlands within the plantation area. Integration of artificial intelligence will be further explored.

Keywords: remote sensing · forest governance · artificial intelligence · remote work

C. Stephanidis et al. (Eds.): HCII 2023, CCIS 1835, pp. 441–448, 2023.
https://doi.org/10.1007/978-3-031-36001-5_56

1   Introduction

This research focuses on remote sensing and forest governance for integrating these land use changes. It makes possible to make assessments related to land vegetation change and improve decision-making by assessing the transformation of land use change. Continued environmental degradation, in the form of land use change, has been a long-standing problem [1, 2]. Referring to the concept of sustainable development strengthens data-based policies in controlling deforestation in Indonesia. Land conversion for oil palm plantations and industrial forest plantations (HTI) causes environmental problems [3–5], especially on the Sumatra Island, Indonesia as the largest expanded area of plantation. Community-based management is considered adequate to support regional growth and development [2, 6]. There are currently various methods for detecting forest land cover based on various remote sensing data and techniques. For instance, utilization of image storages as provided by Worldview 2/3 and UAV data fusion, European Space Agency (ESA) [7–10].

In addition, data-driven research approaches have been widely applied various disciplines, and are also needed in various government sectors [10–12]. Further, there are project artificial intelligence (AI) has been integrated in governmental organizations for instance, data-based governance, data-based monitoring and evaluation, that is in e-participation and e-government systems [9, 13]. A combination of these methodologies and techniques informs the development of forest governance, through multistakeholders approach referred to as collaborative governance [14–16]. The present research utilizes remote sensing data as references to achieve its objectives, for instance, land cover assessment using NDVI, and LAI. In addition, as much of the peat swamp forest, and peatland is in areas of industrial and smallholder oil palm, and industrial timber plantation, remote sensing data has been scarcely applied. Although it has been demonstrated previously it does not clearly distinguish certain land cover types. This methodology offers the potential to provide up-to-date information on changes in peat swamp forests, cultivated land, bare soil, and forestry areas over large areas, and support spatially explicit assessments of land use change. As mentioned earlier, Bengkalis Regency (Rupat and Bengkalis Island)-Riau Provinces is an area prone to deforestation, thus, land use analysis through a remotely sensed data approach is fundamental to analyzing the land cover change in this research.

2   Methodology

Study Area, Data and Methods

This study was conducted in Bengkalis Regency, Riau Province on Sumatra Island, Indonesia. The area is the most vulnerable region for forest fires since 2013 and the province has experienced growing pressure from an expanding palm oil industry and industrial timber plantation [17, 18]. For this research, Sentinel-2 MSI data was accessed through https://scihub.copernicus.eu/ then visualized through SNAP tools and Q-GIS software. The data was processed as shown in Fig. 1. The study analyses biophysical indices as well as vegetation indices that is leaf area index (LAI) and normalized difference vegetation index (NDVI). The characterization of the matrix and the bands is shown in Table 1.

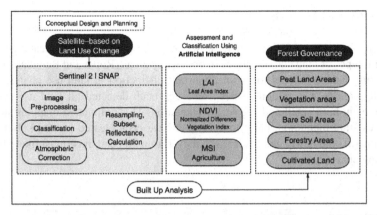

Fig. 1. Overview of the workflow used in this research, and the software used in each step.

Table 1. Sentinel-2 MSI products.

1. Product Name	2. S2 Bands	3. Indices	4. Date of Sensing
Sentinel-2 MSI	B2, B3, B4, B8, B11, B12	NDVI, and LAI	2020 to 2022 (0% cloud cover)

Table 2. Classification and Description

Classification	Description
Peat land	Primary peat land, secondary peat land areas, shrubby land
Water Body	Rivers, canals, sea
Plantation Palm	Industries and smallholders with palm plantations, as a dominant plantation in these areas
Plantation acacia (timber)	Industries timber production and plantation with acacia
Urban	Building and roads
Forest	Primary forest and secondary forest areas
Cultivated land	Cleared land cover in grassland, or peat land areas, bare soil, and fewer vegetation areas

This study assesses the land use cover by combining Biophysical Indices and Vegetation indices for land use change assessment by remotely sensed data. SNAP software was used to characterize and assess land use change by focusing on the spatial, spectral, and temporal resolution of the images, to classify land in the Bengkalis Regency, or as a tool to evaluate the use of land use change, peat land, forestry areas, and palm oil plantation over several years to calculate the land use cover changed (Table 2).

3 Result and Discussion

Analyzing the high-resolution remote sensing data from the SNAP application, resulted in several types of land classifications in both study areas (Rupat and Bengkalis Island), considering land cultivated to be an important distinction in land use change in this research (Fig. 2). The remote sensing data approach detected all land use areas for plantations in both small and big scales plantation. This automated mapping not only detects existing plantation, but also areas that have been cleared (most likely for new replanting (a), and newly cleared areas that overlap with peatlands (most likely for new plantation areas (b).

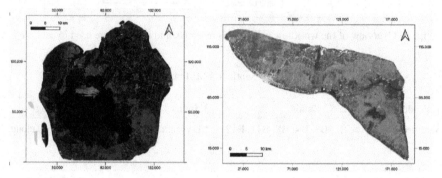

Fig. 2. (a) 2020 (Rupat Island) and (b) 2022 (Bengkalis Island) that used Sentinel-2 image composite in this research, featuring Sentinel 2 MSI natural color (RGB) imagery.

The result of multispectral imager (MSI) natural colors differentiated pixels that assume the cultivated areas respectively. As such, some areas of oil palm plantations that were detected outside of oil palm plantations, through remote sensing visualization data, were found to have new land use changes or land clearing in peatland areas. Using spectral index through band match and expression indicated that Low NDVI value is the blue color more like water, and wet soil. Low NDVI values that are closer to zero, with light green color more likely referred to agricultural land and grassland. The dark green color referred to trees, vegetation, and forests. As mentioned by Acheampong [19]; Belgiu [10] that NDVI was considered a reliable tool for assessing the dynamics of vegetation recovery in the burned land or cultivated land, also suitable for identifying changes in land use cover.

The land cover change displayed in the Fig. 3 shows how forest land transforms around plantation land or forest utilization. In general, the use of remote sensing data approaches improved the sensitivity of detecting cultivated forest cover, providing a better understanding of changes that are usually difficult to map, including fires, smallholders and industrial scale of agricultural areas, peatland cover, wetlands, and barren forest land. Both smallholder and industrial agricultural areas were also clearly detected.

In Bengkalis Regency, the palm oil represents the largest plantation area by type, the bright and dark pink color represents the cultivated land and new palm oil plantation in 2020. In 2022 was greener due to time and period of plantation a year after (Fig. 4 (b, d).

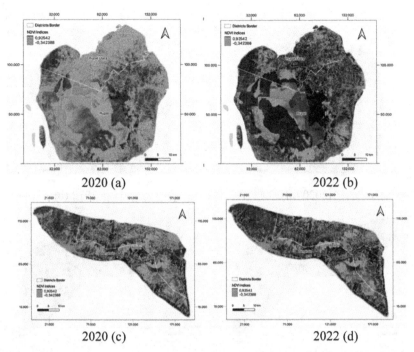

2020 (a)　　　　　　　　　　2022 (b)

2020 (c)　　　　　　　　　　2022 (d)

Fig. 3. Land cover change by NDVI in 2020 and 2022. Note that the significant changes between 2020 and 2022 is not due to natural processes rather it is the growth of the new palm oil plantation.

Palm oil growth indicated land cover change between 2020 and 2022. The images visualization is imperative for government institution to monitor and evaluate land change detection and evaluate policies based on the regulation and raise awareness and public participation in addressing deforestation.

Due to their different but complementary strengths, visualizations of remote sensing data using the LAI approach is also analyzed. However, when analyzed, among the areas that were not classified as palm oil, the classes of "bare soil" were also close to the industrial oil palm areas, in contrast to the peatland areas that still had high values of vegetation indices. However, bare soil cleared land, and grassland or shrubby land are also potentially subject to conversion. Although, the oil palm plantation area also contains shrubby land and bare soil. In this case, an accuracy assessment has been conducted with each land use change classification.

The differentiation of peatlands, oil palm plantations and other land cover types is still challenging, therefore this is still a matter of much research debate. For example, 'peat' is a waterlogged wetland ecosystem where plant matter cannot fully decompose. This can be seen from the results of the analysis using spectral indices by LAI to visualize biophysical parameter. In Fig. 3, the dark orange color may refer to dried soil or certain part of settlements, and bright green color indicates grassland and wet land, dark green color refers to forest or plantation. There is indication that around large-scale plantations are vegetation is water-stressed. Furthermore, the LAI results show that areas of vegetation or barren land have the potential to be converted to community-based land use.

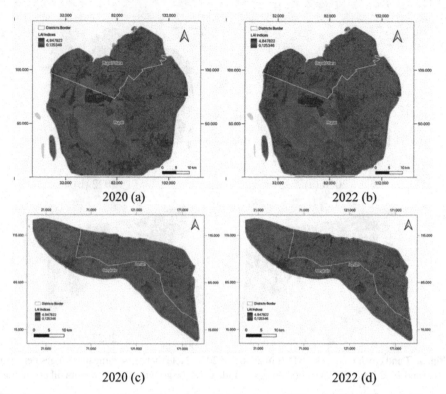

2020 (a)   2022 (b)

2020 (c)   2022 (d)

Fig. 4. Detected changes for Leaf Area Index (LAI) between 2020 and 2022 in Rupat (a, b), and Bengkalis Island (c, d)

Our results are in line with previous publications [20, 21], who assessed and monitored the structure and function of forest ecosystems, the biophysical indicator LAI was used. Kalantar [22] also argued that vegetation indices have highest correlation with LAI.

On the other hand, the sustainability of oil palm production will partly depend on the use of cover crops. For example, cover crops co-exist with oil palm after forest clearance and planting/re-planting, to protect from bare soil. LAI statistics on remote sensing and spectral indices are context-dependent and do not generalize well across different ecosystems [22, 23]. Furthermore, the vegetation index used in this study requires prior knowledge of the parameters to be suitable for the operational monitoring of vegetation cover change. The land cover/land use change detected by remote sensing data shows the classification of land conditions in the study area, ranging from industrial-scale oil palm plantations to smallholder oil palm plantations, and the distribution of peatlands within the plantation area. The resulting resolution demonstrates the potential for land use cover change detection. The data visualization has shown the potential to improve the accuracy of assessing land use change based on the classification function of the analysis that has been conducted.

4 Conclusion

The study concludes that remotely sensed data provides updated information in several types of land cover and vegetation, with multispectral analysis NDVI and LAI assessment showed the importance of environmental condition, where the variable and approach should be developed for monitoring framework on land use change. The effectiveness of this methodology provides an alternative approach for forest governance, which is proven by the result on-the-ground detection and monitoring. In addition, overlapping land function were detected, and land transformation on several areas, such as forest, new land use changes and/or land clearing in peatland areas were detected. The approach is also efficient for government institution to create an operational monitoring in forest governance. Further, the technique can also be relied upon for map land use functions such, palm oil both of smallholder and large-scale, industrial timber plantations, peatlands and burnt land. However, additional detailed mapping could be extended by combining with analysis using more features of Sentinel-3 or Sentinel-2 on land analysis.

References

1. HAdrianto, H.A., Spracklen, D.V., Arnold, S.R., Sitanggang, I.S., Syaufina, L.: Forest and land fires are mainly associated with deforestation in Riau Province. Indonesia Remote Sens. **12**(1) (2020). https://doi.org/10.3390/RS12010003
2. Thoha, A.S., Sofyan, M., Ahmad, A.G.: Spatio-temporal distribution of forest and land fires in Labuhanbatu Utara District, North Sumatera Province, Indonesia. In: 3rd International Conference on Agriculture, Environment and Food Security, AEFS 2019, vol. 454, no. 1 (2020). https://doi.org/10.1088/1755-1315/454/1/012081
3. Helmi, H., Djafri, D., Mutiani, C., Abd Halim, N., Badri, M., Yefni, Y.: Indigenous people in the dynamics of land use changes, forest fires, and haze in Riau Province, Indonesia. In: Natural Resource Governance in Asia: From Collective Action to Resilience Thinking, Andalas University (Universitas Andalas), pp. 291–308. Elsevier, Padang (2021)
4. Burki, T.K.: The pressing problem of Indonesia's forest fires. Lancet. Respir. Med. **5**(9), 685–686 (2017). https://doi.org/10.1016/S2213-2600(17)30301-6
5. Frimawaty, E.: Mapping data on Indonesia's worst forest and land fires of palm oil cultivation lands. In: 1st International Symposium of Earth, Energy, Environmental Science and Sustainable Development, JESSD 2020, vol. 211 (2020). https://doi.org/10.1051/e3sconf/202021105002
6. Aminah, C.Y., Krah, P.P.: Forest fires and management efforts in Indonesia (a review). In: IOP Conference Series: Earth and Environmental Science, vol. 504, no. 1, p. 012013, June 2020. https://doi.org/10.1088/1755-1315/504/1/012013
7. Lim, K., Treitz, P., Wulder, M., St-Ongé, B., Flood, M.: LiDAR remote sensing of forest structure. Prog. Phys. Geogr. **27**(1), 88–106 (2003). https://doi.org/10.1191/0309133303pp360ra
8. López-Andreu, F.J., López-Morales, J.A., Erena, M., Skarmeta, A.F., Martínez, J.A.: Monitoring system for the management of the common agricultural policy using machine learning and remote sensing. Electronics **11**(3) (2022). https://doi.org/10.3390/electronics11030325
9. Deng, X., Fang, Y., Uchida, E., Rozelle, S.: A complementary measurement of changes in China's forestry area using remote sensing data. J. Food, Agric. Environ. **10**(3–4), 1355–1358 (2012). https://www.scopus.com/inward/record.uri?eid=2-s2.0-84873519781&partnerID=40&md5=4ceb36efb3fb0cd80fd7099b82983006

10. Belgiu, M., Drăgu, L.: Random forest in remote sensing: a review of applications and future directions. ISPRS J. Photogramm. Remote Sens. **114**, 24–31 (2016). https://doi.org/10.1016/j.isprsjprs.2016.01.011

11. Liu, G., et al.: Policy factors impact analysis based on remote sensing data and the CLUE-S model in the Lijiang River Basin, China. CATENA **158**, 286–297 (2017). https://doi.org/10.1016/j.catena.2017.07.003

12. Potapov, P., et al.: Mapping the world's intact forest landscapes by remote sensing. Ecol. Soc. **13**(2) (2008). https://doi.org/10.5751/ES-02670-130251

13. Pal, M.: Random forest classifier for remote sensing classification. Int. J. Remote Sens. **26**(1), 217–222 (2005). https://doi.org/10.1080/01431160412331269698

14. Prager, K.: Agri-environmental collaboratives as bridging organisations in landscape management. J. Environ. Manage. **161**, 375–384 (2015). https://doi.org/10.1016/j.jenvman.2015.07.027

15. Sanders, A.J.P., Ford, R.M., Keenan, R.J., Larson, A.M.: Learning through practice? Learning from the REDD+ demonstration project, Kalimantan forests and climate partnership (KFCP) in Indonesia. Land Use Policy **91**, 104285 (2020). https://doi.org/10.1016/j.landusepol.2019.104285

16. Ansell, C., Gash, A.: Collaborative governance in theory and practice **18**(4) (2016). https://doi.org/10.1093/jopart/mum032

17. Dauvergne, P.: Is the power of brand-focused activism rising? The case of tropical deforestation. J. Environ. Dev. **26**(2), 135–155 (Apr.2017). https://doi.org/10.1177/107049651770 1249

18. Enrici, A.M., Hubacek, K.: Challenges for REDD+ in Indonesia: a case study of three project sites. Ecol. Soc. **23**(2) (2018). https://doi.org/10.5751/ES-09805-230207

19. Acheampong, M., Yu, Q., Enomah, L.D., Anchang, J., Eduful, M.: Land use/cover change in Ghana's oil city: Assessing the impact of neoliberal economic policies and implications for sustainable fevelopment goal number one – a remote sensing and GIS approach. Land Use Policy **73**, 373–384 (2018). https://doi.org/10.1016/j.landusepol.2018.02.019

20. Gao, Y., Skutsch, M., Paneque-Gálvez, J., Ghilardi, A.: Remote sensing of forest degradation: a review. Environ. Res. Lett. **15**(10) (2020). https://doi.org/10.1088/1748-9326/abaad7

21. Dainelli, R., Toscano, P., Di Gennaro, S.F., Matese, A.: Recent advances in unmanned aerial vehicle forest remote sensing—a systematic review. Part I: a general framework. Forests **12**(3) (2021). https://doi.org/10.3390/f12030327

22. Kalantar, B., Ueda, N., Idrees, M.O., Janizadeh, S., Ahmadi, K., Shabani, F.: Forest fire susceptibility prediction based on machine learning models with resampling algorithms on remote sensing data. Remote Sens. **12**(22), 1–24 (2020). https://doi.org/10.3390/rs12223682

23. Ferencz, C., et al.: Crop yield estimation by satellite remote sensing. Int. J. Remote Sens. **25**(20), 4113–4149 (2004). https://doi.org/10.1080/01431160410001698870

Industry 5.0: Intelligent Sensor Based Autonomous Control System for HVAC Systems in Chemical Fiber Factory

Jerry Chen[1]([✉]), Rick Chang[2], Bon Peng[2], Willie Liu[2], and Jiann-Shing Shieh[1]

[1] Department of Mechanical Engineering, Yuan Ze University, Taoyuan 32003, Taiwan
s1088701@mail.yzu.edu.tw
[2] Far Eastern Fibertech Company, Ltd., Taoyuan 32853, Taiwan

Abstract. This work presents a human-machine integration approach, which is an autonomous control system that integrates the traditional expert-oriented strategy and intelligent sensor based data-driven strategy. This system offers effective solutions that are able to further improve the energy efficiency and decrease the energy consumption of heating, ventilation and air-conditioning (HVAC) system.

In previous study, it concludes that energy efficient HVAC systems could be obtained by making strategic use and well-structured combination of the existing air conditioning technologies. However, HVAC also have intricate and complex structures that consist of air handler, terminal unit, duct system, compressor, thermostat, etc. Traditionally, the well-tuned proportional-integral-derivative (PID) controller could have well performance around normal working points but its tolerance to variations of process parameter would be seriously affected when the uncertainty is introduced to the environment due to short/long term weather changes from outdoors or events/activities happens indoors. The autonomous system is a novel approach that aims to include all three characteristics of Industry 5.0 (i.e., sustainability, resilience and human-centricity). The system integrated commercialize wind sensor as data collection set which are being widely deploy throughout the HVAC environment. By accessing the detail wind flow data in the HVAC environment, a control model could be used to optimize the air handling unit (AHU) output according to the real-time environment, which enhance the performance on energy conservation.

Keywords: Autonomous Control System · Heating · Ventilation and Air-conditioning (HVAC) · Proportional-Integral-Derivative (PID) · Wind Sensor

1 Introduction

The heating, ventilation air conditioning (HVAC) system is widely studied and used in buildings. The performance of the HVAC greatly relying on good control strategy [1] and sensors [2, 3]. The HVAC unit is responsible for air heating and cooling in the building, and ventilation for air exchanging outdoor. This research aims to develop a data collection system that constantly measures the changes in wind duct (e.g., wind velocity, temperature) to build an autonomous control system over HAVC system which allows it to predict and control the environment under uncertainty.

© The Author(s), under exclusive license to Springer Nature Switzerland AG 2023
C. Stephanidis et al. (Eds.): HCII 2023, CCIS 1835, pp. 449–453, 2023.
https://doi.org/10.1007/978-3-031-36001-5_57

2 Method

To measure the changes in HVAC, a data collection unit is needed. The data collection unit helps to deploy sensors faster. Each data collection unit has at least three components: fixing mechanism, sensor and micro-processor. The data collection unit is placed at the exact point where system information is required; such places could be inside the wind duct or air outlet. The fixing mechanism is where the sensor being installed and wires for data communication and power supply being placed (see Fig. 1).

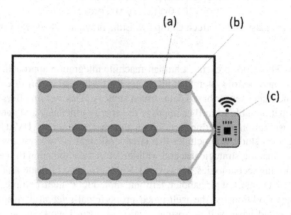

Fig. 1. An example of data collection unit; (a) fixing mechanism; (b) sensor; (c)microprocessor

3 Result

Each placement of the data collection unit is selected carefully according to the expert on site to increase the efficiency of sensor deployment (see Fig. 2). The data collection system is currently put under the endurance test and the protection for data collecting unit would be improved afterward to enhance its longevity. Due to the hazardous of the applied environment, the PCB is coated with epoxy for basic protection from corrosion (see Fig. 3).

Each places for sensor deployment may requires slightly different fixing mechanism. Currently, two kinds of fixing mechanism are designed and deployed for places like wind duct or air outlet individually (see Fig. 4).

The data flow of the above data collection unit is as followed (see Fig. 5). I^2C protocol is used for microprocessor to collect the data from multiple sensors. After retained the data from sensor, the microprocessor would transmit the data package in MQTT to the MQTT broker. Then a self-developed dashboard would subscribe the data from the MQTT broker to display the real-time data. And the data would also be sent to database with the use of node-red platform for historical data review (see Fig. 6).

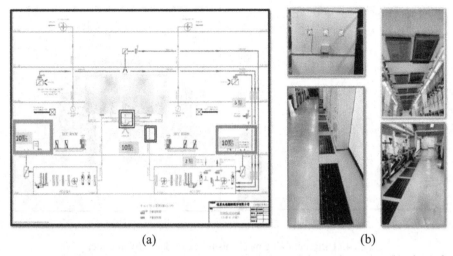

(a)   (b)

Fig. 2. Illustration of sensor deployment: (a) general view of the environment; (b) places for sensor deployment

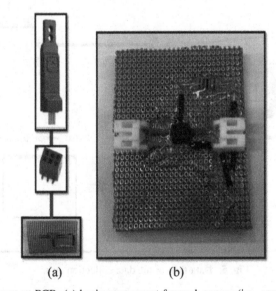

(a)   (b)

Fig. 3. Wind sensor on PCB: (a) basic component for each sensor (i.e., sensor, mount, circuit); (b) the PCB coated with epoxy for corrosion protection

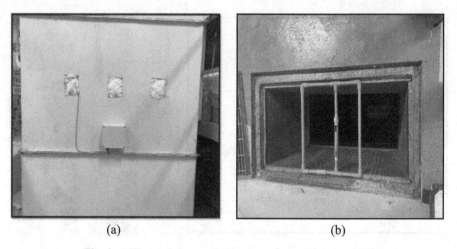

Fig. 4. Different fixing mechanism: (a) air duct; (b) air outlet

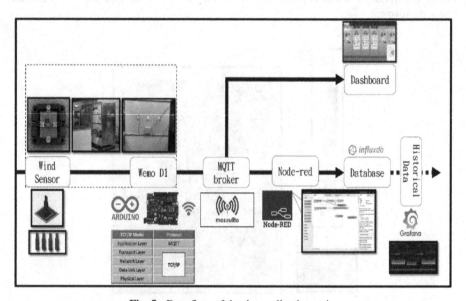

Fig. 5. Data flow of the data collection unit.

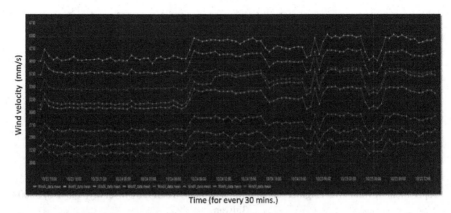

Fig. 6. Wind velocities collected from different data collection unit

4 Conclusion

This research is the first stage of developing an autonomous control system. Customized sensor fixing mechanism is used to optimize the cost efficiency on selected sensor placement in order to further improve the efficiency during the sensor deployment. By developing the data collection system, it allows the parameter of HVAC being studied and modeled for future research.

References

1. Gholamzadehmir, M., Del Pero, C., Buffa, S., Fedrizzi, R., Aste, N.: Adaptive-predictive control strategy for HVAC systems in smart buildings – a review. Sustain. Cities Soc. **63** (2020)
2. Bae, Y., et al.: Sensor impacts on building and HVAC controls: a critical review for building energy performance. Adv. Appl. Energy **4**(19) (2021)
3. Elnour, M., Meskin, N., Al-Naemi, M. Sensor data validation and fault diagnosis using auto-associative neural network for HVAC systems. J. Build. Eng. **27** (2020)

Autonomous System with Cyber-Physical Integrating Features on Public Utility of Chemical Fiber Factory

Jerry Chen[1(✉)], Jiann-Shing Shieh[1], Chi-Yuan Lee[1], Chuan-Jun Su[2], Yun-Chia Liang[2], and Tien-Lung Sun[2]

[1] Department of Mechanical Engineering, Yuan Ze University, Taoyuan 32003, Taiwan
s1088701@mail.yzu.edu.tw, jsshieh@saturn.yzu.edu.tw
[2] Department of Industrial Engineering and Management, Yuan Ze University, Taoyuan 32003, Taiwan

Abstract. This research develops an autonomous system with cyber-physical integrating features on public utility that has potential to stand uncertainty and provide both resilience and sustainability. Funded by National Science and Technology Council (Taiwan) which are promoting collaboration between academic and industry, this research is enabled to transplant the research result on chemical fiber factory. By working with the experts on site, the autonomous system takes the human-centric approach to solve the need of the industry. The developed system collects machine data on public utility (i.e., heating, ventilation and air-conditioning (HVAC), air handling unit (AHU), chiller, boiler, cooling tower and solar powered street light) with both self-made sensor and commercialized sensor, and display them on a panoramic view monitoring system in real-time. The system uses AI approach to model and control energy consumption of the public utility while utilizing hyperparameter optimization features to decrease the model training time cost. Finally, the workers' safety is also insured by analyzing the movement of workers on site and it would set off alarm if any potentially dangerous behavior was detected.

In the early stage of the project, each of the techniques above was developed separately and focused on only part of the public utility; each technique will be integrated afterward. For example, the data collection from self-made sensor and commercialized sensor are tested in HVAC system. Based on the existing solar panel data, hyperparameter optimization is being studied. The worker safety detection is used for indoor closed-circuit television (CCTV) setup around the AHU, air duct and the surrounding of production line. This paper presents the main structure of this autonomous system and general view of each technique.

Keywords: Autonomous System · Cyber-Physical Integration · Hyperparameter Optimization · Fault Detection

C. Stephanidis et al. (Eds.): HCII 2023, CCIS 1835, pp. 454–460, 2023.
https://doi.org/10.1007/978-3-031-36001-5_58

1   Introduction

This integrated research consists of five subprojects. Subproject I develop the architecture of the autonomous intelligent control system [1]. In the early stage, the heating, ventilation air conditioning (HVAC) system of the factory was used as an application, and a corresponding data collecting system which contains collection of data from both wind velocities inside the air duct and the air handling unit (AHU). The data collected by the system would be further used in the industrial system and stored in the database. Subproject II is focused on improving and developing a new all-in-one wind sensor. Validation and calibration of the self-made wireless wind sensor are done by comparing it with the commercial sensor respect to the specification and performance. The self-made wind sensor is produced by the process of micro-electro-mechanical systems (MEMS) and its package is designed to meet the requirement of the application. The subproject III has been built an industrial system that displaying the 360 panoramic images of the facilities on site. Ten kinds of facilities and its relevant device have completed the shooting of 360 panoramic images, with a total of 135 photography (including 5 aerial photography). After the camera shooting is completed, a panoramic viewing system will be built, and it is also an industrial real-time monitoring system which obtained the real-time data of the utility on site. Subproject IV is focused on hyperparameter optimization research. Through steps of data collection, data cleaning, feature selection, machine learning model selection, hyperparameter optimization, model and optimization parameter optimization suggestions, the research has adopted virus optimization algorithm (VOA) as the approach for optimizing the hyperparameters of various machine learning methods. The evaluation of such VOA on various machine learning is made. And data from the solar power generation system was used as the model input for controlling switch of the street light system of cooperated factory. Finally, subproject V is studying the use of Kinects-400 pre-trained SlowFast neural network for action recognition. The purpose of the model is to detect abnormal movements of the workers while operating the machinery. Furthermore, an interactive and cost-efficient platform was also adopted to further improve the level of safety/discipline of workers.

2   Project Approach

2.1   Subproject I

Developing a data collection system for wind sensors in forms of data collection units to reduce deployment costs. Every locations of sensor placement are selected by expert on site, and customized fixing mechanism for sensor is used to optimize the deployment and enhance the endurance of data collection unit.

2.2   Subproject II

Using MEMS techniques to developed a three-in-one sensor which could measure flow rate [2], temperature [3], and humidity [4] in a single set of sensors. The self-made sensor provides a higher cost-performance ratio and better endurance that are customized to the industry environment on site.

2.3 Subproject III

Subproject III constructs a self-made panoramic viewing system [5]. In this system, the data points are displayed on corresponding places to the actual position. This kind of technique gives a comprehensive general understanding of the meaning and easy-to-use features to the user. The system is a virtual representation of the applied factory.

2.4 Subproject IV

This subproject aims to develop a hyperparameter optimization algorithm [6] to improve model result on public utility. By using the hyperparameter optimization, it produces a better result on the output model while greatly reduce the training time. In the early stage, models of classification (i.e., Random Forest, Adaptive Boosting (AdaBoost), neural-like network, support vector machine (SVM), etc.) in supervised learning would be used to evaluate the hyperparameter optimization.

2.5 Subproject V

Subproject V studies the use of Kinects-400 pre-trained SlowFast neural network for action recognition [7]. Due to workers' problems especially at night, it is easy to make a mistake or not follow the normal procedures. Therefore, this subproject is tried to build a model to detect abnormal movements of the workers while operating the machinery. Furthermore, the performance evaluation would be demonstrated in a computer generated animation via metaverse techniques.

3 Result

3.1 Subproject I

The data collection system is already online and under the endurance test. The basic data collection unit includes fixing mechanism, sensor and microprocessors. The microprocessors use I2C protocol to acquire data from multiple sensor and use MQTT to publish data to the storage unit and dashboard. (see Fig. 1). Data regarding to Air Handling Unit (AHU), air duct and air outlet, and indoor pressure difference would be used to build process model and control model (see Fig. 2).

3.2 Subproject II

This research has developed a new three-in-one wind sensor (i.e., air flow, temperature, humidity). Validation and calibration of the self-made wireless wind sensor are done by comparing it with the commercial sensor respect to the specification and performance (see Fig. 3). The self-made wind sensor is produced by the process of micro-electro-mechanical systems (MEMS) and its package is designed to meet the requirement of the application.

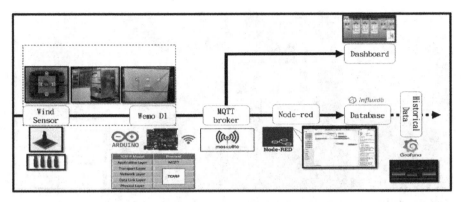

Fig. 1. Data flow of the data collection system

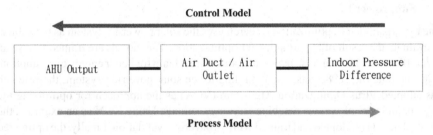

Fig. 2. Progression of building process model and control model

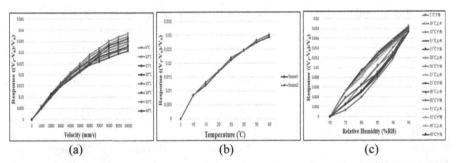

Fig. 3. Calibration of self-made three-in-one wind sensor: (a) Velocity; (b) Temperature; (c) Relative Humidity

3.3 Subproject III

The sub-project 3 has built an industrial system that allow users to experience the 360 panoramic view of the facilities. The information of each machines and equipment would be display in real time. Total up to 135 places/scenes and 563 data points that are ready for user to interact with and could be used for data monitoring (see Fig. 4.).

Fig. 4. Example scene from the 360 panoramic view industrial monitoring system.

3.4 Subproject IV

The hyperparameter optimization research uses the solar powering system as the subject to evaluate the result of hyperparameter optimization. The models are trained to give an on/off (0 for off; 1 for on) instruction to control street lamp for better energy consumption. With the total of 26,986 sets data regarding to the solar powering system, the research has adopted Virus Optimization Algorithm (VOA) as the approach for optimizing the hyperparameters of various machine learning methods. Using KNN as an example, the whole data sets is adopted and trained with 5-fold cross-validation. Finally, the optimized hyperparameters for KNN is given in Table 1.

Table 1. Optimized hyperparameter for KNN (use precision as objective function)

KNN hyperparameter	accuracy	recall	precision
Number of Neighbors, [1, 50]	50	12	50
Leaf Size, [1, 300]	72	22	1
Weights, (uniform, distance)	Uniform	Distance	Uniform
Algorithm, (ball_tree, kd_tree, brute, auto)	Auto	Brute	ball_tree
Metric, (Euclidean, Manhattan, Chebyshev)	Chebyshev	Manhattan	Chebyshev

3.5 Subproject V

This research utilized the pre-trained SlowFast neural network for action recognition to detect dangerous event when worker operates the machinery on site. Once a dangerous event is detected, it would call attention to the administrator to prevent incident. Furthermore, the worker that violate the safety protocol would be recorded in the performance evaluation. The result of performance evaluation would be demonstrated in a computer generated animation that are designed to initiate peer competition (see Fig. 5).

Fig. 5. The computer generated animation that reflect the performance evaluation

4 Conclusion

This poster presents a work of integrated project. Each subproject deliever essential technique for the autonomous system. The entire project involves sensor making using MEMS, sensor deployment with customized fixing mechanism, data collection, real time data display and historical data review for monitoring purpose. Furthermore, this research also applies the collected data to build process and control model while using hyperparameter optimization to enhance the efficiency. The operator on site is also being monitored for any violations of safety protocol; then, it induces performance evaluation to encourage worker to follow the standard operating procedure.

References

1. Chen, J., Abbod, M., Shieh, J.S.: Integrations between autonomous systems and modern computing techniques: a mini review. Sensors **19**(18) (2019)
2. Zhang, Q., et al.: Flexible ZnO thin film acoustic wave device for gas flow rate measurement. J. Micromech. Microeng. **30**, 19551265–19551268 (2020)
3. Shinoda, J., Mylonas, A., Kazanci, O.B., Tanabe, S., Olesen, B.W.: Differences in temperature measurement by commercial room temperature sensors: effects of room cooling system, loads, sensor type and position. Energy Build. **231**, 110630–110642 (2021)
4. Chen, W.J., Teng, T.P.: A compensation algorithm to reduce humidity ratio error due to asynchronous humidity and temperature sensor time constants. Build. Environ. **190**, 107555–107568 (2021)

5. Bucsai, S., Kučera. E., Haffner, O., Drahoš, P.: Control and monitoring of IoT devices using mixed reality developed by unity engine. In: Cybernetics & Informatics (K&I), pp. 1–8. IEEE, Czech Republic (2020)
6. Li, L., Jamieson, K., DeSalvo, G., Rostamizadeh, A., Talwalkar, A.: Hyperband: a novel bandit-based approach to hyperparameter optimization. J. Mach. Learn. Res. **18**, 1–52 (2018)
7. Suris, D., Liu, R., Vondrick, C.: Learning the predictability of the future. In: Proceedings of the IEEE/CVF Conference on Computer Vision and Pattern Recognition (CVPR), pp. 12607–12617 (2021)

Organic Wisdom of Returning to Environmental Ontology in the Context of Urban and Rural Construction: A Case Study of Chongqing, China

Xingyu Chen[1,3] and Hongtao Zhou[1,2(✉)]

[1] College of Design and Innovation, Tongji University, Shanghai 200092, China
hongtaozhoustudio@qq.com
[2] Shanghai International College of Design and Innovation, Tongji University, Shanghai 200092, China
[3] Sichuan Fine Arts Institute, Chongqing 401331, China

Abstract. In the process of accelerating urbanization in China, complex social problems have forced urban and rural design to adopt a broader response strategy, and design methods generally focus on the abstract category dominated by relational design, and lack of design research from the environmental ontology, resulting in a disconnect between design and physical space. Based on the ontology of urban and rural environment, this paper takes industrial site transformation, old city renewal and rural construction as examples, uses observations, fieldwork and case studies methods to observe and study the current situation of space, and takes field evolution, artificial construction and natural integration as the starting point, trying to explore the organic order contained in the environment, so as to put forward the possibility of organic design methods for solving complex social and technical system problems. It is found that the organic order in the environment has the characteristics of adaptability, coherence, coordination and symbiosis, which can better deal with many complex problems within the social system, provide basic basis and relevant ideas, form a more flexible and diversified design method, and help urban and rural transformation.

Keywords: Environment ontology · Organic · Urban and rural construction · industrial site transformation · old city renewal · rural construction

1 Introduction

In the process of accelerating urbanization in China, social civilization and emerging technologies develop rapidly, professional segmentation and cross-field collaboration become more frequent, emerging technologies such as intelligence and big data continue to expand, and the complexity of social resources, capital operation and management levels is getting higher and higher, resulting in continuous changes in the structure of social supply and demand, and the complexity and uncertainties faced in the development of urban and rural systems are far beyond imagination. In this context, The design

C. Stephanidis et al. (Eds.): HCII 2023, CCIS 1835, pp. 461–468, 2023.
https://doi.org/10.1007/978-3-031-36001-5_59

and study of the physical environment is often neglected. So, is there still value in the design study of the physical environment? What kind of ideas can it provide for solving complex urban and rural problems? Based on the above problems, this paper analyzes the hidden order laws in the spatial environment from an organic perspective, taking three representative "complex socio-technical systems" of industrial site transformation, old city renewal and rural construction as examples, and strives to provide basic support for environmental design research in the process of urban and rural construction.

2   The Concept of "Returning to the Environmental Ontology"

2.1   Relevant Theories of Urban and Rural Environmental Design

First of all, social design, as a more integrated, systematic and interconnected relationship network, is becoming an important way to deal with the huge and complex urban environmental problems. Among them, entrepreneurs, capital, enterprises and governments jointly pool resources, participate in management and optimize the ecology for this platform. A sharing and mutual benefit mechanism has been established among the participating members (Lou, 2018), Mutual cooperation and balanced development. At the same time, the category also focuses on the balance between public welfare and business, stimulating new neighborhood relationships in the community, rebuilding social integrity networks, and gradually forming a "warm and nearby" social support system for urban communities (Zhou, 2022). Accordingly, the focus of urban and rural environmental design has gradually shifted to the application of comprehensive collaboration, public participation, and social services.

Secondly, ecological and organic design methods are also commonly applied to the design update of urban and rural environments, and such research mainly explores the design of green ecology, recycling system and ecological network. The environmental design based on green ecology takes the garden as a space symbol and the medium of social governance, and actively guides users to participate in the production of landscape space (Liu&Kou, 2019). At the same time, researchers focus on the way of recycling and regeneration, and systematically integrate and optimize different types of resources in urban and rural environments. In addition, ecosystems are also becoming an emerging driving force for urban and rural environmental transformation, closely link urban and rural environments with natural ecology.

At the same time, Spatial sustainable design of urban and rural environments is also an important research direction, Architects Wang Shu, Zhang Ke, Li Yanbo and others advocate the use of micro-renewal, low-impact, multi-dimensional experience and respect for the historical inheritance of space to carry out urban and rural environment design, focusing on the development of "symbiotic renewal" as the connotation of spatial function replacement mode and perceptual experience shaping (Zhang&Zhang, 2016), as well as the strategic research of sustainable development at the spatial level and historical, social, economic and other cooperative governance (Li, 2019), Adaptive and sustainable strategies that focus on spatial efficiency.

2.2   Reflections on the Ontology of the Environment

In summary, "relational design" focusing on abstract categories is becoming a key design method to deal with complex urban and rural problems (Fig. 1), although there is a response to the huge and complex problems in the process of urban and rural iteration, but in the end, due to the lack of essential traceability of the material space environment, the research cannot accurately anchor the evolution process of the objective environment, resulting in a certain degree of disconnection between design and physical space.Therefore, the exploration of returning to the environmental ontology in urban and rural design will become extremely urgent and important.

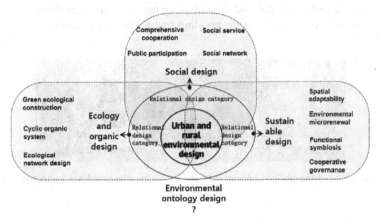

Fig. 1. Research on urban and rural environmental design in China led by "relational design"

3   Research Objects and Methods

Research object: In this paper, Chongqing, was selected as the research object. Chongqing, once a base for heavy industry, has left hundreds of large factories idle as the economy has been transformed..At the same time, Chongqing focuses on the development of new urban areas, and the development of old cities has stagnated. In addition, as the only municipality directly under the central government in southwest China, Chongqing has a huge number of villages and complicated rural construction.

Research Methods: Based on the ontology of urban and rural environment, this paper uses observation methods, fieldwork and case studies to observe and analyze three representative types of urban and rural spaces in Chongqing, such as industrial site transformation, old city renewal and rural construction, in an attempt to sort out the internal evolution law of space, reveal the hidden internal organic order of industrial sites, old city communities and rural environments, and give relevant enlightenment to design methods based on this, so as to solve many complex urban and rural renewal problems. Support the design work and research of urban and rural reconstruction.

4 Exploration of Organics Based on Environmental Ontology

4.1 Spatial Evolution of Industrial Heritage

Spatial Environment Analysis

Taking the single site building of Chongqing Special Steel Mill as an example (Fig. 2), The main body of the factory building is made of reinforced concrete column network structure, steel sloped roof and red brick partition wall, and the wild plants in the factory area are ecologically luxuriant, and the building surface and landscape site have not been renovated at present.Surprisingly, time has taken the texture and aesthetics of this factory building to the extreme, and all kinds of textures, materials, ecology and naturally formed "traces" are imprinted on the building space without exception.

Fig. 2. Photo of the site of a special steel mill in Shapingba District, Chongqing, China

Organic Evolution and Natural Growth

The control and cohesion of nature is fully displayed in this ruin-like building, and presents a subtle aesthetic effect. The brick-filled window holes, the dark brown steel beams and columns, the earthy red walls with a concave and convex texture, and the gray water traces soaked through the exterior walls are just like paleontological fossils in the rock section of the archaeological site, imprinted with the traces of the era of industrial history, they are mixed with each other, fully interpreting the most authentic state of the special steel mill site. Behind this phenomenon is the organic order, Pallasmaa(2016) believes that in the experience of architecture, space, matter and time merge into a single dimension, become the basic essence of existence, and permeate our consciousness. Natural forces act on the surface, structure and shape of buildings, integrating the historical clues and memory aesthetics of industrial sites, and shaping a more poetic spatial experience through the re-creation of imagination.

Natural Organic as a Design Method

People continue to learn from nature and borrow natural abilities to transform, and the whole construction system is not concerned with the fixed eternity of human society, but with the constant evolution of natural relations (Wang, 2012). The accidental participation of nature and organic in industrial sites shows the perfect "debugging power", which can become an important reference for designers to participate in the transformation of industrial sites, this set of "abandonment design" design methods can completely retain the urban ruins and continue the natural growth of the ecosystem, in addition, it can meet the common participation and experience of diverse people, stimulate people's original memories and emotional resonance, further radiate the surrounding environment (Ciqikou Commercial Ancient Town), and promote the coordinated development of the regional economy.

4.2 Man-Made Construction in the Old City Community

Spatial Pattern Analysis

There are a large number of factory unit communities within the urban area of Chongqing, Manzini(2018) proposed that residents are not only users of the city, but also co-designers and co-producers.Through the investigation of the spatial environment of Chongqing Daojiao community, it is found that the "mixed ecology" of traces of human activities can be seen everywhere, such as: self-built space, corner garden, simple tables and stools, storage space, etc. (Fig. 3), interestingly, these very life-oriented "illegal self-made" have almost no pre-planning, in which a variety of material choices, random construction processes and simple construction methods present a complex, chaotic but close to life old city community appearance in the residents' unconscious daily behavior.

Figure 3-1 Self-built space of Daojiao Community, Chongqing, China   Figure 3-2 Corner Garden of Daojiao Community, Chongqing, China   Figure 3-3 Simple table and stool in Daojiao Community, Chongqing, China   Figure 3-4 Storage space of Daojiao Community in Chongqing, China

Fig. 3. Anthropogenic evolution in the Daojiao community in Chongqing, China

Artificially Constructed Logic

Demand-Based Building Activities. The meaning of a thing's existence lies first of all in its usefulness. The simple objects flexibly built fully meet the functional demands of community residents for social communication and daily life, The demand-based construction activities continuously enrich the community space environment, and con-tinue the vital signs of the old community in a slow and suitable evolutionary way, thus shaping a unique "community aesthetics".

Association-Based Chain Reactions. The community space constructed by the autonomous behavior of the inhabitants is intertwined to form a coherent, complex structure, which Gehl(2002) describes as a 'chained' social activity, a dynamic urban environment that in most cases stems from these chain reactions based on necessity and spontaneous activity, in which the elements reinforce each other and ferment together, like notes, communicating and connecting with each other, creating resonant melodies. This is the spatial order that people, space, and time condition each other and interact to build together, fully demonstrating the creativity, imagination and unpredictable vitality created by people in the community environment.

Order-Based Construction Methods. Behind the seemingly random mix-and-match combinations, there are a large number of modular construction and Bricolage with "design logic". Residents will skillfully use scale scaling, morphological evolution, and interchange assembly to systematically organize modular units, at the same time, further enhance the diversity, event, and interest of community life through the mixing of objects at hand and the transformation of the conceptual meaning of objects.

The Method of Renewing Old Cities Inspired by Man-Made Organics

The man-made evolved organic order is anchored in the old city like a "patch", becoming an important medium for regulating the complex problems of many cities. The design method based on the essence of life will realize the sustainable development of the transformation of the old city, make up for the rupture between man and the environment caused by the rapid development of economy and technology, build the relationship between designers, users and the spatial environment, and avoid the collapse of the original environment due to the strong intervention of design and the urbanization process. As Manzini(2018) said, the city is perceived, used and transformed by the inhabitants who live in it, and the city belongs to the people and the community.

4.3   The Natural Integration of the Village Environment

Analysis of the Rural Environment

The rural living environment in Chongqing, which has been developed on the basis of agricultural civilization and natural ecology, has always followed the mysterious and ingenious way of construction, which is generally orderly, partially disorderly, its incomplete and imperfect, reflecting the ingenious reproduction of the chaos of the village world, which is an unexplainable and difficult to copy conceptual method under modern scientific concepts, but it seems that nature itself does not force uniformity, and the village itself is a space for association(jin, 2014), based on the perspective of traditional architecture and design. It may be difficult to fully understand the structure and construction logic of the village.

The Construction Logic of the Village Environment

Spirituality, Beliefs and Rituals. In Liuyin Town, Chongqing, for example, a 43kilometer-long man-made canal runs through the countryside. The canal, which has lost its irrigation function, is shaped like a "snake bone" giant, lying on the top of a rural mountain, subtly stitching nature, life and faith, and becoming an important mythological totem and spiritual protection for the locals. At the same time, the many stone statues of land gods, miniature temples and mountain gods scattered on both sides of the canal and between the arches (Figure 4) have become symbols of daily remembrance and blessing for the villagers. It can be seen that the evolution of villages is just another system parallel to science, and concrete sciences such as myths and rituals are only different from the results achieved by natural science, and the authenticity of their results has not diminished, and they were confirmed ten thousand years ago and will for-ever be the basis of our civilization (Strauss, 2006).

Figure 4-1 Dongsheng Canal, Liuyin Town, Chongqing   Figure 4-2 Land god, mountain god statue, micro temple placed along the Dongsheng canal

Fig. 4. Dongsheng Canal and its surrounding land gods, mountain gods, miniature temples in Liuyin Town, Chongqing, China

Fig. 5. The wall of a house and Bamboo bush bonsai in Liuyin Town, Chongqing, China

The Presentation of Creation and Imagination. The construction of the living environment in Liuyin Town is saturated with a lot of boundless imagination, and there is a precise and reasonable structural order in the seemingly random localized masonry.Taking wall construction as an example, craftsmen use stone blocks of different sizes to construct the texture of porous breathing on the wall, while the walls of individual houses will use a mix of gravel, rammed earth, gray brick and bamboo to form a rich and wonderful visual experience. And at the same time, the bamboo forest outside each house is enclosed by large and small stone walls by residents, and people and animals can enter and exit freely, like a wild bamboo courtyard, or like a giant bonsai that has been neglected, full of conjecture and poetry (Fig. 5).

Natural and Organic Co-ordination. The village environment is a network of life characteristics woven by many complex relationships. Nature connects ecosystem elements such as mountains, streams, flowers, insects, birds and beasts, human elements such as theaters, temples, and cottages, as well as social elements such as farming and ethical beliefs through strong coordination forces. The sequences within the village depend on each other, becoming a state of mutual "symbiosis".

An Organic Design Approach Inspired by Natural Systems
It is difficult to maintain the sustainable development of the rural environment with a single industry, design and technology implantation, and natural systems can consider all design relationships into a unified relationship, thereby avoiding the rupture of the

rural context and allowing the rural "life" to survive. As Strauss(2009) said, "To smell the depths of a daffodil, the fragrance of which may hide more knowledge than all our books combined."

5 Conclusion

This study summarizes a set of construction logic derived from environmental ontology, Reproduce the perceptual construction, structural logic cognition and regional continuation of the spatial environment ontology in the process of urban and rural iteratives. It fully highlights the daily organic characteristics and life conditions of urban and rural environments. Although the organic order implied in the environment is not the design itself, its strong coordination, unifying force and adaptability can be transformed into the elements supporting the design, And reverse support and derive the application of many "relationship design" in urban and rural transformation, At the same time, it can also provide corresponding enlightenment and reference for urban and rural transformation, better deal with many complex problems within the urban and rural environment and social system, promote mutual cooperation, influence, constraint and transformation between various elements, and form a more flexible and diversified design method to help China's urban and rural construction.

References

Lou, Y.Q.: NICE 2035: an experiment of design driven community-supported social innovation. ZhuangShi **5**, 34–39 (2018)

Zhou, Z.S.: Community as a method: building a collaborative platform for urban-rural integration with social design. ZhuangShi **3**, 37–43 (2022)

Liu, Y.L., Kou, H.Y.: Study on the strategy of micro-renewal and micro-governance by public participatory of shanghai community Garden. Chin. Landsc. Architect. **12**, 5–11 (2019)

Zhang, K., Zhang, Y.F.: Symbiotic renewal "MicroYuan'er" by ZAO/standardarchitecture. Times+Architecture **4**, 80–87 (2016)

LI, Y.B.: Siming experiment: the urban, architectural and social perspectives in the case of a historical community redevelopment in Shanghai. Architect. J. **02**, 1–6 (2019)

Pallasmaa,J.: The Eyes of the Skin: Architecture and the Senses, pp.86. China Architecture & Building Press, Beijing (2016)

Wang, S.: We are in need of reentering a nature philosophy. World Architect. **5**, 20–21 (2012)

Manzini, E.: The making of the collaborative city: social innovation and design for city making. ZhuangShi **05**, 12–14 (2018)

Gehl,J.: Life Between Buildings, pp.15. China Architecture & Building Press, Beijing (2002)

Manzini,E., Thorpe, A.: Weaving people and places: art and design for resilient communities. She Ji: J. Des. Econ. Innov. **4**(1), 1–10 (2018)

Jin, Q.Y.: A gaze and a glance. Architect. J. **01**, 18–29 (2014)

Levi-Strauss,C.: The Savage Mind, pp.17. China Renmin University Press, Beijing (2006)

Levi-Strauss,C.: Tristes Tropiques, pp.543. China Renmin University Press, Beijing (2009)

Energy Harvesting Generator
for Human-Computer Interaction

Charisma Clarke[1] ⓘ, Edwar Romero-Ramirez[1](✉) ⓘ, and Kumar L. Vanga[2] ⓘ

[1] Florida Polytechnic University, Lakeland, FL 33805, USA
eromeroramirez@floridapoly.edu
[2] IMS Nanofabrication LLC, Santa Clara, CA 95054, USA

Abstract. Flexible sensors are relevant tools for progress assessment and rehabilitation in healthcare; however, traditional medical equipment is usually tethered to machines that require dedicated personnel. The development of newer materials is making some flexible sensors accessible. Additive manufacturing, better known as 3D printing, is helping to lower the barrier to building such systems with specialized filaments. This makes it possible to design human-computer interaction approaches outside healthcare environments. Still, such systems must be powered by the grid or battery sources. Power consumption tends to be related to physical size, and thanks to the miniaturization of electronics, the trend moves towards lower power requirements. This work explores the power requirements of flexible 3D-printed sensors to evaluate the possibility of employing energy generators to complement, reduce, or eliminate batteries. A sensor was manufactured using an electrically conductive flexible filament and was found to require up to 50 μW. An energy generator composed of two-coil layers and a permanent magnet rotor was designed and tested for power generation. Voltages up to 1 V and power generation up to 12 mW were measured when evaluating the design at a constant speed. Further work needs to be developed to optimize the generator for portable applications.

Keywords: Energy Generation · Flexible Sensor · Additive Manufacturing

1 Introduction

Motion and force sensing capabilities are excellent tools for assessment and rehabilitation in healthcare environments. However, they are mostly limited to specialized equipment requiring dedicated technicians and confined to a few locations. On the other hand, developing flexible sensors for motion and force measurement has reduced costs while allowing accessibility to similar technologies for home use [1]. Many are tethered to large equipment or made portable to be less intrusive but are not designed to be used for extended periods due to power source limitations. In contrast, continuous monitoring and wireless capabilities are highly desirable [2]. Although not exclusively tied to healthcare environments, human-computer interaction demands sensing capabilities from portable electronic devices. Powering these portable electronic devices sometimes

© The Author(s), under exclusive license to Springer Nature Switzerland AG 2023
C. Stephanidis et al. (Eds.): HCII 2023, CCIS 1835, pp. 469–474, 2023.
https://doi.org/10.1007/978-3-031-36001-5_60

is a challenge depending on the energy source. This becomes especially true with the increasing demand for wireless sensor networks with smart processing capabilities. The ever-increasing miniaturization of electronics reduces the energy requirements making it possible to consider energy harvesting technologies to complement or even replace batteries for extended operation. Solar, radiofrequency signals, temperature gradients, and kinetic energy are among the most popular sources to scavenge energy for such endeavors [3, 4]. The utilization of these sources for energy scavenging has been well documented for machine condition monitoring where the physical size of devices has never been a limitation. This paper explores the technology of energy harvesting and its applications toward its use for human-computer interaction for flexible sensors [1, 5–12].

To evaluate energy generation, additive manufacturing of flexible sensors for human-computer interaction was selected as test case in this work [1, 5, 6]. Since stretchable sensors in the form of strain gauges are found often in many fields to serve as force or motion sensors for monitoring systems for human motion, safety, evaluation, or control purposes [1, 2, 5–12], they are chosen as the focus of this study. With advancements in additive manufacturing technologies, it is possible to manufacture strain gauges using composites in order to take advantage of their unique material properties not found in traditional strain gauges. For broad applications in wearable electronics and soft robotics, thermoplastic materials designed for use in additive manufacturing applications are being studied and modified to enhance desirable properties such as elasticity or electrical conductivity [5–12]. Among these materials are various thermoplastic polyurethane (TPU), infused with graphene, carbon nanotubes, or metal nanowires. A traditional metal-based foil-type strain gauge uses the increase in electrical resistance when subjected to a tensile load to determine the strain whereas for a flexible conductive filament, the strain is determined by the reduction in its electrical resistance when subjected to loading. Integrating sensors into a 3D-printed structure can enable the development of embedded force sensors [1]. Within the several available materials, electrically conductive TPU can be found commercially with properties that make it practical for strain sensor applications as reported in the literature [5, 12].

The energy generation effort will be evaluated using an axial flux permanent magnet generator with PCB windings due to the thin profiles for portable applications [13]. The design of these generators require a stator and a rotor [13]. Typically, the rotor is a disk with permanent magnets and the stator is composed of stacked coil windings. A custom design of the generator is presented in this work for energy evaluation.

2 Methodology

A coreless axial flux permanent magnet generator for portable applications [13] was selected to evaluate the energy generated that is needed to power a stretchable sensor. The sensor was fabricated using additive manufacturing (Prusa MK3S+) employing flexible TPU filament and electrically conductive TPU (PI-ETPU 95-250 Carbon Black), as documented [5]. The dimensions of the proposed strain gauge are 20 mm x 50 mm x 0.4 mm, with the sensing element (PI-ETPU) having a linewidth of 1 mm and a thickness of 0.4 mm. Detailed dimensions are shown in Fig. 1. The samples were manufactured using

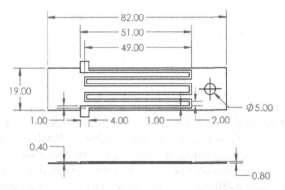

Fig. 1. Geometry of the additively manufactured strain gauge for testing.

the print settings illustrated in Table 1 for 100% infill. The first test studies show the resistance of the sensor changes when subjected to different loads simulating bending. The second experiment subjected the sensor to stretching along the length to observe the change in resistance. The sensor was subjected to bending by varying the applied load from 0 to 50 grams in 10 grams increments. To examine how the sensor's resistance changed with stretching, the sensor was loaded from 0 grams to 2000 grams, and the resistance was recorded after two minutes of loading.

Table 1. 3D printing parameters

Parameter	Value
Infill	100%
Number of shells	2
Layer height	0.2 mm
Extruder temperature	235 °C
Build plate temperature	50 °C
Perimeter speed	40 mm/s
Infill speed	80 mm/s
Raster angle	± 45°
Filament diameter	1.75 mm
Nozzle diameter	0.4 mm

The generator winding was manufactured by photolithography technique, producing features as small as 0.2 mm. This process requires depositing a photoresist on a copper-clad substrate to transfer a pattern using UV light. Once the pattern is created, chemical etching removes the exposed copper to leave the windings. Two layers of these windings were used for experimental evaluation to create the stator design (8 windings, 29 Ω resistance, 34 mm external diameter, 17 mm internal diameter). Sixteen neodymium magnets

(6 x 3 x 2 mm, grade N50) were embedded in a rotor manufactured by stereolithography to complete the experimental setup.

3   Results

The evaluation was completed for the sensor and generator separately to estimate the performance. Experimental results show that the custom-made flexible sensor is useful as a strain gauge. The filament tests performed show predictable elongation over five samples with an average deviation of 6.30% over five data points. Curves of $\Delta R/R$ vs. strain show the same behavior recorded by [10]. Results from loading to simulate bending show decreasing resistance for greater load with an average deviation of 3.47%. Stretching tests show decreasing resistance over multiple runs with an average deviation of 3.53%. Five different test runs were performed to characterize the sensor behavior. This is presented in Fig. 2 for bending and stretching under loading. Preliminary results presented show good repeatability by the sensor when subjected to stretching loads. The resistance follows a decreasing trend with an increased loading with an average deviation of around 3.5% for stretching and bending. The proposed sensor can be evaluated to visualize spatial motion when compared to other strain gauge solutions. Experimental results for the sensor produced resistance values with an average of 0.5 MΩ while using a voltage divider with a supply voltage of 5 V. This leads to power requirements on the order of 50 μW for the sensor operation.

The preliminary generator consisting of two windings and a single rotor was tested at a constant speed to determine the energy generation, as presented in Fig. 3. The generator was tested with multiple loads (7 Ω to 144 Ω) in order to evaluate the maximum power generation experimentally. The testing equipment was set to the lowest speed setting (9,400 RPM), and it was determined that higher power output was observed when the coil resistance matched the external load at 29 Ω, producing 12 mW of power. This is indicated in Fig. 4. A previous study suggests power generation over 50 μW can be obtained from the human body at the ankle and knee while walking, whereas, the elbow and shoulder can provide similar amounts during running [14]. Then, improved designs can provide equivalent power generation from the tested device.

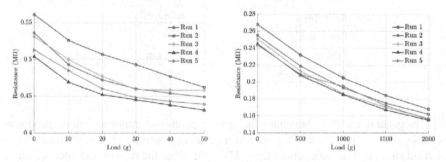

Fig. 2. Resistance vs. load for custom sensor: Bending (left) and stretching (right).

Fig. 3. Generator design: Coil design (left) and testing at constant speed (right).

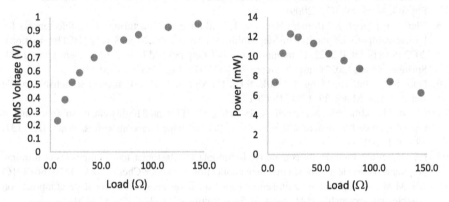

Fig. 4. Results at constant speed: Induce voltage (left) and generated power (right).

4 Conclusion

This paper discusses the design of a portable generator to evaluate the energy production capabilities to power sensors for human-computer interaction. An additively manufactured flexible sensor that uses a TPU base and a conductive PI-ETPU filament as the sensing element was used to test the power requirements. Preliminary results show good sensor repeatability when subjected to stretching loads. The resistance follows a decreasing trend with greater loading with an average deviation of around 3.5% for stretching and bending. These findings demonstrate that an additively manufactured strain gauge shows promise and that the proposed sensor can be evaluated to study spatial motion. The power consumption of the sensor was determined to be on the order of 50 μW. On the other hand, the energy generator presented consists of a two-layer winding and a single permanent magnet rotor for a coreless design. Experimental results show it can provide up to 12 mW of continuous power if connected to a constant rotational source. This suggests that a fraction of rotational speed can provide enough power for the stretchable sensor presented. The proposed generator design is still under development for an optimized design, where further testing is required under regular body motion to evaluate the performance on everyday tasks such as walking or during office work.

References

1. Wolterink, G., Sanders, R., Beijnum, B.J., Veltink, P., Krijnen, G.: A 3D-printed soft fingertip sensor for providing information about normal and shear components of interaction forces. Sensors **21**, 4271 (2021)
2. Bergmayr, T., Winklberger, M., Kralovec, C., Schagerl, M.: Structural health monitoring of aerospace sandwich structures via strain measurements along zero-strain trajectories. Eng. Fail. Anal. **126**, 105454 (2021)
3. Tang, X., Wang, X., Cattley, R., Gu, F., Ball, A.D.: Energy harvesting technologies for achieving self-powered wireless sensor networks in machine condition monitoring: a review. Sensors **18**, 4113 (2018)
4. Romero, E., Warrington, R., Neuman, M.: Energy scavenging sources for biomedical sensors. Physiol. Meas. **30**, R35 (2009)
5. Clarke, C., Steel, K., Romero-Ramirez, E.: Additive manufacturing of flexible sensors for human-computer interaction. In: Stephanidis, C., Antona, M., Ntoa, S. (eds.) HCI International 2022 Posters. HCII 2022. Communications in Computer and Information Science, vol. 1581. Springer, Cham (2022). https://doi.org/10.1007/978-3-031-06388-6_35
6. Guo, S.Z., Qiu, K., Meng, F., Park, S.H., McAlpine, M.C.: 3D printed stretchable tactile sensors. Adv. Mater. **29**, 1701218 (2017)
7. Christ, J.F., Aliheidari, N., Ameli, A., Pötschke, P.: 3D printed highly elastic strain sensors of multiwalled carbon nanotube/thermoplastic polyurethane nanocomposites. Mater. Des. **131**, 394–401 (2017)
8. Liu, H., et al.: Electrically conductive thermoplastic elastomer nanocomposites at ultralow graphene loading levels for strain sensor applications. J. Mater. Chem. C **4**(1), 157–166 (2016)
9. Ali, M.M., et al.: Printed strain sensor based on silver nanowire/silver flake composite on flexible and stretchable TPU substrate. Sens. Actuators, A **274**, 109–115 (2018)
10. Wang, X., Sparkman, J., Gou, J.: Strain sensing of printed carbon nanotube sensors on polyurethane substrate with spray deposition modeling. Compos. Commun. **3**, 1–6 (2017)
11. Dong, W., Yang, L., Fortino, G.: Stretchable human machine interface based on smart glove embedded with PDMS-CB strain sensors. IEEE Sens. J. **20**(14), 8073–8081 (2020)
12. Al-Rubaiai, M., Tsuruta, R., Gandhi, U., Wang, C., Tan, X.: A 3D-printed stretchable strain sensor for wind sensing. Smart Mater. Struct. **28**(8), 084001 (2019)
13. Clarke, C., Romero-Ramirez, E., Kames, E., Soltani, S.: Coreless dual rotor axial flux permanent magnet generator for portable applications. In: PowerMEMS 2022, Salt Lake City, UT, USA, pp. 181-184 (2022)
14. Romero, E., Neuman, M.R., Warrington, R.O. Rotational energy harvester for body motion. In: MEMS 2011, Cancun, Mexico, pp. 1325–1328 (2011)

Web-Based Management for Internet of Things Ecosystems

Paraskevi Doulgeraki[1], Effie Karuzaki[1], Eirini Sykianaki[1], Nikolaos Partarakis[1(✉)],
Maria Bouhli[1], Stavroula Ntoa[1], and Constantine Stephanidis[1,2]

[1] Institute of Computer Science, Foundation for Research and Technology—Hellas (FORTH),
70013 Heraklion, Crete, Greece
{vdoulger,karuzaki,eirinisi,partarak,bouhli,stant,
cs}@ics.forth.gr

[2] Computer Science Department, School of Sciences & Engineering, University of Crete,
70013 Heraklion, Crete, Greece

Abstract. In this paper, we present a front-end User Interface for a secure Internet of Things platform that provides management features as a service on top of heterogeneous Internet of Things ecosystems. The proposed platform is capable of monitoring all the connected devices at various levels, such as remaining energy, uptime, network statistics, quality connection, routing protocol statistics, software bugs, maximum bandwidth, and communication delay.

Keywords: Internet of Things · Management as a service · Service based architectures · Sensor networks

1 Introduction

The Internet-of-Things (IoT) refers to the interconnection of hundreds of smart devices including sensors, smart mobile phones, home appliances, etc. IoT can support a large number of applications, such as environmental monitoring, e-health services, smart agriculture, etc. Its rapid development has led to the creation of various architectures with the contribution of research institutions, but also high-tech companies. This has contributed to their maturation and improvement, but it has also created serious technological fragmentation with isolated platforms that in many cases are incompatible both in terms of software and hardware.

Modern Information Technology (IT) platforms also include other more sophisticated devices, in terms of processing power and available memory, usually referred to as "Gateways", to hyper-connect smart devices to the supporting infrastructure responsible for storing and processing the collected data. Therefore, a modern IT platform includes a large number of heterogeneous hardware devices and software programs. The heterogeneity also extends to the network level, since it is common to use different technologies in different parts of the same platform (WiFi, Zigbee, etc.). Also, devices are often placed in difficult-to-reach locations, and as a result, in the event of a breakdown, it is laborious to locate and repair them. In addition, due to the overconcentration of

C. Stephanidis et al. (Eds.): HCII 2023, CCIS 1835, pp. 475–482, 2023.
https://doi.org/10.1007/978-3-031-36001-5_61

wireless devices, interference is often created which significantly affects the quality of communication.

IT platforms are often the target of successful cyberattacks due to insufficient protection, due to both the lack of knowledge of the relevant personnel and the low computing power of these devices, which make it impossible to use strong cryptographic algorithms [1–3].

Aiming to address the aforementioned challenges, the purpose of the EPOPTIS project [4] is to design, implement and evaluate an interoperable IT architecture that will offer "Management as a Service" to monitor all involved devices in an IoT ecosystem. This service consists of appropriate hardware and software to monitor parameters at various levels 1) remaining energy, 2) uptime, 3) network statistics (e.g. lost packets per protocol), 4) connection quality, 4) routing protocol statistics, 5) software bugs, 6) maximum bandwidth, 7) communication delay, etc.

This paper described the design and implementation of the frontend platform to visualize the devices connected to the IoT ecosystem and their data to present a comprehensive picture of the state of the network and devices. The platform enables monitoring and management using different technologies in a uniform and transparent way to the user.

2 Background and Related Work

2.1 Data Visualization

An integral part of an IoT management system is considered the capacity to sufficiently visualise the infrastructure data, states and alerts. In this context, the term data visualization refers to the representation of data using graphics, animation, 3D rendering, and other multimedia tools [5] to communicate the results of data analysis clearly and efficiently to end users [6]. It has multi-faceted benefits, as it can not only present a wide range of information concisely and understandably but also reveal correlations and patterns between data that are almost impossible to detect otherwise. Essentially, data visualization helps to "make sense" of data and allows the immediate and effective treatment of errors and malfunctions.

In the field of the Internet of Things (IoT), data concerns measurements taken from a large number of sensors and interconnected devices [7–9]. Visualizing them is extremely useful, as it helps to analyze and understand the data collected, which would otherwise have no meaning [10], especially given the endless flow of information collected by smart systems and sensors [11]. In addition, visualization is a cornerstone for IT management and supervision, as it enables the immediate identification of patterns that occur over long periods (e.g. temperature variation in an area) but also the immediate identification of the spatial and temporal points of origin of various malfunctions [12]. For example, through a map, it will be possible to spatially locate the IT points [13] where faults are detected, while through time-based visualizations it will be possible to locate the moment when a fault started.

2.2 Data Visualization for IoT Ecosystems

Visualization tools are instrumental in making IoT network management decisions, as they provide a visual analysis of the data retrieved from the network and highlight patterns that would otherwise remain hidden [7]. Many systems that promise data visualization have been developed and are available today. Among them, some systems support the immersive visualization of data [14] and IoT ecosystems [15]. From a more administrative perspective on the management of IoT ecosystems, several commercial and free systems have become available. For example, CloudRadar is a commercial system for monitoring an IT infrastructure, in which users can monitor data collected by web services [16]. It mainly aims to monitor the performance of these services through predefined metrics, such as the memory they occupy, the CPU load, etc. Another commercial program is Domotz [17], a service for monitoring and managing networks and devices, and notifying users when something does not work properly, enabling remote updates, backup, rebooting and configuring of these infrastructures and devices. One of the most popular commercial platforms for managing and visualizing data received from IT networks is IBM's Maximo platform [18]. Through this platform, the user can monitor the operation of the network, receive notifications when something goes wrong and perform some actions to solve any problems that arise. Google IoT Core [19], in combination with other services on the Google IOT platform, provides solutions related to the collection, processing, analysis and visualization of data resulting from connected IT. Apart from commercial platforms, there are also free ones, such as Freeboard [20], which provides a dashboard in which the user can define what data will be displayed while defining the position, size and title of each element of the dashboard as well as whether it needs one of the predefined display formats (e.g. chart). Contus [21], ThingSpeak [22], TheThings.io [23], and DataDog [24] are among the platforms focusing on data visualization.

2.3 Contribution of This Research Work

Our contribution is summarised as the provision of management as a service on top of heterogeneous IoT ecosystems. In this work, we design and implement a UI that plugs into a service-oriented API that in turn supports the interconnection with various IoT ecosystems through well-defined semantics. Thus, in this work, the heterogeneity of technologies and the plethora of IoT vertical implementations remains hidden under a unique UI layer. Thus, by leveraging existing standards and by supporting API-based integration of IoT ecosystems, this work proposes a platform front-end for basic but important IoT management operations. This is considered the main advantage of this work in conjunction with existing commercial systems and the implementation of this UI is the main contribution of this work.

3 System Overview

The platform supports 3 levels of access for users. These levels are: 'Visitor', 'IoT ecosystem administrator' and 'General administrator'. Visitors can view the devices connected to the respective ecosystem, their position within it as well as the measurements taken from the sensors. They have access to technical features of the ecosystem (e.g. the number of ports, network statistics, etc.) but cannot see potential failures or receive notifications about them.

IoT ecosystem administrators can monitor the state of their assigned ecosystems. In addition to visitors, they can see the status of the ecosystem as well as receive notifications about its smooth functioning and manage the gateways and devices connected to it through a graphical environment. This management includes: (a) editing the elements of an ecosystem (e.g. name, map, etc.) (b) importing/deleting sensors and gateways, (c) processing the technical characteristics of sensors and network gateways, such as name, IP address, communication and data security protocol, and (d) user management.

Their home screen with the control panel is divided into three zones (see Fig. 2). The first is the general information zone where the IoT ecosystem administrator can, in addition to visitors, see how many gateways are down, as well as the number of users who have access to the ecosystem. The second is the notification zone, in which IoT ecosystem administrators can see messages about the operation of the ecosystem at various levels, such as at the level of measurements taken from the sensors, at the network level (faults) and also at the device level (faults and software errors). Finally, the third zone at the base of the page is the monitoring zone of all the portals that belong to the ecosystem as well as the statistical data concerning its operation and the operation of the network. In this zone, the IoT ecosystem administrator can see the map showing the locations where the gateways of the ecosystem are placed. Figure 3 presents the dashboard of an ecosystem and analysis of different information panels.

General administrators have access to all the information of every IoT ecosystem as well as the functions that the IoT ecosystem administrators have, while in addition, they bear the responsibility of managing the platform as well as the users who benefit from the service offered by this system.

4   Implementation

For the design of the EPOPTIS platform interface for the visualization of the measurements collected by IoT ecosystems, an iterative design process was followed aiming to improve the user experience following expert-based evaluation [25–27]. The iterative design was conducted in the form of evolving interactive prototypes to achieve high-quality user interfaces. In this respect, the iteration cycle involved the following phases: (i) problem definition, ideation, and requirements specification; (ii) design of prototypes (evolving from low fidelity to high fidelity mockups, and eventually to functional prototypes); (iii) expert-based evaluation. Evaluation of each prototype was conducted with the participation of domain and usability experts, resulting in identifying problems that should be solved and improvements that should be pursued in the next prototype iteration. The implementation of the system was initiated after concluding the UI design.

The presented platform acts as the front end of a very complex system that integrates IoT monitoring functionality over cloud-based distributed architectures. In this paper, we will analyze the data model and the UI implementation. Graphically, the data model structure is depicted in Fig. 1. At the application level, measurement data is obtained from all sensors participating in the IoT. At the hardware level, data is received from the gateways (which aggregate the information of the individual sensors connected to

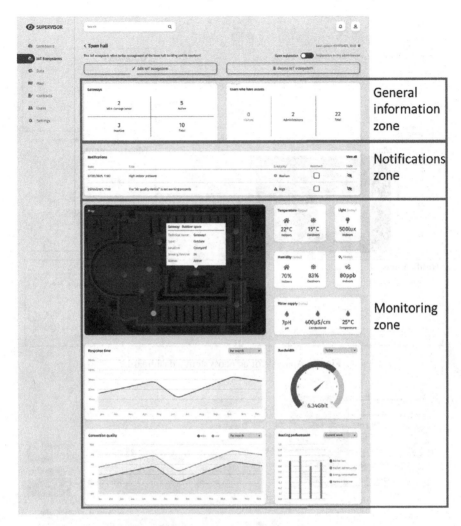

Fig. 1. Supervisor's home page

them) and at the network level, information is received from both the gateways and the individual sensors connected to them. Finally, gateways can detect faults in sensors, which are submitted for visualization.

For the implementation of the user interface, the Angular development platform and framework have been deployed. Angular is an open-source, component-based framework for building scalable web applications, which is supported by Google and a large community of volunteers and companies. Frameworks like Angular allow the fast development of web applications by providing mechanisms to manage and present the data coming from the system's respective data provider. In addition, they ensure high performance and security in applications. The main programming language used in the angular

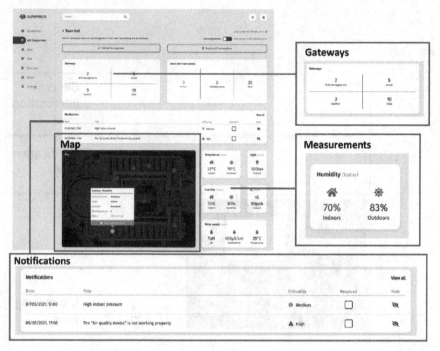

Fig. 2. Analysis of an ecosystem's dashboard.

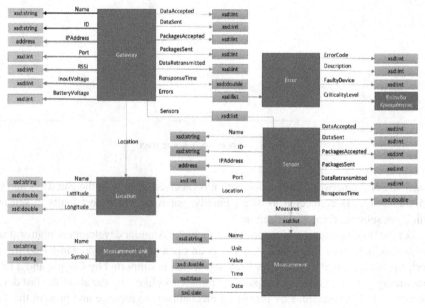

Fig. 3. Data model structure.

framework is Typescript, an open-source language developed by Microsoft. It is a super-set of JavaScript, providing a syntax that allows the optional declaration of variable types, while providing elements of object-oriented programming, such as classes, interfaces, etc. Essentially, Typescript allows for better code organization, better code control for developers, faster performance and better error prevention and handling, making it an ideal choice for large-scale applications as in the case of the EPOPTIS project.

Finally, the HTML5 language and the Bootstrap 5 framework were used for the implementation of the web pages. Bootstrap, being the most popular framework for developing responsive websites, provides mechanisms that control how the web page elements will be shown, rearranged or hidden according to the screen size, ensuring that optimal user experience and usability is offered on all screen sizes (computer screen, tablet, mobile phones). Finally, to control the appearance of web pages, the SCSS language is used - a superset of CSS that offers variables, and nesting features among others to allow better code organization and fine control of the appearance of the interface elements.

5 Conclusion

Summarising this work, we have presented the design and implementation of platform-agnostic web-based management as a service solution for IoT ecosystems. The novelty of this work regards its pluggability to different IoT architectures through a device-agnostic approach that is based on a data model and a generic UI implementation. The proposed solution has been implemented and tested in the context of the research project EPOPTIS financed by the European Union and Greek national funds and has reached a significant level of maturity within the project. The next steps include a user-based evaluation, aiming to assess the usability and usefulness of the proposed solution, with a representative user sample.

Acknowledgement. This research has been financed by the European Union and Greek national funds through the Operational Program Competitiveness, Entrepreneurship and Innovation, under the call RESEARCH – CREATE – INNOVATE (project code: T1EDK-00070).

References

1. Kim, S.H., Wang, Q.H., Ullrich, J.B.: A comparative study of cyberattacks. Commun. ACM **55**(3), 66–73 (2012)
2. Liu, S., Cheng, B.: Cyberattacks: why, what, who, and how. IT professional **11**(3), 14–21 (2009)
3. Bout, E., Loscri, V., Gallais, A.: How Machine Learning changes the nature of cyberattacks on IoT networks: a survey. IEEE Commun. Surv. Tutor. **24**(1), 248–279 (2021)
4. EPOPTIS project. https://www.epoptis-project.gr/en/home/. Accessed 03 May 2023
5. Post, F.H., Nielson, G., Bonneau, G.P. (Eds.): Data Visualization: The State of the Art (2002)
6. Vitsaxaki, K., Ntoa, S., Margetis, G., Spyratos, N.: Interactive visual exploration of big relational datasets. Int. J. Hum.–Comput. Interact., 1–15 (2022)
7. Protopsaltis, A., Sarigiannidis, P., Margounakis, D., Lytos, A.: Data visualization in internet of things: tools, methodologies, and challenges. In: Proceedings of the 15th International Conference on Availability, Reliability and Security, pp. 1–11, August 2020

8. Kalaitzakis, M., et al.: Building a smart city ecosystem for third party innovation in the city of Heraklion. In: Stratigea, A., Kavroudakis, D. (eds.) Mediterranean Cities and Island Communities. Progress in IS. Springer, Cham (2019). https://doi.org/10.1007/978-3-319-994 44-4_2

9. Zidianakis, E., Partarakis, N., Antona, M., Stephanidis, C.: Building a sensory infrastructure to support interaction and monitoring in ambient intelligence environments. In: Streitz, N., Markopoulos, P. (eds.) DAPI 2014. LNCS, vol. 8530, pp. 519–529. Springer, Cham (2014). https://doi.org/10.1007/978-3-319-07788-8_48

10. Allam, S.: Exploratory study for big data visualization in the internet of things. Sudhir Allam, "Exploratory Study Big Data Visualizat. Internet Things", Int. J. Creat. Res. Thoughts (IJCRT) ISSN (2017), 2320–2882

11. Il-Agure, Z., Dempered, J.: Review of data visualization techniques in IoT data. In: 2022 8th International Conference on Information Technology Trends (ITT), pp. 167–171. IEEE, May 2022

12. Yao, L., Sheng, Q.Z., Dustdar, S.: Web-based management of the internet of things. IEEE Internet Comput. 19(4), 60–67 (2015)

13. Karim, F., Karim, F.: Monitoring system using web of things in precision agriculture. Procedia Comput. Sci. 110, 402–409 (2017)

14. Teras, M., Raghunathan, S.: Big data visualisation in immersive virtual reality environments: embodied phenomenological perspectives to interaction. ICTACT J. Soft Comput. 5(4) (2015)

15. Bouloukakis, M., Partarakis, N., Drossis, I., Kalaitzakis, M., Stephanidis, C.: Virtual reality for smart city visualization and monitoring. In: Stratigea, A., Kavroudakis, D. (eds.) Mediterranean Cities and Island Communities. PI, pp. 1–18. Springer, Cham (2019). https://doi.org/10.1007/978-3-319-99444-4_1

16. Cloudradar. https://www.cloudradar.io/. Accessed 10 Jan 2022

17. Domotz. https://www.domotz.com/. Accessed 10 Jan 2022

18. Maximo. https://www.ibm.com/products/maximo. Accessed 10 Jan 2022

19. IoT-core. https://cloud.google.com/iot-core. Accessed 10 Jan 2022

20. Freeboard. https://freeboard.io/. Accessed 10 Jan 2022

21. Contus. https://blog.contus.com/iot-data-visualization-for-iot-platforms-applications/. Accessed 10 Jan 2022

22. Thingspeak. https://thingspeak.com/. Accessed 10 Jan 2022

23. Thethings. https://thethings.io/. Accessed 10 Jan 2022

24. Datadoghq. https://www.datadoghq.com/product/. Accessed 10 Jan 2022

25. Nielsen, J.: Iterative user-interface design. Comput. 26(11), 32–41 (1993)

26. Nielsen, J.: The usability engineering life cycle. Comput. 25(3), 12–22 (1992)

27. Brown, T.: Design thinking. Harv. Bus. Rev. 86(6), 84 (2008)

Analysis of Annotation Quality of Human Activities Using Knowledge Graphs

Shusaku Egami[1] , Mikiko Oono[1], Mai Otsuki[1] , Takanori Ugai[1,2] ,
and Ken Fukuda[1(✉)]

[1] National Institute of Advanced Industrial Science and Technology, Tokyo, Japan
{s-egami,mikiko-oono,mai.otsuki,ken.fukuda}@aist.go.jp
[2] Fujitsu Ltd., Kanagawa, Japan
ugai@fujitsu.com

Abstract. Human activity data from cameras and sensors have potential applications in diverse domains. However, annotation quality varies, and label inconsistency remains a challenge. Annotators' different interpretations also cause other issues. In this paper, we proposed an approach for analyzing the annotation quality for videos of human activities focusing on annotation issues. Specifically, we annotated the same videos using different strategies: (1) fine temporal granularity using primitive action ontology vocabularies and (2) coarse temporal granularity focusing on meaningful action sequences. We then constructed knowledge graphs based on the annotated data and analyzed the relationship between annotation types and noise label tendencies. The results of this study could potentially support the construction of high-quality annotated datasets necessary for understanding human activities in various scenes, from daily life to service operations.

Keywords: Human activity · Video data annotation · Knowledge graphs

1 Introduction

Understanding human activity from data can lead to developing artificial intelligence (AI) systems to prevent injury risks at home and robots that navigate customers in the service industry. Although annotating semantic information to data is necessary to understand human activity, the annotation labels' quality varies. One of the widely known issues is label inconsistency. For example, when annotating a video of turning on the lights in a room, some people annotate the activity as "pressing the light switch," and others annotate it as "switch on the light," resulting in inconsistencies in labels. In previous studies, controlled vocabularies and ontologies [4,5] are recommended to address this issue.

However, there are other issues caused by annotators' different interpretations. Two of those are (1) granularity problem and (2) irrelevant action problem. A video of a person sweeping the floor with a broom may be annotated as "sweeping floor" or may decompose further into three labels: "grasping broom", "walking", and "sweeping floor" (issue (1)). The decomposition can go even further by adding actions that have nothing to do with the purpose of the video, such as "scratching one's head" (while sweeping the floor) or "slightly touching a cup," which typically results in many noise labels (issue (2)). However, it is challenging to identify noise annotations and essential annotations because risk factors of accidents or customer sentiment may be hidden in those irrelevant action patterns (e.g., a customer is tapping the tabletop because of anger). In addition, there is a possibility of a trade-off between the level of detail in time granularity (i.e., machine readability) and the increase of the noise labels.

Our long-term goal is to embody AI in software agents, robots, or cyber-physical systems that can understand the human contextual activity of daily life. To construct the necessary dataset for this goal, in this paper, we aim to investigate to what degree the above annotation quality problems affect the understanding of human activity in specific domains, such as daily life support of older adults and service operations restaurants.

In this paper, we analyzed the quality of annotation data for videos of human activities focusing on annotation issues. Specifically, we first annotated the same videos using different annotation strategies as follows: (1) annotating with fine temporal granularity and eliminating individual interpretations of the annotator as much as possible, and (2) annotating with coarse temporal granularity focusing on the sequence of actions that make sense. We second constructed a knowledge graph based on the annotated data. A knowledge graph is a set of triples SPSVERBc1head, relation, tailSPSVERBc2 consisting of nodes (head and tail) and edges (relation). Finally, we analyzed the relationship between the two types of annotations and the tendency of noise labels (meaningless actions) through various graph searches and visualizations for the knowledge graph.

2 Related Work

Li et al. [3] mentioned the problem of the ground truth annotation quality of datasets in scene graph generation. Specifically, Li et al. focused on the long-tail problem of action labels caused by inconsistencies in the annotation task; however, in this study, we refer to the action labels that are essentially meaningless as "noise." Vizcarra et al. [6] used ELAN[1] [1] to annotate human activity in video data to describe it as a knowledge graph. Although they constructed event-centric knowledge graphs, they did not include activity labels. Nishimura et al. [4] developed the Primitive Action Ontology as a set of vocabularies for fine-grained human actions, excluding the target object and interpretation of the observer from the human activity. Nishimura et al. also investigated the impact on activity recognition accuracy by decomposing the annotation labels into primitive actions and objects. In this study, we adopted the Primitive Action Ontology for annotation.

---

[1] https://archive.mpi.nl/tla/elan.

Table 1. Video data of human behavior

Video	Description	# of videos	Total video length (minutes)
Behavior of older adults	Video footage of older adults' daily activities captured using cameras installed in their homes	48	6
Customer behavior in restaurants	Video footage of customer behaviors captured using cameras installed inside the restaurant	2	142

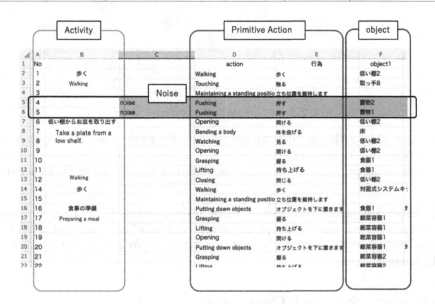

Fig. 1. Example of annotation result

3 Approach

In this study, we annotate video data capturing older adults' daily activities at home and customers' behaviors in a restaurant. We then construct knowledge graphs based on the annotated data to discuss trends and the quality of the annotated data through querying and visualization.

3.1 Data Annotation

Annotation is performed on real video data of human activities shown in Table 1. The annotation target is human activities, and environmental information is not annotated. For each video, the action and activity labels are annotated as follows:

1. annotating with fine temporal granularity and eliminating individual interpretations of the annotator as much as possible, using the vocabularies of Primitive Action Ontology [4], which defines the set of basic human actions,

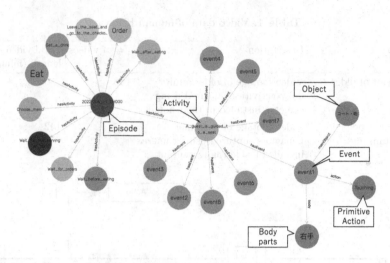

Fig. 2. Part of generated knowledge graphs

2. annotating with coarse temporal granularity focuses on the sequence of actions that make sense, and
3. annotating primitive actions that are irrelevant to the purpose of the activity as noise.

There are four annotators, two of which are responsible for labeling activities and the other two for labeling primitive actions. One of the annotators gives the label "noise" to the irrelevant primitive actions. Figure 1 shows an example of the annotation results.

3.2 Knowledge Graph Construction

We constructed knowledge graphs based on the annotated data. The data format of the knowledge graph adopted Resource Description Framework (RDF)[2], and conformed to the VirtualHome2KG [2] ontology, which structures daily activities as an event-centric knowledge graph as a schema. Figure 2 shows a part of the constructed knowledge graphs. An episode corresponds to a single video and comprises multiple activities. Each activity is composed of multiple events, which serve as more detailed units. Additionally, every event has an associated primitive action.

The constructed KG was stored in Ontotext GraphDB[3], which is a graph database with RDF and SPARQL[4] support. The number of triples was 23,315 (corresponding to the record in the database). The number of activities was 59. The number of events was 3,681. The number of primitive actions was 71.

---

[2] https://www.w3.org/RDF/.

[3] https://www.ontotext.com/products/graphdb/.

[4] https://www.w3.org/TR/sparql11-query/.

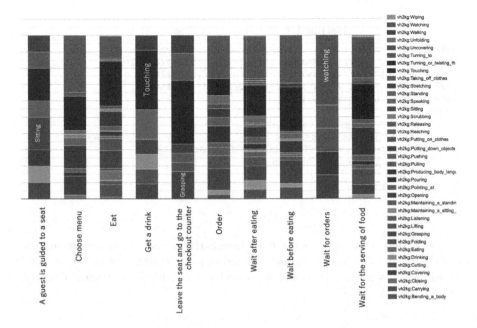

Fig. 3. Percentage of actions included in activities

Table 2. Statistics of noise actions (top 5)

Primitive action	# of primitive action	# of noise	Ratio of noise
Touching	747	102	0.136
Grasping	338	65	0.192
Pushing	96	52	0.541
Putting down objects	298	51	0.171
Lifting	247	44	0.178

3.3   Analysis of Annotated Data Using Graph Queries

The knowledge graph was constructed by clearly distinguishing episodes, activities, events, and primitive actions. Each node was created from annotated data as subclasses or unique instances of these classes and interlinked with each other. Thus, it is possible to perform an analysis that counts multiple nodes of the same type and takes into account the relationships between different types of nodes.

Figure 3 shows the visualization results of a SPARQL query (Listing 1.1) on which primitive actions occur frequently in activities in restaurant videos. We found that whole-part relationships between coarse-grained actions (i.e., activities) and fine-grained actions (i.e., primitive actions), as well as the temporal granularity of activities, were biased.

Table 2 shows the statistics of noise labels (i.e., meaningless actions). We found that the appearance of meaningless actions is also biased. For example,

Listing 1.1. Get activity type and action

```
PREFIX rdf: <http://www.w3.org/1999/02/22-rdf-syntax-ns#>
PREFIX vh2kg: <http://example.org/virtualhome2kg/ontology/>
PREFIX ho: <http://www.owl-ontologies.com/VirtualHome.owl#>
PREFIX rdfs: <http://www.w3.org/2000/01/rdf-schema#>
select ?action ?activity_type
where {
    ?activity vh2kg:hasEvent ?event ;
        rdf:type ?activity_type .
    ?activity rdf:type/rdfs:subClassOf ho:Activity .
    ?event vh2kg:action ?action .
    BIND(RAND() AS ?rand)
} order by ?rand
```

we found that "Touching" is the most frequently judged as a noise action, however, the highest ratio of noise in each action was "Pushing." More than half of
"Pushing" was noise and should be considered in advance if it should be used
as an annotation label.

4   Conclusion

In this study, we annotated video data of human activities with different temporal granularities and constructed a knowledge graph based on this annotation.
We presented the potential for a variety of analyses leading to the interpretation of temporal granularity and meaningless action labels in human behavior.
The results of this study will support the construction of high-quality annotated datasets necessary for understanding human activity and will significantly
impact various scenes from daily life to service operations.

Acknowledgements. This paper is based on results obtained from a project,
JPNP20006 and JPNP180013, commissioned by the New Energy and Industrial Tech-
nology Development Organization (NEDO), and JSPS KAKENHI Grant Number
JP22K18008.

References

1. Brugman, H., Russel, A., Nijmegen, X.: Annotating multi-media/multi-modal
   resources with ELAN. In: LREC, pp. 2065–2068 (2004)
2. Egami, S., Ugai, T., Oono, M., Kitamura, K., Fukuda, K.: Synthesizing event-centric
   knowledge graphs of daily activities using virtual space. IEEE Access **11**, 23857–
   23873 (2023). https://doi.org/10.1109/ACCESS.2023.3253807
3. Li, L., Chen, L., Huang, Y., Zhang, Z., Zhang, S., Xiao, J.: The devil is in the
   labels: Noisy label correction for robust scene graph generation. In: Proceedings of
   the IEEE/CVF Conference on Computer Vision and Pattern Recognition (CVPR),
   pp. 18869–18878 (June 2022)

4. Nishimura, S., Egami, S., Ugai, T., Oono, M., Kitamura, K., Fukuda, K.: Ontologies of action and object in home environment towards injury prevention. In: Proceedings of the 10th International Joint Conference on Knowledge Graphs, pp. 126–130. IJCKG 2021, Association for Computing Machinery, New York, NY, USA (2022). https://doi.org/10.1145/3502223.3502239
5. Nishimura, S., Fukuda, K.: Towards representation of daily living activities by reusing ICF categories. In: Human Aspects of IT for the Aged Population. Supporting Everyday Life Activities: 7th International Conference, ITAP 2021, Held as Part of the 23rd HCI International Conference, HCII 2021, Virtual Event, 24–29 July 2021, Proceedings, Part II. pp. 438–450. Springer-Verlag Heidelberg (2021). https://doi.org/10.1007/978-3-030-78111-8_30
6. Vizcarra, J., Nishimura, S., Fukuda, K.: Ontology-based human behavior indexing with multimodal video data. In: 2021 IEEE 15th International Conference on Semantic Computing (ICSC), pp. 262–267 (2021). https://doi.org/10.1109/ICSC50631.2021.00052

hILDe: AI-Empowered Monitoring System for Vanadium Redox Flow Batteries

Gian-Luca Kiefer[1]([✉]), Alassane Ndiaye[1], Matthieu Deru[1], Boris Brandherm[1],
Laura Gerart[2], Stephan Schulte[2], Bodo Groß[2], Dan Durneata[3],
and Rolf Hempelmann[3]

[1] Department of Cognitive Assistants, German Research Center for Artificial Intelligence,
66123 Saarbrücken, Germany
`gian-luca.kiefer@dfki.de`
[2] Institute for Future Energy and Material Flow Systems, IZES gGmbH, 66115 Saarbrücken,
Germany
[3] Transfercentre Sustainable Electrochemistry, Campus Dudweiler, 66125 Saarbrücken,
Germany

Abstract. The dynamic production of green energy requires capable mediate storage solutions, often in the form of large batteries. Here, a Vanadium Redox Flow Battery is used to collect solar panels' energy and, later, power electric vehicles. Since the balance of the chemical liquids inside the battery can change over multiple loading cycles, a system for predictive monitoring is needed. This paper presents the project "hILDe - Novel, cost-effective and highly accurate indication of imbalance and state of charge of vanadium redox flow batteries using AI-assisted detection of specific colors", which features an absorbance sensor for chemical liquids and an AI-empowered monitoring system to interpret and predict sensory data. The current progress in our lab scenario suggests that the deployment of our sensor and monitoring system enables an accurate and cost-efficient imbalance and state of charge sensor for Vanadium Redox Flow Batteries. In the future, the system will be tested in full-sized batteries to verify its scalability and commercial potential.

Keywords: Artificial Intelligence · Embedded Systems · VRFB

1 Introduction

This paper presents a framework for AI-based state of charge (SOC) and imbalance monitoring of Vanadium Redox Flow Batteries (VRFB). VRFBs (container, see Fig. 1) are suitable for stationary large-scale storage of electricity, e.g., from volatile renewable sources, namely photovoltaics or wind [1]. The energy is stored in two tanks with redox-active vanadium ions of different valences in sulfuric acid. These two liquids are called anolyte and catholyte [2]. The conversion from chemical to electrical energy takes place in the so-called stacks. This separation of energy and power is one of the biggest advantages of this type of battery and enables a flexible adaptation to the individual use case [1]. Currently, one major issue is the in-situ monitoring of electrochemical processes

© The Author(s), under exclusive license to Springer Nature Switzerland AG 2023
C. Stephanidis et al. (Eds.): HCII 2023, CCIS 1835, pp. 490–496, 2023.
https://doi.org/10.1007/978-3-031-36001-5_63

within VRFBs, especially the imbalance [2, 3]. During long-time operation of VRFBs, the vanadium concentration, as well as the volume of the anolyte and catholyte, differs because of various reasons (ion diffusion, gas side reactions, air oxidation, volumetric transfer). Due to these reversible processes, the capacity of the VRFB decreases over time [1]. While the SOC can be easily determined by measuring the potential difference between catholyte and anolyte with an open circuit voltage (OCV) cell [4], the imbalance currently can be determined ex-situ by analyzing the vanadium concentration of anolyte and catholyte [3].

Fig. 1. Typical VRFB setup for charging electric vehicles using renewable energy at IZES [5].

The proposed solution to get both SOC and imbalance in-situ at the same time is the hILDe sensor (see Fig. 2), which measures anolyte and catholyte absorbance simultaneously and uses AI to predict SOC and imbalance. As the measures are not linear but rely on multidimensional parametric curves a dedicated data visualization is necessary to monitor the evolution of data, thus two customizable user interfaces (UI) were implemented.

2 Data Collection and Model Development Based on a Test Rig

The data used for the framework are generated in two test rigs (see Fig. 2) consisting of a lab-scale VRFB equipped with hILDe sensors, OCV cell, and the possibility to take samples during the operation and analyze the vanadium concentration.

The hILDe sensor measures data like the temperature and absorbance at the different wavelengths corresponding to the ultraviolet, yellow, red, and infrared LEDs, respectively 405 nm, 593 nm, 635 nm, and 855 nm. These data are measured on average every 7 s. The vanadium(II) and vanadium(III) concentrations in the anolyte and the

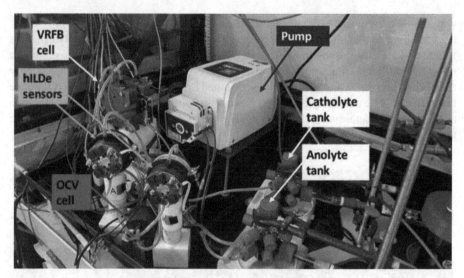

Fig. 2. VRFB laboratory setup at IZES [5].

vanadium(IV) and vanadium(V) concentrations in the catholyte are determined manually by titration of samples which were taken at fixed times. Therefore, the measured concentrations must be interpolated and aligned to the sensor data using linear regression.

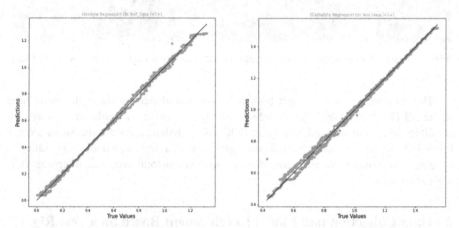

Fig. 3. Scatter plots of prediction accuracy on test data for anolyte and catholyte.

For this purpose and for the following machine learning processes, we use 70% of the data for training and 30% data for model testing. Based on the gathered concentration data, multiple model experiments were conducted to evaluate possible model architectures. These models included neural networks [6] and other machine learning techniques [7–9]. They were implemented using the Python programming language in addition to the Scikit-Learn and Keras frameworks. Eventually, Random Forest Regressors [10] with hyperparameter-tuning were used to create four models, one for each vanadium concentration (vanadium(II), vanadium(III), vanadium (IV), vanadium(V)). The inputs to each model are the LED absorbances of the hILDe sensors and the models then output each vanadium concentration, respectively. The models achieve good prediction accuracy with R2 scores of 0.99. For instance, Fig. 3 shows scatter plots of the prediction accuracy on the test data for vanadium(II) and vanadium(V). The SOC, the imbalance, and the average oxidation state (AOS) are also determined from the predicted concentrations.

3 Architecture

To ensure a distributed architecture, a Flask [11] web service is implemented which provides the previously discussed AI models by offering REST API paths for local network access. Since the compute-intensive model training is already done on specific GPU-accelerated machines, the trained, and therefore lightweight, models can be deployed on cost-efficient hardware (e.g., Raspberry Pi or Mac mini). In our case, a Mac mini is used not only for providing the web service but also for acquiring data generated by the hILDe sensor. The Mac mini is connected to the sensor by a serial communication bus and reads the measurements in real time which enables the service to provide ad-hoc concentration predictions.

A user can now interact with the live data and predictions by using the implemented web applications discussed in the next chapter. These can be used on multiple devices (Desktop, Tablet, Mobile) and, therefore, support the distributed character of the architecture (see Fig. 4).

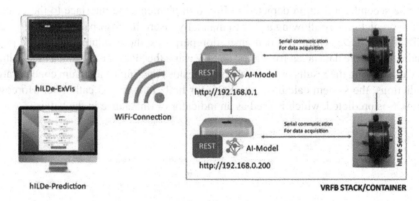

Fig. 4. Simplified view of the hILDe architecture.

4 User Interface of the Monitoring System

For intuitive access to the experiments and predictions, two user interfaces were implemented. The first one, hILDe-ExVis (Experiment Visualizer), is used during the data collection process with the hILDe sensor. It connects to the web service and visualizes the measured experiment data as graphs. Here, it allows us to skip between different experiments and to analyze single loading cycles as well. Intuitive features like a dynamic second y-axis, zoom controls, and individual enabling of different measurements should contribute to the overall usability of the interface (see Fig. 5).

Fig. 5. Screen capture of hILDe-ExVis for monitoring the state of the VRFB.

The second application depicted in Fig. 6 implements the interface to the concentration predictions by allowing a user to manually insert the absorbance values for each LED of the hILDe sensor. For demonstration purposes, these values can also be populated with sample data taken from a test set. By using the "Predict" button, a new column appears showing the results of the prediction: Besides the single vanadium concentration predictions, the system calculates the SOC for both anolyte and catholyte. Moreover, the AOS is predicted, which is used as an indicator of imbalance in the battery.

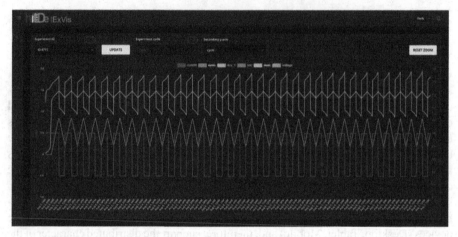

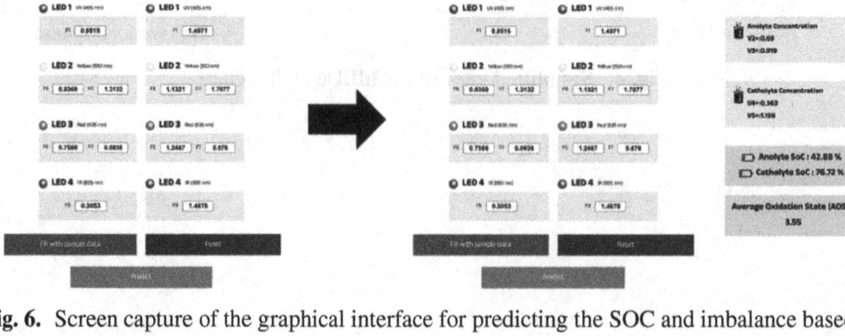

Fig. 6. Screen capture of the graphical interface for predicting the SOC and imbalance based on the collected anolyte and catholyte values.

5 Conclusion

The ongoing hILDe project develops a cost-efficient yet capable VRFB monitoring system which is easy to deploy and gives predictive insights about charging status and possible battery imbalances. To the current date, the hILDe sensor is deployed on a test rig and gathers absorbance data which is then used to train the AI prediction models. Two user interfaces aid both at the data gathering stage and in the production stage, where the prediction of vanadium concentrations gives insights about SOC and the imbalance of the battery.

In the future, the hILDe sensor and the AI-empowered monitoring system will be integrated into a large-scale VRFB to display its real-time state, particularly SOC and imbalance with the two user interfaces. The main purpose is to demonstrate the benefits of the newly developed hILDe sensor and to improve the AI models by training them with data from a commercial VRFB.

Acknowledgements. The investigations were carried out within the joint project "hILDe – Novel, cost-effective and highly accurate indication of imbalance and state of charge of vanadium redox flow batteries using AI-assisted detection of specific colors" (03KB124 A, B & C), funded by

Supported by:

Federal Ministry for Economic Affairs and Climate Action (BMWK).

on the basis of a decision
by the German Bundestag

References

1. Jirabovornwisut, T., Arpornwichanop, A.: A review on the electrolyte imbalance in vanadium redox flow batteries. Int. J. Hydrogen Energy **44**(45), 24485–24509 (2019)
2. Geiser, J., Natter, H., Hempelmann, R., Morgenstern, B., Hegetschweiler, K.: Photometrical determination of the state-of-charge in vanadium redox flow batteries part II. in combination with open-circuit-voltage. Z. Phys. Chem. **233**(12) (2019)
3. Geiser, J., Natter, H., Hempelmann, R., Morgenstern, B., Hegetschweiler, K.: Photometrical determination of the state-of-charge in vanadium redox flow batteries part I. in combination with potentiometric titration. Z. Phys. Chem. **233**(12) (2019)
4. Skyllas-Kazacos, M., Kazacos, M.: State of charge monitoring methods for vanadium redox flow battery control. J. Power Sources **196**, 8822–8827 (2011)
5. IZES gGmbH. https://www.izes.de/en. Accessed 16 Mar 2023
6. Deru, M., Ndiaye, A.: Deep Learning mit TensorFlow Keras und TensorFlow.js. Rheinwerk Verlag, Bonn (2020)
7. Ling, C.: A review of the recent progress in battery informatics. Nat. Partner J. Ser. Comput. Mater. **8**, 33 (2022)
8. Roman, D., Saxena, S., Robu, V., et al.: Machine learning pipeline for battery state-of-health estimation. Nat. Mach. Intell. **3**, 447–456 (2021)

9. Ng, M.F., Zhao, J., Yan, Q., et al.: Predicting the state of charge and health of batteries using data-driven machine learning. Nat. Mach. Intell. **2**, 161–170 (2020)
10. Svetnik, V., Liaw, A., Tong, C., Culberson, J.C., Sheridan, R.P., Feuston, B.P.: Random forest: a classification and regression tool for compound classification and QSAR modeling. J. Chem. Inf. Comput. Sci. **43**(6), 1947–1958 (2003)
11. Grinberg, M.: Flask Web Development: Developing Web Applications with Python, 1st edn. O'Reilly Media, Inc., Sebastopol (2018)

Estimation of Mobility Model Using Limited Mobility Data

Toru Kumagai[✉] [ID]

National Institute of Advanced Industrial Science and Technology, Umezono 1-1-1,
Tsukuba 305-8568, Japan
kumagai.toru@aist.go.jp

Abstract. In Japan rural area conventional public transport does not meet the needs of non-driving population, especially the elderly. To solve this problem, it is essential to obtain precise mobility data. Mobility data refers to measurements of the movements of individuals, including where they come from and where they go, as well as how long they stay at their destinations. However, for privacy reasons, in many cases, projects that measure mobility data do not aim to track specific individuals; instead, they simply describe how many people are present within a larger geographic area during a specific time frame. In addition to that, it is expensive to obtain precise measurements for an entire area. Therefore, this study proposed a method to estimate an area-wide probability model of mobility from precise but limited data. The proposed method generates the origin and destination of a trip in the following two steps. First, the starting point is generated from population density distribution. Next, a conditional probability distribution for the destination at the starting point is derived from the mobility data in the vicinity of the starting point, and the destination is generated. In a concrete manner, the destination is generated by resampling the destination of the mobility data nearby the starting point. The proposed method was demonstrated with GPS mobility data of 106 people. Using the proposed method with geographical distributions of several factor such as population, commercial and public facilities and more mobility data with attributes, more precise area-wide mobility models would be derived.

Keywords: Mobility Model · GPS · Mobility Data · Mobility as a Service · MaaS

1 Background

In Japan rural area there is not sufficient access to public transport. Conventional public transport does not meet the needs of non-driving population, especially the elderly. In addition, the aging and decline of population increase the necessity of efficient transportation systems.

To solve this problem, the local governments and transport operators must consider the drastic redesign of transport systems, and integrate new approaches including ride-sharing, on-demand bus services, and self-driving vehicles, and introduce Mobility as a Service (MaaS) which is an integration of transport and related services [1, 2].

C. Stephanidis et al. (Eds.): HCII 2023, CCIS 1835, pp. 497–502, 2023.
https://doi.org/10.1007/978-3-031-36001-5_64

Such a drastic redesign involves extensive stakeholders including local governments, transport operators, MaaS operators, residents, and related service operators. In order to build a consensus among various stakeholders, and to design effective transport system, it is essential to obtain precise mobility data.

Mobility data refers to measurements of the movements of specific individuals, including where they come from and where they go, as well as how long they stay at their destinations. However, for privacy reasons, in many cases, projects that measure mobility data do not aim to track specific individuals; instead, they simply describe how many people are present within a larger geographic area during a specific time frame. This is insufficient to design transportation systems that consider personal attributes. Even if privacy issues can be overcome, it is expensive to obtain precise measurements for an entire area.

2 Objects

The object of this study was to propose a method to estimate an area-wide probability model of mobility from precise but limited data. This study also demonstrated the proposed method by generating mobility data using real GPS mobility data.

3 Data

3.1 Mobility Data

This study used personal mobility data measured in the Smart Mobility Challenge Project [2] and provided by the Smart Mobility Promotion Council [3]. The data consisted of GPS mobility data of 160 individuals living in or near Tsukuba, Japan over a four-week period. GPS positions were recorded every 3 min. Figure 1(Left) shows a plot of all movement data overlaid on a map of Tsukuba. This study used data for 106 of the 160 individuals, including a sufficient amount of GPS mobility data.

The left and right figures in Fig. 2 show mobility data for two typical subjects, respectively. In both cases, the movement occurred in a star-like pattern from the point where it was thought to be home. Therefore, in this study, we create a mobility model with home as the starting point. This is a reasonable choice considering that the dataset is not so large. This approximation will not be a problem when estimating the demand for travel from the suburbs of the city to the center of the city.

Figure 3 (Left) shows the locations where it was thought to be home of subjects. This is distributed throughout the Tsukuba City area; however, its distribution is different from the distribution of the population of Tsukuba City. Therefore, this mobility data does not represent the distribution of mobility behavior of the city area. The proposed method in this study corrects for the influence of the subjects' omnipresence, making it useful from this perspective.

3.2 Geographical Data

This study used National Land Information System Geographical System (NLIS) [4] which contains a wide range of geographic information such as population, transportation, land use and so on. This study especially used the population distribution around Tsukuba, Japan (Fig. 1(Right)).

The database includes population distribution by age group and future estimates. This information is useful if the mobility data is rich and allows estimation of age-specific mobility models. This information and the proposed model can also be used to predict future demand.

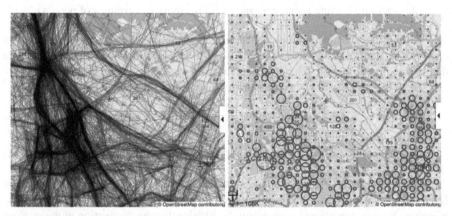

Fig. 1. (Left) Plot of all movement data overlaid on a map of Tsukuba. **(Right)** Population distribution around Tsukuba, Japan. Circles show the population size of each cell of grid. The size of cell is about 500m by 500m. The map is based on data from OpenStreetMap and is licensed under the Open Database License [5]. The map data was downloaded from 'a.tile.openstreetmap.org' using Mapping Toolbox [6].

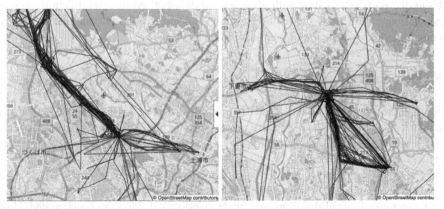

Fig. 2. Mobility data for two typical subjects. In both cases, the movement occurred in a star-like pattern from the point where it was thought to be home.

4 Methods

This study proposed a method to estimate an area-wide probability model of mobility from precise but limited data.

In general, mobility models boil down to the following two conditional probability distributions. In some cases, the model would need to be based on more conditions, such as weather, time of day, etc.

$$p(\text{starting point} \mid \text{geographical information, attributes of person}) \qquad (1)$$

$$p(\text{destination} \mid \text{starting point, geographical information, attributes of person}) \qquad (2)$$

If enough data are available and an appropriate model is assumed, model parameters can be estimated. In many cases, however, it is difficult to obtain large amounts of data that allow this estimation. Therefore, considering the observations in Section 3.1, we propose to use the following two probability distributions in this study.

$$p(\text{starting point} \mid \text{population distribution}) \qquad (3)$$

$$p(\text{destination} \mid \text{starting point}) \qquad (4)$$

The proposed method generates the starting point and destination of a trip in the following two steps. First, the starting point is generated from population density distribution. Next, a conditional probability distribution for the destination at the starting point is derived from the mobility data of subjects whose home is in the vicinity of the starting point, and the destination is generated. In a concrete manner, the destination is generated by resampling the destination of the mobility data as well as the bootstrap method.

The proposed method was demonstrated with GPS mobility data of 106 people. Using the proposed method with geographical distributions of several factors such as population, commercial and public facilities, and more mobility data with attributes, more precise area-wide mobility models could be derived.

5 Demonstrations

We used the proposed method to generate mobility data (Fig. 3 (Right)), with the starting points located in the white rectangular areas shown in both Fig. 3 (Left) and (Right). To generate mobility data for the entire Tsukuba City area, the same process can be applied throughout the entire region.

Figure 3(Right) shows that traffic to Oho, Hojo, and Shimotsuma is heavy. This result is reasonable as follows. Oho is a recently developed shopping district where many commercial facilities from large scale to individual stores are concentrated. Hojo has long been the center of the region, but commerce has declined in recent years. The center of Shimotsuma is close in distance and has a shopping center with a movie theater. On the contrary, there is not so much traffic to and from the central Tsukuba area. Various facilities are concentrated in central Tsukuba, but Tsukuba is far away, so Oho is likely to be preferred for daily shopping. Tsuchiura is one of the political centers of the prefecture and has a terminal station of JR line for Tokyo and prefecture capital Mito. Since there are prefectural and national facilities in Tsuchiura, there is a certain demand for traffic, but it is infrequent.

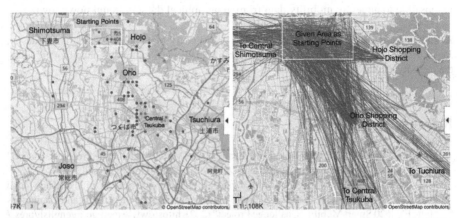

Fig. 3. (**Left**) Locations where it was thought to be the home of the subjects. This map is half the scale of the other maps. (**Right**) Examples of mobility data generation. Mobility data from given area (white rectangle) were generated. There is heavy traffic from the starting points to Oho, Hojo, and Shimotsuma.

6 Considerations and Future Works

The advantage of the proposed method is that it can generate area-wide mobility data from limited mobility data. The generation of mobility data can be done easily even if there are changes in the distribution of the population since generation is based on population distribution. This means that future mobility data can be generated based on the estimation of future population density.

Although person attributes were not accounted for in the demonstrations, the proposed method can easily account for them by generating starting points with population distribution that includes person attributes, and destinations with mobility data that also includes person attributes. However, in that case, the amount of mobility data required will increase.

The proposed method did not account for cases where the trip origin and destination were not assumed to be the subject's home location. To account for such cases, a large amount of data is required, since the number of combinations between destinations other than home is huge. One way to solve this problem might be to use a single probability model for all non-home-related travel for all subjects.

Another problem with the proposed method is that it does not consider the case of frequent visits to places other than one's home. This problem would be solved by considering a model for each frequently visited location.

The proposed method only generates start and destination points and does not predict road routes. Road traffic volumes would be estimated by combining the generated mobility data with the routing system.

One of the other remaining problems is how to use geographical data other than population density to generate starting and destination points. One goal is to create a model that combines mobility data and geographical data. With such a model, it would be possible to generate mobility data from geographical data of an unknown town.

Acknowledgments. This study was supported by Ministry of Economy, Trade and Industry, Japan. We would like to acknowledge Smart Mobility Challenge Promotion Council for providing the mobility data used in this research.

References

1. Ministry of Economy, Trade and Industry, Japan, "Smart Mobility Challenge Project Launched" (2019). https://www.meti.go.jp/english/press/2019/0618_005.html. Accessed 2023
2. Ministry of Economy, Trade and Industry, Japan, "METI Compiles a Collection of Knowledge Useful for Public Implementation and Future Directions Based on the Results and Challenges of the FY2020 Smart Mobility Challenge Project" (202). https://www.meti.go.jp/english/press/2021/0402_002.html. Accessed 2023
3. Smart Mobility Challenge Promotion Council (2019). https://www.mobilitychallenge.go.jp. Accessed 20s23
4. National Land Information Division, National Spatial Planning and Regional Policy Bureau, Ministry of Land, Infrastructure, Transport and Tourism (MLIT) of Japan, "National Land Information System (NLIS)". https://nlftp.mlit.go.jp/index.html. Accessed 2023
5. OpenStreetMap, "Copyright and License". https://www.openstreetmap.org/copyright. Accessed 2023
6. The MathWorks, Inc., "Mapping Toolbox". https://jp.mathworks.com/help/map/. Accessed 2023

Assistance System for AI-Based Monitoring and Prediction in Smart Grids

Thomas Achim Schmeyer[1]([✉]), Gian-Luca Kiefer[1], Boris Brandherm[1],
Albert Klimenko[1], Kai Krämer[1], Matthieu Deru[1], Alassane Ndiaye[1], Jörg Baus[1],
Andreas Winter[2], and Michael Igel[2]

[1] Department of Cognitive Assistants, German Research Center for Artificial Intelligence,
66123 Saarbrücken, Germany
thomas.schmeyer@dfki.de

[2] Power Engineering Saar, Saarland University of Applied Sciences, 66117 Saarbrücken,
Germany

Abstract. The German energy transition confronts the operators of low-voltage grids with new challenges. Local energy producers or large consumers, like, e.g., solar panels, heat pumps, and e-mobility lead to unexpected grid behavior. Because current grids are only sparsely monitored, local unmonitored overloads or violations of the voltage range are possible. To overcome these difficulties a smart monitoring and prediction system is needed. The system must handle different data sources fast and efficiently, so the operators can react to local grid problems. This is solved by using a streaming service to aggregate the data efficiently. Then, the implemented data pipeline is used to train AI-based models to interpolate the unmeasured parts of the grid. These models consider both measured data and predictions, like load profiles and photovoltaic forecasts. Since the grid is not fully observed, a data generator that physically simulates detailed grid scenarios is used to generate large sets of training data. Finally, an interactive GUI is implemented to visualize the data monitoring and predictions in the context of the grid and thus strengthen the user's trust in the system. The presented assistance system is developed in close cooperation with energy experts and grid operators.

Keywords: Machine Learning · Smart Grid · Assistance System · Synthetic Data

1 Introduction

In Germany, current transmission and distribution networks often still correspond to the technical state-of-the-art of one-way energy flow from central power plants to the consumers. The German energy transition plans to phase out nuclear energy by 2023 which forces a renewable energy expansion. This transition confronts the low-voltage grids with challenges like, e.g., unmonitored overloads or violations of the voltage range. Additionally, the volatility of loads and input of renewable energies make it challenging to predict future grid states to apply preventive measures.

Current distribution system state estimation approaches [1] are time- and resource-consuming and, therefore, unsuitable for real-time estimations with a high update rate.

© The Author(s), under exclusive license to Springer Nature Switzerland AG 2023
C. Stephanidis et al. (Eds.): HCII 2023, CCIS 1835, pp. 503–508, 2023.
https://doi.org/10.1007/978-3-031-36001-5_65

Instead, we propose a lightweight AI-based forecast system that allows the estimation of future states, electric current, and voltage loads at utility level for the following day with a granularity of 15 min. Since the grid has only a few measuring points, in some cases only the voltage transformer substations are measured. This results in a lack of training data needed for AI-based models. Therefore, synthetic data are generated using the ATPDesigner [2–5] to train the prediction models. Data generation and training are done offline and need a lot of computing power and resources. But the final online application is light weight using the pretrained models only which makes fast predictions of the grid state possible. While classical approaches to grid state estimation are widely used, current AI-based approaches still lack broad acceptance. Therefore, together with two power system operators, we develop an assistance system for nonlinear systems to increase operators' confidence in AI-based prediction results and facilitate decision-making. Finally, the assistance system will be tested in a real scenario.

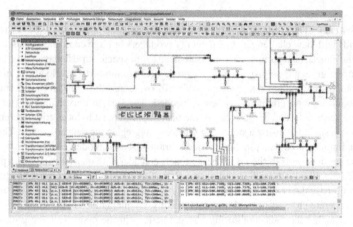

Fig. 1. ATPDesigner for designing and simulating scenarios in electrical power networks [3].

2   Energy Data Pipeline and Forecasting Methods

For our AI-based forecast system [2], we modeled a selected field test area of the existing power grid of 'Stadtwerke Saarlouis' (local energy provider) in the power grid simulation software ATPDesigner with three phases and all operating resources (see Fig. 1).

Once the modeling stage is completed, a specifically designed case generator uses the ATPDesigner technology to generate relevant training cases for the field test area [6]. The samples of the resulting case base serve as input to train the AI-based models [7, 8]. These simulated training cases are needed because actual measurements lack the quantity to train models. To increase the accuracy of the distribution system state estimation, the measurement data of the measuring stations, and, e.g., standard load profiles, solar energy forecasts [9, 10], or electric vehicle user behavior predictions [11], can serve as input data for the models, too. Combining the different models produces the result of the system's AI predictions (see Fig. 2).

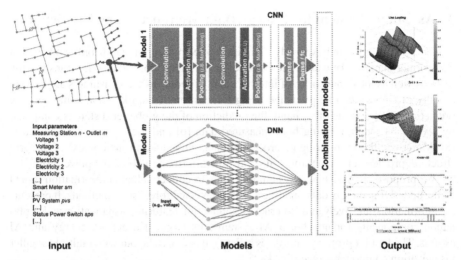

Fig. 2. Transformation workflow starting from the grid structure as Input and the prediction as Output.

Deploying power system software in critical infrastructure is neither cost- nor time-efficient. Therefore, customers request interconnectivity and encapsulation, and our system ensures both (see Fig. 3). Its architecture works with a Kafka service [12] aggregating simulated and measured energy data and bridging it to multiple AI applications and the user interface. Finally, the architecture enables grid operators to have an overview of critical grid situations via the assistance system.

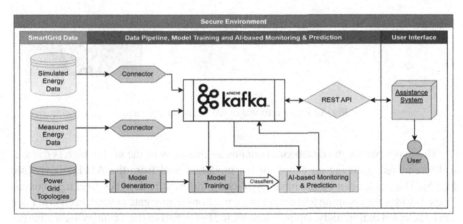

Fig. 3. Architecture of the deployed energy data pipeline.

3   Assistance System for Energy Data Monitoring and Prediction

The energy system is only sparsely monitored since measured data is only collected at transformer stations. However, the physical grid structure of the electric transmission lines, as well as the connections of internal energy producers and consumers are known. Locally, bus nodes can be predicted using forecast methods, like photovoltaic energy predictions [10]. On the other hand, the prediction of the global grid state is computed by several AI methods using both measured data [6] and local PV or load forecasts [8]. Moreover, the monitoring of processed data, embedded in the context of the grid structure, provides grid operators with real-time information about the power grid.

We propose an Assistance System that aims to collect valuable information issued by the underlying energy data pipeline and its connected forecasting methods. It presents the information intuitively as an interactive application featuring visualization and explanation components for non-linear AI systems. Its targeted users are energy and AI experts. The first UI prototype provides a classic dashboard layout with multiple smaller visualization components (see Fig. 4).

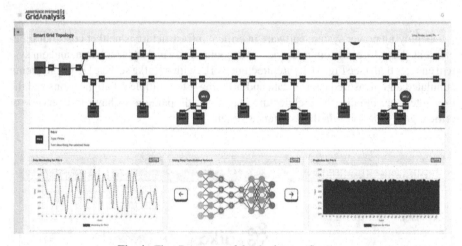

Fig. 4. First Prototype of the Assistance System.

The upper part of the dashboard contains an overview of the grid, which is dynamically rendered by using an export of the modelled grid from the ATPDesigner (see Fig. 5). The render can be modified by filtering different node types like, e.g., busses, loads. Besides the zooming and dragging interactions to navigate around, each grid node can be selected individually. Upon selection, the lower part of the topology view changes to display information about the selected node.

The lower parts of the dashboard display smaller visualization components providing further information for a selected node (see Fig. 6). On the left, it shows a history of the measured data, for example the measured voltage. If there exist no measurements, the data are interpolated by different models taking real voltage measurements of neighboring nodes into account. The next component allows switching the AI-model used

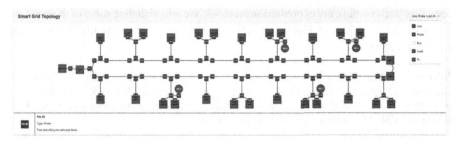

Fig. 5. View of the Grid.

for the node predictions. Moreover, this component will provide information about the prediction accuracy and its explainability in the future. The prediction itself is visualized in the next component on the right and will feature multiple different graph views and annotations.

With this dynamic prediction approach, the user can try different models before deciding on a reasonable action. If external circumstances change, different models could perform better than others. Hence, the system is still designed to be operated with the help of an experienced operator and is not planned to be fully autonomous. Ultimately, the system should increase the operator's acceptance of the AI predictions by making its decision process more transparent and comprehensible.

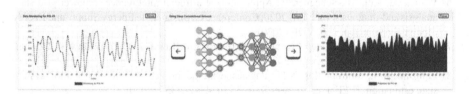

Fig. 6. Data view of a single node.

4   Conclusion

The proposed streaming pipeline allows database access to external services at a low cost of time and resources. Thus, new training data is quickly available for training new prediction models for unique situations. Using the prediction based on live grid data, the grid operator can now monitor the part of his unmonitored network and react to local overvoltage. The Assistance System is developed in close cooperation with experts of the grid operator. While the system is still under development, presentations of the prototype received very positive feedback. This system is an essential building block for transitioning from power grids to smart grids and integrating renewable energy.

We plan to include a broader range of prediction models in further iterations to strengthen the system's prediction abilities. But even more important is the further integration of explainable AI and data analytics components which could increase the grid operators' trust in these novel prediction methods. We will visualize some of the system's outputs in a Mixed Reality HoloLens application which we are currently developing in another project [13].

Acknowledgements. This work was supported by the Project "GridAnalysis" funded by the German Federal Ministry for Economic Affairs and Climate Action (BMWK) under the grant numbers 03EI6034A and 03EI6034D. The authors kindly thank project partners Stadtwerke Saarlouis GmbH and VSE AG for their valuable support and discussions.

References

1. Primadianto, A., Lu, C.N.: A review on distribution system state estimation. IEEE Trans. Power Syst. **32**(5), 3875–3883 (2017)
2. Winter, A., et al.: Künstliche Intelligenz in Stromverteilnetzen – KI-basierte Systemanalyse im Normal- und Kurzschlussbetrieb. In: ew - Magazin für die Energiewirtschaft, pp. 32–35. VDE (2021)
3. FITT - Institut für Technologietransfer an der Hochschule des Saarlandes gGmbH: ATPDesigner Design and Simulation of Electrical Power Networks (2022). http://www.atpdesign er.de/. Accessed 17 Mar 2023
4. Leuven EMTP Center: Alternative Transients Program (ATP): Rule Book. EMTP (1992)
5. European EMTP-ATP Users Group e.V. (2022). https://www.eeug.org/. Accessed 17 Mar 2023
6. Winter, A., Igel, M., Schegner, P.: Application of artificial intelligence in power grid state analysis and-diagnosis. In: NEIS 2020; Conference on Sustainable Energy Supply and Energy Storage Systems, pp. 1–6. VDE (2020)
7. Deru, M., Ndiaye, A.: Deep Learning mit TensorFlow, Keras und TensorFlow.js, 2nd edn. Rheinwerke Computing, Bonn (2022)
8. Zamzam, A.S., Sidiropoulos, N.D.: Physics-aware neural networks for distribution system state estimation. IEEE Trans. Power Syst. **35**(6), 4347–4356 (2020)
9. Stüber, M., et al.: Forecast quality of physics-based and data-driven PV performance models for a small-scale PV system. Front. Energy Res. **9** (2021)
10. Brandherm, B., Deru, M., Ndiaye, A., Kiefer, G.-L., Baus, J., Gampfer, R.: Integration erneuerbarer Energien – KI-basierte Vorhersageverfahren zur Stromerzeugung durch Photovoltaikanlagen. In: Barton, T., Müller, C. (eds.) Data Science anwenden. AW, pp. 147–170. Springer, Wiesbaden (2021). https://doi.org/10.1007/978-3-658-33813-8_9
11. Khan, S., Brandherm, B., Swamy, A.: Electric vehicle user behavior prediction using learning-based approaches. In: 2020 IEEE Electric Power and Energy Conference (EPEC), pp. 1–5 (2020)
12. Apache Software Foundation: Documentation Kafka 3.3 (2022). https://kafka.apache.org/doc umentation/. Accessed 17 Mar 2023
13. Chikobava, M., et al.: Multimodal interactive system for visualization of energy data in extended reality settings. In: HCI International 2023. Springer, Cham (2023)

Immersive Educational Technology for Waste Management Learning: A Study of Waste Detection and Feedback Delivery in Augmented Reality

Qiming Sun[1], I-Han Hsiao[1(✉)], and Shih-Yi Chien[2]

[1] Santa Clara University, Santa Clara, CA 95054, USA
{qsun4,ihsiao}@scu.edu
[2] National Chengchi University, Taipei, Taiwan
sychien@mail2.nccu.tw

Abstract. Artificial Intelligence (AI) and Augmented Reality (AR) techniques have been used by many researchers to improve waste management and promote sustainability. However, waste classification can be complex and confusing for people due to the signs and info-graphics on trash bins may not always be comprehensive. To address this issue, we designed an interactive mobile AR application that detects wastes and provides instant feedback to users on waste sorting. A user study was also conducted, and the results showed that users achieved higher garbage sorting accuracy and their knowledge on recycling was also improved, particularly in discarding complex items. The application also included learning features on sustainability, such as daily recycling tips, waste dictionary, carbon emission estimator, carbon footprint tracer, and carbon footprint data visualization. Our research demonstrated the potential of using immersive educational technology for a sustainable living.

Keywords: Smart recycling · Educational technology · Augmented reality · Waste detection · Carbon visualization · Waste management learning · Sustainable technology

1 Introduction

Waste management is the foundation of sustainable living. Recently, researchers and organizations have undertaken a variety of efforts to support sustainability through improved waste management. For instance, an assortment of Artificial Intelligence techniques have been deployed to facilitate waste sorting: deep learning algorithms to accurately classify trash images [7,10,14]; smart bins and sensors to help waste collection facilities sort garbage [8,11]; and various programs [4,13] undertaken by local agencies or working groups to encourage participation in energy saving or carbon neutrality activities. However, the body of waste knowledge is increasingly complex. Our daily trash is often messy. It consists of a combination of recyclable/non-recyclable or compostable/non-compostable materials. Moreover, the complexity of waste classification can also be very confusing:

C. Stephanidis et al. (Eds.): HCII 2023, CCIS 1835, pp. 509–515, 2023.
https://doi.org/10.1007/978-3-031-36001-5_66

for instance, not all plastic is recyclable, and recycling regulations in the United States may vary by the county, by the city, or even by the organization. According to a national report on municipal solid waste, each one of us produces an average of 4.9 pounds of waste per day [3]. Poorly managed waste creates serious health, safety, and environmental consequences, such as breeding grounds for disease vectors, global climate changes, and long-term economic impacts [5]. Signs, slogans or infographics on trash cans are increasingly used to help people categorize their waste (Fig. 1). However, the graphics of items to trash or recycle may not always be comprehensive or exhaustive. The signs and infographics are not interactive. There is no feedback or guidance to promptly resolve confusion or uncertainty when people are throwing out their waste. A few image classification projects attempt to address the waste classification issue [7,9], but none of them focus on providing feedback to the users with educational resources at the point of disposal. Our work explores emerging technologies by using AI and AR to detect waste objects and to provide instant feedback to facilitate waste sorting.

We designed an interactive mobile Augmented Reality (AR) application to educate users in doing sound day-to-day waste management. Dynamic object detection and instantaneous feedback were provided. A user study was designed and conducted to investigate the effects and the user experiences. We found that the users achieved significantly higher garbage binning accuracy with the technology. The participants improved their recycling and garbage disposal knowledge after using the technology, particularly in discarding complex items. Based on the findings and user feedback, we made subsequent improvements on the application. A range of sustainability learning and awareness features were engineered, including daily learning tips, waste dictionary, carbon emission estimator, carbon footprint tracer, and carbon footprint data visualization. An in depth case study was reported to uncover the potential of learning waste management with our proposed immersive educational technology for sustainable living.

2   Methodology

2.1   The Mobile AR Application

The mobile application we designed incorporates real-time object detection in an AR environment to help users categorize their wastes. Figure 2a shows the homepage of our application, which includes a search bar for quickly search for a garbage's category, a tutorial on how to use the scanner, and a randomly generated recycling tip. The Waste Scanner (Fig. 2b) can be accessed by tapping on the 'Scan Wastes' button on the homepage. The scanner uses real-time object detection to identify the different categories of wastes and highlight them in dashed rectangles with different colors. The object detection model is built using EfficientDet upon multiple public datasets such as TrashNet, Open Image Dataset, and TACO [1,6,10,12]. Moreover, if the application is used near the trash bins, it can detect and track the category labels, e.g. "Recycle", "Landfill", and "Compost", and place an overlay with a green check sign on the appropriate bin while red crosses on other bins (Fig. 2c). In this way, users can have a visual guidance on where they should dispose their trash.

Fig. 1. Common infographics instructions on the trash bins to sort the waste into Landfill, Recycle or Compost bins, which may not be comprehensive and do not provide interactive feedback.

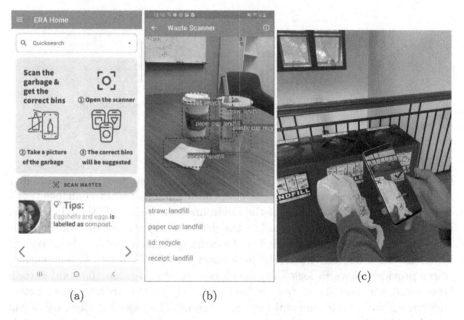

Fig. 2. The app homepage and Waste Scanner. The scanner activates object detection at the center of the camera foci area. The object label and the suggested bin will be presented in the AR view. They are color-coded and aligned with the universal garbage recycling theme: landfill is black, recycling is blue, and compost is green. All the detected objects will be listed under the Detection History panel (b). An use case of getting feedback from the mobile application; the detected waste objects labels will be displayed and the suggested bins will be checked and highlighted in the AR space (c). (Color figure online)

2.2 Usability Study Results

To evaluate the impact of the application on people's waste disposal knowledge, 28 participants were recruited from a computer engineering class for a usability study. The participants were given pre- and post-testings on how to sort five items, including paper, napkin, straw with a cup, hot coffee cup, plastic bag, and receipt. The result showed that the participants gained higher post-knowledge after using the application (t_{27}=-3.471, p<0.01). The effect was particularly notable in disposing complex objects, such as straw and cup, and plastic bag with a receipt on it. Before using the application, the participants' understanding of those complex items was below 50%,. However, with the support of our app, the participants were able to learn on the recycling, resulting in a 20% improvement in disposal knowledge on average (Fig. 3).

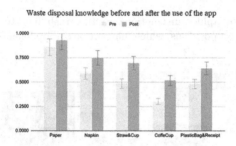

Fig. 3. User's knowledge level before and after using the app.

2.3 Improvements on the Application

Based on the feedback from the usability study, we added a set of Sustainability Awareness Technologies (Fig. 4) that offers additional features to enhance user's experience and understanding of the environmental impact of their behaviors. In the waste scanner, users can select the detected objects and add them to the carbon footprint tracer (Fig. 4a & 4b). An estimated amount of saved carbon will be calculated based on the Waste Reduction Model (WARM) [2]. The carbon tracer provides views in logs and calendars with statistics on the total carbon been saved and how many trashes been correctly sorted, to help users better understand their environmental impact. Through the calendar view, users can get a high-level overview of their footprint overtime, allowing them to see trends and patterns in their behavior (Fig. 4c). In cases that the waste scanner is unable to detect a particular item, a waste dictionary is also provided for users to directly search for wastes and add the items into the carbon tracer (Fig. 4d).

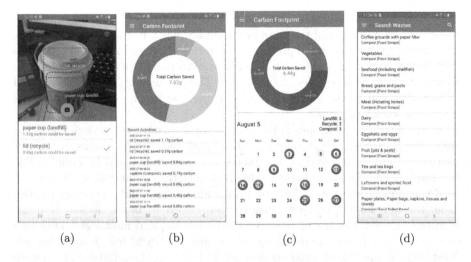

(a)   (b)   (c)   (d)

Fig. 4. Sustainability Awareness Technologies: The detected objects can be selected to user's personal carbon footprint tracer (a & b); the carbon footprint tracer also illustrates the estimated carbon emission with logs and calendar visualization views (b & c); user can search for any undetected waste from the waste dictionary (d).

2.4   Case Study on the Improved Application

A case study was then conducted to explore and evaluate the user experience on the application's improvements in the real-world setting. Two participants, A and B, were recruited to use the app for at least one week. User A was instructed to use the app on every disposal for one week; user B was asked to use it when it was needed over two weeks. Our application recorded the usage data, including the time and the detected wastes. Only textual data is uploaded and stored in the cloud. Pictures taken by users were used solely for object detection and were deleted once the detection was completed. After the trial, a survey and exit interview were administered to each of the participants to gather feedback.

3   Evaluations

3.1   Behavior Analysis

Based on the data collected during the study, we could have a sneak peek of how the users utilize the app in daily life. On average, user A opened the application 2.6 times each day and user B opened it 1.8 times per day. As for the function usages, user A used the waste scanner the most times (24 times) and took 24 photos. The participant also manually refreshed the tips for 19 times. However, searching (3 times) and footprint functions (2 times) were barely used by this user. The other case, user B tended to use the search-and-add function (42 times) more than the scanner (opened for 7 times, took only 2 pictures). The user checked the footprint records (10 times in total) and refreshed tips (9 times) every day. According to these observations, we found that users were capable of using both core functionalities to obtain feedback when it was needed. However, they may have their personal preferences in terms of operating it, and tended to stick to the their comfortable method, either took a picture or direct searching, to look up for correct categories of the wastes. The participants also demonstrated to pay attention to the auxiliary functions, such as tips and footprints, as the additional knowledge input.

Both participants demonstrated a good consciousness of garbage classification: user A disposed 19 recyclables, 10 compostable, and 6 landfills during her usage while user B disposed 18 recyclables, 14 compostable, and 11 landfills. The two participants demonstrated two different patterns during the study. User A used the application mainly for look up the knowledge - did one search or scan using the app for the correct category then closed it, barely looked into the footprints record. Her list of waste was more unique, and most items appeared only once. User B was more like using the app to 'track' his disposal history. Most items in his list repeated many times and most of them (30 out of 43) were daily consumables such as utensils, paper products, and bottles. He navigated the footprint tracker on a daily basis to check his progress.

3.2   Feedback and Future Work

Both participants demonstrated an overall satisfaction and willing to continue using the application in our feedback survey. The application could be improved in some ways based on the study results. Firstly, due to the limitations of the object detector, some objects may not be detected correctly and require users' manual modifications. However, when users were trying to change the result by themselves, there was a high chance they cannot decide the garbage category correctly. According to our study, the user's self-labels only had an accuracy of 63%. Thus, a better detector shall be introduced to avoid users labelling garbage on their own. Such demands were also presented in the users' feedback. In addition, there was still a 20% error rate when we tested the users about the correct categories of the garbage they disposed in the past week. Thus more educational features could be added in order to intensify the user's memory on recycling.

4   Conclusions

In this paper, we presented a mobile application integrated object detection and augmented reality to improve users' recycling knowledge and behaviors. In our first usability study, which involved 28 participants, the application demonstrated its ability to train and improve the users' recycling knowledge, particularly in disposing of complex waste items. We then adopted some feedback from the participants and made several improvements to the application. The updated app could estimate the carbon been saved and gave visualizations on personal carbon footprint. The follow up case study was conducted with two participants in depth for one to two weeks. The findings suggested that the application had the potential to encourage proper waste sorting and contribute to our daily sustainable life. In the future, we prioritize to improve the waste detection model's accuracy, add more educational features, and conduct studies that facing a wider and larger group of users thus make the application become more inclusive and easier to use.

References

1. trashnet. https://github.com/garythung/trashnet (2022) Accessed 27 Sept 2022
2. Containers, P., Good, N.D.: Documentation for greenhouse gas emission and energy factors used in the waste reduction model (warm) (2016)
3. EPA: national overview: facts and figures on materials, wastes and recycling. https://www.epa.gov/facts-and-figures-about-materials-waste-and-recycling/national-overview-facts-and-figures-materials
4. Jacobsen, R.M., Johansen, P.S., Bysted, L.B.L., Skov, M.B.: Waste wizard: exploring waste sorting using AI in public spaces. In: Proceedings of the 11th Nordic Conference on Human-Computer Interaction: Shaping Experiences, Shaping Society, pp. 1–11 (2020)
5. Kaza, S., Yao, L., Bhada-Tata, P., Van Woerden, F.: What a waste 2.0: a global snapshot of solid waste management to 2050. World Bank Publications, Washington (2018)
6. Kuznetsova, A., et al.: The open images dataset v4. Int. J. Comput. Vis. **128**(7), 1956–1981 (2020)
7. Lin, W.: Yolo-green: a real-time classification and object detection model optimized for waste management. In: 2021 IEEE International Conference on Big Data (Big Data), pp. 51–57. IEEE (2021)
8. Longo, E., Sahin, F.A., Redondi, A.E.C., Bolzan, P., Bianchini, M., Maffei, S.: A 5g-enabled smart waste management system for university campus. Sensors (Basel) **21**(24), 8278 (2021)
9. Narayan, Y.: Deepwaste: applying deep learning to waste classification for a sustainable planet. arXiv preprint arXiv:2101.05960 (2021)
10. Proença, P.F., Simões, P.: Taco: trash annotations in context for litter detection. arXiv preprint arXiv:2003.06975 (2020)
11. Reif, I., Alt, F., Hincapié Ramos, J.D., Poteriaykina, K., Wagner, J.: Cleanly: trashducation urban system. In: CHI'10 Extended Abstracts on Human Factors in Computing Systems, pp. 3511–3516 (2010)
12. Tan, M., Pang, R., Le, Q.V.: Efficientdet: scalable and efficient object detection. In: Proceedings of the IEEE/CVF Conference on Computer Vision and Pattern Recognition, pp. 10781–10790 (2020)
13. Thieme, A., et al.: We've bin watching you" designing for reflection and social persuasion to promote sustainable lifestyles. In: Proceedings of the SIGCHI Conference on Human Factors in Computing Systems, pp. 2337–2346 (2012)
14. Wahyutama, A.B., Hwang, M.: YOLO-based object detection for separate collection of recyclables and capacity monitoring of trash bins. Electronics (Basel) **11**(9), 1323 (2022)

Research on Architectural Space Design of Digital Youth Community Based on Transition Design Concept

King Sing Sze, Meng Meng Du, and Yu Zhai[✉]

Xiamen Academy of Arts and Design, FuZhou University, Xiamen 361021, Fujian, China
miazhai@fzu.edu.cn

Abstract. In recent years, with the development of digital information technology and the combination of architectural design field and other fields, architectural design methods and processes are constantly changing, and architectural generative design methods appear. Building generation design is a self-generated design of building space units based on different complex models and algorithm logic. Among them, the main function of computers is to calculate and screen, and to visualize complex and abstract problems. By designing related programs and algorithms, the optimal solution is sought in different constraints. As a new social group, youth groups have many inconveniences at the beginning of community life, and we lack of community architecture research for this group. This paper puts the Transition Design theory into a conceptual youth community architecture scheme, and tries to solve the problems of optimal path, architectural modeling and spatial layout in the scheme by combining theory with digitization, so as to provide thinking and reference for the design of digital youth community architecture.

Keywords: Transition Design · Digitization · Youth Community · Stakeholders · Architectural Space

1 Introduction

Youths represent the hope and future of the country. It is very important for the community space to meet the living needs of contemporary and future youth groups. While the construction of digital city in China has promoted the development of economy and technology, the large-scale inflow of population has led to the unprecedented test of limited land resources in cities. The construction of community has increased greatly, but the digital coverage level is low, which leads to the poor quality of community service and the inability to meet the conditions for all stakeholders to live together. How to create a living environment that can improve the quality of life, promote the neighborhood communication and enhance the sense of belonging for the young people living in today's digital age and developing into the future has become an important issue. Based on the emerging Transition Design theory, this paper solves the architectural space problem of digital youth community, and promotes the whole design scheme to a more sustainable and ideal future transformation (Fig. 1). The digital community space is no longer limited to the traditional meaning, function and form, but pays more attention to the influence of urban environment and user group behavior, pays attention to the optimization process of space, and gradually rises to the transition of perception level. Re-imagine how to involve multiple stakeholders and make it unique and satisfied with the future by using unlimited design conditions.

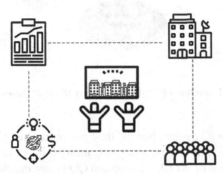

Fig. 1. Future Digital Youth Community (source: photo created by the author)

2 The Research Background

2.1 Digital Community and Youth Groups

In a broad sense, "Digital City" refers to the information of a city [1]. It is not only a general description of urban information, but also the purpose of urban information. It uses digital means to inspect, analyze and govern the whole city, so as to promote the smoothness and coordination of people flow, logistics, capital flow and other factors in the city. The design and construction of digital community is the foundation for the formation of "Digital City". Among modern urban buildings, digital communities and intelligent buildings have developed rapidly. Nowadays, more and more young people and laborers gather to work and live in big cities, and digitization has become an indispensable part of social life. As the main force in the digital age, young people are not only the guides of technological change, but also the leaders in the future. They should understand, experience and apply digital technology and actively participate in the wave of digital development. The youth groups in cities are expanding, so the digital living space suitable for young people has become a great social demand.

The construction of digital youth community is a huge demand and an important development direction both at present and in the future. The birth of digital community is based on the birth of intelligent building, and the emergence of intelligent building achieves the digitization of community life. It is characterized by smooth communication network system links, complete information network system, centralized management of building equipment monitoring system, automatic fire alarm and linkage between fire protection system and communication facilities, etc. [2], forming a healthy, safe, efficient and comfortable digital community (Fig. 2). This kind of data collection, data transmission, data display, etc. can be presented centrally, and can achieve the goal of integration and sharing of these data, providing the greatest convenience for residents' lives.

Fig. 2. Organizational structure of digital community (Source: photos made by the author)

When the user group is young people, they pay more attention to the convenience brought by digitalization. Home repairing and utility bill can be paid through mobile phones; The construction of We Chat Group and QQ Group enables residents to interact with managers and give timely feedback on service quality. This requires coordination of designers, youth and other stakeholders in the community to participate many times, so as to develop the community enough to meet future needs. Moreover, youth participation in the community is regarded as a favorable way to develop the partnership between youth and other residents, and promote the integration of youth's social resources through partnership, thus showing positive youth development expectations [3, 4]. However, the existing research on youth community participation holds that the reasons for the low youth community participation mainly include the following aspects: long working hours, great pressure, insufficient supply of community volunteer service, low community satisfaction and community recognition [5–7].

2.2 Digital Community and Youth Groups

From the concept of time and space, "transition" can be interpreted as a process or state in which things gradually develop from one stage to another and extend to "from here to there". Transition Design draws lessons from social science methods to understand the social roots of anti-solution problems, and puts the attention and joint design of stakeholders at the core of the problem-solving process [8]. More social and environmental problems are caused by market speculation, unfair distribution and waste of resources. At the same time, there are also "transitional period" and "transitional stage" when looking at people's life, production and environment from the perspective of social development. Therefore, the position and mode of confirmation need to be changed and upgraded to a transitional design mode more suitable for the present or the future (Fig. 3).

In the past decades, China's urban and rural areas have undergone unprecedented changes, and after entering the post-industrial era, the design has also undergone a transformation. In this context, we are faced with the problem of designing the environmental space of different regions after continuous comprehensive consideration, or carrying out secondary development and transformation. In order to build a relatively harmonious

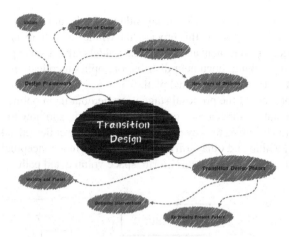

Fig. 3. Transition Design program diagram (Source: photos made by the author)

design system, we should dynamically understand the social development and cultural forms in different regions and different times, and use new ideas and technologies to intervene in design. For example, the Ferrous Foundry Park Project in Massachusetts, USA, this project is to transform a polluted brown land in the post-industrial period into a regenerated urban park with dense green plants and a large population. From early conception to long-term planning and management of the project, stakeholders have a high degree of autonomy in making decisions about the future development of the community. At the same time, through frank and transparent discussion of community history to support a series of projects, including coordinating planting programs and developing riverside greenways, this participation model is reestablishing the relationship between residents and the environment they create and the natural environment. Ultimately, Ferrous Foundry Park is a successful example of fully engaging stakeholders and transforming neglected industrial sites into unprecedented landscape experiences. Through the participation of stakeholders, it is more advantageous to break through the restrictive forces in the original environment and better maintain, protect and develop satisfactory relations. We should study the concepts and methods of transitional environment design, think about what problems to solve, how to solve problems, what objects to serve and what objects to exclude, and finally achieve a certain goal. And carefully consider the ethical principles involved in environmental design, so as to make it optimal in dealing with the relationship among people, things, technology, society and culture.

3   The Research Methods and Demonstration Construction

3.1   Research Methodology

Based on the Transition Design theory, the vision of stakeholders such as young and middle-aged residents, managers, business operators, government and designers in the community is obtained by combining online and offline, and the new design method is jointly confirmed. Secondly, we will continue to Re-frame present and future through digital means such as the Internet, We Chat and Facebook, and set new design interventions at specific nodes (Fig. 4). In this process, the whole community and its surrounding residents, managers, government and other stakeholders are driven to participate in it for many times, from docking, document distribution, opinion collection, post-adjustment and other activities to confirm the final plan.

The whole process of the proposal stage is carried out in an online and offline way, so the wishes of stakeholders are recorded in digital form, and how to implement such digital information becomes the key point. In this study, the collected data are visualized by Grasshopper, Rhino and other software, and applied in a conceptual design scheme to solve the generation of architectural form, space volume and path.

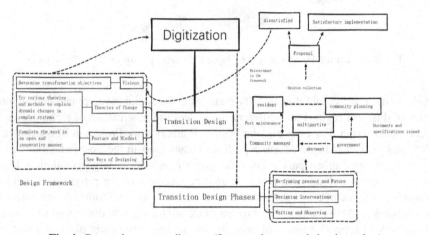

Fig. 4. Research program diagram (Source: photos made by the author)

3.2 Research Process

The scheme is located in a residential area in Baoshan District, Shanghai, China, and the main residential area is two buildings. Through online questionnaire interviews with young people around the project in the early stage, it is concluded that their ideal residential community needs service functions, commercial catering, entertainment, social and public supporting facilities besides residential functions. Based on these basic reference conditions, functional planning is carried out according to the existing layout of the two buildings. Clustering Categorical Data is adopted in architectural modeling and spatial layout, which transforms residential functions, service functions and supporting facilities functions in batches, replaceability, free connection and controllability, and then inputs specific parameters, such as the number of living rooms and the demand of youth space volume, so that the design of the whole discrete building construction will be full of changeable possibilities in spatial mode and form. Clustering Categorical Data in Grasshopper's algorithm program as shown in (Fig. 5), based on the determination of the red line of the building range, the three-dimensional lattice is generated by using Populate 3D arithmetic unit, and each three-dimensional lattice is established into a space box by combining OcTree arithmetic unit, and its shape change will be changed with the adjustment of Seed parameters of Jitter random arithmetic unit. The path between the two buildings is evolved by using FreiOtto's famous Wool Experiment. Its algorithm program in Grasshopper, such as (Fig. 6), divides the functional areas in the building into control points, and then divides them into point one and point two according to the two buildings. Each point is connected by VB Script with these two groups of points, and different types of line-bending effects can be obtained by adjusting different percentages of repulsion and tension.

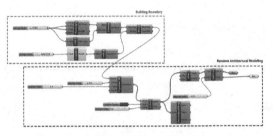

Fig. 5. Clustering Categorical Data Process diagram (Source: photos made by the author)

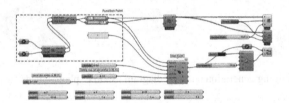

Fig. 6. Wool Experiment Process diagram (Source: photos made by the author)

3.3   Results of Study

After the path connection between 27 building function control points below and 36 building function control points above, 8 different levels of tension and repulsion are input by Grasshopper with Wool Experiment for path control, and it is concluded that the route with the most aggregation is the main path of the two buildings (Fig. 7). Secondly, the optimal path result is not only two-dimensional, but also the optimal path of the upper and lower staggered floors of the whole building (Fig. 7).

In terms of architectural modeling and space division, Grasshopper and Rhino are used to carry out Clustering Categorical Data according to the data of site youth demand and space residential volume size, and the internal layout of space is divided by multi-objective restriction rules or probability distribution, which makes the internal organization of architecturalspace changeable and rich in levels (Fig. 8).

After the spatial layout and path of the building are determined, the generation of residential buildings is coming to an end. The glass curtain wall encloses the discrete space, which makes the building appear as a whole and deals with the subdivision surface of the atrium. The paths of the two buildings are set in the form of air corridors, and grille structures are added outside the corridors to assist in bearing loads and help maintain greening and ecological functions. Through the combination of data such as functional flow point, requirements and volume in the early stage and the application of algorithms, a set of conceptual youth community architectural designs (Fig. 9) is finally obtained.

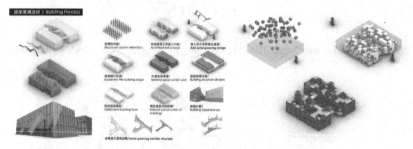

Fig. 7. Path composition process diagram (Source: photos made by the author)

Fig. 8. Building generation analysis diagram (Source: photos made by the author)

Fig. 9. Architectural Renderings (Source: photos made by the author)

4 Conclusion

At present, the construction of digital youth community is not paid enough attention in China, but it is an important way to solve the housing problem of youth groups in the future. With the help of the Transition Design theory, this paper tries to promote multi-stakeholder participation, deeply understand the vision and needs of local young residents for residential buildings, and collect information and data for the living patterns and living needs of digital youth community buildings. Under the condition of perfect data, building space is generated by modeling software and parameter processing software. Such generated buildings not only have changeable possibilities in form, but also rely on data positioning, and the interior of the space is rationally laid out. This paper provides a new design direction.

Fund Projects. 2022 Research Project of the Provincial Association for Science and Technology Innovation Think Tank (Project No: FJKX-2022XKB004).

References

1. Lv, J., Li, W.: Research on the development mode of the chinese digital city. Inf. Sci. (05), 672–675 (2006)
2. Shi, S.: Digital residential quarter and intelligent building. China Housing Facil. (Z1), 92–95 (2015)
3. Watts, R., Flanagan, C.: Pushing the Envelope on Youth Civic Engagement: a developmental and liberation psychology perspective (2007)
4. Cicognani, E., Zani, B., Fournier, B., et al.: Gender Differences in Youths' Political Engagement and Participation. The Role of Parents and of Adolescents' Social and Civic Participation. Academic Press (2012)
5. Jinqiao: Urban youth's community participation: a holistic analysis based on sociology. Youth Res. **146**(02), 56–60 (2019)
6. Zhang, W., Chen, F., Liu, X.: Reasons for youth absence in community volunteer service: based on a community survey in Beijing. China Nonprofit Rev. (1) (2018)
7. Deng, L.: Cognition, action and influencing factors of young people in community governance – based on a survey in Shanghai. J. China Youth College Politic. Sci. (5), 23–29 (2015)
8. Irwin, T.: Transition design: design for systems-level change. Art Des. (10), 12–22 (2018)

Defining How to Connect Nature and Digital World to Decrease Human Impact

J. Valerio[✉] [ID], J. Piña[ID], D. Peña[ID], M. Ávila[ID], R. García[ID], B. Parra[ID], D. Méndez[ID], and A. Núñez[ID]

Universidad Autónoma Metropolitana, Vasco de Quiroga, 4871 Mexico, Mexico
adrianvalerio731@gmail.com, {rgarcia,bgarcia,dmendez, anunez}@cua.uam.mx

Abstract. Human impact in forests and natural protected areas seems to be a consequence of the lack of environmental awareness of visitors and the population who live nearby areas [1]. This paper presents the process of analysis to determine which tool or digital platform would be useful to promote information related to conservation of natural areas, to achieve this, different elements and moments of the process of communication are considered to identify key points to study the media as a possible digital output in order to assess their effectiveness. Three possible digital outputs are considered: visual identifiers, such as augmented reality elements linked through a mobile application; electronic devices such as NFC's or an off-site installation. The project seeks to develop a communicational process that facilitates ecologically responsible behavior, through useful informative content that promotes the appropriation of the space, based on the understanding of the motivations of the users and their behaviors. In order to carry out the analysis process and the understanding of the problem, three theoretical supports are considered that fit with the research approach. Two of them are related to the interaction of people with the physical space; while the third explores the inference process behind a behavior.

Keywords: Conceptual Design and Planning · Heuristics and Guidelines for Design · Audio-visual Artificial Environment

1 Introduction

During the pandemic of COVID-19 people resorted to open spaces as a synonym of safety [2]. Dieter Helm [3] argues that this event will change the way people act with respect to natural environments, both individual and collective, however, it is difficult to understand whether these changes will be for the well-being of the environments and its preservation or their deterioration and consumption.

The research process has lead the investigation to the identification of three theoretical supports that fit with the focus of the problematic. Two of them are related to the interaction of people with physical space—appropriation of space and way-showing—; while the third—attribution theory—explores the inference process behind a behavior.

The original version of this chapter was revised: The ORCID number has been added for the author Peña D. The correction to this chapter is available at
https://doi.org/10.1007/978-3-031-36001-5_89

C. Stephanidis et al. (Eds.): HCII 2023, CCIS 1835, pp. 524–532, 2023.
https://doi.org/10.1007/978-3-031-36001-5_68

The combination of them applied to the object of study in question has provided solid support to the flow of information development for which it has been contemplated a digital system as output.

According to Eurrutia, P. [4], "the appropriation of space is the generation of links with 'places', which facilitates ecologically responsible behavior, as well as involvement and participation in the environment itself". In such a way that the links that are established between the visitors and the places, have their origin in the relationship set up between them, therefore, the "appropriate" environment becomes and develops a fundamental role in cognitive, identity and relational processes, which explains dimensions of behavior beyond what is merely functional [4]. Mollerup, P. [5] defines wayshowing as "the professional activity of planning and implementing guidance systems in buildings or outdoors", an act in which a conception of location, path layout and information on the route -whether artificial or natural- arise. Finally, for psychology the concept of attribution is reserved for the way in which the causes of a behavior are perceived; either due to an external factor—situational—or internal—dispositional—[6]. Consequently, attribution theory is concerned with the information that people use in making causal inferences about events; and the way in which this cognitive perception influences their motivations and behaviors [7].

Since some years ago, the development of technology has increased, and accordingly with it the number of developers interested in improving user experience, personalizing interaction based on a dataset requirement, experiencing different interaction design methods and technologies, etc. However, the main purpose of this article is to identify and expose the characteristics, advantages and limitations of three possible solutions applied in a context that offers different limitations for technological implementations [8], either because of internet access or lack of electricity. Thus, this research seeks to generate information on how users behave in protected natural areas and how we can encourage them to make environmentally responsible decisions, while this research article is based on the theoretical framework proposed to analyze the problem, as well as the interaction needs that have been identified during the process in order to promote an environmental behavior in natural protected areas.

1.1 Protected Natural Area Where the Study is Being Conducted Sample

This research is being conducted in the Mexican protected natural area called Desierto de los Leones, which is located in the west of Mexico City. The reasons why this place was chosen are that it has great social, cultural and, above all, ecological relevance [9]; since many urban communities depend on the forest for drinking water supply and count on to serve as a natural lung to improve the air quality of the city. This place was designated as the first national park in the country, however, poorly implemented public policies caused a series of fires in 1998 that resulted in the loss of 400 hectares of forest [10]. More than 20 years after this event, the affected area has not fully recovered because visitors carry out careless activities in the area due to a lack of knowledge of the park's internal regulations and specialized environmental education in the area. Therefore, we believe it is essential to integrate these two thematic axes into the proposal in order to have both a regulatory and an educational dimension in the technological proposal.

2 Interaction Definition

2.1 User Selection

There are various types of problems in this study area, which come from different sources and involve different users. But hiking is identified as the most careless activity—due to misinformation—that have prevented the recovery of the forest, however most of them have shown interest in improving their relationship with the environment [11].

2.2 Methodology

The process of analysis is briefly describing in the subsequent section. Firstly, it was carried out a brainstorming to generate the first draft of the system, as a result of this process were detected the following need: the definition of the interaction system characteristics is crucial to accomplished the objective of the project. There were selected five possible technological solutions that offer different limitations for the implementation. The information and ideas spill after the research process made it possible to filter options and choose only three possible technological outputs. Since it is very difficult to generate a concrete user in these environments, we re-sorted to the design thinking methodology [12] in order to start designing the three pro-posed solutions. In this way, four basic concepts of the methodology will be applied: empathize, define, ideate and prototype—evaluation will be a later step in the re-search—always thinking about the users and their relationship with the natural environments. In this way, we aim to satisfy the visual and functional needs in the communicative requirements for the conservation of the park, in a useful and meaningful way for the users. And, subsequently, to provoke the expected change of attitude.

3 Results

3.1 NFC technology

Near Field Communication (NFC), it is a short-range wireless communication technology, the transmission process depends on the reader device generating a magnetic field by passing an electric current through a coil. When another magnetic field is brought nearby, it induces an electric current that wirelessly transmits the data to the reader [13]. This technology has different modes of operation, this project considerer two.

On Site: Natural Areas. The first one, the peer-to-peer mode enables sharing information between NFC-enabled devices. For this matter, the NFC tag on the park's sign is the device with which the visitor can interact by passing their cell phone near (see Fig. 1), allowing the hiker to carry accurate information on his phone the rest of the way, and to know what actions take in that area without harming the environment. Each signage with NFC tag activates information.

The Interaction Experience for the Visitor. Previously the visitor has downloaded the application on their mobile phone, this operates offline. Once on site, visitor walks the route preplanned and find signage with the NFC tag at different points of the way, to which must get closer the mobile phone. The NFC acts as a signal emitter that trigger the preloaded application, this identifies the geographic location of the visitor and display tips and warning for taking care of the forest. Then, the visitor will be able to consult the information and continue the way to the next signage with NFC tag.

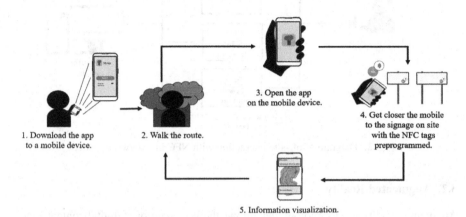

Fig. 1. Diagram of on-site interaction with NFC in peer-to-peer mode.

Off Site: Interactive Installation. The second one, the read/write mode, with which is possible to storage data on a computer, the data can be used later to produce information about the interaction. It is worth highlighting that the proposal for this installation has its basis in interactive, digital and installation art. As explained by Edmonds and Candy, digital art media can be applied to various forms of art, including painting, performance, cinema, and participation. In cases where the medium is static, such as print, the technological issues related to output devices, such as printers or video projection, are well-defined [14]. In terms of the level of interaction that we aim to achieve, we refer to the taxonomy proposed by Cornock and Edmonds [15], which is divided into four categories: static, dynamic-passive, dynamic-interactive, and dynamic-interactive (variant). The category that will be implemented is dynamic-interactive, which is based on the human "viewer" taking an active role in influencing the changes in the artistic object.

The Interaction Experience for the Viewer. Firstly, each visitor receives a NFC bracelet. Secondly, the spectator can choose to approach to any of the four signages, which are receivers, it is necessary that the spectator bring the bracelet closely to a NFC receiver to initiate the interaction. Finally, once the tour has concluded, the collected data is storage in a computer (see Fig. 2).

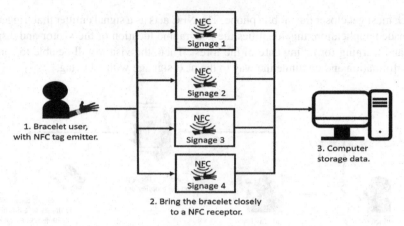

Fig. 2. Diagram of off-site interaction with NFC in read/write mode.

3.2 Augmented Reality

Augmented reality is a technology that allows the visualization if digital content superimposed on a video stream of reality, to achieve it is necessary a preprogrammed application that identify and associate the markers that trigger the content. The software uses computer vision technology to recognize the marker when it is pointed with the camera-equipped device.

To design the experience certain stages must be completed (see Fig. 3). The first stage implied the definition of the requirements, restrictions, functionalities and characteristics, that conduct the design and development of the animated elements, the programming of the application with all its functionalities, and the markers creation. The second stage consist in the integration of the previous parts, this include an evaluation of units and components and the possible evolution of the software functions. To continue at the final

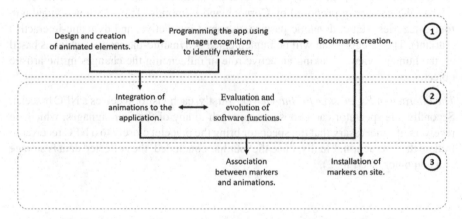

Fig. 3. Diagram of the experience design process with augmented reality.

stage with the association between markers and animations, the revision of its operation and finally the installation of markers on site.

The Interaction Experience for the Visitor. Initially the visitor has downloaded the application on their mobile phone, that operates offline. Then, once on site, the visitor walks the route preplanned and find signage with the markers at different points of the way, when a marker is identified the visitors opens the application mobile and points the mobile phone at it, this triggers the content and initiate the visualization of the augmented reality interaction, the process repeats as many times as the visitors wants (see Fig. 4).

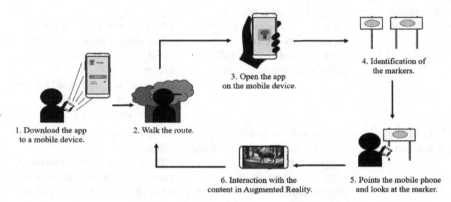

Fig. 4. Diagram of interaction with augmented reality.

4 Discussion

The three proposals have strengths and limitations during the interaction experience, Table 1 shows some of the considerations made during the analysis process, other aspects related to the technology functionalities were considered, but are not included in this article.

Table 1. Interaction systems strengths and limitations.

Interaction system	Strengths	Limitations
NFC on-site	– No power supply required – The NFC tag works regardless of the state of the signage – The information provided depends on visitor location	– Short range – No dialogical data processing – The visitor must have a recent cell phone model to interact with the system – The user is disconnected from the environment by focusing his attention on the phone screen
NFC off-site installation	– It is possible to re-signifying an object (signage) through an active interaction by the user – Alternative participation by viewers (photographs, videos, etc.) – The experience is not linear, it depends on decisions viewer	– The development, is designed for a single user – There will be little and no direct interaction between spectators who are not active participants and the installation – It has an established time to interact with the piece (finite experience)
Augmented reality	– Non-invasive – The application can include music, sound effects and visual elements – A story can be told	– The user loses sight of the environment – Keeps user attention on the mobile phone – User experiences alone – Users must wait a delay of data processing of the marker

5 Conclusions

After this, we conclude that the system that most closely aligns with the ideals of the project, and with the three theoretical axes presented in the introduction, is the interactive off-site installation. We consider it propitious to have a technological contribution in our research, however, most of them are opposed to the ideals of natural environments, or in other words, the temporary disconnection of the screens. This is why, as a result of the discussion, we realized that the technologies placed on site would force users to use their devices during the tour, causing a loss of contact with the place.

In terms of human-computer interaction, on-site technologies have a greater number of limitations due to the characteristics of the environment itself, so the user would have a higher level of frustration when not being able to access all the information at the time. On the other hand, off-site interactive installations are a system that would have a greater reach among users and would facilitate a change in their behavior by presenting visual and narrative elements that would have a greater impact on them. In this way, we would comprehensively promote the appropriation of the space by avoiding technological distractions on site, while promoting information on environmentally responsible behavior that they can acquire before visiting the natural area.

From here on, the research and the project will focus on generating the contents of the interactive installation according to the proposed theories, detected user needs and the strengths and weaknesses of the system in question; and, subsequently, usability tests will be carried out with control groups. Therefore, the conclusions of this article cannot be definitive, since it is research in progress, and the conclusive results will be obtained later.

References

1. Cruz, J., Gómez, O.: Descripción y análisis de la situación actual del turismo de naturaleza en la Reserva Forestal Protectora quebrada Honda, caños Parrado y Buque en Villavicencio, Meta (Colombia). Turismo y Sociedad vol. XXXI, pp. 199–226 (2022)
2. López, A., et al.: COVID-19: impactos en el medio ambiente y en el cumplimiento de los ODS en América Latina. Desarrollo y sociedad 1(86), 104–132 (2020)
3. Helm, D.: The environmental impacts of the coronavirus. Environmental & Resource Economics. Environ. Resource Econ. **76**(1), 21–38 (2020)
4. Vidal, T., Eurrutia, P.: La apropiación del espacio: una propuesta teórica para comprender la vinculación entre las personas y los lugares. Anuario de psicología **36**(3), 281–297
5. Mollerup, P.: Wayshowing > wayfinding: Basic and interactive, 1st edn. BIS Publishers, Amsterdam, The Netherlands (2013)
6. Kassin, S., Fein, S., Markus, H.: Social Psychology. edn. Wadsworth Publishing Company, California, United States (2010)
7. Heider, F.: The Psychology of Interpersonal Relations, 1st edn. Wiley, New York, United States (1958)
8. Dix, A., Gill, S., Hare, J., Ramduny-Ellis, D.: Connecting Physical and Digital Worlds. In: TouchIT: Understanding Design in a Physical-Digital World 1st edn. Oxford University Press, Oxford, United Kingdom (2022)
9. Secretaría del Medio Ambiente y Recursos Naturales: Desierto de los Leones, https://www.gob.mx/semarnat/articulos/desierto-de-los-leones. Accessed 6 Sept 2018
10. Comisión Nacional de Áreas Naturales Protegidas: Programa de conservación y manejo. Desierto de los Leones. CONANP-SEMARNAT (2006)
11. Secretaría del Medio Ambiente: Trabajan Sedema y CONANP para mejorar el suelo del desierto de los leones. https://www.sedema.cdmx.gob.mx/comunicacion/nota/trabajan-sedema-y-conanp-para-mejorar-suelo-en-el-desierto-de-los-leones. Accessed 6 Nov 2021
12. Hasso, P.: Guia del proceso creative: Miniguía: una introducción al Design Thinking + Bootcamp bootleg. Universidad sigo 21 (n.d.)
13. Islam, M., Islam, S., Ling, T., Hooy, K.: NFC-based mobile application for student attendance in institution of higher learning. In: 2022 1st International Conference on AI in Cybersecurity (ICAIC), pp. 1–5 (2022)

14. Edmonds, E., Turner, G., Candy, L.: Approaches to interactive art systems. In: Proceedings of the 2nd International Conference on Computer Graphics and Interactive Techniques in Australasia and South East Asia, pp. 113–117 (2004)
15. Cornock, S., Edmonds, E.: The creative process where the artist is amplified or superseded by the computer. Leonardo 1(6), 11–16 (1973)

Movement Monitoring in Commercial Areas Using Internet of Things

José Varela-Aldás[1,2](✉) ⓘ, Belén Ruales[2], and Gedeoni Bastidas[2]

[1] Centro de Investigaciones de Ciencias Humanas y de la Educación - CICHE, Universidad Indoamérica, Ambato 180103, Ecuador
josevarela@uti.edu.ec
[2] SISAu Research Group, Facultad de Ingeniería, Industria y Producción, Universidad Indoamérica, Ambato 180103, Ecuador
belenruales@uti.edu.ec

Abstract. The Internet of Things has been a trend in the last decade and is now found in countless applications, solving problems in almost any field. Specifically, in the commercial area, there is an effort to apply this technology to facilitate the control of services or processes. This work presents the movement monitoring of commercial areas. The proposal uses the ESP32 board that, using passive infrared sensors located perpendicular to each other, covers two areas of interest for commercial premises with multiple products. The collected data travel to the ThingSpeak Platform, where there are graphs with the states of the sensors, allowing identify the active area. The results present the motion state readings in the two areas, indicating the correct functioning of the system. Finally, we use a technology acceptance model to analyze this proposal, determining an acceptance of 69.6% that is not favorable for this proposal.

Keywords: Internet of Things · ESP32 board · Passive Infrared sensor · ThingSpeak · technology acceptance model

1 Introduction

The Internet of Things (IoT) can be viewed as a widespread, worldwide neural network of interconnected devices in the cloud. This allows intelligent machines to communicate and interact with one another and with objects, infrastructure, and the environment. This leads to the generation of an enormous amount of data, which can be processed into actionable insights that have the potential to automate and optimize various aspects of our daily lives, thus making them more convenient [1]. The IoT has emerged as a trend and found widespread applications, offering solutions to problems across various fields [2–4]. In addition, significant strides have been made toward fulfilling the technological prerequisites for integrating smart devices with the Internet. Despite these advancements, the IoT paradigm grapples with difficult obstacles concerning implementing security and access control measures within resource-limited environments [5, 6].

In the commercial sector, in particular, a concerted effort has been made to leverage this technology and streamline the management of services and processes [7]. The

© The Author(s), under exclusive license to Springer Nature Switzerland AG 2023
C. Stephanidis et al. (Eds.): HCII 2023, CCIS 1835, pp. 533–539, 2023.
https://doi.org/10.1007/978-3-031-36001-5_69

IoT is driving a significant transformation in residential and commercial buildings. With IoT technologies, buildings are becoming more intelligent, efficient, and secure. Researchers have already applied IoT in various applications and settings to convert traditional buildings into smart ones [8].

This document details the evaluation of a monitoring system to detect movement in commercial areas. For this, the ESP32 board and the ThingSpeak web server are used. The objective is to analyze the acceptance of the proposal through a technology acceptance model. The document has been organized into 5 sections: Sect. 1 presents the introduction to the topic; Sect. 2 describes materials and methods; Sect. 3 shows the results; Sect. 4 presents the discussion; and, Sect. 5 contains the conclusions obtained.

2 Materials and Methods

Figure 1 presents the scheme of this proposal. The objective is to monitor movements in commercial areas. The central component is the ESP32; this controller receives information from the passive infrared (PIR) sensors. The acquired information travels to the web server for remote monitoring of variables; in this case, the data is sent to ThingSpeak. At the other extreme is the user, who receives information on the status of the detected movements.

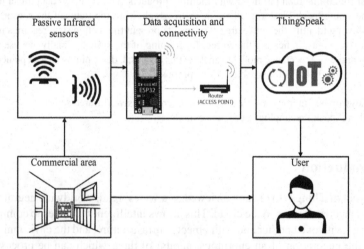

Fig. 1. General outline of the proposal.

2.1 Electrical Connections

The required electrical connections are based on ESP32 Development Module. The controller is connected to PIR sensors through digital ports. These elements are installed in a case to monitor the movement of the commercial areas.

2.2 Web Server

ThingSpeak is an IoT platform that allows the user to manage local site variables through a web interface; this server offers the web service to interconnect the devices through its web page. Configuring the channel with the two required fields (State 1 and State 2), see Fig. 2. ThingSpeak also graphs the variables created as it receives new data.

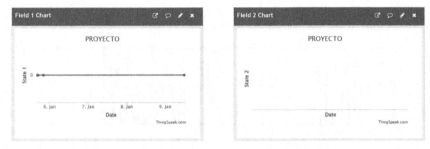

Fig. 2. Channel configuration in ThingSpeak.

2.3 Programming the ESP32

For the programming of the ESP 32, the WiFi connectivity library (WiFi.h) is required, which allows the device to establish communication with the Internet through a WiFi network. And the ThingSpeak.h library enables it to connect the device to the web service as a client. The data received from the sensors are sent to the web server every second because we have the ThingSpeak license.

3 Results

The proposal is installed in establishments with multiple commercial services. Figure 3 shows the installed proposal, observing that the sensors are located almost perpendicularly to cover two commercial areas.

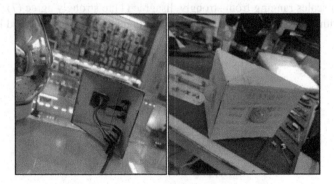

Fig. 3. Photos of installed monitoring system.

3.1 Measurements of Motion States

The recorded data in Fig. 4 illustrates the movement readings over a period of time in the two commercial areas, where multiple activations were registered in a short time due to the concurrence operation of the commercial establishment. This indicates the effective functioning of the proposed system.

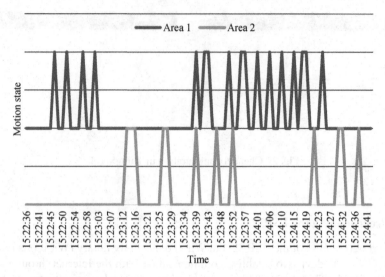

Fig. 4. Movement readings in the 2 areas obtained from ThingSpeak.

3.2 Acceptance Analysis

In the acceptance analysis, a technology acceptance model is applied, specifically, the consumer acceptance of internet of things technology [9]. Applying the components of perceived usefulness, perceived ease of use, social influence, perceived enjoyment, and perceived behavioral control. All items of model acceptance were measured via seven-point scales ranging from strongly disagree (1) to strongly agree (7). The results obtained with the administrator user of the commercial areas are presented in Table 1.

Table 1. Results of technology acceptance model.

Indicator	Score
Perceived usefulness	
- Using the monitoring system would enable me to supervise more quickly.	4
- Using the monitoring system would make it easier for me to supervise in commercial areas.	5
- Using the monitoring system would significantly increase the quality or output of my life.	5
- Overall, I would find using the monitoring system to be advantageous.	5
Perceived ease of use	
- Learning to use the monitoring system is easy for me.	7
- I find my interaction with the monitoring system clear and understandable.	5
- I think using the monitoring system is easy.	6
Social influence	
- People who are important to me would recommend using the monitoring system.	3
- People who are important to me would find using the monitoring system beneficial.	4
- People who are important to me would find using the monitoring system a good idea.	4
Perceived enjoyment	
- I have fun with using the monitoring system.	4
- Using the monitoring system is pleasurable.	5
- Using the monitoring system gives enjoyment to me.	4
Perceived behavioral control	
- Using the monitoring system is entirely within my control.	5
- I have the resource, knowledge and ability to use the monitoring system.	6
- I am able to skillfully use the monitoring system.	6
Total	78/112 (0.696)

4 Discussion

It is evident that there are many related works in the literature. For example, [10] implements a smart system using a PIR motion sensor that integrates with AWS cloud technology using the BeagleBone Black controller. Another work implements an intelligent human traffic monitoring system based on IoT using Raspberry Pi; the objective is to notify in real-time and interact with the system remotely [11]. People have also been tracked through sensors and IoT technology, aiming to monitor soldiers through the communication module and give them the status of other soldiers [12]. On the other hand, home automation systems also use PIR sensors to detect movement and, accordingly, control devices [13]. But few works analyze the acceptance of technology from the user's perspective; specifically, in our work, we found an acceptance of 69.6%, evidencing that the social influence and the perspective of enjoyment need to improve significantly.

This work is limited by an individual case and the need for a custom user interface to visualize the movements.

5 Conclusions

This work presents the development of a movement monitoring system for commercial areas. Thus, it is possible to graphically observe the states of movement of two areas of interest with an update of one second. Although the correct functioning of the system is achieved, the results of the acceptance model indicate the need for improvements to approve the use of this proposal.

In future works, a custom mobile application or web application can be developed that allows better interaction with the system.

References

1. Bhardwaj, S., Kole, A.: Review and study of internet of things: It's the future. In: 2016 International Conference on Intelligent Control Power and Instrumentation (ICICPI), pp. 47–50. IEEE (2016). https://doi.org/10.1109/ICICPI.2016.7859671
2. Kumar, S., Tiwari, P., Zymbler, M.: Internet of Things is a revolutionary approach for future technology enhancement: a review. J. Big Data 6(1), 1–21 (2019). https://doi.org/10.1186/s40537-019-0268-2
3. Varela-Aldás, J., Silva, S., Palacios-Navarro, G.: IoT-based alternating current electrical parameters monitoring system. Energies 15, 6637 (2022). https://doi.org/10.3390/en15186637
4. Toapanta, J., Miranda, M., Andaluz, V.H., Palacios-Navarro, G., Varela-Aldás, J.: Control of a security door through the Internet of Things. In: Communications in Computer and Information Science, pp. 391–397 (2022). https://doi.org/10.1007/978-3-031-06388-6_52
5. Ouaddah, A., Mousannif, H., Abou Elkalam, A., Ait Ouahman, A.: Access control in the Internet of Things: big challenges and new opportunities. Comput. Networks. 112, 237–262 (2017). https://doi.org/10.1016/j.comnet.2016.11.007
6. Misra, N.N., Dixit, Y., Al-Mallahi, A., Bhullar, M.S., Upadhyay, R., Martynenko, A.: IoT, big data, and artificial intelligence in agriculture and food industry. IEEE Internet Things J. 9, 6305–6324 (2022). https://doi.org/10.1109/JIOT.2020.2998584
7. Bayer, S., Gimpel, H., Rau, D.: IoT-commerce - opportunities for customers through an affordance lens. Electron. Mark. 31(1), 27–50 (2020). https://doi.org/10.1007/s12525-020-00405-8
8. Lawal, K., Rafsanjani, H.N.: Trends, benefits, risks, and challenges of IoT implementation in residential and commercial buildings. Energy Built Environ. 3, 251–266 (2022). https://doi.org/10.1016/j.enbenv.2021.01.009
9. Gao, L., Bai, X.: A unified perspective on the factors influencing consumer acceptance of internet of things technology. Asia Pacific J. Mark. Logist. 26, 211–231 (2014). https://doi.org/10.1108/APJML-06-2013-0061

10. Patoliya, J.J., Patel, S.B., Desai, M.M., Patel, K.K.: Embedded linux based smart secure IoT intruder alarm system implemented on beaglebone black. In: Patel, K.K., Garg, D., Patel, A., Lingras, P. (eds.) icSoftComp 2020. CCIS, vol. 1374, pp. 343–355. Springer, Singapore (2021). https://doi.org/10.1007/978-981-16-0708-0_28
11. Musharaf Hussain, M.M., Rahman, M.M., Uddin, M.S., Arefin, M.S.: IoT Based Smart Human Traffic Monitoring System Using Raspberry Pi. Presented at the (2023). https://doi.org/10.1007/978-3-031-19958-5_34
12. Sabarimuthu, M., Krishna, M.P., Sundari, P.M., Aarthi, L., Juhair, P.M., GowthamRaj, G.: IoT based soldier status monitoring using sensors and SOS switch. In: 2022 Second International Conference on Computer Science, Engineering and Applications (ICCSEA), pp. 1–6. IEEE (2022). https://doi.org/10.1109/ICCSEA54677.2022.9936125
13. Darji, M., Parmar, N., Darji, Y., Mehta, S.: A Smart Home Automation System Based on Internet of Things (IoT) Using Arduino. Presented at the (2022). https://doi.org/10.1007/978-981-19-5037-7_19

Remote Monitoring of Electrical Parameters Using M5Stack Core2

José Varela-Aldás[1,2(⊠)] ⓘ and Fernando Saá[2]

[1] Centro de Investigaciones de Ciencias Humanas y de La Educación - CICHE, Universidad Indoamérica, Ambato 180103, Ecuador
josevarela@uti.edu.ec
[2] SISAu Research Group, Facultad de Ingeniería, Industria y Producción, Universidad Indoamérica, Ambato 180103, Ecuador
fernandosaa@uti.edu.ec

Abstract. The Internet of Things applications have benefited from the new integrated systems available on the market and the monitoring of electrical variables has become a necessity in the domestic and industrial fields. For this reason, this work presents the monitoring of electrical parameters using an M5Stack Core2 device. To obtain the electrical parameters, PZEM 004T V3.0 is used, this sensor allows reading voltage, current, active power, power factor, and active energy. For remote monitoring, the web service of the ThingSpeak platform is used. On this page, the information is presented graphically with a sample time of 15 s. The tests are carried out by monitoring the operation of a 3D printer while it manufactures a part. To validate the measurements, a commercial meter is used as a control instrument. The results show the online data and the comparative graphs between the proposed meter and the commercial meter, obtaining an error of 0.176% for the voltage and 7.085% for the current, which allows the proposal to be validated.

Keywords: Electrical measurements · M5Stack · IoT · remote monitoring · web server

1 Introduction

1.1 Motivation

For several years, the monitoring of electrical parameters has been an important requirement in automated systems, installing devices dedicated to the collection and sending of information to the main computer [1]. This need became more evident with the appearance of industry 4.0, where all components of the industry must report their status continuously, taking advantage of all this information to prevent damage [2]. This implies the connectivity of industrial systems, requiring new communication technologies that facilitate connection with the cloud [3].

Currently, the internet of things (IoT) is in the focus of interest of researchers and developers from all over the world intending to extend this technology on a large scale, obtaining the greatest amount of possible benefits [4]. For this, there are still several

C. Stephanidis et al. (Eds.): HCII 2023, CCIS 1835, pp. 540–548, 2023.
https://doi.org/10.1007/978-3-031-36001-5_70

problems to solve, such as privacy, security, standardization, ethics, scalability, reliability, quality, and more [5]. In addition, the IoT not only provides services but also offers real-time data availability in the so-called knowledge age. This allows making precise decisions that feedback on the operation of the system to continue improving the performance of the same IoT system [6]. For this to be possible, electronic devices with higher performance are required to facilitate the implementation of new proposals.

In electronics, embedded systems are defined as devices that contain peripherals and firmware for local processing of digital data, often on a single board. This equipment is becoming easier to program and configure, reducing development time and allowing focus on the study of the impact in application and research environments [7]. An example of this trend is the M5Stack Core2 ESP32 IoT integrated system, this device allows including several sensors and performing local processing, as well as more advanced data processing via WiFi or Bluetooth connection [8, 9]. These characteristics allow the development of portable proposals for remote monitoring through the Apps combined with artificial intelligence techniques such as Machine Learning [10]. In developing countries, it is still difficult to access low-cost technologies that allow remote monitoring using IoT [11], which is why proposals are required to facilitate the expansion of this technology.

1.2 Related Works

In related works, [12] develops an IoT-based system to remotely monitor the location, activity, and health of your pets. The measured variables are speed, heart rate, and location, this data is sent using an M5Stack Core2 board and the activity is predicted by a custom machine learning algorithm. All of this information is displayed on a user-friendly website including information related to the breed of the pet.

Concerning the remote monitoring of electrical energy, in [13] the authors develop an active energy meter using the PZEM-004T sensor. In this work, they use different devices for reading and uploading information. The data is uploaded to the internet using a NODE MCU board and then viewed from a mobile application developed for the Android operating system. The variables presented are voltage, current, active power, power factor, and energy.

In the same context, [14] presents an electrical energy meter based on IoT, this device was developed to monitor the electricity consumption in a building. The main components are the PZEM-004T sensor, an Arduino Nano Mini microcontroller, and the ESP8266 board, the latter received the data by serial communication to send it using WiFi. The meter collected electrical energy data for a week. The authors conclude that the results support the proper functioning of this proposal and indicate that these electrical energy data are useful for efficient energy management.

This document details the design, implementation, and evaluation of a remote monitoring system of electrical parameters based on the IoT. For this, an M5 Stack Core2 device and the ThingSpeak web server are used, and the measurements are validated using commercial multimeters. The document has been organized into 5 sections: Sect. 1 presents the introduction to the subject including the related works; Sect. 2 describes materials and methods; Sect. 3 presents the results of the operation tests; Sect. 4 presents the discussions; and, Sect. 5 contains the conclusions obtained and the future works.

2 Materials and Methods

The scheme of this proposal is presented in Fig. 1. The central component is the M5Stack Core2, this controller receives information from the PZEM 005T V3.0 sensor. The acquired information is sent to the web server for remote monitoring of electrical variables. On the other hand, this study uses commercial multimeters as control instruments. The control measurements serve as a reference to determine the measurement error of the proposed device. For the tests, the electrical measurements of a machine in operation are acquired using the proposed meter and the control instruments.

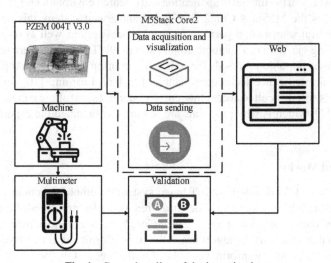

Fig. 1. General outline of the investigation.

2.1 Electrical Connections

The required electrical connections are presented in Fig. 2. The M5Stack Core2 device is connected to the PZEM 004T V3.0 sensor through TTL configuration since the sensor uses serial communication to deliver electrical measurements. On the other hand, the sensor has 4 sockets for power connection, 2 sockets are connected directly to AC voltage and 2 sockets are connected to the current measurement clamp. The machine to be supervised is a 120 Vac single-phase 3D printer with live-neutral connection.

2.2 Web Server

The IoT platform used for the connection between the two stations is ThingSpeak, this server offers the web service to interconnect the devices through its web page. Configuring the channel with the 5 required fields (voltage, current, active power, power factor and active energy). By using the third version of the sensor, power factor is obtained, unlike its predecessors that did not offer this electrical measurement. In addition, ThingSpeak graphs the variables created as it receives new data.

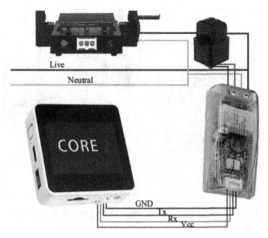

Fig. 2. Electrical connections.

2.3 Programming the M5Stack Core2

For the programming of the M5Stack Core2, the Arduino IDE software is used, installing all the required libraries. The M5Core2.h library allows you to use the features of the embedded system, including the LCD. The PZEM004Tv30.h library implements the Modbus RTU protocol to obtain data from the sensor. The WiFi.h library allows you to establish communication with the Internet through a WiFi network. And the ThingS-peak.h library allows you to connect the device to the web service as a client. For the connection to the server, the channel number and the writing key (ApiKey) generated when configuring the channel are used. Although the data is updated every second on the LCD, it is only sent every 15 s due to web server restrictions in the free mode.

3 Results

The proposed system is installed in the power supply of the 3D printer; this machine is programmed to print a piece with a duration of 25 min. Figure 3 shows the proposed system in operation, observing a voltage of 125.6 V for this instant, as well as the other electrical measurements presented on the LCD screen.

3.1 Measurements of Electrical Parameters

Figures 4, 5 and 6 present the measurements of some electrical parameters recorded by the meter of this proposal. Figure 7 shows the active power values recorded during the 25 min of the experiment, obtaining a maximum value of 210.7 W, a minimum value of 7.8 W, and an average value of 56.052 W with a standard deviation of 64.557 W.

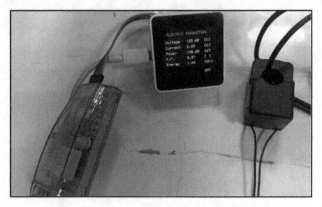

Fig. 3. Picture of the measuring system in operation.

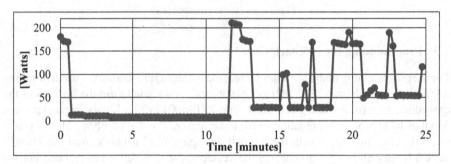

Fig. 4. Active power measurements obtained by the proposed meter during the experiment.

Figure 5 shows the power factor values recorded during the 25 min of the experiment, obtaining a maximum value of 0.59, a minimum value of 0.41, and an average value of 0.468 with a standard deviation of 0.0567.

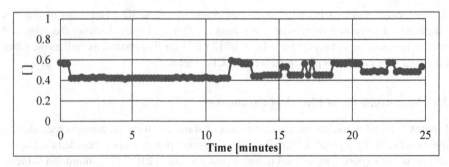

Fig. 5. Power factor measurements obtained by the proposed meter during the experiment.

Figure 6 shows the active energy values recorded during the 25 min of the experiment, obtaining a maximum increase of 0.878 Wh, a minimum increase of 0.0325 Wh, and an average increase of 0.234 Wh with a standard deviation of 0.269 Wh. Concluding experiment with a consumption of 23,355 Wh.

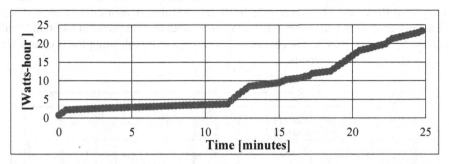

Fig. 6. Active energy measurements obtained by the proposed meter during the experiment.

3.2 Comparison of Measurements

To validate the measurements, the data is compared with control instruments. To measure current, a TRUPER brand clamp multimeter (MUT-202) is used and a conventional multimeter of the same brand (MUT-39) is used to measure voltage. The recording of control measures is done manually.

Figure 7 shows the voltage values recorded by both meters during the 25 min of the experiment, Voltage 1 belongs to the proposed meter and Voltage 2 belongs to the control instrument. For the proposed meter, a maximum value of 126.4 V, a minimum value of 125.3 V, and an average value of 125.89 V with a standard deviation of 0.261 V are obtained. For the control instrument, a maximum value of 126.5 V, a minimum value of 125.5 V, and an average value of 126.1 V with a standard deviation of 0.273 V are obtained. Comparing the measurements, an absolute mean error of 222 mV and a relative error of 0.176% are obtained. This result allows validating the proposal for this electrical variable.

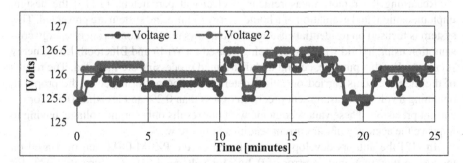

Fig. 7. Comparison of voltage measurements between both instruments.

Figure 8 shows the current values registered by both meters during the 25 min of the experiment, Current 1 belongs to the proposed meter and Current 2 belongs to the control instrument. For the proposed meter, a maximum value of 2.884 A, a minimum value of 0.145 A, and an average value of 0.847 A with a standard deviation of 0.888 A are obtained. For the control instrument, a maximum value of 2.89 A, a minimum value of 0.19 A, and an average value of 0.911 A with a standard deviation of 0.882 A are obtained. Comparing the measurements, a mean absolute error of 64.56 mA and a relative error of 7.085% are obtained, this result allows validating the proposal for measurements of high currents.

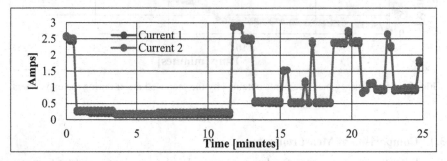

Fig. 8. Comparison of current measurements between both instruments.

4   Discussions

In the literature there are few proposals based on the M5Stack Core2 integrated system, requiring more studies of its applications to determine the advantages and limitations of this technology. In [8] the authors use an M5Stack board to analyze air samples by installing sensors to detect various volatile organic compounds. The results show a correct operation of the system with a response and recovery time of 10 min. This time is much longer than that achieved in our work for the website, which guarantees better control of the monitored states.

Regarding the remote measurement of electrical parameters, in [15] the design, implementation, and evaluation of a home energy monitoring system are presented. This system is focused on residential customers and allows remote monitoring of energy consumption using hybrid wireless technology based on Wi-Fi and Bluetooth Low Energy standards. For this purpose, central and distributed processing are included. The results of the measurements carried out allow determining the performance of the proposal, obtaining a voltage measurement precision of less than 0.2% and less than 0.5% for the current precision. These values coincide with our results only for the voltage, having to improve the accuracy of our current readings in future works.

In [13] the authors develop a meter based on the PZEM-004T sensor. Based on the test results, they find an error of 0.29% for voltage, 4.63% for current, 4.92% for active power, 1.36% for power factor, and 3.3% for total energy calculation. Compared with our proposal, we obtained voltage measurements with a lower error and current measurements with a higher error, and for both indicators, the difference is not significant. This allows us to validate our measurement of electrical parameters for the 2 variables.

Finally, in [14] the authors use similar components to implement their proposal, sharing the sensor and the server with our proposal. The main difference is in the acquisition and sending of data, which is done by combining 2 boards, one board for acquisition and another for communication with the server. The parameters measured were voltage, current, power, and energy, lacking the power factor, which is measured in our work, because an older version of the PZEM 004T sensor is used. There is also no evidence of control measurements using other devices for the measurement of electrical parameters. In addition, this work does not allow the information to be displayed locally, making it difficult to monitor the electrical parameters in situ, especially in cases of disconnection from the internet.

5   Conclusions and Future Works

This work presents the development of an electrical parameter meter using the M5Stack Core2 integrated system for remote monitoring through the web. Obtaining a functional system that allows the acquisition of voltage, current, active power, power factor, and active energy observable from anywhere in the world through the internet with a sampling time of 15 s. In addition, voltage and current measurements were validated using control instruments with an error of 0.176% and 7.085%, respectively.

In future works, it is intended to include more sensors with the possibility of monitoring multiple power lines simultaneously. In addition, it is planned to validate more electrical parameters using measurements in buildings and for a long time analyzing the results concerning commercial devices for remote monitoring of electrical energy based on the Internet of Things.

References

1. Khera, N., Jain, S.: Development of LabVIEW based electrical parameter monitoring system for single phase supply. In: 2015 Communication, Control and Intelligent Systems (CCIS), pp. 482–485. IEEE (2015). https://doi.org/10.1109/CCIntelS.2015.7437964
2. Kudelina, K., Vaimann, T., Asad, B., Rassõlkin, A., Kallaste, A., Demidova, G.: Trends and challenges in intelligent condition monitoring of electrical machines using machine learning. Appl. Sci. 11, 2761 (2021). https://doi.org/10.3390/app11062761
3. Peraković, D., Periša, M., Zorić, P.: Challenges and issues of ICT in industry 4.0. In: Ivanov, V., et al. (eds.) DSMIE 2019. LNME, pp. 259–269. Springer, Cham (2020). https://doi.org/10.1007/978-3-030-22365-6_26
4. Behrendt, F.: Cycling the smart and sustainable city: analyzing EC policy documents on internet of things, mobility and transport, and smart cities. Sustainability 11, 763 (2019). https://doi.org/10.3390/su11030763
5. Kumar, S., Tiwari, P., Zymbler, M.: Internet of Things is a revolutionary approach for future technology enhancement: a review. J. Big Data 6(1), 1–21 (2019). https://doi.org/10.1186/s40537-019-0268-2
6. Astill, J., Dara, R.A., Fraser, E.D.G., Roberts, B., Sharif, S.: Smart poultry management: Smart sensors, big data, and the internet of things. Comput. Electron. Agric. 170, 105291 (2020). https://doi.org/10.1016/j.compag.2020.105291
7. Carminati, M., Scandurra, G.: Advances in measurements and instrumentation leveraging embedded systems. Rev. Sci. Instrum. 92, 121601 (2021). https://doi.org/10.1063/5.0070073

8. Kwiatkowski, A., Drozdowska, K., Smulko, J.: Embedded gas sensing setup for air samples analysis. Rev. Sci. Instrum. **92**, 074102 (2021). https://doi.org/10.1063/5.0050445

9. Varela-Aldás, J., Silva, S., Palacios-Navarro, G.: IoT-based alternating current electrical parameters monitoring system. Energies **15**, 6637 (2022). https://doi.org/10.3390/en1518 6637

10. Varela-Aldás, J., Toasa, R.M., Baldeon Egas, P.F.: Support vector machine binary classifiers of home presence using active power. Designs. **6**, 108 (2022). https://doi.org/10.3390/design s6060108

11. Lopez-Vargas, A., Fuentes, M., Vivar, M.: Challenges and opportunities of the internet of things for global development to achieve the United Nations sustainable development goals. IEEE Access **8**, 37202–37213 (2020). https://doi.org/10.1109/ACCESS.2020.2975472

12. Harshika, G., Haani, U., Bhuvaneshwari, P., Venkatesh, K.R.: Smart pet insights system based on IoT and ML. Presented at the (2022). https://doi.org/10.1007/978-981-16-7167-8_53

13. Andriana, A., Zuklarnain, Z., Baehaqi, H.: Sistem kWH Meter Digital Menggunakan Modul PZEM-004T. J. TIARSIE **16**, 29 (2019). https://doi.org/10.32816/tiarsie.v16i1.43

14. Wasoontarajaroen, S., Pawasan, K., Chamnanphrai, V.: Development of an IoT device for monitoring electrical energy consumption. In: 2017 9th International Conference on Information Technology and Electrical Engineering (ICITEE), pp. 1–4. IEEE (2017). https://doi.org/10.1109/ICITEED.2017.8250475

15. Jebroni, Z., Afonso, J.A., Tidhaf, B.: Home energy monitoring system towards smart control of energy consumption. In: Afonso, J.L., Monteiro, V., Pinto, J.G. (eds.) GreeNets 2018. LNICSSITE, vol. 269, pp. 40–53. Springer, Cham (2019). https://doi.org/10.1007/978-3-030-12950-7_4

IoT-Based System for Web Monitoring
of Thermal Processes

José Varela-Aldás[1,2]([✉]) [ID], Pedro Escudero[1,2] [ID], and Sandra Casa[2]

[1] Centro de Investigaciones de Ciencias Humanas y de la Educación - CICHE, Universidad Indoamérica, Ambato 180103, Ecuador
josevarela@uti.edu.ec, pescudero2@indoamerica.edu.ec
[2] SISAu Research Group, Facultad de Ingeniería, Industria y Producción, Universidad Indoamérica, Ambato 180103, Ecuador

Abstract. The thermal processes are characterized by generating a slow first-order response; these are stable systems. This characteristic favors controlling and monitoring the temperature in all ranges, dispensing with expensive devices to automate these processes. Thus, multiple low-cost proposals meet the technical requirements and include industry 4.0 features. This work presents a web monitoring system for thermal processes. To collect the temperatures, DHT22 sensors and an ESP32 board are used. The proposal includes Internet of Things technology, sending the data to the ThingSpeak server for remote viewing. The tests are carried out in a cold room heating process using a heater; Fig. 1 shows the temperatures of both components, observing how the temperature in the room stabilizes. The temperatures in the cooling room range from -1 [°C] to 27 [°C], and in the heater from 25 [°C] to 59 [°C]. Finally, the applications and limitations of the monitoring system are analyzed.

Keywords: Web monitoring · temperature sensor · IoT · thermal processes · cold room

1 Introduction

The slow first-order response generated by thermal processes is a defining characteristic of stable systems [1]. This property facilitates the control and monitoring of temperature across all ranges, eliminating the need for costly automation devices [2, 3]. As a result, various low-cost solutions that fulfill the necessary technical requirements and incorporate industry 4.0 features are available [4]. As one of the main features of Industry 4.0, the Internet of Things (IoT) enables remote monitoring of nearly any process [5, 6].

The IoT platform is a crucial component of the IoT, as it hosts data from the local site and sends it to consumers, typically through mobile or web applications [7, 8]. Various IoT platforms offer programmatic tools that can integrate a wide range of functionalities through multiple APIs. IoT application developers or administrators face the challenging task of selecting an IoT platform that best suits their requirements based on factors such as cost, the number and type of available APIs, programming language, and device

C. Stephanidis et al. (Eds.): HCII 2023, CCIS 1835, pp. 549–553, 2023.
https://doi.org/10.1007/978-3-031-36001-5_71

compatibility [9]. Although mobile apps offer attractive features for remote viewing, web apps are still widely used for monitoring remote processes [10].

This paper introduces a low-cost system that utilizes temperature sensors to collect data for display in a web application. Its purpose is to monitor thermal processes in real-time, utilizing an ESP32 board and temperature sensors in the electronic circuit. The system is built on the ThingSpeak platform"s plugin, which receives and graphs data for reading. The document is divided into five sections, with the first providing an introduction to the topic. The second section describes the materials and methods employed in the work, while the third illustrates the results. The fourth section contains a discussion, and the fifth presents the conclusions that have been obtained.

2   Materials and Methods

Figure 1 depicts the thermal process monitoring system proposed, with the main objective of tracking low-range temperatures in industrial processes. This system utilizes the ESP32 board as a controller to gather data from temperature sensors, which is then sent to the IoT platform, ThingSpeak, for remote monitoring of variables. Additionally, a web application has been created to enable users to monitor the process from their web browsers.

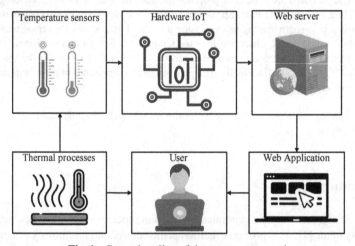

Fig. 1. General outline of the system proposed.

2.1   Electronic Circuit

To operate, the hardware necessitates an electronic circuit utilizing the ESP32 Development Module. Through digital ports, the controller is linked to temperature sensors. The DHT22 sensor is a cost-effective and efficient option that measures both temperature and relative humidity. It employs a thermistor to gauge the ambient air and has a temperature measurement range of −40 °C to 80 °C, a resolution of 0.1 °C, and a sensing time of 2 s.

2.2 Programming and Web Application

To operate the system, several tasks need to be completed within the software. These include programming the controller, configuring the IoT platform, and developing the web application. In order to program the ESP32 board, the libraries WiFi.h, ThingSpeak.h, and DHT.h are required. The DHT.h library is responsible for receiving sensor data via serial communication. Once the data is obtained from the sensors, it is sent to the web server every 2 s using a ThingSpeak license.

ThingSpeak is an IoT platform that provides a web interface for managing local site variables. The platform offers web services that allow devices to be interconnected through its website. Finally, the web application is developed using the Google Gauge plugin, which enables the creation of the interface using HTML code.

3 Results

The system is tested in different low range thermal processes. As shown in Fig. 2, the web application displays the readings of the two temperatures in separate graphs. The user interface also includes a refresh button and a button to export the data. In addition, the user accesses the application using ThingSpeak credentials.

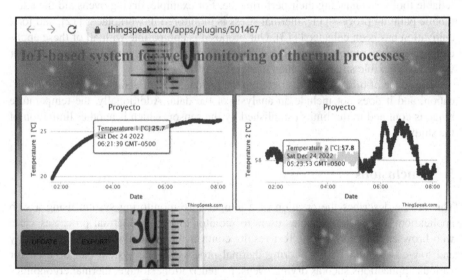

Fig. 2. Web application user interface.

3.1 Measurement of a Thermal Process

Figure 3 depicts the temperature of both the system"s components during a cold room heating process, wherein a heater is utilized. The temperature stabilization of the room can be observed during the almost nine-hour process. The cooling room temperatures range from −1 [°C] to 27 [°C], while the heater temperatures range from 25 [°C] to 59 [°C].

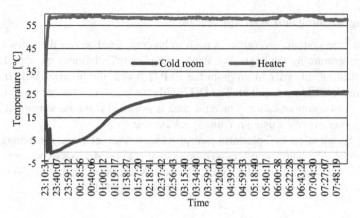

Fig. 3. Temperatures of the thermal process in a cold room.

4 Discussion

Various industrial processes use low-range thermal processes, and the IoT has been a reliable tool for enhancing their performance. For example, drying ovens aid the auto-mobile painting process [11], thermal stress is monitored in workplaces [12], and food cultivation has been enhanced [13]. Our proposal is compatible with all of these applications, enabling remote monitoring of the temperature at two points of interest, and our work has a flexible structure, which makes it easy to expand.

The scope of this work is restricted to the presentation of data through a web application, and it does not include an analysis of the data. Additionally, the temperature range is confined to the limits established by the sensor, which is another limitation of the study.

5 Conclusions

This article describes the creation of a temperature monitoring system using a web application. The system enables users to monitor low-range thermal processes via a web browser from anywhere. Test results confirm the system"s proper functionality and low-cost option for monitoring thermal processes. The system can be used for various applications such as drying ovens, pasteurization, storage, thermal ergonomics and more. In future research, data analysis algorithms could be employed to identify abnormal temperature changes.

References

1. Wijayanti, H.B., Bansal, N., Deeth, H.C.: Stability of whey proteins during thermal process-ing: a review. Compr. Rev. Food Sci. Food Saf. **13**, 1235–1251 (2014). https://doi.org/10. 1111/1541-4337.12105

2. Sánchez, C., Dessì, P., Duffy, M., Lens, P.N.L.: OpenTCC: an open source low-cost temperature-control chamber. HardwareX **7**, e00099 (2020). https://doi.org/10.1016/j.ohx.2020.e00099
3. Mollocana, J.D., Jorque, B.S., Varela-Aldás, J., Andaluz, V.H.: Temperature control of an electric through virtual hardware in the loop technique. In: Mesquita, A., Abreu, A., Carvalho, J.V. (eds.) Perspectives and Trends in Education and Technology. SIST, vol. 256, pp. 689–701. Springer, Singapore (2022). https://doi.org/10.1007/978-981-16-5063-5_56
4. Saini, J., Dutta, M., Marques, G.: Sensors for indoor air quality monitoring and assessment through Internet of Things: a systematic review. Environ. Monit. Assess. **193**(2), 1–32 (2021). https://doi.org/10.1007/s10661-020-08781-6
5. Manavalan, E., Jayakrishna, K.: A review of Internet of Things (IoT) embedded sustainable supply chain for industry 4.0 requirements. Comput. Ind. Eng. 127, 925–953 (2019). https://doi.org/10.1016/j.cie.2018.11.030
6. Sharma, A., Burman, V., Aggarwal, S.: Role of IoT in industry 4.0. In: Bansal, R.C., Agarwal, A., Jadoun, V.K. (eds.) Advances in Energy Technology. LNEE, vol. 766, pp. 517–528. Springer, Singapore (2022). https://doi.org/10.1007/978-981-16-1476-7_47
7. Fahmideh, M., Zowghi, D.: An exploration of IoT platform development. Inf. Syst. **87**, 101409 (2020). https://doi.org/10.1016/j.is.2019.06.005
8. Bansal, S., Kumar, D.: IoT ecosystem: a survey on devices, gateways, operating systems, middleware and communication. Int. J. Wireless Inf. Networks **27**(3), 340–364 (2020). https://doi.org/10.1007/s10776-020-00483-7
9. Babun, L., Denney, K., Celik, Z.B., McDaniel, P., Uluagac, A.S.: A survey on IoT platforms: communication, security, and privacy perspectives. Comput. Networks **192**, 108040 (2021). https://doi.org/10.1016/j.comnet.2021.108040
10. Alulema, D., Zapata, M., Zapata, M.A.: An IoT-based remote monitoring system for electrical power consumption via web-application. In: 2018 International Conference on Information Systems and Computer Science (INCISCOS), pp. 193–197. IEEE (2018). https://doi.org/10.1109/INCISCOS.2018.00035
11. Svejda, P.: Smart paint shops — improving quality, flexibility and efficiency. IST Int. Surf. Technol. **10**, 16–19 (2017). https://doi.org/10.1007/s35724-017-0029-8
12. Varela-Aldás, J., Buele, J., Mosquera, H., Palacios-Navarro, G.: Development of a WBGT index meter based on M5Stack Core2 (2022). https://doi.org/10.1007/978-3-031-21704-3_23
13. Najmurrokhman, A., Daelami, A., Nurlina, E., Komarudin, U., Ridhatama, H.: Development of temperature and humidity control system in internet-of-things based oyster mushroom cultivation. In: 2020 3rd International Seminar on Research of Information Technology and Intelligent Systems (ISRITI), pp. 551–555. IEEE (2020). https://doi.org/10.1109/ISRITI51436.2020.9315426

Detection System for Domestic Environmental Pollutants Based on ThingSpeak

José Varela-Aldás[1,2]([✉]) [ID], Mario Miranda[2], and Guillermo Lasluisa[2]

[1] Centro de Investigaciones de Ciencias Humanas y de la Educación - CICHE, Universidad Indoamérica, Ambato 180103, Ecuador
josevarela@uti.edu.ec
[2] SISAu Research Group, Facultad de Ingeniería, Industria y Producción, Universidad Indoamérica, Ambato 180103, Ecuador
mariomiranda@uti.edu.ec

Abstract. Internet of things platforms is essential components for project development with connectivity. Thus, these have positioned themselves in the market by offering multiple cloud services, such as a database, application programming interface, and more. This paper presents a system that collects data from air concentration sensors to detect the presence of pollutants. The electronic circuit uses a system-on-chip with WiFi connectivity and the MQ2 and MQ3 sensors, which detect liquefied petroleum gas and alcohol concentrations in the air, respectively. The system is based on the ThingSpeak platform, which receives and graphs data to see readings outside expected ranges. The results present the concentration levels of the MQ2 and MQ3 sensors, indicating the correct functioning of the system, and future applications of the proposed design are discussed.

Keywords: ThingSpeak · gas sensors · IoT · system on chip · domestic environmental pollutants

1 Introduction

The development of projects with connectivity requires essential components, namely Internet of Things (IoT) platforms. These platforms have established their presence in the market by providing various cloud services, including databases, application programming interfaces, and more [1, 2]. The IoT has become a trend, finding applications in different fields, and offering solutions to numerous problems. The integration of smart devices with the Internet has also made significant progress technologically. However, the IoT paradigm faces challenges in implementing security and access control measures in environments with limited resources [3–5].

A focused attempt has been made, particularly in the domestic sector, to utilize this technology and enhance the quality of life for tenants [6, 7]. The IoT is catalyzing a significant revolution in both residential and commercial buildings. Thanks to IoT technologies, buildings are evolving into more intelligent, effective, and safe structures.

C. Stephanidis et al. (Eds.): HCII 2023, CCIS 1835, pp. 554–559, 2023.
https://doi.org/10.1007/978-3-031-36001-5_72

Researchers have already deployed IoT in diverse applications and environments to convert conventional buildings into intelligent ones [8, 9].

On the other hand, gas sensors are extensively utilized for advanced engineering purposes such as medical, environmental, industrial, automotive, and agricultural applications. The gas sensor market is projected to reach $1,336.2 million by 2027, making it one of the largest markets in the sensor technology industry. To generate real-time multivariate data sources, gas sensors must operate without any spatiotemporal limitations. Thus, integration of gas sensors with the IoT is essential [10].

This work presents a system that collects data from air concentration sensors to detect the presence of pollutants. The electronic circuit uses an ESP32 board and gas sensors. The system is based on the ThingSpeak platform, which receives and graphs data to see readings outside expected ranges. The document has been organized into five sections: This Sect. Presents the introduction to the topic; Sect. 2 describes materials and methods; Sect. 3 illustrates the results; Sect. 4 describes the discussion; and Sect. 5 contains the conclusions obtained.

2 Materials and Methods

The proposed detection system for domestic environmental pollutants is illustrated in Fig. 1. Its primary goal is to monitor gases within residential areas. The system employs the ESP32 board as the controller, which collects data from the gas sensors. The acquired information is transmitted to the IoT platform, ThingSpeak, for remote monitoring of variables. On the other end, the tenant receives updates on the detected gas levels.

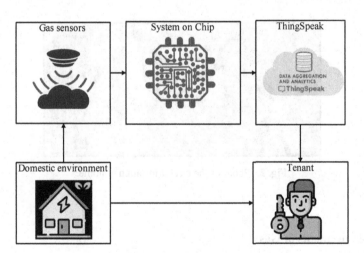

Fig. 1. General outline of the system.

2.1 Hardware

The hardware requires an electronic circuit based on the ESP32 Development Module. The controller is connected to gas sensors through analog ports. The MQ2 sensor is suitable for detecting LPG, propane, methane, alcohol, hydrogen, and smoke, with higher sensitivity to LPG and propane. The MQ3 sensor is very sensitive to alcohol and less sensitive to benzene, and also detects gases such as LPG, hexane, CO, and CH4 with very low sensitivity. These sensors are installed in domestic environments to monitor air contaminants.

2.2 Software

In the software, programming the controller and configuring the IoT platform is required. To program the ESP32 board, the WiFi ammunition library and the ThingSpeak library are used. The analog value is converted to a scale from 0 to 100%. Data obtained from the sensors is sent to the web server every second, thanks to the ThingSpeak license.

ThingSpeak is an IoT platform that enables users to manage local site variables through a web interface. The platform provides web services for interconnecting devices via its web page. The user can configure the channel with two required fields, one for the MQ2 sensor and one for the MQ3 sensor, and ThingSpeak graphs the variables as it receives new data.

3   Results

The installation proposal is intended for a domestic environment, specifically in the kitchen of a home. As shown in Fig. 2, the sensors are mounted high on the wall.

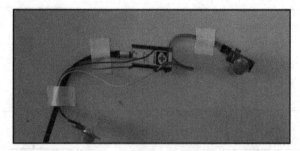

Fig. 2. Photo of the circuit installed at home.

3.1 Measurements of Gas

Figures 3 and 4 depict the gas readings collected over an 8-h period, showing a noticeable decrease as time elapsed, particularly with the MQ3 sensor. It is noteworthy that the kitchen features a small bar utilized by the occupants. On average, the MQ2 sensor recorded a reading of 29.19%, while the MQ3 sensor registered an average reading of 22.08%. These results demonstrate the successful operation of the proposed system.

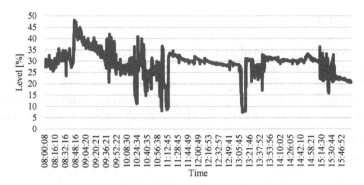

Fig. 3. Gas concentration levels (MQ2) collected in ThingSpeak.

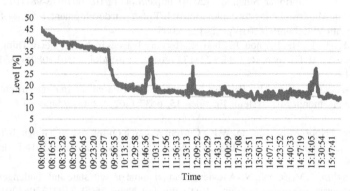

Fig. 4. Air alcohol concentration levels (MQ3) collected on ThingSpeak.

4 Discussion

This work enables the residents of a home to visually monitor the readings of two gas sensors, and this monitoring can be performed remotely from anywhere in the world through the ThingSpeak website. Prior literature includes similar proposals [11], but those were restricted to a single sensor. Unlike those works, our approach has the potential to incorporate multiple gas sensors without major modifications. Some other proposals utilize sensor data to automatically reserve gas cylinders [12], while others identify gas spills, fires, and gas leaks, and mitigate gas concentration levels through automatic ventilation [13]. Additionally, a hybrid kitchen security system utilizing embedded devices and sensors to detect abnormal events via IoT has been implemented using artificial intelligence [14]. A recent work proposes gas leak detection using the MQ2 sensor and an IoT-based alert system [15]. While our proposal may not be as comprehensive as some of the more recent works, it offers an affordable starting point for further research into air pollutant detection.

The limitations of this study stem from the data collection process, as it did not undergo analysis with conventional methods or artificial intelligence. Moreover, it is imperative to implement alerts that notify the user when values exceed the normal range.

5 Conclusions

This work details the creation of a gas monitoring system designed to detect household pollutants. The system allows for real-time graphical observation of gas levels in a home's kitchen and bar. The findings demonstrate the system's efficacy, revealing high gas concentrations during morning hours via both sensors. Future studies may apply data analysis algorithms and incorporate alerts to notify tenants of dangerous gas levels.

References

1. Guth, J., et al.: A detailed analysis of IoT platform architectures: concepts, similarities, and differences. In: Di Martino, B., Li, K.-C., Yang, L.T., Esposito, A. (eds.) Internet of Everything. IT, pp. 81–101. Springer, Singapore (2018). https://doi.org/10.1007/978-981-10-5861-5_4
2. Fahmideh, M., Zowghi, D.: An exploration of IoT platform development. Inf. Syst. **87**, 101409 (2020). https://doi.org/10.1016/j.is.2019.06.005
3. Wang, F., Hu, L., Hu, J., Zhou, J., Zhao, K.: Recent advances in the Internet of Things: multiple perspectives. IETE Tech. Rev. **34**, 122–132 (2017). https://doi.org/10.1080/02564602.2016.1155419
4. Varela-Aldás, J., Silva, S., Palacios-Navarro, G.: IoT-based alternating current electrical parameters monitoring system. Energies **15**, 6637 (2022). https://doi.org/10.3390/en15186637
5. Mohamad Noor, M.B., Hassan, W.H.: Current research on Internet of Things (IoT) security: a survey. Comput. Networks. **148**, 283–294 (2019). https://doi.org/10.1016/j.comnet.2018.11.025
6. Almusaylim, Z.A., Zaman, N.: A review on smart home present state and challenges: linked to context-awareness internet of things (IoT). Wireless Netw. **25**(6), 3193–3204 (2018). https://doi.org/10.1007/s11276-018-1712-5
7. Wang, Z., et al.: A survey on IoT-enabled home automation systems: attacks and defenses. IEEE Commun. Surv. Tutorials **24**, 2292–2328 (2022). https://doi.org/10.1109/COMST.2022.3201557
8. Lawal, K., Rafsanjani, H.N.: Trends, benefits, risks, and challenges of IoT implementation in residential and commercial buildings. Energy Built Environ. **3**, 251–266 (2022). https://doi.org/10.1016/j.enbenv.2021.01.009
9. Varela-Aldás, J., Miranda, M., León, J., Gallardo, C.: Analysis of electrical energy consumption in the home using IoT. Presented at the (2022). https://doi.org/10.1007/978-3-031-19682-9_71
10. Jung, H.-T.: The present and future of gas sensors. ACS Sensors. **7**, 912–913 (2022). https://doi.org/10.1021/acssensors.2c00688
11. Santiputri, M., Tio, M.: IoT-based gas leak detection device. In: 2018 International Conference on Applied Engineering (ICAE), pp. 1–4. IEEE (2018). https://doi.org/10.1109/INCAE.2018.8579396
12. Shrestha, S., Anne, V.P.K., Chaitanya, R.: IoT based smart gas management system. In: 2019 3rd International Conference on Trends in Electronics and Informatics (ICOEI), pp. 550–555. IEEE (2019). https://doi.org/10.1109/ICOEI.2019.8862639
13. Anika, A.M., Akter, M.N., Hasan, M.N., Shoma, J.F., Sattar, A.: Gas leakage with auto ventilation and smart management system using IoT. In: 2021 International Conference on Artificial Intelligence and Smart Systems (ICAIS), pp. 1411–1415. IEEE (2021). https://doi.org/10.1109/ICAIS50930.2021.9395774

14. Chen, L.-W., Tseng, H.-F.: DeepSafe: a hybrid kitchen safety guarding system with stove fire recognition based on the Internet of Things. In: IEEE INFOCOM 2021 - IEEE Conference on Computer Communications Workshops (INFOCOM WKSHPS), pp. 1–2. IEEE (2021). https://doi.org/10.1109/INFOCOMWKSHPS51825.2021.9484547

15. Rekha, V.S.D., CH, N.S.M., Sravya, A.: Condition monitoring and detection of hazardous gas leakage using smart device. In: 2022 International Conference on Electronics and Renewable Systems (ICEARS), pp. 396–400. IEEE (2022). https://doi.org/10.1109/ICEARS53579.2022.9751937

Design Goals and Feasible Design Logic of Meta Smart City

Haoqi Wang(✉)

Wuhan University of Technology, 122 Luoshi Road, Wuhan, Hubei, People's Republic of China
15226983938@163.com

Abstract. The technology concept of "metaverse" has been closely related to urban space since its birth. In particular, the development of metaverse-related technologies and the support policies issued by the governments of major cities around the world have opened the door to the transformation of digital intelligence in the 21st century, making the current urban development face a new situation of transformation from informationization and digitalization to intelligence and wisdom. The deep integration of metaverse technology and urban space will likely open up a new urban development space, which will have a profound impact on the reconfiguration of urban digital intelligence, governance level and digital economy development. However, the current digital construction of smart cities has encountered some problems with digital characteristics. These problems are also the starting point for the involvement of metauniverse technology in the construction of smart cities. This study proposes the concept of "meta smart city" by sorting out the stages of smart city development, and makes a holistic framework for its connotation, necessity, design goals and feasible design logic, so as to provide guidance for future scientific research and development of meta smart city governance.

Keywords: Meta Smart City · Urban Digital Construction · Design Logic

1 Generation of Meta Smart City

To discuss the generation of meta smart cities, it is necessary to understand the development path of smart cities. The development of smart cities is essentially a process that evolves dynamically with the social changes brought about by science and technology. In the decades when the Internet took off, it was invariably technology that led the development. That is, first there are smart devices, and then start to consider the network construction, followed by the formation of the Internet, a variety of applications debut, is a gradual process.[1] Rather than the integrated application of a variety of technologies, smart cities are the next stage in the development of a kind of information technology. In this stage, not only the smart city, but also the industrial Internet and the meta-universe are included, and the three present a parallel development pattern.

Therefore, the city form can be divided into two stages: the first stage is driven by information technology and biotechnology, and the technology in this stage mainly follows the "tandem" development mode of "smart devices → network construction →

C. Stephanidis et al. (Eds.): HCII 2023, CCIS 1835, pp. 560–566, 2023.
https://doi.org/10.1007/978-3-031-36001-5_73

application debut" and is based on two-dimensional information presentation. In the second stage, the meta-universe technology is the driving force of the city development, as "smart devices + non-smart devices" and "Internet + Internet of Things" have emerged in this stage. In the second stage, metaverse technology is the driving force of urban development, because of the multi-mode form of "smart devices + non-smart devices" and "Internet + Internet of Things", and the network construction to support smart cities and metaverse devices is not mature, diverse applications have already appeared, forming a "parallel" development mode of devices, network and applications, which mainly relies on This stage can be called the "three-dimensional metaverse era", and there are two types of urban forms: smart cities and meta smart cities.

The "digital twin" governance model from Xiong'an New Area in China indicates that the initial stage of the meta smart city is the digital twin governance stage, which focuses on using digital twin technology to instantly sense and connect everything in the real world with the twin world, forming two parallel worlds with precise mapping. The virtual and fault-tolerant nature needed to guide the manifestation of the hidden order of the city is the greatest characteristic of the metaverse. At present, the metaverse is in its initial stage and the related technology is not mature, but we can be sure that digital twin technology is the basic technology of the metaverse. As the metaverse achieves the integration of virtual world and real world in the future, it is believed that the smart city will also come to the stage of virtual-real integration governance, that is, the meta smart city form.

2   Why to Develop Meta Smart City

With the development of information technology, especially the mobile Internet, the threshold of using the network is getting lower and lower, and more convenient wisdom services could have radiated to more and more people in the city. However, the current information construction of most cities is limited to the technical level of cloud computing, big data, Internet of Things, etc., ignoring the fact that a smart city is a vision of the ideal future city state for the current problems of the city, rather than a city construction model brought about by a specific new technology. The application of digital technology in urban construction has made obvious achievements, but the problems with many "digital features" have also come to the fore.

2.1   Current Bottleneck of Urban Digital Construction

First of all, due to the influence of the compartmentalized administrative management system and administrative operation mechanism, government departments at all levels usually have their own intelligent governance platform, and the problem of repeated construction of smart city platform is more serious. There are certain differences in the information collection methods and data storage formats of each smart governance platform, making it difficult to achieve free exchange and rapid transmission of data and other information between smart governance platforms, which in turn affects the level of smart city operation and governance effectiveness. [2] Smart city is a system engineering, each subsystem of the "wisdom" simple sum does not achieve the "wisdom" of the whole city. But the current smart city construction due to the lack of top-level design system support, still can't form a wisdom synergy.

Second, in the process of urban wisdom, there is often a "digital divide" phenomenon. This is a problem that has always existed in the information age, and is an old worldwide problem. The "digital divide" is related to age, education, economic income and other factors. Affected by these factors, some specific groups of people have become "information poor", and it is difficult for them to enjoy the convenience brought by wisdom. In the wave of wisdom, there are more elderly people who are "information poor", and many of them do not know how to use the Internet, and do not know how to use or are not willing to use smart devices. [3] With the influx of older, less educated population in the city, even if the city is wisdom construction, this part of the group may not be able to benefit from it, and may even add to the trouble of life.

Third, the current wisdom construction of cities still focuses on the introduction of advanced technology, investment in advanced equipment, and the creation of advanced experiences, and less on the wisdom city construction as a catalyst to promote the integration of human resources and humanistic spirit development. In the process of accelerated urbanization, in order to expand and extend on a large scale, they all imitate international and modern metropolises to varying degrees, making urban architecture large-scale and uniform, resulting in homogenized buildings all over the place. Essentially, it is a lack of clarity in the positioning of the city, neglecting the natural and historical origins in urban construction, so that the uniqueness of the city is missing in the appearance of the city, reducing the imagination of the residents of the city.[4] This in turn causes some modern cities to have insufficient cultural drive for residents, making it difficult to obtain a psychological perception beyond the physical function of the city and to achieve the residents' resonance with the city culture.

2.2 Design Goals of the Meta Smart City

First, meta smart city will build an open and decentralized system. As a digital smart city space, meta smart city inherits the dynamic gene of "scale" of the city, and through blockchain technology, it builds an innovation-driven model of ecological openness and cross-border co-creation, so that meta smart city has the ecological attribute of "open source and common governance" and allows It allows each city resident to participate in the process of governance, maintenance and operation of the city system to ensure the long-term stability and growth of the city system, thus achieving the purpose of optimizing, upgrading and continuously creating the traditional city system.

Second, to follow the "people-oriented" city concept. Through 3D engine, blockchain, artificial intelligence, virtual reality and other key technologies, meta smart city builds the infrastructure ecosystem of meta smart city, emphasizing various application scenarios of human interaction and human-computer interaction, thus creating various products and services to enhance the living experience of city residents and finally realizing people's pursuit and aspiration for a better city life.

Thirdly, preserve historical memory and urban characteristics. The future meta smart city will have unpredictable novel applications and devices, but it cannot bypass the spiritual temperament, historical laws and cultural system of the city in the past. All these past historical memories and urban temperament will be semantic and digitalized by computers into a basic capability for urban development, which will help the city reach the goal of digital transformation and provide better intelligent resident services for future city residents.

2.3 Elements of Meta Smart City Design

In order to achieve the proposed design goals of the meta smart city, the design elements of the meta smart city need to be sorted out. The design elements of the meta smart city include the resident, services, and information (see Fig. 1). Whether it is the duplicate construction of wisdom platforms in city management, obstructed data circulation, convenient digital facilities that do not consider audience characteristics, or the loss of city cultural characteristics and blind pursuit of quick results and high fault tolerance of technological showmanship, all of them are not balanced with the resident, service and information. When the city construction ignores data sharing and resource decentralization, it will create information silos, slow down the efficiency of the city's government management, and then affect the people's experience of government activities and government services; when the city construction ignores the physiological and psychological characteristics of the people, it will reduce the enthusiasm of the people to participate in the construction and development of the city's wisdom, and will bring troubles to the people's life, even if the city has the best services and efficient information transmission. Even if the city has good services and efficient information transmission, it will not help; when the city construction ignores the regional nature of the service experience, then it will cause a uniform city experience, which is not conducive to cultivating people's city loyalty, and the information will be limited to rational data.

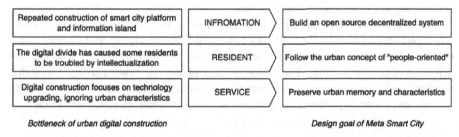

Bottleneck of urban digital construction   Design goal of Meta Smart City

Fig. 1. Sorting out design elements from the dilemma of digital construction and goals

The reason why meta smart city is proposed, in addition to the objective reason that the rise of meta-universe technology will certainly promote the new form of smart city, more importantly, the various problems with digital characteristics in the current city construction reveal that the current process of urban wisdom relies only on technological upgrades, technological revolution and ignore the management of social relationships. As an open, interwoven whole of multiple systems, especially with the addition of "people" as a complex variable, the city becomes a huge socio-physical information system. Such systems are full of amplified randomness, which poses a great challenge for trying to generalize laws or predict dynamics with static models. The development of information technology and Internet ecology has broadened the construction dimension of urban digitalization and provided technical feasibility for smart management of cities.

3 Feasible Design Logic of Meta Smart City

3.1 Diversified Participation Platform Based on Residents

The future meta smart city should place more emphasis on "resident-centeredness" and divide into two deeper meanings: centering on all residents and centering on resident participation. The former emphasizes multiple user subjects, i.e., the meta smart city should be open to all people living in the city; the latter means that users should not only be the service recipients of the meta smart city, but also the planners and feedback providers of the city.

Centered on all residents, i.e., it cannot be designed only for those residents who are good at using digital products. The intervention of meta-universe technology stimulates the qualities of information media mobility. The current construction of smart cities still focuses on urban public services, and the information medium for residents to access these services still relies on smart terminals. Information media, as an extension of people, is the link that connects people to social relationships.[5] However, the limitation of smart terminal makes information confined to the screen. The mobility of information media can make objective objects become the transmitter and processing platform of information, and then become the connecting link between people and people, people and things, and things and things. Information should be liberated from the screen, that is, information exists where it should exist. A combination of real and virtual information display is more in line with human cognitive intuition and is conducive to the enhancement of experience for all residents.

Centered on resident participation, i.e., activating the group wisdom of residents and applying it to the city. Participatory governance of cities is the core essence of the European Commission's connotation of smart cities and one of the key words in the definition of new smart cities. The reason for the emphasis on public participation is that residents are the end-users of smart cities, they know best where the problems of the city lie and can give an important evaluation of "whether the smart city is smart or not".

3.2 Contextualized City Services Based on Scenarios

The future meta smart city should emphasize the construction of humanistic contexts. People do not exist in isolation, but must live in a certain context. According to habit theory, we can presume that the construction of the future meta-universe will not be beyond the real world, and the habits formed by people in the socialization process will be brought from the real world to the meta-universe, which will also produce a context similar to the real society.[6] The reason why the meta-universe is called the universe is that there must be various scenarios of human life presented. And contextuality is also common between the meta-universe and the real world. In the real world, urban services need to analyze the problems of service recipients from the context, and also solve problems from the context.

A humanistic smart city is not a simple pile of top technology, but a collection of livable places built with the core of serving the resident. Therefore, the construction of a meta smart city should start from the interests of the resident, fully consider the cultural and spiritual needs of the resident, and adopt reasonable and advanced technology to build this new city. Only when technology and humanities are coordinated, the power of technology is brought into play to the utmost. Combining the technological path of the metaverse into the physical city scene provides residents with a new type of leisure and entertainment place where virtual and reality interact. The virtual scene should be constructed based on the local cultural lineage of the city as well as specific realistic scenes.

3.3 Industry-Based Domain-Based Information Sharing

The future meta smart city should emphasize the top-level design of the system of resources and eliminate information silos. At present, each industry under the smart city still takes the institution as the main body of information production, and there are certain information barriers that limit the information exchange between each other. In the meta-universe era, individuals exist as individuals of digital production, enjoying the convenience of communication, interaction facilitation and embodied experience brought by the digital production of the meta-universe, and also participating in the digital production of the meta-universe platform economy as the sharers and contributors of digital productivity.[7] The future meta smart city will establish domain meta-universes by industry categories, such as education meta-universe and medical meta-universe, which not only break the information barriers among institutions, but also realize cross-industry information linkage.

As a highly technically integrated complex giant system, the meta smart city empowers the physical city through technologies such as the Internet, Internet of Things, blockchain, cloud computing, and edge computing to link material entities such as energy environment, transportation and logistics, commercial entities, social organizations, government organizations, infrastructure, and human behavioral activities in the city to build a wise urban ecological complex giant system. For the occurrence of uncertain events in this system, the sharing and circulation of data can realize a new model of simultaneous reporting by multiple people and global confirmation by multiple parties. The government's management services and coordination capabilities in the city are comprehensively enhanced.

4   Conclusion

From information city, digital city to smart city, and then to meta smart city, meta-universe carries the vision of human for the future city form and urban life. As the largest virtual carrier of future human digital intelligence, meta smart city will carry more thoughts and behaviors of human users with the rapid development of meta-universe-related technologies, providing more diverse and realistic experience effects, and will certainly feed back to the real physical city and promote its comprehensive digital intelligence transformation and upgrading. However, the meta smart city is still in the exploration stage, and the problems of digital features exposed in the current city development actually point out the direction for us to build the meta smart city. Seizing the three elements of resident, service and information and keeping the balance of the three is a feasible path to build a livable and ecological city.

References

1. Ma Long, F.: The development of smart cities, industrial Internet and the metauniverse from the perspective of the history of information technology. Inf. China **349**(1), 41–43 (2022). (in Chinese)
2. Chen Peng, F.: Present difficulties and optimization paths of smart city construction. J. Ningxia Communist Party Inst. **24**(1), 93–101 (2022). (in Chinese)
3. Li Haoming, F.: The wisdom Dilemma and Countermeasures of old Urban communities from the perspective of unbalanced development. Popular Stand. **336**(1), 122–125 (2021). (in Chinese)
4. Xue Yabo, F.: Analysis of urban culture communication based on algorithmic city. J. News Research **12**(13), 239–241 (2021). (in Chinese)
5. HU Y.F., Yao Q.S.: Metaverse: meta-media, involuntary interaction and the singularity of subjectivity evolvement. Stud. Cult. Art **15**(1), 56–64 (2022). (in Chinese)
6. Zhao Yufeng, F.: The metaverse and the virtual turn of social work. Sci. Econ. Soc. **40**(3), 8–15 (2022). (in Chinese)
7. Cao, K.F.: The metaverse "digital community": decentralization or constructing centralization. Yuejiang Acad. J. **14**(2), 78–88 (2022). (in Chinese)

Based on User Experience Design Strategy of Intelligent Kitchen Waste Recycling System - A Case Study of Chinese Communities

Zhiyun Yang and Han Han[⊠]

Shenzhen University, Shenzhen, China
han.han@szu.edu.cn

Abstract. In recent years, comprehensive smart kitchen waste recycling systems have emerged in some urban communities in China. However, there are problems with the human-machine interaction experience, which has led many residents to continue to use traditional waste disposal methods, resulting in poor application results for smart kitchen waste recycling systems. This article takes user needs as the core and proposes five design strategies for smart kitchen waste recycling systems based on the user experience dimension model and feedback from the application of intelligent kitchen waste recycling systems in Chinese communities. The design strategies aim to meet the functional, usability, and pleasure needs. Among them, two design strategies address functional requirements, and three design strategies focus on usability, including the addition of a "bag-breaking" function, the implementation of a multifunctional design, adherence to ergonomic principles, ease of use principles, and consideration of the characteristics of middle-aged and elderly users. The final design strategy aims to improve the reward mechanism to increase user participation and satisfaction.

Keywords: kitchen waste · intelligent recycling system · user experience · design strategy

1 Research Background

1.1 Definition and Overview of Kitchen Waste

Kitchen waste is the organic waste produced from food processing and consumption, such as vegetable leaves, leftover food, fruit peels, and expired food. It contains organic matter and nutrients that can be recycled into animal feed, organic fertilizer, and bioenergy. However, it is prone to rot, acidification, and odor, which can cause environmental pollution and health hazards if not properly handled during collection, storage, and transportation [1]. Therefore, an efficient kitchen waste recycling system that separates it from other domestic waste can help maintain ecological sustainability and generate economic benefits.

Community is the main place where citizens generate and aggregate domestic waste. In China, kitchen waste accounts for the main part of urban community domestic waste,

© The Author(s), under exclusive license to Springer Nature Switzerland AG 2023
C. Stephanidis et al. (Eds.): HCII 2023, CCIS 1835, pp. 567–576, 2023.
https://doi.org/10.1007/978-3-031-36001-5_74

about 60% of the total amount, but the final recycling rate is only about 18% [2]. Solving the problem of kitchen waste classification and recycling has always been the focus and difficulty of urban domestic waste recycling work (Fig. 1).

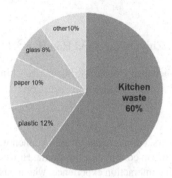

Fig. 1. Proportion of different types of urban community household waste in China

1.2 Development Status of Intelligent Kitchen Waste Recycling System in Chinese Communities

In recent years, China's progress in technologies such as big data, artificial intelligence, and the Internet of Things has provided technical support for functions such as garbage recognition, data collection, flow monitoring, and intelligent management in kitchen waste recycling systems. The kitchen waste recycling in a few cities in China has moved from the traditional manual sorting mode to the initial intelligent sorting stage. Comprehensive and high-intelligence classification recycling systems for kitchen waste have emerged in some urban communities in China, including intelligent machines and equipment for front-end residents, such as "intelligent kitchen waste recycling bins," "intelligent kitchen waste recycling rooms," "smart points cards," "smart garbage trucks" for the middle-end [3], and "big data supervision platforms" for the terminal.

Currently, intelligent kitchen waste recycling systems have not been widely used in communities, only being promoted and used in some city communities. At the same time, there are some communities where intelligent recycling equipment is idle shortly after being put into use, and residents are more accustomed to using traditional garbage bins. A survey showed that only 8% of residents are satisfied with the intelligent recycling bin, while 65% of residents believe that the design of the intelligent recycling bin is unreasonable and the human-machine interaction experience is poor [4] (Fig. 2). In addition, some communities' intelligent recycling systems do not have efficient operation support, and there are often situations where the garbage in the bin overflows but is not cleaned up in time.

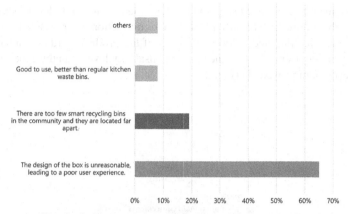

Fig. 2. Survey on the use of kitchen waste recycling bins

2 Research Objectives

The objective of this research is to analyze cases of intelligent kitchen waste recycling systems applied in Chinese communities, and summarize an intelligent kitchen waste recycling process. Based on user feedback, including positive and negative feedback, the existing problems of intelligent kitchen waste recycling systems are addressed, with the aim of improving the human-machine interaction experience for users and promoting the efficiency of kitchen waste recycling. The research explores design strategies for intelligent kitchen waste recycling systems in Chinese communities under the context of the Internet of Things and artificial intelligence, in order to make kitchen waste recycling more humane, intelligent, and efficient.

3 Research Methodology

This study adopts qualitative research and literature theory research methods, with case study as the main research strategy. The user experience dimension model and human-computer interaction experience demand principles provide the theoretical foundation for this paper, and the relevant literature on the application of intelligent kitchen waste recycling systems provides the basic perspective for case sampling in this study. By analyzing the intelligent kitchen waste recycling systems adopted by some communities in China in recent years, this study summarizes the interactive behavior of residents in the intelligent recycling system and the intelligent technology involved, and discovers the problems that exist in it. Finally, based on the user experience dimension model and human-computer interaction experience demand principles, this study proposes the design strategy of intelligent kitchen waste recycling system, aiming to improve the user-human interaction experience.

3.1 User Experience Dimension Model

Jordan's user experience dimension model consists of three levels: functionality, usability, and pleasure. In this model, the functional level is the most basic, ensuring that the product can meet users' basic needs and expectations; the usability level focuses on the usability of the product and the efficiency of task completion; the pleasure level includes the appearance, feeling, and emotional effects of the product. Jordan emphasizes that only after meeting users' needs at the basic and usability levels can the experience at the pleasure level be improved [5] (Fig. 3).

Fig. 3. User Experience Dimension Model

3.2 Principles of Human-Computer Interaction Experience Demand Design

When designing human-computer interaction systems, attention should be paid to user needs and expectations to ensure that the system provides a high-quality user experience. Human-computer interaction experience requirements are divided into three levels and six needs, including presentation design and information quality needs, information structure fluency needs and interaction usability needs, system quality needs, and humanization needs. Intelligent product design should follow these requirements, such as simplifying interface design, ensuring information security and authenticity, complying with user mental models, providing users with a sense of control and freedom, ensuring system stability, avoiding error situations, and providing reasonable information prompts and operational constraints to enhance the user's human-computer interaction experience [6].

4 Analysis and Summary of Processes for the Application of Intelligent Kitchen Waste Recycling Systems in Chinese Communities

4.1 Analysis of Chinese Community Intelligent Kitchen Waste Recycling System Application Cases

This research selected Yue Gui Community, Huoxing Street, Furong District, Changsha, Balizhuang Street, Chaoyang District, Beijing, and Shenlan Jiezuo Community, Haxi Street, Nangang District, Harbin as case study objects, and analyzed relevant literature and reports to understand the usage and residents' feedback of the intelligent kitchen waste recycling systems in these communities. The application of intelligent kitchen waste recycling systems in Chinese communities has both feasibility and limitations.

Positive feedback from residents includes the bag-breaking function of the intelligent recycling bin, the point or cash reward system, the closed environment of the box, and the sterilization design, which incentivizes residents to actively deliver classified kitchen waste, effectively reducing the odor of kitchen waste and improving the recycling efficiency, and receiving recognition from residents. However, negative feedback from residents indicates problems with the design and use of intelligent recycling bins, such as insufficient capacity or too small a throw-in port, and inconvenient operation. Especially for the middle-aged and elderly groups, they may feel that the operation of the intelligent recycling bin and mobile app interfaces is cumbersome, which creates resistance towards the machine and still prefer to use traditional recycling bins. Therefore, the design of intelligent kitchen waste recycling systems needs to comprehensively consider users' needs (Fig. 4).

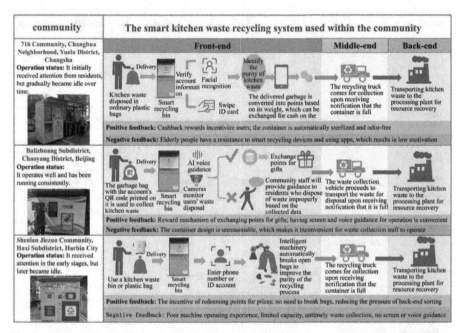

Fig. 4. Analysis of community-based intelligent kitchen waste recycling system application case

4.2 Summary of the Process of Intelligent Kitchen Waste Recycling System in Chinese Communities

This study presents the complete process of the intelligent kitchen waste recycling system based on a detailed analysis and summary of the application cases in three Chinese communities. The process consists of three stages: the front-end intelligent waste delivery and collection, the mid-end intelligent transportation, and the back-end big data platform recycling feedback. In each stage, it is essential to consider user behavior, intelligent terminal products, intelligent hardware/software technology, and user feedback, both positive and negative. Among them, the front-end delivery stage is a critical human-machine interaction behavior carrying stage of the intelligent recycling system, integrating the most advanced intelligent technologies such as RFID radio frequency identification technology [7], intelligent image recognition technology, and infrared automatic induction, and also receiving the most user feedback. Therefore, this study emphasizes improving the front-end human-machine interaction experience of the intelligent kitchen waste recycling system and puts forward targeted design strategies (Fig. 5).

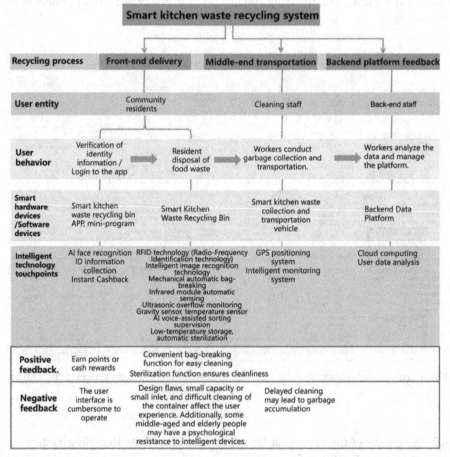

Fig. 5. Summary of the process of intelligent kitchen waste recycling system in Chinese communities

5   Based on User Experience: Design Strategies for China's Smart Kitchen Waste Recycling System

This article takes user needs as the core, based on the user experience dimension model, combined with the Chinese community kitchen waste intelligent recycling system, and considers the positive and negative feedback and application of intelligent technology, proposing five design strategies for intelligent kitchen waste recycling systems that should meet the basic, usability, and pleasure needs. In terms of functional requirements, this article proposes two design strategies, namely, adding a "bag-breaking" function and implementing multi-functional design to meet the special needs of kitchen waste recycling. In terms of usability, this article proposes three design strategies, including considering ergonomic principles, following usability principles, and considering the characteristics of middle-aged and elderly users to improve the usability and acceptability of intelligent kitchen waste recycling bins. In terms of pleasure, this article proposes a design strategy to improve the reward mechanism to enhance user participation and satisfaction. Figure 6 shows the derivation process of the design strategies.

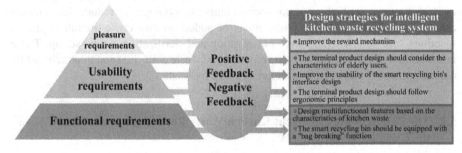

Fig. 6. Derivation Process of Design Strategies

5.1   Smart Kitchen Waste Recycling System Should Meet the Functional Requirements

The Intelligent Recycling Bin Must have the "Bag-Breaking" Function Added. Currently, most community residents still use disposable plastic bags to hold kitchen waste. These plastic bags are difficult to degrade and if mixed with kitchen waste, they will increase the workload of back-end sorting and affect the recycling and utilization of waste. Therefore, "bag-breaking" is a necessary requirement for delivering kitchen waste, which can improve the purity of waste collection. Currently, residents mainly use two methods for "breaking bags" when disposing of kitchen waste: one is to open the bag and pour the kitchen waste into the trash can, and the other is to use a metal tool to cut the bag and let the waste fall into the bucket. However, both of these methods are easy to dirty the hands or clothes of residents [8]. Therefore, many residents are unwilling to perform the "bag-breaking" action without supervision, resulting in many plastic impurities in the kitchen waste collected and transported to the terminal.

As front-end collection of kitchen waste requires high purity and no impurities, but there is a reality that residents are unwilling to manually break bags when disposing of kitchen waste. The design of intelligent kitchen waste collection system needs to add "bag-breaking" function at the front end of intelligent collection box. The design of intelligent kitchen waste collection box should include two functional components: one is the image recognition module, which can analyze the composition of kitchen waste in real-time during the process of residents' disposal, and judge whether there are other impurities such as plastic bags; the other is the mechanical automatic bag-breaking device, which can realize bag-breaking operation by the combination of mechanical arm and blade, and separate plastic bags from kitchen waste for recycling [9].

Multi-functional Design of Smart Recycling Bins Based on the Characteristics of Kitchen Waste. The biggest difference between kitchen waste and other household waste is that it is easy to rot and affects the subsequent utilization of resources. There-fore, under the premise of easy classification and storage, the intelligent kitchen waste collection box should be designed with multiple functions, considering its two main characteristics: high moisture content and easy spoilage. To reduce the moisture con-tent, a drainage or drying function can be added; to slow down the rate of decay, functions such as low-temperature preservation and sterilization can be set up. These measures can effectively improve the efficiency of waste collection and treatment, while reducing the odor and hygiene problems caused by waste.

5.2 The Design of the Intelligent Kitchen Waste Recycling System Should Meet the Usability Requirements

The Design of the Smart Kitchen Waste Recycling Bin Should Consider Ergonomic Principles. Following ergonomic principles can result in more user-friendly smart kitchen waste recycling bins, improving efficiency and comfort. When designing, the height should be suitable for the average person's height to avoid users having to bend over or raise their arms too high. The opening should be large enough to facilitate waste disposal, and the angle of the opening should be suitable for the user's throwing angle, reducing muscle fatigue and discomfort. Additionally, the recycling bin should provide visual or auditory feedback indicating whether the waste has been successfully deposited, and whether further classification or waste treatment is required. Furthermore, the inner liner design should be easy for cleaning personnel to remove, and the bin's shape and material should be easy to clean.

The Interface Design of the Smart Recycling Bin Should Follow the Principles Of Usability. The interface design should provide simple and clear operation feedback and explicit interactive guidance, such as using interactive graphics, colors, texts, and dynamic elements to guide user operations, and adding explanatory control functions to make it easier for users to master the system's operation process and overall architecture. In addition, the design should minimize cognitive difficulty and use standardized design language to convey information. Providing guidance to users at critical points can avoid the learned helplessness caused by task failure. For example, by providing help through voice prompts and visual or auditory feedback after successful operation, and by providing reasonable information prompts and operation constraints, users can avoid erroneous behaviors. Finally, to ensure a good user experience, the human-computer interaction interface design must have high security, stability, and operational performance to ensure that there are no crashes, malfunctions, or information leaks in the underlying system [10].

Design of Terminal Products in Smart Waste Management Systems Should Consider the Characteristics of Elderly Users. As community aging becomes more severe, the design of terminal products in smart waste management systems should take into ac-count the characteristics of middle-aged and elderly people who deposit garbage. Due to the low acceptance of smart devices and mobile applications among most middle-aged and elderly people, the design of smart devices should simplify the usage process and ensure that the system response speed matches the neural response speed of the elderly. In addition, logical operations and steps should be minimized as much as possible, and a physical restriction logical approach should be adopted to make it easier for users to adopt instinctive or habitual behavior, thereby improving the user experience [11].

5.3 The Design of Smart Kitchen Waste Recycling Systems Should Meet the Emotional Needs for Pleasure

Improve the Reward Mechanism in the Intelligent Kitchen Waste Recycling System. Based on incentives, recycling systems are considered as one of the practical systems to improve recycling rates and maintain public participation in waste recycling activities [12]. Therefore, when designing an intelligent recycling and classification system, emphasis should be placed on improving the reward mechanism to encourage residents to actively participate in the classification and disposal of kitchen waste. Specific design strategies include: 1) setting up a gravity sensor, which updates residents' cards with corresponding points based on the weight of kitchen waste deposited every time; 2) adding intelligent image recognition technology, which can analyze the components and purity of deposited kitchen waste in real-time; 3) improving the interface design of the resident's mobile terminal app or mini-program, optimizing the points accumulation and withdrawal page, making it clear and concise, reducing understanding costs, and simplifying the operation steps, so that residents of different ages can easily operate.

6   Conclusion

The Five specific design strategies proposed in this article aim to meet the basic functional requirements, usability requirements, and emotional needs of users. Design strategies based on user needs can effectively improve the user experience and enhance residents' enthusiasm for kitchen waste classification and recycling. These design strategies provide useful ideas and directions for the design and optimization of intelligent kitchen waste recycling systems. However, the design strategies proposed in this article still have certain limitations. Firstly, due to the regional and cultural differences in community residents' living habits and kitchen waste composition, personalized design and adjustments are required based on actual situations. Secondly, with the development of technology and social changes, users' demands for intelligent kitchen waste recycling systems will also constantly change, thus requiring continuous follow-up of user needs and optimization.

References

1. Teng, J., Dong, Y.: Design exploration of kitchen waste recycling bin under the background of garbage classification. Art Obs. **3**, 144–145 (2019)
2. Development direction of kitchen waste treatment under garbage classification policy. NetEase News, 27 April 2021. https://www.163.com/dy/article/G8K5JFEG05509P99.html
3. Yu, H., Chen, Y.: Design and application of intelligent garbage classification and recycling system. Packag. Eng. Art Ed. **39**(18), 154–159 (2018)
4. Beijing Daily Group. Why beautiful garbage classification recycling bins are not popular. Beijing Daily Client, April 13 2021. https://baijiahao.baidu.com/s?id=16969001403817530408&wfr=spider&for=pc
5. Jordan, P.W., Persson, S.: Exploring users' product constructs: how people think about different types of product. CoDesign **3**(S1), 97–106 (2007)
6. Zhu, X.: Cognitive research on interface design based on emotional experience. (Master's thesis, Southeast University) (2018)
7. Mao, C.: Design of intelligent garbage classification and recycling system based on RFID. Inf. Syst. Eng. (2022)
8. Li, S.: Research promotes the use of end-breaking bag technology to prevent dirty hands when disposing of kitchen waste. Shenzhen Special Zone Daily, A04, 28 October 2022
9. Xie, S., Luo, W., Lou, Z.: Design and simulation of a garbage bin with automatic separation of garbage bags. Mech. Electr. Technol. **2020**(04), 5–7 (2020). https://doi.org/10.19508/j.cnki.1672-4801.2020.04.002
10. Chen, D.: Design and research of urban life garbage classification and recycling system based on IoT. (Master's thesis, Qingdao University) (2021)
11. Liu, Z., Zhang, F., Guo, W.: Research on the design of interactive products for the elderly from the perspective of user experience. Packag. Eng. **36**(2), 63–66 (2015)
12. Zhou, J., Jiang, P., Yang, J., Liu, X.: Designing a smart incentive-based recycling system for household recyclable waste. Waste Manage. **123**, 142–153 (2021)

(Smart) Product Design

Research on Public Seating Design of Scenic Spots Based on Kansei Engineering

Yuhan Cheng and Yi Jin[✉]

East China University of Science and Technology, No. 130 Meilong Road, Xuhui District,
Shanghai, China
1362200456@qq.com

Abstract. The impact of the new crown epidemic on the tourism industry is unprecedented. Research on public facilities in scenic spots has far-reaching significance for the development and operation of the tourism industry in the post-epidemic era, and can help the tourism industry more reasonably adapt to the development needs of the post-epidemic era. Based on the theory of Kansei engineering, this paper collects and screens suitable sensibility vocabulary and samples of public seats in scenic spots, and conducts sensibility evaluation experiments. Through factor analysis, the key factors and related physical elements that affect the sensibility evaluation of seat design are obtained, providing a basis for the design practice of public seats in scenic spots basis. In the end, the main needs of users for seats are summarized into three aspects: (1) sensory factors - special and fun, which mainly affect the appearance style and interactive design of seats; (2) functional factors - durability, sense of security, which mainly affects the functional design of the seat; (3) emotional factors - warmth and comfort, mainly affect the experience of using the seat.

Keywords: Scenic spots · Public seats · Kansei engineering

1 Introduction

Tourism-related industries, which have been hit hard by the epidemic in the past three years, urgently need to be revived and restored. The impact of the new crown epidemic on the tourism industry is unprecedented. Research on scenic spots has far-reaching significance for the development and operation of the tourism industry in the post-epidemic era, and can help the tourism industry more reasonably adapt to the development needs of the post-epidemic era [1]. At the same time, in recent years, domestic and foreign scholars and industry experts have conducted valuable academic discussions and industrial practice research on public facilities in scenic spots. Public seats have the characteristics of publicity and communication. Under this, understanding tourists' new perception and demand for seats in scenic spots can effectively help the renewal and design of public seats in scenic spots, and help the recovery and development of scenic spots.

Based on the theory of kansei engineering, this paper collects and screens suitable sensibility vocabulary and samples of public seats in scenic spots, and conducts sensibility evaluation experiments. Through factor analysis, the key factors and related physical

C. Stephanidis et al. (Eds.): HCII 2023, CCIS 1835, pp. 579–590, 2023.
https://doi.org/10.1007/978-3-031-36001-5_75

elements that affect the sensibility evaluation of seat design are obtained, providing a basis for the design practice of public seats in scenic spots basis.

2 Public Seats

2.1 The Concept and Classification of Public Seats

Public seating is an appliance that meets people's needs for "sitting" outdoors, that is, seats, stools in the traditional sense, flower racks, gallery stools, pavilions, etc. in public spaces., Items based on demand, including steps, big stones, edge of flower beds, etc. Public seating is an important part of urban furniture, which has the characteristics of publicity and communication [2].

There are many kinds of public seats, and the classification methods are also various. The more common classification methods are: (1) According to the setting method, it can be divided into permanent fixed seats and movable seats. This paper mainly focuses on the fixed seats in scenic spots; (3) According to the style, there are Ming-style seats, Western-style seats, Southeast Asian-style seats, post-modern style seats, etc. It is found that outdoor seats are common in domestic communities, and the most common ones can be roughly divided into five categories, except for individual cases: (1) tree-enclosed chairs: (2) gazebo seats; (3) leisure benches; (4) stone pier, Stone benches; (5) Edges of flower beds, etc. Among them, leisure benches and gazebo seats are the most utilized. [3].

2.2 Research Status of Public Seating

Xiaofeng [4] believes that public furniture has the characteristics of publicity, durability and artistry, and believes that the design of public furniture should follow the principles of landscape, locality and integrity with the environment. Weiping [5] believed that human beings are accustomed to judging the material of the seat by direct contact, so more suitable materials should be used in the design. Tingcui [6] conducted related research on the color of public furniture. She believed that the factors affecting the color of public furniture include material factors, regional factors, and humanistic factors. She believed that the color of public furniture should be in harmony with the overall color of the environment.

Most of the recent research studies the design of public seating from the perspective of interaction. Liya [7] put forward the interactive experience strategy and method of urban seating by observing people's behavioral psychology in public space, and explained and verified it through the case of interactive experience urban seating design. To sum up, the design of public furniture should fully consider people's physiological and psychological needs, and at the same time maintain coordination with the environment in which it is located.

Research and discussion on public seats are mostly limited to the urban public living environment, and there are few studies on public seats related to the tourist environment of scenic spots.

3 Kansei Engineering Research Theory

Kansei Engineering was proposed by Kenichi Yamamoto, the former president of Mazda Corporation, and it is one of the commonly used measurement methods for product emotion. As the name suggests, Kansei Engineering is a research between art and science, Kansei and Engineering. It is based on the analysis of the perceptual cognition of the characters and serves as the theoretical basis for product design and product improvement. The biggest feature of Kansei Engineering is to quantify perceptual cognitive behaviors in the way of engineering. The main experimental method is to conduct qualitative and quantitative analysis through the selection of perceptual vocabulary, corresponding to product characteristics, and compare and analyze the experimental data and samples obtained from the measurement, so as to find out which design elements affect the perceptual evaluation. It is often used in the test and development stage of industrial products, providing designers with a more scientific design basis [8].

Kansei engineering is often used to study seating products.Lei [9] took high-speed train seats as the research object, proposed a theoretical framework based on Kansei Engineering system, conducted research on product image modeling and color design, and effectively identified the modeling and color design elements that affect product image. Zhenpeng [10] explored the design elements and priority order of the anchor chair modeling image, and provided designers with guidance and reference for the anchor chair modeling design. Cheng [3] used the theory of kansei engineering to obtain the key factors and related physical elements that affect the sensibility evaluation of seat design through factor analysis, which provides a basis for the practice of seat design. To sum up, it is feasible to analyze the seat design of scenic spots based on Kansei Engineering.

4 Experiment Design

4.1 Collection of Kansei Words

The selection of kansei words directly affects the design results and the accuracy of design evaluation. Therefore, when collecting kansei words, it is necessary to choose the adjective that best expresses the user's true feelings about the community seat. There are many ways to collect kansei words, such as observation, interview, questionnaire, reading of literature and collection of related websites. Taking time and other factors into consideration, this article mainly uses desktop research to collect sensibility vocabulary through literature and websites: at this stage, it mainly collects by reading literature related to kansei engineering and public seats, and searching for community seat keywords on major seat-related websites.

(1) Books and magazines: "Engineering Design of Sensibility" by Tsinghua University Press, "Public Facilities and Environmental Art Design" by China Architecture and Architecture Press, "Research on Urban Public Facilities System Design" by China Architecture and Architecture Press, and related papers on outdoor seating Literature, etc.;
(2) Forum community categories: duitang.com - Seat Zone, Puxiang Industrial Design Station, Sina Home, Landscape.com, Building Materials.com, etc.;

A total of 102 groups of kansei words were collected at this stage.

4.2 Screening of Kansei Words

This project uses the mathematical statistics method to count 102 groups of kansei words collected, exclude 82 groups of repeated words, analyze the remaining words, and remove words with similar meanings and words that are not very relevant to this experiment There are a total of 40 perceptual adjectives in the vocabulary, which are divided into 20 groups according to the opposite meaning (Table 1).

Table 1. Table of kansei words

Modern-Traditional	Smooth - Rough	Round - Sharp	Warm - Cold
Interesting - Boring	Streamline - Geometric	Dexterous - Clumsy	Tidy - Messy
Beautiful - Ugly	Innovative - Old-fashioned	Professional-Amateur	Refined - Crude
Concise - Complex	Coordinated - Abrupt	Environmentally friendly - Polluted	Special - Normal
Safe - Dangerous	Thick -Thin	Durable - Vulnerable	Cozy - Uncomfortable

Then, 20 sets of emotional vocabulary were conducted in a questionnaire survey. A total of 20 users were recruited, and they were asked to choose 8 sets of words that best describe public seats. The number of times each set of words was selected is as follows (Table 2).

Table 2. Table of Perceptual Vocabulary Scores

Kansei words	The number of times selected	Kansei words	The number of times selected
Modern-Traditional	15	Professional-Amateur	5
Interesting - Boring	17	Environmentally friendly - Polluted	4
Beautiful - Ugly	7	Warm - Cold	10
Concise - Complex	5	Tidy - Messy	5
Smooth - Rough	3	Refined - Crude	3
Streamline - Geometric	12	Special - Normal	13
Innovative - Old-fashioned	7	Safe - Dangerous	14
Coordinated - Abrupt	4	Thick -Thin	3
Round - Sharp	5	Durable - Vulnerable	12
Dexterous - Clumsy	3	Cozy - Uncomfortable	13

Through the statistics of the selection results, the 8 groups of words with the highest number of choices are finally obtained (Table 3).

Table 3. The final Kansei words selected

Cozy - Uncomfortable	Streamline - Geometric	Modern-Traditional	Durable - Vulnerable
Safe - Dangerous	Warm - Cold	Special - Normal	Interesting - Boring

4.3 Screening of Experiment Samples

A total of 82 samples of public seats in scenic spots were obtained through network research, and the sample types covered common public seats in scenic spots at home and abroad, and 12 of the most representative ones were selected as experimental samples (Table 4).

Table 4. Final selected sample pictures

4.4 Establishment of the Semantic Difference Scale

The 8 groups of perceptual vocabulary determined by the above screening are used to establish a 7-level semantic difference scale, as shown in Table 4–5. The scores include -3, −2, −1, 0, 1, 2, and 3. Take " uncomfortable-comfortable " as an example, −3 is very uncomfortable, −2 is uncomfortable, −1 is slightly uncomfortable, 0 is no feeling, 1 is generally comfortable, 2 is relatively comfortable, 3 is very comfortable, the score The smaller the score, the closer to the adjective on the left, and the larger the score, the closer to the adjective on the right.

5 Results and Analysis

5.1 Summary of Experimental Data

The method of online questionnaire survey was adopted, and the interviewees were invited to rate the 12 seat samples through 8 groups of adjective pairs on the semantic difference scale. A total of 74 questionnaires were distributed and 68 valid questionnaires were obtained. Table 6 is obtained by calculating the average score of valid questionnaires.

Table 5. Semantic Difference Scale

Uncomfortable	−3 −2 −1 0 1 2 3	Cozy
Dangerous	−3 −2 −1 0 1 2 3	Safe
Geometric	−3 −2 −1 0 1 2 3	Streamlined
Cold	−3 −2 −1 0 1 2 3	Warm
Traditional	−3 −2 −1 0 1 2 3	Modern
Normal	−3 −2 −1 0 1 2 3	Special
Vulnerable	−3 −2 −1 0 1 2 3	Durable
Boring	−3 −2 −1 0 1 2 3	Interesting

Table 6. The average of the sample score

	Cozy - Uncomfortable	Safe - Dangerous	Streamline - Geometric	Warm - Cold	Modern-Traditional	Special - Normal	Durable - Vulnerable	Interesting - Boring
Sample 1	.28	1.07	.75	−.44	−.90	−1.74	−.01	−1.41
Sample 2	−.24	−.74	−.94	−.28	−.21	.59	−1.03	.47
Sample 3	−.41	.93	−.63	−.49	−.22	−.71	.50	−.62
Sample 4	.72	1.31	1.16	.34	1.03	.34	.79	.78
Sample 5	−.53	.51	−.19	−1.40	−1.29	−1.53	.96	−.68
Sample 6	−.49	.32	−.66	−.85	.60	−.06	.75	−.40
Sample 7	−.32	−.22	.22	−.32	−.06	.01	.22	.06
Sample 8	.44	.97	−.28	.00	1.78	1.22	.63	1.18
Sample 9	.29	.38	.04	−.09	1.56	1.59	.66	1.41
Sample 10	.29	.60	1.38	−1.10	2.03	1.81	1.26	1.49
Sample 11	.75	.75	1.35	.32	1.69	1.41	1.04	1.13
Sample 12	1.00	1.03	1.04	.88	1.49	1.38	.75	1.54

5.2 Analysis of Experimental Data

Import the mean scores (Table 7) of ten samples for each pair of perceptual vocabulary into SPSS statistical software for factor analysis, and obtain the gravel map, explained total variance and component matrix.

Table 7. KMO and Bartlett's test

KMO Sampling Suitability Quantity		.650
Bartlett's test for sphericity	Approximate chi-square	95.972
	Degrees of freedom	28
	Significant	.000

Table 8. Common Factor Variance

	Initial	Extract
Cozy - Uncomfortable	1.000	.968
Safe - Dangerous	1.000	.875
Streamline - Geometric	1.000	.716
Warm - Cold	1.000	.914
Modern-Traditional	1.000	.942
Special - Normal	1.000	.995
Durable - Vulnerable	1.000	.941
Interesting - Boring	1.000	.963
Extraction method: principal component analysis		

It can be seen from Table 7 that the significant value of the Bartlett test for sphericity has a P value of 0. At the significance level, the null hypothesis should be rejected and the correlation coefficient matrix is considered to be significantly different from the identity matrix. At the same time, the KMO value is 0.650. According to the KMO standard, we can know that the questionnaire items can be used for factor analysis. As can be seen from Table 8, it can be seen from the table that the extracted values of most variables are greater than 0.85, and the variables can be well expressed by common factors.

The abscissa of the gravel diagram (Fig. 1) represents the factor components that affect the index of the seat, and the ordinate represents the characteristic value. It can be seen from the figure that the eigenvalue (variance contribution) of the first factor is very high, which contributes the most to explaining the original items; the eigenvalues of the third and later factors are all small, and contributes a lot to explaining the original items is small and can be ignored, so it is more appropriate to extract three factors.

It can be seen from the total variance (Table 9) explained that based on the eigenvalue greater than 1, after extracting 3 factors, the 3 factors together explained 91.420% of the total variance of the questionnaire items, and the contribution rate of component 1 to the result was 56.269%. The contribution rate of 2 is 21.302%, and the total contribution rate

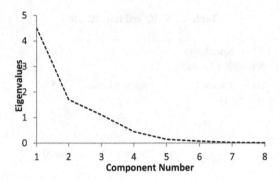

Fig. 1. Gravel map

Table 9. Total Variance Explanation

Element	Initial eigenvalue			Extract loading sum of squares			Rotational load sum of squares		
	Total	Percent variance	Accumulation%	Total	Percent variance	Accumulation%	Total	Percent variance	Accumulation%
1	4.501	56.269	56.269	4.501	56.269	56.269	3.108	38.851	38.851
2	1.704	21.303	77.571	1.704	21.303	77.571	2.338	29.222	68.073
3	1.108	13.848	91.420	1.108	13.848	91.420	1.868	23.347	91.420
4	.446	5.574	96.993						
5	.144	1.805	98.799						
6	.074	.920	99.718						
7	.019	.236	99.954						
8	.004	.046	100.000						

Extraction method: principal component analysis

of component 3 is 13.849%. In general, the information loss of the original questionnaire items is less, and the factor analysis effect is ideal, which has research significance.

It can be seen from the Table 10 that "tradition-modern", "mass-personality", and "boring-interest" have higher loads on the first factor; "danger-safety", "geometry-streamline", "fragile-durable" There is a higher loading on the second factor; "sad-comfortable" and "cold-warm" have a higher loading on the third factor.

It can be seen from the Table 11 that the principal components are analyzed through the loading matrix, and the size of the value represents the mutual coefficient between the perceptual vocabulary and the principal components, and the larger the value, the closer the relationship between the two. It can be seen from the table that the highest scores of principal component 1 are "individual", "interesting", and "modern", and the highest scores of principal component 2 are "durable" and "safe". Therefore, it can be obtained that the first five perceptual needs of target users for community seats are: individuality, fun, modernity, durability, and safety.

Table 10. Composition matrix after rotation

	Element		
	1	2	3
Cozy - Uncomfortable			.744
Safe - Dangerous		.869	
Streamline - Geometric		.713	
Warm - Cold			.907
Modern-Traditional	.895		
Special - Normal	.976		
Durable - Vulnerable		.860	
Interesting - Boring	.938		

Extraction method: principal component analysis
Rotation method: Kaiser normalized maximum variance method

a. The rotation has converged after 5 iterations

Table 11. Component score coefficient matrix

	Element		
	1	2	3
Cozy - Uncomfortable	−.036	.093	.383
Safe - Dangerous	−.227	.418	.141
Streamline - Geometric	−.047	.286	.113
Warm - Cold	−.091	−.143	.602
Modern-Traditional	.315	.039	−.102
Special - Normal	.383	−.122	−.084
Durable - Vulnerable	.134	.456	−.435
Interesting - Boring	.342	−.083	−.039

Extraction method: principal component analysis
Rotation method: Kaiser normalized maximum variance method
Component score

6 Discussions

From the above analysis, the main needs of users for seats can be summarized into three aspects: (1) sensory factors - special and fun, which mainly affect the appearance style and interactive design of seats; (2) functional factors - durability and sense of security, which mainly affects the functional design of the seat; (3) emotional factors - warmth and comfort, mainly affect the experience of using the seat.

Table 12. Sample factor scores

	Sensory factor	Functional factor	Emotional factor
Sample 1	−2.05	.46	.89
Sample 2	.11	−2.67	.44
Sample 3	−.96	.02	−.41
Sample 4	−.17	.96	1.06
Sample 5	−1.16	.45	−1.56
Sample 6	−.10	−.22	−1.26
Sample 7	−.14	−.86	−.24
Sample 8	.69	.04	.24
Sample 9	1.07	−.32	−.08
Sample 10	1.41	.96	−1.30
Sample 11	.74	.71	.63
Sample 12	.56	.46	1.58

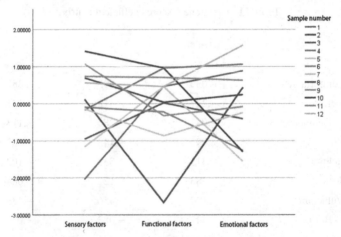

Fig. 2. General chart of sample factor scores

According to Table 12 and Fig. 2, it can be seen that sample 10 has the highest sensory factor score, followed by sample 9, and then sample 11 and sample 8. Through comparative analysis of seat samples, both sample 10 and sample 9 have The expression of more rhythmic lines also has the characteristics of free and irregular shape. Sample 11 has a clever rounded shape, and at the same time, it uses the same white marble material as sample 8, which is very modern.

The highest functional factor score is sample five, followed by sample ten, and again sample eleven. Through the comparison and analysis of the seat samples, the use of sample 5 stone, the enduring traditional shape and placement make its safety and durability highly unified. The clever use of light-colored metal materials in sample ten makes people feel solid and trustworthy. Sample 11 has a white wide and thick panel, a stable base, and a wider seat overall, which can be used for reclining or sitting, giving people a sense of stability and safety.

The highest score of emotion factor is sample 12, followed by sample 4, and again sample 1. Through the comparative analysis of the seat samples, both sample 12 and sample 4 have relatively round shape expressions, and at the same time, the use of color gives people a warm and simple feeling.

To sum up, in the subsequent design process, we should learn from the modeling advantages, functional advantages, and experience advantages of several samples with higher scores in the key influencing factors. For example, the wide and thick seat panel, the irregular overall shape, and the rounded design form conform to the seat width and height of the man-machine. Therefore, in the future design of public seats in scenic spots, we should start from the two aspects of key influencing factors—sensory factors, functional factors, and emotional factors, absorb the shape, interaction and functional advantages of several samples with higher scores in key influencing factors, and avoid low design flaw of few samples.

This study also has some limitations. First of all, there is no empirical investigation on the existing scenic spots, and there is a lack of understanding of the seating conditions in the actual scenic spots. Secondly, the seats collected in this paper are mainly fixed seats in scenic spots as the research object. At the same time, the samples did not collect the situation of intelligent scenic seats. Finally, in terms of perceptual vocabulary screening and questionnaire collection, the number of interviewees and categories are concentrated in the youth group, and there is a lack of perceptual evaluation of seats by the elderly. In the future, on the basis of this research, we can explore the differences between groups of people and the perceptual evaluation differences of users in specific scenic spots for seats, so as to help scenic spots realize personalized seating facilities design. In general, how to better improve the tourism experience and create a warm scenic spot through the improvement of the seats in the scenic spot, I hope this article can be used as a guide to provide some ideas for future design.

References

1. Jiawei, Y.: Study on the change of tourism market behavior intention in the post-epidemic era. Bus. Exhib. Econ. **55**(09), 39–42 (2022)
2. Weiguang, W., Liyun, L.: Urban Environmental Facility Design, 1st edn. Shanghai People's Fine Arts Publishing House, Shanghai (2017)
3. Lucheng, L.: Research on community seat design based on emotional interaction. Shanghai University of Engineering Technology (2022)
4. Xiaofeng, F.: The current situation and prospect of urban furniture research. Furniture **43**(02), 1–7 (2022)
5. Weiping, D.: Research on the form design of outdoor seats. Jiangxi Normal University (2018)
6. Tingcui, L.: Research on color design of public outdoor furniture. J. Chifeng Univ. (Natural Science Edition) **31**(03), 71–72 (2015)
7. Liya, L.: Research and design of urban seats with interactive experience based on behavioral psychology. Packag. Eng. **40**(06), 213–216 (2019)

8. Lixian, L., Ling, H.: Kansei Engineering Design, 2nd edn. Tsinghua University Press, Beijing (2015)
9. Lei, X., Xiao, Y.: Research on image modeling and color design of high-speed train seats. Mech. Design **36**(03), 139–144 (2019)
10. Zhenpeng, L., Lejing, S., Jinhua, X., Jiaqi, N.: Research on the modeling image of anchor chair based on Kansei engineering. Packag. Eng. **42**(18), 239–246 (2021)

Building Sustainable Design System to Achieve Digital Sustainability of Enterprise Products

Anirban Dey[✉], Devashree Marathe[✉], and Anand Karelia[✉]

SAP Labs India Pvt. Ltd., Bangalore, India
{anirban.dey03,devashree.marathe,anand.karelia}@sap.com

Abstract. 'Carbon Footprint' has become a commonplace word but is rarely fully understood. It has become synonymous even with 'Global Warming' and the immediate picture that forms in the mind about probable causes of it, is of evil agendas and larger than life actions such as drilling into the ocean floor for oil, imagery of burning forests, large wastelands after wastelands of useful thrown away bulk load of stuff, all pointing towards the grossly unsustainable habits of the entire human population.

This easily imaginable crime-scene is incomplete, though not inaccurate.

As of now, the only place where sustainability is imaginable is at what a business undertakes, and the physical resources, that get utilised within its processes. **However, this poster aims to bring to light the rather non-obvious player in sustainability – the User Interfaces themselves.**

For instance, in any sustainable enterprise scenarios where solutions convey the carbon emission details, enable the industries to track their carbon footprints or other such metrics. **Ironically, what is not considered in these calculations is the emissions from the illuminated screens on which these solutions are consumed.** Thus, we aim to look into the sustainability of the UI & the backend code that runs these 'sustainable' solutions.

There are ways to design UI in a more sustainable way through building design system, guidelines & interactions by keeping sustainability in the core.

This poster aims to demystify carbon emissions and make them more understandable and tangible for the every-man, identify the precise relations between UI design and carbon emissions, and suggest a starting point for a solution as also **a stepping stone towards changing the user behaviour by improvised UI approaches from the UX community as a whole.**

1 Introduction

Since the 1990s with technology showing up in more instances of human activity than ever imagined before, there's also been a certain awareness that's developed about the impact of this technology on our environment. It came naturally maybe, to measure the impact caused by these technology-enabled activities, and study its effects on the surroundings – people, animals, soil, trees, skies, water, you name it. Most times, the effect was noticed first, then came the analysis of what is causing this, and sometimes, it pointed to technology.

C. Stephanidis et al. (Eds.): HCII 2023, CCIS 1835, pp. 591–597, 2023.
https://doi.org/10.1007/978-3-031-36001-5_76

We do not intend to remain oblivious to the fact that carbon emission and its impact on earth, is a much debated topic. There's a line of thought that would argue human activity is too insignificant, and the changes the planet is going through, are completely irrelevant to our existence here. We choose to not partake in this conversation.

For the purpose of this paper, we will leave aside this debate of what exactly carbon emissions from human activity are doing to the environment, to what degree, etc. and focus solely on bringing to notice, which all human activities are even contributing to these emissions in the first place.

1.1 Carbon Emissions from the Perspective of 2023

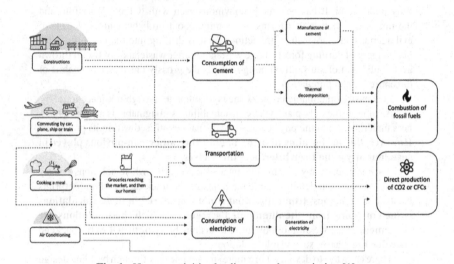

Fig. 1. Human activities leading to carbon emission [1]

Often times, when imagining 'carbon emissions' the immediate image that comes to mind is a big factory on some distant field, puffing out clouds of thick brown smoke. Although carbon emissions by definition are "carbon dioxide emissions or CO_2 emissions that are stemming from the burning of fossil fuels and manufacture of cement – including carbon dioxide produced during consumption of solid, liquid, and gas fuels as well as gas flaring", the activities leading to these emissions are not limited to only these scenarios (Fig. 1).

Another definition mentions "carbon emissions mean carbon dioxide emitted when fossil fuels are burned in vehicles, building, industrial processes and so on." This one seems to cover a broader range of activities, but as per our understanding, is still incomplete [3, 4].

The technology being used here, to write, review and consume this content, is playing its role in carbon emissions too!

According to a study conducted by University of Oxford8, there are three major ways in which the screen-based technology we are using on a regular basis, has an impact on the amount of carbon emissions in the atmosphere –

1. Manufacture of this technology
2. Usage of this technology
3. Disposal of this technology

The study mentions, "for a standard PC and screen, operated over a 6 year period, the annual GHG impact (carbon footprint) will be around 778 kg CO_2e. Of this, around 85% results from manufacture and shipping, and the remaining 15% from electricity consumption while in use" [1].

We propose to take into consideration a further detail when thinking of the emissions from usage of technology perspective – that during usage, it isn't only electricity that is a contributing factor in carbon footprint of the activity of operating device – the internet, and type of device, also affects the carbon footprint, and can have if not larger, an equal impact as electricity consumption does.

Up until a decade ago, internet usage wasn't as expansive as seen in 2023.

Studying its effects and implications on emissions, may not have been too relevant even 10 years ago, but perhaps these numbers help understand why it matters now, more than ever.

Date	Number of users	World population (%)
December, 1995	16 Millions	0.4
December, 1996	36 Millions	0.9
December, 1999	248 Millions	4.1
December, 2004	817 Millions	12.7
December, 2009	1,802 Millions	26.6
December, 2018	4,313 Millions	55.6
December, 2022	5,544 Millions	69.0

Fig. 2. Usage of internet [2]

Today the internet continues to grow day by day. The above table shows the incredibly fast evolution of the internet usage from 1995 to 2022 (see Fig. 2).

Internet is a dynamic factor in carbon emissions – it isn't as binary as electricity. When anyone anywhere on the planet, plugs in their device to charge the battery, the electricity being consumed isn't varying based on how the user chooses to charge the device. It is in that sense a factor beyond the control of the user herself. Internet usage on the other hand, can be dependent on how the user is choosing to interact with the screen-based technology, and this is precisely the area we believe change in carbon footprint is possible – for the power lies in the hands of the user!

And it is not a small number of users anymore, but an exponentially growing one.

If we look at the human population growth patterns, it is evident that the carbon footprint of screen-based technology is no longer a minor contribution to the overall carbon emissions, considering almost 69% of the population – around 5,544 million people – use this technology on a regular basis as of now (Fig. 3).

Year	Total World Population	Ten-year growth rate (%)
1950	2,556,000,053	18.9
1960	3,039,451,023	22.0
1970	3,706,618,163	20.2
1980	4,453,831,714	18.5
1990	5,278,639,789	15.2
2000	6,082,966,429	12.6
2010	6,956,823,603	10.7
2020	7,794,798,739	8.7
2030	8,548,487,000	7.3

Fig. 3. World Population

2 The (Hidden) Emissions

2.1 Screen Time

The current modes of entertainment for consuming image-based content or watching videos on laptops and mobile phones are only a glimpse of how technology can play a role in our recreational time. Our collective screen time could be unknown for now, but it is possible to already establish connections between that and carbon emissions. **Consider what may seem like a minor fact right now – that watching half an hour of video content creates emissions equivalent to driving almost 4 miles (approx. 1.6 kg of CO_2 emissions)** [5] – taking into consideration the projected population of 2030 as per the earlier chart, this fact will surely seem not so minor anymore, as it could be the reality of 8 billion individuals.

When we talk about screen time in general it does not limit to only watching content on various platforms. It comprises of using the screens for day-to-day work besides social networking, sending/receiving messages through freeware, cross-platform communications, emails, video calls etc. And all this may or may not always have the perfect interface to minimize or reduce carbon emissions during usage. **As per some reports, it is concluded that an average person spends almost 6 h and 58 min per day on screens while staying connected to the internet** (Fig. 4) [7, 9].

The prolonged wait we experience while data loads in certain instances of a user interface, is because the system is taking a longer time to complete the task, and this reality substantially impacts the emissions we are talking about. Even the browsing behaviors of users bring out some statistics like, **a typical website produces 6.8 g of carbon emissions every time a page loads, which is roughly the same as the emissions produced during boiling water in an electric kettle for a cup of tea** [6].

Activity	Average Daily Screen Time
Watching TV/Videos	3 Hours 16 Minutes
Gaming	1 Hour 46 Minutes
Social Media	1 Hour 27 Minutes
Browsing Websites	51 Minutes
Video Chatting	20 Minutes
E-Reading	15 Minutes
Content Creation	14 Minutes
Others	29 Minutes

Fig. 4. Average daily screen time of US Teens

2.2 The User Interfaces

The user interfaces of various platforms that enable a user to browse, watch, create or monitor content are not always the happy part of the experience. These user interfaces too have an implication on the way they interact to the time they keep the users interested or attached to them. We are all quite aware of the infrastructure running constantly behind every internet activity such as network devices, data center machines, ISP routers, etc., which consume energy on their own too. The growing number of internet users and social media trends have contributed majorly to the increase of carbon footprint. Besides these, the user interfaces are also at times not the best optimized or designed to make the activity less emissive. And if they are optimized, these optimization techniques aren't clearly communicated to the users. One example is that of the 'notifications' on any smart device – laptops/phones/tabs/watches, etc. – how the user chooses their settings around these notifications, can determine the number of emissions occurring in the instance of receiving one single message! **Users are not always aware of the behavioural changes that could help them in getting the best out of technological interactions,** hence it's the responsibility of the technology owners too, to help and guide towards this change.

When we investigate the enterprise products where organizations have been creating/developing products to help maintain the sustainability of their customers, the irony lies in rarely providing details of the emissions behind projecting that report on the user interfaces. **These user interfaces along with the architecture lying beneath might not be the greenest of products** that are creating awareness and trying to project the reality of climatic emissions. These kinds of transparency and awareness in understanding the big picture of the full cycle of emissions are essential for any organization to be a front-runner in the sustainability of enterprises.

3 How a Design System Can Help Users to Be Carbon Efficient

A design system is usually put in place to shape the larger part of interaction paradigms. Because of the similarities in interaction patterns defined by design systems, the user habits get cemented during application usage. These newly formed habits can either lead to positive or negative impact on the carbon footprint. There are commonalities in habits across the user groups using identical design systems. A bigger design system creates a proportionately larger impact because of the scale of its consumption – the higher number of users, and the longer committed periods for which they utilize the software.

3.1 Positive Impact Through Design Systems

Let us understand some positive impact of design systems with an example of the 'SAP Fiori' design system. There are multiple reusable components in the Fiori design system. 'Responsive table' is one such reusable component. It consists of a 'lazy loading' feature which loads only 20 items upfront instead of loading all 1000s of records the table contains in reality. Upon scroll into the last row, the table simply loads the next 20 [10, 11].

Table settings also allow users to skim through all the available columns of the table, and hide the low priority columns from view. (This stems from another purpose – that each user might be functioning differently, and this feature allows for some easing of the UI on the eyes as well.) Columns can be configured to sort the desired attribute during display. E.g., if user needs to take an action on the 'in progress' statuses, the table can be configured to sort & display the rows with 'in progress' status on the top & users don't need to scroll further to look for rows with 'in progress' statuses from the long lists. On top of this, the system also allows users to save the unique configuration of the table as their personal 'variant'. With all optimizations of such reusable components if 'x' amount of carbon emission is reduced & the components are consumed by 'y' number of users, total positive impact on the carbon emission can be x * y.

3.2 Negative Impact Through Design Systems

On the contrary, if a component defined in the design system is not carbon efficient & consumes 'a' amount of data due to inefficiency, & is consumed by 'b' number of users, total negative impact can be a * b. Designers need to be mindful about the carbon emissions while shaping the user behavior through design systems & patterns.

3.3 Prioritizing Interactions Based on Carbon Footprint

Pagination Over Infinite Scroll. Because of the 'infinite scroll' feature, users are encouraged to scroll endlessly without any clear purpose. Interaction started with the lower interaction cost & better adaptiveness to the mobile device interaction. But it established the habit of scrolling infinitely & users end up consuming more data every time they interact. Apart from implications like addiction, information overload & increased screen time it also increases carbon emissions. Pagination is relatively older but a more beneficial interaction in this context. It breaks the infinite scroll into smaller pages & user can take a conscious decision while loading the next page [12].

Manual Play over Auto Play. Auto play of next video after ongoing video ends & auto playing the video while scrolling the video content in video streaming app is becoming popular. With such features, user ends up consuming more carbon footprint with continuous streaming of videos. A small change in a design system like asking user to take a conscious decision to play next video can reduce carbon emissions to considerable amount. It also takes care of user's consent.

Let's understand this with examples from some of the famous social media applications. In Facebook's default settings, video adds begin to play automatically as soon they appear on the screen however, on Twitter, the video ads begin after a tap. Just one small design decision can leave a huge impact on the data consumption & carbon footprint for platforms with a massive userbase.

Static Image over Animated Content.   Currently, there is a heavy usage of visual content in applications. With more usage of animated content, carbon footprint is increasing. By keeping the static visual content as the default option & animated content as a secondary option, the system can effectively decrease the usage of animated content, thus also minimizing the carbon footprint.

Tabs over Long List.   Long lists load entire content during the launch. If the content is divided into multiple tabs, content gets loaded based on the selection of the tabs. This can result into greener browsing.

4 Conclusion

At a theoretical level, we have put together some ideas of what heuristics can be followed for a 'green' UI.

We aspire to explore further and look forward to the possibility of bringing real-time carbon emission metrics while applications are being used, for our study, as well as for the users of the applications, allowing them an informed decision on whether they want to scroll further on Instagram or not, and what the impact of that decision will be like, perhaps in terms of something relatable, such as the health of a tree, or a favorite animal!

References

1. https://www.it.ox.ac.uk/article/environment-and-it
2. https://www.internetworldstats.com/emarketing.htm
3. https://ec.europa.eu/eurostat/statistics-explained/index.php?title=Glossary:Carbon_dio
   xide_emissions
4. https://www.lawinsider.com/dictionary/carbon-emissions
5. https://www.goodbyecar.uk/blog/emissions-of-daily-activities
6. The Carbon Cost of Googling. https://www.theguardian.com/environment/ethicallivingblog/
   2009/jan/12/carbon-emissions-google
7. https://www.livemint.com/companies/news/half-hour-of-netflix-leads-to-emissions-of-1-
   6kg-of-co2-equivalent-climate-experts-11572240109579.html
8. For more Average Screen Time Statistics (2023) Worldwide. https://explodingtopics.com/
   blog/screen-time-stats
9. Carbon Footprint of Most Popular Social Media Platforms. https://www.mdpi.com/2071-
   1050/14/4/2195
10. https://www.sap.com/products/technology-platform/fiori.html
11. https://experience.sap.com/fiori-design-web/responsive-table/
12. https://gulfnews.com/special-reports/deadly-scroll-without-end-how-infinite-scroll-hacks-
    your-brain-and-why-it-is-bad-for-you-1.1676965239566

Development of Multi-objective Optimal Design Method Using Review Data with Kansei Items as the Objective Function

So Fukuhara[1], Saerom Lee[2], and Masao Arakawa[2(✉)]

[1] School of Science for Emergence, Kagawa University, Takamatsu, Japan
[2] Faculty of Engineering and Design, Kagawa University, Takamatsu, Japan
arakawa.masao@kagawa-u.ac.jp

Abstract. In product design, it is important to understand user's kansei values and reflect them in the product. We then need to identify the relationship between kansei evaluations and product features. A large amount of text data including users' impressions and kansei evaluations of products are stored on the Web as review data and various indices have been developed to evaluate products sensitively based on these. However, no method has been established to regress these evaluation indices on the design proposal using optimization. In this study, we propose the rudimentary design method for obtaining design proposal (product features) that satisfy users' kansei requirements by using multi-objective optimization with regression models and validate effectiveness of the proposed method through experiment on real products.

Keywords: Product Design · Multi-objective Optimization · Regression Model

1 Introduction

Computer design support technologies that incorporate optimization analysis, such as CAE, have developed rapidly against the backdrop of faster CPU speeds and increased storage capacity. In recent years, as users' needs have diversified in the design field, attention has also been focused on kansei (sensory) requirements such as usability and comfort, in addition to conventional values such as functionality and reliability. However, conventional technologies treat physical parameters, such as mass and size, as objective functions, making it difficult to reflect the ambiguous needs of customers, such as their kansei requirements. To reflect kansei requirements in the design, it is necessary to analyze the relationship between customers' kansei evaluation of the product and its feature values. For kansei evaluation, indexing methods based on subjective experiments [1] and customer kansei indexing methods based on review data [2] have been developed, and we can obtain customer kansei evaluation values for products. On the other hand, the method of translating customers' kansei evaluations back into product design has not yet been clearly established and has only just begun. In this study, we focus on customers' kansei evaluation in product reviews, propose a design method that reflects

C. Stephanidis et al. (Eds.): HCII 2023, CCIS 1835, pp. 598–606, 2023.
https://doi.org/10.1007/978-3-031-36001-5_77

customers' kansei requirements in product design, and verify the effectiveness of the method. Specifically, we first calculate product kansei scores (kansei evaluation values) from review data of products described in Japanese using existing methods [2], and then solve a multi-objective optimal design problem using regression models and optimization methods to obtain design proposal that satisfy customers' kansei requirements.

2 Proposed Method

In this section, we introduce our proposed design method. The proposed method is divided into four main phases.

1. Preprocessing
2. Calculation of Kansei Score
3. Regression Model Building
4. Optimization

2.1 Preprocessing

In order to calculate kansei score of products from review data, it is necessary to extract the kansei evaluation words (kansei words) from the review data. Therefore, morphological analysis and filtering are performed on the review data as preprocessing. Morphological analysis divides Japanese sentences without word boundaries into word-wise segmented data suitable for analysis. Here, we use Mecab 0.996 [3] as the morphological analysis engine. In filtering, words that meet the following conditions are extracted from the word set as a set of kansei words. The conditions are: 1) the part-of-speech is adjectival independence, 2) the part-of-speech is the adjective stem of a noun, 3) the word is included in the Evaluative Expression Dictionary [4], and 4) the word is included in the words with the attribute "evaluation" in the Japanese Evaluative Polarity Dictionary [5, 6].

2.2 Calculation of Kansei Score

In this phase, existing methods are used to calculate kansei score of the products. To calculate kansei score, topic extraction is performed on the set of kansei words in the previous section, and Kansei score of each product are calculated based on the topics obtained. Hierarchical Dirichlet Process LDA (HDP-LDA) is used for topic extraction, and the input value is a document for each product that is a concatenation of all reviews (set of kansei words) for the same product. After extracting the topics, kansei score for each topic for each product is calculated using the frequency of occurrence of kansei words for each review and term-score. Term-score is a measure of the importance of a word in a topic. Term-score of a word v in a topic k is calculated by the following equation, where β is the probability of occurrence of the word in a topic, where K is the total number of topics.

$$term - score_{k,v} = \hat{\beta}_{k,v} \log \left(\frac{\hat{\beta}_{k,v}}{\left(\prod_{j=1}^{K} \hat{\beta}_{j,v} \right)^{\frac{1}{K}}} \right) \tag{1}$$

Kansei score of a product is obtained by scoring each topic for each review of the product and taking the average of these scores. Then, Kansei score $Score_{p,k}$ of topic k of product p is calculated by the following equation, where n_p is the number of reviews of the product, $KanseiWords$ is the total number of kansei words, $freq_{r,w}$ is the frequency of kansei word w in review r, and $term - score_{k,w}$ is the term-score of word w in topic k.

$$Score_{p,k} = \frac{1}{n_p} \sum_{r=1}^{n_p} \left(\sum_{w=1}^{KanseiWords} term - score_{k,w} \cdot freq_{r,w} \right) \tag{2}$$

Since the same scaled values are obtained for Kansei scores in each topic, the maximum and minimum values of Kansei scores in each topic are used to scale the $Score_{p,k}$ in each topic for each product as follows. This scaling process causes $Score_{p,k}$ to take on values in the range $[0,5]$.

$$Score_{norm_{p,k}} = 5 \cdot \frac{Score_{p,k} - \min(Score_k)}{\max(Score_k) - \min(Score_k)} \tag{3}$$

2.3 Regression Model Building

The regression model is used to model the relationship between Kansei score and product features. In detail, the objective variable of the regression model is Kansei score of each product, and the explanatory variables are the product features. Since features may take both quantitative and categorical data, we use extended mathematical quantification theory class I as regression models. In addition, Kansei scores are assigned to each topic of the product, regression models will be constructed for each topic.

Extended mathematical quantification theory class I is a method based on multiple regression analysis in which the objective variable is quantitative data and the explanatory variables are both categorical and quantitative data. Applied to the target data, the following relationship equation between the objective variable y and the explanatory variables $x_i (i = 1, 2, \ldots, p)$ can be constructed, where $\beta_i (i = 0, 1, \ldots, p)$ are the regression coefficients.

$$y = \beta_0 + \beta_1 x_1 + \beta_2 x_2 + \ldots + \beta_p x_p \tag{4}$$

2.4 Optimization

In this phase, a design proposal is derived based on the customer's sensible requirements. In detail, the topics extracted in Sect. 2.3 are used as evaluation items, and the product features that satisfy the customer's required frequencies for each item are calculated. Such a design problem can then be defined as an error minimization problem between the customer's kansei requirements for the product and the response value of the regression model, with the product's features as design variables. In this study, the satisfying trade-off method [7] and Particle Swarm Optimization (PSO) [8] are used to solve such a design problem.

The satisfying trade-off method can be formulated as follows using the customer's requested frequency f_{aspk}, the worst requested frequency f_{worstk}, and the response value f_k of the regression model for each evaluation item k.

$$\text{find } x \tag{5}$$

$$\text{minimize} \left\{ max \left(\frac{f_{aspk} - f_k}{f_{aspk} - f_{worstk}} \right) \right\} \tag{6}$$

$$\text{subject to } x \in X \tag{7}$$

PSO is a metaheuristic optimization method developed by Kennedy and Eberhart in 1995 through the simulation of social interactions in the foraging behavior of a group of birds. In this study, PSO is used as an optimization method to solve the problem formulated by Eqs. (5)–(7), where the position and velocity of each search point in PSO are updated according to the following equations

$$x_d^{k+1} = x_d^k + v_d^{k+1} \tag{8}$$

$$v_d^{k+1} = wv_d^k + c_1 r_1 (p_d^k - x_d^k) + c_2 r_2 (p_g^k - x_d^k) \tag{9}$$

where x_d^t and v_d^t are the position and velocity of search point d in the tth search, x_d^{t+1} and v_d^{t+1} are the position and velocity of search point d in the $t + 1$st search, p_g^k is the best solution for the search point group and p_d^k is the best solution for search point d. r_1 and r_2 are random numbers in [0,1], and w, c_1 and c_2 are parameters.

3 Verification Problem

In this section, we present the results of applying our proposed method to actual review data. The validation target is a wristwatch as in the previous study [2]. We used text review data from a purchase support site where user reviews are posted for each product and products with an extremely small number of reviews are considered to have low reliability in product evaluations, so the target products in this verification were those with 20 or more reviews posted. As a result, the total number of wristwatches produced is 84. The following three points were verified.

- Confirmation of kansei words with the highest term-score for each topic

- Confirmation of the top scoring products in each topic
- Study of the proposed design using the proposed method

3.1 Kansei Words with the High Term-Score

HDP-LDA was applied to the set of kansei words extracted from the target review data. Table 1 shows the top four kansei words in the term-score for six of the extracted topics and the results of the authors' interpretation based on these sensible words. Those words that cannot be interpreted are marked with an "X".

Table 1. Result of topic extraction.

Topic	Top 4 Kansei Words	Interpretation
1	かっこいい(Cool), タフ(tough), 完璧(perfect), 重厚(imposing)	頑丈で頼もしい (Robust and dependable)
2	プロフェッショナル(professional), 特別(special), 美(beauty), 角(square)	際立っている (conspicuous)
3	色気(sexy), ハンサム(handsome), 大人(adult), 無垢(innocent)	大人な色気(mature sex appeal)
4	爽やか(fresh), 若い(young), 艶(charming), 感動(impression)	若くて爽やかな (young and fresh)
5	懇意(friendly), 正月(New Year), 大げさ(overdone), 波(wave)	X
6	お門違い(impression), 粗い(allowances), お陰(country), 一目瞭然(happy)	X

Table 1 shows that topics 1, 2, 3, and 4 can be interpreted as a set of kansei words related to wristwatches. However, topics 5 and 6 contain words such as "正月 (New Year's)" and "波 (wave)" that are not kansei words, making it difficult to interpret them as a set of kansei words.

3.2 Top Scoring Products

Table 2 shows the processed sample photos of the wristwatches with the highest kansei score for each topic for which a set of kansei words was obtained in Sect. 3.2.

Table 2. Product with the highest kansei score.

Topic	Interpretation	Product image		
1	頑丈で頼もしい (Robust and dependable)	sample1	sample2	sample3
2	際立っている (conspicuous)	sample4	sample5	sample6
3	大人な色気 (mature sex appeal)	sample7	sample8	sample9
4	若くて爽やかな (young and fresh)	sample10	sample11	sample12

3.3 Design Proposal

To verify the effectiveness of the proposed method, a design proposal was derived using the sensory evaluation values of actual products. In detail, we refer to the kansei scores in topics 1–4 of the actual product that have characteristic Kansei scores, and derive a design proposal by using values close to that values as the customer's required frequency f_{asp} in the proposed method. We then compared the derived features of the design proposal with those of the referenced product to confirm the reproducibility of the design proposal derived by the proposed method. We chose as our reference object sample 1, shown in Fig. 1. Sample 1 has the largest kansei score in Topic 1 and is one of the products with characteristic evaluation values for the entire product, and kansei score of sample 1 ($f_{sample1}$) in each topic are shown in Table 3. We then used these values to determine the customer's requested frequency f_{asp} in this verification as shown in Table 3.

Fig. 1. Sample product.

The features in Table 4 were selected as the design variables for the problem. Table 5 shows the coefficients of determination for the regression model with these features as

Table 3. Kasei Score.

	Topic1	Topic2	Topic3	Topic4
$f_{sample1}$	5.00	3.97	2.56	3.80
f_{asp}	5.00	4.00	2.50	4.00

Table 4. Design variables

ID	Parameters (Type)	ID	Parameters (Type)
x1	Width (numerical)	x8	Chronograph (category)
x2	Height (numerical)	x9	Bezel color (category)
x3	Power (category)	x10	Belt color (category)
x4	Dial display format (category)	x11	Dial color (category)
x5	Case shape (category)	x12	Character color (category)
x6	Case material (category)	x13	Case color (category)
x7	Belt material (category)	x14	Color of character on bezel (cat)

Table 5. Coefficient of determination of regression model.

	Topic1	Topic2	Topic3	Topic4
R^2	0.811	0.768	0.752	0.713

explanatory variables and kansei score for each topic as objective variables. The model was constructed with a good fit for all topics.

Table 6 shows the optimization results of the proposed method based on the aforementioned conditions.

Table 6. Optimization result

	X1	X2	X3	X4	X5	X6	X7	X8	X9	X10	X11	X12	X13	X14
ref	49.3	43.2	4	5	2	1	1	4	1	1	1	5	1	1
opt	49.9	41.9	4	5	1	2	5	4	5	1	3	5	1	5

Although there are category discrepancies in six of the features, the other features are consistent. Figure 2 also shows that the design proposal has value similar to value of sample 1 for the feature that have value that are significantly different from those of many other products.

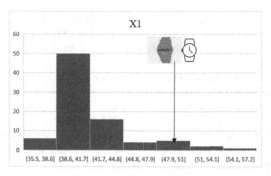

Fig. 2. Distribution of X1

4 Future Work

We cite incomplete preprocessing of the review data and the redundancy of the regression model as issues found through the validation presented in this paper. For the former, Table 1 in Sect. 3.2 shows that the extracted topics include words that are not sensible words, making it difficult to interpret them as a set of sensible words. We believe that this is caused by insufficient preprocessing of the review data. In fact, this study did not perform any processing such as unification of distortions or filtering using an aplausible dictionary, and we believe that it is necessary to introduce more robust preprocessing. For the latter, the regression model constructed in the validation does not take variable selection into account at all, making it a redundant model that also includes explanatory variables whose influence on the objective variable is quite small. In the optimization process, the values of the objective variables do not change much even if the values of those variables change, so those variables are redundantly factors that increase the number of design variables. From this perspective, variable selection in regression models is important and should be implemented in the future.

5 Conclusion

In this paper, we proposed a rudimentary design method to reflect customers' kansei requirements in product design and verified its effectiveness. The proposed method uses text mining to calculate product kansei evaluation values from product review data, and uses regression model and multi-objective optimization to derive product features that satisfy customers' kansei requirements. In the validation, the reproducibility of crucial features values derived by the proposed method was confirmed through a comparison of the derived design proposal and the actual product. On the other hand, issues such as insufficiency of preprocessing and redundancy of the regression model were also observed.

References

1. Akiyama, S., Suzuki, K., Gehrmann, A., Nagai, Y., Ishizu, S.: Noun based kansei image retrieval system by the use of MTS method. Int. J. Affect. Eng. **8**(4), 1171–1178 (2009)

2. Yamada, A., Hashimoto, S., Nagata, N.: Automatic impression indexing based on evaluative expression dictionary from review data. Int. J. Affect. Eng. **17**(5), 567–576 (2018)
3. MeCab: Yet Another Part-of-Speech and Morphological Analyzer, https://taku910.github.io/mecab/. Accessed 17 Mar 2023
4. Kobayashi, N., Inui, K., Matsumoto, Y.: Designing the Task of Opinion Extraction and Structurization. IPSJ SIG Technical Reports, NL171-18, pp. 111–118 (2006)
5. Kobayashi, N., Inui, K., Matsumoto, Y., Tateishi, K.: Collecting evaluative expressions for opinion extraction. J. Nat. Lang. Process. **12**(3), 203–222 (2005)
6. Higashiyama, M., Inui, K., Matsumoto, Y.: Learning sentiment of nouns from selectional preferences of verbs and adjectives. In: Proceedings of the 14th Annual Meeting of the Association for Natural Language Processing, pp. 584–587 (2008)
7. Nakayama, N., Sawaragi, Y.: Satisficing trade-off method for multiobjective programming. In: IFAC Proceedings Volumes 17, pp. 183–210 (1984)
8. Kennedy, J., Eberhart, R.C.: Particle swarm optimization. In: Proc. of IEEE Int. Conf. Neural Networks, vol. 4, pp. 1942–1948 (1995)

Revamping Interior Design Workflow Through Generative Artificial Intelligence

Ziming He[1](✉) [iD], Xiaomei Li[1], Ling Fan[1,3], and Harry Jiannan Wang[2]

[1] Tongji University, Shanghai 200092, China
zim0409@gmail.com
[2] University of Delaware, Newark, DE 19716, USA
[3] Tezign, Shanghai, China

Abstract. This paper presents some preliminary results on how generative AI (Artificial Intelligence) can transform key tasks in a typical interior design workflow, namely, ideation, schematic drafting, and layout planning. We show via examples how targeted fine-tuning and deliberated prompt engineering can jumpstart the creative process and improve the overall workflow efficiency and effectiveness. Ideation by collecting targeted reference designs to fine-tune a Stable Diffusion model and cranking out various ideas by simply engineering prompts. Schematic drafting is to test design ideas in the actual environment, where designers model the space structure with specific design elements. We used an actual photo of a plain office as a guidance and teach the model to generate images with specified features, such as different styles, materials, décor objects, while maintaining the underlying spatial configuration. Layout Planning is to organize the functions with comprehensive consideration of functional relationships and layout design principles. The generative model is fine-tuned using selected layout plans, which can accommodate different functional strategies, such as private rooms, large open areas, etc. and provide viable layout options.

Keywords: Interior Design Workflow · Generative AI · Generative Design

1 Introduction

Interior design business today requires more direct articulations on justifying the design decisions. However, much of the design process depends on intuitive judgment and implicit knowledge, a clear presentation needs to be structured through systematic methodologies [1]. Designers are constantly challenged for both addressing the problems strategically with knowledge and purposing solutions ingeniously with creativity. Generative design as a new paradigm for design research facilitates designers with much wider solution space, automated and digitally adaptive design approaches, and evolutionary design thinking [2]. Common generative systems in architecture are generally developed based on the principle of defining interactions between elements upon rules and operations to address various design problems, including formal pattern language, massing/zoning, layout/circulation planning, and performance-based optimization, etc.

© The Author(s), under exclusive license to Springer Nature Switzerland AG 2023
C. Stephanidis et al. (Eds.): HCII 2023, CCIS 1835, pp. 607–613, 2023.
https://doi.org/10.1007/978-3-031-36001-5_78

[3]. Related studies tend to employ a single technique to solve a specific problem, resulting in outcomes that require further finalization and lack integration with the overall workflow.

Deep learning enables generative design to handle complex tasks and produce superior outcomes. Generative Adversarial Network [4] in particular, has been instrumental in many scenarios, its capability of learning significant features and their relationship with large image-based datasets [5] are employed from basic house designs [6] to even more complicated planning strategies [7]. The effectiveness of proposed methods is evident in many problems that are formalizable, yet the limitation remains with implicit factors such as culture or aesthetics, subjective interventions from designers are still crucial to the design process [8].

Recent development in generative AI has shown promising progress. Compared to earlier machine learning systems, the key distinctions of the novel generative models are their architectural capacity in modeling complex data and the enormous amount of data they are fed with [9]. The generative models can map the latent high dimensional semantic space of multi-media input and generate new contents in any format as output. The ability of extracting sophisticated semantics from implicit information is of great significance for design scenarios. The practical implementation also shows great potential with models generating design-oriented digital content, such as Stable Diffusion [10]. However, the results produced by current models are not stable enough, and lack effective controls for necessary stability factors such as composition, perspective, and spatial structure. ControlNet [11] proposes methods for adding additional control during the image generation process, enabling results to be constrained as needed. For interior design, the new generative techniques present significant opportunities, but to meet more specific demands in design practices will require additional fine-tuning and integration.

Therefore, our research focus on specific methods of utilizing generative AI into the interior design workflow. The implementation is targeted towards relatively earlier stage in a typical interior design project, which involves intensive needs of outputting materials while communicating with clients, processing ideas, and kicking start the project. The work revolves around the aspects of fine-tuning the generative model to accommodate interior related features and incorporating additional operations to facilitate the design workflow.

2   Materials and Methods

The study uses Stable Diffusion's text to image framework as infrastructure. However, the base model has limitations in flexibility and effectiveness for interior design. To adapt into the design tasks more effectively, the base model requires further modifications in two key aspects: model fine-tuning to capture interior-specific features, and stability controlling to maintain the structural parameters of interior space.

Fine-tuning is implemented base on LoRA [12], which dramatically reduces the training costs while maintaining or even improving the model's quality. The dataset used for training contains a set of selected images and caption files that describes each image. The image captioning is automated through BLIP [13], which efficiently retrieves texts from images. Users are also allowed to customize the captions by adding specific contents. With given dataset, the trained model can be generated under 10 min with reasonable GPU hardware such as Tesla V100, which is applicable in the fine-tuning works toward various design tasks.

The stability control employs various models from ControlNet [11], such as canny edge, depth and M-LSD. ControlNet models extract the structural features from input image, and use that as guidance for the final generation. Canney edge model is suitable for inputs like user sketches, while depth and M-LSD models work better with photos or initial renderings.

Regarding the characteristics of interior design workflow, the study focuses on 3 main tasks that can be dramatically transformed by generative AI: Ideation, schematic drafting, and layout planning.

2.1 Ideation

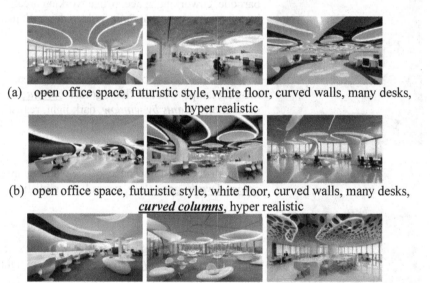

(a)   open office space, futuristic style, white floor, curved walls, many desks, hyper realistic

(b)   open office space, futuristic style, white floor, curved walls, many desks, ***curved columns***, hyper realistic

(c)   open office space, futuristic style, white floor, curved walls, **yellow chairs** many desks, hyper realistic

Fig. 1. Generated Design Idea Variations

Ideation in interior design is the combination of conceptual ideas, formal styles, and functional arrangements. In the traditional workflow, sketches and reference images are typical means, which can also be seamlessly linked with generative AI producing more appealing outcomes. The sketches can be taken as inputs for guiding the generation, and reference images can be used as the dataset for training the model. After fine-tuning with specified features in given references, and necessary guidance, the model then can generate massive outcomes with synthesized styles and prompted details. Figure 1 demonstrates with 3 distinctive styles and detailed variations.

2.2 Schematic Drafting

Initial Guidance Image

Baroque Style

baroque, coworking space, office working area, hanging lamps, ***marble floor***, golden decorations, dark light, realistic

baroque, coworking space, office working area, hanging lamps, wooden floor, golden ***baroque*** decorations, ***plants by window***, dark light, realistic

Maximalist Style

maximalist, coworking space, office working area, ***colorful walls***, ***gray floor***, warm light, realistic

maximalist, coworking space, office working area, ***color strip walls***, ***clean concrete floor***, warm light, realistic

Fig. 2. Generated Drafts from Initial Image

At schematic design stage, ideas and styles are tested within actual environment to concretize the design, draft options in more depth are required. Designers normally start modeling the space structure and design elements. With generative AI, designer can input a background image as guidance, either a photo of the site or an initial render from the digital 3D model. The model generates new images while holding the underlying structural configurations. This allows designers to quickly test visual performance of ideas under meaningful contexts. This feature is demonstrated in Fig. 2 with different style variations from the original plain office space.

2.3 Layout Planning

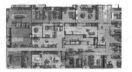

(a) office layout, floorplan, meeting rooms, ***many private rooms***, ***long walls***, colored drawing, light color ground, illustration)

(b) office layout plan, meeting rooms, ***large open areas***, colored drawing, light color ground, illustration

Fig. 3. Generated planning with different organizational strategies (private vs open)

Layout planning requires comprehensive consideration among many functional parameters. Generative AI also shows potential of learning from the planning strategies and generates new options through training the model with a set of layout plans as samples. Designer can use a plain layout drawing as input, and control the planning with text prompts. This study demonstrates this feature in Fig. 3 with different planning strategies.

3 Preliminary Evaluation

To validate the proposed methods, we conducted a use study with three professional designers. The evaluation metrics include productivity, effectiveness, and generalizability. Three designers are invited to produce design options within eight hours simulating a typical working day. The subjects including office design, home design and furniture design. Each user is required to train the models for above subjects, the dataset can be created with 20–30 images from either the internet or their previous works. For the generation process, users are also required to document the prompts they used, the time consumption, the overall results using both trained and untrained models, as well as the finest ones in each batch of generation. From the test result, the designers can generally produce over 20 viable design options for each subject that can be further developed, which is a significant leap in productivity comparing the traditional workflow, where the normal amount of production with given time is around 2–5 according to their experience. For the effectiveness, users generally gave positive responses to the trained model, most of the results can reflect the features from given dataset, around 30% from them are picked as fine results by users. While with untrained model, specific features are less tangible with prompts, the picking rate goes down to around 10%. However, the model is not accurate enough for positional prompts such as "by the window" or "at the center". Also, the results of layout planning are still rough for identifying specific elements. Regarding the distinctive design subjects in the test, the methods performed well generalizability on handling common issues in the domain of interior design.

4 Conclusion

In this article we proposed a series of methods of utilizing generative AI in interior design workflow, including the training mechanisms on various design related features, and controlling mechanisms for stabilizing the spatial parameters. The characteristics of interior design are taken into full consideration, which ensures the usability in the most common scenarios of the design practice. A preliminary evaluation is conducted with professional interior designers, the result reveals the performance of the system on aspects of productivity, effectiveness, and generalizability. However, the limitations in recognizing positional prompts and clarities in layout planning requires elaborated dataset with more detailed captions, the model in general should also be fine-tuned for interior-specific features, extended utilities such as in-painting/out-painting and integrated renderings with 3D models are also to be further developed.

References

1. Haddad, R.: Research and methodology for interior designers. Procedia Soc. Behav. Sci. **122**, 283–291 (2014). https://doi.org/10.1016/j.sbspro.2014.01.1343
2. McCormack, J., Dorin, A., Innocent, T.: Generative design: a paradigm for design research. In: DRS Bienn. Conf. Ser. (2004)
3. Singh, V., Gu, N.: Towards an integrated generative design framework. Des. Stud. **33**, 185–207 (2012). https://doi.org/10.1016/j.destud.2011.06.001
4. Goodfellow, I., et al.: Generative adversarial networks. Commun. ACM. **63**, 139–144 (2020). https://doi.org/10.1145/3422622
5. Isola, P., Zhu, J.-Y., Zhou, T., Efros, A.A.: Image-to-image translation with conditional adversarial networks. In: 2017 IEEE Conference on Computer Vision and Pattern Recognition (CVPR), pp. 5967–5976. IEEE, Honolulu, HI (2017). https://doi.org/10.1109/CVPR.2017.632
6. Nauata, N., Chang, K.-H., Cheng, C.-Y., Mori, G., Furukawa, Y.: House-GAN: relational generative adversarial networks for graph-constrained house layout generation. In: Vedaldi, A., Bischof, H., Brox, T., Frahm, J.-M. (eds.) Computer Vision – ECCV 2020. LNCS, vol. 12346, pp. 162–177. Springer, Cham (2020). https://doi.org/10.1007/978-3-030-58452-8_10
7. Chaillou, S.: ArchiGAN: Artificial intelligence × architecture. In: Yuan, P.F., Xie, M., Leach, N., Yao, J., Wang, X. (eds.) Architectural Intelligence, pp. 117–127. Springer, Singapore (2020). https://doi.org/10.1007/978-981-15-6568-7_8
8. Krish, S.: A practical generative design method. Comput. Aided Des. **43**, 88–100 (2011). https://doi.org/10.1016/j.cad.2010.09.009
9. Gozalo-Brizuela, R., Garrido-Merchan, E.C.: ChatGPT is Not All You Need. A State of the Art Review of Large Generative AI Models (2023). http://arxiv.org/abs/2301.04655

10. Rombach, R., Blattmann, A., Lorenz, D., Esser, P., Ommer, B.: High-Resolution Image Synthesis with Latent Diffusion Models (2022). https://doi.org/10.48550/arXiv.2112.10752
11. Zhang, L., Agrawala, M.: Adding Conditional Control to Text-to-Image Diffusion Models (2023). https://doi.org/10.48550/arXiv.2302.05543
12. Hu, E.J., et al.: LoRA: Low-Rank Adaptation of Large Language Models (2021). http://arxiv.org/abs/2106.09685
13. Li, J., Li, D., Xiong, C., Hoi, S.: BLIP: Bootstrapping Language-Image Pre-training for Unified Vision-Language Understanding and Generation (2022). http://arxiv.org/abs/2201.12086

Innovative Brand Design for Traditional Cantonese Soup

Zhiqian Hu[1(✉)], Mo Qin[1], Wenting Hou[1], Caihong Huang[2], and Longqi Chen[1]

[1] Tongji University, No. 281 Fuxin Road, Yangpu District, Shanghai, China
zhiqianhu@tongji.edu.cn
[2] Jiangnan University, Lihu Road 1800, Wuxi 214122, China

Abstract. Guangdong soup is a conventional delicious, nutritious, and medicinal cuisine Guangdong area in China. With the development of society, the improvement of people's living standards, and the enhancement of health consciousness, it has been rapidly promoted. Traditional Cantonese soups need more novel and aesthetic enjoyment, but the development is limited due to slow development, few varieties, poor taste, and obsolete packaging. In order to meet the challenges of sustainability and overcome cultural fragility, this paper focuses on the possibilities of integrating traditional soup culture with technology in current socio-historical conditions and tries to apply the theoretical research results to the development of the brand "Master Soup" in Kaiping, Guangzhou. This paper provides a new perspective on the sustainable development of traditional soup culture and has some guiding significance for promoting soup-product development in China.

Keywords: Cantonese soup culture · cultural sustainability · innovation in technology application · service design

1 Background

China's soup culture has a long history, in which Guangdong soup is the most famous. Cantonese soup is also known as "old fire soup." It is a healthy recipe inherited in Guangzhou for a thousand years and one of the critical cornerstones of Guangdong's food culture. It has been included in the next group of national intangible cultural heritage submissions [2, 4, 6]. However, old fire soup is mainly famous in Guangdong and Guangxi provinces and barely recognized in others. The overall scale is small, which is hard to form a degree of industrial scale [5]. The situation reflects that although the traditional brand has deep cultural accumulation, it has different degrees of product aging and regional brand differences, resulting in the unexplored potential of traditional soups in the consumer market [1].

The existing problems are also opportunities: (1) Traditional Chinese soups need a private brand. Although Cantonese soup has a long history, the market is still "small, scattered and chaotic," having prominent regional characteristics but not forming a wide range of consumers. (2) There is a conflict between young people's personalized soup demand and outdated traditional brands. (3) The soup market is still developing, with a huge market gap and demand.

In this project, we plan to start with a new brand concept, standardize soup production through technological innovation, tap into people with high-frequency consumption through marketing innovation, and expand consumer groups through soup retailing [8, 9]. The traditional culture can be further expanded with the help of transmission of Chinese traditional soup culture among young people because the core group of health food consumers tends to be younger, and the consumption scenario tends to be routine. We reviewed the current development of Guangdong's old fire soup. We proposed the brand concept of "master soup", which includes service, technology, culture, and other elements, aiming to provide design solutions for the future industry of soup marketing.

2 Guangzhou Soup Market Demand Insights

In order to better understand the culture of Guangzhou soup and find the pain points and needs of Guangzhou soup, this paper adopts two research methods: the field research method and the user interview method. We observed the environment of Guangzhou soup restaurants, soup varieties, dining consumers, and consumption behaviors to get Cantonese soup's pain points and opportunity points. We also interviewed young people with a soup-drinking habit of profoundly understanding the influence of traditional Cantonese soup on Generation Z and their exact needs for soup.

2.1 Field Research

This study conducted field research by visiting Guangzhou, the most representative city in Guangdong Province. By observing and interviewing the most well-known soup restaurants (e.g., Dayang Original Soup and Dade Soup, etc.), we gained authentic data on the soup-drinking habits of the local population.

According to the inspection of these soup stores (see Fig. 1), we got the following pain points for Guangdong soup.

- Soup stores are old, small, and shabby, forming an uncomfortable and attractive space for customers to dine in.
- It is not very attractive to the young group, making it difficult to sustain the Cantonese soup culture long-term. At present, it attracts mainly the elderly, some of whom will bring their grandchildren to have soup as a daily healthcare habit; in addition, tourists, mainly influenced by online information, take it as a tasting experience whose repurchase rate is low, lacking in-depth understanding of Cantonese soup culture.
- It takes work to meet people's demand for customization. For customers who try Canton soup for the first time, choosing a suitable soup for themselves is difficult due to a lack of understanding of food functions [1].

2.2 User Interviews

Because the background of the study is based on the cooperation project between the Guangzhou Kaiping government and Tongji University, the aim is to empower

Fig. 1. The Authentic Guangzhou Traditional Soup Store

Guangzhou's cultural tourism industry through design power and help Guangzhou's cultural tourism industry development with high quality. Therefore, we expand the customer's scope from Guangzhou to nationwide. Secondly, the younger generation has an urgent need for healthcare, and they can be the main force of consumption in the next generation, but they need more than traditional Cantonese soup. In order to find the root cause, we organized semi-structured interviews with 8 Generation Z, aged between 20–26 years old with a soup-drinking habit, living in Fujian, Zhejiang, and Shandong. After the interviews, these insights were summarized in Table 1.

In conclusion, although Guangzhou's soup culture has a strong regional identity, the sustainability of its transmission still needs to improve. Such as the following:

- Old traditional stores with timeworn environments. Although popular in the local area, once it leaves the soil where roots are planted, they lack a way to spread the culture nationally.
- Only taking "health" as a selling point is not attractive to new generations. The overall image of the Guangzhou soup brand is old-fashioned and lacks high recognizability. It needs to create more communication with young people.

To summarize, if we want to promote Cantonese soup culture to young people throughout China or the world, we need to reshape the image of Cantonese soup at the brand level, especially in three ways: more intelligent technology, a more innovative service experience, and more profound cultural creation.

3   A New Perspective on the Brand Innovation of Cantonese Soup

There are many bottlenecks in developing quality soup manufactory in Guangdong, such as the traditional soup varieties and the promotion of soup to the outside world. These are limited by regional culture and technology, the need for more attractiveness to young

Table 1. User Interview Insights

Insights summary	Insights	Interview Excerpts	Interviewees
Young people demand more personalized and convenient soups	Add ingredients with the appropriate effects to adjust the body condition	"For example, recently my mother will put a herb called 'ginger root' into the soup to help us reduce the inner heaty caused by hot weather."	Lan
		"Since dad has high blood lipid, mom will also put goldenrod in the soup, which has the function of lowering blood lipid."	Wang
		"Will focus on the benefits and nutrition of the soup."	Ding
		"I don't know what kind of soup to eat to regulate the body."	Zhao
	Young people have more inconvenience in making soup at home	"Boiling meat soup will take me several hours, using the pressure cooker might be faster."	Lan
		"Sometimes I am too busy to make them then I will order take-out soups."	Xi
Canton soup restaurants have a traditional, outdated brand image and lack new images to occupy the minds of young people	Awareness base of Cantonese soup image	"I tried Lo Foh Tong only once in Guangdong province in traveling. There are tons of traditional soup restaurants there."	Qin
		"Cantonese soup is quite famous, I knew it through the food documentary."	Liu
	Lack of cognitive base for soup brands	"Never heard of a particularly well-known soup brand, does the instant hot-pot count?"	Ding

(*continued*)

Table 1. (*continued*)

Insights summary	Insights	Interview Excerpts	Interviewees
		"I usually cook soup myself and will order take-out soup from time to time. I have no brand preference."	Qiu

people, and outdated soup brands. To solve the contradiction between young people's demand for personalized soups and the aging of traditional Cantonese soup brands, the "Master Soup" brand was built. The brand's core value includes service, technology, and cultural innovations.

3.1 Brand Rejuvenation Transformation

Heritage is the foundation; innovation is the means. The advantage of traditional brands lies in the "old," old reputation and old technology, but the dilemma also lies in the "old," outdated marketing concept and old business model. Only through innovation can we keep up with the trend of the times and activate the traditional Cantonese soup brand [3]. To enhance the uniqueness of traditional Cantonese soup brands and the sense of identity of young consumers, give full play to the synergistic innovation advantage of cooperation between industry and research, create personalized and convenient soup instant products that are more attractive to young consumers, and promote the communication between traditional brands and young consumers.

3.2 Building a Soup Ecosystem

Build a perfect user service experience through product, interaction, and exhibition design. Through advanced technological means, soup enterprises can strengthen their ability to innovate on their own to play a more significant role in promoting the social and economic development of the region and achieve symbiotic development with stakeholders from the soup brand community to the soup brand ecosystem [1].

3.3 Cultural Marketing Builds Brand Stories

For the marketing of the "Master Soup" brand, it is crucial to tell the brand story through culture and extend the cultural attributes of the brand. From the marketing point of view, through the school-enterprise cooperation resources such as the cooperation project with the Kaiping Municipal Government of Guangdong Province and the Cantonese Cuisine Master Project, the Master brand story is created to increase the authenticity of the brand and create a professional, healthy, delicious and nutritious brand perception image.

4   Brand Design of "Master Soup"

4.1   Service System for Generation Z: A Pop-Up Store in Shanghai

The brand cooperated with Kaiping's famous chefs. It took technological development as the starting point, targeting contemporary wellness and emotional needs to create a future "Chinese style + technology" restaurant business based on researching future life scenarios in Road Renewal of Shanghai. We have therefore integrated the features of functional soup, the physical and mental health, traditional ingredients and national style elements, virtual personalities, and NFT soup recipes to create the New Age Master Beauty Soup.

The construction of the service system covers brand design, product design, interaction design, and exhibition design. The active AI virtual personality market provides new fertile ground for the IP economy. The construction of the service system covers brand design, product design, interaction design, and display design. In this speculative design, the virtual IP Meng will provide customized functional soup recipes as an NFT in Metaverse according to the user's needs and situation. (see Fig. 2) Users can buy the one customized for them in our virtual store and redeem the physical soup in the pop-up store in reality.

Fig. 2. "Meng Po" The Virtual IP Of "Master Soup"

4.2   Branded Products Combined with Technology for Innovative Design

This product uses elements of acid and cyberpunk in its visuals. It strives to be international and youthful while carrying forward the elements of traditional Chinese culture. The product design highlights the concept of "the ritual of holding the soup in your hand" (see Fig. 3). Based on the ancient Chinese vessel, the product is designed as FMCG (fast-moving consumer goods), which is portable and allows instant consumption by a wide range of consumers. Also, they will own the recipe data generated by the AI. Traditional Chinese colors and ingredients will be used to divide the recipes into different categories according to the following functions (calming the mind, warming the body, enhancing immunity, and awakening vitality).

In the mass production stage, in order to integrate nutrition knowledge with the master formula, actively seeking OEMs is necessary. We use small-scale trials to sample the product and invite target users to conduct taste tests and interviews to adjust the flavor and taste. With positive feedback, mass production will be implemented, a new product will be created, and an offline shop will be set up in Shanghai on Chifeng Road as a pilot. The technologies applied in the preparation of soups include the following four points.

Fig. 3. The Instant Soup Products Of "Master Soup"

- Using a time-step stewing process to avoid nutrient loss and further optimizing the nutrient extraction process (amount added, high temperature and pressure reaction time, and temperature) and enzymatic digestion technology (amount added, enzymatic digestion time, enzymatic digestion temperature, enzymatic digestion pH) to improve the nutritional value of the soup;
- Separation of oil, water, and ingredients, individual sterilization, and concentrated/freeze-dried portioning to extend the shelf life of the soup without adding preservatives;
- The use of different functional medicinal foods as core ingredients.
- The establishment and implementation of an information-based traceability system.

4.3 Interaction Design & Exhibition Design: 5 Experience Zones, 8 Service Touchpoints

The exhibition space is divided into five experience zones (see Fig. 4): the attraction zone – the tunnel; the interactive zone – the Meng Po diagnosis area; the product zone – the digital ingredients and efficacy display; the exhibition zone – the world view display in the age of "friendly" technology; finally, the purchase zone – the robotic arm area. A sense of technology and mystery are the textures sought throughout the design of the space.

As shown, this paper will create a service and interaction design in a future Chinese-inspired cyberpunk tone, using mainly AI generation and radio frequency identification technology (RFID). Users will first be attracted by the branding in the tunnel and interact with the AR installation to capture their social capital. Once users arrive at the central art installation, they can interact with the AI Meng Po, inputting their emotions and experiences at the moment, and feel the change and soup pool color in the pipeline during ingredients selection. After visiting the multi-screen product display, users can collect or purchase unique customized recipes and soups from the robotic arm area. After purchase, they can also access the Soup Geniverse community for follow-up interaction. Through AI technology and the theory of synaesthesia, Meng Po adds emotional recall variables (Mood, Physical condition, and Memory nouns) and Restricted variables (Kaiping Master Production Memories, Function of soup ingredients, and Emotional Associative Perception) into AI and generates the customized soup recipes.

To sum up, the whole design has a total of 8 touch points: 1. Users will get RFID identification interactive signage in the tunnel; 2. Users will engage in AR photo interaction in the immersive brand story projection tunnel; 3. Users will interact with the main installation IP Meng Po; 4. Users will use RFID to interact with the visual mood board; 5. Users will have a tour of the digital ingredients and efficacy in the product area; 6. Users will interpret the speculative design worldview in the display area; 7. Users will receive NFT recipes and soups in the purchase area; 8. Users will share and interact with other users in the soup community. (Fig. 5, the green labels in the diagram show the technical applications corresponding to each functional area.)

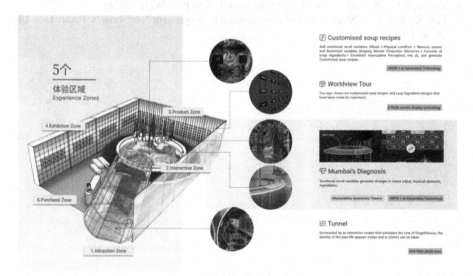

Fig. 4. Concept Store of Master Soup with the Intelligent Interactive Space.

5 Summary

The "Master Soup" brand aims through service design solutions to improve the competitiveness of Guangzhou soup products. Secondly, it promotes the spread of the Guangdong soup culture by combining advanced marketing methods with scientific technology. Leading to the formation of a youthful, national, and international brand for this traditional health food.

References

1. Chen, J., Zhang, LX.: Study on the construction of smart tourism ecosystem in Guangdong-Hong Kong-Macao greater bay area. In: China Environmental Science. The Journal of Chinese Society for Environmental Sciences **1** (2018)
2. Ding, J., Guo, J., Shenghua, P., et al.: Cantonese soup culture. Guangdong Sci. Technol. **15**, 4 (2008)
3. Li, P., Xie, Y., Li, J., Yang, K.: Study on the rejuvenation strategy of time-honored brands – taking Pien Tze Huang as an example. J. Finance Econ. Theory **3**, 11 (2021)
4. Zeng, X.F., Chen, H.G., Zhou, S.Y., Yu, L.M.: The cultural evolution of Cantonese soup. Anhui Agric. Sci. **45**, 32 (2017)
5. Qin, Y., Bai, W.D., Zhao, W.H., Qian, M.: Thinking about the industrialization of Cantonese old fire soup. China Season. **37**(10), 4 (2012)
6. Xu, Y.C.: Canton soup. Popular Sci. Technol. **2** (2001)
7. Li, L., Su, Y.: China's soup industry, when to be big? New Food **26**, 2 (2007)
8. Zhang, H.C.: Marketing innovation of old brands. New Bus. Wkly. (2018)
9. Pan, X., Ren, Z.H.: Marketing the future: cultural redemption of "old" brands. Future Dev. **10**, 94–96 (2011)

Toys for Kidult: The Cross-Cultural Study of Customers' Behavior Process of Designer Toys Online Visual Merchandise Display

Xiu-Qi Hung$^{(\boxtimes)}$ [ID] and Tseng-Ping Chiu [ID]

National Cheng Kung University, No.1, University Road, Tainan City 701, Taiwan
{p36114050,mattchiu}@gs.ncku.edu.tw

Abstract. The study investigates the cross-cultural customers' behavior towards designer toys online visual merchandise display. Designer toys are created by independent designers and attract hobbyists to collect. Online stores are important access for customers to purchase designer toys. To find an expressive way of online displaying, the study divides designer toy photography into three parts, focal character, background, and dioramas. Uses the AIDMA model to evaluate the customer behavior process in four online display scenarios. And assess customers' preferences for each scenario. The result reveals that although there has no signified effect with the AIDMA model, having backgrounds and dioramas indeed increases customers' preference for the designer toy, and East Asians tend to prefer toys with backgrounds more than Westerners.

Keywords: Cross-cultural · Designer toys · Visual display

1 Introduction

"Designer toys", are toys created by independent designers or artists. They use elements such as painting, sculpture, or art on the toys to show their personality. Today, manufacturers display designer toys online and sell them through E-commerce platforms such as Amazon, Shopee, etc. for customers to access easier. Thence visual merchandise displays become vital.

The target customers of designer toys are aged between 15 to 40 years old. They are no more a child but still indulge in toys, and be named Kidult. Kidults engage in re-creating an imaginative world, building dioramas, or taking toys outside to build a fantasy ambiance for toys. The phenomenon is applied to the designer toys exhibit, in the online store, the toys usually arrange in dioramas or real-world backgrounds, it building the context to the toys, and add stories to them.

The cross-cultural study indicates that the attention to the context of East Asians and Westerners is different. East Asians prefer a context-inclusive style while Westerners prefer an object-focused style. The study aims to understand the difference between East Asia and Western customers on different designer toys' online visual displays. And evaluate the influence of background and dioramas on consumers' behavior and preference for designer toys. Finally, points out an expressive methodology for designer toys online visual displaying for cross-cultural consumers.

C. Stephanidis et al. (Eds.): HCII 2023, CCIS 1835, pp. 623–630, 2023.
https://doi.org/10.1007/978-3-031-36001-5_80

2 Literature Review

2.1 Designer Toys

Define Designer Toys. Designer toys, also known as art toys, are three-dimensional figures designed by the artist or designer. They are usually made from materials such as vinyl, resin, plush, and wood [1]. Designer toys are 'limited edition, relatively expensive figures aimed at niche collectors'[2]. Unlike most toys that are translated from media like televisions, films, comics, or video games, designer toys are original characters, which blend art, graphic, and toys to create novel items.

Movement. Designer toys first emerged in Hong Kong, in 1997. Eric So and Michael Lau were the founders. Tokyo also had designer toys designers at the same time, the representative is Bounty Hunter designed by Hikaru Iwanaga. Designer toys quickly spread to the UK, North America, and Southeast Asia [2, 3]. Designer toys were experimentation in character production, they found a new medium mixture of character merchandising and art hence encouraging the consumer to become a collector [4].

Target Customer. According to the Frost & Sullivan report, more than 95% of designer toys consumers are young people aged between 15 to 40. About half of them are Generation Z [5]. Generation Z describe youth born in the mid-1990s through the late 2010s. They are familiar with technology, such as smartphones, cameras, television, and social media, at a young age [6].

Marketing. Global consulting company Frost & Sullivan estimates the size of the global designer toys retail market has grown rapidly. It stands at US$8.7 billion in 2015 and reaches US$30 billion in 2021, the annual growth rate is 34.6 percent. The global designer toy market is estimated to exceed US$65 billion in 2027 [7].

Online Stores provide a shopping environment with no limit on time and geography. Designer toy brands have opened official online stores and sell products through E-commerce platforms such as Amazon, Shopee, etc. [8].

2.2 Adult and Toys

Kidult. The postmodern adult is characterized by an unprecedented infantilism nature, especially in the age between 20–40 years old. They are named the kidult. Those who are interested in entertainment intended for children such as toys, computer games, television programs, etc. [9]. As Neil Postman says in "The Disappearance of Childhood", the boundaries of adulthood become indefinable. Toy play is no longer exclusive to children, but for an adult with childish innocence [10].

Adults Play Toys as Nostalgia and Escapism. Adults who acquire toys and play with them have explained their activities as nostalgia. Toys are considered objects that provoke a memory of childhood happiness. Surrounding with toys can be associated with imaginary worlds and act as escapism. When playing with toys, adults can have a short escape from reality and indulge in the wonderful imagination [11].

Adults' Interaction with Toys. Toy play traditionally means children use various physical materials in their play. However, adults are also involved. They not only play but collect toys as hobbies. Adult collectors don't buy everything., they buy the given kinds they like [11]. World play is a feature when adults play with toys. They devote time, space, and various materials to organize displays, build dioramas, or create doll dramas for different toys [11].

Backgrounds and Dioramas. The background is the scene in the real world. Adults will take their toys to public spaces, finding places similar to television series and films. They use digital devices to take photos of toys (see Fig. 1). The photograph will re-create popular scenes as if they are in the film's world [11]. Building dioramas is a usual way adults play with toys either. Dioramas (see Fig. 2) is a depiction of reality, it is a small-scale representation of a scene [12], in which three-dimensional figures or objects are displayed. Dioramas can help viewers propose hypotheses, and create a narrative for themselves [13].

Fig. 1. Adults re-create the Star Wars scene in the real-world background.

Fig. 2. Dioramas is a small-scale representation of a scene.

2.3 Cross-Cultural

"Culture" is everywhere, it can be counted as geographically based and focus on familiar distinctions, such as the East versus the West on the global, social class, gender, race, ethnicity, and so on. A cultural context influences the social members to share ideas, and practices and organizes one's experiences and behavior [14].

Holistic Thought Versus Analytic Thought. Nisbett and his colleagues have proved that East Asians and Westerners are different in cognitive and perceptual orientations [15]. Western civilizations are oriented from Greece, which emphasized thinking analytically and being more focused on the object. By contrast, China traditions such as Taoism and Confucianism pay more attention to the relationships between the focal object and the field. It influences East Asian to think holistically [16].

Cultural Variations in Aesthetic Preferences. Masuda and his teams conducted a study on investigated contemporary cultural aesthetic preference differences. Found that as East Asians tend to have a holistic thinking style, they are sensitive to the context in artistic domains, and emphasize contextual information at the expense of the figure. As for Westerners, they are accustomed to analytic patterns of attention, therefore more likely to exhibit a predilection to focus on salient objects [17].

2.4 Consumer Behavior

The AIDMA model designed by Hall [18] is widely used by media advertisers. The model depicted the consumer purchasing process through the five stages, Attention, Interest,

Desire, Memory, and Action. Attention is the first step in the AIDMA process. Once attention is gained, the next step is to arouse the consumer's interest in the advertised product. Soon the consumer might desire to have the product and keep it in his or her memory. Finally, the consumer acts to purchase the product [19, 20].

3 Hypotheses

In this study, the study exhibit designer toys online in different world play scenarios and examine the variety of customer behavior, preference, and cross-cultural influence. The study anticipated that (H1) In the online store, designer toys with backgrounds would arouse consumers' behavior and (H2) In the online store, designer toys with dioramas would arouse consumers' behavior. As for the culture, we suppose (H3) Easterners would prefer designer toys with backgrounds or dioramas to Westerners.

4 Study 1

The study use the online questionnaire to conduct Study 1. The participants were presented with 30 pictures of different kinds of designer toys, and be asked to answer the two questions by using the seven-point Likert scale, ranging from 1 = strongly disagree to 7 = strongly agree. The questions are adapted from Mackenzie's research [21]. Question 1 is "Do this toy favorable to you?" and the following is "Do you think this toy is interesting?" We average the score of the two questions and select the toys that score above the mean as materials in Study 2.

4.1 Method

Participants. 71 East Asian participants, most of them Taiwanese. 8 participants were Westerners, coming from The United States, the Czech Republic, and so on.

Materials. 30 photographs of different designer toys are selected from designer toys online stores, Artoyz in France, Jinart in Taiwan, and Pop Mart in China. The toys are under two limits, first, they need to be the original characters. Second, the background of the picture needs to be blank, and without any object there.

Procedure. The study use the online questionnaire to conduct this study. This questionnaire includes the following three parts. First, evaluation of customers' preference for designer toys. Second, personal information, and finally, customers' experience of purchasing designer toys.

4.2 Result and Discussion

According to the 79 participants' replies, the study analyzed the average of favorable and interesting (see Fig. 3), and the M = 4.23, SD = 0.47. There were fifteen designer toys scored above the mean, they were selected as materials in Study 2.

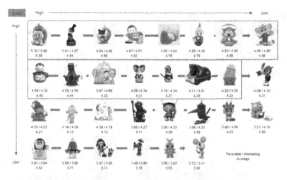

Fig. 3. The score of the toys in Study 1

5 Study 2

The study use the online questionnaire to conduct Study 2. There are four different scenarios (see Fig. 4), and each participant would enter one scenario according to their birthday. In Scenario 1, the participants would present with designer toys exhibited with both backgrounds and dioramas. In Scenario 2, the designer toys here are displayed in the backgrounds and with no dioramas. Scenario 3 has dioramas but without backgrounds. In Scenario 4, there only have one focal character in the pictures.

Fig. 4. The example of the four scenarios in Study 2.

The participants were presented with 15 pictures of different kinds of designer toys, and be asked to answer five AIDMA questions. The questions are adapted from Wei's research [20]. Question 1 is about attention "I think this toy attracts me." Question 2, Interest, "I feel an interest in the toy.". Question 3, Desire, "I want to have the toy.". Question 4, Memory, "I think this toy is impressive.". And finally, Action, "I think I am willing to buy the toy." We used a seven-point Likert scale, ranging from 1 = strongly disagree to 7 = strongly agree, to evaluate the participants' behavior process on toys.

5.1 Method

Participants. The study had receive 243 reliable replies. 135 East Asians were a participant, most of them are Taiwanese. 108 participants are Westerners, coming from The United States, Canada, Germany, and so on. The participants were divided into four scenarios. Scenario 1 has 35 East Asians and 30 Westerners. Scenario 2 have 27 East

Asian and 33 Westerners. There are 34 East Asians and 25 Westerners in Scenario 3. As for Scenario 4, 39 East Asians and 20 Westerners took a part.

Materials. 15 kinds of designer toys are selected according to the result of Study 1. The study use Photoshop to attach or erase the background and dioramas to them. Figure 5 shows the designer toys pictures we presented in the four scenarios.

Fig. 5. The materials in Study 2 are divided into four scenarios.

Procedure. The study use the online questionnaire to conduct this study. This questionnaire includes three parts evaluation of customers' behavior process for designer toys, personal information, and customers' experience of purchasing designer toys.

At the end of the first part, the study prepared a manipulation check. There had a simple introduction about backgrounds and dioramas. Participants are asked to evaluate if they perceive that these toys have "backgrounds" or "dioramas" in the former study. This part is to make sure the materials were reliable.

Since designer toys are niche to hobbyists to collection [2]. The study anticipant having background and dioramas will increase the preference. At the end of Study 2, subjects will see toys in four different states (Fig. 6), and sort them from $1 =$ dislike to $4 =$ like.

Fig. 6. The same toy in four different states.

5.2 Result and Discussion

According to 234 participants' replies. The result of the manipulation check is significant $F(3,239) = 20.239$, $p < .05$). Subjects have perceived backgrounds and dioramas in the former research.

As for H1, the study anticipate in the online store, designer toys with backgrounds would arouse customers' behavior, but the result is unobvious. There is no significant effect in each dependent variable and their average.

H2 expects designer toys with dioramas would have higher scores in the AIDMA model from customers. However, there's no significant difference in AIDMA and their average whether designer toys with dioramas or not.

H3 refers to cross-cultural, the study anticipate that Easterners would pay more attention to designer toys with backgrounds or dioramas than Westerners. But the result reveals Westerners (M = 4.68) have a higher score than East Asians (M = 4.10) in each scenario.

In the experiment on preference. The average score of the four states from high to low is State 4 (M = 3.42), State 2 (M = 3.00), State 3 (M = 2.90), and State 1 (M = 1.92). The result proves that compare to the toy in blank, participants tend to prefer the toys with backgrounds or dioramas. Significantly, State 2 gain more preference from East Asians than Westerner (F = 8.84, p < .05), and Westerner prefer State 3 more compared to East Asians (F = 6.64, p < .05). It supports Masuda's theory that East Asians are context sensitive while Westerner is focus on object [17].

6 General Discussion

The study aims to investigate the cross-cultural consumer behavior of designer toys online visual merchandise display to find an expressive way of online displaying. First, we found 15 toys gain higher preference from the customers. Second, we divided the designer toys' photography into three parts, focal character, background, and dioramas. And evaluate the customer behavior process in four online display scenarios. Finally, ask about the preference of each scenario.

The study reveals that designer toy customers might have less cognition about the toy background and dioramas, this supposes also supported by the AIDMA model since there is no significant effect between having a background, dioramas, or not.

As for preference, having backgrounds and dioramas will increase participants' favor for designer toys. The study also prove the tendency that East Asians tend to prefer toys with a background and having dioramas will improve Westerners' preference for the toys.

The study proves that having background and dioramas will make the toy more favorite to both Eastern and Western consumers. While selling designer toys online, the toys could exhibit in the world play scenarios, it is a better methodology than displaying designer toys in the blank. Having background and dioramas not only conveys the story of the toys but triggers the consumers' hearts.

References

1. Pro, I.: Vinyl Will Kill: An Inside Look at the Designer Toy Phenomenon (2004)
2. Phoenix, W.: Plastic Culture: How Japanese Toys Conquered the World (2006)
3. Baudrillard, J.: The System of Objects (1996)
4. Vartanian, I.: Full Vinyl: The Subversive Art of Designer Toys (2006)

5. Ma Xiao, S.S.J.: From digital content to toy products in entertainment consumption, Pop Mart brings IP to the offline scene of Z Generation (2020)
6. Turner, A.: Generation Z: technology and social interest. J. Individ. Psychol. **71**, 103–113 (2015)
7. Ci, Z.C.: Analysis of the Market Size and Development Trend of the Global Trendy Game Industry in 2022 (2022)
8. Gu Sheng, H.X.Y.: From the perspective of globalization, an in-depth discussion on the space, pattern and business model of designer toys (2022)
9. Bernardini, J.: The Infantilization of the Postmodern Adult and the Figure of Kidult (2014)
10. Postman, N.: The Disappearance of Childhood (1982)
11. Heljakka, K., Harviainen, J.T.: From displays and dioramas to doll dramas adult world building and world playing with toys. Am. J. Play **11**(3), 351–378 (2019)
12. Tunnicliffe, M.J.R.S.D.: Dioramas as depictions of reality and opportunities for learning in biology. Curator Mus. J. **54**(4), 447–459 (2011)
13. Zhong, N., Li, M., Wu, Y., Lu, S.: The impact of different forms of statistical information on reading efficiency, effect, and mental workload: an eye-tracking study, pp. 97–102 (2011)
14. Dov Cohen, S.K.: Handbook of Cultural Psychology (2019)
15. Nisbett, R.E., et al.: Culture and systems of thought: holistic versus analytic cognition. Psychol. Rev. **108**(2), 291–310 (2001)
16. Masuda, T., Nisbett, R.E.: Attending holistically versus analytically: comparing the context sensitivity of Japanese and Americans. J. Pers. Soc. Psychol. **81**(5), 922–934 (2001)
17. Masuda, T., et al.: Culture and aesthetic preference: comparing the attention to context of East Asians and Americans. Pers. Soc. Psychol. Bull. **34**(9), 1260–1275 (2008)
18. Hall, S.R.: Retail advertising and selling (1924)
19. Sumita Ushio, I.R.: Development of e-marketing contract structure based on consumer-generated contents and its optimal strategy. Department of Social Systems and Management Discussion Paper Series (2009)
20. Wei, P.S., Lu, H.P.: An examination of the celebrity endorsements and online customer reviews influence female consumers' shopping behavior. Comput. Hum. Behav. **29**(1), 193–201 (2013)
21. Mackenzie, S.B., Lutz, R.J., Belch, G.E.: The role of attitude toward the ad as a mediator of advertising effectiveness - a test of competing explanations. J. Mark. Res. **23**(2), 130–143 (1986)

Research on Product Modeling Image Prediction System Based on Support Vector Machine

Tao Li[✉] and Meiyu Zhou

School of Art Design and Media, East China University of Science and Technology, No. 130, Meilong Road, Xuhui District, Shanghai, People's Republic of China
787305111@qq.com

Abstract. With the continuous improvement of modern manufacturing level, the concept of user-centered product design has been gradually attached to enterprises. The functional and technical features of products can no longer meet the needs of users, and consumers pay more and more attention to the emotional experience brought by products. As a very important part of the design, product image is crucial to the emotional experience of users.

In order to promote the development of product image design, the research proposes a product modeling image prediction system based on Kansei Engineering, which predicts the overall product modeling image by constructing a Support Vector Machine (SVM) model.

Firstly, determine the representative samples and perceptual images of the product; Secondly, combined with the morphological analysis method to analyze the design elements of the product, and combined with the semantic difference method to make a questionnaire to construct the product modeling image feature evaluation scale; finally, Preprocess the data collected by the questionnaire, divide the training set and test set, use the Support Vector Machine to establish the correlation model between the design elements and the perceptual image, and verify the effectiveness of the model.

The research takes a hand-held vacuum cleaner as a case for verification, and builds a hand-held vacuum cleaner modeling image prediction system based on the Support Vector Machine model, which proves the effectiveness of the prediction method and provides effective assistance and support for product image optimization.

Keywords: Product image design · Kansei Engineering · Prediction system · Support Vector Machine

1 Introduction

1.1 Research Background

With the improvement of people's consumption level and aesthetic concept, people's consumption needs are no longer limited to the pursuit of product functions, but become more personalized and diversified [1]. The development trend of product design is toward

C. Stephanidis et al. (Eds.): HCII 2023, CCIS 1835, pp. 631–639, 2023.
https://doi.org/10.1007/978-3-031-36001-5_81

more efficient, intelligent and systematic development, and the concept of design is gradually shifting to "form follows emotion", and user perception-centered design will become an important factor influencing product design [2]. Therefore, on the basis of satisfying the function of the product, it is also necessary to comprehensively meet the user's physiological and psychological multi-dimensional emotional needs, improve the user experience, and optimize the overall product design level.

Product image is a kind of psychological symbol given to users by the product, and it is also a psychological image or concept obtained through association and imagination, which has certain subjectivity and ambiguity [3]. The formation of product modeling image is derived from the direct experience of the user's five senses on the product's shape, such as lines, colors, textures, and structures. The user's satisfaction with the product shape is an important factor that triggers the user's perceptual identification and purchase behavior [4]. In traditional design practice, designers need to combine user's image preference with product shape. Accurate image expression can improve the effective communication between product and designer, product and consumer. Therefore, using engineering methods to study the relationship between users' perceptual images of products and product modeling elements will help designers objectively analyze the perceptual images presented by different product shapes, so that they can be used as much as possible in design practice. Design products that meet consumers' feelings and perceptions.

1.2 Kansei Engineering

Kansei Engineering, as a representative method in emotional design, guides and evaluates design schemes by obtaining users' perceptual images of specific product attributes and connecting them [5]. Using this method, people's ambiguous emotional needs and images can be transformed into product design elements, which makes it widely used in the field of design.

Current research on Kansei Engineering in product design is often used to analyze single or multiple styling elements that influence product imagery, but quantitative research methods for determining overall product styling imagery are lacking. With the rapid development of information technology, a series of algorithms represented by machine learning have shown advantages in the statistical analysis of perceptual data. Lai et al. [6] applied gray correlation analysis and a neural network model based on a perceptual engineering framework to investigate the direct mapping relationship between cell phone shape form elements and the semantic vocabulary of perceptual imagery. Wang [7] built a product form optimization system using SVM and IGA to optimize the form of electric bicycles. Hsiao [8] applied genetic algorithms and neural networks to reorganize the elements of the product shape to obtain an optimal image of the product.

In this study, we propose a new method that can scientifically predict the overall product styling imagery, combined with the Support Vector Regression (SVR) model in machine learning, take many styling elements in products as the research object, and build a product styling imagery prediction system based on Kansei Engineering experiments.

2 System Framework

2.1 Product Image Prediction System

The construction of the product styling imagery prediction system is divided into two main processes, and Fig. 1 shows the experimental process. The first is to construct the product styling imagery evaluation scale, collect the user evaluation data, and then construct the mapping relationship between product styling design parameters and product perceptual imagery based on the regression model in SVM.

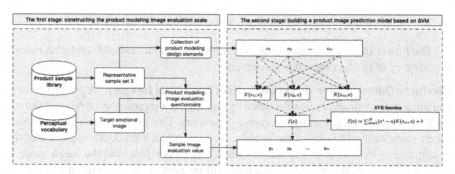

Fig. 1. Product modeling image prediction process

2.2 Kansei Engineering Experiment

Collect and Screen Out Representative Product Samples. Collect a large number of sample images of the products to be studied through various channels such as e-commerce platforms, the Internet and magazines, invite designers to delete some samples with duplicate forms or high similarity after group discussions, and Finally select a representative product sample set X:

$$X = \{X_1, X_2, \ldots, X_M\} \tag{1}$$

Determine the Perceptual Semantic Vocabulary to Describe the Product Shape. The perceptual semantic vocabulary can visually reflect the perceptual imagery of the product. A large number of perceptual semantic words are collected through user surveys and aftersales evaluations on ecommerce platforms, and the large number of collected perceptual words are initially screened and analyzed, and designers are invited to screen the perceptual semantic words to obtain a perceptual vocabulary group that describes the product to be studied.

Extracting Product Form Design Elements. Use the representative sample set X as the base data for decomposing the product form elements. Use morphological analysis to list the various styling elements that make up the product [9]. In the process of decomposing the product styling elements, the group members can discuss with the designer or conduct interviews for consumers to analyze and summarize the styling design elements that have a strong influence on the product imagery. For each representative product sample, the set of its morphological design elements can be obtained as:

$$x = \{x_1, x_2, \ldots, x_N\} \tag{2}$$

A representative set of product samples X can be represented as a matrix:

$$X = \begin{bmatrix} x_1^1 & x_2^1 & \cdots & x_N^1 \\ x_1^2 & x_2^2 & \cdots & x_N^2 \\ \vdots & \vdots & x_n^m & \vdots \\ x_1^M & x_2^M & \cdots & x_N^M \end{bmatrix} \tag{3}$$

The matrix in which m represents the number of product samples and n represents the category of product form design elements.

Conduct a Questionnaire Survey on Product Perceptual Imagery. A product perceptual imagery questionnaire was designed by combining a representative product sample set X with a screened perceptual semantic vocabulary. This questionnaire uses a 7-point Likert scale method to collect the evaluation value of each product sample under the description of the target perceptual semantic vocabulary pair, and the mean value is derived from the data statistics. These data will be used as the training set and test set for training the product image prediction model.

Result Analysis and Verification. The morphological design elements of the product samples are encoded as the input items of the model, and the average evaluation value of the perceptual image corresponding to each product sample obtained from the questionnaire survey is used as the output item of the model, and part of the sample data is randomly selected as the training set training the regression model in SVM, the remaining sample data is used as the test set to verify the accuracy of the model.

3 Method

3.1 Support Vector Regression

Support Vector Regression (SVR) is a kind of supervised learning algorithm based on statistical learning theory. It combines the advantages of SVM classifiers and extends the ideas of SVM to regression problems, which can handle small samples, nonlinearity, classification and regression analysis well with good generalization ability. It performs very well in various practical applications such as face recognition, image classification and text classification. In the field of Kansei Engineering research, SVR is often used to construct association models between design elements and product imagery.

In this study, SVR will be used to evaluate the product image as a way to construct a product image prediction model. Some samples are randomly selected in the sample set as the training set D_1.

$$D_1 = \{(x_i, y_i)\} \tag{4}$$

where $i = 1, 2, 3 \cdots, m$, $x_i \in R^d$, $y_i \in R$, x_i represents the feature vector to be input, d represents the dimension of x_i, y_i represents the evaluation value of a certain sample, introduce the kernel function:

$$K(x_i, x) = \varphi(x_i) \cdot \varphi(x) \tag{5}$$

The relationship between the product design elements x_i and the perceptual evaluation value y_i is fitted with $f(x)$, and the expression is:

$$f(x) = \sum_{i=1}^{m} (\alpha_i^* - \alpha_i) K(x_i, x) + b = \omega \cdot \varphi(x) + b \tag{6}$$

where α_i^*, α_i represent Lagrange multipliers not less than 0; ω represents the normal vector of the hyperplane; and b represents the bias constant.

Introduce the relaxation factor ξ_i^*, $\xi_i \geq 0$, the penalty factor $C > 0$, the penalty factor indicates the degree of penalty for samples that exceed the error to avoid the phenomenon of overfitting, the loss function uses the insensitive function ε. The optimization objective is:

$$min \frac{1}{2}\omega^2 + \frac{C}{m} \sum_{i=1}^{m} (\xi_i + \xi_i^*) \tag{7}$$

By introducing Lagrange multipliers α_i^*, α_i, α_j^*, α_j, for constrained optimization, the nonlinear SVR can be transformed into a pairwise quadratic optimization problem to be solved as follows:

$$\begin{aligned} \max &\left(\alpha_i^* - \alpha_i\right) \\ &= \sum_{i=1}^{m} (\alpha_i^* - \alpha_i) - \varepsilon \sum_{i=1}^{m} (\alpha_i^* + \alpha_i) - \frac{1}{2} \sum_{i=1}^{m} \sum_{j=1}^{m} (\alpha_i^* - \alpha_i)\left(\alpha_j^* - \alpha_j\right) K(x_i, x) \end{aligned} \tag{8}$$

Based on the KKT condition, the SVR problem is transformed into a convex quadratic programming problem, and the final regression function of the nonlinear SVR is obtained as:

$$f(x) = \sum_{i=1}^{m} (\alpha_i^* - \alpha_i) K(x_i, x) + b = \omega \cdot \varphi(x) + b \tag{9}$$

3.2 Experimental Procedure

In this section, a handheld vacuum cleaner is used as a research case to train the SVR model to predict the imagery of handheld vacuum cleaners. The specific implementation of support vector regression in building a product stylistic imagery prediction model is illustrated through this case, and the practicality and reliability of the method is verified.

A total of 130 product samples were collected from e-commerce platforms, product brochures, etc. Nine designers with more than 3 years of experience in product design were invited to make preliminary arrangements in a group discussion to eliminate samples with low resolution, high similarity, and large differences in proportion and size. The final 50 experimental samples are shown in Fig. 2.

Fig. 2. Handheld vacuum cleaner sample set

The perceptual semantic vocabulary describing the handheld vacuum cleaner was collected extensively from relevant user reviews, books, product brochures and the Internet. The KJ method was used to identify main relevant words, and the designers were invited to consider and discuss the product based on its stylistic features to filter out four representative perceptual words, and finally formed an adjective pair as shown in Table 1, selecting [simple-complex] as the perceptual imagery to describe the stylistic features of the handheld vacuum cleaner.

Table 1. Perceptual Vocabulary Group

Vocabulary1	Vocabulary2	Vocabulary3	Vocabulary4
Simple-Complex	Lightweight-Heavy	Rounded - Squared	Dynamic - Stable

Based on the shape characteristics of handheld vacuum cleaners, a group of nine experienced designers was formed to decompose the shape elements of handheld vacuum cleaners based on the morphological analysis method, and summarize the morphological design elements that have a great influence on the shape imagery of handheld vacuum cleaners and are representative of the design elements, which are divided into four categories according to the product structure. The results are shown in Table 2.

Table 2. design elements of hand-held vacuum cleaner

Category	Design elements
Base outline x_1	1 2 3 4 5 6 7 8 9
Top profile x_2	1 2 3 4 5
Vacuum cup x_3	1 2 3 4 5 6
Fuselage cross-section x_4	1 2 3 4

Using a 7-point Likert scale, 50 handheld vacuum cleaner samples were combined with perceptual vocabulary [simple-complex] to create a semantic difference questionnaire and distributed on the Internet. 37 questionnaires were collected back, with up to 78% of the respondents being design students, teachers, designers or product managers. The mean value of the collected imagery was calculated and normalized to construct a handheld vacuum cleaner modeling imagery evaluation scale, as shown in Table 3. The evaluation value is in the range of 0 to 1.The larger the evaluation value, the more complex the product imagery, and the smaller the rating value, the simpler the product.

Table 3. handheld vacuum cleaner modeling imagery evaluation scale

Sample	x_1	x_2	x_3	x_4	Evaluation value
01	3	3	4	4	0.69
02	5	2	5	3	0.16
03	4	3	4	4	0.41
⋮	⋮	⋮	⋮	⋮	⋮
50	3	1	4	4	0.46

Based on python language for program development, the SVM module in Scikit-learn is imported to train the SVR model by coding the decomposed handheld vacuum cleaner modeling features as the input values of the SVR model and the user's perceptual evaluation values as the output values.

In order to train the SVR model with higher accuracy, the optimal parameter values of the model need to be selected: kernel function and relaxation factor. Using grid search, 50 samples are used as the base data, divided into 10 mutually exclusive subsets with the same number, and each subset is used as a test set for 10-fold cross-validation, and the model performance is measured by the mean square error (MSE). The optimal parameters of the model are selected by this method: the kernel function is rbf, and the relaxation factor ε is 0.02. The penalty factor C has a default value of 1.0. Finally, 90% (45) of the product samples are randomly selected as the training set, 10% of the samples are selected as the test set, the kernel function is rbf radial basis function, the relaxation factor ε is 0.02, and the penalty factor C is set to the default value of 1.0, and the SVR model is trained and the accuracy of the model is verified. The validation results are shown in Fig. 3.

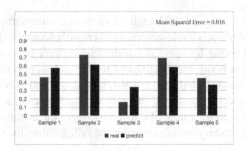

Fig. 3. real and predicted values of the test set

The 50 samples were used as the test set and predicted with the trained SVR model, and the results are shown in Fig. 4.

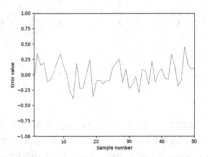

Fig. 4. real and predicted values of the test set

4 Result

The accuracy of the SVR model was evaluated using the MSE. The results are shown in Table 4.The MSE of the test set is 0.016 and the MSE of all samples is 0.037, thus indicating that the model constructed based on the support vector machine model for predicting the styling imagery of handheld vacuum cleaners has a high accuracy and a good ability to fit the experimental data, and the model can be used for predicting the styling imagery of products.

Table 4. SVR model prediction results

	Test set	All sample set
MSE	0.016	0.037

5 Conclusion

In this study, we propose a product modeling imagery prediction system based on perceptual engineering, which uses a SVM model to predict the overall product modeling imagery, and validate it with the imagery prediction of a handheld vacuum cleaner as an example. The results show that the system can be used to predict the imagery of relevant products. However, there are shortcomings in the experiment, as the material and color of the product can affect the product's perceptual imagery, and this experiment only takes the morphological elements as the research variables, so the scope of the study is not comprehensive. In addition, the imagery of products is multifaceted, and the relationship between multiple perceptual imagery and product design needs to be considered comprehensively.

References

1. Maruca, R.F.: Mapping the world of customer satisfaction. Harv. Bus. Rev. **78**, 30 (2000)
2. Zheng, P., Yu, S., Wang, Y., Zhong, R.Y., Xu, X.: User-experience based product development for mass personalization: a case study. Procedia CIRP **63**, 2–7 (2017)
3. Xue, L., Yi, X., Zhang, Y.: Research on optimized product image design integrated decision system based on kansei engineering. Appl. Sci. **10**, 1198 (2020)
4. Pentus, K., Mehine, T., Kuusik, A.: Considering emotions in product package design through combining conjoint analysis with psycho physiological measurements. Procedia Soc. Behav. Sci. **148**, 280–290 (2014)
5. Levy, P.: Beyond kansei engineering: the emancipation of kansei design. Int. J. Des. **7**(2), 83–94 (2013)
6. Lai, H.-H., Lin, Y.-C., Yeh, C.-H.: Form design of product image using grey relational analysis and neural network models. Comput. Oper. Res. **32**, 2689–2711 (2005)
7. Wang, T., Zhou, M.: A method for product form design of integrating interactive genetic algorithm with the interval hesitation time and user satisfaction. Int. J. Ind. Ergon. **76**, 102901 (2020)
8. Hsiao, S.-W., Tsai, H.-C.: Applying a hybrid approach based on fuzzy neural network and genetic algorithm to product form design. Int. J. Ind. Ergon. **35**, 411–428 (2005)
9. Cluzel, F., Yannou, B., Dihlmann, M.: Using evolutionary design to interactively sketch car silhouettes and stimulate designer's creativity. Eng. Appl. Artif. Intell. **25**, 1413–1424 (2012)

Exploring Sustainable Product Design Framework Based on Responsible Consumption and Production

Shuo-fang Liu and Ru-chun Huang[(✉)]

National Cheng Kung University, No. 1, Daxue Road, East District, Tainan City, Taiwan
(R.O.C.)
liusf@mail.ncku.edu.tw, p36101049@gs.ncku.edu.tw

Abstract. According to the SDGs, more and more research has come out. There are countless methods for sustainable product design, but most of the actual usage and results are not as significant as expected. In order to understand the more commonly used sustainable design methods in recent years and the sustainable design framework proposed by researchers, such a huge and comprehensive information is suitable for using literature review method to compare their differences and similarities, and analyze them from it. A good design of human-computer interaction can improve the efficiency of product use and reduce the waste of energy and resources. Based on the twelfth goal "Responsible Consumption and Production" of SDGs, this article aims to understand the framework of sustainable product design, different applications in different scopes, and its relevance to human-computer interaction.

Keywords: Responsible Consumption and Production · Sustainability · Product Design Framework · Literature Review

1 Introduction

1.1 Issue Promotion

With the intensification of global warming and the gradual increase in population, natural resources are overrun each year. The United Nations promotes the SDGs between 2015 and 2030 vigorously, which is also be expected to solve the challenges facing human beings and the planet without affecting the basic needs of human beings. Among those, the twelfth goal is "Responsible Consumption and Production", hoping to significantly reduce the generation of waste through prevention, reduction, recycling and reuse [1].

It also encourages large-scale or multinational companies to incorporate sustainability information into their periodic reports. Take ASUS for example, its 2021 Sustainability Report details the company's implementation of material and energy management, packaging design, and metal recycling. These strategies and outcomes for their corresponding objectives are described as well [2].

© The Author(s), under exclusive license to Springer Nature Switzerland AG 2023
C. Stephanidis et al. (Eds.): HCII 2023, CCIS 1835, pp. 640–646, 2023.
https://doi.org/10.1007/978-3-031-36001-5_82

Moreover, The Earth Overshoot Day is advancing year by year, but only 8.6% of resources can be totally recycled [3]. The issue of sustainability has received more and more attention and have gradually become an indispensable part of people's lives.

In sustainable product design, human-computer interaction is regarded as one of the important design factors. For human-computer interaction, it can improve the ease of usability, learnability, reliability, and safety of product design and product-service systems. And further to achieve efficient, inclusive and sustainable applications.

1.2 Current Development

There are many terms on sustainable design issues, the most common ones are: sustainable design (SD), sustainable product design (SPD), green design, eco design etc. Although there are still some differences between each term, the purpose is to reduce the harm and impact on the environment, and take economic benefits into one of the design considerations, and develop the best design method [4]. In terms of overall development, from the early design for X (DfX) and eco-design to the current product service system (PSS), it is also moving towards sustainability-product service system (SPSS) [5], and even Smart-PSS [6, 7] directions prevail.

Recently, Kar et al. [8] pointed out that corporate strategy is one of the factors driving sustainable consumption. Besides, green marketing innovation and sustainable consumption are highly correlated terms, and they are also one of the feasible development methods for enterprises to face the global economy. Moreover, Shaharuzaman et al. [9] explored the choice of materials for sustainability, and widely been used in the product innovation field. Delaney et al. [10] actively studied different approaches to sustainable product design. Kong et al. [11] proposed a new framework based on the integration of different dimensions among product procedures, lifecycles, and related tools.

Undoubtedly, there are countless methods for sustainable product design; however, scholars have used existing design methods to participate in the product design process, and it is found that most of the actual usage and results are not as significant as expected. There are still flaws and contradictions in judging whether the criteria for sustainable behavior are met.

2 Methodology

2.1 Literature Review

The literature review belongs to secondary research. Mishra [12] believes that the literature review not only presents data, but also needs to include research models, research future trends, and other related extension topics, to provide more comprehensive reference content.

In addition to helping to establish a research framework, analyze, and integrate, literature review can illustrate the correlation between research more clearly. Besides, it also proves that there will be meaningful extension and contribution in the academic research [13].

2.2 Research Design

In order not to miss any literature that can be included in the research, this study planned each research step in the following Fig. 1 and screening criteria (see Table 1.). The data search mainly divided into two parts: the first part is the inquiry and screening of the literature; and the second part is related websites and quotation document search (see Fig. 1).

The first part of literature search is mainly based on EBSCOHost, Scopus and Web of Science, select literature from 2018 to 2022, and search for matching titles, keywords and journal names, including: sustainability, sustainable product design, green design, product design framework…etc. When all the conforms of the literature lists are exported, this research will remove duplicate literature, read abstracts, and search for the full text by EndNote. After reading the abstract, delete the literature that is not related to product design, the final step is to read the full text in detailed and incorporate as a literature that can be further analyzed.

To be more systematic and efficient when screening titles and abstracts, this study also established five levels of screening criteria. The order of relevance to the research design is highly relevant, moderately relevant, partially relevant, including indeterminate, partially mentioned but not relevant, and not at all relevant.

And in the second part, relevant websites are searched with keywords such as the United Nations SDGs, sustainability-related reports, sustainable consumption and production, etc. Moreover, the references in the first part are extended for targeted search and reading. Finally, entering the statistics and analysis stage of literature review.

Table 1. Preliminary setting of research design (made by this research)

Criteria	Research item and filter
keywords	((sustainab* OR green OR eco*) w/3 (product* OR cultur*) w/3 design*) AND (framework* OR ((method* OR process* OR development*) w/3 design*))
Databases	Academic: Academic Complete Search [EBSCOhost], GreenFILE [EBSCOhost], Scopus, and Web of Science
	Non-academic: Web-pages and reports from research organizations, governmental agencies, and citation searching
Geographic scope	Worldwide
Publication years	2018–2022

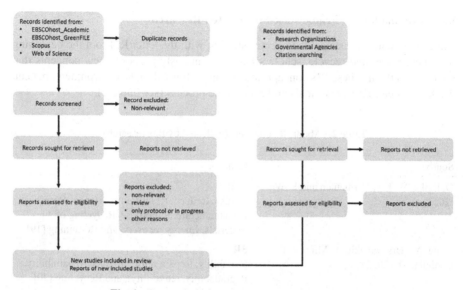

Fig. 1. Research design step (made by this research)

3 Findings

From a broad perspective, the fields of research on sustainable product design include packaging, furniture, automobiles, home appliances, electronics, etc. Product service systems, strategies in company, and education in academic are also the touch points that can be studied in detail. And in the current existing framework, product life cycle sustainability assessment, assembly and disassembly design, etc., are important tools and elements that continue to emerge and affect the design framework.

3.1 Sustainability in Human-Computer Interaction Research

Some research use the help of software, such as using Sustainable Xpress (or Sustainability) in SOLIDWORKS to evaluate whether the product meets the standard of sustainability [14, 15]. The software analysis standard quantifies the carbon footprint, total energy, air acidification degree and water eutrophication consumed in the four stages of material, manufacturing, transportation and end of life respectively. Apart from this, some may put forward a new application method by combining CAD software with LCA to evaluate the environmental impact [16] or use TechOptimizer to improve the process [17].

For designers, it is convenient for evaluating; however, most of them are mainly focused on environmental impact. Especially, Ahmad et al. [18] found that most of previous studies from 2007 to 2017 mainly focused on ecological design tools, while sustainable design should be different from it. Three aspects, environment, social, and economic, should be considered comprehensively, and the term confusion should be minimized.

3.2 Sustainability in Framework-Formulated Research

There are countless sustainable concepts starting with the letter R. From the beginning of reduce, reuse, and recycle, scholars have continuously proposed new concepts that extend from them. These 'Rs concept' are no longer limited to the environment, but can also be applied to different fields and even in the process (see Table 2).

Table 2. About 'Rs concept' (collected by this research)

Source	Concept
D. Reike, W. J. V. Vermeulen and S. Witjes (2022)	**10R** Refuse, Reduce, Resell/re-use, Repair, Refurbish, Remanufacture, Repurpose, Recycling of materials, Energy recovery, and Re-mining [19]
Wang, Y. Harsuvanakit, A. Mincey, T. Cordella, M. (2022)	**3R** Reliability, Repair, reuse, upgrade (repairability, upgradability, reusability), and Recycling [20]
Rihar, L. and Kusar, J. (2021)	**6RE** rethink, repair, replace, reuse, reduce, and recycle [21]
Liu, C.; Zhao, Y. (2020)	**7R** Reduction, Reuse, Recycling, Redesign, Revalue, Renovate, and Regenerate [22]

In the industry, moreover, Fairphone [23], a Dutch electronic manufacturer founded in 2013, is committed to using fair and recyclable materials, as well as a structure that is easy to assemble and disassemble. While providing consumers with a 5-year warranty period, it even proposed a strategy that another mobile phone will be reborn when the consumer buy a Fairphone to create a longer lifespan for the mobile phone.

4 Discussion

Although this research is still ongoing, there is no doubt that improving the efficiency of product use, reducing waste and resource consumption, and prolonging the life of products are common points of human-computer interaction design and sustainable product design. Both of them are in pursuit of reducing the negative impact on the environment and achieving sustainable development.

In order to meet the new human-computer era, good human-computer interaction design can help product designers better understand the needs and habits of users, and then design products that better meet the needs of users, reducing the waste and disposal of products that do not meet the needs of users.

Literatures also show that people's perception of sustainability and consumption habits are important influencing factors in product design process. It is suggested that further research can be done on how to enhance users' cognition and understanding of sustainable products through human-computer interaction design, and even promote users' positive behavior and choices for sustainable products.

And lastly, according to current findings, we deeply believe that a good design of human-computer interaction can improve the efficiency of product using and reduce the waste of energy and resources.

References

1. United Nations. Take Action for the Sustainable Development Goals. https://www.un.org/sustainabledevelopment/sustainable-development-goals/. Accessed 04 Aug 2022
2. ASUS. 2021 ASUS Sustainability Report. https://csr.asus.com/english/index.aspx. Accessed 01 Sept 2022
3. Circle Economy. The Circularity Gap Report 2022. https://www.circularity-gap.world. Accessed 17 Aug 2022
4. Hong, M.Z.: Investigation and Research on Green Design Technology. Environment and Development Foundation, Taipei City, Taiwan, ROC (2002)
5. Shokohyar, S., Mansour, S., Karimi, B.: A model for integrating services and product EOL management in sustainable product service system (S-PSS). J. Intell. Manuf. **25**(3), 427–440 (2014)
6. Carrera-Rivera, A., Larrinaga, F., Lasa, G.: Context-awareness for the design of smart-product service systems: literature review. Comput. Ind. **142**, 103730 (2022)
7. Li, X.Y., Wang, Z.X., Chen, C.H., Zheng, P.: A data-driven reversible framework for achieving sustainable smart product-service systems. J. Clean. Prod. **279**, 123618 (2021)
8. Kar, S.K., Harichandan, S.: Green marketing innovation and sustainable consumption: a bibliometric analysis. J. Clean. Prod. **361**, 132290 (2022)
9. Shaharuzaman, M.A., Sapuan, S.M., Mansor, M.R.: Sustainable materials selection: principles and applications. In: Sapuan, S.M., Mansor, M.R. (eds.) Design for Sustainability, pp. 57–84. Elsevier (2021)
10. Delaney, E., Liu, W., Zhu, Z.C., Xu, Y.C., Dai, J.S.: The investigation of environmental sustainability within product design: a critical review. Des. Sci. **8**, e15 (2022)
11. Kong, L., Wang, L.M., Li, F.Y., Guo, J.: Toward product green design of modeling, assessment, optimization, and tools: a comprehensive review. Int. J. Adv. Manufact. Technol. **122**(5–6), 2217–2234 (2022)
12. Mishra, S.: Reviewing the literature. In: Methodological Issues in Management Research: Advances, Challenges, and the Way Ahead, pp. 11–25 (2020)
13. Tang, P.C., Wu, M.M.: From literature review exploring thesis' innovative writing phenomena. J. Libr. Inf. Sci. **39**(2), 4–25 (2013)
14. Subharaj, C., Jerin Leno, I., Vivek, S., Joe Patrick Gnanaraj, S., Appadurai, M.: Sustainable manufacturing system applying on eco-design products. Mater. Today Proc. **68**, 1528–1535 (2022)
15. Effendi, M.S.M., et al.: Sustainability analysis and integration with Dfma and Fea: a case study of radio design. In: AIP Conference Proceedings (2021)
16. Ben Slama, H., Gaha, R., Benamara, A.: Proposal of new eco-manufacturing feature interaction-based methodology in CAD phase. Int. J. Adv. Manuf. Technol. **106**(3–4), 1057–1068 (2019). https://doi.org/10.1007/s00170-019-04483-7
17. Frizziero, L., Francia, D., Donnici, G., Liverani, A., Caligiana, G.: Sustainable design of open molds with QFD and TRIZ combination. J. Ind. Prod. Eng. **35**(1), 21–31 (2018)
18. Ahmad, S., Wong, K.Y., Tseng, M.L., Wong, W.P.: Sustainable product design and development: a review of tools, applications and research prospects. Resour. Conserv. Recycl. **132**, 49–61 (2018)

19. Reike, D., Vermeulen, W.J.V., Witjes, S.: Working with the new conceptualization of circular economy 3.0: illustrating the ten value retention options. In: Csr, Sustainability, Ethics and Governance, pp. 71–97 (2022)
20. Wang, Y., Harsuvanakit, A., Mincey, T., Cordella, M.: Towards a digital knowledge base of circular design examples through product teardowns. Procedia CIRP **105**, 314–319 (2022)
21. Rihar, L., Kusar, J.: Implementing concurrent engineering and QFD method to achieve realization of sustainable project. Sustainability **13**(3), 1091 (2021)
22. Liu, C., Zhao, Y.: The application of lifecycle design strategies in the interaction design. In: Goonetilleke, R.S., Karwowski, W. (eds.) AHFE 2019. AISC, vol. 967, pp. 369–376. Springer, Cham (2020). https://doi.org/10.1007/978-3-030-20142-5_37
23. Fairphone official website. https://www.fairphone.com/en. Accessed 26 Sept 2022

How Service Design Thinking Could Help Preserve the Institutional Knowledge for Social Problems Solvers: A Case Study of Stray Dog Population Management Planning Guidelines

Wei-Ting Wang⬤, Hsien-Hui Tang[✉]⬤, and Jia-Yun Li⬤

National Taiwan University of Science and Technology, Taipei City 106335, Taiwan
{drhhtang,M11110101}@gapps.ntust.edu.tw

Abstract. With the increasing problems of stray dogs in Taiwan, societies have been raising their awareness to discuss the issue. The complex perspectives amongst stakeholders, poor communication, the difference between regional environments, and even the resources contribution all result in the dog TNR (Trap, Neuter, and Return) implementation lack of standard operating procedures. The situation influenced the effectiveness of preserving practical and tacit knowledge of the related implementation. Although the public and private sectors have spent a significant amount of time and resources for years, the problems of stray dogs have yet to be solved due to the lack of institutional knowledge.

Therefore, the research question is how to apply service design thinking to solve this complex social issue from a knowledge viewpoint. This study explored how service design thinking can resolve the obstacle of preserving institutional knowledge through the *"Stray Dog Population Management Planning Guideline"* case study. The three objectives are the followings. Firstly, to analyze the problems that affect the implementation of dog population management—secondly, to devise the best solution utilizing service design thinking. Thirdly, to discuss how service design thinking impacted the preservation of institutional knowledge through study cases. The research results are insights into applying service design for complex knowledge preservation and conversion through an innovative social case. The research provides a revolutionary mindset on solving a complex social problem, encouraging stakeholders to take a knowledge communication approach.

Keywords: Service Design · Institutional Knowledge · Stray Dog Population Management · Social Issues

1 Introduction

Due to beliefs in animal equality and religions, stray dogs can be seen in the cities and countryside in Taiwan, and the problem has been dramatically concerned and discussed in recent years. Stray dogs living close to the communication where people live can cause problems with sanitation, noise, the environment, traffic accidents, or even people's safety. On the other hand, if stray dogs live in desolate mountain and forest areas, it

© The Author(s), under exclusive license to Springer Nature Switzerland AG 2023
C. Stephanidis et al. (Eds.): HCII 2023, CCIS 1835, pp. 647–654, 2023.
https://doi.org/10.1007/978-3-031-36001-5_83

would overlap with the living area of wild animals, causing conservation animals to be attacked or infected by the canine distemper. In 2019, it was estimated that the number of stray dogs in Taiwan was about 155,869 (Council of Agriculture, Executive Yuan, 2019). To cope with the severe problem, domestic governments and animal rights organizations have spent plenty of time and resources to propose policies and plans for dog population management. However, dealing with the problem related to stray dogs is considerably hard, leading to severe social problems.

Several factors result in the problems of stray dog population management, SDPM, such as the education of pet owners, dog neutering, and dog housing and disposal. Among the abovementioned factors, dog neutering is the essential method for managing stray dogs. However, its practical experience is tacit and hard to preserve. It is hard to record the emergency or uncertainty in the field compared to the explicit knowledge that can be preserved by specified format and regulation. The tacit knowledge tends to be preserved through word of mouth or apprenticeship, which is hard to record on paper and diffused, making the implementation can only be conducted in a specific group or region. In this case, it is difficult for multiple parties to communicate and exchange their practical experience effectively. In the long term, lousy communication would make the practical experience in the field unable to be organized and preserved systematically.

The study first explained the complexity of stray dog management and the difficulty of knowledge transformation through literature reviews. Second, it analyzed the case of "SDPM Planning Guideline" to present how service design thinking and method can transfer the practical experience into a learnable guideline, resolving the problems of SDPM. Finally, the study analyzed the critical factors of how service design impacts the preservation of the practical experience of stray dog neutering through the semi-structured interview.

In this case, the service designers transformed and preserved the best practical experience of SDPM, establishing an operating procedure that can be referred to and learned. It aims to increase the effectiveness of Taiwan's SDPM and to make the overall population under control, ending up with a learnable reference book, "Stray Dog Population Management Planning Guideline".

2 The Difficulties of Social Problem Solving

Social Problem Solving (SPS) is the process by which people try to discover or invent an effective solution to social problems. The problem of stray dogs mainly comes from the overwhelming number and the need for more management capacity. SDPM is a kind of SPS. The following will describe details of the difficulties of this SPS and its relations to knowledge.

2.1 Difficulties in Achieving Strategic Collaboration Between Organizations

Collaborative relationships between organizations can also be described as integrating resources; however, it is challenging to balance the public and private sectors during SDPM practice. In seeking a qualified partner, the government tends to expect the ideal candidate to stand out in a diverse and competitive environment. Nevertheless, in issues requiring experience and continuity, only a few private sector departments often meet the standards, and governments are prone to generate inertia dependence as a result. On the other hand, the private sector needs help partnering with the government due to the tedious process of reimbursement or administrative work. The collaborative relationship has consequently changed from positive encouragement to harmful prevention. Knowledge of collaboration is needed.

2.2 Difficulties in Communication and Diffusion When Organizational Knowledge Keeps Expanding Over Time

Knowledge of animal protection is accumulated and updated over time, and the main treatment of stray dogs has also changed from sheltering to neutering. The knowledge of stray dog sterilization has been accumulated through the attempts and implementation by various organizations. Yet, not all organizations can expand their mindset over time. Most organizations implement neutering programs independently within a defined region, and the methods and practices would differ due to environmental and cultural differences. However, as the scope of implementation expands, overlap in the scope of activities between organizations is inevitable. Nevertheless, the lack of knowledge exchange and communication platforms between organizations makes it difficult for each of them to flow with the other, leading to a knowledge gap or even confrontation. As a result, stray dog management in Taiwan is mostly formed within a single organization and is hard to spread and implement in other places. Transferable knowledge is needed.

2.3 Difficulties in Properly Allocating and Integrating Resources due to the Organization's Lack of the Appropriate Knowledge

Stray dogs are generally defined as dogs that are not under human supervision and are not restricted in their activities. According to International Companion Animal Management Coalition's definition (2019), the composition of stray dogs can be subdivided into four types: owned roaming dogs, owned lost dogs, community dogs, and unowned dogs. The key to the ethnic group conversion of a stray dog is the scope of care provided by the human and whether the caregiver is the owner. The resources and the neutering programs will differ according to each type of dog.

Although roaming and private breeding are illegal, the government lacks the workforce to inspect and punish them, leading to behaviors still quite common in Taiwan's rural areas. Only some owners have the right concept of dog breeding or even the financial ability to spay or neuter a dog. In terms of owned lost dogs, unowned dogs, and community-owned dogs, they need more supervision from owners, so animal protection groups or offices will trap and neuter them. However, the three groups of dogs have different difficulties in trapping. On the other hand, people who feed stray dogs are less likely to be recognized by society due to the sanitary problems from feeding, making them unwilling to cooperate with trapping to some degree. Knowledge of execution is needed.

3   The Complexity of Knowledge Conversion in Social Problem Solving Using Service Design in Terms of the SECI Model

The implementation of SDPM worldwide is fraught with variables, including the executors, the measures, and the one being executed (Smith, 2019). In Taiwan, due to the difference in the operation mode of SDPM and the allocation of resources, each party has developed various types of sterilization operations of several scales. Among them, only large-area and large-scale operations have the opportunity to achieve the benefits of TNvR, and the scale of the neutering operation will also restrict the range of areas and types of stray dogs.

Although most SDPM is implemented in a publicly available way, the large-scale and strategic neuter operation usually contain highly personalized tacit knowledge, such as the context in which leaders plan operations, the experience of personnel implementation, and the collaboration between internal organizations, and the above contents are difficult to be understood without a personal experience. However, transforming from tacit knowledge to explicit knowledge plays a key role in SDPM.

The SECI model of knowledge dimensions proposed by Nonaka (1994) explains the interaction between tacit knowledge and explicit knowledge, in which the process of externalizing tacit knowledge to explicit knowledge could be used to examine the case. SECI model could better interpret the background of SDPM problems and the urgency of its solution. It describes the whole knowledge generation and conversion process, which eventually becomes common knowledge in the organization. The SECI model is presented as Fig. 1.

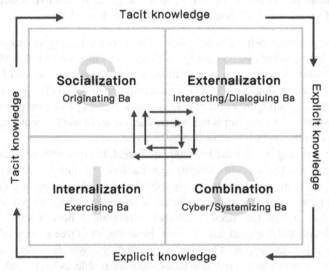

Fig. 1. SECI model of knowledge dimensions (Nonaka, 1994)

In this case, the practice of service design is the tool used to transform the SDPM knowledge among different stages of the SECI model. Service design is a measure that can attract diverse stakeholders to provide their experiences and integrate a series of knowledge to become the foundation of a new service. With the balance of perspectives from many parties, they can co-create innovative services and solutions which are more comprehensive (Patrício et al., 2018).

The existing circumstance of SDPM in Taiwan is consistent with the construction of service design thinking. Transferring knowledge through service design methods is suitable to make them circulate between organizations. The study case followed the triple diamonds process of service design (Wang et al., 2022). The first stage (Problem Distillation) defined the core problem through exploration. The second stage (Design Iteration) began with design ideating and ended with convergence and integration. The third stage (Practice Diffusion) practiced and developed the solution by service evaluation. The complex issues can be analyzed with the triple diamond stages, constructing a new service with solutions. The service design thinking's impact on knowledge transformation can be seen by comparing the triple diamond process of service design against the SECI model (see Fig. 2).

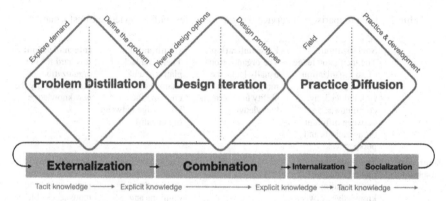

Fig. 2. The comparison of the triple diamonds process and SECI model

In the stage of problem distillation, the researcher collected related second-hand information in a wide range and gained a deeper understanding of professional knowledge through interviews, observations, and other methods. At the same time, the texts, figures, or videos could record tacit knowledge, which can be externalized and converge with core problems.

The design iteration stage proposed innovative solutions and a systematic knowledge structure based on the restructures and reorganizations of explicit knowledge. With those, the knowledge turned into a combination stage, and the final design outcomes are the collection of explicit knowledge.

In the practice diffusion process, the design outcomes were turned into practical applications and evaluated to determine the design's impact and effectiveness on the issue. Iterating existing knowledge by real application and feedback made knowledge reach internalization. The evaluation process transferred the new knowledge into shared knowledge in the organization and kept preserving it, achieving the socialization stage finally.

Service design features could include emphasizing stakeholders, sequence, holistic view, realism, and evidence (Lee & Tang, 2022). This research added co-creation as the last feature. Service design could integrate diverse perspectives and practical experiences to clarify the problem through the opinion of a trusted third party and explore and discuss the core solution systematically. The case proposed intelligible operating principles according to the stakeholder's needs and finally achieved knowledge preservation, reducing the number of stray dogs under control.

In this case, the researcher had to conquer the complexity of the four processes of knowledge transformation mentioned above. Therefore, service design could be regarded as the method that can assist in transferring knowledge and summarizing the final operating principles. With the six principles of service design, this study categorized how to support knowledge transformation and construct the solution. Table 1 is the particial comparison of service design principles with the complexity of knowledge transformation. It illustrates how individual principles of service design can cope with the complexity of knowledge transformation separately. The results showed that the three features of

Table 1. The comparison of service design principles with knowledge transformation.

	Socialization: The tacit knowledge of an organization would preserve isolated, lacking communication between different organizations and perspectives	Externalization: The organization usually lacks the motivation and ability to externalize knowledge	Combination: There is a lack of platform and character to combine the knowledge between organizations	Internalization: It is hard for the organization to accept or apply the new knowledge
Emphasize stakeholders	The researcher gained a deeper understanding of tacit knowledge between organizations based on a stakeholder-centered mindset	-	The researcher acted as a platform that received opinions and information between organizations can collect the data comprehensively	The new knowledge balances several perspectives and is more accessible for organizations to learn
Sequence	-	The researcher analyzed the complete journey through the skills of interviews and observations	The researcher integrates the lengthy knowledge of the journey into the visualized operating key points	-
Holistic view		The researcher had to record the diverse and cross-disciplinary knowledge completely to result in detailed research	The researcher considered all knowledge to analyze a learning structure	

service design (Emphasizing Stakeholders, Sequence, and Holistic view) assisted a lot when externalizing and combining knowledge.

For example, emphasizing stakeholders in service design can promote the internalization of knowledge, changing the fact that the organizations used to close their knowledge. The stakeholders could move from a confrontational position to a consensual and collaborative partnership, raising the possibility of acceptance of new knowledge by organizations. The sequencing emphasizes the service journey and the integration across channels. Therefore, time-wise and system-wise knowledge was noted for preservation. The holistic view would ensure the completion of the knowledge from a macroscopic view. With those features, service design can help the conversion of tacit knowledge and the combination of explicit knowledge in organizations.

4   Conclusions

Social problems would change over time, and solutions must evolve and increase new knowledge, just like SDPM. The knowledge within social problem solvers should break through the scope of tacit knowledge, integrate and refresh with explicit knowledge, and thus generate new core knowledge, finally diffusing throughout the organization. When service designers intervene in social issues from a third-party position, it can serve as a platform to gather the knowledge of multiple stakeholders, clarify their common goals, gradually reach a consensus, promote the exchange of knowledge among multiple parties, and improve the operation among organizations.

To sum up, this case study is a practical example of using service design on social problems to transform knowledge in the SECI model. The case study illustrates the complexity of knowledge preservation as one of the solutions to social problems and as a response to the context of knowledge preservation through the service design process. Service design can effectively break through the situation of knowledge closure, converting experience and providing a way to preserve knowledge for SDPM and other social problems.

References

Council of Agriculture, Executive Yuan: Estimation results of Taiwan stray dogs' quantity (2019). https://www.coa.gov.tw/theme_data.php?theme=news&sub_theme=agri&id=8463

International Compaion Animal Management Coalition (ICAM). Humane Dog Population Management Guidance: 2019 Update (2019)

Lee, Y., Tang, H.H.: How to apply service design thinking on designing accessibility apps: a case study of public transportation for the visually impaired (2022)

Linder, S.H.: Coming to terms with the public-private partnership: a grammar of multiple meanings. Am. Behav. Sci. **43**(1), 35–51 (1999)

Nonaka, I.: A dynamic theory of organizational knowledge creation. Organ. Sci. **5**(1), 14–37 (1994)

Patrício, L., Gustafsson, A., Fisk, R.: Upframing service design and innovation for research impact. J. Serv. Res. **21**(1), 3–16 (2018)

Smith, L.M., Hartmann, S., Munteanu, A.M., Dalla Villa, P., Quinnell, R.J., Collins, L.M.: The effectiveness of dog population management: a systematic review. Animals **9**(12), 1020 (2019)

Wang, D., Hsieh, W.A., Chen, S.Y., Tang, H.H.: The complexities of transport service design for visually impaired people: lessons from a bus commuting service. Int. J. Des. **16**(1), 55–73 (2022)

Exploring Smart Sportswear for Sit Skiers - Human-Centered Design Approach

Jia Wu[✉], Jung Hyup Kim, and Li Zhao

University of Missouri-Columbia, Columbia, USA
jw7ff@umsystem.edu, {kijung,zhaoli}@missouri.edu

Abstract. This research explores the development of smart sportswear for sit skiers, utilizing a human-centered design approach. Sit skiing is a challenging and physically demanding sport, and there is a need for high-performance clothing that can enhance the skier's comfort and performance while also providing safety. The study explores how smart sportswear can meet the needs and preferences of sit skiers, as well as the difficulties and challenges when sit skiers choose smart sportswear. The study involved a qualitative research method, including observation, textual analysis, and in-depth interviews with open-ended questions. The results of the study indicated that smart sportswear could provide valuable feedback and information to sit skiers, helping them to real-time monitor their health indicators, reduce risk, prevent injuries, and improve their overall performance. Further research is needed to explore the effectiveness of smart sportswear in real-world settings and to address the challenges of cost, maintenance, and integration with other technologies.

Keywords: Smart Sportswear · Sit Skier · Human-Centered Design Approach

1 Introduction

Sit skiing is a Paralympic sport that makes skiing possible for people with lower body disabilities. People who practice this sport use a special aid called a sit-ski, made of a personalized molded seat attached to a single ski [1]. In addition, sit skiing is widely regarded as an extreme sport that elevates the risk of skiers suffering from traumatic injuries due to the combination of high speeds, intense external forces, and a competitive environment [2–4] that can increase the risk to the health, safety, and performance of athletes [5]. Hence, sportswear lies in its ability to fulfill various needs of athletes, including physical, psychological, biochemical, physiological, safety, performance, and ergonomic requirements [6]. The creation of personalized smart sportswear specifically tailored for athletes with unique requirements could potentially offer a groundbreaking solution in meeting their diverse needs. [7, 8].

Recent research has shown that wearable sensors in sportswear could help skiers by providing real-time data on their physical activity, such as heart rate, body temperature, and movement patterns. This information can be used to monitor performance, prevent injury, and optimize training programs [9, 10]. For example, real-time feedback on

C. Stephanidis et al. (Eds.): HCII 2023, CCIS 1835, pp. 655–663, 2023.
https://doi.org/10.1007/978-3-031-36001-5_84

physical status can be used to coach athletes in the appropriate way to train motor skills. Integrating multiple sensors into the fabric allows for instant analysis of vital signs in real-world situations and helps athletes improve their performance [11].

However, existing research has focused on applying smart sportswear to able-bodied athletes. Academics have neglected to explore research on smart sportswear for people with lower body impairments. Therefore, This study investigates the potential of incorporating sensors, electronic textiles, high-performance materials, and flexible designs into smart sportswear to address the needs and obstacles faced by sit skiers with lower body impairments, with a focus on enhancing their health, comfort, safety, and performance.

2 Literature Review

2.1 Human-Centered Design Approach

Human-centered design (HCD) is a design methodology that involves understanding the user's needs and preferences to create a functional and useable product by applying human factors/ergonomics and usability knowledge and techniques [12]. When it comes to smart sportswear designed for sit skiers, taking the HCD approach would entail conducting research on the unique requirements and difficulties experienced by sit skiers to create a product that provides to their individual needs [13–15]. By employing an HCD approach, a sit skier's experiences encompass the sportswear's effectiveness, comfort, safety, and the skiers' emotional contentment [16].

2.2 Research Considerations for Smart Sportswear for Sit Skiers

A sit skier is an athlete who participates in adaptive skiing, which is a type of skiing that is modified to accommodate individuals with disabilities. Sit skiing enables athletes with lower body impairments to participate in skiing, reaching high speeds and navigating challenging terrain with a high level of control [17]. The sport of sit skiing has evolved significantly over the years, with advances in technology and gear making the sport more accessible to a wider range of athletes [8].

Smart sportswear integrates sensors and other electronic components into clothing or accessories, enabling the monitoring and tracking of diverse aspects of the wearer's health and performance [18, 19]. These wearable sensors and electronic textiles can assist athletes in preventing risk and injury, measuring important health indicators, enhancing performance, powering team progress, forming interaction platforms, and providing real-time feedback [8, 20]. For example, sensors integrated into smart sportswear may aid in minimizing risks and preventing injuries [21]. Research shows that smart sportswear allows athletes to perform their sports unencumbered while physiological (heart rate, respiration), performance (posture, movement), and environmental (temperature, humidity) data are acquired in real-time [22]. This advantage is especially significant in extreme sports, where athletes often have to make quick decisions and perform acrobatic maneuvers in challenging environments, and any unforeseen obstacles or reactions could pose a significant risk to their safety [8]. Another example is electronic textiles, which could measure athletes' health indicators [23]. Due to disabled ski athletes suffering from acute or chronic injuries, which require continuous monitoring by health care personnel [24], electronic textiles, which measure body temperature, heart rate, blood pressure, and vital signs [11], can help to constantly understand the health status of the athlete [24]. Furthermore, because of the softness, comfort, and breathability of electronic textiles [11], they can be used as undergarments or base layers to improve the skiers' comfort [23].

2.3 Smart Sportswear for Sit Skiers in Scholarship

The versatility of smart sportswear has led to numerous proposed applications to improve training, recovery, and safety. According to the study [25], wearables providing real-time biofeedback can offer insights on enhancing movement and minimizing human errors. Also, the study [26] suggested that the integration of electronic textiles and smart sensors into fabrics has resulted in the development of intelligent clothing systems that can remotely monitor an individual's health. Moreover, the study [27] explains that sportswear can enhance an athlete's performance and provide the desired wearing comfort through the special features of high-performance fabrics. However, existing research on smart clothing has predominantly concentrated on developing sportswear for able-bodied athletes. Little research has been done to integrate smart sportswear with ergonomics to design sportswear for people with lower body impairments. To address the gap in the literature, the researchers developed the following research questions:

Research Question 1: What are the needs of smart sportswear for sit skiers?
Research Question 2: What are the difficulties and challenges that sit skiers face in smart sportswear?

3   Method

3.1 Interviewees Recruitment

Ethical approval was obtained from the university IRB prior to beginning recruitment or data collection. Researchers sent emails to eight international and national disability sports committees, providing information about the research project and recruiting sit skiers. Subsequently, six sit skiers expressed interest in the study. Ultimately, three sit skiers were interviewed based on the time available. One sit skier had spinal cord injury, another one had spina bifida, and the third one had spinal cord injury. In addition, the researchers contacted one designer and one manufacturer of sportswear for the athletes of the Chinese National Team for the 2022 Paralympic Winter Games in Beijing, to understand their challenges in meeting the sportswear needs and wants of sit skiers. They were interviewed separately, bringing the total number of interviewees to five.

3.2 Data Collection

The data for this study stems from three rounds of fieldwork. A variety of data-gathering methods were used, which ensured construct validity through triangulation of data [28].

First, the researchers went to the snow park and observed sit skier A for an hour to obtain field data on the skier's performance and challenges during sit ski training. A week later, the researchers interviewed sit skier A via video call.

Second, prior to interviewing the sit skiers, the researchers gathered available information from websites, promotional materials, news reports, and online videos from committees such as the International Paralympic Committee to collect secondary information about sit skiers and sportswear. This allowed the researcher to construct a basic framework for the needs of sit skiers' sportswear, providing further information to determine the role of smart sportswear in meeting the needs and challenges of sit skiers.

Third, to better understand the needs of smart sportswear for sit skiers (and the resulting challenges to develop it), the researchers conducted in-depth interviews with open-ended questions, and the five interviewees were asked to share their thoughts on smart sportswear and its effect on performance, comfort, safety, accessibility, and ergonomics. Each interview lasted approximately 45 to 60 min. After the interviews, the researchers compiled field notes from the recordings and emailed them to the interviewees for confirmation to ensure the accuracy of the transcripts. For questions requiring further clarification and confirmation, the researchers contacted the interviewees via email, telephone discussions, and instant messaging. Table 1 shows an overview of the completed data.

Table 1. Overview of the data

Interviewees	Category	Gender	Age	Country	Duration of the interview	Date
Sit Skier A	Spinal Cord Injury	Male	30	Dublin	60 min	February 2023
Sit Skier B	Spina Bifida	Male	42	United States	45 min	March 2023
Sit Skier C	Spinal Cord Injury	Male	25	United States	60 min	March 2023
Sit Skiwear designer	/	Female	/	China	45 min	January 2023
Sit Skiwear manufacturer	/	Female	/	China	60 min	March 2023

3.3 Data Analysis

This study followed the process of qualitative thematic analysis for analyzing the data. Thematic analysis is useful for summarizing key features of a large data set [29] and examining the interviewees' perspectives, identifying their similarities and differences and unanticipated insights [30]. The researchers analyzed the data by connecting interviewees' responses to questions exploring skiers' needs and challenges. After identifying initial themes, the researchers reviewed data for overlap within the themes and attempted to condense the data into themes that best reflect the totality of the data [31].

4 Findings

4.1 Research Question 1: Sit Skiers' Needs for Smart Sportswear

The researchers' analysis found that comfort was frequently mentioned as a priority for sit skiers when choosing smart sportswear. Interviewees generally agreed that comfort features are one of the most important factors when looking for skiwear. In addition, regarding the comfort category, interviewees said that some smart fabrics and the way ease of putting them on or taking off all let them feel comfortable. With regards to smart fabrics, the capacity to balance temperatures between the wearer's body and the surrounding environment is a crucial aspect. Given the cold conditions encountered while sit skiing and the dampness induced by sweating during training and exercise, the interviewees stressed the significance of waterproofing and insulation functions in smart sportswear. This is because if the skiers become wet or cold while skiing, it can hamper their training and risk their health. It is important to consider accessibility when developing sportswear for people with lower body impairments, especially when putting on and taking off items. Skiers with disabilities or mobility issues may have difficulty dressing independently. Therefore, they need to have their sportswear adapted for participation in skiing activities. For example, easy-to-use closures, fabrics with elasticity or stretch, front closure options, and adjustable sizing would be beneficial. Sit Skier B expressed that "not having seams or very flat seams in the bottom area of the ski pants" and "having a higher waist at the back" can be helpful and useful.

Second, interviewees generally agreed that different types of sensors would be beneficial for athletes in monitoring health, preventing risks, and improving training in real time. Smart sportswear has the potential to incorporate sensors capable of detecting diverse physiological signals, such as body temperature, blood pressure, heart rate, and more. This capability is particularly crucial for individuals with lower body impairments. In addition, since sit skiing is an extreme sport, athletes are exposed to risks during fast skiing and are prone to injuries. These technologies can provide real-time feedback for skiers' physical condition, which sit skier B said, "it is very useful and makes me feel safe." Also, the intricate terrain of a ski resort, including steep slopes and rocks, increases the risk of falls and collisions, which can result in severe injuries for sit skiers. For example, in the researcher's observation of sit skier A's one-hour training, when sit skier A was accompanied by his coach to take the magic carpet (incline ramp or conveyor belt that assists sit skiers up the slope), he lost his balance and fell into the gap between the magic carpet and the snowfield due to his body imbalance. However, the magic carpet was still in progress, did not stop (Fig. 1). The hazardous situation continued for approximately 30 s, as the control room (staff member responsible for managing the incline conveyor belt) was unable to promptly determine the skier's predicament. After the training, the researcher asked sit skier A what considerations he had when he was falling. He mentioned that "I hope the control room can notice me in time, or there are some safety protection gears available." In this case, when he falls, it would be better if the signal was transmitted to the control room in time so that the control room can stop the magic carpet the first time to prevent risk. Moreover, sit skier A mentioned that "if the sportswear can have a function like an airbag, that means when I am about to fall, the sportswear can eject an airbag, that is also a great protection way."

Fig. 1. Sit Skier A Fell in the Gap Between the Magic Carpet and the Snowfield

In addition, interviewees expect that smart sportswear can help athletes to improve teams' performance as well. Smart sportswear can collect and analyze an athlete's physical data continuously, generating large metrics that coaches can use to design training programs and make informed decisions.

Finally, the interviewees suggested that the smart sportswear platform should integrate multiple functions such as real-time health monitoring, injury prevention, and performance improvement in a single garment. Smart sportswear with comprehensive functions is valuable when it combines comfort, mobility, accessibility, and timely health, safety, and training instructions. Smart clothing with integrated features can boost skiers' confidence while skiing. Additionally, smart sportswear has the potential to drive technological advancements that enable communication between the garment and control rooms in real-time, ultimately maximizing the safety of athletes on the ski slopes.

4.2 Research Question 2: Difficulties and Challenges in Smart Sportswear for Sit Skiers

Smart sportswear and wearable sensors have the potential to significantly improve the performance and safety of sit skiers. However, there are several difficulties and challenges that must be addressed to realize the full potential of these technologies.

The first is the complexity of the sport. Sit skiing involves a wide range of movements and requires athletes to adjust their body position and weight distribution in response to changing terrain. This complexity presents a challenge in developing smart sportswear that can effectively monitor and respond to the athlete's movements.

Second, developing smart sportswear can be expensive, particularly when incorporating advanced sensors and electronics. This cost may be prohibitive for some athletes, which could limit the adoption of the technology.

Third, it is difficult to balance comfort and usability. Smart sportswear for sit skiers must be comfortable and easy to use. However, skiers are often required to wear multiple layers of clothing to stay warm, which can make it difficult to incorporate smart technology into their clothing without compromising comfort or usability. Finally, there is the issue of data security and privacy. The use of wearable sensors in smart clothing can result in the generation of a substantial amount of personal data, posing significant challenges in terms of data security and privacy for athletes and teams.

Overall, the development and adoption of smart sportswear and wearable sensors for sit skiers requires a multidisciplinary approach to address technical, social, and economic challenges. Addressing these challenges will require collaboration between athletes, coaches, engineers, the apparel industry, and other stakeholders in the sports industry.

5 Significance and Limitations

The significance of research on smart sportswear for sit skiers lies in its potential to improve the performance, safety, and accessibility of sit skiing. Smart sportswear can provide real-time feedback and information to sit skiers, helping them to optimize their technique, avoid injury, and improve their overall performance. It can also provide additional safety features, such as crash detection and emergency notifications, which can be especially important for sit skiers who may be at a higher risk of injury.

However, several limitations exist in developing and integrating smart sportswear for sit skiers. These limitations include a lack of available data on sit skiers and their movements, limited opportunities for testing due to the need for specialized equipment and environments, and the high cost of technology development and integration into sportswear. Additionally, smart sportswear requires regular maintenance and may need to integrate with other technologies, which can present further challenges. Addressing these limitations is important to ensure that smart sportswear for sit skiers is effective, safe, and accessible. More research is needed to gather data on sit skiers and their movements, as well as to develop and test smart sportswear in real-world conditions. The cost of smart sportswear also needs to be addressed to ensure that it is affordable and accessible to all sit skiers. Finally, design and development must consider the maintenance and integration challenges of smart sportswear to ensure that it is practical and usable in a real-world setting.

References

1. Tweedy, S.M., Beckman, E.M., Connick, M.J.: Paralympic classification: conceptual basis, current methods, and research update. PM&R **6**, S11–S17 (2014)
2. Flørenes, T.W., Bere, T., Nordsletten, L., Heir, S., Bahr, R.: Injuries among male and female World Cup alpine skiers. Br. J. Sports Med. **43**(13), 973–978 (2009)

3. Flørenes, T.W., Nordsletten, L., Heir, S., Bahr, R.: Injuries among World Cup ski and snowboard athletes. Scand. J. Med. Sci. Sports **22**(1), 58–66 (2012)

4. Pujol, N., Rousseaux Blanchi, M.P., Chambat, P.: The incidence of anterior cruciate ligament injuries among competitive Alpine skiers: a 25-year investigation. Am. J. Sports Med. **35**(7), 1070–1074 (2007)

5. Jordan, M.J., Aagaard, P., Herzog, W.: Anterior cruciate ligament injury/reinjury in alpine ski racing: a narrative review. Open Access J. Sports Med. 71–83 (2017)

6. Damuluri, R., Babel, S.: Review of functional and protective clothing for sports. Network **8**, 9 (2023)

7. Haladjian, J., Reif, M., Brügge, B.: VIHapp: a wearable system to support blind skiing. In: Proceedings of the 2017 ACM International Joint Conference on Pervasive and Ubiquitous Computing and Proceedings of the 2017 ACM International Symposium on Wearable Computers, pp. 1033–1037 (2017)

8. Allen, T., Shepherd, J., Wood, J., Tyler, D., Duncan, O.: Wearables for disabled and extreme sports. In: Digital Health, pp. 253–273. Academic Press (2021)

9. Tang, S.L.P.: Wearable sensors for sports performance. In: Textiles for Sportswear, pp. 169–196. Woodhead Publishing (2015)

10. Syduzzaman, M.D., Patwary, S.U., Farhana, K., Ahmed, S.: Smart textiles and nanotechnology: a general overview. J. Text. Sci. Eng **5**(1), 1–7 (2015)

11. Memarian, F., Rahmani, S., Yousefzadeh, M., Latifi, M.: Wearable technologies in sportswear. In: Materials in Sports Equipment, pp. 123–160. Woodhead Publishing (2019)

12. IS09241-11: Ergonomic requirements for office work with visual display terminals (VDTs) Part 11: Guidance on Usability. ISO (1998)

13. Gasson, S.: Human-centered vs. user-centered approaches to information system design. J. Inf. Technol. Appl. (JITTA) **5**(2), 29–46 (2003)

14. Boy, G.A.: The Handbook of Human-Machine Interaction. A Human-Centered Design Approach. Ashgate, Farnham (2011)

15. IS09241-21O, Ergonomics of human-system interaction - Part 210: Human-centered design for interactive systems. ISO (2010)

16. Kuniavsky, M.: Smart things: ubiquitous computing user experience design. Elsevier, Burlington (2010)

17. Gastaldi, L., Pastorelli, S., Frassinelli, S.: A biomechanical approach to paralympic cross-country sit-ski racing. Clin. J. Sport Med. **22**(1), 58–64 (2012)

18. Yanfen, L., Pu, H.: Smart sportswear. In: 2011 International Conference on Future Computer Science and Education, pp. 135–138. IEEE (2011)

19. Keogh, J.W.: Paralympic sport: an emerging area for research and consultancy in sports biomechanics. Sports Biomech. **10**(3), 234–253 (2011)

20. McCann, J., Bryson, D.: Smart Clothes and Wearable Technology. Woodhead Publishing (2022)

21. Bere, T., Bahr, R.: Injury prevention advances in alpine ski racing: harnessing collaboration with the International Ski Federation (FIS), long-term surveillance and digital technology to benefit athletes. Br. J. Sports Med. **48**(9), 738 (2014)

22. Scataglini, S., Moorhead, A.P., Feletti, F.: A systematic review of smart clothing in sports: possible applications to extreme sports. Muscles Ligaments Tendons J. (MLTJ) **10**(2) (2020)

23. McCann, J.: Environmentally conscious fabric selection in sportswear design. In: Textiles for Sportswear, pp. 17–52. Woodhead Publishing (2015)

24. Gilgien, M., Reid, R., Raschner, C., Supej, M., Holmberg, H.C.: The training of Olympic alpine ski racers. Front. Physiol. **9**, 1772 (2018)

25. Lam Po Tang, S.: Wearable sensors for sports performance. In: Textiles for Sportswear, pp. 169–196 (2015). https://doi.org/10.1016/b978-1-78242-229-7.00008-4

26. Ahsan, M., Teay, S.H., Sayem, A.S.M., Albarbar, A.: Smart clothing framework for health monitoring applications. Signals **3**(1), 113–145 (2022)
27. Manshahia, M., Das, A., Alagirusamy, R.: Smart coatings for sportswear. In: Active Coatings for Smart Textiles, pp. 355–374 (2016)
28. Golafshani, N.: Understanding reliability and validity in qualitative research. Qual. Rep. **8**(4), 597–607 (2003)
29. King, N.: 21—using templates in the thematic analysis of text—. In: Essential Guide to Qualitative Methods in Organizational Research, vol. 256 (2004)
30. Braun, V., Clarke, V.: Using thematic analysis in psychology. Qual. Res. Psychol. **3**(2), 77–101 (2006)
31. Wimmer, R.D., Dominick, J.R.: Mass media research. Cengage Learning (2013)

Research on Innovation of Jewelry Display Design Mode Based on Virtual Reality Technology

Ziqiong Yang[1], Rui Xu[1,2(✉)], and Jinmeng Zhang[1]

[1] School of Art and Design, Fuzhou University of Foreign Languages and Trade, Fuzhou 350200, China
635524937@qq.com
[2] The Graduate Institute of Design Science, Tatung University, Taipei 104, Taiwan

Abstract. In modern society, with the development of science and technology and the emergence of various innovative products, people are no longer limited to the feelings brought by ordinary display forms. Publish posters, newspaper static display, window static display, star endorsement dynamic display, network dynamic special effects display, and multimedia dynamic demonstration to convey the design concept and significance of new products. The traditional display design mode and display means have become the resistance to the development of jewelry industry [1].

The research method of this paper: This paper attempts to overcome some disadvantages of the current traditional lacquer jewelry display in the modern and contemporary digital design, ① Use the case analysis method to take the lacquer jewelry display design as the main research object, and investigate the application of virtual reality technology in the market ② The advantages and significance of the application of virtual reality technology in jewelry display are obtained by analyzing the application of virtual reality technology in jewelry display design. ③ On the basis of virtual reality technology, a virtual display design mode is proposed, and it is applied to the display of lacquer jewelry by analyzing the shape, matching method, and wearing effect of lacquer jewelry in advance. This article will also analyze the framework of the system to create a virtual visual model of lacquer jewelry by using modern modeling and engraving software and 3D network technology, and put forward ideas for the display design and display of lacquer jewelry, and propose a visual and dynamic model for people. How lacquer jewelry is displayed.

Keywords: Virtual reality technology · Virtual display system · Immersive interaction

1 The Main Purpose and Results of the Study

Jewelry is a kind of jewelry that can carry people's perception and thoughts, and has its unique symbolism. In daily life, people will choose jewelry according to their favorite style and mood. With the change of technology in our country, people's insight, perception, understanding and experience of real objects have changed, and they are no longer

C. Stephanidis et al. (Eds.): HCII 2023, CCIS 1835, pp. 664–670, 2023.
https://doi.org/10.1007/978-3-031-36001-5_85

simply satisfied with the status quo. The existing display methods can no longer meet people's needs for the whole process of jewelry from design to display. Thomas Michel pointed out that the previous visual culture has departed from the language-centered rationalism and increasingly turned to the image-centered, especially the image-centered perceptualism [2]. For jewelry designers to display their works after incubation, the more difficult things for designers are: 1. Use limited manpower, material resources and technology to maximize the beauty of the designed products. 2. The promotion of jewelry design is a big problem. The products designed by jewelry designers need to quickly attract consumers through special product experience when consumers buy them in online flagship stores or offline specialty stores, so as to increase product sales. 3. The designed products should be advanced and realistic at the same time, in line with contemporary fashion trends. According to the above research, the purpose of this paper is: 1. Using virtual reality technology to study the system framework of lacquer jewelry display design as a starting point, the obtained system framework can be used in lacquer jewelry display design and as a new type of e-commerce platform to obtain user needs medium. 2. To enhance the domestic design community's understanding of lacquer and lacquer craftsmanship, which is conducive to the cultural dissemination of lacquer, and to promote the research and application of the combination of lacquer jewelry display and virtual reality technology. The results of this study: Through the previous research and related experiments, the results show that jewelry display on the market plays a very important role in promotion, scene construction, cultural and design thought dissemination, product experience and final sales process. Conferences, exhibitions, and exclusive stores all pay great attention to the design and innovation of jewelry display. The framework of this lacquer display design system can be used in jewelry display in the future, helping designers find the entry point so that virtual reality technology can be integrated and used in design. The innovative virtual reality display system will help jewelry break free from the original display restrictions. As a carrier, virtual reality technology can better promote this Chinese intangible cultural heritage to people, and to a certain extent, it can improve the economic and social benefits of lacquer jewelry. Therefore, this article will take lacquer jewelry as an example to illustrate the promotion of the application of virtual reality technology in lacquer jewelry display to the design and display of lacquer jewelry.

2 Theoretical Basis

2.1 Overview of Virtual Reality Technology

In the 20th century, the emergence of virtual reality technology can solve this big problem. It breaks the limitations caused by external factors in reality and makes intangible cultural heritage more possibilities. Virtual reality technology (English name: Virtual Reality, abbreviated as: VR) is a technology involving computer graphics, artificial intelligence technology, simulation technology, human-computer interaction technology and other fields. A brand-new practical technology developed [3]. The so-called analysis from a narrow perspective can divide virtual reality technology into four categories: desktop VR systems, immersive VR systems, enhanced VR systems, and distributed VR systems [4]. From a broad perspective, it is to use 3D software or 3D information to construct a space that allows people to operate conveniently, bringing users an immersive experience, breaking the scale of the original object, and interpreting the object itself with a new visual experience to re-establish the relationship between objects and people, it can also be called a virtual reality system.

2.2 The Application of Virtual Reality Technology in the Field of Jewelry Design Display

BAVLO jewelry virtual reality JVR was officially released in 2016. It is based on binocular stereo vision, and what you see is real three-dimensional jewelry, just like a 3D movie, and the picture can be carried out with the head movement. People can switch and interact according to their own preferences. This system is directly connected to Baolong's style library. In this way, you can complete style selection, DIY virtual try-on, and match at any time.

Fig. 1. Virtual Jewelry Display of Baolong JVR System

2.3 The Necessity and Advantages of Applying Virtual Reality Technology to the Display Design of Lacquer Jewelry

The emergence of virtual reality technology is a communication bridge between carbon-based space (reality) and silicon-based space (virtual), which can restore the real objects in carbon-based space with high precision and high precision. It was first proposed by Palmer Lackey, which greatly broadened the field of people's exploration of reality and virtuality. Designers apply virtual reality technology to jewelry display design based on people's physiological and psychological characteristics such as vision and hearing, combined with 3D modeling image generation technology, multi-sensor interaction technology and high-resolution reality technology, opening up different possibilities for jewelry designers. The traditional immersive path to display design.

In the past, jewelry designers had to go through concept transformation first, and then carry out a long process of physical production experiments. They could only imagine the final effect of this work with imagery. The disadvantage of this is that it will consume a lot of manpower and material resources and the final product may be unsatisfactory, the construction period is long, and the time cost is high.

Therefore, the necessity of applying it to the display design of lacquer jewelry is mainly reflected in: ① The designer first defines the problem and then transforms the market demand, and the concept extraction is simpler and more efficient; ② Output the image for sketching; The object image construction is combined with the written program to try more possibilities, which can save materials and manpower, improve the success rate of jewelry designer design, use 3D object image construction to make optimization plans and decision analysis in advance, so as to avoid waste of materials and time, and reduce (Fig. 1) ④ put the designed jewelry into the market, and obtain user feedback through the immersive experience of consumers (virtual try-on, DIY customized lacquer jewelry, making the overall decoration style of the specialty store more distinctive) and purchase. Improve ⑤ to carry out the design of the exhibition space, which greatly provides people with a better visual experience and visual image sense. ⑥ A brand-specific online interactive platform can be set up to showcase the uniqueness of the product. After opening, merchants of related products can settle in later, making the communication between merchants and consumers more convenient and smarter, and it can also increase the sales of jewelry. The advantages are: ① Stronger sense of substitution. The use of virtual reality technology can better convey the design concept of jewelry designers, and let people experience the product's shape, proportion, and simulated usage scenarios and wearing effects most directly from the visual and auditory perspectives of the five senses., with sound effects (you can find suitable sound effects through the idea that the product wants to convey, so that the scene is more immersive), bringing users an immersive experience. ② Strong inclusiveness, which can contribute to the promotion, continuation and progress of traditional culture or intangible cultural heritage. The virtual image presented is actually the real image of jewelry. ③ Make it easier for consumers to remember the brand. The unique experience method and the exquisite online interactive system can make the brand it acts on more deeply in the minds of consumers (Fig. 2).

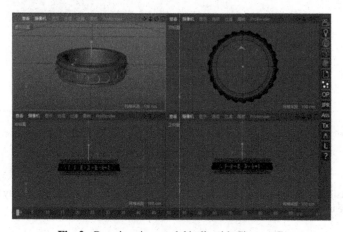

Fig. 2. Rotating ring model built with Cinema4D

2.4 Feasibility Analysis of the Application System of Virtual Reality Technology in the Display of Lacquer Jewelry

New technologies is complementary to contemporary art - for example: lacquer craft. The lacquer used in the lacquer craft, also known as natural lacquer, is a milky gray secreted from the lacquer tree. It will oxidize and mature into a brown viscous liquid when exposed to air. The lacquer craft, an ancient traditional technique, has a profound cultural heritage. Creators often use homemade hairbrushes, oil brushes and other materials to paint, and combine techniques such as splashing paint, twisting, and layering to create. The lacquer itself, including the lacquer jewelry made, has the characteristics of anti-corrosion, waterproof, moisture resistance, wear resistance, insulation, anti-boiling water, acid resistance, alkali resistance, environmental protection, and non-toxic characteristics, and the finished product will not cause allergies to users. Nowadays, in order to better adapt to the young people's market, the designer has innovated the production process, adding silver wire, mother-of-pearl, and opal to the design, after polishing and polishing, and then using cooking oil and flour after repeated kneading, it will Gives off a pleasing glow. Make lacquer jewelry from handicraft to product, and gradually enter the vision of young people. Most of the lacquer jewelry on the market is sold offline, and most of them use static pictures and texts as promotional posters and WeChat group chats to promote online. The traditional marketing methods prevent people from knowing the materials and product details intuitively. It further restricts the cultural transmission of lacquer, an intangible cultural heritage, and limits the development of its market.

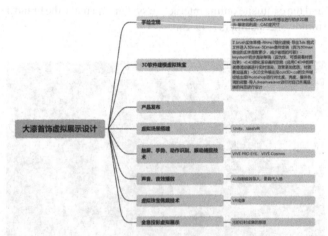

Fig. 3. Feasibility analysis: the technologies required for the lacquer jewelry display system and the software used for the corresponding technologies

3   Design System for Virtual Display of Lacquer Jewelry

First use Rhino7 for preliminary modeling (as shown in Fig. 3). The designer uses 3D software to create ideas according to the concept transformation, and uses the different visual feelings presented by modeling to enrich the shape and texture of objects and realize geometric, organic and The effect of digitization is presented. Rhino can cut the target object at the fastest speed to show its effect (Figs. 4, 5 and 6).

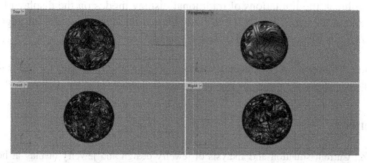

Fig. 4. Use Rhino7 to refine the modeling and take paint beads as an example

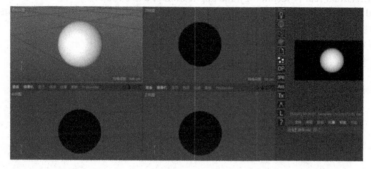

Fig. 5. The final version can be modeled in Cinema 4D (also available in 3Dmax)

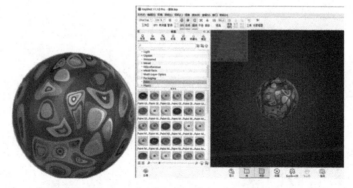

Fig. 6. Render using keyshot11 to render faster, and the Arnold renderer of Cinema 4D can be used for high precision

4 Conclusion

Virtual reality technology recreates the beauty of lacquer jewelry in a narrative field, which can break the limitations of traditional display modes on the display of lacquer jewelry, and at the same time make technology and intangible cultural heritage and its related art fields Fusion produced different sparks.

Fund Name. Campus level longitudinal research project topic "Promoting the fusion design of traditional lacquer and jewelry in the process of sublation and inheritance" (FWXXS21126).

References

1. Wei, Z.: Current situation and analysis of jewelry design and jewelry display at home and abroad
2. Erli, Z.: Michel's "image turn" theoretical analysis. Lit. Art Res. 1, 30–38 (2012)
3. Hu, X.: Virtual reality technology and application practice (2004)
4. Visual touch out of "real"—Exploring a new mode of artistic jewelry creation in digital virtual space

Interactive Design of Children's Creative Furniture in Urban Community Space

Dingwei Zhang⑩, Tanghao Gao⑩, Jingwen Tian⑩, and Hongtao Zhou⁽✉⁾⑩

College of Design and Innovation, Tongji University, Shanghai, China
zhangdingwei@tongji.edu.cn, lifeisfurniture@gmail.com

Abstract. Children's creative furniture intervention in urban space, the development of society and the active exploration and research on the functionality of urban space presenting a diversified urban development model and actively creating a child-friendly city is a typical urban development sample. It can solve the counting problems of functional failure and demand misalignment of child-friendly urban public space, re-examine the inclusiveness and diversity of urban neighbourhood space, create a child-friendly city, drive social power, realize children's design dreams in a new mode, and construct a child-friendly future community. The design team conducted joint workshops and children's furniture creative curriculum design for social experiments in conjunction with Fengjiao Yuan Primary School. Using the streets of Fengpu District in Shanghai as the research site, the team conducted a creative activity of localization and creative storm translation, exploring the localization and inclusiveness of urban space and residents through children's creativity and activating the vitality of urban community space. The four-dimensional social innovation model of participation in learning - participation in design - participation in construction - participation in maintenance is constructed to explore the role of children's creative furniture in the process of urban renewal and the research path. A series of children's creative furniture design activities realize children's participation in urban construction in the form of urban masters, and creativity and imagination add vitality and temperature to the city. Creative design from children's perspective is an effective methodological strategy for empowering and reshaping community space. Children's innovative furniture design provides a rich spatial experience design, allowing residents to feel the effect of spatial expansion and improve the inclusiveness, interactivity and entertainment experience of urban community space. The in-depth exploration of spatial resources of urban neighbourhoods and urban furniture design needs, adhering to the innovative development model of adapting to local conditions and designing for needs, provides design ideas and empirical references for the development of the functional expansion of urban community space.

Keywords: Interaction Design · Creative Furniture for Children · Urban Community Space · User Experience · Innovative Design

C. Stephanidis et al. (Eds.): HCII 2023, CCIS 1835, pp. 671–677, 2023.
https://doi.org/10.1007/978-3-031-36001-5_86

1 Introduction

With the development of society and active exploration and research on the functionality of urban space, diversified urban development models are presented, and actively creating child-friendly cities is a typical urban development sample. Actively advocating the principle of child-first design, expanding the space for children's growth, building an urban spatial environment suitable for children's healthy physical and mental development, detailed in every aspect of urban construction, and looking at a different urban landscape from a one-meter-high perspective. A child-friendly city must have the full participation of children, listen to their voices, let them become the little masters of the town, and add vitality and temperature to the city with the creativity and imagination of children.

Urban community public space is an important field for exploring spatial environment design research for children's growth. Community creation is an essential theme for urban space construction, especially for urban public space construction in the context of the new crown epidemic. Community space upgrading is used to enhance the resilience, adaptability and inclusiveness of community public space and to explore community micro-renewal design strategies that are creative, childlike, and at the same time scalable. The project seeks to shape community space from children's perspective, stimulate children's sense of ownership, cultivate children's artistic creativity, explore social innovation models, drive social crowdfunding, guide industrial co-build, and help children's dreams come true.

2 Content

2.1 Urban Furniture Design Issues

Seating is the micro-facility that can best reflect the temperature of a city and carries the city's care for its citizens. "Urban elements", "street furniture", "urban components", and "pedestrian street furniture"......, since its appearance in the 1960s, urban furniture has been called by different names in different countries [1]. With the rapid development of the urban process, the current urban furniture design suffers from two extreme criticisms. The plan pursues the use of function too much, and the form could be more exciting, or the form is pursued obsessively, and the functional effect is lost. The architect Wright advocates the dialectical unity of function and form rather than having to sacrifice the other for the sake of one at the expense of the other. In addition, contemporary urban furniture design elements are scattered and inconsistent with the surrounding environment, resulting in a lack of human and cultural characteristics and a lack of innovative interaction and social participation of children. Urban furniture is one of the constituent elements of urban space, and humanized, interesting and interactive urban furniture plays an essential role in creating a healthy and livable city.

2.2 Children's Creative Furniture Design in Urban Neighbourhoods

As the carrier of children's inner creative ideas and unique elements of creative urban renewal construction, children's innovative furniture should maintain and present children's innocence, simplicity, imagination and expectation. As designers, parents and social forces, we must explore the relationship between urban creative transformation development and children's healthy growth. Children's creative ideas should be felt and experienced, and children's emotional needs must be considered in place. Emotional engineering design is the core content of the current design field, Professor Donad·A·Norman of the United States divides emotional design into three levels [2]: the instinctive level that focuses on visual observation and understanding of the design appearance; the behavioural level that focuses on the pleasure and utility of the user's use; and the reflective level that a design changes and recalls the user's self-image. Emotional design can close the emotional distance between design and users, and creative design based on human instinct, behaviour and reflection will create a pleasant, warm emotional experience for users.

2.3 Design Case

The project is an experimental project of children's creative practice between Tongji University designers and Shanghai Fengjiao Yuan Primary School, jointly promoting the construction of micro-renewal of urban communities with well-known social enterprise units. Taking urban children's furniture design activities as a touch point, the idea of children's creative furniture is realized gradually from point to line and from line to surface. The team focuses on tapping the actual needs of community residents for street furniture and expands the depth of the project based on the children's creative practice project. At the end of 2021 and the beginning of 2022, the "100 Chairs Building Dreams" activity was held in Fengxian District, Shanghai, which is an inclusive child-friendly urban neighbourhood creation activity with children as the main body and designers and residents working together, fully respecting the needs of different groups and constructing a learning-involvement-design-involvement-build-involvement-maintenance system. It is a multi-dimensional social innovation model of participation in learning - participation in design - participation in construction - participation in maintenance, and it explores the role and research path of creative furniture in the process of urban neighbourhood renewal.

Practice Path

(1) *Pre-planning and design selection*

The "Hundred Chairs for Building Dreams" activity was themed on children's creative seats. First of all, Tongji University, Fengpu Street, Clover Hall, and Fengjiuyuan Elementary School, together with local enterprises, concentrated human resources on the streets and schools to carry out project planning and promotion activities for several hundred children and families. Secondly, a chair creative design competition, "Chair by Dream, Foresee the Future", was held to collect creative design concept works for public furniture in urban neighborhoods. Through several sessions of creative workshops between young designers and children from local primary and secondary schools and communities, thousands of creative chair designs were collected. The designers then categorized and selected the seating designs, digitally organized them, and assembled them into a booklet to hold displays, presentations, and exhibitions for the art and creativity of the children in Fengpu District in their communities and schools (Fig. 1).

Innocent children have extraordinary imagination and creativity that adults do not have, producing a batch of works that are full of novelty and fun but not lacking in practicality [3]. Some of the excellent chair designs will be integrated into the streets and alleys of Fengpu Street, community shopping malls and schools to truly convey the "temperature" of the chair. Among them, the design works such as "Little Wooden Horse" painted by Hu Youti, a first-grader of Fengjiu Academy Annex Primary School, "Caterpillar" by Xu Qiang, a sanitation worker, and "Smiling City" designed by Xi Wangqi, a student, was all well received by everyone.

Fig. 1. Chair Creative Design Competition Design Selection and Arrangement

(2) *Design transformation*

The designer team further selected typical children's creative seats with expandable cases and worked with the children to deepen the design and optimize the children's creative ideas in the form of 3D modelling. While keeping the children's simple ideas, the children's seats were designed and created with the possibility of practical operation. The artistic dreams of children, sanitation workers, construction workers, delivery boys and other types of people were transformed from two-dimensional drawings into three community public artworks (Fig. 2).

Some children participated as little community planners; some students drew their own works through their understanding of the city and life; children of different ages and citizens participated in the public art process, combining the warm seats with actual needs. Student Hu Youti said, "Because my zodiac sign is the horse, I painted a wooden horse seat, 'horse' means success in Chinese proverbs".

(3) *Art exhibition activities*

By taking the initiative to optimize the design, our team tried to conduct local corporate crowdfunding, combining children's dreams with street visions, convening design and manufacturing power to transform children's artistic dreams from two-dimensional drawings into three community public artworks, and landing the first batch of children's creative seats. At the same time, online crowdfunding is opened to allow more caring people and public welfare projects to be funded by the community. Let the transformation of urban children's dynamic space and urban industry combine to introduce social resources to help realize children's design dreams. On October 31, 2021, more than 100

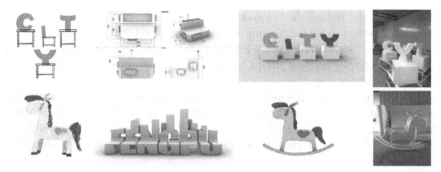

Fig. 2. From left to right, the child seat design, 3D modelling, effect drawing and physical production respectively

children's creative seats with urban temperature were presented at Fengpu Xiangyuan Downton Abbey (England Little Theatre), and thousands of whimsical seat designs were partially realized out (Fig. 3). Fengxian children have an unprecedented sense of pride and belonging, and the project urgently needs to get more children's creativity off the ground and create children's own creative neighbourhood.

Fig. 3. "100 Chairs Building Dreams" activity poster and activity site

(4) *Children's seat drifting touring activities*

After the end of the 100 chairs building dreams to action, the excellent creative seat furniture works for the follow-up funding activities and excellent children's creative seats for the second phase of community drifting activities. Eight groups of representative creative seats were selected to enter the Hanchun Road floating exhibition, with new wall painting scenarios suitable for children's seats (Fig. 4) to enhance the immersion of children's dreams, immersive experience of the fantasy reality of childhood, making the seats situational, and turning the street into a children's seat paradise. The "pony chair" brings happiness to those who ride it and also implies success. The wall painting is full of children's memory elements, such as the carousel, children's slide, Ferris wheel, and circus performance are all images of children's imagination for a better life; the starry sky behind the "Moon Chair" expresses the desire for a better future with Van Gogh's "starry sky" style. Behind the "Flower Bed Chair" is the growth of everything, with the scene of flowers lining the painting and the Fengpu seat behind the Fengxian Youth Activity Center "Sea Flower" and the Fengpu Four Seasons Ecological Park "Downton Abbey" characteristic building groups, representing the new city of Fengpu District and the future of Fengpu (Fig. 5).

This Children in Seats community drifting activity is an effective attempt at urban micro-renewal. By means of online crowdfunding, other suitable children's creative furniture designs will continue to be selected for subsequent implantation into different urban neighborhood public spaces to explore the path of furniture design in urban spaces.

Fig. 4. Children's seat Hanchun Road drifting program effects

Fig. 5. The second phase of the 100 chairs exhibition activities - creative seat community drifting activities real scene

3   Conclusion

This collaborative co-creation of participatory creative seating design activities, looking at community space renewal from a child's perspective, inspired residents to actively participate in innovation and human needs were respected. October 2021, the team planned the 100 Chairs Art Exhibition in Fengxian Fengpu Four Seasons Ecological Park in Shanghai, a large-scale children's urban seating collection, an exhibition designed to stimulate the creativity of Fengpu children, as well as the later community drift. Bringing social power to realize children's design dreams in a new mode and constructing a child-friendly community of the future.

In the new era, especially in the context of the epidemic, the importance of community is highlighted, and the diversity of forms of community renewal is explored. And the way of children's creative perspective has great potential, and children become one of the best links among many elements. Through the creative design activities of children's creative furniture implanted in the community environment, interactive urban street furniture can better elicit mutual communication among residents and provide a rich spatial experience design. Children's creative design is a new perspective and an effective methodological strategy for reshaping the environment of old communities [4].

Children's creative furniture attaches importance to the interactive experience, which can also enhance the interactive experience between people and people, people and urban street furniture, and people and living environment [5].

Acknowledgments. We would like to thank Shanghai Fengpu Street and Tongji University and Creative Experimental Teaching Center, the public welfare organization Clover Hall and other participating organizations for their support, as well as all participants. We also thank Professor Zhou Hongtao and the students for their guidance and help writing the thesis.

References

1. Bao, S.D., Shi, H.: A study on the theory of urban furniture in China. Decoration **07**, 12–16 (2019)
2. Norman, D.A.: Design Psychology 3: Emotional Design. M. Translated by He X.M, Ou Q.X. CITIC Press, Beijing(2012)
3. Zhou, X.M.: Research on creative and interesting furniture design. Packag. Eng. **02**, 242–244 (2018)
4. Han, B., Dai, M.L.: Optimization of urban community play space based on children's perspective. Shaanxi Preschool Teachers Coll. **02**, 44–51 (2022)
5. Lin, D.: Parent-child furniture interaction experience design. Ind. Des. **07**, 139–140 (2018)

Research on Interactive Packaging Design Based on User's Emotional Experience

Dingwei Zhang⃝, Jingwen Tian⃝, and Hongtao Zhou(✉)⃝

College of Design and Innovation, Tongji University, Shanghai, China
zhangdingwei@tongji.edu.cn, lifeisfurniture@gmail.com

Abstract. The innovative application of intelligent interaction technology based on user experience in modern packaging design improves the interaction between consumers and packaging to achieve a more interesting and intelligent packaging innovation design, thus improving human consciousness and consumer experience. Taking the user's emotional experience as the research perspective and interactive packaging as the research object, the three levels of emotional Through the analysis of interactive application design scenarios of packaging, we explore the interactivity, sharing and sustainability of intelligent interaction in modern packaging design, analyze the interaction design experience of packaging at different levels, and highlight the human-oriented design concept of smart packaging. Novel packaging materials, avant-garde design concepts and advanced intelligent interaction technologies can not only ensure the essential functions of modern packaging but also enhance the interactive experience between consumers and creative packaging and meet or even stimulate consumers' deep-seated emotional needs and experience consumption patterns. Designers always need to keep their sensitivity to design. With the user as the core and the integration of modern intelligent technology, they can realize the upgrade of consumers' emotional demands and interactive experience of contemporary packaging and explore the multiple possibilities of interactive packaging design based on emotional experience.

Keywords: Emotional Experience · Intelligent Interaction · Packaging Design · Experience Design

1 Introduction

New technological materials such as the Internet of Things and 3D printing have enabled modern packaging design to achieve innovative development. People's demand and concern for product packaging have gradually shifted from the material layer to the spiritual and emotional level. People are willing to engage and interact with the packaging [1]. The protection, transportation and storage functions can no longer meet people's demands for packaging. The improvement of packaging technology, the progress of intelligent technology, and the emergence of new materials have provided the possibility for packaging innovation. The Internet of Things, information technology and other elements are changing consumers' aesthetics of packaging, operators' marketing concepts and

© The Author(s), under exclusive license to Springer Nature Switzerland AG 2023
C. Stephanidis et al. (Eds.): HCII 2023, CCIS 1835, pp. 678–686, 2023.
https://doi.org/10.1007/978-3-031-36001-5_87

designers' perception of packaging design. In particular, the packaging we come into contact with every day not only has the function of transportation and protection but also is the object of emotional interaction with consumers in the pursuit of quality of life. The packaging design should reflect humanistic care, meet people's emotional needs, and combine marketing, consumer psychology, technical aesthetics, and other scientific content [2].

2 Emotional Design of Packaging

Emotional design is a human-centred design that takes the user's emotional experience as the main content. Packaging design, if only the function and appearance of the design, can no longer meet the needs of consumers. The user's emotional demands must be recognized and satisfied, and emotional design has become the core of the design field. American Professor Donald-A-Norman divided expressive design into three levels [3]: instinctive level, which mainly refers to human observation and understanding of product appearance from instinct; behavioural level, the user's pleasure and utility when using, function, ease of reading, usability and feel are the four main aspects of the behavioural level; reflective level, the design of the user's self-image change, personal satisfaction in a particular part and recollection. This level is related to the customer's long-term feelings and the need to establish the brand's or product's long-term value. I don't care what the designs look like. I only care about the emotions they inspire in the user," says designer Philippe Starck. Starck believes that in design, one should pour all the designer's experiences and feelings into one thing - design should not be understood, but felt and experienced!" [4]. The three levels of emotionality theory are used to analyze and explore the user's emotional experience path for interactive packaging. From visual, tactile, and gustatory experiences to analyse of the user's perceptual characteristics to elucidate the user's emotional experience influences the user's purchase intention. Explore the real needs that can meet both the psychological changes of consumers and the new forms of intelligent product packaging design nowadays.

3 Intelligent Interactive Design of Packaging

3.1 Intelligent Interactive Packaging Design

Intelligent technology is a critical element of emotional experience design. Intelligent interaction technology is the process of exchanging specific information between humans and computers. Intelligent interaction design is the study of product function, interaction behaviour and "external product visual design" to serve the user's needs [5]. In packaging design, circulation and use, an interactive communication relationship is established between the product, the producer and the consumer, making the packaging more human, intelligent and emotional. The "emotional interaction" of packaging design refers to the interactive communication behaviour of consumers when contacting the packaging [6].Intelligent interactive packaging uses modern information technology to meet the experience process of consumers' needs for products in many aspects.

Intelligent Design of Packaging Interaction. According to a recent study by Technavio, the smart packaging market is growing at a rate of 11% globally and is expected to exceed \$50 billion in value by 2025 [7]. Intelligent interactive packaging focuses on the emotional interaction between consumers and packaging with information transparency and mutual trust. Designer Li Yafan's team's "farmer file" series of intelligent fruit packaging uses QR code and RFID technology through the cell phone to scan the QR code or label of the fruit. You can browse the fruit's characteristics, the environment's origin, the growth cycle, distribution channels and other information, but also directly with the farmer through online communication and interaction. It is even possible to communicate among consumers, group purchases, share shopping experiences, and improve the satisfaction of users' emotional interaction process.

Intelligent Packaging Sharing. The development of intelligent technology and the sharing lifestyle inspires the concept of sharing product packaging. Packaging sharing is to simplify the procedure as much as possible, reduce time and money costs, realize the behaviour of consumers interacting with packaging repeatedly for multiple uses, improve the efficiency of human-object interaction and increase consumer interaction experience. Packaging shareability is considered from multiple perspectives: (1) Shared packaging design can optimize the interactive allocation of resources and promote industry innovation and sustainable development. (2) For packaging enterprises, how the same product packaging can provide the same packaging design service for multiple enterprises and reduce enterprise costs? (3) For consumers, the sharing of the subsequent recycling of packaging and the interactive experience process of multiple consumers using the same packaging multiple times and recycling. In terms of logistics recycling and the use of intelligent technology, shared packaging continues to explore new industry standards. Shanghai Jielong Group has developed a new model of "shared packaging" and "box sharing" storage and logistics recycling packaging sharing. It has become an attempt to transform the packaging and logistics industries (Fig. 1).

Fig. 1. Different Shared Package Boxes

Smart Environmental Sustainability. The sustainability of intelligent and environmentally friendly packaging is a reflection of the designer on the environmental and ecological damage caused by human activities and a firm commitment to professional ethics. It can be considered from these aspects: (a) intelligent environmental protection of packaging. The combined application of biodegradable materials and new technology materials can reduce pollution and improve the recycling rate of waste packaging, providing material support for green packaging design. New structural designs can also achieve sustainable use. As shown in Fig. 2, the corrugated paper shared packaging design, a modified hanging structure packaging, when not in use, will be flattened and stored; when in use, the round fruit can be stacked and turned, and the paper material can be degraded and recycled. The packaging structure has the advantages of being simple and portable, easy to disassemble, environmentally friendly and inexpensive, and can be used repeatedly [8], which increases consumer participation and interactive experience. (B) Innovative application of original packaging materials. Such as wicker, bamboo, wattle, rattan, wheat stalks and other raw materials prepared into the transport vending containers, reflecting the regional style of the product and increasing the local sentiment. Not only does it have ecological recycling value, but it is also full of solid country feeling, strengthening the human-centred emotional communication and interaction of the design.

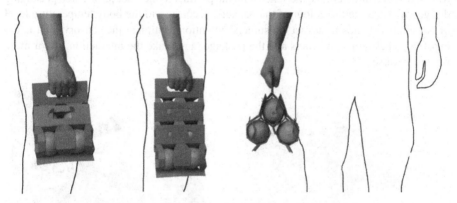

Fig. 2. "Farmer's Archives" fruit sharing package design

3.2   Intelligent Interactive Packaging Experience Design

Intelligent interactive experience refers to the experience of communication and interaction between consumer users and product packaging, mainly from the subjective emotional experience of consumers in the three time periods before, during and after the purchase of products. In the whole process, consumers pay more attention to the material (quality) and spiritual (emotional) level of the intelligent interactive packaging experience to achieve a higher level of consumer perception identity.

Initial Interaction Experience Design. Initial interaction experience is a communication experience in which consumers get in direct contact with the packaging before purchasing the product, and they get this interaction experience through visual, tactile, and olfactory senses [9]. Entering the supermarket, the first thing we can quickly get is information about fresh fruits and vegetables from the shape, tone, material and touch of the outer packaging of fresh fruits and vegetables. Those exaggerated, characteristic packaging shapes direct display the product's actual quality of transparent packaging design so that consumers have a direct sensory experience. To facilitate the convenience of customers in the whole box to buy fruit to check the freshness of the fruit, part of the transparent structure of the packaging design not only can increase the aesthetic value of fruit packaging but also can improve the desire and credibility of both buyers and sellers [10]. Figure 3 packaging design is a combination of transparent packaging and creative labelling, fresh fruits and vegetables are directly presented to give consumers real visual enjoyment, focusing on the visual interaction between consumers and fresh fruits and vegetables, stimulating consumers' strong desire to buy.

For example, in Fig. 4, designer Naoki Hirota designed a meat freshness indicator label to show consumers the freshness of meat. When the heart in the package is in the fresh stage, the indicator is shown as white at the top and bottom. As the freshness of the meat decreases over time, the lower part of the funnel-shaped indicator label changes from white to blue. This freshness indicator allows consumers to easily and intuitively see the quality status of the product inside the package, increasing consumer trust and visual interaction experience with the product. Other tactile-oriented packaging designs will change the colour of the package according to the body temperature level of consumers' hands to attract consumers' attention, optimize the sensory interaction experience between consumers and the package, and make the interaction full of more fun and diverse.

Fig. 3. Fruit packaging design

Fig. 4. Label design of indicator of freshness preservation

Process Interactive Experience Design. Interactive packaging focus on the consumer in the use of behaviour in the process of the unexpected sense of joy. The interactive process of using, carrying and opening the package affects the user's emotional experience. Intelligent technology assistance can be achieved to enhance the interactive communication and entertainment of packaging and consumers, which enhances the interactive experience of consumers [11]. Pan tiger design team launched Chu orange 2.0 version (Fig. 5), special Chu orange gift box set structure design, to pull outward packaging, orange automatically rise, convenient to put the orange to take, increase the consumer and packaging use process interaction experience, also implies Chu old life of the ups and downs [12]. Figure 6 The "17.5° Orange", which is being sold by Farmers' Spring, applies modern intelligent traceability technology to give consumers an in-depth understanding of the product at the time of purchase. By scanning the QR code on the surface of the orange and entering the cell phone interface, it is possible to trace the base of this class of oranges as well as the information on the length of sunshine, the temperature difference between day and night, and the amount of rainfall for planting. Modern technology for the visual representation of the fruit information architecture is open and transparent and has the nature of interactive entertainment to enhance the consumer experience [13].

Fig. 5. Chu orange design of version 2.0   **Fig. 6.** The packaging and tracing of 17.5° orange in the farmer's mountain spring

Experience Design of Subsequent Derived Functions. The following functions of the package give the package a second life and satisfy consumers' demand for subsequent use and entertainment of the package. Designer Li Yaeven's team developed a visualized and intelligent programming interactive App software for "Farmer's File" fruit packaging to realize the combination of packaging and consumers at the front end and packaging and recycling at the back end. Users can take the initiative to participate in environmental protection actions by scanning the QR code label on the packaging through the intelligent terminal and getting recycling advice and scientific information on the packaging materials so that consumers can participate in the action experience of intelligent packaging waste classification and recycling. Figure 7 shows from left to right the material composition of the packaging, the recycling suggestion of the material and the location of the surrounding automatic recycling machine. This application interconnects "consumer-package-recycling", enhances the cognitive experience and presents the new era of packaging recycling.

Figure 8 shows the packaging design of a fun fruit and vegetable platter in the famous FRESH'N'FRIENDS organic supermarket chain. By realizing children's active participation in the creative packaging activities of fruit and vegetable platter, the problem of children disliking fruits is solved. Children can also do their favourite fruit puzzles electronically through the online APP, and the staff will make the same fruit platter for them. The child's initiative to participate in the production process and the intervention of intelligent design software has increased the fun of shopping and improved the problem of children not loving fruit, which many parents have affirmed. The future of packaging design is not just a simple superposition of pattern functions. The intervention of intelligent interaction with children in this fun-filled puzzle creation activity to experience a different kind of fun.

Fig. 7. Application of "farmer file" package design system and RFID tag

Designers need to combine intelligent technology and consumers' material and spiritual needs with packaging design, strengthen the interactivity of packaging based on emotional experience, improve the efficiency of intelligent packaging and consumer recognition, and enhance the concept of interactive packaging design; in addition, in-depth consideration of the interaction between consumers and packaging, from intuitive feelings, action experience and follow-up design of three dimensions of interactive design, to strengthen The integration of fun, intelligence and interactivity in fresh fruit

Fig. 8. Interesting fruit platter packaging interactive experience design

and vegetable packaging to meet consumers' higher level of spiritual and emotional needs identity and enhance packaging branding[9].

4   Conclusion

Emotional interactive packaging design can close the distance between the product and the user and make the consumer feel surprised or warm. Through the innovative application of intelligent interactive technology, new packaging materials, two-dimensional code and other technologies, it can not only ensure the basic functions of the packaging, but also enhance the good interactive experience between consumers and intelligent packaging to meet or even stimulate consumers' emotional needs and consumption experience. Designers must adhere to the user as the core, the integration of information intelligence technology, to achieve the upgrade of the consumer's interactive packaging experience, to explore the integration of emotional experience in interactive packaging design and design optimization, to achieve packaging design to meet people's emotional needs and improve the effectiveness of interactive packaging design. Closely combined with new technologies, we actively explore the development of the packaging design industry.

References

1. Huang, X.: Research on interesting food packaging design based on consumer psychology. Ind. Des. **06**, 83–84 (2018)
2. Wang, C.H.: Function and innovation of fruit packaging. Yantai Fruit Tree. **39**, 14–16 (2018)
3. Norman, D.A.: Design Psychology 3: Emotional Design. M. Translated by He X.M,Ou Q.X. CITIC Press, Beijing(2012)
4. Yi, J., Wu, Z.J.: Exploration of methods and trends of product emotional design. Hunan Univ. Sci. Technol. (Soc. Sci. Ed.) **01**, 161(2013)
5. Wu, Z.H.: Research on the Interactive Packaging Design. Hunan University of Technology, Changsha (2013)

6. Wu, Y.L.: Emotions and Experiences: Research on Interaction of Packaging Design Based on Consumer Psychology. Southeast University, Nanjing (2015)
7. Li, T.: Technology innovation helps food/drug intelligent packaging rise to prominence. Screen Print. Ind. **01**, 51–56 (2018)
8. Li, Y.F.: An Integral Molding Process of A Spherical or Global-Like Fruit Package, China, CN107934199A, vol. 04, p. 20 (2018)
9. Luo, X.Y., Hao, Y.C.: Research on food packaging design based on interactive concept. Packag. Eng. **40**(16), 67–71 (2019)
10. Zhang, J., Guo, M.Q.: Overall packaging development of featured fruits in pan zhi hua from the perspective of green ecology. Art Sci. Technol. **28**(10), 69 (2015)
11. Chen, X.T., He, X.: Interactive packaging design analysis. Packag. World **03**, 24–26 (2017)
12. Pan, T.: Chu Orange Design 2.0 I Pass on Orange, Inheritance (2019). https://www.douban.com/note/735351945/
13. Gathered by choosing: Small "Orange" Big Dreams, 17.5° in Orange with Micro Store Web Celebrity Trip (2019). https://mp.weixin.qq.com/s?__biz=MzI0MTk2MzQzNw%3D

Research on Urban Subway Public Space Design Based on Regional Culture Dissemination

Shiyuan Zhu[1], Ying Chen[1($\boxtimes$)], and Yawen Yang[2]

[1] Changsha University of Science and Technology, Changsha, China
15707293368@163.com

[2] Hunan International Economics University (Hunan University), Changsha, China

Abstract. The purpose of this study is to explore the user perception of the display of major cultural elements in urban subway public spaces, and to provide design reference for improving the cultural expression of subway space design. Through a user questionnaire survey, this study conducted a relatively detailed exploration of the cultural needs of subway public space users and the expression status of regional culture, using the method of questionnaire survey to obtain and analyze data. The results show that there are some problems in the public space of urban maps, such as insufficient coordination of display regional cultural space, monotonous architectural space, single regional cultural communication function, and less design of cultural interactive devices. Propose plans such as interactive forms of new media, innovative regional cultural concepts, enriching spatial interface color design, and highlighting sculpture sketch design, to provide reference for the design of regional cultural expression in urban subway public spaces.

Keywords: urban subway · public space design · regional culture dissemination

1 Introduction

Subway, as a common public transportation in modern urban life, is the "best space" for deducing and inheriting urban culture because of its "double high" of mobility and aggregation. Subway effectively extends the above-ground space and develops the underground space, which plays an important guiding role in the development of urban pattern, urban style and human environment. With the functional trend of complex subway buildings, subway space has gradually become a gateway space to understand the connotation of urban culture, as well as an important carrier to highlight the regional culture and urban style of the city. It's importance is self-evident.

In the high-speed construction of urban subways in China, subway cultural construction between lines and regions is neglected. Currently, the spatial design of subway stations in China is transitioning from addressing basic functional needs to enhancing the cultural value of the city. How to create a subway architectural space with "regional urban cultural imagery" from a cultural perspective and an artistic perspective will inevitably become a key issue for the sustainable development of urban subway construction.

According to the survey, problems during the construction of regional culture in Chinese urban subway stations are as follows:

1.1 Lacking of Coordination in Displaying Regional Culture

There are nearly 30% of passengers believe that the regional cultural expression in subway stations is inconsistent with the urban environment, and the interaction with the urban cultural axis and the echo with regional culture need to be improved. On the one hand, the design of the subway station has a weak connection with the surrounding environment. Entrances and exits have many problems regarding the volume and location selection. On the other hand, the underground space environment of each site is the same, which fails to interact with the urban regional style and is monotonous in displaying the regional culture.

1.2 The Style of Subway Spaces is Monotonous

Data show that the regional culture of the current space of Chinese urban subway is insufficient in terms of style, volume, color and so on. The artistic processing of guiding signs within the station is simple, and there is no consideration of regional cultural characteristics. The style of infrastructures, such as seats and bins, are common and can be applied everywhere.

1.3 The Function for Cultural Communication in Subway Areas is Simple

With the development of subway stations, it have evolved into a "synthesis" with multiple functions rather than just a space to meet only traffic functions.The survey shows that current public space of Chinese urban subways only provide simple type of behavior and activities. Many subway's waiting halls do not even have "cultural walls". Instead, large-area of advertisements or empty walls are difficult to realize the function of regional culture transmission.

1.4 There Are Few Interactive Devices for Cultural Communication in Subway Spaces

Interactive installation art is a comprehensive art form that it can endow avant-garde art with the characteristics of marketization and popularization..It uses computer and communications technology, e.g., video, images, audio and text, etc. to respond to the viewer's commands. Interactive devices in the subway public space can help local passengers to understand the history and culture, and enhance their sense of national identity. At the same time, it can help foreign tourists to feel the local characteristics of culture, effectively spread regional culture. In our country, the public space of the subway lacks the interactive device design, especially the interactive device design demonstrating the regional culture.

2 Method

Through questionnaire design, this study conducted an online questionnaire survey on "Cultural Expression of Urban Metro Public Space" among 1015 subway riders of different ages, focusing on the expression of regional culture in the subway station space with the subway public space design as the entry point. The questionnaire survey involves user portraits of subway riders, cultural concerns in public space and evaluation of the effect of regional cultural communication in subway public space. It explores the current situation of regional culture in subway public space, and how to combine new technologies, new ideas, new materials and diverse ways to shape the public space of urban subway in China, so as to better disseminate regional culture.

3 Experiment

The survey involved subway riders from all over China and from all walks of life. The questionnaire strives for authenticity and objectivity, providing reliable and reliable research data and questionnaire design and feedback for the planning and design of subway public space bearing regional culture.

3.1 Basic Information About Users

As of March 2023, the total passenger flow of subway in China reached 59.8031 million, and the number of operating stations reached 5683. After sorting out the survey data, the gender of users participating in the survey is basically the same, with 45.32% and 54.68% for men and women respectively; Users participating in the survey span all age groups, of which passengers aged 31 to 40 account for 34.68%; They come from different regions such as Northeast China, North China and East China, among which South China accounts for the highest proportion; The education background of users is mainly undergraduate, junior college and senior high school, with 76.16% of the respondents; 50% of the surveyed users are company employees, and other industries are also involved.

3.2 Activities in the Subway Station Area

It can be seen from the investigation of the public space activities of the urban subway that people have a strong demand for subway space. According to the data, excluding occasional subway passengers, frequent subway passengers accounted for 82.46% of the total number of people surveyed, indicating a high frequency.

People use subway as a means of transportation for a variety of purposes, involving low-carbon travel experience, scenic spots, shopping, as a transit tool, etc. Passengers will also engage in a variety of personal activities and communication activities in the urban subway space, among which 56.65% are engaged in recreational reading and 43% are engaged in space appreciation, indicating that users hope to have some understanding of urban culture. The activity forms of passengers correspond to the needs of passengers, and the activity types are relatively rich. People gradually begin to pay attention to the activities that can be provided in the subway space (Fig. 1).

As the carrier of public transport activities, people in the urban subway space hope to interact with the surrounding environment. They usually stay in the waiting space of the platform, the rest space of the station hall, the shops in the connecting channel station

Fig. 1. Word frequency graph of passengers' activity in subway public space (Self-Designed Form)

and the subway entrances and exits, or enjoy the cultural walls and buildings alone, or talk with their families, friends, classmates, and colleagues.

The survey results show that people go out to take the subway for activities very frequently. Accordingly, the demand for the use of public space in urban subway is also very strong, and the use efficiency and quality of subway station space should also be widely paid attention to.

3.3 Understanding and Satisfaction of Cultural Expression in Subway Public Space

According to the survey data, nearly 20% of passengers think that the construction of urban subway space needs to optimize the experience. Decoration and beautification, cultural communication, aesthetic education, advertising promotion and commercial commerce are the important functions of the subway space. Passengers also say that the cultural expression of urban subway public space has an important impact on their travel. However, in terms of the current construction of public space of urban subway, only less than 30% of the passengers think it is beautiful and comfortable, and the passengers who think the subway space is not consistent with the urban environment, too much advertising, and monotonous accounted for 26.4%, 17.83% and 15.96% respectively. As for the expression of regional culture in subway public space, more than half of the people think that there are some echoes and no echoes, indicating that the construction of urban subway public space needs to be optimized and the expression of regional culture needs to be improved.

In general, users believe that the cultural expression of subway public space is an important factor affecting their communication and travel, and only the subway public space with strong regional culture can bring better travel and communication experience to passengers and other users.

The score order of satisfaction at the level of station connection is: access space climate adaptability > surrounding architectural style regionalism > rationality of square outside station > coordination of surrounding environment. At the level of connection, satisfaction with coordination of surrounding environment is low, and people believe that coordination between subway ground space and surrounding environment needs to be strengthened, so as to better reflect regional culture. The satisfaction of access space adaptability and building space regionalism is high, which are 4 and 3.95 respectively. However, the highest evaluation is given to the climate adaptability of the entrance and exit space, because it is the most basic requirement for the regional climate adaptability of buildings, no matter shading from the sun, wind or rain and snow.

People are satisfied with the design of the urban subway public space, but it still needs to be improved at the level of urban areas such as regional echo and station scene matching. In some cities with prominent cultural characteristics, the space of some special stations tries to echo the culture, but it is far from enough. At the same time, at the level of underground space, the guide system, folk business facilities and other aspects are not enough, resulting in the lack of vitality of the underground public space of the subway station, poor identification, affecting the travel of passengers.

4 Conclusion

Subway station is one of the public spaces with the largest flow of people in the city, and it is a kind of artificial place. Due to its relatively closure and publicity feature, passengers will have a different reaction from those in the ground space both physically and psychologically. Therefore, the transformation of subway spaces by adding function of cultural communication to eliminate its sense of closure and urgency is impending.

Designing strategies of subway spaces which combined with the function of cultural communication could be summarized as follows:

4.1 New Media Interaction as New Expression Form

The survey found that current urban subway public space have very poor performance regarding cultural expression, no matter in the pespective of type distribution of regional culture or the art expression form aspect. To enrich the diversity of art expression form in spaces can be started from two aspects: on the one hand, regional culture could be summing up as a system firstly, and then be merged into subway spaces by design strategies; On the other hand, regional culture could be displayed by multiple forms in subway spaces, e.g., murals, reliefs, sculptures, mini museums, new media screens, cultural interactive devices and the holistic construction of the whole space. Historical memory is displayed to meet the needs of different passengers.

4.2 Integrating Regional Culture into Urban Activities and Planning Behavior Paths

Organizing rich urban activities in the station space not only promotes the city's personality, but also plays an important role in prospering the city's economy and culture, becoming an important marketing tool for a city. In the vicinity of the station with enough space for activities, music performance, ethnic characteristic performance, square dance, characteristic exhibition and other activities with a smaller scope of activities can be organized, and recreational facilities can be set up at the boundary of the site, which can not only meet the needs of citizens for rest, but also experience the regional culture of the city. In terms of behavior path planning, it is first necessary to conduct underground functional zoning design. By analyzing the use functions and traffic flow lines of underground space, it is determined that regional culture can be expressed at a certain node and location in the space, in order to achieve a perfect combination of functional space design and cultural expression. Secondly, it is necessary to organize and plan behavior paths and clarify spatial orientation. Based on the analysis of passengers' behavioral psychology, the path planning of subway space should be convenient, safe, easy to identify, and rich in diversity.

4.3 Rich Spatial Interface and Color Configuration Design

For the interface design of urban subway space, the concrete performance is the ceiling design, wall design and ground design of underground space. The design style of ceiling, wall and ground of underground space in the same station space should be unified, and the symbols of local regional culture should be extracted, abstracted and deformed, and applied to the interface processing of underground space. The color selection of subway public space should be bright and comfortable to relieve the depression brought by underground. As the underground space is closed and boring, color is the first sensory impression to people, which can give people a head start. Different places can choose different colors according to the local climate and other environmental factors to create colors in the station space, which not only satisfies people's psychological needs, but also plays a good decorative effect.

4.4 Highlight the Sculpture Logo and Facility Design

At the level of guiding signs, it is necessary to achieve the regionalization of logo design. The prerequisite for visual guidance design on subway station signage is to coordinate with the surrounding environment. Decorative techniques such as the color and shape of vertical signage can be used to design, combining visual guidance signs with vertical signage. At the same time, decorative patterns representing local regional characteristics can be added to subway guidance design, which can not only meet people's guidance and recognition needs and habits, but also achieve the purpose of guiding passengers, It plays a role in transmitting information and reflects the local regional cultural characteristics. At the same time, regional storytelling design can be utilized to continuously integrate the entire underground space through the display of murals on the walls on both sides of the space, the transmission of sculptures in the rest space of the station, and the embodiment of cultural walls. After completing the series of actions from entering the station, buying tickets, waiting for the train, and taking the train, passengers also have a certain understanding of the cultural story and historical context of the region.

Admittedly, there are still many problems to be solved deeply in the research on the performance of subway station public space based on regional culture, which are mainly divided into the following aspects:

1. There are various kinds of regional culture in China. Besides historical culture, industrial culture and campus culture, there is also immigrant culture, folk culture and intangible cultural heritage culture. It is suggested to strengthen the careful study of Chinese regional culture, to provide more themes for the cultural expression of subway public space.
2. The research on the expression of decorative art in subway public space involves psychology, architectural space, aesthetics, and other disciplines, which requires a variety of knowledge reserves. Due to the limited personal time and knowledge reserve, the research on some specific issues is not thorough enough and needs to be improved in the future.
3. Consider how to combine subway public space with souvenirs with regional cultural characteristics, bring subway decorative art into people's daily life by combining with modern design, and strengthen the publicity of regional culture. The characteristics of each subway station are studied deeply, and the public space of subway station is designed with one standard.

References

1. Shu, Y.: Urban Underground Space Environmental Art Design. Tongji University Press, Shanghai (2015)
2. Beijing Planning Commission. Beijing Subway Public art. China Architecture and Building Press, Beijing (2014)
3. Yang, Z.: Art Entry: Public Art of Rapid Transit. Beijing Institute of Technology Press, Beijing (2005)
4. Wu, D.: Subway Public Art Creation: From Viewing to Practice. China Ocean Press, Beijing (2016)
5. Deng, Y.: Analysis on the diversity and function of Art Forms in Public Space. West. Leather **16**, 24–25 (2019)

Correction to: Defining How to Connect Nature and Digital World to Decrease Human Impact

J. Valerio⬤, J. Piña⬤, D. Peña⬤, M. Ávila⬤, R. García⬤,
B. Parra⬤, D. Méndez⬤, and A. Núñez⬤

Correction to:
Chapter "Defining How to Connect Nature and Digital World to Decrease Human Impact" in: C. Stephanidis et al. (Eds.): *HCI International 2023 Posters*, **CCIS 1835, https://doi.org/10.1007/978-3-031-36001-5_68**

In the originally published version of chapter 68 the ORCID number of the author Peña D. was missing. The ORCID number has been added.

The updated original version of this chapter can be found at
https://doi.org/10.1007/978-3-031-36001-5_68

Author Index

Printed in the United States
by Baker & Taylor Publisher Services